"Friedrich Schleiermacher's *On Religion: Speeches to Its Cultured Despisers* (1799) took on the major arguments of the enlightened intelligentsia of his day. He, thereby, revived Christianity and enabled it to thrive in the rise of reason and science. So Schleiermacher is known as the father of modern theology. Scott Shay's *In Good Faith* has picked up that historic baton and bridges believers and non-believers, of all religious persuasions, into a compelling twenty-first century story about why faith matters for healthy human communities today."

—PROFESSOR DWIGHT N. HOPKINS, University of Chicago Divinity School

"*In Good Faith* is a tour-de-force! Scott Shay considers a wide array of scholarly and popular arguments, sources, narratives, and conversations regarding religion, morality, and text in making a modern case for the plausibility and rationality of religion. In reading through its pages, I felt I was examining a twenty-first century companion to Schleiermacher's classic *On Religion: Speeches to Its Cultural Despisers*. Written in a clear and engaging fashion, *In Good Faith* will deservedly capture the attention of thoughtful persons interested in questions of faith and doubt, good and evil. I recommend it highly!"

—RABBI DAVID ELLENSON, Chancellor Emeritus of Hebrew Union College, Jewish Institute of Religion

"Scott Shay invites you to a friendly but serious conversation with someone who is honest, learned, and sincere on a topic that requires far more nuanced exchanges than mere tweets and sound bites at a time when idolaters, both atheists and monotheists, are misusing and misrepresenting religions, misinterpreting and misappropriating the Bible to further their base ambitions while ignoring God's rational and compassionate visions for humanity and the world that are articulated in the Bible and practiced and valued by rational and modern believers. Whether one is a skeptic, Jew, Christian, Muslim, atheist, humanist, spiritual but not religious, or non-affiliate, you are in for an intellectual and spiritual treat if you dare to be open and honest about your own rationale for and experience of your belief or unbelief."

—PROFESSOR URIAH Y. KIM, Dean of Graduate Theological Union

"Scott Shay, in a deeply personal, yet academically rigorous study, shows why it is rational to believe in God, especially in this modern era. Modernity is deeply grounded in the great monotheistic religions, which created and inspired societal structures that value equality, justice, morality, ethics,

Advance Praise for *In Good Faith*

"I can't think of another book with which I disagree so strongly that has engaged me as deeply as this one. Scott Shay makes the case for religious belief with deep scholarship, clear logic, and great civility. It would be wonderful if other advocates on both sides would take up this discourse in a similarly civil manner."

—BARNEY FRANK, Former Member of the House of Representatives

"*In Good Faith* is an extraordinary and beautifully written book, which offers an important new perspective. *In Good Faith* sets the stage for a fruitful dialogue between believers and nonbelievers in the discussion of faith and scientific rationality. Scott Shay argues that monotheists and atheists can be on the same side and combat idolatry together. His definition of idolatry as a dangerous deification of finite beings and ideas clarifies that modern rational critiques of religion can actually be helpful in clearing monotheism of its idolatrous streams."

—MONSIGNOR TOMAS HALIK, Professor of Sociology, Charles University and President of Czech Christian Academy

"This book is an inspired and profound exposition on the pitfalls of the idolatries of our age. What a remarkable manifesto on the rationality and indeed the beauty of faith as well as the ugliness and betrayals of idolatry! I hope that my fellow Muslims will give this book a fair hearing. It will only strengthen their own faith in the One and Only God who we all worship."

—PROFESSOR KHALED ABOU EL FADL, UCLA School of Law

"Sit down with Shay as he speaks of his faith, and the reasons he is a serious Jew. Here is an honest account of how a modern person finds meaning and purpose in a thoughtful consideration of ancient texts."

—PROFESSOR LAURIE ZOLOTH, PH.D., Dean and Margaret E. Burton Professor of Religion and Ethics, The University of Chicago Divinity School

"Scott Shay has written a vigorous, well-informed, and highly readable defense of faith in a secular age. Impressive in its scope and depth, it should be read by Jews, Christians, and Muslims, as well as skeptics, for they will find in it the reflective wisdom of one who has thought long and hard about the human struggle against idolatry in all its forms."

—RABBI LORD JONATHAN SACKS, Professor of Law and Ethics, Kings College and care for the needy. This book defends those foundations against the common atheist argument that our modern values have emerged from secularism. Shay demonstrates why both faith and reason are necessary in our era. Whether from the political left or right, deeply religious or secular, readers will benefit from Shay's insights as to how good faith can help heal our fractured society."

—PATRICK MCHENRY, U.S. Congressman, North Carolina

"*In Good Faith* is written with sincerity, honesty, and intelligence. The book presents ideas in a straightforward manner without overbearing theological and philosophical language and without a dogmatic tone. *In Good Faith* reveals a depth of knowledge by Shay of the religious situation in contemporary western society and especially in America. I hope that many readers take advantage of this resource. They will be intellectually rewarded for having done so."

—PROFESSOR SAYYED HOSSEIN NASR, Islamic Studies, Washington University

"Meticulously researched, Scott attempts to answer the age-old question: whether you can be a person of science and reason and a believer in God. Scott answers that question with a resounding yes. The reader of this book will have an opportunity to examine their own faith journey and square their understanding of the rational world with our spiritual selves."

—HEIDI HEITKAMP, U.S. Senator, North Dakota

"Scott Shay brings an important contribution and perspective to the current cultural conversation regarding religion and atheism. Well researched and engagingly written, *In Good Faith* reintroduces discussion surrounding a term we don't hear of much anymore…'idolatry.' The author has done extensive research across a wide range of viewpoints, and presents rational and compelling arguments that any thinking person will be forced to reckon with. I believe this volume will give clarity and voice to those who feel that religion is 'under assault.' I highly recommend this book!"

—PASTOR ROBERT STEARNS, Executive Director of Eagles Wings

"*In Good Faith* should encourage those who believe in God that their faith is well founded and rationally consistent, while challenging atheists to reexamine the rationality of their own position."

—REVEREND DR. JOHN CARLINI, President of the Center of Spiritual,
Personal, and Relationship Growth

"Scott Shay has written a remarkable, inspiring, and informative book that offers a serious and sustained alternative to the common, familiar way of defending the reasonableness of transcendental faith. The argumentative strategy adopted by the author relies on showing that present-day neo-atheism, by conflating idolatry and monotheism, is unable to understand why and how monotheistic religions radically break with idolatry, the root of evil. Written in a non-technical language accessible to non-specialist readers, *In Good Faith* argues that the three religions of the Book, far from constituting an impediment to the advancement of scientific knowledge, actually encourage it. This finely argued book will enhance the use of the Bible in a variety of fields. It is essential reading for economists concerned with the foundations of their discipline and for policy makers seeking to cope with the challenges of the so-called hyper-modernity, as well as for historians, moral philosophers, and theologians. Through a careful theological, exegetical, and hermeneutical method, Scott's account is at once timely, novel, and provocative. A captivating read."

—STEFANO ZAMAGNI, Professor of Economics, University of Bologna and Pontifical Academy of Social Sciences

"Kudos to Scott Shay for tackling atheism's staunchest and most vocal adherents with sensitivity, accessibility, humor and intelligence. His is a committed voice of faith, shaped by erudition and experience, unafraid to stand up for his convictions in a time of persistent doubt."

—DR. ERICA BROWN, Associate Professor, George Washington University School of Education and Development and Director, Mayberg Center for Jewish Education and Leadership

"Scott Shay sets out to prove that one could believe in God and read the Bible as a modern and rational person. In a lucid and engaging fashion—using sources ranging from Hammurabi to Plato to Constantine to Shakespeare to Freud to the Maori—he tackles the concept of idolatry, the morality of the Bible, the problem of evil, the existence of God, the historicity of the Bible, and faith and prayer. I believe that line by line, chapter by chapter, Shay has not only given the New Atheists a run for their money, but has emerged victorious. *In Good Faith* is a tour de force."

—RABBI DAVID GOLINKIN, Professor of Talmud and Jewish Law, The Schechter Institute and President Emeritus, The Schechter Institute

"Scott Shay invites everyone to the table: Jews, Christians, Muslims, scientific rationalists, and skeptics of all stripes. But it's for the serious purpose of showing how belief in the God of the Abraham religions can be an ally of scientific inquiry and efforts to build bridges of understanding in today's multi-religious and secular age. Undergraduates and adult learners in faith communities will find here much food for thought, as well as some delightful storytelling."

—Bishop James Massa, Catholic Diocese of Brooklyn, Former Executive Director of the Secretariat for Ecumenical and Interreligious Affairs, United States Conference of Catholic Bishops

"Shay presents a sensitive reading of the Hebrew Bible. Using stories from his own life and from history, he argues persuasively that we must all join forces to resist the evils of idolatry in our own time."

—Claire E. Sufrin, Associate Professor of Instruction and Assistant Director of Jewish Studies, Crown Family Center for Jewish and Israel Studies

"Scott. A. Shay has made an invaluable contribution by his most readable and logically compelling *In Good Faith*. He demonstrates why the Bible is still—after thousands of years—one of the most well read books in every generation, why to be a religionist is at least as relevant and intellectually satisfying in our modern age as it is to be an atheist, and how belief in God can direct an intelligent and sensitive person towards a more meaningful and ethically-charged life. It is a must-read especially for every sensitive young adult thinking about how to live his or her life!"

—Rabbi Shlomo Riskin, Founder and Chancellor of the Ohr Torah Stone Institutions

"Scott A. Shay is neither an academic nor a theologian, but he thinks and writes like one. A banker, he could have been a lawyer as well, presenting a formidable defense and a critical, rational analysis of faith and reason to eliminate the idolatry within them. With a touch of humility and a sense of humor, with a multidisciplinary perspective, he takes us on an intellectual journey towards believing in God and reading the scriptures in good faith. Through *In Good Faith*, Scott A. Shay 'places us at the intersection of what needs to be done and what we can do to achieve a better world in light of perfect truth.'"

—Saliba Sarsar, Professor of Political Science, Monmouth University

"In his book *In Good Faith*, Scott Shay reminds us that faith is as much a journey of the mind as of the heart. Shay's passion for defending religion and belief is rigorously argued with traditional texts, excerpts from conversations with religious leaders, and anecdotes from his life experiences."

—RABBI DEBORAH JOSELOW

"Monotheism has generated astonishing leaps of ethical consciousness from Moses to Rumi to Martin Luther King Jr. for reasons this book seeks to understand. This book contains the foundational truths as to why a Monk, Imam, Rabbi, or Bible Rapper would dedicate their lives to Ethical Monotheism. In my work as an educator, I encounter people daily who struggle with their faith. Shay's book will give them doubts about their doubts."

—MATT BARR, Bible Rapper and Educator

"*In Good Faith* is extremely powerful and thought provoking and is a must read for anyone interested in trying to comprehend the interchange between religion, society and social justice. In highlighting how actions in the name of religion have been abused, he dissects the real differences between belief, atheism and idolatry and thereby provides a fresh, new take on these conversations which were previously stuck in a rut. Scott Shay, systematically in easy prose untangles the misconceived perception that religion lays at the root of idolatry, of self-interest, self-enrichment and aggrandizement and shows that the reverse is true. Shay successfully describes how religion has been misinterpreted and abused to justify the behavior of idolatry in the name of religious piety."

—NICHOLAS WOLPE, CEO, Liliesleaf

IN GOOD
FAITH

Questioning Religion and Atheism

SCOTT A. SHAY

A POST HILL PRESS BOOK

In Good Faith:
Questioning Religion and Atheism
© 2018 by Scott A. Shay
All Rights Reserved

ISBN: 978-1-68261-792-2
ISBN (eBook): 978-1-68261-793-9

Cover Design by Tobi Kahn
Cover Composition by Cody Corcoran
Interior Design and Composition by Greg Johnson/Textbook Perfect

Post Hill Press
New York • Nashville
posthillpress.com

Published in the United States of America

*This book is dedicated to my wife Susan
and our wonderful children—
Benjamin, Ariel, Alison, and Abigail.*

CONTENTS

ILLUSTRATIONS

INTRODUCTION

God and Sushi

"I'll have a dragon roll."

My business acquaintance placed his sushi order with our waiter one rainy afternoon in May 2013 before returning his attention to me: "As for you, well, as a believer you have it all wrong. Why should anyone in his or her right mind believe in God? We should be enthroning man instead."

A successful businessman, my lunch companion was also a proudly self-proclaimed atheist. Fussing with his hoisin sauce, he went on to say that humankind is all there is, and that we should act to honor and improve man and woman through science and reason, not religion. "We humans can figure out right from wrong for ourselves without the help of some nonexistent god or his or its imagined laws," he asserted confidently. "We should not waste our time on worshipping some made-up god."

His argument seemed reasonable enough, even seductive. Still, I couldn't help think—between the appetizers and a tantalizing seared tuna steak—that I just did not share his point of view.

Are we earthly inhabitants of Carl Sagan's Pale Blue Dot really knowledgeable enough to dismiss the idea of God and to substitute ourselves atop the cosmic pyramid? What does it really mean "to enthrone man," anyway? I couldn't help but picture gilt-framed portraits of pompous French kings. Most of all, I couldn't accept my colleague's visceral dismissal of religion. Religious teachings are the foundation of my personal and communal morality as a Jew, and of most of modern global morality too, or so it seems to me. Because we had other items to discuss, I kept these reflections to myself, but I did take the opportunity to respond to my companion with H. L. Mencken's famous quip: "For every complex problem, there is an answer that is clear, simple, and wrong."

I don't embrace Mencken's views on God; he was, after all, a well-known nonbeliever. But his words on problem solving are peerless. At minimum, they helped steer the encounter back to business issues.

Doubt Is in The Air

As I went back to my office after the lunch, I felt somewhat overwhelmed. Before the lunch, I had just come off a week in which a fellow congregant at my synagogue told me that after all these years of showing up faithfully to daily prayer services, he still wasn't sure whether there was a God—and in which a Christian colleague who had made serious financial sacrifices to send his children to a private Catholic school told me he goes back and forth as to whether all the God stuff is just bunk. I had also just finished reading James Kugel's bestselling *How to Read the Bible* for the second time, which a good friend had pointed out to me had so little to say about the Bible's contemporary relevance that he was unwilling to recommend it to others. I enjoyed reading *How to Read the Bible* and was intrigued by its philological and historical critical explanations as well as its description of many types of traditional interpretations. But like my friend, I was struck with what *How to Read the Bible*—like many books that approach the Bible from a historical perspective—could not explain. Namely, why so many great modern figures—from Martin Luther King Jr., to Nelson Mandela, or even the founders of feminism like Frances Willard—would find such inspiration for their life's work in the Bible. I was not sure why a reader of *How to Read the Bible*, unfamiliar with the Bible's stories and not primarily interested in historical biblical criticism, would actually want to read the Good Book or consider it good.

"Mind If I Ask You A Question?"

For me, though, this particularly dramatic week of religious confessions actually fit a familiar pattern. These were far from the first conversations in which an acquaintance had volunteered a view about God or the Bible to me. After years of volunteer work for Jewish charities, and having authored a book on the subject of American Jewry, I evidently come across as a usual suspect in whatever gin joint I enter.

Initially, I was surprised that so many people chose to "talk God" with *me*. I'm not a rabbi, nor could I play one in community theater. Though I'm known in my circles as a believer, my previous book did not address Judaism as a set of teachings, so at first I was baffled that God kept entering the conversation. I was left wondering what was going on, until one day it dawned on me that for many American Jews, doubts about God spill over into feelings about the Jewish people. After all, if there is no God, then we ought to shelve the Bible in the folklore and mythology section of the local library, between Hans Christian Andersen and the Brothers Grimm. So why bother with all the fuss about strengthening the Jewish community? Sure, an argument could be made for keeping the Jews around as a distinct people with distinct values for the sake of global cultural diversity. That's a worthy enough cause, but it hardly ranks with working against nuclear proliferation or fighting poverty. As for preserving the Jewish community as a means of preserving a Jewish religion based on an ancient and outdated fiction—really? Not to mention holding on to the baggage of some politically incorrect myth about covenant and chosen-ness? Don't those concepts smack of chauvinism, perhaps even racism?

Further, since I proudly practice my Judaism, many Christian and Muslim friends, colleagues, and acquaintances over the years have felt comfortable sharing their personal views and doubts about their own religions with me, whether at the annual holiday party (often after one too many Heinekens) or even at a New York Knicks game (surely a test of anyone's faith in its own right, given their on-court performance in the last few decades).

In the course of these conversations, I came to understand that people held one of three perspectives.

The first perspective goes something like this: "You seem like such a reasonable fellow, so how is it that you buy all this God stuff? Please don't tell me you believe in Santa Claus and the Tooth Fairy, too?" "…Come on, haven't we civilized moderns outgrown all of that?" Or this: "And the Bible is just so primitive and obscure, it is no longer relevant to educated adults." These people believe that the book *Religion for Dummies* should have been titled *Religion Is for Dummies*.

The second perspective sounds like this: "I definitely believe in God, but I know it's completely irrational." It's as if they are confessing to parking their reason at the door simply because their hearts tell them to do so. As if they agree that there is no distinction to be made between belief in the God of Abraham and belief in superheroes, since most got their religious education from after-school and Sunday school lessons that were about as convincing as infomercials.

The third perspective is more like this: "I think you can be modern and educated and religious, but the atheists are right—you don't necessarily need religion or God to be good, and frankly some aspects of the Bible seem more than a little questionable to the modern reader." I count myself as a fellow traveler in this third group. But it was not always so.

There was a time I would not have picked up a Bible voluntarily either, and God was frankly irrelevant. I was one of many refugees from Hebrew school in the 1970s who had a truly terrible experience—alleviated only by intense daydreaming about hockey in the winter and baseball in the spring. After six years of class four afternoons a week for two hours each, I learned how to decode and pronounce Hebrew words but little else other than that we Jews believed in one God and that the Bible was very long and very boring. I was much more positively challenged by secular public school, where the movies, classics, and Superman and Batman comics sparked my imagination along with books like *The Adventures of Huckleberry Finn* and anything written about the Chicago Cubs. Nor did I get much reinforcement for the value of the Good Book at home. I didn't come from a bookish family. Neither of my parents graduated college, although my mother took two courses at community college after she graduated high school. My father, who was a survivor of the Holocaust, had a view of God that I'll detail later in the book, but did not press it on me or anyone, and we certainly did not learn the Scriptures together. Yet as a junior in high school I punctuated my more-or-less-happy secular equilibrium partially thanks to an encounter with a marvelous science teacher, who probably didn't realize the importance of the encounter to me. I decided to enroll myself in a Jewish school. (A bit more about this later as well.) And from that point on in my life, I continued to have a number of talented teachers in university and even as a working adult who, well versed in biblical criticism, opened up the great wisdom of the Bible to me and led me to ponder seriously what it meant to believe in God.

While I could name many, I must name two teachers who left the greatest imprint on how I read the Bible and relate to God. As a year-abroad student at Hebrew University, I had the opportunity to take a class with Professor Nehama Leibowitz, who is now recognized as one of the great Jewish biblical commentators of the modern period. She was as tall and sharp in Bible as one could be in contrast to her diminutive physical stature. I tried to register for the class but I could not get in, such was the popularity of this teacher—even among hormonal twenty-somethings. I contacted her and she said it would be okay for me to audit the class, but I had to prepare like everyone else. She closely interrogated every word, every story, every subpart of a story, and every contextual allusion of the text for discrepancy, inconsistency, or usage elsewhere in the Bible or even at times elsewhere in ancient literature, or for parallels in modern thought. In her classes, the philosophical, ethical, and psychological dimensions of the text came alive, not only rivaling the insights about the human condition from great classics of literature and philosophy, but even surpassing them. I was hooked.

Rabbi David Silber was my teacher for several years as an adult. I was introduced to his teaching when I was selected as a Wexner Heritage participant and continued to learn with him long after the program was over. He taught me, and countless others, to carefully read the Bible without coming to the text with any preconditions. At my Jewish high school, I had learned the Bible with the help of the many medieval commentators, but they also sometimes obscured the text as well. With Rabbi Silber the heroism of female figures came alive, the humanity of the patriarchs all too apparent, the dilemmas of the leaders palpably real. He invited us to consider the ethical dimensions of each story and to question, question, question the text. Not only was reason not the enemy, it was essential to reading the text and wrestling with God. He, too, understood biblical criticism well. While I was too scared to challenge Professor Leibowitz about anything (she was intimidating to say the least), as an adult, I was more comfortable asking Rabbi Silber tough questions or about contradictions in the text that bothered me. I learned how to approach these difficult passages not by fearing them but rather by welcoming them to deepen my understanding of the text's wisdom. It was because of these teachers that I could read the Bible, like one of my role models Dr. King did, as a work I could relate to my own life, to my choices, and to what I thought worth fighting for.

The many years of Torah study I have undertaken with amazing teachers have shored up my view that the Bible is as relevant a text as ever and that it is perfectly rational to believe in God. Yet, I have felt increasingly alone in this view. In the last decade, fewer and fewer people I know are as certain as I am. All these talks about God have made this all too apparent to me. The so-called New Atheists have come on the scene, and they are having a profound influence on skeptics and believers alike. They question how anyone could believe in God in good faith.

Atheists Can Be Awesome

In recent years, atheists have made their voices heard loud and clear, and their views resonate with a lot of people. I first encountered the celebrated Oxford evolutionary biologist and prominent atheist Richard Dawkins in 2009 when I read his manifesto, *The God Delusion*. His biting wit and turns of phrase kept me turning the pages. But that book was a success for more than its style. The events of September 11, 2001, the rise of religious extremism and violence, and the political polarization in the United States have inspired Dawkins and a new generation of atheists to condemn belief in God, the Bible, and religion on the grounds that they are not only *irrational* but *immoral as well*. And with everything from violence against abortion clinics to ISIS, more and more people feel they have a point.

Since 2001, several atheist authors, most famously the American journalist and neurobiologist Sam Harris (*The End of Faith: Religion, Terror, and the Future of Reason*), Dawkins himself (*The God Delusion*), the late British-American journalist Christopher Hitchens (*God Is Not Great*), the Tufts University philosopher Daniel Dennett (*Breaking the Spell: Religion as a Natural Phenomenon*), and the French philosopher Michel Onfray (*Traité D'athéologie: Physique de la Métaphysique*, translated as *Atheist Manifesto: The Case Against Christianity, Judaism, and Islam*) have written books denouncing religion as a form of irrational enslavement and advocating atheism. Together, these authors, among others, have been called the New Atheists. All of these authors have achieved considerable commercial success. In the last few years, others have added to the conversation. Steven Pinker, a psychologist and author of *The Better Angels of Our Nature: Why Violence Has Declined*, and Yuval Harari, a historian and author of *Sapiens: A Brief History of Humankind*, have taken an outspokenly atheist approach to their sweeping accounts of human nature and history, also with tremendous commercial success.

These books are but the most well known that have influenced a new and more strident atheist movement in North America and Western Europe. While all somewhat different in emphasis, these books make the case that polytheistic and monotheistic religions alike have proven to be historically suspect, patently false, and immoral at their sources. In other words, belief in God, or any gods, is irrational and immoral. They claim it is irrational because believing in one God is no different than believing in fairies, because science disproves God, and because faith and prayer are just forms of magical thinking with no scientific basis. And it is immoral because the Bible—like other ancient texts of its time—justifies many crimes, because the nonexistent God monotheists believe in is a sadist given the evil in the world, and because religions just lead to violence and intolerance. But most of all, the authors of these books claim that modern secular societies like Scandinavia are among the most tolerant and moral places the world has ever seen. The New Atheists attribute our modern social justice to the modern philosophical and sometimes literal rebellion against religion. They view themselves as finishing the job.

A Gallup poll found that belief in God among Americans declined to 86 percent in 2014 from 98 percent in 1967; Gallup also found the portion of those polled answering "none" for their religion rose to 17 percent in 2015 from 8 percent in 2000.

As has been the case for many Americans, the New Atheists intrigued me. Yet as I read Richard Dawkins or listened to other atheists, I had a paradoxical response. I could agree with them that religion has wreaked far too much havoc in the world, that religious observance has not curbed some individuals' enthusiasm for crime, that some religious practices seem downright superstitious, and that you don't need belief in God to be moral. Yet I just could not accept their dismissal of religion, but nor did I have a ready answer for their criticisms—and I wanted to.

It was after that one lunch in 2013 that the ball finally dropped for me. I needed to write a book. It seemed that so much of my upbringing and life experience was leading me to grapple with these issues that I simply had to begin. I felt I owed it to all those who had not been exposed to the teachers I had to offer up the alternative view that one could believe in God and read the Bible as a modern rational person. As we will further discuss in part VI, being at the intersection of what needs to be done and what you have the ability to do is the most consequential place to be. Too often we pass up the power of such places because these require hard choices. I realized that I had come to just such a junction. After making my decision, I gave up bicycling and cut back deeply on my communal volunteering and just about everything else except family, work, and wine. I began to start collecting my ideas culled from years of study into words and to gather further research from across the disciplines to respond to the atheists' challenge.

Twilight of Idols and Dawn of a New Discourse

This book is thus primarily the result of my thinking about whether the atheists' criticisms of Religion with a capital "R" are correct. It is the outcome of my decision to follow my initial paradoxical response to these criticisms, wherever it would take me. While many books have been written from a variety of perspectives in response to such atheist claims about God and monotheism,[1] I can say after becoming a favored customer at Amazon that, despite having learned a lot, none have gotten to the heart of why I felt the atheists were both "right" and "wrong." Yet thanks to these books, many conversations, and much reflection, and the cumulated years of studying the Bible, modern Jewish thinkers, and the works of modern scholars in varied fields, I came to an answer that satisfied me, and which is the premise of this book. Namely, the atheists have it backwards. Far from being identical to the polytheism of old, Judaism, Christianity, and Islam *actually largely align with humanist atheism* in that they are rational and moral and oppose idolatry. The atheists' criticisms of religion all ring true as criticisms of idolatry, but not of Abrahamic monotheism, which they misrepresent. Instead of the notion that we must rid the world of religion, both monotheism and reason can align in the name of the true and the good. Atheists and monotheists can actually be on the same side!

The heart of this book, and the source of the atheists' confusion, is that most modern people no longer understand what is meant by the concept of idolatry. Idolatry is not just the worship of imagined gods ranging from the benevolent to the bizarre. Idolatry, simply put, is a lie about the power and authority of finite things, whether elements, animals, or people. This lie is usually used for selfish and unjust aims: it is the root of evil. Because our human default is idolatry, we have to work intellectually and morally to overcome it. The Bible and the monotheistic religions it birthed revolutionized the world because they totally exposed the irrationality, deceptiveness, and injustice of idolatry and replaced it with a just and rational view of God, man, and the world.

While this book argues that idolatry and monotheism are opposite, the atheists' incorrect equation of monotheism and idolatry has much to teach us. Monotheistic cultures have fallen into idolatrous patterns and severely distorted monotheistic ideals, with devastating consequences. Monotheists, in fact, become idolaters anytime they assume the role of the solely correct spokesperson for God. By doing so they take His name in vain. Atheists also rightly claim that reason and moral intuition alone can lead to equality and justice, without resorting to God or a Bible. While I agree that reason can lead to justice, the historical record demonstrates that reason alone is neither necessarily just, nor sufficient.

This book is therefore also a blanket rejection of the atheist claim that secularism and atheism have been the primary drivers of political, social, and intellectual progress in the modern age. Rather, the values most cherished by atheists actually—and ironically—find their basis in monotheistic teachings. Yet modern rational critiques of religion have also helped to clear monotheism of its idolatrous streams. The Bible still has much to instruct us, religious and secular people alike. But one does not have to believe in God to reject idolatry or appreciate the Bible. This book is therefore not an attack on atheism, a completely rational intellectual position to maintain. Rather, what you will find here is a challenge to the broadsides fired by leading atheists against monotheism in their persistent confusion of monotheism and idolatry. Once these misunderstandings are cleared away, the encounter between atheists and monotheists, far from being a polemical battle, can be friendlier and mutually enriching.

While this book claims that monotheism has revolutionized the world, it nonetheless rejects in no uncertain terms the view that *only Jewish, Muslim, and Christian civilizations* have anything to teach us. Cleary, this is not observably true. Rather it argues that the cardinal prohibition by these three monotheistic religions—the prohibition against idolatry—has already changed the world for the better and deserves a central place in our conversations about global justice today. It is however, as I will explain, a gross misunderstanding to conflate idolatry—lies about the power and authority of finite things—with the cultural values of many traditionally polytheistic cultures today, such as respect for family, for one's heritage, nature, place, the mystery of life and other values, which are also alive in the Bible, New Testament, and Qur'an. It is an even worse misunderstanding to use this prohibition to destroy other cultures wholesale, something which monotheistic societies have unfortunately sometimes tried to do. Rather the prohibition against idolatry is, I will claim, the key to discerning the dividing line between the good and the evil in any culture, past or contemporary, secular or religious, and therefore the key to achieving pluralism without moral relativism.

Authorial Aspirations: Admit It, We All Have Them

I have four hopes for this book. None of them are particularly modest, but all are genuine.

My first hope is that the reader will conclude that it is as rational to be a monotheist as to be an atheist.

My second hope is that readers will come truly to understand the concept of idolatry. The deification of a finite being, idea, or thing poses many social, political, and intellectual dangers. Atheists, monotheists, and agnostics may not ever agree on God, but they can agree on idolatry and work to combat it together.

My third hope is that readers, whether they are atheists or believers, will gain a newfound respect for the religious texts, especially the Bible, as the gateway to our understanding of monotheism. Whatever the reader concludes about God, it should be clear that these texts have shaped our entire way of seeing and being in the world and are a vital part of any conversation about creating a better human future.

My final hope is that, despite the rationality of both monotheism and atheism, readers will come to the conclusion that the existence of the God of the Bible—who is omnipresent, omnibenevolent, omnipotent, and listens to our prayers—is consistent with evidence available to us.

This Book in 900 Words or Fewer

This book is divided into six sections that address the atheists' primary arguments. Atheist authors conflate idolatry and monotheism. They do not recognize monotheism's radical break with idolatry, which was the primary purpose of the Bible. Further, they ignore the important commonality between monotheistic and rational critiques of idolatry—which, if they had understood, would reveal to them how their worldview is much closer to monotheism than they previously thought, setting aside belief in God. Indeed, part one describes how the Bible brought radical new ideas about man's relationship with God, man, and the world. Those ideas transformed the ancient world and continue to inform us today. Among them, monotheism introduced the notion that man is made in God's image, with sweeping consequences.

The atheist authors also claim that it is impossible for us moderns to get our morality from religion, particularly from the Abrahamic faiths of Judaism, Christianity, and Islam. In their view, the values of our modern enlightened era, which they consider to be moral, arose from a radical break with religion. In contrast, part two shows that monotheism not only informs our modern model of moral relationships, but that reason alone can lead us to moral conclusions that many contemporary atheists would find abhorrent. At the same time, modern critiques of religion have challenged those so-called monotheists who are in reality idolaters. While atheists consider religion to be the major cause of war, the historical record shows that untempered greed and lust for power, two drivers associated with idolatry, are the greater culprits.

Further, atheists argue that they have an even stronger moral allegation against the notion of God—namely, the question of how an omnibenevolent God, the source of all love, could let man inflict so much suffering in the world. Part three claims that the existence of evil is the means by which we humans can have free will and therefore decide whether to become partners with God in perfecting the world. Here, too, it also shows that with reason alone our view of evil would be very different. An argument I sadly hear all too frequently, one that is often repeated by atheist authors, is that the prevalence of religious criminals taking a perp walk down screen on the six o'clock news proves that religion is not a source of morality. How, it is asked, can one pray in the morning and then spend the rest of the day preying on people? From pedophile priests, to Ponzi schemes, to inflammatory imams, to red-handed rabbis, religious folks need no lesson in giving religion a bad name. We'll examine these issues by showing how the Bible defines evil much like the Golden Rule.

We'll also have a look at how the Big Bang and evolution squares with the idea of a creator deity. Part four argues that there is no scientific proof or disproof of God, only two rational arguments for and against different views of the origins of nature. In other words, reason does not require us to make a choice between evolution and a creator God who hovers over creation like a helicopter parent.

Part five explores what archaeology has to say about whether the events in the Bible actually took place. It claims that archaeologists and biblical scholars are far from unanimous. Instead, they can be divided into three main groups: those who deny the Bible is based on actual events, those who think it is partly based on actual events, and those who think it is mainly based on actual events. Part five explores the evidence for all three positions. Given these disagreements, I argue that it is rational to accept that the events similar to those described in the Bible actually could have taken place based on archaeology (though the Bible takes poetic license in describing them).

For atheists, faith is by definition irrational and prayer nothing more than an outmoded superstition. In contrast, part six explains that both to accept the existence of God or to reject His existence requires a step of faith. I explore how taking this step for faith in one God has changed and still can change the lives of people for the better. I also argue that prayer is not, like incoming 800-numbers on a cell phone, always ignored but rather, like faith, a practice that can lead us to improve our relationships and transform the world.

This book is written with all three Abrahamic faiths in mind, since Judaism, Christianity, and Islam have all been routinely subject to attack by atheists. That said, most of this book focuses on the Hebrew Bible, in part because much of the firepower of the atheists is targeted toward this original source for the Abrahamic concept of God. In this book, when I mention the Bible, I am referring primarily to the Five Books of Moses, otherwise known as the Torah or the Pentateuch.[1] I also discuss the Books of the Prophets, which I identify separately. I will refer to the Oral Law (what is often called the Talmud in Hebrew)[2] as the compendium of commentaries on the Bible and rabbinic discussions of the law. When I invoke the Christian Scriptures or the Qur'an, I will cite these books as such.[3] I will use the pronoun He for God in following with the mainstream convention, even though the God of the monotheistic religions is beyond gender. Likewise, I will sometimes use the word "man" to refer to all of humanity. In addition, when I use the term monotheism, I am referring to Judaism, Christianity, and Islam. I will use the words idolatry and polytheism interchangeably.

Other Voices

I am most familiar with the Hebrew Scriptures and other Jewish texts. So as part of the research for this book, I interviewed eight leading Christian and Muslim thinkers. They helped me understand how their faith traditions view the issues presented in this book.

These religious leaders all gave generously of their time. It was a privilege to meet with them. I sensed in each case that I was in the presence of individuals whose faith guides every aspect of their lives. Throughout the book, I quote some key excerpts from these interviews.

---

[1] This book includes footnotes as well as endnotes. In the text, all footnotes will be notated with black superscript numerals, and all endnotes will be notated with grayscale superscript numerals. All quotations from the Pentateuch and other sources of the Hebrew Canon will be quoted from the *JPS Bible* (Philadelphia: Jewish Publication Society, [1985], 2008). I have however taken the liberty to adapt the translation where I disagreed with the JPS's text based on my reading of the Hebrew.

[2] Quotations from the Talmud and Midrash are my own translations or my own adaptations of online translations.

[3] Quotations from the Christian Scriptures will be from New Revised Standard Version of the Bible, *Holy Bible: New Revised Standard Version* (New York: American Bible Society, 1989) which is available online through www.bibligateway.com. The quotations from the Qur'an will be quoted from *The Qur'an*, trans. M. A. S. Abdel Haleem (Oxford: Oxford University Press, 2008).

For quite a few of the religious leaders, I had the opportunity to see them in action or to meet them outside the context of a formal interview. I had the pleasure of hearing Chaplain Tahera Ahmad's incredibly spiritual Qur'an chanting at a baccalaureate ceremony at Northwestern University, where she serves as a chaplain of my alma mater. She is among the best-known and most-respected female Islamic leaders in the United States. Raised in a suburb of Chicago, Chaplain Ahmad received her Islamic religious training in prestigious institutions both in the United States and Egypt. Chaplain Ahmad has had the distinction of being invited to the White House and was the first woman to deliver the Qur'an recitation to open the convention of the Islamic Society of North America.

Many New Yorkers will recognize Imam Shamsi Ali from his appearance at Yankee Stadium just a few days after September 11, 2001. He helped with the healing the city and the country so urgently needed. Imam Shamsi is a renowned Muslim scholar, author, speaker, and interfaith advocate. He heads the Jamaica Muslim Center in Queens and is one of the leading voices of interfaith dialogue in New York. He grew up in Indonesia in a very poor village, whose modest ambition was simply for him to be able to read the Qur'an and nothing more. From this humble background, he grew to become a significant Islamic scholar and faculty member studying Islam in Saudi Arabia and also earning a PhD in the United States. A polyglot, Imam Shamsi does much of his work in languages beyond the first two he learned. The Royal Islamic Strategic Studies Centre of Jordan named him one of the most influential Muslims in the world today.

Reverend Chloe Breyer is the director of the Interfaith Center of New York. I looked forward to meeting Reverend Breyer because of my interest in her book *The Close: A Young Woman's First Year at Seminary*. In it, she describes the journey she took from a secular upbringing to ordination as an Episcopal priest. Under Reverend Breyer's leadership, the Interfaith Center of New York has led the partnering of community faith groups with the New York Police Department and assisted broken families. In addition to her work in New York, she has traveled multiple times to Afghanistan on humanitarian missions, with a special focus on educating girls in the Wardak Province. Reverend Breyer seeks to infuse spirituality in local and international social action.

Reverend Dr. Calvin Butts serves both as senior pastor of the Abyssinian Baptist Church, one of the most historically important African American churches in the nation, and as president of State University of New York at Old Westbury. He is also the founder and force behind the Abyssinian Development Corporation, which has spearheaded Harlem's economic revival since the 1980s, and serves additionally on two New York State economic development corporations. Reverend Dr. Butts accomplishes more in a day than most people do in a week, and just listening to his assistant run through his list of varied and impactful events on the morning of my interview wore me out. I'd been told that visitors lined up to get into Abyssinian's services but dismissed this as urban legend until I saw the crowd, queued up along 138th Street one Sunday morning, with my own eyes. Abyssinian has become a bona fide tourist attraction (to the dismay of some congregants). I knew I needed to speak with Reverend Dr. Butts after I heard him deliver a guest sermon in Temple Emanu-El at a Friday evening Shabbat service commemorating the life of Martin Luther King Jr.

Timothy Cardinal Dolan is the tenth archbishop of New York. His flock numbers 2.5 million Catholics and he oversees a huge array of social services, hospitals, schools, colleges, and, of course, churches. But Cardinal Dolan does not just administer to his huge community; at heart, he is a parish pastor. During a break in our interview, he unassumingly asked if I'd mind giving him feedback on a point he was trying to make in the sermon he was preparing, and he spoke animatedly about a group of nuns he was looking forward to meeting later that day. I was impressed that everything he discussed seemed framed to put other people first. Though an eagerly sought-after public figure with a grueling schedule, Cardinal Dolan regularly makes time to visit the sick and the poor. I have personally watched him work in a soup kitchen as part of a joint UJA-Federation–Catholic Charities USA project. The Cardinal displays a perfect balance between gregariousness, mindfulness, spirituality, and service.

Reverend Dr. Katharine Henderson is president of the Auburn Seminary. She is a "pastor's pastor" who helps to train other clergy in social justice and community building. Even more impressive are her extensive efforts to bring active faith and an ethical compass to the business community, filling a critical need. We will later hear her inspiring story, a personal journey that took her from stagnant nonbelief to a resilient religious life as a leading light among Presbyterians. Reverend Dr. Katharine Henderson is one of those rare folks who speaks in perfect paragraphs: topic sentence followed by supporting sentences with a concluding sentence at the end setting up a transition to the next paragraph. I was struck by her remarkable mental and verbal organization and her sharp clarity of thought, both during our meeting and, even more so, when I later read the transcript.

Father Alexander Karloutsos is the spiritual advisor to the Order of St. Andrew and is the clergy leader of Faith: An Endowment for Orthodoxy and Hellenism. Father Karloutsos is an articulate and energetic spokesman for the theology of the Greek Orthodox Church. During my interview with Father Karloutsos, a true scholar at heart, he offered me a steady stream of sources I should check out, articles I should at least scan, and books I *had* to read. As we spoke, he would frequently jump from his chair in search of a quote in a book buried under a stack of others. Invariably, he would find the citation somewhere in the middle of the book and pass it to me with satisfaction while his lightning mind had already moved the conversation onto another topic. I left Father Karloutsos with several books in hand and a long list of homework assignments.

Bishop William Murphy led the Diocese of Rockville Centre on Long Island until his retirement in 2016. He has an extensive background in Catholic theology, having served as undersecretary for the Pontifical Council for Justice and Peace after earning a doctorate in sacred theology and teaching in two seminaries and two universities. I first met Bishop Murphy at a fundraising dinner for St. John's University where a friend was receiving an award. I was sitting at a table next to an empty chair when a waiter came up and deposited a stack of double-wrapped food containers on my plate (apparently, I seemed to be the only person among the thousand or so at the event who had ordered a kosher meal). At that precise moment, Bishop Murphy (whom I had not previously met) took the empty chair next to me and, before exchanging a word, the two of us broke out in laughter. We both sensed there was a joke here somewhere—"A bishop and this one kosher guy in the banquet hall are sitting down to a gala dinner…" All we needed was a punch line. And then, to my surprise and delight, Bishop Murphy provided it by starting to speak in Yiddish. Needless to say, our interview together many months later was entertaining and illuminating.

My interviews with all of these faith leaders were truly a special pleasure, providing me not only with information but with the inspiration that spurred this project forward. That being said, other than the actual words uttered by these wonderful thinkers that I have quoted from these interviews, all views expressed in this book are mine (for better or worse), and no one else should be held responsible for any content herein.

Now that the book is written, I promise you—whether you are a believer, undecided, or an atheist—that going on this intellectual journey with me will be worth it, because it will be a chance to discover a path trodden across the ages by many great thinkers, leaders, personalities, all people like you and me, who changed the world for the good because they were rational, critical people who believed in God and read the Scriptures—in good faith.

December 1, 2017

PART ONE

What Is Idolatry and Who Cares?

INTRODUCTION

Is Religion Bunk?

The Bible displays undisguised contempt for the gods and idols of other nations. This attitude leaves true believers with the unenviable task of having to reconcile God's overt hatred of competing deities with His more loving attributes of benevolence, compassion, and mercy. Richard Dawkins and like-minded critics have no such problem. Of course, they have resolved from the get-go that "God is the ultimate jealous narcissistic maniac,"[1] an unjust bully obsessed with personal power and glory just waiting to take down anyone who bends a knee to another divinity. But where's the harm if an ancient Egyptian entreated one of many native deities to protect her flock of sheep in 1200 BCE? What is the problem if a modern adherent of the Wiccan religion in 2018 chants an original magic spell for a peaceful new year?

And just why should belief in *one* god trump belief in many? A quantitative difference, to be sure, but qualitative? Monotheism or polytheism, we're being asked all the same to submit to imagined superpowers. Not to mention that, like other religions, monotheism is nothing more than an invention of the royal and priestly classes, dead set on boosting their advantage and bolstering their power. Rather than capitulating to the supernatural, shouldn't we be embracing secularism as the preferred force for fashioning a more rational and just world?

I raise the above questions ironically. If our goal, in fact, is to establish a society that is lasting, just, and free, then we must turn our focus to idolatry and its contemporary manifestations across the globe. To understand the true nature of idolatry is to condemn it, and this part of the book explains why. Contrary to the view of the atheists, idolatry is neither an innocent nor an innocuous case of divine possessiveness, consecrated statues, and calisthenics in the buff. *Idolatry has always been, and today continues to be, the most divisive and dangerous ideology in the world. It promotes lies about power and relationships in society. It deifies—that is, falsely attributes superior and inexplicable powers to—finite natural processes, animals, and people. It also bestows the authority—that is, falsely attributes the right—to these finite beings to use those powers as they choose, simply because they have them.* Thus, across time, it has led to the widespread exploitation of the many by the deified few.

Ancient societies first imagined natural elements, flora, and fauna as gods because of the seemingly mysterious and arbitrary sway they held over people's lives. As chieftains acquired political and economic control, they fashioned gods in their own images and compelled the people to serve these gods as well. Though the elites justified their domination of the people, their power and manipulative worldview did not go unchallenged. Across the ancient world, brutal elites faced challenges to their power in practice in the form of revolts. In Greece and Rome in particular, philosophers and moral leaders stepped forward to confront idolatry in theory as well. Their writings appealed to reason and moral intuition, and they retain their clarity and cogency even today. Similarly, the great philosophies of the East, particularly Taoism, Buddhism, Confucianism, and philosophical currents in Hinduism, demonstrated the reach of reason and moral intuition. Like Greek philosophy, they spread far and wide, persisting to this day. The same can be said of the wisdom of oral cultures from around the world, from Ibgo to the Inuit, passed down particularly in proverbs and stories.

But, in the end, it was the Hebrew Bible that proved far more effective than any popular revolt, Hellenic writing, or any other wisdom tradition in radically disrupting idolatry's distortions about power and relationships. From the very beginning, the Bible proffered the message that there exists only one superior power: a single God all powerful and all good. According to the Bible's worldview, neither human beings, elements of nature, nor invisible spirits should be worshipped. Unlike the imagined gods that idolatry draws on to justify the subjugation of populations, the one true God expresses power through justice. He demands that we humans follow suit. In adopting these transcendent ideas and

4

ideals, the three major monotheistic religions have transformed the world for the better. Whether we choose to believe in God or not, we moderns are heirs to and beneficiaries of the monotheistic revolution.

Atheist critics will point out, and rightly so, that monotheism is not without its own elites—groups who oppress others, even if only in the name of one God instead of many. Still, this argument falls short of the mark, for it fails to acknowledge that the Bible has already anticipated the problem. The third of the Ten Commandments, following logically from the first two against idolatry, forbids taking God's name in vain. Among other interpretations, this prohibits declaring oneself an unauthorized spokesperson for God, a form of self-idolization. Still, atheists will go on to say, despite this prohibition, numerous Christian, Muslim, and Jewish elites have persisted in repressing others in God's name. By the seventeenth century, such abuses had become so widespread that modern Western thinkers began to reject monotheism on the same rational grounds that ancient thinkers rejected idolatry. Precursors of today's atheists, they demanded people reject God and revelation. Instead, they called on reason alone for paving the path to a good society. But reason, as we have learned all too well from modern experience, comes with its own brands of misuse. It can be turned against innocent human beings as easily as it was against imaginary gods.

The Bible's prohibition against idolatry, including taking God's name in vain, is the great insight of monotheism. Atheists and monotheists would do well to recognize its profound relevance to their lives today. God's harsh threats against idolaters cannot be dismissed as morally meaningless. One need not believe in God to believe in the Bible's message that, in the fight for justice, the enemy is idolatry.

One God, Two Gods, Three Gods More

Atheist writers just don't get idolatry. In misjudging the Bible, they conflate idolatry and monotheism under a joint banner, emblazoned with the intended insult "irrational." You can hear Michel Onfray chuckling between the lines as he catalogs his examples: Some worship stones— from the most primitive tribes to today's Muslims walking around the Black Stone in the eastern corner of the Kaaba. Others venerate the moon or the sun, some an invisible god who cannot be represented on pain of idolatry, or else an anthropomorphic figure—white, female or male, Aryan of course. Another, a thoroughgoing pantheist, will see God everywhere, while another, an adept of negative theology, nowhere. By some he is worshipped covered in blood, crowned with thorns, a corpse; by others in a blade of grass, Eastern Shinto fashion. There is no man-made foolery that has not been dragooned into the ranks of putative divinities.[2] Daniel Dennett and Sam Harris, likewise, view all religions as equally superstitious and inane. Christopher Hitchens goes further, contending that idolatry and monotheism are equally unjust as well:

> Whether we examine the oriental monarchies of China or India or Persia, or the empires of the Aztec or the Incas, or the medieval courts of Spain and Russia and France, it is almost unvaryingly that we find that these dictators were also gods, or the heads of churches. More than mere obedience was owed them: any criticism of them was profane by definition, and millions of people lived and died in pure fear of a ruler who could select you for a sacrifice, or condemn you to eternal punishment, on a whim.[3]

Some atheists find classical polytheistic cultures, particularly ancient Greece and Rome, superior to monotheistic ones. In Onfray's view, centuries after the Greeks performed the welcome intellectual feat of developing working systems of philosophy, fanatic Christians did all they could to suppress it. He writes:

> Vandalism, autos-da-fé, and the culture of death. Like Paul of Tarsus, Christians were convinced that academic learning hindered access to God. All books (not just books by authors accused of heresy, such as Arius, Mani, and Nestorius) were at risk of being burned. Neo-Platonist works were condemned as books of magic and divination. People who possessed libraries feared for their safety.[4]

The New Atheist authors discern no thematic connection whatsoever between the Bible's prohibition against idolatry and its avowed principles of justice. What's more, Dawkins views the prohibition as morally absurd and destructive:

> If we took the Ten Commandments seriously, we would rank the worship of the wrong gods, and the making of graven images, as first and second among sins. Rather than condemn the unspeakable

vandalism of the Taliban, who dynamited the 150-foot-high Bamiyan Buddhas in the mountains of Afghanistan, we would praise them for their righteous piety.[5]

In my view, the atheists' arguments about idolatry demonstrate a total misunderstanding of the concept, a confusion extending to some monotheists as well.

Why Everyone Needs a Primer on Idolatry

In December 2015, I had the pleasure of taking a family vacation in New Zealand. (If you've not yet done so, book a flight as soon as you finish this book.) North and South Islands are among the most gorgeous places on earth. Hobbiton is a hoot, and unique spots like White Island seem to hail from another planet. Though our visit included its fair share of scenic sights, it put a special emphasis on Maori culture. The Maori arrived on the New Zealand islands in the 1200s CE. They brought with them the polytheism of the Polynesian peoples of the time.

We were privileged to meet Maori individuals involved in preserving traditional Maori culture and practices, much of which I could appreciate and relate to as a member of my own community with similar concerns. I was deeply impressed by the Maori connection to the land and spirit of the islands of New Zealand. As Maori describe their traditional gods and legends, one senses the deep warmth with which they embrace their traditions and the wisdom that they impart. To be introduced in a personal way to a Maori individual is to learn of the *whakapapa* of that individual. This is the link through the generations by which Maori trace their lineage back to one of the seven original canoes that arrived at Aotearoa, now known as New Zealand. Reverence for ancestors is yet another aspect of the people's connection to the land and to each other. As the Ngai Tahu tribe put it, "*Whakapapa* is our identity [...] our feet on the ground." The Maori language is a bubble bath for the ears when pronounced with the correct cadence, one syllable after another sharing the same emphasis. For those who have only seen the New Zealand national rugby team, the All Blacks, perform a *haka*, be advised that there are many different *haka*, all hypnotic and impossible to stop watching. The culture of the *marae*, the Maori's communal gathering places, both preserves these traditions and carries them forward, catering to the evolving social and political realities confronting the Maori people. If Maori religion is idolatrous, it's fair to wonder, "Hey, what's so bad about idolatry?"

The question, though, is not who dismisses idolatry today, but who takes it seriously. Bowing to idols and sacrificing nubile virgins may have gone mainstream in the ancient world, but it's gone the way of Sony's Betamax tapes today. It would seem not only absurd but even deeply wrong to imagine that the current religious observances of a polytheistic society such as the Maori could be dangerous. Many monotheists pay little attention to idolatry at all, despite the role it plays as a core concept in the context of monotheism. For many Hebrew school teachers, pulpit rabbis, and ministers, it's enough if they can convey the idea of just *one* God.

Not that monotheists do such a great job of understanding their own beliefs. Some of the most devastating blows to monotheism are self-inflicted. Consider that the formal Jewish education, such as it is, of an overwhelming majority of non-Orthodox Jews culminates with their bar/bat mitzvah, prior to eighth grade at best. Christians in many denominations fare no better, generally concluding their religious studies soon after confirmation, if that. Imagine if we were to similarly abandon our children's secular education at age thirteen. This bizarre, self-defeating approach to religious training is not the only problem. Mainstream Jews and Christians are both intellectually and spiritually shortchanged when they learn the tenets of monotheism about human relationships without any serious grounding in the sacred texts. They are similarly shortchanged when the focus is so much on the words of the texts that any meaningful connection to the way we conduct our own modern relationships only comes as an afterthought.

It is impossible to understand monotheism without comprehending the Bible's worldview and gaining insight into the practices the Bible so emphatically opposes. The prohibition against idolatry is arguably the Bible's primary contribution to humanity. In exposing the seductive and persistent lies of idolatry and baring their oppressive consequences, the Bible offers in its place a just and rational view of God and man. It does so in a language that was comprehensible to the ancient Israelites, who lived surrounded by idolatrous practice. To us, who bring a modern sensibility to the text, the Bible seems sometimes very alien, even offensive.

This is all the more true since we today—whether monotheists, atheists, or traditionalists such as the contemporary Maori—have already so much inherited and taken to heart the Bible's message that we have difficulty understanding the nature of what it was actually combatting way back when. Yet, as I argue above and will explain below, understanding idolatry today is as relevant as ever. We will focus on the ancient Near East, the Middle East and North Africa, and Europe, where monotheism first challenged idolatry.[1]

---

[1] A note on the references for part one. The references in this section have two functions: sources for data and sources for arguments. This chapter refers to the many historical surveys that have been used to fact-check the historical data used to make my arguments. The historical argument or interpretations of these surveys do not however necessarily accord with the arguments I make in this section. The secondary historical sources that have been used as a source for my arguments are mentioned explicitly in the text as well as referred to in the endnotes.

CHAPTER 1

The Prison of Idolatry

Wander through the Egyptian galleries at the Metropolitan Museum of Art, ponder the graceful curves of the Greek amphorae at the J. Paul Getty Museum in the Malibu Hills, lose yourself in the epic tale of *The Odyssey*, the heroic Icelandic sagas, or the lyrical verses of Arabic love poetry and it's easy to imagine that the ancient world was as culturally advanced and enlightened as our own. Consider some of the accomplishments of civilizations in the ancient Near East and Mediterranean. They created cuneiform, built the pyramids, authored tragedies like *Oedipus Rex*, invented philosophy, and devised Hammurabi's Code and Roman legal systems. They recorded celestial phenomena in astronomical catalogs and calculated from multiplication tables on clay tablets. We may live in an age of digital tablets and Mars Exploration Rovers, antibiotics and internet, but it's important and intellectually honest to acknowledge that our advanced society is founded upon and continues to be inspired by the ancient world's dizzying array of achievements. At the same time, and despite our tendency to often romanticize and identify with the ancient world in our popular entertainments from *Gladiator* to *Vikings* and *Xena: Warrior Princess*, it's important as well to recognize that these societies were very different from our own. A fundamental abuse of power pervaded the very structure of these societies.

The myths, gods, laws, and wisdom of each ancient society reflected the priorities of that group's local elites. They reflected, too, an inherited body of archaic beliefs about the power of natural processes. Despite the cultural gulf between ancient civilizations, between the empire of ancient Babylon and the chiefdoms of ancient Scandinavia for example, broadly similar patterns emerge regarding the nature of the gods, man, and the world and the relationships existing between them. These patterns reveal that those select few who comprised the elite of idolatrous societies developed a systematic body of lies and propaganda integral to maintaining their hold on power and imprisoning the people in a false reality. The false reality became so entrenched that both the oppressors and the oppressed thought it was true.

The Fictional Prison Guards of Idolatry

The elites of the ancient Near East commandeered ancient gods for political purposes. The first gods were imagined as the spirits of places and natural processes.[1] As the societies in the region became more organized, leaders refashioned gods in their own image for their own gain.[2] By the time of the Bible, the ancient Near Eastern gods in Mesopotamia, Egypt, and Canaan were projections of the earthly rulers who described them[3] in the myths they wrote and guarded.[1]

These fictional gods competed fiercely to assert dominance in the heavenly court just like their counterpart earthly kings. In Mesopotamian mythology, for example, the god Marduk battles his rival Apsu.[4] Ancient Near Eastern peoples did not trust their gods, who could make your crops flourish or kill your cows in spiteful punishment if they felt neglected,[5] or even if they just felt like it.[2] They also randomly abused others simply because they could. The Canaanite god Baal, for example, was rampant in his lust for bestiality and incest.[6]

The gods of other nations were often no better role models. Our appreciation for marble statues of physically ideal Greek gods in luscious gardens should not fool us. Zeus inspired the Giant Porphyrion with a mad passion for Hera so that he could kill him with a thunderbolt as he raped her. With this "operation," Zeus thereby takes his place as king of the gods.[7] The warrior elites of the Germanic and Celtic world created

---

[1] Berman, *Created Equal*, chapter 4. Berman explains how Mesopotamian myths were written by and for the elites.

[2] In ancient Mesopotamia, the gods were represented as essentially unreliable and capricious. Holland, *Gods in the Desert*, 188.

gods whose personal traits reflected their own claim to power: battle prowess. Most Irish goddesses, whatever their primary role, were also deities of war[8] just in case! Of all the gods in the Germanic pantheon, Thor, the god of war, was most popular by far.

Thor deserves our attention for a moment. Our main sources about Thor mainly reorder the Norse pantheon and their exploits along classical and Christian models.[9] Hence, Thor's father becomes one of the twelve chieftains of Troy![10] This reworking of ancient Norse idolatry explains how Thor has been turned into one of the "good guys" in comic books and Hollywood movies, when, to those who worshipped him in actuality, he represented domination by military might. Today, amazingly, children can buy Thor dolls in Disney stores, and this once savage warrior is depicted on screen as a sympathetic superhero who would "rather be a good man than a good king"! (Full disclosure: I also fork over twenty-three dollars to see Marvel's *Avengers* films in IMAX.)

In sum, the gods of ancient idolatry were akin to comic book thugs with superpowers and a readership who believed the fiction to be a reality. But here's a crucial detail—like human rulers, these gods were not all-powerful and were subject to fate, an arbitrary force that organized the hierarchical order of the world.[3] The idea of fate, thus, both justified the injustice of the world and discouraged people from imagining an alternative.

The True Prisoners of Idolatry

Propagandizing for political purposes, ancient Near Eastern elites likewise adapted and manufactured myths about the nature of humankind. According to one Mesopotamian myth, human beings were created with one intention only: to serve and attend to the gods. Thus, gods could enjoy unhampered eternal leisure and engage in unmitigated mischief.[11] But when, like some raucous crowd of Saturday night revelers at a bar below a bedroom window, the humans grew too boisterous and noisy, disgruntled gods sent a roaring flood to destroy them.[12] Yet as floodwaters

---

[3] The notion of fate is an important feature of ancient religions. Some ancient cultures, like the Etruscans, were particularly focused on it. See Michelle Renee Salzman et al, *The Cambridge History of Religions in the Ancient World* vol. 1 (Cambridge: Cambridge University Press, 2013); and Holland, *Gods in the Desert*.

failed to exterminate all the denizens of earth, the gods devised infertility and disease in order to limit the human population. Surviving mortals were expected to serve the gods with increased trepidation if they hoped to avoid divine wrath.[13]

The Greek gods acted no differently. In the words of Homer: "Thus have the gods spun the thread for wretched mortals: that they live in grief while they themselves are without cares; for two jars stand on the floor of Zeus of the gifts which he gives, one of evils and another of blessings."[14] And, most importantly, not all men were created equal. Great leaders could not only claim descent from the gods directly; they might also, like the pharaohs of Egypt, be or become gods themselves. At the very least, the leaders and priests enjoyed a special relationship with the gods and a privileged place above other men.[15] Even Plato, for all the thought he gave the matter, divided men by the quality of their souls, acceding to the bias of an ancient myth.[16] Man's inequality was just another way that fate ruled man. And fate conveniently ascribed to the elites their place in the social hierarchy of men.

A Self-Serving Code of Conduct

The elites in ancient idolatrous societies unabashedly established laws that would reinforce their own power. Ironically, the problem societies faced was not lawlessness but rather the injustice of the law. Law codes in Mesopotamia—such as the Code of Ur-Nammu (ca. 2060 BCE) attributed to the king of Ur; the Code of Lipit-Ishtar of Isin (ca. 1934–1924 BCE); or the famous Code of Hammurabi—as well as the later codes of Greece and Rome, provided widely different punishments for similar crimes depending upon the social status of the criminal being charged.[17] Financial laws were manipulated so that the state (i.e., kleptocratic kings) possessed the power to seize people's assets, even their children, as penalty for default on a loan.[18] Loans themselves were outrageous: exploitative interest rates reflected a cunning loan shark ruthlessness and could be as high as 20 to 33 percent.[19] (Where is the Consumer Financial Protection Bureau when you really need them?) Ancient Near Eastern kings not only wrote the laws—no one claimed that, like the Bible, they were divinely revealed—but they then appointed the judges who administrated the courts.[20] Among the tribal societies of Northern Europe and

13

pre-Islamic Arabia, where elites had not reached such heights, the tribal councils of elder men decided the law.[21] Indeed, everywhere, the legal system reinforced a powerful patriarchy.[4] In both the ancient Near East and in the classical world, fathers had the power of life and death over their children according to the law.[22] The Greeks of Sparta added their own special flourish for infanticide by dispassionately throwing their children off of cliffs.[23] In Athens, women had no legal personhood at all. In polytheistic Northern Europe, women fared somewhat better, but it is a fantasy to think that more than a harem's full were warriors like Queen Boudica or the legendary shieldmaiden (the Viking women who may or may not have fought alongside men).[5] Legal, political, and social equality between men and women was simply nowhere to be found in idolatry's mindset or moral landscape.

Prison Rituals

The earliest forms of idolatrous worship were popular and widespread across the community, but, by the time of the Bible, ancient Near Eastern worship fell under the control of kings and priests.[6] These hierarchs held sway over centralized cults, the purpose of which was essentially to provide flattery and bribes to the gods as one would to a fearsome king. All costs, of course, were paid for by the plebs, and much of the offerings was pocketed by the priests.[7] People still venerated personal and household gods, but the ruling class made it clear that the central cult was what really mattered, and they gave their gods prime real estate in magnificent temple complexes.[8] The ancients did not just fashion statues of their gods as symbolic artifacts; they truly believed that living gods inhabited these statues.[24]

---

[4] For more on women in the ancient world, see Sharon L. James and Sheila Dillon, *A Companion to Women in the Ancient World* (Malden: Wiley-Blackwell, 2012).

[5] For women in ancient Northern Europe, see Barry Cunliffe, *The Ancient Celts* (Oxford: Oxford University Press, 1997); Malcolm Todd, *The Early Germans*, 2nd ed. (Malden: Blackwell Pub., 2004); T. Douglas Price, *Ancient Scandinavia: An Archaeological History from the First Humans to the Vikings* (New York: Oxford University Press, 2015); and Judith Jesch, *Women in the Viking Age* (Woodbridge: Boydell Press, 1991).

[6] Worship was especially centralized in the ancient Near East, even compared with other ancient civilization. See Salzman,*The Cambridge History of Religions in the Ancient World.*

[7] Though individuals might still have fireside idols, the temple worship was what counted.

[8] See the essays on the Sumerians, Assyrians, Babylonians, and Egyptians inSalzman, *The Cambridge History of Religions in the Ancient World.*

Legions of priests encouraged this belief by means of an elaborate charade of washing the mouths of idols, dressing and feeding these statues, and providing them with glittering entertainments, multicourse banquets, and musical performances. No one ever actually saw the idols eat, since they would only do so behind a curtain—yes, an essential part of the ritual, of course.[25] These ancient gods could be voracious in their appetites. A daily meal for the god Anu in the city of Uruk might include, among other nourishment: twelve vessels of wine, two vessels of milk, 108 vessels of beer, 243 loaves of bread, twenty-nine bushels of dates, twenty-one rams, two bulls, one bullock, eight lambs, sixty birds, three cranes, seven ducks, four wild boars, three ostrich eggs, and three duck eggs.[26] If the priests failed to show proper strict submission or neglected a ritual, the people could expect calamity visited upon themselves and their community.

The widespread ancient idolatrous practice of human sacrifice also served to reinforce the elites' domination over people's lives. The pharaohs of Egypt expected to maintain their lavish royal lifestyle in the underworld by pre-ordering the murder of slaves, servants, and even officials to keep them company in the afterlife, the so-called retainer sacrifice.[27] In Mesopotamia, this was accomplished by officials who drove sharp pikes into the heads of unenviable court musicians, slaves, guards, and courtiers so that these members of the retinue could enjoy the privilege of continuing to provide their services to their king in the netherworld.[28] (A fate that would sorely test the loyalty even of Bruce Wayne's devoted butler Alfred.)

Nor did Greece and Rome, the second birthplace of Western civilization, exhibit any qualms in this regard. The Celts, in what is modern-day France, conducted human sacrifices, hoping to persuade the gods to preserve the lives of their soldiers in battle, the irony of their practice clearly eluding them.[29] Germanic tribes around the Elbe would take their earth goddess for a jaunty drive in a cattle-drawn cart, after which the slaves who washed the dusty wagon would be promptly drowned.[30] In addition to such divine sacrifices to the gods, the power elite of these idolatrous societies performed retainer sacrifices as well. An Arab chronicler writing about the Norsemen, for example, describes a "lucky" servant girl who, before accompanying her master to a fiery death on his funeral pyre, was first allowed to drink herself silly and sexually cavort with as many people as she liked before, in a drunken stupor, she was simultaneously strangled and stabbed[31] (since clearly one form of murder would not do). The Qur'an, too, in Surah 6:137 mentions the practice of child sacrifice among pre-Islamic Arabian tribes, though here, thankfully, we are spared the gory details.

That Old Black Magic

Magic was another deceit the elites used to assert control over the populace. Magic is a core element of idolatry, which wreaks havoc on society. Egyptian rulers, for example, habitually employed displays of magic for purposes of controlling everyone and everything around them.[32] It's hardly surprising, then, that pharaohs and priests kept the secrets of their supposed magic close to their tunics.[33] Pyramid texts record how pharaohs practiced ritual cannibalism to ingest the magical powers of others:

> *The king orders sacrifices, he alone controls them,*
> *the king eats humans, feeds on gods,*
> *he has them presented on an altar to himself,*
> *he has agents to do his will. He fires off the orders!* [...]
> *The king eats their magic, he gulps down their souls,*
> *the adults he has for breakfast,*
> *the young are lunch,*
> *the babies he has for supper,*
> *the old ones are too tough to eat, he just burns them on the altar*
> *as an offering to himself.*[34]

Whether pharaohs actually ate humans or not, the fact that they proudly proclaim to do so is bad enough. Nor did "the glory that was Greece, the grandeur that was Rome," those great classical forebears of Western civilization, break the black magic habit (although there, it was less in the hands of elites). Curse tablets were a particular favorite. One of the more amusing curse tablets I've come across originates in the Roman city of Bath in present-day England. It prosaically curses the people who stole a bather's clothes.[35] Ancient Norsemen had their magic, too. Some favorite weapons of Viking warrior leaders included hag-riding, possessing someone else's body and eyesight, and the raising of corpses.[36] Warriors also used magic "war-fetters" to paralyze their enemies (this might actually have been a sonic technique disguised as magic).[37] In both cultures the elites tried to hold the reins of magic, though its use was widespread beyond their circle. For example, Nordic societies frequently killed women for practicing black magic.[38] More broadly, magic wreaked havoc with man's relationship with the world and the development of the ancient mind. As will be explored further in part four, belief in magic impeded the development of reason and discouraged people from relying upon their own rational observations about the world.

O Oracle, My Oracle

Divination was another technique used to exert power and insidiously reinforce oppression. In ancient Egypt, consulting oracles was an essential aspect of decision-making.[39] Like medical doctors practicing their specialties and subspecialties today, the ancient Mesopotamians were "certified" in unique forms of divination. Historians have named some of these: *extispicy* (the reading of organs of sacrificed animals); *lecanomancy* (interpreting signs in water in a dish); *libanomancy*, also known as *knissomancy* (interpreting incense smoke); and *aleuromancy* (observing heaps of poured flour).[40] (Note to the reader: if your spouse is a historian, I suggest *you* be the one to name the kids.) Zealously guarding the means of interpreting the will of the gods greatly reinforced the power of the priests who recorded and reported the divine messages.[41] To understand the seriousness of these circumstances, try to imagine our global leaders handing over their decision-making and political power to telephone psychics.

The Romans had their own personal favorite divinatory style: bird-watching.[42] Before undertaking any important enterprise, Roman custom required the formal sanction of augurs, priestly bird-watchers. The famed Roman lawyer Cicero described the augurs' power:

> There are many forms of religious authority in the state, but the highest and supreme authority is that of official augury. For what power, legally considered, is greater than the ability to dissolve assemblies and councils appointed by the highest authorities in possession of their full powers, or to rescind the decisions of those bodies? What authority carries more weight than the augur's power to dismiss any undertaking, simply by saying "Postponed to another day"? What power is greater than deciding when consuls must resign from their office? What power is more sacred than that of granting or withholding the right of assembly to the people and

the plebs? Indeed, without an augur's authority, no act by a magistrate either at home or in the field has validity for anyone.[43]

Cicero also claimed that the Arabians' tribes were accomplished bird-watchers.[44] A similar obsession with divination pervaded Northern Europe. Germanic tribes loved divination with marked twigs.[45] A large number of women claimed to have psychic abilities and worked magic to see into the future.[46] As in many polytheistic societies, Scandinavian women performed ceremonies of trance seership.[47] In essence, divination was an attempt by the powerful to trick the fate to which human beings were subjected. In practice, it gave rulers a false sense of control, reinforcing their megalomania and buttressing the influence of the priests.

Prison Pecking Order

So how did all these lies start, and why did they stick? Originally, chieftains established dominion by means of very earthly power strategies. They accumulated wealth, allies, and military strength so as to destroy their opposition.[48] As chiefdoms grew into states, however, the kings retained power in two ways. They maintained these political strategies and justified their rule through the myths about the relationships of gods and man[49] described above. In Egypt, attributing divine character to the king meant that he was "the only human" being who mattered.[50] He then acted that way. Pharaohs of old certainly exploited the people economically in the name of their special status. They mustered forced labor simply to build overblown mausoleums, where they hoped to be magically catapulted into the abode of the gods after death.[9]

The palace and temple held most of the real estate and therefore controlled the means of production, the source of economic power.[51] The king collected taxes from the people to sustain the palace and the temple for his own benefit and that of the priests. The priesthood not only relied on similar myths but created an aura of power with their magic and costly illusions. With elaborate rituals and tricks worthy of David Copperfield, these holy men hoodwinked the people (and likely even themselves) into

---

[9] While historians are no longer of the opinion that the pyramids were built strictly by slaves, they believe that builders owed labor to the pharaoh. Mark Lehner, *The Complete Pyramids* (New York: Thames and Hudson, 1997).

believing in fabricated gods. The ancients understood the power of pageantry well before Hollywood rolled out its red carpet. Once in power, as we've discussed, the elites justified the culture of oppression they created as divinely ordained. In the ancient world, the common folk, not to mention the slaves, had little by way of defense against such structural domination. The people's only raw power strategy against their rulers seemed to be to rise up in rebellion. They sometimes did rise up, but usually at great cost and loss.[10]

In Greece, the elites had a harder time establishing their hegemony, though not for lack of trying. Unlike their counterparts in the ancient Near East, Greek rulers were initially unable to carve out large-scale empires. Instead, the Greek islands were ruled at first by petty kings. They soon turned into oligarchies after nobles devised political strategies to monopolize rule. Though divesting power from the king, these nobles withheld independent rights from the poor and the otherwise disenfranchised.[52] Still, even the oligarchs' rule did not go uncontested. The aristocracy's oppression of the Athenian people led to civil war.[53] The Greek reformer Solon restored the peace by cancelling all debts of the impoverished and setting up assemblies. These gained concessions formed the basis of Greek democracy. Further reforms followed in the wake of struggles between the people and the aristocrats.[54] The elites' lack of total power explains why Greek religion, unlike ancient Near Eastern religion, was never a state cult but rather a city and civic one.

Yet, despite the limitations imposed upon them by circumstances, the elite families still basically ran the city (polis). Voting privileges were only available to those citizens who had completed military service.[55] Further, slaves (30 percent of the population), along with foreigners and women, were excluded from citizenship altogether. Greek myths describe class differences and extol the exploits of heroes. And while they say less about royal and priestly connection to the gods, they still reflect the privileges of elites. The appeal Athenian democracy held for the elite class of men

---

[10] In the ancient world, some slaves revolted—as did oppressed peoples such as the Jews during the Roman period for example, as did common people. Wikipedia has a useful list of ancient revolts and rebellions: Wikipedia contributors, "List of Revolutions and Rebellions," *Wikipedia, The Free Encyclopedia*, en.wikipedia.org/w/index.php?title=List_of_revolutions_and_rebellions&oldid=839151797. See also Jack A. Goldstone, *Revolutions: A Very Short Introduction* (Oxford: Oxford University Press, 2014), which includes a section on revolutions in the ancient world.

who enjoyed its privileges was undeniable. How's this for nine-to-five? A wealthy male Athenian citizen could start his day at the gym, indulge in sex (often with a preadolescent boy), enjoy a hot bath and massage, spend the afternoon hours discussing deep philosophical ideas or debating local politics, and return home to his wife (herself rarely permitted to leave the house) for some marital sex and a wine-soaked feast served by his large estate's staff of many slaves (with whom, well—why not?—he could have a nightcap and even more sex).[56]

But the Greeks hardly stuck by democracy for long. Alexander the Great of Macedon came along, traversed the Mediterranean to India, and created one of the ancient world's largest empires. Rather pleased with himself, he proclaimed his desire to be honored as a god.[57] But then, as fate and a high fever would have it, he died. As for the tribal societies of Northern Europe, don't let anyone hoodwink you into thinking they were any more egalitarian. Kings were able to impose themselves among a number of Germanic peoples as the embodiment of a divine ancestor.[58] Not that this always worked in the kings' favor. Anglo-Saxon kings were meant to bring luck to their people as mediators between heaven and earth, but if their luck failed, they were executed.[59] The elites' relative power in establishing hegemony is reflected in the idolatrous myths of ancient peoples.

Despite mixed results in establishing total political domination, all ancient elites championed the institution of slavery. Inhabitants of Italy who predated the Romans would force the slaves of recently deceased masters to do battle to the death and then be buried with their master.[60] This practice was a likely precursor to gladiator fights.[61] The Romans themselves, of course, famously enjoyed cheering on slaves and criminals as they were being mauled to death by wild animals, and these same Roman citizens, done with the work of attending circuses, thought nothing of raping slaves in their leisure time.[62]

Prison Annexation

Ancient idolatry deified its leaders, glorified their power, and held the little people in contempt. It fostered expansion and constant warfare.[63] King Sargon of Akkad (24th–23rd century BCE) desired ores for the production of metal goods, so he simply decided to conquer and steal the lands of others. You think he could have tried his hand at trading goods for metal like a civilized fellow. His court chroniclers wrote of Sargon's "splendor": "[Sargon] had neither rival nor equal. His splendor, over the lands it diffused. He crossed the sea in the east. In the eleventh year he conquered the western land to its farthest point. He brought it under one authority. He set up his statues there and ferried the west's booty across on barges."[64] These types of leaders knew no rules of war, no Geneva Conventions, no bounds. From Akkadians to Assyrians, Babylonians, neo-Assyrians, and neo-Babylonians, every single ancient empire waged unjust offensive wars of conquest. They committed mass murder, enforced displacement, and even wholesale genocide.[65] Carrying their own gods with them into battle, they would frequently steal their victims' gods as a sign of victory.[66] This ancient version of capture the flag was fatal to the loser. Wandering Hittites even invented germ warfare—or, in contemporary parlance, bioterrorism—by releasing infected sheep into the territories they conquered.[67]

The ancient Greeks and Romans, for all the laurels of culture with which their Western heirs have crowned them, exhibited an undiminished appetite for conquest and domination. And why not? Hadn't the gods promised victory? Weren't foreigners lesser beings than themselves—*barbaroi*, as the Greeks called them? Even before Alexander's empire, the Greek city-states fought incessant and costly wars. The Romans for their part, on the global path to conquest, would ritually beseech local deities to change sides and come join Rome.[68] If the local deities proved reluctant, more's the pity, as Caesar may have shrugged when he destroyed the sacred grove near Marseilles.[69] During the time of its empire, Rome experienced virtually constant military expansion and civil war.[70]

Similarly, the Celts and Germanic peoples invaded and conquered for booty and slaves. In other words, they stole and murdered others for a living. The ancient Viking warriors known as berserkers were notorious for a chaotic fighting style, inspired by indulging in copious amounts of alcohol and hallucinogens, which serves as the origin of the English word "berserk."

The pre-Islamic Arabian tribes, of whose gods and mythology we know much less, specialized in violent anarchy. This disordered host of tribal groups and clans, each with its own gods, reveled in vendettas, internecine quarrels, and attempts to dominate one another.[71]

But not all was lost.

The Philosophers' Football Rematch:
The Greeks Against the Gods[11]

Ancient Greek philosophers used common sense and reason to criticize the gods. Elites of the ancient Near East, as far as we can ascertain, maintained their traditions of idolatry until foreign invaders decisively put an end to their cultures. And as to the oral hunter-gatherer societies or agricultural chiefdoms on all continents, without records we may never know who criticized those gods before the arrival of monotheism. The philosophers in Greece, in contrast, took a different tack, as did philosophers in India and China at roughly the same time and likewise through reason, though a discussion of Hindu theology, Chinese Philosophy, and atheism is beyond the scope of this book.[72] Even before the appearance of the two giants of Greek philosophy, Plato and Aristotle, the pre-Socratics—men such as Thales and Anaximander—argued, based on observations, that the world operated by certain fixed laws. As historian of science Andrew Gregory shows, many of these thinkers held views close to pantheism, which attributes a soul or intelligence to nature.[73] We shall explore the connection between science and the concept of one God in more detail in part four. More germane to the discussion about idolatry right now is the view of the Greek playwright Aristophanes. According to Aristophanes, the gods were not real entities but rather irrational human projections: "The gods, my dear simple fellow, are a mere expression coined by vulgar superstition. We frown upon such coinage here."[74] The philosopher Xenophanes pointed out that the gods of different peoples tended to mirror the personality characteristics of those very peoples.[12] Unsurprisingly, Plato was not fond of magic, that bread and butter of so many idolatrous elites. He insisted that magicians were a low-life sort of people and demanded that they be strictly regulated by laws. Playwright

---

[11] For the original match, please see the Monty Python sketch "Greece vs. Germany, Monty Python Philosophers' Football Match." The sketch can be viewed on Youtube. https://www.youtube.com/watch?v=7E_8EjoxY7Q.

[12] For an exploration of the Greek philosophers' critical view of the gods, see Jon D. Mikalson, *Greek Popular Religion in Greek Philosophy* (Oxford: Oxford University Press, 2010); and Tim Whitmarsh, *Battling the Gods: Atheism in the Ancient World* (New York: Alfred A. Knopf, 2015). Mikalson emphasizes the concessions the philosophers made to religious customs despite their criticism, and Whitmarsh distinguishes between materialist critics of the gods and Plato and Aristotle, who cannot be considered atheists.

Aristophanes and the epic poet Homer also found occasion to poke fun at oracle-mongers.

In place of the unjust and irrational pantheon of Greek mythology, these philosophers imagined one omnipotent and omnibenevolent God. Xenophanes espoused a belief that "One God, greatest among Gods and men, entirely dissimilar to mortals in nous and body."[75] He thus maintained that this God comprehended all things within himself, moved all things, and, most significantly for the ancient world, bore no resemblance to human beings. Both Plato and Aristotle endorsed a connection between the notions of absolute intellect and absolute good with a notion of Godliness, and even, to varying degrees, a concept of one God.[76] For Aristotle, absolute good and absolute intellect are part of the essence of God; for Plato they are the highest principles.

Plato's and Aristotle's rational and just vision of God mirrored a similar vision of the ideal society.[77] Idolatrous elites described an ideal world as one in which they got to rule for their own benefit. To achieve this, they would con people into serving a panoply of gods and control society at large by maintaining an occasionally prudent political leadership. In contrast, both Plato and Aristotle connected the notion of a good society with the idea of justice based on the "common good." Plato's *Republic* is concerned with the definition of just actions and a just city-state.[78] Likewise, Aristotle's *Politics* inquires into individual and collective justice.[79] From both we learn of abuses of royal, aristocratic, and popular power. Both philosophers concluded that a just society must be based on good *for all*, not just on the selfish interests of an elite. That being said, Plato also believed that a just society would be ruled by philosopher kings, an elite group of its own. Though elitist, Plato's society would be marked by access to the truth about what is just and good for all. For Plato, universal good was the natural result of all people exercising their specific talents and roles in harmony. Aristotle advocated a "mixed constitution," a combination of aristocracy (the rule of aristocrats) and polity (the rule of the people) under law. Despite a lingering elitism, both philosophers saw the law playing a central role in keeping the elites in check within their proposed just societies. Plato considered the state subservient to the law. Aristotle argued that people became just by following the law. Plato's and Aristotle's views of humankind prevented them from advocating total political equality. However, their preoccupation with a just society for all based on rational reflection and the rule of law was eons away from unfettered elite hegemony. Yet, the rejection of the gods could lead in another direction.

Some philosophers not only rejected the gods, they discarded the divine and the just, touting instead the virtue of brute human power. James Thrower suggests, in his history of Western atheism, that the same rejection of idolatry that led many to the concept of one God and universal justice led other philosophers to become radical skeptics.[80] Protagoras not only rejected the gods, but he and other Sophists claimed that *nothing* was absolute. The naturalistic, anthropocentric, and relativistic vision of the Sophists also affected their view of justice. They considered the law to be nothing more than an expression of either the arbitrary will of the ruler or the will of the strongest party.[13] According to Plato, for example, the Sophist Callicles argued that justice was not natural. First, because it differs so radically among different peoples, and second, because it conflicts with wisdom, which urges us "to rule over as many people as possible, to enjoy pleasures, to be powerful, to rule, to be a lord."[81] This new skeptical criticism of idolatry had much in common with the critique of scholars inclined toward a more monotheistic view, such as that of Plato and Aristotle. However, as Plato himself would explain, the Sophists' view could lead to radical moral relativism and worship of power that also resulted in the banishment of justice.[82] These philosophers shared the focus of idolatry's elites on power as the ultimate objective in life. They simply saw no need to justify it by recourse to supernatural phenomena.

It is amazing how the ancient Greeks, by force of pure reasoning, came to anticipate most of the fundamental issues that we still grapple with today. One God makes most sense, certainly better than many. At the same time, the power of reason, while it can expose the falsehood of idolatry, can also lead to a "logical" abandonment of all morality. As with the *Monty Python* sketch, the match goes to the Greek philosophers.

Before we return to our history of the cradle of monotheism, we must take a small detour to the Far East. The epoch that saw the flowering of Greek philosophy also saw the appearance of the great philosophers

---

[13] Plato is a great critic of the Sophists' cynicism. See Balot, *Greek Political Thought*, 189. See also John M. Dillon and Tania Gergel, *The Greek Sophists* (London: Penguin, 2003).

of the East, including Confucius, Laozi, and Siddhartha Gautama, aka the Buddha. And like Greeks, who influenced the entire Christian and Muslim world, their ideas would cross nations from India to Japan, from Thailand to Korea, at much the same time and continue to be influential today. This success is no accident. In the words of Bishop Murphy:

> The human heart is seeking to know who he or she is, where they came from, and where they are going. Sometimes they put together a pretty high set of standards by which they live. The Buddha did that. In all great religions, the more deeply you study and go into Hinduism you realize that there is an innate human stirring to know, a foundation there that has some extraordinarily wonderful ideals. Confucianism is the same—you go through the whole thing to discover that the human heart is always seeking.

Although there is no place to discuss the matter here, the great philosophers of India and China espoused teachings that, like those of the Greeks, lessened the idolatrous nature of ancient Chinese and Indian society and increased social justice.

But whether in Athens or in China, the reasoning employed by philosophers was not enough to emancipate the world from idolatry or to create a just society. Monotheism arrived on the scene in the form of the Bible. It, not Greek philosophy, would bring the rejection of idolatry to the masses, though not without difficulty.

Humanity's Lowest Common Denominators

We have focused above on the presence of idolatry in the Middle East and Europe, as these regions are the cradle of monotheism. But idolatry is the default mode of humanity; it is like a sinister melody with many variations around the globe. The tribal Vikings' penchant for human sacrifice can be found in pre-Buddhist Tibet as well, or among tribal peoples in Iroquois country. The Aztec Empire, like the Babylonian, promoted ritual murder of human beings. The pugnacious Celts might have found their match fighting the Maori and other Polynesians, not to mention the Zande in Central Africa. They might have given the Mongols, too, a run for their money. Nor were the Apache ones to shrink from a good fight.

25

As for imperialism, it's hard to choose between the Greeks and the Aztecs. I mean, is it better to sacrifice tens of thousands of people to strengthen your empire or to wage wars of conquest and declare oneself a god as Alexander did? Across the world, the animistic beliefs of hunter-gatherer societies often gave way to those personified gods that the elites used in order to maintain power. Some of these societies, like those in Greece or in ancient Sweden, nonetheless maintained a relatively egalitarian political structure. Others quickly became highly hierarchical societies distinguished by nobles and kings, as in medieval Japan, China, and the Inca Empire. But nowhere did these societies—not even those that produced wisdom literature or proverbs exhorting kings and chiefs to act magnanimously—preach human equality before the law.

Polytheistic peoples across the world also produced wisdom, as we have seen with two major non-Abrahamic classical Indian religions—namely, Hinduism and Buddhism. Thus the Vedas speak of Brahman, the source of all.[83] Buddhism teaches about karma, that our actions have consequences.[84] The same can be said for Taoism and Confucianism as well as for wisdom traditions in smaller agricultural societies such as the Igbo in Nigeria and the Pueblo peoples of the Four Corners. The forms of idolatrous societies around the globe have been as varied as has been their level of injustice, deception, and inequality, but all defended to a greater or lesser extent the domination of elites (whether pharaohs of great empires or chieftains of smaller clans) based on lies about power. While animist hunter-gatherer societies across the world from Africa to Oceania, from South America to Siberia tended to be more egalitarian than idolatrous chiefdoms and kingdoms, these cultures were nevertheless mired in magic and divination, often controlled by shamans. Further, they did not develop the principle of equality before the law or juridical structures, which often led to violence as a means of conflict resolution between individuals and groups.[85]

Prison Has Its Appeal

So why did idolatry last so long? Despite the rampant injustice and abuse in idolatrous societies, these cultures still held some attraction. For the elites, the advantage was obvious. Even if they were at times to fear the gods of their own making, the notion that service and sacrifice would appease them reduced the anxiety. Certainly, on occasion, all was not rosy for the elites. They might be overthrown at any moment by rivals or, more rarely, by underlings or the people at large who understood the game, but, for the most part, once acquired, power only begot more power. Even the folk who toiled for the elites found that idolatry had a certain appeal. As Steven Pinker argues in *The Better Angels of Our Nature: Why Violence Has Declined*, ancient idolatrous states like Egypt or Babylon proved much safer for people than the more egalitarian animistic hunter-gatherer societies that battled and murdered at alarming rates, since the states used their power to create order even when that order was based on an unjust hierarchy.[86] Some elites tried to better the people's lives out of self-interest. Not all ancient leaders were brutal tyrants. As mentioned, many books of wisdom from the ancient Near East, not to mention proverbs from around the world, encouraged kings to act with prudence and good will toward their people.

Early cults of nature spoke to man's sense of wonder at the natural world. The privilege of honoring and sacrificing to spirits of place and the ability to worship natural processes gave the common people a sense of control over a worryingly uncertain world. Colorful festivals in honor of the gods added a spirit of zest, fun, and diversion to otherwise drab lives. In ancient Rome, crowds attended breathtaking chariot races as part of religious services. Or they attended high-spirited festivals dedicated to the god Mars with the same enthusiasm you might find today at a college football game or a Radiohead concert.[87] Celtic Iberians enjoyed all-night dance parties following the sacrifice of a wild animal outdoors under the spell of a glowing full moon.[88] In pre-Islamic Jordan, singing girls were the toast of elaborate banquets.[89] In addition, people believed that their gods, oracles, and magic would provide them with benefits if they were careful in their performance of the appropriate rituals. If the gods would reveal the results of a battle beforehand, all the more power to you. But since the people believed that the gods could only be won over with sacrifices, then the alternative seemed rather grim. Indeed, the Romans came down hard on Christians precisely because they feared that the adherents of the new religion were offending the gods. Such an insult jeopardized the empire of Rome. Idolatry worked its circular logic. Few had the courage to confront it openly.

The ancient world, from Egypt to Scandinavia, was a livable, albeit often horrible, place. Idolatry held a strong appeal and indomitable influence, and its chains would not be cast off without a revolution. If idolatry, thus, seemed to be the default mode of humanity, it would take a forced reset to change that mode.

CHAPTER 2

The Prison Break

*When you present the idea of one God, it actually causes friction
and challenges the powers-that-be.*

—CHAPLAIN TAHERA AHMAD

The great innovation of the Bible was to challenge the lies about
power that defined ancient idolatry. The story of the Exodus was
that challenge. As the Bible tells it, the migration of the descendants of
Jacob to the center of the ancient world, Egypt, served God's ultimate
purpose. It led to a confrontation between the Israelites and what was
then the greatest idolatrous nation of the time in the greatest showdown
in history. In the narrative, the actions each of Joseph, Moses, and God
in sequence directly contest the idolatrous worldview of the Egyptians.
God's revealed laws at the time of the Exodus were meant to provide a
blueprint for a just society. Unlike what Yuval Harari claims in *Sapiens*, or
Steven Pinker writes in *The Better Angels of Our Nature*, the Exodus (and
the entire Bible for that matter) is not like any other ancient idolatrous
myth in the service of selfish elites. One would never know, though, from
their writings, or from those of other atheists, that many scholars hold
this view. Thus for those who want a challenge to this widely held but
demonstrably false perspective (and many false ideas have had a long
shelf life, even among very clever people), this chapter is for you. For
skeptical readers, the question of whether the events of the Bible could
have occurred will be addressed in part five, but even if they did not, the
message is still revolutionary.

Exodus: Liberation Demonstration and Performance Art

The Exodus story actually begins in the Book of Genesis with the story of Joseph. Sold by his brothers into slavery and left to rot in an Egyptian jail, Joseph came to bring the first ray of light of Abrahamic monotheism to the rest of the ancient world. Having been told of Joseph's gift for interpreting the dreams of his cellmates accurately, Pharaoh offered Joseph an opportunity to take his talents to the palace. Dream interpretation was a form of omen-reading familiar to the priestly classes, but Joseph was quick to distinguish between his outlook and that of the court magicians:

> And Pharaoh said to Joseph, "I have had a dream, but no one can interpret it. Now I have heard it said of you that for you to hear a dream is to tell its meaning." Joseph answered Pharaoh, saying, "Not I, but God will see to Pharaoh's well-being." (Genesis 41:15–16) Joseph continued to explain how, through the dream, "God has told Pharaoh what he is about to do." (Genesis 41:25)

Joseph's intent was to chip away ever so subversively at the magicians' power by introducing the idea of God's omniscience and Pharaoh's subordination to God. Jacob's other sons soon settled in Egypt where, initially, they lived in peace and multiplied thanks to Pharaoh's magnanimity and sense of indebtedness to Joseph. However, as the Bible records, with Joseph's death, a new pharaoh quickly and all too conveniently forgot his predecessor's debt of gratitude to Joseph and to God. (Reminds me of some folks I met on Wall Street.) The new king, as idolatrous leaders do, began to exert his power through abuse and enslavement of the Jews under the pretext that they had become too numerous and might rebel. (Exodus 1:10) He decreed death to all newborn Hebrew boys and enlisted the entire Egyptian population, fearful and compliant, in his murderous plan. Nonetheless, an independent-minded Pharaoh's daughter (likely skeptical of her father's divinity) was unafraid. One day she plucked out of the water an Israelite boy hidden in a basket among the reeds and raised him in the palace.

Only two others, both Hebrew midwives, feared God's power more than Pharaoh's and refused to murder the children. But when the midwives had to answer to Pharaoh, they did not argue that it was wrong to murder the infants. They simply pleaded that they had been thwarted by the speedy birthing methods of the Israelite mothers who just kept popping them out (Exodus 1:19), while the midwives only arrived in time to collect the fee. Had they protested more openly, they would have been executed. Pharaoh's lust for power and its accompanying political and social ills were in full swing. Unbeknownst to him, though, his daughter had brought into the royal household an infant who would grow into the royal house's greatest adversary. "Moses," she had named him. The monotheistic revolution that would see full bloom when the child grew to adulthood, though as of yet underground, had now begun.

Ultimately, Moses would challenge Pharaoh to let the Israelites worship God. Egypt turned into the scene of an awe-inspiring demonstration project against idolatry—think Super Bowl, World Cup, and Olympics all rolled into one. Moses became the center of this revolution. Unlike today's slick politicians, he was neither arrogant nor a great public speaker. He needed no Gallup Organization to poll-test his platform. Moses had guts. He dared to question Pharaoh, the god-king, in the name of the one true God, and all for the sake of a slave population, no less. Moses's staunch opposition to the status quo, in favor of the lowest of all social groups and in the name of the one all knowing, all powerful, and all good God, undercut the presumed legitimacy of Pharaoh's oppressive political and social system. Pharaoh refused and refuted Moses as expected, charging, "Who is the Lord that I should heed Him and let Israel go? I do not know the Lord, nor will I let Israel go." (Exodus 5:2) Pharaoh understood only his own will and power.

The showdown had begun and God's purpose was clear. The Biblical text is explicit—the Israelites' deliverance from the Egyptians had a two-fold purpose: that both Israel (Exodus 6:6) and Egypt should know that "I am the Lord." (Exodus 7:5) As events unfolded, Moses began demonstrating God's power through signs and wonders. This strategy was necessary to prove the extent of God's strength, or omnipotence, to a society obsessed with magic. And it worked, with tragic results. Pharaoh refused God's request and therefore allowed his own people to be harmed. But even more shockingly, he asked his magicians to harm them a second time to show that they were just as powerful as God. The competition between Moses and the court magicians ended with the magicians unable to replicate the plagues. (The Bible was so allergic to magic that, as we shall see in part four, Moses lost his right to enter the land when he gave the false impression of drawing water from a rock by magic, by failing to invoke God's name.) Yet Pharaoh still did not relent, and so God punished the Egyptians measure for measure for their complicity in upholding such an idolatrous society. The plagues, thus, delivered a foreboding message to the Egyptians in the very heart of world idolatry: your Pharaoh is not a God. The one true God exacts retribution for abuse of power against others for gain. Those who do not oppose idolatry in fact support it.

After the last of the plagues, the Israelites feasted on slaughtered lamb, considered an Egyptian deity, and thereby put a nail in the coffin of Egyptian idolatry. But, according to Jewish tradition, this demonstration of divine power was still not enough for Pharaoh. Only when his army drowned in the sea did the king of Egypt finally admit defeat. Each step along the way in the process of the Exodus undermined the idolatrous matrix of Pharaoh's deifications, the priests' power, and their combined oppression of others. In the end, freedom defeated domination, justice overwhelmed raw power, and human initiative coupled with divine assistance dispelled the myth of fate.

Yet, even the disruptive message of the Exodus was insufficient to inculcate the Israelites, the Egyptians, or bystander nations with this revolutionary new worldview. Idolatry remained too powerful in the imagination and served too many interests. Thus, to further propound the message of monotheism, the one God soon revealed to the Israelites the laws and teachings that make up the content of the Bible. The idea was simple enough. The Israelites would follow these laws and teach the rest of the world their moral efficacy through example. Among the first of these revealed laws came the Ten Commandments. They were short and snappy, easy for the Israelites to remember. Once learned, they were intended to be applied unreservedly to all circumstances of life and society.

The first of the Ten Commandments, according to Jewish tradition, is the declaration that God brought the Israelites out of Egypt; the second (or first in Christian traditions) is a blanket prohibition against idolatry. This ban against the worship of "other gods" also appears as one of the traditional seven Noahide laws applicable to all humankind. No, the prohibition against idolatry is not, as Dawkins would have us believe, the narcissistic hissy fit of a jealous god and eternal egotist disguised as a divine decree. It is, however, perhaps the most radical and definitive dividing line that could have been drawn in the ancient world. It is the line between one true, just, and all-powerful God and a numberless host of fictional deities created in the image of the fickle pharaohs and flawed elites for their own benefit.

The commandment begins with the prohibition of the worship of another god. "I the Lord am your God who brought you out of the Land of Egypt, the house of bondage. You shall have no other gods besides Me." (Exodus 20:2–3) This interdict ensured that mortal beings remembered that the only God worth worshiping is all good and all powerful, not subject to whims, self-serving, and bound by fate. The commandment continues by forbidding the Israelites in the most concrete way from attempting to fashion statues of gods in the image of powerful men, the very essence of idolatry. The third commandment prohibits oppression under the false guise of God's will. Taking God's name in vain in this way is idolatry in another form. Far too many *monotheists* in history have aped the claims of idolatrous priests and god-kings who attempted to rule others by asserting a special conduit to God's desires. So, yes, when atheist writers criticize this dangerous manipulation of monotheism, you'll certainly find me singing in their amen choir.

Extreme Makeover: The God Edition

The Bible created a theological revolution. The God of the Book of Exodus enters history as the antithesis of the gods of idolatry. Unlike the gods of the Egyptian pantheon, fashioned in their own image by a political elite eager to justify their hold on power, the God of the Exodus proves to be just in essence and consumed with justice for everyone. The proof? God liberated the enslaved Israelites from the oppression of the Egyptian elites. God sought to liberate the Egyptians themselves, elite and common folk alike, from their own idolatrous ways by giving them the chance to release the Israelites of their own free will. When Pharaoh not only refused God's request (calling on his magicians to replicate the first two plagues against the Egyptian people), and when the people in turn still did not rebel (knowing of their leader's insane attack against them), God took away Pharaoh's free will and punished the Egyptians through ten coercive plagues. Just as the Germans and Soviets did not rebel en masse against Hitler or Stalin, the Pharaohs of their day, since they either could not imagine such a rebellion or feared to do it, so too the Egyptians acquiesced to their own suffering. More than anything, the God of the Exodus serves as a model of just and liberating power in contrast to Pharaoh's unjust and imprisoning power. The difference between the God of the Bible and idolatrous gods becomes even clearer when we examine God's relationship with man.

There is no reciprocal relationship, for example, between the gods of ancient Near Eastern myths and the dwellers on earth. These gods toy with common folk at their will; on occasion they might develop a liking for a particular mortal who has attained power and privilege. The God of the Bible, on the other hand, has give-and-take bonds with commoner and king, rich and poor, enfeebled and empowered, and develops reciprocal pacts with all of mankind. These pacts are called covenants. The first is made with all of mankind after the flood, when God commands Noah and his sons to be fruitful and multiply, not to commit murder nor condone those who might. (Genesis 9) In return, God vows never to destroy mankind or the world again. In the covenant with the Israelites after the Exodus (Exodus 19–24), God promises they will become a kingdom of priests and a holy nation—a nation privileged only in that it will possess the capacity to teach others by example, if its own people keep God's laws. Neither of these two covenants serves the particular interests of any given leader or class.[1] Nor even, as we shall see in more detail in part two, do they privilege any given nation. On the contrary, both are established in such a way that human beings can only keep their side of the bargain if they adhere to laws requiring them to treat others justly. There you have it—God's reciprocal connection with man, based on a whole new understanding of human dignity and worth.

Liberated Man

The Bible's revolutionary new view of man is heralded front and center when, in the very first chapter, humanity is created in no less than God's image. If in ancient Mesopotamian myths, man is created as a lowly afterthought, a deck boy to the leisure-loving gods, in the Bible men are created to "share in his glory and his dominion over the world,"[2] in partnership with God.[3] But, more to the point, all men and women are created in God's image. Not that the Bible did away with sexism, the

Faiths and Societies in the World in 1000BCE

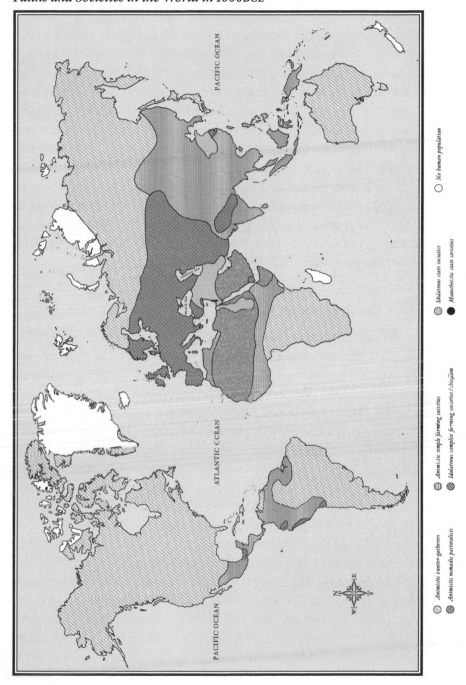

oldest hierarchy in the world. (We will address this issue in part two.) Still, the point remains that both men and women accepted the covenant with one God. The Bible does not multiply its origin stories like alternate comic book universes. No biblical human being descends from a goddess like Aphrodite, none are children of a divine ancestor, no one belongs to a special race of otherworldly beings. Because all people are of common ancestry, no one individual can lay claim to some privileged relationship with the gods because of pedigree. Similarly, given this view of mankind, no one group or nation stands to gain political advantage or power based on birth. Instead, what we find here is the foundation for an egalitarian order based on just relations[4] rather than a hierarchical society based on abuses of authority. There are those who might bring up the old canard, protesting (wrongly as I will show) that Abraham became the father of a racially superior "chosen people." To them, I ask, hold that thought for part two as well.

A Free Community

The Bible initiated a profound political revolution. It subordinated all people to the same law by limiting the influence of the power elite. Whereas, as we have seen, idolatry pointed to mythology to justify continued dominance by the elite, the Bible, on the other hand, painted a picture of a society where all people were bound to the covenant of Noah and, later, all Israelites became equally bound to an extended covenant with God. There were no exceptions made for kings or priests, blue bloods or VIPs, and no extra-charge Disney FASTPASS Service to skip lines.

In fact, the very concept of a king originally existed only at the fringe of acceptability in the Bible. The Israelites did not initially have a human monarch. When the people later appealed for one, acquiescence to their choice was couched as a concession to the weakness of that generation and not as an ideal. The Israelite model of kingship that finally emerged was sharply limited. The king was as equally obligated to abide by the laws of the Torah as any of his people. To use a contemporary term, he was a constitutional monarch. What a contrast to the neighboring nation-states in the ancient Near East, whose kings regulated the laws to accord themselves monopoly of all power.[5]

To emphasize this point, the Bible required every monarch to own a Torah scroll and read from it daily:

> When he is seated on his royal throne, he shall have a copy of this Torah written for him on a scroll by the levitical priests. Let it remain with him and let him read in it all his life, so that he may learn to revere the Lord his God, to observe faithfully every word of this Torah as well as these laws. Thus he will not act haughtily toward his fellow or deviate from this commandment to the right or to the left, to the end that he and his descendants may reign long in the midst of Israel. (Deuteronomy 17:18–20)

In addition, as a built-in curb to any Israelite king who might have been bitten by a bug for royal arrogance, the palace was answerable to the prophets. These visionaries and moral voices of their generations were themselves kept in check by strict laws.[6] They also coexisted with the separate power base of the high priest. This mandated arrangement was the original form of what Americans recognize as the system of checks and balances for a government. When an Israelite king violated these strictures, his whole royal line could be removed or punished. Such was the case with Saul, who inaugurated and lost the first kingship. Years later, Rehoboam, the son of Solomon, forfeited his reign over ten of the tribes of Israel because of his arrogance toward his subjects and his unjust taxes. Thus, while not living in a democracy—since the majority could not legislate their own laws—the people of ancient Israel did possess an ultimate voice in politics and a veto over the kingship. They were also held responsible as a collective for the types of leaders who came to rule the nation.[7] Inspired by the Bible's call for higher allegiance to the King of Kings, the community could derive strength not only to identify and oppose oppressive leaders, but even to rebel against them on grounds of principle.

The Bible also reined in the power of the priestly class. They were forbidden to own land, could not be appointed kings, and were not permitted to hoard tithes for themselves. Further, a whole independent construct was added to the power structure—namely, a system of courts. Judges were appointed by the people[8] independently from tribal or class affiliations. And they held office outside of the authority of either the king or the priests.[9] Judges, too, had to follow a divinely ordained law code, one that was beyond royal or priestly manipulation.[10] Finally, the Bible also challenged a form of power seen in tribal societies—namely power-sharing arrangements that were limited by kingship and tribal supremacy. In contrast, the Bible rejected tribal hierarchy and extended citizenship to all Israelites.[11] The most amazing part of the famous story of Solomon deciding on splitting a baby claimed by two prostitutes was that two prostitutes were allowed in the palace at all. The Bible, thus, broke the monopoly over political power of the elites in both idolatrous states and idolatrous tribal societies. Women became prophetesses, leaders, and judges in Israel's history, though women's unequal role within the Bible's governing structure is also a topic we shall address in part two.

The Bible also empowered all men economically. By contrast, the elites of idolatrous nations established themselves as the class to whom others owed tribute. They used their economic dominance to also ensure political dominance. This abuse was justified by recourse to idolatrous mythology and maintained by effective strategies of power. The Bible, for its part, uniquely and humanely upends the whole notion of one class of people that produces without enjoying while a second class benefits without working. First and foremost, the Bible provides for economic equality. It ensured that its citizenry came into possession of land and was able to remain economically secure.[12] Neither king nor priest owned large tracts of land in the Bible.[13] In addition, no land is fully salable in perpetuity, though land is held by individual families and even women can inherit land. As a result, the risk of monopoly is all but eliminated, as is the potential for political injustice resulting from it.[14] Even slavery, often a consequence of failure to repay debt in the ancient world, is strictly regulated in the Bible, though not abolished outright (another topic we will address in further detail in part two). What greater contrast is there to the monopoly of land by king and priest in the ancient Near East?

The Bible's view of taxation is also radically innovative. Rather than collecting tribute payments for the sole benefit of the elite, the Bible offers a model of taxation dedicated to meeting social needs and purposes.[15] Furthermore, the Bible taxed everyone, no exception.[16] Biblical laws forbade charging interest, a proud token of civic sensibility and communal responsibility.[17] Again, what a contrast this presents to the elites of the ancient Near East, who charged up to 30 percent interest.

To cite one last example, though I could go on, in the Bible debt release was mandated every seven years. This law was not created as a means for the political leadership to buy off the people,[18] but rather as a means to ensure that no permanent underclass should develop.[19] Whereas the elites formed the nucleus of power in many idolatrous societies, there is simply no word to designate "class," "caste," "noble," or "landed gentry" in the Bible.[20] As Joshua Berman writes, the Bible created "a law based society with curbs on the corruptive influence of power as an integral part of the system."[21]

The Free Man's Rule Book

The Bible created a legal revolution by protecting all members of society. The first difference between the biblical laws and the laws of idolatrous societies is their putative source. Whereas rulers in ancient idolatrous societies created their own laws, which ranged in character from the very cruel to the reasonably just, biblical law was considered divinely ordained. This was true not only for the biblical laws pertaining specifically to the Israelites but for the Noahide laws as well, the universal code of moral behavior that God expected of humanity. The Noahide laws, or Seven Laws of Noah, imparted an absolute legal standard to which all nations continued to be beholden. As a result, they markedly influenced the development of modern international law, as will be explored further in part two. The biblical concept of law as divine revelation[22] thus further limited the power of the king and other possible usurpers to control or change the law.

And let's not forget, we are talking here of the Bible. Not only are all people, commoner and king alike, equally beholden to the law, but the very content of the law reinforces the equality of all human beings before God. The clearest example of this is the fact that, according to the Bible, murder of a human is considered a crime, no matter the status of the person who was murdered. (Leviticus 24:17)[23] Further, the law applied to Israelite and non-Israelite residents alike,[24] just as it applied to all humans after the flood. The biblical code even made important provisions for strangers, who found themselves among the most vulnerable people in other cultures. No statement is repeated more often in the Bible than the reminder to the Israelites of their obligation, "Be kind to the stranger because you yourselves were strangers in Egypt." As will be described in part two, even the laws related to the treatment of slaves and women, which indeed perpetuated several inequalities, nonetheless significantly improved the lot of these two groups compared to other cultures of the time. The egalitarian nature of the Bible's vision even extended to the people's access to the laws themselves. In contrast to legal texts in other parts of the ancient Near East, the Bible was meant to be available and taught to all Israelites.[25] As the text itself prescribed, "Write down this poem and teach it to the children of Israel." (Deuteronomy 31:19) The entire nation, and not just the elites, was meant to know God's laws and transmit the culture.[26] And the purpose for doing so is clear—in order that the people become a metaphorical kingdom of priests. As Berman writes, in the biblical view a "kingdom of priests" means a "holy and educated nation."[27] The fact that the Bible is written in an alphabetic and not symbolic script makes it that much more accessible.[28]

Not that biblical law was totally rigid. Times change, economies and technologies change, and laws need to evolve as well. The Bible permits laws to change with the times, provided the changes are grounded in the precepts of the Almighty God. In Deuteronomy 17:9, the Bible counsels to go to the judges in charge "at the time." The law codes of the ancient rabbis are replete with references to laws that used to be implemented one way but were later modified. These innovations occurred due to changes in society or as adjustments to different norms in different geographical regions. The Bible thus envisioned a balance between the concept of universal, divinely revealed absolutes and a necessary mechanism for adapting them.

A Temple of Freedom

Last but not least, the Bible brought about a cultic revolution. True, the Bible did prescribe sacrifices, a common practice among idolaters in the ancient world. However, the biblical sacrificial rituals were much more limited in scope than those of the neighboring polytheistic religions. In the view of some ancient and medieval Jewish commentators, the Jewish sacrificial cult existed only in concession to normative expectations of the surrounding cultures. The Bible limited the stuff of sacrifices to produce and farm animals that were relatively low in cost. Each Jew was expected to donate the modest sum of a half shekel per year to the Temple, and there was a tax to the priests of about 2 percent, not an excessive sum. (Parenthetically, the larger 10 percent, or tithe, that was taxed was used to pay Levite teachers and ritual stewards for their communal activities.) Sacrifices were intended to atone for certain sins or to express thanks; they were never meant to appease God's anger through gastronomic bribery. Further, the human participants on the giving end of the sacrifices were often on the receiving end as well. For the immediate families of participants consumed the overwhelming majority of the meat, such as from the Passover and *chagigah* offerings. Priests ate most of the rest. Very few of the sacrifices were fully burnt on the altar. Jewish law also was diametrically opposed to the sexual nature of many rituals that accompanied the sacrificial practices in idolatrous societies. It required anyone going to the Temple to be purified from sexual activity or emissions via the *mikvah* (ritual bath) and to wait overnight before being allowed to enter.

Every few weeks, "watches"—groups of priests from across the nation—made their way to Jerusalem for stints at the Temple. No one group of priests held the Temple under its total control. While, clearly, some permanent supervising priests were always on hand, even the high priest was guided by the high Jewish court, the Sanhedrin. All in all, the sacrifices served theological purposes such as atonement, purification, thanksgiving, or commemoration of holidays. They symbolized the constant devotion of the Jewish People to God via daily sacrifice, every morning and afternoon. There is simply no record in the Bible of any sacrifice brought manifestly to induce any specific behavior on the part of God. Most importantly, sacrifices were never the main means of divine service. Unlike the many gods of idolatry who demanded appeasement from wayward humans, the one God of the Bible sought positive social relations founded upon ideals of justice. The words of Isaiah could not ring more clearly:

> "What need have I of all your sacrifices?" says the Lord. "I am sated with burnt offering of rams, and suet of fatlings and blood of bulls; And I have no delight in lambs and he-goats" [...] Learn to do good. Devote yourself to justice. Aid the wronged. Defend the orphan. Fight for the rights of widows. The Bible declared, "Justice, justice you will seek" (Isaiah 1:11, 17)

Contrary to what atheist authors argue, monotheism is not just another idolatrous superstition. The Bible provided nothing less than a template for a radical revolution in how man related to God, other men, and the world. In place of a hegemony of elites, the Bible called for the common good. (For those readers who object, saying the Bible actually privileges men and Jews, please hold off until part two.) This new template, as we shall now see, has changed the world, though through a very long, uneven, and complicated process.

CHAPTER 3

3,300 Years In and Out of Prison

When the Israelites form the calf because Moses was busy talking to God, they decided to create their own god, and what happens when we create our own gods? We become slaves to them.

—BISHOP WILLIAM MURPHY

It's Not Easy Being Free

Despite the Exodus and God's laws, both the Bible and archaeology provide evidence that the Israelites continued to worship idols. The overwhelming appeal of idolatry and the root impulses that nourish its practice is a topic we shall discuss in part three. For the moment, suffice it to say that even the Israelites, who had suffered miserably under the idolatrous Pharaoh only to be liberated by God, were still not immune to its attractions. Despite periods of unity and faithfulness to the law, Israelite kings were especially vulnerable to the wiles of idolatry. Ahab, the king of northern Israel, and his infamous wife Jezebel brought Baal worship to the Northern Kingdom, where the Prophet Elijah preached against their evil ways.[1] For despite the Bible's exhortations, many of Israel's kings were not immune to power politics as the numerous palace coups recounted in the Book of Kings attest. Nor were the monarchs always just in their attitudes and ways. In chapter 12 of the Book of 1 Kings,

God told Rehoboam not to contest the will of the people, who sought lower taxes and more lenient labor requirements. Rehoboam ignored the Lord and chose to follow his advisers' counsel instead, rebuffing the people and increasing their burdens. The Prophet Amos railed in the mid-eighth century BCE against the exploitation of small farmers by the wealthy. This was proof positive that the biblical ideals of equality and justice had not taken deep root among the Israelites of that time.[2] Prophets of the First Temple period warned the Israelites of their idolatrous ways and of their injustice. The Israelites would not listen. According to Jewish tradition, the Israelites suffered exile to Babylon for breaking the covenant, as the Bible had warned. Even in exile, the Israelites were slow to learn their lesson. The Book of Esther recounts how the Jews exiled to Persia participated in banquets, during which King Ahasuerus used utensils taken as booty from the Temple in Jerusalem in order to mock Judaism. The benevolent Persian emperor, Cyrus, who conquered Babylon and much of the ancient Near East and central Asia, however, allowed the Jews to return, rebuild the temple, and exercise autonomy, though not sovereignty.

During the Second Temple period, the Jews initially rededicated themselves to following God's law, but failed again to uphold it. Jewish tradition recounts that the Israelites, who now called themselves Jews,[3] accepted the law a second time, under the leadership of the Prophet Ezra. After his defeat of the Persians and conquest of the area of Israel (333 BCE), Alexander allowed the open practice of Jewish laws.[4] However, this state of affairs did not last for long. By the time of the Maccabees, the title of high priest could be bought from the Greek rulers, as occurred with Jason.[5] An ensuing fight between Jason and an even more radical priest, Menelaus, led the Hellenistic Greeks under Antiochus IV to clamp down. He prohibited the Jews from following their own laws and compelled them to serve the Greek god Dionysus.[6]

The Jews loyal to the law were not, however, defeated. Resistance coalesced around the Hasmonean family, who rebelled against their overlords.[7] This victory is celebrated in the Jewish holiday of Hanukkah. Yet under Simon, the Hasmoneans usurped two roles by becoming both high priests and political leaders.[8] (One descendant, Aristobulus, would later declare himself king.)[9] The problems continued. Sectarian factionalism became rampant. Jews fought each other over the meaning of the law.[10] The Essenes withdrew altogether from society, certain that the end of the world was nigh. The people were equally divided into two camps. There were those who wished to ingratiate themselves to their imperial and idolatrous overlords, first Greek and then Roman. And there were those who wished to follow exclusively in the ways of the Bible. Ultimately, the idolatrous Romans would not tolerate the expressed loyalty of the Jews to God over Rome.[11] The Romans besieged Jerusalem, destroyed the Temple, and ended any and all semblance of Jewish self-rule. By 130 CE, Hadrian had built a pagan temple on the very spot where the Jewish Holy of Holies once stood. Idolatry had vanquished monotheism, or so it seemed. Yet, by the time the Romans had crushed the Jews, the message had already spread differently.

First Escapees Out of Rome

The Jews failed to fulfill the creation of an exemplary society founded on biblical law. However, they experienced greater success in spreading the message of monotheism, both directly and indirectly. As noted earlier, Greek and Roman philosophers had developed ideas of their own that resembled biblical concepts of God, man, and justice. In addition, after the Bible had been translated into Greek via the Septuagint, it became better known.[12] A number of Greek and Roman philosophers also made the connection between the one God of the classical thinkers and the God of the Bible.[13] Others, who had encountered Jews, personally praised their laws,[14] justice,[15] and wisdom,[16] and the leadership abilities of Moses.[17] Of course, many philosophers scorned monotheism. Apion, in particular, would repudiate the Jews for mocking the gods[18] and allege that Jews hated those outside their faith.[19] Jewish thinkers who had close ties to the Romans, such as Josephus, sought to counter these attacks.[20]

Philosophers were not the only ones intrigued by the Bible. Many people in the Roman Empire became "God-fearers."[21] These were people who had not gone through a formal conversion to Judaism but who embraced a monotheistic worldview. According to Louis Feldman, the overall number of God-fearers is unclear, but they were numerous. Judaism owed its appeal to the Jews' high regard for the law, their ethical behavior, their philanthropy, and their functioning community.[22] Some Romans even turned to Judaism as a protection against magic![23]

These Romans recognized and appreciated the superiority of monotheism's moral and social codes over idolatry's systematic irrationality and social injustice.

Despite the advance of monotheistic ideas, Rome's encounter with Judaism did not transform the empire. The God-fearers constituted only one of many groups in an empire awash with a myriad of religious groups and attitudes, ranging from Stoicism to mystery cults, whose name reveals about as much as we know of them. Christianity began as a Jewish sect but later, after the innovations of Saint Paul, opened its doors to all people. This move shifted Christian leadership from Jewish apostles to Roman bishops and preachers. In retrospect, this last innovation was the crucial step in bringing monotheism to the world's attention. Still, a growing interest in monotheism among some Romans was hardly going to uproot idolatry, especially among the leadership who benefitted from it most. The period of the first century was a time of heightened emperor worship. And while the second century was more stable, the third saw increasingly drastic forms of abuse of power and violence.[24] Between the time of the first flowering of popular monotheistic movements, especially Christianity, in the first century CE, and the final Christianization of the Roman Empire in the fourth century, polytheism and various forms of monotheism coexisted. Sometimes this coexistence was peaceful and sometimes it was bitter, hostile, and deadly. Some Roman emperors, Diocletian for one, attempted to eradicate the Christians by wholesale destruction of churches and beheading of bishops.[25]

Only after Rome had become an officially Christian empire did monotheism's global revolution take hold. This revolution would lead to the spread of monotheism in the East as well, in the form of a second monotheistic empire, the Islamic caliphate, some three centuries later.

New Manuals for a Global Jail Break

For Jews and Catholics, for people of the book, we have a God who cries. We have a God who has a heart. We have a God who is as the father of the family who watches His children fighting in the backyard and saying "this is not the way it is supposed to be." So what does that give us? It gives us immense humility. This sense gives us tremendous sense of repentance and a constant seeking of

46

Spread of Christianity from 100 to 1500 CE

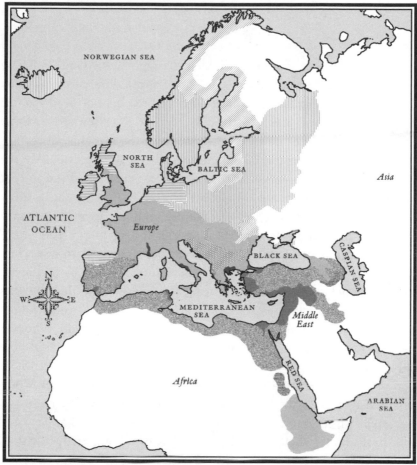

Nestorian Christians (Eastern Christians) expanded east from Mesopotamia to Iran, sending missions and establishing communities throughout central Asia to China as well as coastal towns in India from the 600 to 1500 BCE. These Christians had broken with the rest of the Christian world in 427 CE. Most Nestorian communities in Central Asia, China, and India collapsed by 1500. Only those in Mesopotamia remained.

● Christian by 100 CE, remains Christian

● Christian by 100 CE, but later becomes Muslim with Christian minorities or switches between Christianity and Islam

○ Christian by 400 CE, remains Christian

◉ Christian by 400 CE, but later becomes Muslim with Christian minorities or switches between Christianity and Islam

◉ Christian by 400 CE, but later becomes polytheistic and then re-Christianized

○ Christian by 800 CE, remains Christian

◉ Christian by 800 CE, but later becomes Muslim with Christian minorities

▥ Christian by 1200 CE, remains Christian

▧ Christian by 1500 CE, remains Christian

Jewish communities and/or Jewish merchants existed in most of the areas that were Christianised in this period. Though these communities were also expelled and subject to forced conversion at various times.

renewal because we know what happens when religion gets selfish or even cocky. That's when horrors start.

—TIMOTHY CARDINAL DOLAN

Christian Scriptures spread the Bible's message about God and man throughout the Roman world. The theological differences between Christianity's and Judaism's conceptions of God cannot be discussed here at length, and they are treated exhaustively elsewhere.[26] These differences should not detract, however, from the fact that Christianity drew heavily upon the Bible's message about God, particularly the first three commandments. Christian Scriptures confronted the gods of ancient cultures: "Since we are God's offspring, we ought not to think that the deity is like gold, or silver, or stone, an image formed by the art and imagination of mortals." (Acts 17:29) Their Scriptures urged Christians to reject idolatry and the submission it demanded: "Formerly, when you did not know God, you were enslaved to beings that by nature are not gods." (Galatians 4:8) Now, instead, the Apostle John described an omnibenevolent God: "Beloved, let us love one another, because love is from God; everyone who loves is born of God and knows God. Whoever does not love does not know God, for God is love." (1 John 4:7–8) The early Christians taught their followers that man lives in a world where God rewards the good and punishes the wicked, rather than a world capriciously ruled by fate. "For all of us must appear before the judgment seat of Christ, so that each may receive recompense for what has been done in the body, whether good or evil." (2 Corinthians 5:10) Christian Scriptures explained how God created all human beings from the same parents. "From one ancestor he made all nations to inhabit the whole earth, and he allotted the times of their existence and the boundaries of the places where they would live, so that they would search for God and perhaps grope for him and find him—though indeed he is not far from each one of us." (Acts 17:26–27) In the teachings of Jesus and the apostles, Christians could find reiterations of the Bible's model of just and equal relationships. The Christian Scriptures exhorted men to treat each other well and preached the lesson that all humans have value and deserve compassion: "Let love be genuine; hate what is evil, hold fast to what is good; love one another with mutual affection; outdo one another in showing honor." (Romans 12:9–10) Slaves, women, and common people could aspire to an afterlife of joy and freedom in the kingdom of heaven. Many took encouragement from the words of Saint Paul: "There is no longer Jew or Greek, there is no longer slave or free, there is no longer male and female; for all of you are one in Christ Jesus." (Galatians 3:28) Roman people joined Christian communities, which taught them the basic laws necessary for cooperative relationships. "The commandments, 'You shall not commit adultery; You shall not murder; You shall not steal; You shall not covet'; and any other commandment, are summed up in this word, 'Love your neighbor as yourself.'" (Romans 13:9)

The holy writings of Islam followed in the spirit of the Bible and the Christian Scriptures. The Qur'an, the central religious text of Islam revealing the word of God, echoes the Bible's view of God, man, and just social relations. As Chaplain Tahera Ahmad describes, "Consider Islam—the pre-Islamic Arabian Society was at the brink of utter chaos, clans were destroying each other in tribal warfare, and so Mohammad arrives on the scene; and this is the consensual understanding of Mohammad in that he comes in a time and place at the brink of destruction."

Historians agree, the Arabian Peninsula was in a state of flux, pagan rulers were trying to push back the influence of Christians from Ethiopia, and general instability affected the oasis region of Hijaz where the Prophet Mohammad was born.[27] The Prophet brought the message of the God of Abraham to the Arabian people through his teachings and the Qur'an. "Say, 'He is God the One, God the eternal. He begot no one nor was He begotten. No one is comparable to Him.'" (Qur'an 112:1–4) The Qur'an also presents an exalted view of man and spreads the notion that God rewards and punishes people based on their behavior toward others. "Goodness does not consist in turning your face towards East or West. The truly good are those who believe in God and the Last Day, in the angels, the Scripture, and the prophets; who give away some of their wealth, however much they cherish it, to their relatives, to orphans, the needy, travelers and beggars, and to liberate those in bondage; those who keep up the prayer and pay the prescribed alms; who keep pledges whenever they make them; who are steadfast in misfortune, adversity, and times of danger. These are the ones who are true, and it is they who are aware of God." (Qur'an 2:177) Its message of mercy also rings loud and clear: "Allah will not give mercy to anyone, except those who give mercy to other creatures." As Chaplain Tahera Ahmad explains, "Mohammad

Spread of Islam from 634 to 1500 CE

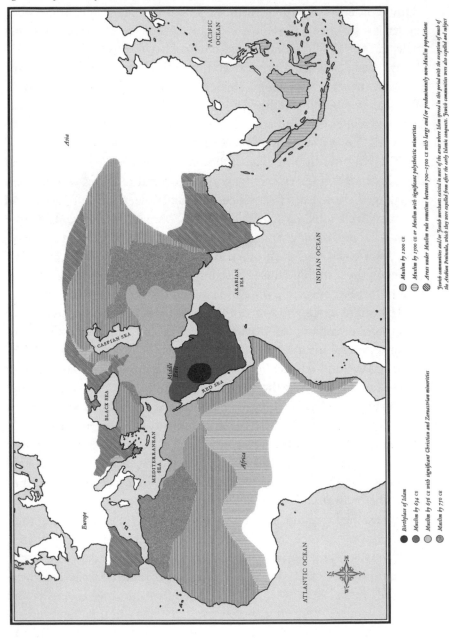

revived the message of Abraham and this is what the Qur'an in its early passages expands upon. That this project was about reviving humanity, and was about giving people equal opportunities. Not burying women alive for example, as was previously common and just the beginning."

Christianity and Islam changed how the ancients viewed the afterlife. Both Christianity and Islam communicated the message that the afterlife was a reward for a life lived according to ethical and moral precepts. This teaching had important social consequences as well. Chaplain Tahera Ahmad explains:

> For a mainstream Muslim to be considered a Muslim or be part of the tradition, the afterlife is one of the main tenets. The pagan Arabs of pre-Islamic Arabia did not believe in the afterlife. One reason that there was a resistance to the message of Mohammad was because he would say that the daughters being buried alive will ask for justice in the afterlife. That the infant female girl that you have buried alive, will ask for what sin was she killed. You have these big questions being asked of the men of the community about the way that they are treating the weakest members of society. And when they know that there will be an afterlife, they know that this all will come to justice. Then they stop committing these crimes.

Christianity and Islam so upended idolatrous concepts of God and man that we no longer grasp the transformation that they accomplished.

Early Christian and Muslim Scriptures rejected idolatrous notions about the gods and man, but, like the Bible, they did not eliminate all injustice and inequality. These remaining discrepancies would affect Christian and Muslim communities until our day. They would also frequently be invoked and, not surprisingly, even distorted by unscrupulous elites to bolster their own power. The Christian Scriptures, for example, displayed an even more ambivalent attitude to earthly powers than the Bible or the Qur'an. Some texts argued that "[…] 'We must obey God rather than any human authority'" (Acts 5:29), while others encouraged Christians to obey political leaders since they were "instituted by God" (Romans 13:1–5). In general, the apostles took a less political approach to justice and equality than the Bible. This would have lasting consequences. Though Saint Paul advocated equality before God, he also called on Christians to respect earthly power structures.[28] Christian ideas about slavery proved similarly ambiguous. The Scriptures spoke of the fact that man was always internally free (Galatians 3:28), but they also called on slaves to obey their masters (Ephesians 6:5). Masters, in turn, were encouraged to treat their slaves well (Philemon 15–18). Attitudes toward women were also ambiguous. On one hand, Saint Paul counsels that there is neither man nor woman in the Christian community. On the other hand, we have letters that call upon women to be subject to their husbands completely (Colossians 3:18). Similarly, we find the following in Saint Paul's own letter to Timothy: "I permit no woman to teach or to have authority over a man; she is to keep silent." (1 Timothy 2:12)

The Qur'an, too, includes equally mixed messages. Many passages reject violence against unbelievers, yet others specifically provoke it, as in Qur'an 8:12: "Your Lord revealed to the angels: 'I am with you: give the believers firmness; I shall put fear into the hearts of the disbelievers—strike above their necks and strike all their fingers.'" At the same time, we find the following verse: "There is no compulsion in religion: true guidance has become distinct from error, so whoever rejects false gods and believes in God has grasped the firmest hand-hold, one that will never break. God is all hearing and all knowing." (Qur'an 2:256) The Qur'an advised rulers to consult with the people in what is called the *shura* or consultation with people affected by a decision (Qur'an 3:159 and 42:36). Over time, the *shura* came to be interpreted by some as consultation with scholars alone. The Qur'an's view of women also presents an ambiguous message: "[Divorced] women have [rights] similar to their [obligations], according to what is fair, and [ex-]husbands have a degree [of right] over them: [both should remember that] God has the power to decide." (Qur'an 2:228)

Early Christian and Islamic Civilization: Close but No Cigar

The teachings of Christianity profoundly changed the Roman world. After the destruction of the Temple, the Jews were bereft of political power and would take a decidedly back seat to Christians in the spread of monotheism.[1] Christian groups organized at the grassroots level. They

---

[1] For a general history of the spread of Christianity, see Charles Freeman, *A New History of Early Christianity* (New Haven: Yale University Press, 2009).

erected hospices for the sick and orphans.[29] Early Christian communities may have also included both men and women leaders.[30] Christian ideas also led to greater economic equality in the empire, though only through voluntary action. Pious Roman nobles might give away whole fortunes[31] or, with lesser zeal, practice routine Christian charity. Constantine did not appoint Christianity the official religion of the empire. This would not occur until 380 under Theodosius. But he did sanction it, did favor the Christians, and did implement measures in accordance with Christian concepts of human dignity. Constantine banned infanticide[32] and demanded that the Roman state care for those children whose parents could not provide for them.[33] He also outlawed gladiator shows and subsequent emperors upheld this ban. As the Church expanded, Christian bishops not only preached to the wealthy but also spread the message to the lower classes.[34] Sources from that period indicate that Christian notions of equality and justice before God led to greater attention to the poor and to women.[35] By the seventh century, people from what is today Ethiopia to Ireland, Armenia to Saudi Arabia, were Christians. In Arabia in particular, where Jews, Christians, and polytheists mixed, the second global monotheistic religion was born thanks to the teachings of the Prophet Mohammad.

Islam transformed Arabia. The introduction of Islamic law curbed the exploitation of the poor and improved the treatment of slaves.[36] It limited polygamy and afforded women legal status. It sought to end the proliferation of false contracts and theft. Islam prohibited blood feuds in favor of payment in money rather than spilling of blood. And it led to the outlaw of practices such as female infanticide and adultery.[37]

Christians and Muslims officially banned many of the most egregious polytheistic religious practices, such as magic and divination. Yet they also, to their great credit and our great appreciation, preserved much of the Greek scientific and philosophical writings, something we shall have more to say about in part four.

Monotheists' Self-Sabotage

So we've now reached a point at which the three major monotheistic religions are on the map. On behalf of humankind, I would love to have been able to tell you here that, from this point forward, humanity began to work together for the benefit of all mankind. They cooperated in gratitude and acknowledgment of one omnibenevolent God, who everyone recognized in one form or another. I would love to have been able to go on saying that henceforth all monotheists recognized they were brothers and sisters…established equitable relations between each other without regard to race, gender, or differences in theology…inspired those outside the cradle of Judaism, Christianity, and Islam to adopt the tenets of equality of justice freely, while at the same time preserving their own cultural uniqueness.

Alas, as you know, that's not quite what happened. The reality is much uglier. But the reason is not what the atheists suppose. No, the reason is that too many monotheists did not truly embrace those first three commandments of the ten. No other gods. No graven images. No taking God's name in vain. Together, these three commandments represent one integrated idea, and that idea has to do with the usurpation of power in the name of gods or God. Arrogating such power to oneself always leads to a slippery slope of domination and oppression.

What follows is a brief summary of the messy history of monotheists. They paradoxically spread both justice and injustice down the corridors of time, and all in God's name. Perhaps a few lightning bolts striking down anyone who violated the first three commandments might have struck the fear of God in people and made history a lot neater? For the monotheist, the answer is no. As parts III, IV, and VI of the book will explain, from a believer's perspective, that sort of alternative would have derailed the whole point and purpose of humanity.

The problem started early on. Rabbinic commentaries exceed the Bible in sexist undertones[38] and in taking a conciliatory approach to unjust governments.[39] Both early Christian and Muslim thinkers sometimes exploited God's name and misinterpreted ambiguous passages in Scriptures as a means to bolster the power of elites. Saint Augustine, one of the most important Christian theologians during the Roman Empire, supported secular law with all its inequality in order to prevent anarchy.[40] Christian emperors no longer deified themselves openly. However, they did champion the idea that God had appointed them to a special status, one more closely resembling that of a Roman emperor than a biblical king.[41] Nobles held fast to their political privileges. In addition, although the early Christian church was quite egalitarian, by the fourth century, it too had developed a highly structured hierarchy inspired by imperial pomp and practices.[42] When the emperor officially adopted Christianity, he politically empowered and privileged the Church and its priestly class—most of whom were nobles anyway.[43] This development would affect the institution for the rest of its history.

In early Islam the picture is similar. Succession in the early caliphate is a story of murder and intrigue as three of the first four caliphs were murdered.[44] Later caliphates soon consisted of familial dynasties.[45] Ethnic and tribal ties still determined one's station within the empire, and non-Arab Muslims such as Berbers, Egyptians, Iranians, and others were given a distinct and inferior status as *mawla*[46] and expected to Arabize. These peoples responded in return by forming movements to preserve their cultures in a movement called Shu'ubiyyah. True, Islam demanded that rulers consult with scholars and the people in a process called *shura*, but this consultation became limited to the scholarly class.[47] Slavery continued to play a major role in the economy.

Early thinkers in both religions showed ambivalence towards nonbelievers, and the elites knew how to exploit such tensions for personal political gain. Unlike Judaism, which sought to spread monotheism by example, Christian and Muslim thinkers assumed a more proactive approach. Some strongly condemned forced conversions, while others were more tolerant of the intolerant practice, pointing to apparently contradictory passages in their Scriptures.[48] Harsh measures were enacted against idolaters in both Christian Rome under Justinian[49] and under the military expansion of the first three caliphates.[50] Suffice it to say that early thinkers of both religions developed an ambivalent relationship toward the Jews. They both officially tolerated the earlier religion, but each proclaimed its own respective and superseding superiority.[51] This particular conflict would continue to characterize relations between the monotheistic faiths for centuries to come. Jews, in turn, would adopt an ambivalent attitude to the religions that succeeded them, at times viewing them positively, at others condemning them.[52] That being said, judging by the members of society most likely to be subjected to oppression and abuse, a person was far better off in Christian Rome than in Imperial Rome and in Muslim Arabia than in pre-Islamic Arabia.

Christianity and Islam in the Middle Ages:
Still a Work in Progress

The expansion of Christianity and Islam during the Middle Ages improved the lot of the idolatrous peoples of Europe and Africa. Invasions by idolatrous peoples continued to devastate Europe and the Middle East in the course of this period. In northern France in the eighth century, Vikings created a state of virtual anarchy. The region now called Normandy took its name from these invaders, Norman being a variation on Norse men. The bishops and Christian kings of Europe absorbed and Christianized idolatrous peoples in the north and east, often by first influencing the king to convert.[53] In fact, vast swaths of Europe and many European peoples, including the Hungarians, Scandinavians, Slavs, Balts, and many Germanic tribes, did not adopt Christianity until the Middle Ages. In some cases, such as Lithuania, Christianity only took hold in the fourteenth century. Dehumanizing practices like infanticide and human sacrifice were then outlawed.[54] Throughout the Middle Ages, people of all stations could go to court to be heard.[55] Though still deprived of political power, Jews in both Christian and Muslim lands could, during good times, act as advisors to kings, though they acted at their mercy and for their benefit. Or they could hold, as did Rabbi Yitzchak of Troyes, friendly scholarly exchanges with Christian priests.[56] Christianization also shepherded the economies of these Northern and Eastern European peoples away from pillage and slave raiding toward mutually beneficial trade and self-sustaining agriculture.[57] In the medieval courts and cathedral schools in Europe and in the madrasas in the medieval caliphates, scholarship flowered.[58] Muslim traders brought Islam to West Africa and Indonesia during this period, where the kings and people largely adopted it voluntarily. However, Muslims, like their Christian counterparts, were not averse to waging wars of conquest.[59]

At the same time and in a less generous spirit, medieval Christian leaders and thinkers twisted religious ideas into support of greater power grabs on the part of the clergy and elites. European medieval kingdoms fell far short of the biblical model in their systems of justice and notions of equality. Society was now unashamedly divided among kings, a landowning elite, and peasants, the latter sometimes free, often serfs.[60] The medieval Church justified these inequalities by rationalizing that society was naturally divided between those who prayed, those who fought, and those who worked. Medieval kings engaged in endless wars between each other or against groups of nobles. One interminable period of hostilities lasted a whopping one hundred years. Medieval society's emphasis on the hereafter, public artistic displays of punishments of hell, and obscure, exhaustive arguments about the nature of God focused medieval minds elsewhere. These diversions thus effectively forestalled the true establishment of justice in the here and now.[61] The Church replaced pagan rites with many questionable practices, such as the multiplication of miraculous relics. There were enough relics of the "original" cross, for example, to make up hundreds of crosses. Selling indulgences—that is, bribes to get into heaven—was another medieval clerical invention. In their zeal to eradicate polytheism, Christian kings conducted bloody wars against idolatrous peoples in the north.[2] However, as the Middle Ages progressed, the clergy also became increasingly intolerant of Christian dissenters and other monotheists such as Jews and Muslims, leading to violent crusades in the south of France and in Germany.[62] The abuse of the nobility and clergy was such that peasants revolted in many areas in late medieval Europe.[63]

Islamic theologians and leaders were guilty of similar excesses. They too justified them as God's will. Even during Islam's golden age, social hierarchy reigned. Imperial ambitions did too: the Fatimid dynasty moved hundreds of thousands of Arabs into North Africa. The goal was to crush the political power and Arabize the culture of the Zirid (an Amazigh, often called Berber) kingdom in a form of settler and cultural colonialism. The Almohads conquered Granada in the twelfth century and forced the previously tolerated Jews and Christians to convert, leave, or face death. The Christians returned fire with the unashamedly named Reconquista.

Squabbling between emirs and sultans was typical of the Islamic Middle Ages. In the Indian subcontinent, the Muslim conquests were often brutal and violent. Scholars abused their clerical clout and intellectual talents to retroactively justify political assassinations via Islamic law.[64] Muslim slave trade was also in full swing during the Middle Ages,

---

[2] See Rosenwein, *A Short History*; and for a more detailed account, Anti Selart, *Livonia, Rus', and the Baltic Crusades in the Thirteenth Century*, trans. Fiona Robb (Boston: Brill, 2015).

offering masters a dizzying choice of humans for sale from as far as West Africa and the Ukrainian steps.[65] Still, small consolation though it may be—compared relatively with the violence and inhumane practices of idolatrous groups of the time, such as the Mongols and Vikings—the Abrahamic faiths improved the lives of most humans that came under their rule. Put simply, it was better to be an Irish milkmaid than a Viking sex slave. The forward march of monotheistic societies, though admittedly far too slow and extremely flawed, continued into the Renaissance.

Revising the Escape Plan and Liberating the World

In the fifteenth and sixteenth centuries, Christians, increasingly divided, used God's name for opposing purposes. On the one hand, many old elites sought to achieve new heights of oppression. On the other, intellectuals, merchants, and some common folk appealed to the Bible and reason to challenge Christian rulers' use of religion for their own gain.[3] Among the old elites, Catholic kings and popes grew emboldened by the exploration of the Americas to propose converting polytheistic peoples.[66] In actuality, this was little more than excuse for the conquest and exploitation of the new lands being discovered across the ocean. The papal bull Romanus Pontifex of 1455, which granted the Portuguese the right to grab land in Africa and enslave Africans and other polytheists, was a low point in Christian history. And yet, these pronouncements were made in the name of God—another sad and clear example of taking God's name in vain. In 1493, Pope Alexander VI asserted King Ferdinand and Isabella's right to claim dominion of the conquered lands. The Treaty of Tordesillas the following year somehow awarded the Spanish and Portuguese crowns the "right" to divide the non-European world between them. But just as Europeans were bringing a brand of Catholicism to millions outside Europe, the Church was about to face a massive challenge on its home ground.

A number of thinkers critical of the misuses of religion by king, nobility, and the Church itself turned to the Scriptures themselves to

---

[3] A great survey on religious movements in this period is R. Po-chia Hsia ed., *A Companion to the Reformation World* (Malden: Blackwell Pub., 2006); and William R. Estep, *Renaissance and Reformation* (Grand Rapids: Eerdmans, 1986). On the politics and society of the period, see Euan Cameron ed., *Early Modern Europe: An Oxford History* (Oxford: Oxford University Press, 2001).

raise the alarm. As none other than Michel Foucault writes: "[F]rom the second half of the Middle Ages onward, the Bible was the great form for the articulation of religious, moral and political protests against the power of kings and the despotism of the Church..."[67] After all, wasn't that what the Bible was always meant for? Already in the fourteenth century, theologians such as the Oxford-educated John Wycliffe advocated greater political equality and justice based on the Scriptures, which he had translated into English.[68] His followers became known as the Lollards and posted their manifesto, "The Twelve Conclusions of the Lollards," on Westminster Hall. In it they demanded, among other things, that the Church renounce its wealth and political power and that the priesthood be reformed. They also rejected the veneration of images and railed against the idolatry of the Church, claiming that "God alone was Lord."[69] The Lollards' radical challenge to the Church hardly endeared them to the ecclesiastical hierarchy. The Church in fact excommunicated them as heretics, though they had friends among anticlerical nobles. The Lollards' message was picked up in the early fifteenth century by a young Czech theologian named Jan Hus. He established similar groups in the Czech lands, called the Hussites. Hus not only criticized Church corruption—he rejected the sale of indulgences and questioned the legitimacy of the Crusades.[70] The Church, in turn, burned him at the stake.

But Martin Luther, a German monk, was already next in line.[71] Luther was eager to criticize the Church hierarchy, condemn the pope, denounce usury and indulgences, and demand a return to the teachings of the Bible. He did so by posting his manifesto, a somewhat more long-winded Ninety-Five Theses, on the door of the Wittenberg Cathedral. German peasants, chafing under the nobility's attempt to turn them into serfs, took Luther's message as a call to greater political and economic equality.[72] They produced a parallel manifesto, "The Twelve Articles." In it they demanded an end to unfair taxes established by the nobles; access to fish, game, and wood in common lands confiscated by the nobles; and access to real justice, not the arbitrary whims of the nobles. Unlike the Lollards and the more radical factions, Luther definitively redirected the bourgeoning Protestant movement away from political equality. He reaffirmed political hierarchy in his subtly named pamphlet, *Against the Murderous, Thieving Hordes of Peasants.*[73]

John Calvin, another Protestant reformer, began as a humanist lawyer. His studies led him to break with the Catholic Church and
create a church structure that empowered lay members to a large degree
and demanded more rights for citizens. At the same time, the reforms
Calvin instituted in Geneva were so strict that he was asked to leave
the city. Erasmus of Rotterdam, who remained Catholic, sanctioned
the power of kings and the Church but emphasized their need to serve
the people.[74] Like the Protestants, Erasmus also appealed to reason and
Scriptures to condemn superstitious practices within the Church, which
he denounced in his pamphlet *In Praise of Folly*.[75] From the Reformation
onward, the Catholic Church would be divided between those bishops,
priests, and orders who buttressed royal power and those who appropriately devoted their ministry to the people. Reformers increasingly relied
upon the Bible for their arguments. This led, on occasion, to greater dialogue with Jewish rabbis, but it could degenerate as well to bitter hostility,
as in Luther's case. The Jews, for their part, often found themselves cozy-
ing up to unjust and exploitative nobles and kings. Their motives were
divided between a bid for self-preservation, since these figures of authority were the ones most likely to protect them,[76] and self-interest, since
the elites had all the power and money. Further, in Jewish communities
across Muslim and Christian lands, Jews in exile were themselves controlled by their own elites, who did not always serve them.

The bitter contests over the true model of church and society from
the fourteenth to the seventeenth century did not lead to political justice
or equality for the masses.[77] They did, however, permanently diminish
absolute royal and church authority, a necessary first step. The challenge
of Protestantism to papal and royal authority was such that, over the
course of the sixteenth and seventeenth centuries, the continent became a
battlefield between religious and political factions. While Protestants tri-
umphed in Germany, England, and the Netherlands, these were victories
of the rulers against the pope. In Germany, the Reformation strengthened the power of the emperor, while in England the nobles made gains,
as did the wealthy merchants in Holland. In all three countries, radical Protestants were outlawed, and many fled to the American colonies.
Unfortunately, nowhere did the peasants or workers see political gains.

Catholic priests and royals in France and Spain increased their
power and turned to absolute rule. As pushback against the Protestants'

challenge to both papal and royal authority,[78] French and Spanish absolutist leaders, like Philip II and Francis I, continued the expansionist and colonial policies of these countries. They arrogantly seized other people's land and territories.[79] Philip, for one, modestly named a group of islands in the Pacific the Philippines! Francis I ruled over "New France." Nevertheless, the Reformation irrevocably changed Europe.

In the Muslim world, imperial expansion was the rule. The Ottoman expansion continued with the empire's conquest of the Balkans.[4] The Safavid Empire of Persia expanded into Georgia, Armenia, and the Caucuses, deporting hundreds of thousands of subjugated Georgians, Armenians, and Circassians to Persia itself. Mughal emperors, with the exception of Aurangzeb, ruled somewhat less hostilely over Hindus and others in the Indian subcontinent, although income inequality was extreme. Few dared question the sultan's, the shah's, the emperor's, or scholars' authority during this period. In contrast, the consequences of the Protestant critique of the Church's political authority and doctrines could not be reversed. In reaction to this period of turmoil within the monotheistic, mainly Christian world, a number of thinkers went from denunciation of the excesses of the Catholic Church to a denunciation of monotheism itself. They spurned faith in the one God as an irrational belief that promoted injustice.

Before describing the rise of secularism, it is important to note one matter. Monotheistic ideas spread to the world in a manner quite different from that often portrayed by nineteenth-century European colonizers. When the Germanic peoples of Scandinavia were burning slave girls on funeral pyres, Ethiopian Jews and Christians were preaching that man was created in God's image. While Japan was still ruled by a warrior caste and Lithuania still practiced polytheism, Muslims in the Mali Empire had devised a constitution and a working government in the form of an imperial federation. This is not to suggest that access to monotheistic teachings necessarily triggered instant change or significant technological and scientific advantage. The Irish could write of the Bible and its wisdom, though they surely lagged behind the Chinese, Aztec, and Incas in luxury, technology, and grandeur. But more to the point, it is hard to

---

[4] For a general history of the Ottoman Empire, see Lapidus, *Islamic Societies;* and on the topic of conquest and conversion, see Marc David Baer, *Honored by the Glory of Islam: Conversion and Conquest in Ottoman Europe* (New York: Oxford University Press, 2008).

argue that the seventeenth-century imperial French and English were more just than the Iroquois confederacy—who incidentally believed in one Great Spirit—since both were bent on expanding their territory.

The Philosophers Take on Monotheism

Starting in the seventeenth century, a growing number of philosophers claimed that the God of the Bible, like the gods of old, was nothing more than a human projection. These same philosophers were the first to conflate the monotheistic concept of taking God's name in vain with actual idolatry. This was an unfortunate but frankly understandable mistake. In previous centuries, European philosophers had largely fought over the nature of Christian teachings, arguing the character of an ideal Christian society. In the seventeenth century, and even more so in the eighteenth, a number of them began to abandon the notion of God altogether.[80] The first atheists, such as Baruch Spinoza, whose Jewish family had been forced to convert to Christianity under the Portuguese, actually advocated something closer to pantheism and deism than full-blown atheism. In this respect, they were not unlike the pre-Socratics.[81] According to this scheme of things, God existed in nature but did not interfere with the natural laws that ordered the world. Philosophers after Spinoza felt free to dispense with the notion of God altogether. The material world was all there was, period. (We will explore this materialistic viewpoint more in part four on science and God.) The seventeenth-century Polish philosopher Kazimierz Łyszczyński argued in his treatise *On the Non-Existence of God* that God existed as an idea because man created him in his image.[82] His perspective echoed the ancient view of Xenophanes, who argued that the gods were just a projection of man.

In the nineteenth century, the philosopher Ludwig Feuerbach would likewise declare that God was a projection of man's inner nature.[83] In the twentieth century, Sigmund Freud joined the debate, adding a psychological twist. God was simply the projection of our understanding of the father figure. And if God was but a fiction, then, of course, so was the Bible. Indeed, it was no big leap from rejecting the authority of the Church to repudiating biblical authority altogether.

As early as the seventeenth century, philosophers like Spinoza had begun to question the idea that the Bible was a divinely revealed text.

They maintained instead that it must have been composed by many authors at different times. Other philosophers, such as Thomas Hobbes, also raised doubts about the authorship and message of the Bible. (We will deal with these two issues in much greater detail, mostly in part five but to some degree in part two.) Most importantly, Enlightenment thinkers promoted reliance on reason alone as a tremendous leap forward.[84] As Immanuel Kant expressed it, "Enlightenment is man's emergence from his self-incurred immaturity." In Kant's view, this immaturity did not result from a lack of understanding; rather, it was from a lack of courage to use one's reason, intellect, and wisdom without the guidance of another.

In the minds of many of these modern philosophers—as in the minds of their ancient Greek predecessors—the clerical and royal elites created the fiction of God as a means to oppress the masses. Reason was the antidote, offering a way to liberate them from religion's mind control. Yes, the Protestants had begun to question clerical authority, but many, as we saw, merely substituted new authorities in place of the Catholic Church. Atheists, however, rejected the authority of all religious institutions and dismissed the very need for religion itself.[85] Łyszczyński argued that the concept of God and religion was not only illegitimate, it was implemented with sinister intentions: "the cunning oppressed the simple with their concept of God." Denis Diderot, the eighteenth-century French philosopher, exclaimed, "Man will never be free until the last king is strangled with the entrails of the last priest." In the nineteenth century, Karl Marx branded religion the opium of the people and derided its purpose as no more than to drug the masses out of their misery. Accusations that the Church oppressed the people certainly rang true in places such as Poland and France, where the power of the Church, king, and nobility remained strong. But even where Church authority weakened and atheism could blossom, tolerance did not always follow suit. In places where the atheists' rejection of the Church offered Jews freedom from Christian oppression, it was, nonetheless, often accompanied by demands for assimilation and rejection of their identity as a people and religion. (More on this in part two.)

This enlightened turn toward reason by modern thinkers could, as in the classical period, also be used to justify oppression. Machiavelli's *The Prince* offered another rational take on society.[86] Not unlike the

Sophists of ancient Greece, Machiavelli extolled the merits of power.[5] Like many of his contemporaries, he exiled God and the Bible from his political writings. However, unlike other thinkers, Machiavelli showed little concern for social justice or the general good. What Machiavelli deemed "virtue" was not the application of justice but the liberal use of deception, cunning, strategy, and all forms of violence to acquire and maintain power. Machiavelli did advise that one ought to *appear* honest and good. Machiavelli was widely read by political leaders from Henry VIII to Joseph Stalin and would revolutionize modern political thought.

Starting in the eighteenth century, European elites would also appeal to "scientific" arguments about the "inferiority" of certain peoples to justify their domination. Like Machiavelli and the Sophists, but now armed with the "reason" of "biological" evidence, they claimed that nature divided its creatures into the rulers and the ruled. Thus, in the modern period as in the classical world, reason could be used to justify a political order based on justice, law, and human equality. But it could also be martialed to defend a political order based on the very power machinations observed in classical idolatrous societies, simply without any explicit reference to the gods.

---

[5] For a discussion of Machiavelli's thought and influence see: John M. Najemy ed., *The Cambridge Companion to Machiavelli* (Cambridge: Cambridge University Press, 2010); and Timothy Fuller ed., *Machiavelli's Legacy: The Prince after Five Hundred Years* (Philadelphia: University of Pennsylvania Press, 2016).

CHAPTER 4

The Rise of Atheism and the Revenge of the Idols

Atheists Say Freedom Can Do Without God

Many atheists today claim that history has proven them right. Atheism is progress. Their smoking gun? Scandinavia! The Nordic countries, once the source of formidable warriors, now score among the highest in the world in social welfare, in equality, and in GDP. They also score among the lowest in crime and in government and business corruption. They observe the separation of powers and take political equality for granted. Indeed, not only do they believe in the equality of all human beings, but Scandinavians have developed the most gender-equal societies in the Western world. They allow a free market to operate, engendering healthy economic competition, and they possess one of the most generous welfare systems in the world, all paid for, as with the biblical model, with the people's taxes. Scandinavians are also among the most prosperous and happiest people in the world and not just because they can eat meatballs at IKEA. For many atheists, Scandinavia seems to offer proof positive that you need neither God nor religion to create the good society. But hold on: Are all modern secular societies as wonderful as the Scandinavian?

Freedom to Oppress

> *When Jehovah made the covenant with Abraham, that required accountability and we live in a world where we don't want to be accountable. We just want to be successful, we want to be admirable, but our finiteness comes when we also have accountability. So we don't like to have bosses and we want to have gods if we create them in our own image. So if the playboy model becomes the kind of figure I want to be, I will say and do what I need to. If I want to be a powerful political person, then I might subject myself to the political bosses who will get me to the top. If I want to be a very rich businessman, I might compromise my ethics to become a very rich businessman, and be in those circles. If I want to be a religious figure, I might compromise my ethics to become a powerful religious figure. So we tend to create our gods. The enablers become for us the idols of which the Old Testament tells us to beware, as they are idols. Jesus, following the prophets, condemned these sorts of idols. This is a core teaching of monotheism.*
>
> —FATHER ALEXANDER KARLOUTSOS

Religious people can counter the atheists' claims by pointing to the many modern secular societies ruled by elites who use their political power to defend their own selfish interests. I had personal experience learning this particular outlook as the result of a series of conversations I had with a middle-level trader on his way up in the early 1980s.

In those days, I was working for Salomon Brothers in the mergers and acquisitions department. Every morning I took the Lexington line subway from Ninety-Sixth Street to Bowling Green. No one I know is nostalgic about the Lexington line of that era. In the summer, the then-not-air-conditioned line was so hot that I arrived to work drenched in sweat. In the winter, depending on the subway car I found myself in, I was either overheated and sweating on arrival, or in full hypochondriac mode from all of the coughing and sneezing of my fellow passengers—or both. So when a particular trader honked his horn as I was making my way to the Ninety-Sixth Street station and offered me a ride downtown, I was very happy.

As we traveled south along FDR Drive, he suggested that if I waited in a certain spot any morning that he was driving down to Wall Street, he would pick me up. He was pretty fastidious about leaving at a precise time, so I could more or less know if he was traveling downtown on any specific day and, if not, jump on the subway. For the next several months, I happily made it a habit to be there whenever I wasn't traveling. The price for the trip was having to listen to his philosophy of the world, which he loved to expound—don't forget these were the antediluvian days before cell phones.

This trader's totally secular philosophy consisted of the idea that his comfort and self-interest came first. He believed every one of us was on our own. Power was all that mattered. He was not a racist, but he did not believe in the equality of man, since not all people were equally powerful. As for God? Irrelevant as Zeus. He articulated what I have come to recognize as a common mash-up of Peter Singer's philosophy (more about him later), a good dose of "we know what's best" elitism, along with a dash of "What's good for the size of my wallet?" Success for him was all about being on top, not about justice for all, because certainly not everyone counts the same. And why should they? She who has the power should use it. No absolute law, no absolute right, no absolute good. However, like so many other direct disciples of Machiavelli, he didn't think it was a good idea to publicly admit any of this. As for government policy, he thought it best to nod with concern when problems of inequality and income disparity arose, but not to try to fix them, especially not with any taxes. When it came to getting ahead in business, or on Wall Street specifically, he did not want to break any laws, because that could have consequences. But any loophole was fair game for exploiting. In his mind, the spirit of the law and regulation was irrelevant; the detailed words were what counted.

My ride's approach to life goes a long way toward explaining why only one person took the hit for the 2008 mortgage crisis, and no top executive at that. One would have expected far more convicted parties, given that millions of American people lost their homes and their livelihoods, and measureless financial damage was inflicted on countless others around the world. Yet only one person in the financial service sector by the name of Kareem Serageldin was punished, who even the sentencing judge acknowledged played a tiny role not central to the crisis. The reason is simple: many actors with highly priced lawyers scrupulously followed the letter of the law and regulation, because they knew that both were toothless.

The one exception to this rule was also a semi-idolatrous act. In 2012, New York county prosecutors who had not charged any Wall Street firm with criminal acts in connection with fraudulent mortgages felt under pressure to do something, so they found a sacrifice and indicted a small Chinatown bank with 240 criminal charges. The case dragged on for three years and finally the bank and the seventy-nine-year-old owner were acquitted on all 240 charges. Perhaps the fact that the supposed victim, the Federal National Mortgage Association (FNMA), testified that it had not experienced any actual losses and that the bank had self-reported the alleged violations had something to do with that. Nevertheless, the case drained the resources of the owner's family and of the community bank. The tragedy is depicted in a well-done documentary, *Abacus: Small Enough to Jail* (2017). Think of the prosecutors as priests who attempted to appease the people's anger by finding an unrelated, seemingly defenseless sacrifice. This was a lot easier than going after any central, well-funded culprits. What no one did on any side, including the prosecutors, was to set up a fair, simple, and transparent system.

In fact, it was the very technical and opaque nature of mortgage rules and regulations that made the massive and unjust profits possible in the first place. For example, some underwriters waived through mortgage applications without proper due diligence, even though they knew the risk to foreclosure was meaningful. The underwriters' compensation was based on volume, not an individual client's ultimate ability to repay. The Wall Street conduits that sliced and diced these mortgages for sale to investors also waived in a lot of mortgages that they "kind of sort of" knew weren't so good. Since they weren't keeping any risk on the books and since everything was disclosed (as required, usually on page 413 in an appendix or a footnote, font size four), they were good to go. After all, the rating agencies had given these bonds investment-grade ratings. The few voices that warned of the coming debacle, including that of Lew Ranieri, the inventor of the modern mortgage-backed security, were drowned out by the happy noise of the money-making machine.

By the way, plenty of home buyers were also complicit by knowingly applying for so-called "liar's loans" and by claiming multiple homes as a primary residence. There were too many people purchasing four or seven or eleven homes with no money down because they once attended a seminar explaining how to do this. Also, Congress and successive administrations grew accustomed to the lobbying dollars from FNMA and the Federal Home Loan Mortgage Corporation (FHLMC, better known as Freddie Mac). This money deflected appropriate legislation or regulation that would have guarded against this duopoly from taking massively excessive risk, which was ultimately on the taxpayers' tab. In short, once a culture where not everyone is equal takes hold, then only power matters. In such a Machiavellian climate, it is hard to demand that people look out for one another or create laws that prevent exploitation.

From those rides, I came to believe the opposite of what the trader was telling me. We needed fewer regulations and more clarity about what is just. We needed the appropriate laws to back it all up and thereby make people accountable. As Ranieri has argued, just as a stockbroker is held legally responsible for selling a bad stock, so too should the sellers of these other financial products be held to account by law.

Now and then I did gently argue with the trader who was kind enough to let me join him. I did push him to think, but since those car rides to Salomon Brothers were so much nicer than the 4, 5, or 6 trains, I must admit I didn't push too hard. Some months later I moved to York Avenue, where I could catch a nice, if slow, express bus to Wall Street. I just read the paper and put those conversations in the back of my mind.

My carpool host was not alone. Today's world is full of secular leaders who believe power trumps justice. They rule in the interest of the oligarchies they represent, power for themselves and their own groups' advantage at the expense of the people and at the cost of justice. Times have changed, so these elites no longer feel the need to refer to any supernatural ideology. In the early twentieth century, elites denied women and minorities the vote due to their "feeble nature" when in fact they just wanted to hold on to their political power. On the right, legions of South American dictators shared the profits of their countries' resources among themselves and foreign investors. On the left, Communist Party cronies used cadres to enrich themselves, all the while proclaiming the dictatorship of the proletariat. In the United States, business and political interest groups gave political leaders outrageous campaign contributions to make sure that their interests were looked after. Across the globe, oligarchies have also ensured their continued economic dominance through imposing "tribute" on one class without significantly contributing themselves.

Today, we call this corruption and it is ubiquitous. Many Western countries rail against offshore banking and yet permit it on their own shores for foreign citizens. They also draft legislation to protect their own environment while allowing their elites to degrade the environment in the developing world. Monopolies are, of course, far from a thing of the past. As Machiavelli so cleverly advised, many of these political leaders disavow their selfish interests and cosmetically appear good. I will have more to say about all of these forms of injustice in part three. In addition to those who exploit their power while seeking to appear good, there are those secular leaders who openly flaunt their power.

Modern Idolatry: New and Not Improved

Most criminal states of the twentieth century were secular, and they adopted practices common to ancient idolatrous regimes. Tyrants such as Stalin, Hitler, Mao, Pol Pot, Saddam Hussein, and present-day Kim Jong-un not only seized power, eliminated justice, and started wars, but, to varying degrees, they outlawed religion. Yet, like the idolatrous leaders of old, they all had fetishes for building statues of themselves everywhere. Stalin famously ordered the Soviet space agency to project an image of his face into the sky.

Infamously, the 1934 Nuremberg Rally reached its climax with Rudolph Hess exhorting the masses that "the party is Hitler. But Hitler is Germany, just as Germany is Hitler. Hitler! Sieg Heil!"[1] This succinct summary of power could have been used by any Egyptian pharaoh or Mongol khan. Kim Jong-un accused his uncle of corruption and, as punishment, claimed to have had him stripped naked and fed to hungry dogs. A Roman would have attended this sort of event at the Colosseum. Today you can see this sort of thing on YouTube. Kim Jong-un's father, Kim Jong-il, used the standard idolatrous practice of destroying over two thousand Buddhist temples and Christian churches to show that he was the new god in town. The Kims fostered the belief that their patriarch, Kim Il-sung, actually had something to do with the creation of the world. This explains the need to erect 40,000 statues in his honor and an additional 3,200 obelisks, which are called Towers of Eternal Life. All of this statue building took place in a country that cannot feed its people. These are priorities that would have been common in the ancient world. Another dictator, Saddam Hussein, won two elections with 100 percent of the vote, an amazing achievement even in its articulation. Papers reported happy voters shouting that they "give their blood and lives to Saddam, their leader."[2] The cult of personality was extremely powerful in maintaining impressive military and police discipline in Iraq. The power of idolatry cannot be underestimated. In the words of Reverend Dr. Calvin Butts, "The Nazis clearly didn't believe in God. They kept the Catholic Church and they made deals with certain churches, but they clearly didn't believe in God."

Even black magic has made a comeback in modern secular rogue states. The SS leader Heinrich Himmler was so obsessed with witchcraft that he looted 140,000 books on the subject from libraries across Europe. He also set up a unit to investigate and publicize the issue. According to researchers, he was trying to prove that the persecution of witches in the seventeenth century represented the Church's attempt to destroy the German race. It is believed that he deployed his SS teams to discover traces of an old Germanic culture that survived the witch hunts.[3] Nor were the Nazis alone. The reviled Haitian dictator François "Papa Doc" Duvalier was widely believed to practice black magic against Haitians. He dressed himself up as the vodun god of the underworld, and his secret police were widely known as "Tonton Macoute," a boogeyman figure known for stealing innocents.[4] As viewers learned in the film *The King of Scotland*, Idi Amin's idolatrous irrationality, not to mention geographical confusion, became abundantly clear on the world scene. Russian authors in the 1920s often wrote of Stalin's occult powers, something neither Stalin nor Communist Party cadres denied.[5] Further, he used occult symbols in Soviet propaganda. Saddam carried a blue stone for immortality around with him. While bizarre, these dictators' fascination with the occult follows the pattern of idolatry we have seen thus far. In response to these examples, atheist authors have of course pointed to the modern abuses of power in religious countries.

"God" Can also Lead the Way to Slavery

Many atheists will counter that modern monotheistic societies oppressed others in the name of God to unprecedented degrees. The most glaring example of this is the European colonial project that continued well into the twentieth century.[1] The so-called "scramble for Africa" (1881–1914), which represented the last wave of European imperialism, consisted of Christian European nations competing to colonize the most African territories for their own purposes. The imperialists partly justified their actions by proclaiming that it was "the white man's burden" to bring Christianity and modern ideas to the world. In fact, Christian European nations primarily exploited these colonies economically, often with unspeakable brutality.

One horrific example of this is the systematic maiming of child rubber plantation workers after the Belgians conquered what is now the Democratic Republic of Congo. Then there was the German genocide of the Herero and Namaqua in modern-day Namibia so that Deutschland could use *their* land. European colonization—especially in the Americas and Africa—but generally everywhere Europeans conquered from the fifteenth century onward, also led to cultural decimation. In the name of spreading Christianity and civilization, Europeans destroyed indigenous communities and cultures, when not killing indigenous people outright. In the "kind" nation of Canada, the government was taking children away from their parents to forcefully assimilate them into Canadian, that is to say European, culture as late as the 1970s. Finally, the breathtaking injustice of the European colonial powers makes idolatrous nations seem tame. One could argue, for example, that the Hopi, otherwise known as the Pueblo peoples of Arizona, although polytheistic, created a more just and egalitarian society than the Americans who revered the Bible and took the Pueblo land.[6]

Not that Muslim governments have a clean record. As we saw through the Middle Ages, the Empires conquered and Arabized North Africa. Subsequent Muslim Empires also oppressed their subjects. The early modern Ottoman and Safavid Empires used massive population

---

[1] For a good survey on European imperialism, see George Raudzens, *Empires: Europe and Globalization, 1492–1788* (Thrupp: Sutton Pub., 1999); and James R. Lehring, *European Colonialism since 1700* (Cambridge: Cambridge University Press, 2013).

transfers to consolidate their power. The Ottomans transferred conquered peoples such as the Turkmen, Tatars, Balkan Christians, and Greek (Ottomans) en masse while the Safavids did the same with the Armenians, Georgians, and Circassians, many of whom died in the process—the Armenian genocide being the worst of such policies. They also settled their own populations in newly conquered regions to strengthen their rule. In the contemporary Islamic Republic of Iran and Saudi Arabia, the most Muslim states, clerical elites routinely imprison and execute citizens who oppose the regime. Perhaps the modern atheists who criticized monotheism as unjust and in the service of the elites who advocated it have a point.

Atheists argue that, since modern religious societies have perpetuated large-scale injustice, religion is irrelevant. On the other hand, religious critics often respond that the existence of unjust secular societies proves that atheism is dangerous. Neither answer is in fact satisfactory. It is only when we apply the concept of idolatry and those first three commandments that we can gain clarity. The issue is not whether a country declares itself secular or monotheistic; the question is whether it is in actual fact idolatrous or not.

Why Condemning Idolatry Trumps Believing in God

I am not judging anyone here, but I think there is a humility that is involved with valuing something that has remained a huge part of how human beings have lived throughout centuries. I think for those who say, "That was great but we are more advanced now, we don't really need the values of religion," we should recognize this as a rejection of our own history.

—CHAPLAIN TAHERA AHMAD

Any confusion about the role that religion and atheism might play in acts of oppression in modern times is cleared up when we apply the category of idolatry. Take Scandinavia. Its success is not so much due to its secularism as it is to its rejection of idolatry. In fact, Scandinavian society's view of humanity and its relationships firmly rejects the deification of any person. Scandinavians elevate man, while refusing to place some people above others. In Scandinavia, all people are beholden to a law that treats them equally and prevents monopoly of power. Scandinavian laws are meant to facilitate cooperation and mutual respect rather than domination. Scandinavians thus resist the idolatrous view of power in all the ways that we have seen outlined by the Bible, even though they do not attribute their laws to God. And, it should come as no surprise that, as a recent study shows, most Scandinavians generally hold a positive view of biblical ethics, even if they do not believe that the Bible is divine or maintain a faith in God.[7] Scandinavian societies are the product of many centuries of Christian and monotheistic ideas, which still, albeit in a secularized form, inform their culture. In the words of Father Alexander Karloutsos:

> The values of the community do prevail. And are they being undermined by this mindset that you can be anything you want, you can practice anything you want, create your own morality? Yes, but because there is such a strong reservoir of spiritual and intellectual growth from the Judaic Christian experience, we still resist idolatry.

If they stay at their current equilibrium, these societies may in fact remain just, as their secularism is anti-idolatry. However, we just don't know yet if this will be the case. Father Karloutsos once again:

> If everyone is creating his or her own morality, there is no morality. Where is the defined line? We are in a society where our freedoms are given to us despite our not having earned them. We have no understanding to maintain them, and we have not fought to preserve them.

Without the prohibition against idolatry, man naturally tends to deify himself. There is no recourse, no principle with which to fight this deification. This is evident in societies where Machiavellian elites oppress the masses for their own gain. Without openly deifying themselves, they are in fact claiming to be greater than the people they dominate. As a result, they arbitrarily give themselves the power to impose laws on others to their benefit. As Timothy Cardinal Dolan explains:

> You know that the world would only be worse without religion, because every person would have a god, and more often than not it would be the god you are looking at in the mirror when you shave in the morning. Then you have an unrestrained tyranny of

subjectivism and self-willfulness that leads to the morality of the bunker, and that is really bad.

These elites reject human equality and therefore egalitarian justice without openly admitting it. We must compare the laws, the government structures, and the views of man in such societies with biblical ones if we truly want to comprehend the extent that idolatry reigns free in those places. The Bible's description of idolatry is even more helpful in analyzing the nature of open dictatorships. The fact that modern tyrants deified themselves with the same tricks as their ancient predecessors provides clear warning for all those who might be taken in by their charisma or false charm. The Bible's description of idolatry is as relevant as ever as a guide to judging the worth of secular societies.

Measuring themselves against the prohibition of idolatry is also essential for those who consider themselves monotheists. Monotheists must examine their own history through the lens of those same first three commandments. Any time biblical commentators exaggerated the obedience people owe to rulers, as Luther did, they are elevating some men above others, and yet are not all men and women made in God's image? Any time the king and priestly class began to concentrate power and issue decrees and taxes to their own benefit, as occurred before the German Peasants' War for example, they have taken God's name in vain and become idolaters. Any time monotheists speak of people's use of unseen satanic forces, or of "magic" as they did during the Salem witch trials, we are talking about idolatry. Any time elites claimed explicitly or implicitly that men were *not* all made in God's image, as occurred during the conquest of the Americas, they betrayed monotheism and became idolaters. Any time kings assumed absolute power, as did Louis XIV, they betrayed monotheism and took God's name in vain and became idolaters.

We can go further. Understanding the atheists' critique of monotheism can also be useful to monotheists who would cleanse their religions of idolatry. One of the most poignant articulations of this idea can be found in an essay from the 1920s called "Pangs of Cleansing." In it, Rabbi Abraham Isaac Kook argued that we should view the atheist critique of monotheism as a fair means for purifying the latter from idolatrous tendencies, more specifically the tendency to create the God of Abraham in our own image. Most monotheistic leaders today agree. In the words of

Chaplain Tahera Ahmad, "We live in a time and space where we need to look at how the nature of God as well as the references to God and the scriptures reflects how God is understood by us."

Atheist criticisms do, indeed, underscore the necessity of returning to traditional prohibitions against idolatry and a traditional humility about our notions of God. As Reverend Dr. Katharine Henderson says:

> No one can make God into his or her own image. People try to all the time and that is when human beings get into trouble as groups or individuals of trying to make God in our image, whether it is Christians, Jews, and Muslims or even joining nonbelievers in making God very small. I think that transcendences of God should keep us from doing this. This is a check against our hubris as human beings. But often God is so completely present in moments of doubt or tragedy or loss or grief or love that I think that people feel God in an indescribable way.

Father Alexander Karloutsos put it slightly differently, but shares the same message:

> In the Orthodox Church, which is probably consistent with the Hebraic experience, we don't have a problem with the perfect concept of God. But to go further is to make an idol. We do not know.

Rabbi Kook's embrace of the atheists' criticism challenges believers to face difficult questions rather than to censor them. Imam Shamsi Ali says something of the same:

> When people ask about God, some say, "Just believe. Don't discuss religion or talk about it." And I think even our young Muslims don't accept religion that way. Thirdly, because of the general environment, it has become easy for people to accept ideas without deeper analysis and because some stop thinking when it is said that this is the view of science. People sometimes don't ponder enough.

For many monotheists, the atheists' critique of the injustices perpetrated by monotheistic societies are also salutary reminders. Because atheists are not committed to the church in any way, they force monotheists to be totally honest about the damage done in the name of God. As Cardinal Dolan points out:

One of the reasons atheism is so popular today is that believers get cocky and arrogant. When atheists say, "you know organized religion has been the cause of some of the greatest horrors in the history of humanity," we need to respond, mea culpa. I am afraid they are right. But we can add it has also been the cause of some of the greatest philanthropy and some of the greatest affirmation of human progress and charity and works of justice to humanity. We can say these positives with the same certainty, but there is no denying harsher realities as well. We can also say no to the charge that religion is abusive. Religion itself is not abusive. But one has to admit organized religion has not lived up to what it should be.

Imam Shamsi Ali offers a few insights on this question as well:

The number one reason I think is because of the misrepresentation of the religion by their followers. In the case of Islam, the increase of violence and terrorism in the name of religion certainly decreases the trust of the religion, including the young Muslim generations.

Wiping Idolatry's Hard Drive: A How-To Guide

Atheists have claimed that monotheism is by its very nature a kind of imperialist project. It is true that monotheism largely spread through the structure and power of the Roman (later Byzantine) and then Arab/Muslim and finally English, French, and Portuguese Empires. It is also true that monotheists have committed cultural genocides and atrocities for which there can be neither rationale nor repentance. But it needn't be this way. The biblical prohibition against idolatry can provide a means for societies to recover and preserve their cultural specificity while also promoting justice.

I saw this process in person during that family vacation in New Zealand. Even as many proud Maori recounted those parts of their traditions they dearly loved, they also spoke to me about those parts of their tradition they no longer practiced and believed were appropriate to deemphasize. My Maori guides described how their people were once hardened warriors whose clashes between tribes and subtribes were fierce, bloody, and brutal. War possessed a sacred nature. Victors would eat the bodies of defeated warriors to consume their spirit as well as to provide sustenance. Sometimes warring groups would abduct their enemies and break their legs to preserve the captives' lives until they were ready to eat them. Today's Maori no longer advocate those practices. They have rejected this part of their tradition, partly in response to their encounter with Christianity, and partly as a result of rational considerations. Now they are a milder bunch whose warrior tradition has morphed into a talent for sports like rugby.

My guides were also open about the fact that the Maori gods did not provide any moral legacy by tradition. Like the gods of the ancient Near East, the Maori gods were no moral exemplars for human or humane behavior, nor did they bequeath their people anything like a Bible to provide moral guidance. If anything, the stories of the gods were a guide as how *not* to behave with those outside the clan. According to Maori traditions, the creation of the world of humans was a result of the children of the founding gods conspiring to murder their parents. Maui, a Maori demigod (and a frequent personage of other Polynesian pantheons), was a troublemaker whose consequences had to be dealt with by humanity. According to my Maori guides, the Maori no longer accept the moral message of these myths, with the important exception of the ideas they purvey about bravery and loyalty to fellow warriors.

In present-day *marae* (the Maori's place of meeting), the values taught are a combination of traditional and monotheistic ideas. For example, *marae* today accept members of other tribes and those who move to the area. The origins of the *marae* were much more particularistic. Outsiders were only sometimes welcomed as guests, rarely as new members. None of this is to denigrate the Maori or to set aside the gross injustices that they endured after the arrival of the Europeans. However, the Maori story is an example of how we moderns lose sight of the dangers of idolatry because our encounter with polytheism has occurred among traditional societies whose traditions are very beautiful and commendable in many respects. In so doing we forget that most traditional societies have rejected many of the idolatrous parts of their traditions. More to the point, the case of the Maori provides a clear example of how rejecting idolatry can lead cultures to retain cultural diversity without moral relativism. The Maori's recovery of the beautiful parts of their tradition and their rejection of the more troubling parts shows how each culture can use monotheistic and rational notions of a just God, just relationships, and human equality in order to adjust their own cultures appropriately without destroying them. This is a process that all peoples should do for themselves by themselves—from the Maori in New Zealand, to Pueblo Indians in New Mexico, to Buddhists in China, to monotheist Christians and Muslims and Jews, everyone has to deal with their own idolatry. The same process has occurred in other parts of the world. In India, for example, Hinduism's encounter with both Islam and Christianity strengthened monotheistic trends within the religion. It has also opened Hindus to question practices such as *sati* (burning the wife on the funeral pyre of her dead husband) and to reevaluate the caste system. Likewise, Tibetan Buddhism no longer advocates a rigid class system since its encounter with the West. Today, the Maori, like many other traditional peoples, are reclaiming the positive aspects of their heritage in a way that demonstrates how all peoples should reexamine themselves. With such a process, the texts, idols, artifacts, even pyramids of old can be disarmed of their power, transferred to the realm of art, where they can be studied. While these remnants are a witness to the darker side of human beings and their imagination, they also tell us about human drives that lead to idolatry, a theme we will explore in part three.

Resistance Is Not Futile

The Bible teaches humanity that we need to resist and reject our natural inclination toward idolatry. The Bible leads us to the conclusion that idolatry is an ideology that brings on a dangerous game of domination and submission, which inevitably ends in misery and destruction through structural oppression, exploitation, and abuse. This is no surprise, as philosophers Moshe Halbertal and Avishai Margalit demonstrate in their book on idolatry, that critics of political ideologies such as racism have much to gain from analyzing their subjects as analogous to idolatry.[8] What other concept could these philosophers use? Idolatry can best be summed up as the exact opposite of what makes life constructive and meaningful. For this reason, both atheists and monotheists who reject idolatry are positive forces for the good; likewise, both monotheists and atheists who fall prey to idolatry become tools for degrading humanity. If we can't create religious societies founded on justice, at least let's strive for creating non-idolatrous Swedens and preventing the development of future idolatrous North Koreas.

Defeating the Data Gods

Opposing secular idolatry is even more pressing today in our age of data collection. Back in the 1990s, Lew Ranieri and I became intrigued by the idea of credit scoring. As it had for some time, Fair, Isaac and Company dominated the credit scoring market with its eponymous FICO score. Lew and I and the rest of the team thought that FICO scores were good tools but flawed. After all, a FICO score could not accurately rate a spouse who was reentering the job market or a recent immigrant or a recent graduate. This was the so-called "thin file" problem. There just was not a lot of credit history for these sorts of folks. So, we invested in a company called Neuristics, which ended up mimicking FICO scores more than being an improvement.

Fast-forward to 2014–2015. Lew and I started speaking again about the whole idea of credit scoring in an age of artificial intelligence. The world had changed in several important ways, and continues to change today. The amount of data available on every individual has mushroomed. And for data that can't be directly determined, in many cases it can be surmised. The rise of social media has produced myriads of free data and even where individuals keep their profiles and other information "private," the mass of individuals and linkages makes estimates ever more accurate. Further, many people are willing to permission their data for imaginary trinkets. Read page seven, paragraph three of the next privacy policy to which you click "I agree." Ninety-nine percent of people reading this book have already signed away a vast quantity of their personal information in just such a way. Cookies, they are everywhere.

The bottom line is that very few people have a thin file anymore. Coupled with this is the power of artificial intelligence. With a thick social file on everyone and more credit history than in the history of mankind available automatically from credit bureaus, a whole host of data can be linked with credit outcomes. All of this could make new, more powerful credit scores a great boost for loan and other financial instrument providers.

But there is a great downside to such data collection as well. An artificial intelligence tool that took into account a person's whole history and make-up could intensify all sorts of discrimination even with the best intentions. Let's assume that no facial recognition or race, creed, or gender data is permitted to be absorbed by the AI credit scorer. That is not enough. After all, AI is by definition very, very smart. It could start to pick up all sorts of other data points that could relegate historically discriminated groups to further discrimination. Of course, the AI credit score tool won't know race, creed, or gender per se. But it would quickly figure out groups that have had historically worse than average credit performance and will make it even harder for them to move up the economic rungs even though it is no fault of the individual. The first person from a family to attend college will find herself held back in accessing credit and paying higher insurance fees and the like because of her ethnic and familial connections. Perhaps people she has links to have poor credit history. That might impact her for her entire life.

The parallel between AI and the utilization of pure reason unfettered from principles of justice is clear. If AI were to know everything about someone, it is highly likely that AI would indeed make use of race, creed, and gender markers in making decisions without doing so by name. Would we really like an AI tool to decide on who has access to credit or to career opportunities or to college entrance? Certain ethnic minorities might have lower graduation rates, so the AI tool would generalize and turn all those who share the same characteristics away from college. Men generally have lower college graduation rates these days, so they too as a group might find it harder to be accepted in the first place. If we lived in a pure AI reason world, discrimination would be heightened and could not be overcome. The tricky thing about AI or any similar tool is that it quickly becomes part of the air. Who questions the driving instructions coming from a GPS device? I generally find that even when I have already driven to a certain destination several times, the GPS tool often has a slightly better suggestion. While this is not truly analogous to credit scoring, so goes the slippery road in which we might use the convenience of an AI tool to make decisions for us as a society without fully thinking through the implications.

The dangers of AI's potential concentration of power are clearly described in the Bible. While the Bible never mentioned Facebook, an oft misunderstood allegorical story makes the point. We noted previously that chapter 11 of the Book of Genesis provided a caution to too much homogenization in decision-making as an idolatrous act. Between the time of Genesis 10:5—in which there were many peoples, languages, and lands—and the beginning of chapter 11, the situation had transformed. A mass globalization had taken place, probably via some tyrant, with everyone speaking and thinking the same way, though it isn't clear exactly why they are thinking that way, nor do they seem very self-aware other than having "one common purpose." In this generally misread story, it is not, as most assume, that the people begin by wanting to build a tower to the heavens. First, they come together in 11:1–2 on one common platform. Then they come up with a tool, namely bricks, which seems to be a new technology, and finally after prototyping them, the people arrive at an efficient process to make and use them with mortar, also a new creation, in 11:3. In the first part of the verse of 11:4, the goal is to build a city. Only afterward is the tower mentioned as if it were the icing on the cake. God does not like this process, as technological progress dangerously leads to more and more homogenization. If we all use Google, Microsoft, Facebook, Amazon, or Apple products everywhere on earth, we risk sacrificing something of our differentiated humanity. Once the technological tools became available to the people of Babylon, they could not resist using them even as they weren't sure where it would lead them.

It is no pun to say that the danger of artificial intelligence is that we will idolize it. Recall that we defined idolatry as blind belief in the power of a finite person or thing. From the perspective of the Bible, the real danger is not that some sort of Terminator artificial intelligence will rise up to dominate humanity. Rather, the danger is that humanity will place its belief in decisions made by artificial intelligence, and there is no end to the harm that we would thereby self-inflict on our humanity. Properly used, artificial intelligence is a tool. Improperly used, we begin to bow down to it. Like the ancient Babylonians, we have a tool but don't have a vision as to where it will lead us and it can lead us anywhere. Combine autonomous vehicles, facial recognition, and AI together—a platform, mortar, and bricks. It is not hard to imagine a dystopian future in which our cars will only take us where the authorities are willing to let us go. Plus, anyone using a vehicle will be immediately identifiable. We won't be better off than those Babylonians building a tower.

At the beginning of part one, we asked whether it is rational that an omnibenevolent God would demand draconian punishment for such a seemingly petty offense as the worship of other gods. The answer is yes and deservedly so. While the ancient Jewish court system did not attempt to punish even a miniscule fraction of idolaters, the concept that idolatry was a punishable offense established a vital principle. The greatest rationalists of the classical world, the Greek philosophers, recognized idolatry's dangers, too. Without this theological prohibition, who knows if monotheism could have spread, given the entrenched position of idolatry in the surrounding societies? Throughout the past two millennia, idolatry crept into politics and social relations, particularly through the vehicle of taking God's name in vain as we have explained it. As Timothy Cardinal Dolan said, when religions get cocky, horrors happen. Idolatry remains the most potent existing threat to social justice, freedom, and world peace. The severe and inflexible message of the Bible in combating idolatry is no less timely today than it was millennia ago. But we have to bear in mind all aspects of the first three commandments. Claiming to speak authoritatively for God is the monotheistic equivalent of the danger of idolatry.

PART TWO

Is the Bible Unjust and Is Progress Secular?

Is the Good Book Good?

The atheist writers tell us that the Bible's laws and principles are grossly inferior to the systems of justice and guaranteed freedoms in the modern Western secular world. Too many passages in the Bible strain the modern moral compass even if they are a modest step up from the myths of Babylonia and the Code of Hammurabi. We moderns advocate universal justice, yet the Bible invents racism—the *chosen* people—and advocates genocide. We moderns uphold equality and social justice; the Bible sanctions slavery and oppression of women. We moderns extol the impartiality of the law; the Bible exhorts collective punishment for the crimes of the few. We moderns defend freedom of religion; the Bible turns harmless rituals into capital violations. With such a violent holy book, no wonder monotheism has been the major cause of war in history, allege the atheist writers.

Only when we moderns abandoned religion, the atheist argument concludes, have we *really* made strides in freedom, justice, and equality for all. Simply put, the Bible is, at best, hopelessly out of date and utterly irrelevant. At worst, it is an intractable impediment on the path to liberty and justice.

Too often, modern believers find themselves struggling to respond to this line of attack. They take the atheists' claims about the Bible at face value without scrutinizing them. As a result, they believe—as the atheists claim—that they have to pick and choose those biblical passages that appear more rational and morally balanced. Or they shrug, saying, "You just can't expect human beings to understand God's commandments." Or acquiesce to the superiority of modern secular morality. Most frightening of all, some believers swayed by the atheists' arguments feel compelled to acknowledge that our relationship with God demands that we behave irrationally and unjustly. But, in fact, believers do not have to make these concessions. The entire premise of the atheists' argument about the Bible is wrong.

Here in part two, I claim that an honest appraisal of the biblical text reveals a document that is just and fair. *The Bible is the first ancient text to advocate universal justice.* It does so consistently from the universal stories about mankind to the particular story of the people of Israel. Even biblical passages that seem most particularistic and racist—the conquest of the Promised Land and the destruction of the Canaanites for example—or those that seem most cruel and unjust—collective punishment, and capital punishment for ritual violations—are proven to be just under the circumstances. You simply have to read the text. Reading these passages shows that they actually defend what atheists wrongly consider to be modern concepts of universal justice. These include land and sovereignty for all people, collective responsibility for implementing justice, and respectful human relationships.

Let me emphasize that we will be doing a careful reading of the text. We will not resort to rhetorical gymnastics to avoid unpleasant obstacles. To offer one example, when the Bible metes out the death penalty, it is less a function of cruelty than a catalog of the seriousness of certain offenses at a time when the death penalty was ubiquitous. Yes, the Bible bends to its time, although the ancient rabbis would be among the first to limit the application of the death penalty. Likewise, and contrary to atheist accusations, the Bible neither celebrates slavery nor the oppression of women, as did other ancient cultures. Rather it confines and implicitly condemns them, at the same time opening the way to their gradual demise. The Bible defends personal freedoms to an extent unheard of in the ancient world, an epoch in which people were confined to class, customs, and occupation from birth. Biblical personalities consistently shatter social molds, practices, and even niceties. The Bible's stories may herald from an era almost alien to us. Yet modern readers still find in their message an inspiration to fight against the injustices they see around them.

This is why, contrary to atheist claims, modern emancipation movements have often found inspiration in the Bible and monotheistic teachings. These movements have, in turn, enabled monotheists to recover their tradition from those who had oppressed in the "name of God" through distorted and selective use of the Bible. They have also inspired many modern monotheists to reexamine biblical passages and interrogate traditional interpretations that contradict the Bible's overall message of justice and equality, especially with respect to women. The Bible's purpose was to expose lies about power and transform society. This is why it is so tragic to find its message purposefully distorted. The Bible remains civilization's most powerful moral text, if we only read it as it was meant to be read.

The Bad Book

The atheist writers all agree that the Bible and the Abrahamic religions are antithetical to contemporary justice. They promote the chauvinism, violence, and senseless punishments that form the core of monotheistic teachings. In the atheists' view, monotheists who claim otherwise simply turn a blind eye to the biblical text. On chauvinism, Michel Onfray writes: "Let us give credit where it is due. The Jews invented monotheism and everything that went with it. First divine right and its mandatory correlative: the chosen people exalted, other peoples discounted; a logical enough sequence."[1] Further, according to the atheists, the Scriptures take chauvinism to its logical end. They justify collective punishment and, worse, genocide for the benefit of the chosen nation, whether Jews, Christians, or Muslims. As Dawkins explains: "The ethnic cleansing begun in the time of Moses is brought to bloody fruition in the book of Joshua, a text remarkable for the bloodthirsty massacres it records and the xenophobic relish with which it does so."[2] From Onfray's perspective: "The Catholic, Apostolic, and Roman Church excels in the destruction of civilizations. It invented ethnocide, the spiritual rather than the physical extinction of cultures."[3] In the atheists' view, the extent of war and destruction perpetrated by monotheists in the name of God proves this point. As noted earlier, the atheists believe that the Scriptures not only promote violence but also perversely urge draconian punishments for behaviors that harm no one. In Dawkins' words: "My purpose has been to demonstrate that we (and that includes most religious people) as a matter of fact *don't* get our morals from scripture. If we did, we would strictly observe the Sabbath and think it just and proper to execute anybody who chose not to. [...] We would execute disobedient children."[4]

According to the atheist writers, it is inconceivable that our cherished contemporary commitment to justice and freedom for all humans derives from the Bible or monotheistic religions. Those who disagree simply deceive themselves. Hitchens argues, "Then there is the very salient question of what the commandments do *not* say. Is it too modern to notice that there is nothing about the protection of children from cruelty, nothing about rape, nothing about slavery, and nothing about genocide? Or is it too exactly 'in context' to notice that some of these very offenses are about to be positively recommended?"[5] In Dawkins' words: "All I am establishing is that modern morality, wherever else it comes from, does not come from the Bible."[6] For the atheist writers, attempts to dispute their reading of the Bible and religion are deceitful "apologetics." Dawkins writes: "If we reject Deuteronomy and Leviticus (as all enlightened moderns do), by what criteria do we then decide which of religion's moral values to *accept*? Or should we pick and choose among all the world's religions until we find one whose moral teaching suits us?"[7] The atheist authors contend that we should confront the objectionable scriptural verses on their plain reading. If we don't, we are being dishonest. If we do, then we modern Western people must acknowledge that the Bible's message is based on standards of inequality and domination and submission. This would make the Bible no different than idolatry.

CHAPTER 5

How Not to Read the Bible

The way I would answer this is that you would have to analyze the text in question and critique text with text and so instead of taking an isolated text from the Bible out of context such as a particular story where God is commanding the Israelites to attack another group or whatever, that you need to look at both the context and other texts, too.

—REVEREND DR. KATHARINE HENDERSON

The atheists' criticisms of the Bible would be a fatal blow to monotheism if they actually emanated from a correct reading of the Bible. But they don't. The atheist writers satisfy themselves with select biblical passages to make their point. They ignore many others that would contradict their argument. As an example, Dawkins writes that biblical morals are "just plain weird."[1] This is too glib. Does Dawkins find the biblical prohibitions against murder and theft weird? How about its provisions for the use of fair weights and measures? Treating strangers with kindness?

To better illustrate the atheists' methods of misinterpretation, consider the following. A friendly Martian lands on Earth. He covers his antennas with a hipster hat, commences to learn English, and investigates this planet we humans call home. Our Martian visits the library, where he comes across an article in a legal journal specializing in the most problematic American statutes. He reads about the USA Patriot Act (which authorizes unprecedented surveillance and detention and allots powers akin to martial law to the president), the "three-strikes law" in certain states (whereby after three convictions a defendant is sent to prison for life without the possibility of parole), and virtually any law or treaty related to Native Americans prior to the last half century. This friendly Martian might well conclude that the United States is a terrible, immoral place beset with evil rulers. And yet, had this same Martian come across an article discussing the Bill of Rights and other constitutional protections, he would certainly have a different opinion. In selectively choosing the biblical passages they present as evidence, the atheist writers limit the understanding of their audience at the outset. They tell them only what they want them to believe.

The atheist authors also practice a decontextualized reading of disturbing biblical passages, thereby altering their meaning. What does such a decontextualized reading look like? Let's say our same friendly Martian picks up an American history text and reads that the president had ordered the capture and killing of Osama bin Laden. He learns that Americans celebrated that action. His conclusion? The United States was comprised of rabid people who reveled in their leaders randomly ordering the killing of other humans. However, any helpful Earthling librarian could offer the Martian some articles on September 11, 2001, which would put the president's order in perspective. The Martian might still object to the American government's actions but would comprehend the context and circumstances in which they were taken. Omission of crucial information about context is at the heart of the problem with the atheists' reading of the Israelite's conquest of the land of Canaan, which we will consider later in this section.

The atheists, further, appear insensitive to how literary style impacts the meaning of the texts. Or, perhaps, they purposely choose to ignore it. This distorts their readings. They fail, for example, to differentiate between what the Bible reports and how the Bible expects its readers to react to that narrative. In many instances, the biblical text clearly disparages the actions of the actors it is chronicling. Returning once again to our friendly Martian, suppose he picks up a copy of *The New York Times* to read. He would hopefully recognize that just because the *Times* recounted certain stories of mayhem, criminality, war, or bad public policy, it does not mean that the *Times* editorial board endorsed those actions. In fact, our helpful librarian might offer to explain that the

Times' decision to report certain stories actually demonstrated its moral concern. Yet, here we have the atheists making just this error. Dawkins cites the story of the concubine at the end of the Book of Judges—an admittedly gruesome, bloody, and profoundly disturbing narrative—as evidence of the Bible's cruelty.[2] But this unwarranted cruelty is precisely what the Bible wants to drive home to its readers. The Book of Judges concludes with this horrifying event and then tags on the following ominous coda: "In those days there was no king in Israel; everyone did as he pleased." (Judges 21:25) The added verse contains a pointed double entendre. The phrase "there was no king" refers both to a human king, anticipating the Book of Samuel, in which the anointment of a king is condoned and chronicled, and to the Heavenly King, God, since "everyone did as he pleased." There could be no harsher biblical indictment of the Israelites than that they had set aside God's teachings, the Torah, with its blueprint of justice, and opted, instead, for a lawless society.

The atheist authors also accuse religious thinkers of simply interpreting the Bible to suit their agenda. This view is a gross distortion of the interpretive traditions within the three monotheistic religions, all of which maintain rules of interpretation, not unlike the rules for interpreting law, literature, philosophy, or science for that matter. Once again, imagine our friendly Martian handed the American Constitution cold turkey, no commentary, no indication of its interpretation, implementation, or intent. His views of the Constitution would surely be skewed. He might think the Fifth Amendment allowed for all accused parties to remain silent in court and therefore no case could reasonably move forward. Or he might understand the First Amendment as permitting someone to shout "fire" in a crowded theater.

Without delving into the technicalities of the three monotheistic religions' interpretation of Scriptures, their general parallels with legal interpretations and academic source analysis are revealing. For example—and unsurprisingly—all three monotheistic religions require an accurate reading of the words of the text. They also demand the kind of consideration of context and narrative style that I have described above. In addition, each of the Abrahamic faiths are in possession of compendia of traditional interpretations for the texts, which serve as a starting point for scholars. In the case of Judaism, the primary interpretive aid to the Bible is the Oral Law, or the Talmud. In brief, the Talmud contains earlier additional laws and interpretations of the Bible, called the *Mishna*, as well as later extensive rabbinic discussions of the *Mishna* and the Bible, called the *Gemara*. There are two Talmuds, one compiled in Jerusalem and the other in Babylon. Another source for scriptural exegesis consists of a collection of rabbinic stories and interpretations called the Midrash. Islamic scholars refer to the compendia of Mohammad's interpretations as the *hadith*. Both the Talmud and the hadith are often referred to as oral tradition because they were, indeed, originally passed down orally. Both expand upon and specify meanings in the written texts. The Christian Church fathers provided some of the first written commentaries on the Bible and New Testament. These continue to be authoritative in many Christian denominations, though they do not hold the same status as the oral tradition in Islam and Judaism. For Jews and Muslims, the written word cannot be interpreted without the Talmud or hadith, respectively, yet the atheist authors ignore the oral tradition. This flaw will become apparent when discussing capital punishment in the Bible, whose application in Judaism draws almost exclusively from interpretations recorded in the Talmud. Monotheistic religious scholars and theologians throughout the ages have borne the responsibility for translating scriptural verses into humanly performable and enforceable laws. Monotheistic traditions have always read the principles and stories of the Bible in relation to their intuitive morality and to their lived experience.

No discussion of the monotheistic traditions of Scriptural interpretation can fail to note that the Bible and Scriptures are also works of art. They are written with literary craftsmanship and techniques that enrich the text and deepen the reader's understanding of its message. If our friendly Martian visited in the summertime and was patient enough to stand in line for hours and land a ticket to a free performance of Shakespeare's *Henry V* in Central Park, he could easily conclude that he was privy to an eyewitness report of events. The helpful librarian might refer him to a Google search. Here he would learn that Shakespeare took great poetic license in representing the events and the words of the protagonists he portrayed. The Bard chose the literary genre of drama and employed the literary devices of humor, rhyme, and poetry, even while adhering to the contours of historical events relatively accurately.

This book claims that, in the case of the Bible, the first eleven chapters of Genesis venture beyond literary license, certainly into the realm of metaphor, but never into the realm of myth. There is a big difference. These early Genesis tales in the first eleven chapters are super-compact stories. They describe extremely complex and long-term historical processes, such as the creation of the world and the development of the first human civilizations, in a largely poetic way. This style is intended to highlight essential ethical and theological points. As the Bible unfolds, relating stories of the patriarchs and the Exodus, the narrative increasingly shifts into a historical account. That being said, the Bible continues to make extensive use of poetic forms. Among them, repetition of turns of phrase, puns, word games, and symbolic numbers convey the theological and moral points of the stories in creative and effective ways. These forms also make the Bible's stories memorable, just as the poetic lyrics and rhythmic patterns of accomplished songwriters linger in the minds of their listeners. Literary devices underscore the message of the text, and their presence in no way reflects upon the text's historicity outright. The Battle of Agincourt certainly took place, but perhaps without Henry V's speech happening precisely as depicted by Shakespeare. As Shakespeare has Henry V say:

> Old men forget; yet all shall be forgot,
> But he'll remember, with advantages,
> What feats he did that day. Then shall our names,
> Familiar in his mouth as household words
> Harry the king, Bedford and Exeter,
> Warwick and Talbot, Salisbury and Gloucester,
> Be in their flowing cups freshly remember'd.
> This story shall the good man teach his son.

So perhaps the Bible, as Shakespeare explains, makes "household" names with literary "advantages" that make them unforgettable.

The atheist authors base their judgments on a highly selective view of historical processes. Here's our friendly Martian taking a coffee break at the library vending machine and overhearing a group of people discussing the Ku Klux Klan. Curious, he uses his newfound knowledge to google the Klan and sees it self-described as a Christian group. He might conclude being Christian means being racist and violent. Yet, the historical record clearly establishes that the Ku Klux Klan is a fringe group within the history of Christianity. The same would be true if the

Martian were informed of the Taliban's destruction of the world's largest Buddhas in the Hindu Kush mountains or encountered details of the assassination of Yitzhak Rabin by Yigal Amir. When the atheists accuse religion of being the major cause of war, and when they contend modern morality is exclusively secular in origin, they are committing two basic fallacies: (1) of generalizing based on extreme, unrepresentative examples, and (2) of taking at face value what people say they are even if their actions say otherwise.

Let's examine the texts and historical record regarding monotheistic morality based on the above-mentioned rules for reading the texts. As we do so, I suggest that the Bible be read simultaneously in two ways. First, as a text of its time, tailored to its first readers who emerged from a world of radical inequality and injustice. Second, as a source of timeless principles and concepts about the nature of justice and equality. This duality explains how the Bible could both generate a revolution in the ancient world and continue to inspire people in the modern one. It also explains why monotheists are increasingly ready to extend equality and justice to all, even beyond the biblical parameters; for these parameters are, in some cases, limited by the context of ancient realities that no longer apply.[1]

---

[1] A note on the references for part two. The references in this section have two functions: sources for data and sources for arguments. This chapter incudes the many historical surveys and case studies of legal phenomenon that have been used to fact-check the data used to make my arguments. The main arguments and/or interpretations of these sources do not necessarily accord with the arguments I am making in this section. The sources that have been used as a source for my arguments are mentioned explicitly in the text as well as referred to in the endnotes.

CHAPTER 6

The Bible Is About Each of Us

God said, "Listen, take it from the Adam story, if you follow God's instructions as to what to do, you will be all right." But the people always seem to eat from the tree and do everything God tells them not to do. God comes back, never questioning, always in love with them. "I love you. I forgive you. You are going to pay for some of this foolishness, but remember, it is your own doing. I told you not to do it." God is faithful, even if we are not faithful.

—REVEREND DR. CALVIN BUTTS

Genesis and the Big Bang of Universalism

One has only to open the Bible and start reading to discover its concepts of human equality and universal justice. The first eleven chapters of the Bible begin with Adam and Eve, continue with Cain and Abel, lead up to Noah, and finish with the fractious citizens of the Tower of Babel. These multilayered early chapters profoundly address the human condition and relationships. It's no wonder that these stories have captured the imagination of writers, artists, and philosophers, as well as theologians, for almost two millennia. They have come to form the archetypical narrative of Western and Islamic culture.[1]

The Bible asserts that God created man and woman in His image: "And God created man in His image, in the image of God He created him; male and female He created them." (Genesis 1:27) Scripture further tells us that, because all human beings are descendants of the first human, consequently we are all brothers and sisters.[1] At the risk of stating the obvious, the meaning of this passage is clear. Humans, both men and women, are inextricably connected with each other no matter what side of a border they live on, how they worship, the color of their skin, or their sex. Such assertions are a radical departure from the received wisdom of ancient idolatrous cultures, where station, ethnicity, and gender determined your worth, your right to life, or even your ability to claim the status of a god.

The story of Adam and Eve describes the universal human condition. Adam and Eve succumbed to the temptation of eating from the tree of the knowledge of good and evil, which God had forbidden. This led to their fall from perfection, resulting in the flawed world we know. The story communicates a universal message: good and evil are always before us, and the knowledge and desire for both are within us all. We humans are neither omnipotent nor omniscient—and certainly not gods. But we do possess the power to discern good from evil, to make choices, and to channel our drives—as anyone faced with a pint of Ben & Jerry's Chunky Monkey ice cream already knows. (More about these drives in part three, which deals with evil.) Our choices, made under imperfect circumstances and with limited information, literally create our world. In this way, the Bible defines humans by their moral choices, and not, as in idolatrous cultures, by fate, station, nor the whims of the gods. The most foundational and enduring biblical narratives concern men and women's choices and the effect they have on individuals and on society at large.

The story of Cain and Abel (Genesis 4) is a weighty tale about human relations and choices. Cain and Abel fought, as many brothers do, but this sibling rivalry only turned lethal when the subject turned to pleasing God—in other words, religion. The two brothers both made offerings; God favored Abel's. Cain became furious with God's refusal to accept his offering and took his anger out on his brother, the world's first case of

---

[1] The rabbis have a lot to say about the fact that the Bible includes two creation stories of man. The first of man and woman and the second of Adam and Eve. I recommend the discussion of these two stories in Joseph B. Soleveitchik, *The Lonely Man of Faith* (Jerusalem: Maggid, 2012). And for Kabbalistic commentaries on the creation stories and their implications for gender and the relationship between the sexes see Sarah Yehudit Schneider, *Kabbalistic Writings on the Nature of Feminine and Masculine* (Jerusalem: Devora, 2009).

fratricide. Cain is confronted by God, and his response gives us one of the most memorable quotes of Western culture: "Am I my brother's keeper?" (Genesis 4:9) Here the Bible describes the problem of jealousy and pride. It reveals at the outset humankind's inability to show mutual respect and failure to cooperate. Instead of working together with Abel, Cain becomes so consumed by pride that he eliminates his perceived competition for God's attention. He then denies his responsibility for his brother.

Based on this tale, we can infer that the Bible wants us to respond to the question "Am I my brother's keeper?" with a resounding *Yes! Yes! Yes! I am absolutely my brother's keeper.* Whether his offering is better than mine or worse, my responsibility for my brother rises far above my selfish pride. I *am* my brother's keeper. Such a message of responsibility for one's fellow stands in stark contrast to the idolatrous culture of dogged competition with and ruthless power over others.

The Bible's universal messages about human relations continue in the stories of Noah and the Tower of Babel (Genesis 6–11:10). This time the story extends beyond the family to the social and political level. Cain's murderous example to mankind led to the degenerate generation of Noah's lifetime. The Bible notes, "the earth became corrupt before God; the earth was filled with lawlessness." (Genesis 6:11) Human beings certainly knew there was a God and understood the difference between good and evil. Yet, they ignored this knowledge and chose instead to fulfill their drives at any cost. This attitude devolved into a self-destructive spiral of murder, thievery, and abuse. Humanity was on a course to destroy itself. To prevent this, God decreed a reboot with Noah. Subsequently, according to the story, God made a covenant with Noah that all of humanity would never in the future be destroyed, no matter what their sins. (Genesis 6:18 and 8:21) But this covenant, the first one in the Bible, came with an explicit moral command. God prohibited murder. The text reads:

> Whoever sheds the blood of man,
> By man shall his blood be shed;
> For in His image did God make man. (Genesis: 9:6)

A simple law. Should any person take another's life, the killer will pay for it. This law asserts the most basic freedom, that every individual has a God-given right to life. In addition, it affirms that reward and punishment exist in the world to protect that freedom. Can we imagine such a law in effect in the ancient world, where fathers could sacrifice or murder their newborn children or where one could pay off a victim's family to excuse punishment for murder? According to oral tradition, though not recorded in the Bible, God repeated five other laws to Noah as well. These included no idolatry, no blasphemy, no stealing, no incest or bestiality, and the positive commandment to set up a court system. (Babylonian Talmud Sanhedrin 58b) The list was completed by the command not to eat from living animals prior to their ritual slaughter which, like the prohibition of murder, was mentioned in the Bible. (Genesis 9:4) The Noah story reminds us that certain absolute and universal laws must be *constantly remembered* if humanity is to avoid creating a culture of abuse that only ends in destruction. Yet, so often we fail. At a certain level, we seem to yearn for divine intervention. This lesson is even more poignant in our modern age in which multiple countries possess nuclear weapons that could set off literal and figurative chain reactions capable of obliterating all of civilization and the natural world. In ancient times, the Bible was already warning us of the power we possess to destroy all of humanity if we let evil prevail.

The first eleven chapters of the Bible conclude with the story of the Tower of Babel, a brief but potent tale of political hubris. All of humanity is forced to band together in its prideful attempts to build a tower that will allow man to touch the very heavens and conquer the realm of God. It is often overlooked that in the story, the people were coerced to have one language and one purpose. (Genesis 11:6) In essence, this presents a paradigm for all totalitarian regimes that follow, from Caesar to Mao. Previously in Genesis (10:5), we had learned that different peoples had already developed different languages and lived in different lands.[2] Somehow a tyrant or tyrannical elite group had managed to subjugate humanity and impose one purpose and one language on them. Thus, by chapter 11 the Bible already shares Onfray's viewpoint about ethnocide. While commonly understood as a punishment for humanity's arrogance, in the story God merely restores the previous status quo: to each people a different language and a different piece of land to call home. (Genesis

---

[2] Although this point is clear in the Bible, almost everyone I have talked to has such a preconceived view of the story of the Tower of Babel in the Bible that they miss the point of how humanity lived before.

11:7–8) The story thus explains that man's purpose is not universal totalitarianism, nor is it cultural uniformity; rather, our purpose is to create a good society and to get along with other societies.

The early chapters of Genesis thus contain universal messages for humanity. They have inspired a vast amount of written commentary and creative art. With the conclusion of the Noah and Tower of Babel parables, the Bible transitions from archetypical moral stories about the human condition to more naturalistic depictions of the day-to-day world. It does so by focusing on one branch of humanity.

Abraham—A Man with a New Plan

The atheists' accusation that the Bible is a racist text obsessed with the power and glory of one people could not be further from the truth. Even after the events of the Tower of Babel, men yet again tended toward abuse and oppression of one another. God decides to provide humanity a leader to serve as a role model for all. The universal scope of Abraham's mission becomes clear from God's first encounter with him:

> I will bless those who bless you
> And curse him that curses you;
> And all the families of the earth
> Shall bless themselves by you. (Genesis 12:3)

God does not abandon the world for Abraham. Nor does He set Abraham on a course of world domination through promises of smashing military victories, oodles of exotic booty, or legions of foreign slaves. Instead, God is intent upon teaching the world about justice and love of humanity through the perfect example of Abraham. Because Abraham is not just for Abraham. Abraham is for everyone, the antithesis of the idolatrous leader. He eschews any plans for world conquest. He voluntarily prays from his own conscience and from the heart for the wicked people of Sodom to be spared destruction. (Genesis 18:23–33) Abraham not only foresees a world of justice and cooperation, he wants to enable people to learn how to bring it into being. Abraham possesses the courage to enter a potentially deadly war to rescue his nephew Lot. He makes this decision even though the two had earlier parted under not-so-friendly circumstances. (Genesis 14)

As Abraham grows old, he passes on his mission to teach just and cooperative relationships to his children. God blessed all of the descendants of the Abrahamic line. Jacob's children are given instructions about the right way to live. Like Jacob, Esau and Ishmael are endowed with a special mission to father their own nations, take possession of their own lands, and found unique kingdoms. Jewish tradition considers Ishmael and Esau the archetypical fathers of Islam and Christianity, respectively. Both traditions endeavor to carry on the moral message of Abraham—admittedly, not without considerable sibling rivalry. For their part, Christians and Muslims see themselves in a universalistic role, as well. However, the Bible's universal message does not end with Abraham's descendants.

The Demonstration Nation

Thus, according to the Bible, the purpose of the Israelite nation was to serve as an example to other nations. The Israelites were to model an alternative society founded on laws that promote justice and equality. You can look high and low for a hierarchical order of kings, nobles, and slaves among the Bible's laws, but to no avail. All you will find is the Israelites, divided into tribes of equal standing and equal status before the law. True, priests are entrusted with special functions, but few special privileges, and strangers, elsewhere exposed, fall under the protection of the law. The Israelites are awarded one homeland, but they are also under a divine mandate not to conquer any others. Understood in this light, the Bible's depiction of Israel's laws is no more racist or condescending to other nations than the description of a person's exemplary principles is to other individuals. For, at the end of the day, both examples are human. Before the Israelites entered the land, God had the following words to say:

> See, I have imparted to you laws and rules, as the Lord my God has commanded me, for you to abide by in the land that you are about to enter and occupy. Observe them faithfully, for that will be proof of your wisdom and discernment to other peoples, who on hearing of all these laws will say, "Surely, that great nation is a wise and discerning people." For what great nation is there that has a god so close at hand as is the Lord our God whenever we call upon Him? Or what great nation has laws and rules as perfect as all this Torah that I set before you this day? (Deuteronomy 4:5–8)

This message demonstrates without any room for doubt that the tenets and laws of the Bible are a gift intended for the Israelites to share with the world. If the Bible were as particularistic and racist as the atheists claim, it would ignore the other nations and denigrate their capacities. Yet the Bible does just the opposite. As the text indicates, "When they hear all these statutes, they shall say: 'Surely, that great nation is a wise and discerning people.'" Thus, in contrast to the rest of the ancient world, whose nations sought to inspire fear of their unfettered power, the Israelites were appointed to inspire emulation of God's laws. Their purpose in entering the land is to establish a model polity there and only there. In place of a domination nation, the Bible aspires for the Israelites to be a demonstration nation.

At the same time, the Bible is not offering up hagiography. The Israelites are depicted with gross warts and all. The people betray God on a whim, kings are depicted as adulterers and idolaters, and the high priests even forget the Bible. But, most shockingly for the ancient context, no one in the history of the Israelite nation is considered a god or god descendant. Moses, the greatest figure in the Bible, is a mere mortal whose very burial place is obscured lest people worship his remains.

We Can All Be the Dude that Makes a Difference

The Bible is concerned that not only the Israelites but all other nations learn to act justly. This idea pervades the later prophetic writings, as well. The Books of Job and Jonah explicitly concern the well-being and fate of non-Abrahamic and non-Israelite peoples. The Bible's description of God's fury against nations that practice idolatry and oppress their own and others provides a sign of His concern for all humans. If God did not care about other peoples, He would have little reason to reward or punish them. Yet the Bible leaves little doubt of its intent that all people treat each other justly and learn to cooperate for the greater good.

Other books of the Hebrew Scriptures—such as Psalms, Ecclesiastes, and Song of Songs—communicate the message of God's concern and kindness for all His creation. The recurring theme in Psalms is that God will bless and protect all *good* people: "He will bless the House of Israel; He will bless the House of Aaron; He will bless those who fear the Lord, small and great alike." (Psalm 115:12–13) The words of the prophets such as Amos, Micah, and Hosea demonstrate the Bible's concern for universal justice. Here is the Prophet Amos:

"To Me, O Israelites, you are
Just like Ethiopians"—declares the Lord.
"True, I brought Israel up
From the Land of Egypt,
But also the Philistines from Caphtor
And the Arameans from Kir." (Amos 9:7)

Isaiah shares his vision for a utopian world in which

In the days to come,
The Mount of the Lord's House
Shall stand firm above the mountains
And the tower above the hills;
And all the nations shall gaze on it with joy.
And the many peoples shall go and say:
Come,
Let us go up to the Mount of the Lord,
To the House of Jacob;
That he may instruct us in His ways,
And that we may walk in His Paths. (Isaiah 2:3)

Man will live in peace and harmony when he discards the desire to dominate, abuse, and oppress others. The Bible and its prophetic writings are the first books to describe an alternative to the abuse of power: the acceptance of monotheism's moral tenets and laws.

The prophets' specific admonishments to the Israelites are also meaningful for all peoples and have been interpreted as universal refrains. Reverend Dr. Katharine Henderson comments on Isaiah's message:

You could take a prophetic text, from Isaiah 58, for example, the "repairs of the breach" text, which has very specific language about how to live a moral life. "Is this not the fast that I choose, to loosen the bonds of injustice and to set the oppressed free, to bring the homeless poor into your home, to clothe the naked, to visit the imprisoned" and it connects those activities on behalf of the most vulnerable in a society with belief in God? If you do these things, these moral things, then God will be present with you, you will feel the spirit of God as a presence in your life and you will be called the repairer of the breech, the restorer of streets where we live. So in that one prophetic text you have a pretty full picture of the kind of moral life that God intends for our action in the world, our behavior in the world on behalf of others, our service to others with God's presence, feeling, being in touch with God's presence and our identity in the world as individuals who repair breaches instead of creating them, a repairer of the breach, a restorer of streets to live. That is very tangible thing, it is called infrastructure. It is not just the food and the mouth of the hungry, it is clearing a path and creating an infrastructure for a just society.

It comes as no surprise that the soaring words of the later prophets are overlooked by the highly selective readers of the atheist camp. Although this book focuses primarily on the five books of Moses and the early prophets, since that is where the atheists concentrate their firepower, the overall arc of the Scriptures is universalistic. In the later prophetic texts, as in the Five Books of Moses, the role of the Jews is neither to dominate the world nor to exclude themselves from it. Rather, like Abraham himself, their role is to be a nation of righteous trailblazers and teachers by example. As Isaiah writes: "I will also make you a light of nations, that My salvation may reach the ends of the earth." (Isaiah 49:6) The goal is for each nation to create a more just society by their own initiative, while at the same time retaining their own distinct identity.

The Bible's concern for other nations is not only unique in the ancient world, it distinguishes it from most modern secular movements, whose outlook with regard to their neighbors has been economic and political self-interest. How many modern nations take as their goal the creation of a model society that others can emulate? Modern nations that claimed to show a concern for the prosperity of other countries have often used this claim selfishly. They imposed their preferred model of government and economy on others for their own material gain. Thus, the colonial French, for example, who claimed to help "uncivilized" Africans, imposed their legal and educational system, not to mention their language, throughout West Africa. At the same time, they exploited the native populations and their resources. In contrast, the Bible wants the world to willingly embrace the wisdom of the moral precepts it advocates, not to submit resentfully to compulsion nor require cultural assimilation.

CHAPTER 7

The Bible and Genocide

To those who accept the idea that the Bible *begins* with an overture of universal moral import, the atheists are eager to point out that what follows is anything but. God's gift of the land of Israel to Abraham and the command to wipe out the seven Canaanite nations that inhabit it is proof of how deeply racist and unjust the Bible really is. God promises the land to Abraham and his descendants (Genesis 12:1–8) and later commands the Israelites to conquer the land in the books of Numbers and Deuteronomy. Joshua executes the mission. In Hebrew, this commandment is referred to as the *herem*. In chapter 6 of the Book of Joshua, the Israelite army destroys the city of Jericho, killing all but one family. Joshua chapter 11 depicts the total destruction of Hazor, with not one survivor. Chapter 12 lists thirty-one defeated local kings, their subjects either slain or dispossessed. It is not difficult to see how readers of a modern sensibility—who find themselves barraged daily with gruesome reports and disturbing images of homeless Syrian and Yemenite refugees or, not long ago, the victims of genocide in South Sudan and similar global catastrophes—might find these biblical events a little too close for comfort. The atheists play off of our world in upheaval. They leverage current events to bolster their argument that God's very promise of land to Abraham is a sure indication that God is racist. Worse still, they add, the *herem* is a clear instance of genocide motivated by racial supremacy and imperialistic greed with a veneer of divine sanction committed against defenseless innocent indigenous people. According to this reading, the origin of racist imperialism and genocide is to be found in the biblical *herem*. The following discussion will consider each element of this claim.

A few readers may imagine some inferences from this discussion about the modern state of Israel and its present conflict with the Palestinians. This would be an error. Our discussion here focuses uniquely on the Bible's commandment with respect to the seven idolatrous groups that populated the land of Canaan *more than three thousand years ago.* Ancient and modern, rabbinical interpretations of this text are unanimous in their understanding that these seven nations no longer exist, or are no longer identifiable, and that these commandments no longer apply in our modern world.¹ The fact that these commandments have lapsed, however, does not alleviate the need for modern readers to wrestle with the question, "Why would a benevolent God ever enact such decrees?"

Is God a Racist?

God does not just care about the Israelites. The Bible depicts God as the sovereign of the universe, who awards land to all peoples. Atheists who claim otherwise are not simply misinterpreting the text but misreading it. As we have seen, leaders in idolatrous cultures had no qualms seizing any parcel of land that captured their fancy. Contrast this with the Bible's view that all people have been granted a rightful place in the Creator's world. In the story of God's promise of land to Abraham and the conquest of Canaan, we are meant to find one illustration among many of God's sovereignty over the world. We are meant, also, to understand the conditional nature of all human land ownership. We are not meant to raise a banner of blind chauvinism and nationalism in the name of the Israelite nation, nor celebrate one ancient people's power.

You don't have to read between the lines to get this. The Book of Joshua opens with preparations "to cross the Jordan, together with all this people, into the land that I am giving to the Israelites." (Joshua 1:2) The punch line: God apportions land to all peoples. Earlier, in Deuteronomy, God admonishes the Israelites not to disturb the groups to whom He has promised other lands, such as the descendants of Esau:

> And charge the people as follows: You will be passing through the
> territory of your kinsmen, the descendants of Esau, who live in Seir.

Though they will be afraid of you, be very careful not to provoke them. For I will not give you of their land so much as a foot can tread on; I have given the hill country of Seir as a possession to Esau. What food you eat you shall obtain from them for money; even the water you drink you shall procure from them for money. (Deuteronomy 2: 4–6)

The same holds true of Moab:

And the Lord said to me: Do not harass the Moabites or provoke them to war. For I will not give you any of their land as a possession; I have assigned Ar as a possession to the descendants of Lot. (Deuteronomy 2:9)

The point of the text is clear: God allots land to everyone, not only the Israelites, and God keeps his promises to everyone. Indeed, God does not just dispossess others for the Israelites, he does it for other peoples to whom he promises land. Regarding the Moabites, for example:

It [the land of the Moabites] was formerly inhabited by Emin, a people great and numerous, and as tall as the Anakites. Like the Anakites, they are counted as Rephaim; but the Moabites call them Emim. Similarly, Seir was formerly inhabited by the Horites; but the descendants of Esau dispossessed them, wiping them out and settling their place, just as Israel did in the land they were to possess, which the Lord has given to them. (Deuteronomy 2:10–12)

Still, we cannot escape asking, even if God apportions land to all peoples, why by means of gross injustice and death of civilians? Surely a benevolent God, like any doting parent, could arrange for every child to receive their portion at the table in peace.

Is God a Colonialist?

The *herem* is an instance of a universal rule: *God is the global realtor, and the mortgage is moral behavior.* When a people fail to behave morally, they forfeit their sovereignty, land, even their lives to another people. The *herem* makes this point. When God first promises Abraham that his descendants will inherit the Promised Land, He tells him, "they [your descendants] shall return here in the fourth generation, for the iniquity of the Amorites [one of the seven Canaanite nations] is not yet complete." (Genesis 15:16) Abraham's offspring would first have to go into exile in Egypt and subsequently survive as slaves simply so the Canaanites would have time to repent. Only failing such repentance could God justify the destruction of the Canaanites and the transfer of land to Abraham's descendants.

The implication of this statement is clear. First, Abraham's neighbors were up to no good. In fact, not only do the children of Jacob have to get out of Dodge, but all of Abraham's children—Ishmael and the children later born to Ketura, as well as his grandchild Esau—are hustled out of Canaan, as well (see Genesis 21:14, 25:6, and 36:6). The second implication of the statement is that God does not play favorites, dispossessing and destroying one creation for the sake of another willy-nilly. Nor are evil societies randomly punished, but only when they have reached a point of no return. This notion is made explicit in the following text: "And when the Lord your God has thrust them from your path, say not to yourselves, 'The Lord has enabled us to possess this land because of our virtues'; it is rather because of the wickedness of those nations that the Lord is dispossessing them before you." (Deuteronomy 9:4–5)

The Canaanites are far from the only people who risk destruction and/or exile if they sink into moral corruption. The same universal law applies to Israelites. If they fulfill their divine responsibilities, they reap reward; if they fail, they risk punishment. This is just another example of the atheist authors neglecting a text that clearly contradicts their claims:

> "When you have begotten children and children's children and are long established in the land, should you act wickedly and make for yourselves a sculpted image in any likeness, causing the Lord your God displeasure and vexation, I call heaven and earth to this day to witness against you that you shall soon perish from the land that you are crossing the Jordan to possess; you shall not long endure in it, but shall be utterly wiped out." (Deuteronomy 4:25–26)

In another passage, God promises untold calamities to the Israelites if they abandon His laws: "The Lord will let loose against you calamity, panic, and frustration in all enterprises you undertake, so that you shall soon be utterly wiped out because of your evil-doing in forsaking me." (Deuteronomy 28:20) Among these curses, which include pestilence, disease, and many forms of suffering, God also promises foreign invasion and destruction: "The Lord will bring a nation against you from afar, from the end of the earth, which swoop down like the eagle—a nation whose language you do not understand, a ruthless nation, that will show the old no regard and the young no mercy." (Deuteronomy 28: 49–50) God also threatens exile: "The Lord will scatter you among all the peoples from one end of the earth to the other, and there you shall serve other gods, wood and stone, whom neither you nor your ancestors have experienced. Yet among those nations you shall find no peace, nor shall your foot find a place to rest." (Deuteronomy 28:64–65)

The conquering Israelites live under the same threat as the Canaanites. Such moral equivalency was unknown in the ancient world. Empires came and went because of the raw power they wielded, not because of their virtuous ways. The Bible also recounts how God made good on his threats. The books of Kings and Chronicles describe how the united monarchy under King Solomon disintegrated after a fight over succession. Jeroboam created his own kingdom in the north and erected two temples, one of which included golden bulls at the entrance. Ahab and his infamous wife Jezebel allowed Baal worship to become a national religion (1 Kings 16:31). The Prophet Elijah (1 Kings 18–21; 2 Kings 1; 2 Chronicles 21) and his attendant and then successor Elisha (1 Kings 18–21) called the Jews of the Northern Kingdom to repent and reject idol worship, but to no avail. The Jews in the Kingdom of Judah behaved marginally better. The Prophet Jeremiah demanded that the people of Judah repent from their idolatrous practices (Jeremiah 1–2, 6, 11, 14, 23, 27, 28), again to no avail. God enforced his stated conditions and unleashed destruction and exile on the Jews. Sennacherib finished the conquest, which included the deportation of the Jews from the Northern Kingdom and some of the Jews from Judah. The ten tribes that lived in the Northern Kingdom were lost forever. (2 Kings 17–18) The remaining Jews of Judah, who had still not learned their lesson, were deported a second time and Solomon's temple destroyed by Nebuchadnezzar II. (2 Kings 24–25 and 2 Chronicles 36; Jeremiah 52) Though some of the Jews of Judah returned to Judah after repenting (Book of Ezra), ultimately God also exiled them again and destroyed the Second Temple.

Elsewhere in the Bible, as atheists again omit, God punishes all nations for the injustices they commit against their own and against others. In Amos chapters 1 and 2, the prophet catalogs the sins of the kingdoms of Damascus, Gaza, Tyre, Edom, Moab, Amnon, Judah, and Israel, thus illustrating how God punishes cruelty and moral transgressions against other nations, not simply against the Israelites. Against Damascus he writes: "Thus said the Lord: For three transgressions of Damascus, for four, I will not revoke it. Because they threshed Gilead with threshing boards of iron." (Amos 1:3) He also criticized Moab for their crimes against Edom.

> Thus said the Lord:
> For three transgressions of Moab,
> For four, I will not revoke it:
> Because he burned the bones
> Of the King of Edom to lime.
> I will send down fire upon Moab,
> And it shall devour the fortress of Kerioth.
> And Moab shall die in tumult,
> Amid shouting and the blare of horns;
> I shall wipe out the ruler from within her
> And slay all her officials along with him—said the Lord.
> (Amos 2:1–3)

This is all well and good, someone might say, but still, why did God command the Israelites to kill Canaanite civilians?

Is God Genocidal?

The biblical *herem* is an instance of harsh justice against the immoral Canaanites who refused to mend their ways. It is not an example of racial genocide. Here again, atheist critics simply fail to read the text. The Bible is staunch in its assertion that in this world there are some crimes so heinous they deserve death, some societies so criminal they warrant extinction. (Later in this chapter we will discuss whether we moderns still believe this.) Contrary to atheist apologetics, the Bible emphasizes that the *herem* is all about the actions of the Canaanites and their crimes. It is not about the essence of the people. The Canaanites were granted the entire period of the Israelites' Egyptian exile to mend their ways. But even after the Exodus, which itself should have provided a clear and

111

uncomfortably close warning, the Canaanites continued in their corrupt ways. While the Israelites wandered in the wilderness for forty years, making no attempt to hide their goal to conquer the land (Numbers 10:29–30), the Canaanites squandered the opportunity to repent. But those few who did repent were later allowed to remain, and no one who left was ever hunted down on racial grounds. One major example of a repentant Canaanite is Rachav, the woman who housed the Israelite spies before the conquest. Her words to them are instructive:

> I know that the Lord has given the country to you, because dread of you has fallen upon us, and all the inhabitants of the land are quaking before you. For we have heard how the Lord dried up the waters of the Sea of Reeds [...] When we heard about it, we lost heart, and no man had any more spirit left because of you; for the Lord your God is the only God in heaven above and on earth below. Now since I have shown loyalty to you, swear to me, by the Lord that you in turn will show loyalty to my family. (Joshua 2:9–12)

Rachav recognized God's sovereignty over all the world as the basis for the Israelite claim to the land. As a result, she and her family were saved and allowed to stay. The Bible's implicit lesson is that any people or individual righteous enough to recognize God's sovereignty—which in this case means the Israelite right to possess this particular land, just as the Moabites possessed their particular land—will be spared. Further, the Bible commanded the Israelites to kill only those Canaanites who, despite all warning and opportunity, defiantly chose to remain in the Promised Land. (Deuteronomy 20:16–18) The Israelites were not sanctioned to hunt down any Canaanites who elected to depart. Self-exile was itself a punishment, but a lesser one than death. Self-exile symbolized acquiescence to God's decision to give the land to the descendants of Abraham. The Gergashites did just that and were spared.[1] Another nation, that of the Gibeonites, made a fraudulent offer to the Israelites. They contended deceitfully to be from a far distant land and proposed to become their servants. On this basis, they remained. (Joshua 9: 3–27)

---

[1] While the Gergashites were among the seven Canaanite nations that God had ordered the Israelites to drive out when taking the land, the Bible never mentions the Israelites warring with them. From this omission, one can surmise that they fled the land, leaving the Israelites no reason to wage war against them.

When King David conquered Jerusalem, he permitted the remaining Jebusites to stay and bought rather than took the future site of the Temple. (1 Samuel 24:18–25, 1 Chronicles 21: 18–27) The Jebusite seller acted piously and ultimately the other Jebusites must have as well, as they eventually assimilated into the Israelite community. The *herem* reveals a slow-motion process designed to allow anyone who so wished the time to effect an escape or repent. The Bible's assessment of most of the Canaanites, however, was that they were a people who refused to repent. As a nation steeped in decadence, they deserved the punishment they brought down upon themselves.

Are the Israelites Imperialists Just Hiding Behind God?

Some atheists suggest that the biblical depiction of the *herem* is a ruse to cover up standard imperialism. One might argue, for example, that the Israelites intended on their own to kill the Canaanites and then justified their plan by attributing it to the will of God. Some academic biblical scholars and atheists (as will be explored in greater detail in part five) go so far as to say that the Israelites wrote the Bible and did so in order to justify their actions *ex post facto* like other ancient chronicles. But if this were the case, then the biblical narrative makes no sense. As shown in part one, ancient Near Eastern empires had little need for either a divine gift of a homeland as reward for good behavior or for a justification of their brutal conquests.[2] Even if, as atheists and some biblical scholars claim, the Bible were written much later than the period of events it reports, the point remains. The Israelites' later neighbors were just as ruthless, gloating over imperial conquests *outside their homelands*, with no moral qualms. Nebuchadnezzar II, the neo-Babylonian emperor, felt no need to justify his many conquests in ancient Syria, Judah, and Egypt, which inspired terror throughout those lands.[3] The wise men of ancient Athens had no philosophical equivocations about utterly destroying Melos during the Peloponnesian War, even as Melos proclaimed its neutrality.[4] The Romans eviscerated Carthage and waged brutal wars of conquest against tribal groups and centralized states with the singular goal of enlarging their empire.[5]

In light of all this warfare in the region, how do atheists explain the fact that only the Israelites should be forbidden from taking any booty or capturing women as sex slaves? None of these prohibitions are logical if the *herem* is just a standard form of imperialism. As the Athenian diplomats explained to the people of Melos: there is no concept of right and wrong when it comes to conquest, there is no weighing of human life or worth, there is no sense of mercy; there is just strength and ruthlessness.[6] For the biblical narrative to mirror ancient tales of imperialism, conquest, and genocide, the story would have been completely different. It would have begun with a depiction of Abraham as a great warrior leader whose descendants slaughtered the Canaanites right away. Subsequent campaigns would lead to the creation of an Israelite empire, replete with relief statues and chronicles depicting the fate of the victims of the ambitious Israelites. If this hypothesis were true, what need would there have been to record a divine edict warning the Israelites that their lease on the land was subject to their good behavior? Ancient empires certainly interpreted current or future misfortune and losses as the result of cultic neglect.[7] None, however, recorded preemptive warnings about the consequences of an entire people's disobedience of ethical laws.

Finally, irrespective of the Bible, the human race was already familiar with genocide and ruthless in its execution. Claiming that the Bible introduced these sorts of practices is not only nonsense, it is slander. By contrast with ancient imperialism, the Bible makes it eminently clear that the Canaanite conquest was a one-time command that could never be carried out again. The Israelites were not to embark on imperial campaigns beyond the borders of the land promised to Abraham. More to the point, they did not gloat over their exploits with relief statues of massacres, nor was the conquest of Canaan commemorated as a national holiday. Rather, some rabbis considered this a tragic outcome that could have been avoided.[8]

Imperial actions of modern European Christians guilty of idolatrous ideologies of racism and supremacy highlight the difference between modern imperialism and the *herem*. Let's start with a comparison to the conquest of the Americas. The Bible depicts how the Israelites received the land from God as their *only homeland*, yet they were forced into exile to give the Canaanites time to repent or leave so as not to be punished. After the conquest, the Israelites even allowed righteous Canaanites to stay, not requiring they convert to Judaism. In contrast, the British, French, Spanish, Portuguese, and others who conquered and settled the Americas took the land of others on their own initiative *when they already had a homeland* in Europe.[9] They conquered with the official justification of converting natives to Christianity, buttressed by claims of supposed racial superiority. They made false pacts with the indigenous Americans, never intending to live up to their promises—in many cases resorting to mass murder instead.[10] In the 1850s, the Yuki Native Americans were almost wiped out in US government raids, their population dropping from 20,000 to 168 by the 1880s.[11] By the 1870s, after its land mass was firmly under the control of the government, the US still waged a ruthless war against the Apaches. The government murdered them, displaced them, broke previous treaties, and relegated them to desolate reservations.[12] If that weren't enough, it also forced them to adopt European culture. Even during the twentieth century, Americans, Australians, and Canadians of European ancestry continued to forcibly take indigenous children from their parents and place them in distant schools to assimilate them, thereby hoping for total cultural, if not physical, annihilation in three countries where the native peoples posed no serious political threat.[13]

The history of the Muslim empires has similar dynamics, also tinged with the idolatry of racism and supremacy. The Arab-dominated Islamic leadership who, like the Europeans, *already had a homeland*, in this case in the Arabian Peninsula, also conquered other lands and peoples. They dominated Assyrians in what is modern-day Iraq, and Copts in Egypt, as well as the Persians in Iran, as well as Berbers (Amazighs) in North Africa, Nubians in Sudan, and many others through military and imperial expansion. They too justified their actions by the spread of Islam. Though on the whole less brutal and racist than the later European imperialists, they nonetheless created a two-tiered society. Non-Arab populations were treated as *mawla* (clients), an inferior status even after their conversion to Islam,[2] and were taxed separately. Jews and Christians were also given an inferior status and required to pay special taxes. Indeed, throughout the Middle Ages, the Islamic Arab dynasties sought to end Amazigh (Berber) political independence in particular. To this end, the caliphate imported Arabs from the peninsula to North Africa to

---

[2] Lapidus, *Islamic Societies*, 50–53. For a concise history of minorities in the Islamic world, see Mordechai Nisan, *Minorities in the Middle East: A History of Struggle and Self-Expression* (Jefferson: McFarland, 2002).

alter the population on the ground and promote Arabization.[3] As with indigenous people in the Americas, the Amazigh are only now seeing political and linguistic recognition across North Africa. Farther south, the Islamic conquest of what is today Sudan had a similar ethnic dimension that is only now being addressed.[14] Several centuries later, the Turks would control the Islamic empire, subjugating the Arab peoples in turn, along with other Christian nations, and forcibly transferring populations. The Safavid Persians would likewise transfer hundreds of thousands of Armenians, Georgians, and Circassians. In the early seventeenth century, only 20 percent of the population of Armenia were Armenians as the result of Shah Abbas I's deportations. Even as late as the twentieth century, secular Arab states such as Egypt encouraged Egyptian Arabs to repopulate the areas cleared by the Aswan Dam so as to further Arabize the region.[15] In Mauritania, Arab Mauritanians continued to enslave African Mauritanians well into the twentieth century, as well.[16] Several governments in the region have the shared "honor" of trying to erase the Kurds. This imperial and colonial aspect of both the spread of Christianity and Islam—carried out as they were by specific peoples, who claimed superiority—still trouble modern-day adherents of both religions.

The reverse was true of the biblical Israelites. Though duped into a treaty with the Gibeonites using false pretense and trickery, the Israelites honored it and refrained from exiling or killing them. (Joshua 9:3–27) And over time, as the *Mishna* recounts, descendants of the Gibeonites embraced many Jewish traditions, though they were not compelled to do so. After the conquest of the Promised Land, the Israelites received no further divine command to go to war for additional territory. This, too, stands in sharp, painful contrast to the American experience. The Americans of European ancestry continued their imperial march to the Pacific Ocean based on the vision of manifest destiny. One can add the Americans' conquest of Hawaii and the Philippines to the list of territorial ambitions in the age of imperialism.[17]

Nor was the Israelite conquest marred by the kind of cruelty nineteenth-century Americans exhibited. As a "sport," American soldiers cut out Apache women's genitals, stretched them on saddles, and then wore

---

[3] For a history of the Berbers, see Michael Brett and Elizabeth Fentress, *The Berbers* (Oxford: Blackwell, 1996).

them as hats.[18] There is no evidence in the Bible of the Israelites gloating, displaying body parts, or boasting of destruction. However, even Theodore Roosevelt (admired for his trust busting, his regulations on food and drugs, and his support for the preservation of nature) blithely declared the Apache campaign "as righteous and beneficial a deed as ever took place on the frontier."[19] The carnage during the conquest of the Americas was not just the specialty of the British and their US and Canadian descendants. Western-colonizing nations perpetrated them in almost all of their colonies. Examples include the mines in Potosi, Mexico, or in Huancavelica, Peru, where the Spanish, *hardly lacking any territory*, literally worked the Native Americans to death for gold and silver.[20] In all of these cases, European Americans never questioned their sense of superiority, nor did they fear that they would suffer defeat if they did not uphold a higher moral standard. Even if Europeans, in particular, referred to the Bible to justify their actions, they certainly did not follow it, or they would never have acted with such avarice and cruelty.

The *herem* also differed from modern genocides. The Israelite conquest was not about revenge. By contrast, revenge has played an important role in modern genocides. The Israelites were not allowed to conquer Moab, as we have already seen, or to make war with the Moabites. This prohibition held even though the Moabites plotted to thwart Israel through the prophet Balaam's curses and then Balak's plot of the mass seduction of Israelite men by Moabite women. (Numbers 22–26) The Armenian genocide, however, was carried out by many Turkish Muslims who had been expelled from the recently independent Christian lands[21] (one might add the Turks had previously conquered and subdued these very lands). The Hutus slaughtered the Tutsis during the Rwandan genocide with the justification of revenge for Tutsi privilege during the colonial period.[22] Nor was it about racial extermination, as occurred with the Nazi and Rwandan genocides, as explained earlier.[4] For even the biblical call to destroy the Amalekites, was not about their "race," but rather about a collective retribution for their collective goal of destroying Israel.

Even with this background, some readers might argue, the killing of men, women, and children is always inexcusable, at least in modern

---

[4] On racial genocides, see Jones, Genocide; and Ben Kiernan, Blood and Soil: A World History of Genocide and Extermination from Sparta to Darfur (New Haven: Yale University Press, 2009).

times. No matter what the crimes of the Canaanites, no matter how much warning they were given, the *herem* was unjustifiable.

What is the Modern Take on Genocide?

Despite claims to the contrary, modern people actually describe some historical episodes of genocide in terms of "just punishment." These justifications reflect attitudes and values similar to those of the Bible. This historical fact is not immediately apparent. The official definition of genocide, according to the United Nations, reads as follows:

> *Any of the following acts committed with intent to destroy, in whole or in part, a national, ethnical, racial or religious group, as such: killing members of the group; causing serious bodily or mental harm to members of the group; deliberately inflicting on the group conditions of life calculated to bring about its physical destruction in whole or in part; imposing measures intended to prevent births within the group; [and] forcibly transferring children of the group to another group.*

No wiggle room here for right or wrong or the concept of collective punishment. Nonetheless, when subjugated peoples rose up in violent and even genocidal revolt against their European colonizers—such as the Native Americans in Upper Bolivia around the time of the American Revolution, or the Mayans led by Cecilo Chi and the African slaves in Haiti, both in the nineteenth century—historians have found justification for their behavior.[23] Nat Turner, who led a slave rebellion in Virginia, and Pompey, who did so in the Bahamas, were both responsible as leaders for the slaughter of many whites, some complicit and some not. Yet both men are regarded today as heroes who helped free their people from the yoke of unjust oppression. As genocide scholar Adam Jones suggests, C. L. R. James, the famed historian of the Haitian Revolution, "excuses the genocide of the Haitian whites based on past cruelties."[24]

In general, modern people distinguish between genocides and genocidal assaults that contain a morally plausible element of retribution or takeover by a formerly subjugated group. The latter are not only less likely to be condemned, they are often welcomed.[25] Other examples abound, including the expulsion of the Germans from the Sudeten lands and Poland after World War II and the Bosnians' retribution against the

Serbs for the atrocities at Srebrenica.[26] Contemporary morality, thus, does in the estimation of some experts concede some measure of collective punishment. It can be reasonably argued that the war against the Canaanites, and the underlying reasons for waging it, resembles the above-referenced scenarios more than it does those of modern imperialism and genocide.

Although the Canaanite conquest may fall under the rubric of a historically excused genocide, we must note the unique circumstances. The Israelite attack against the Canaanites is a punishment, at least at first, for the Canaanites' atrocities against God and themselves—that is—humanity. It is a sanction meted out only after the Canaanites were given time to change their ways and a forty-year final warning. Unlike the above-mentioned modern genocidal attacks we tend to excuse, the Israelites were not taking a swift revenge against former oppressors. The Bible also asserts that Canaanite culture stood as an impediment to the Israelites' mission to be a demonstration nation. Would any modern atheist reader have had moral qualms with the strategic annihilation of the Nazis in Germany in the 1920s, particularly the leaders, who would eventually lead the German people to commit mass murder? Would we not rather have given democratic leaders and groups a chance to lead Europe's largest nation to a better future? There is simply no basis for the atheists' claims that the *herem* is a precursor to modern imperialism and racial genocide.

Far from an epic of nationalistic pride, the Bible presents the history of the Israelite nation as a universal lesson for all peoples. The major difference between God's apportioning out lands to the Israelites and to other nations is that, in the case of the Israelites, *public miracles* in Egypt are associated with their departure to acquire their national homeland. The purpose of both the miracles and the redemption from Egypt was to inspire Israel's neighbors to understand, as did Rachav and Jethro and likely many unnamed others, that God was the sovereign of the world.

> You have but to inquire about bygone ages that came before you, ever since God created man on earth, from one end of heaven to the other: Has anything as grand as this ever happened, or has its like ever been known? Has any people heard the voice of God speaking out of a fire, as you have, and survived? Or has any god ventured to go and take for himself one nation from the midst of another

by prodigious acts, by signs and portents, by war, by a mighty and outstretched arm and awesome power, as the Lord your God did for you in Egypt before your very eyes. (Deuteronomy 4:32–34)

The story of the Israelites' acquisition of the Promised Land is God's way of demonstrating, through the example of one people, that no empire has the right to dominate other peoples. Nor can societies that descend into total corruption survive. Each nation has their sovereign place on earth, each is accountable for its actions, and each plays a distinct and important role in perfecting the world.

The Whole Class Will Have Detention

Contrary to the atheists' claim, the Bible condemns unwarranted collective punishment. Here again, the Bible stands in stark contrast to the rest of the ancient world. As shown in part one, the peoples of the ancient Near East considered it normal for the gods to punish entire populations for even minor infractions.[27] In this regard, Assyrian and Babylonian prophets largely railed against cultic neglect.[28] The prophets of the Bible, on the other hand, had the chutzpah to question God, even reproach him, when he prepared to punish his creation for sins against other people.[29] In a dramatic reversal to the notion of collective punishment, Abraham called for a collective *second chance* for the entire people of Sodom if even there could be found only ten righteous individuals among them. Moses also quarreled with God, after the Israelites' sin of the golden calf. As the text states:

> But Moses implored the Lord his God, saying, "Let not Your anger, O Lord, blaze forth against Your people, whom You delivered from the land of Egypt with great power and with a mighty hand. Let not the Egyptians say, 'It was with evil intent that He delivered them, only to kill them off in the mountains and annihilate them from the face of the earth.' Turn from Your blazing anger, and renounce the plan to punish Your people. Remember Your servants, Abraham, Isaac, and Israel, how You swore to them by Your Self and said to them: I will make your offspring as numerous as the stars in the heaven, and I will give to your offspring this whole land of which I spoke, to possess forever." And the Lord renounced the punishment He had planned to bring upon his people. (Exodus 32:11–14)

The prophets begged, cajoled, and cried out to the Israelites and other nations to repent so as to avoid the destruction warranted by their behavior. The story of Jonah describes the sins of the people of Nineveh as "violence that is in their hands" and "evil way." (Jonah 3:8) The desperate pleas of Jeremiah ring loud and clear. Later rabbinic tradition continues to question the morality of collective punishment. It faults the biblical Noah for not doing more to persuade his fellow human beings to atone before the flood.[30] The atheist writers rightly point out that, in places, the Bible prescribed capital punishment for individuals as well as groups, but there is a lot more to the story and a lot more defining context to that charge than the atheists admit.

CHAPTER 8

The Bible
and the Death Penalty

Can the Bible Outdo a Texas Governor's Enthusiasm for the Death Penalty?

Atheists who decry capital punishment in the Bible forget the historical context. Among ancient and even early modern texts and cultures, the Bible is quite restrained in its application of the death penalty for individual crimes. Any discussion about the death penalty in the Bible, therefore, must take this into account. The idolatrous ancients had a far more extensive and more disturbing death penalty list than the Bible. The Draconian Code of seventh-century BCE Athens—from which we have the adjective "draconian"—made such minor offenses as idleness and stealing certain vegetables punishable by death.[1] The Code of Hammurabi includes in its relatively shorter list of capital crimes death for the mere suspicion of cursing another person, stealing temple property, or buying certain goods from the son or slave of a third party without a witness. Yet murder, with the exception of a wife killing her husband and lover, is conspicuously absent as a crime punishable by death.[2] The ancients revised their laws. They sometimes meted out the death penalty for minor crimes and sometimes limited the number of crimes punishable by death. These revisions demonstrated the highly political, rather than moral, nature of the death penalty, which served to preserve the interests of the powerful.[3]

In contrast, the Bible calls for the death penalty for just twenty-three acts. Among them, the leadoff crime is murder. Notably, this punishment applies to all the people, no matter their place in society, nationality, or gender. Other crimes include kidnapping, rape of a betrothed woman, and bearing false witness in a capital case. Islamic and Christian writings have generally followed the biblical lead in limiting the nature of crimes deemed capital offenses to those which harm others. Historically, however, Christian and Muslim countries have nonetheless applied it more frequently than their own teachings warranted. A discussion of this history is, however, beyond the scope of this book, which will focus on the Bible and its Jewish commentaries.

Despite the general thrust of capital punishment in the Bible, all of these crimes seriously harm the victims. The atheist authors will claim, however, that death was also prescribed for harmless activities.

Death for Choosing the Wrong Decaf

Many atheists point to the Bible's imposition of capital punishment for ritual violations as far from just. This characterization is misleading. Take, for example, the prohibitions against witchcraft and false prophecy. These are not proscriptions against someone exercising freedom of expression. They are not the equivalent of a green light to executing a loud and ranting orator on a soapbox because he's interrupting your Sunday morning latte in Central Park. Rather, these are injunctions against those who are truly harming the community. Witchcraft and false prophecy are the equivalent to modern cults. They enslave people to ideals that are psychologically and socially destructive. They place people at the mercy of leaders/god kings/priests. Yes, the intent of biblical laws against witches and false prophets were most certainly and often abused. A historical case can be made that men exploited witchcraft trials to assert domination over women.[4] But again, corrupt implementation does not discredit the principle behind the proscription.

Atheists also find unacceptable authoritarianism in the Bible's insistence on capital punishment for sexual crimes. Another misreading. The Bible's prohibition against incest and sexual relations between family members or with animals reflects a matter of broad societal concern. Its purpose is not the criminalizing of private, consensual conduct. The viewpoint of the Bible and monotheistic religions is that certain sexual relations are destructive of the very fabric of the family. They attack its foundation, which is built on trust and safety from abuse. Do the atheists really believe that a daughter ought to consent to sexual abuse at the hands of her father? It is neither prudish nor overly constraining to establish boundaries on abusive sexual practices. As for sex in general, the Bible and Jewish tradition consider it to be a holy expression of love and pleasure.

By contrast, the ancient world, especially Greece and Rome, was rife with abusive sexual relations.[5] The Roman emperors seem to have specialized in coercive sex. The emperor Nero, for his part, found pleasure in dressing up as a wild animal and attacking the private parts of slaves attached to poles.[6] The emperor Tiberius was known to receive oral pleasure from toddlers who confused his member with a woman's breast.[7] (Today he would find his name on a sex offender registry website.) In each case, the emperor's unchallenged power permitted and sustained sexual exploitation and depravity at the expense of others. Can we blame the Bible for taking a stand against this perverted use of power on pains of death?

The death penalty for breaking the laws of Sabbath may be the command we moderns arguably find most difficult to accept. The ancient rabbis already in their day supplied a mitigating loophole. It became necessary to find two witnesses who had both warned the Sabbath desecrator beforehand *and* had then heard his/her acknowledgment of their warning—a most rare occurrence. Jewish law treats ritual infractions far less harshly than infractions against individuals and certainly less harshly than the ancient polytheistic cultures treated them. The Mesopotamians condemned someone to death for disturbing temple property.[8] The prophets of Israel are unequivocal that one's conduct toward others far outweighs any offering of sacrifices. But even for crimes worthy of the death penalty, according to the Bible, rabbinic commentators showed a radical leniency in their interpretations of the text.

The Ancient Rabbis Were the First Anti-Capital Punishment Activists. Why?

The ancient rabbis actually shared many of the concerns we moderns have about the death penalty in principle. Atheist authors wrongly assert that Jewish tradition celebrates executions. If atheists understood how monotheists read the Bible, they would look to the rabbinic commentaries on it, especially in the Talmud. Babylonian Talmud Makkot 7a records that Rabbi Elazar ben Azariah declares, "Any Sanhedrin [the highest Jewish court] that executed one person every seventy years was deemed a violent court." His colleagues, Rabbi Tarfon and Rabbi Akiva, are quick to add that, had they been members of the court, there would have been no executions at all. When Rabbi Shimon ben Gamliel retorts that a total abolition of the death penalty would raise the number of murders, he refers specifically to the capital punishment for murder and not for ritual infractions. Most astonishingly of all, Hillel actually outlawed the death penalty during part of the Second Temple period. He did not believe the courts could be rigorous enough. This decision was taken due to the corruption under the Roman client King Herod and the Roman emperor Augustus. Hillel doubted that the courts of his day could act in the impartial, dispassionate, and thoroughgoing way required to execute the death penalty in a just fashion. This is not all that far from the reasoning expressed by the US Supreme Court in the 1972 case of *Furman v. Georgia*, which led to a timeout in the imposition of the death penalty in the United States. Subsequent to Hillel's decree, the Sanhedrin never reinstated the death penalty. It remained, however, a theoretical right, had the Sanhedrin reentered the Hall of the Hewn Stones, which never happened. Far from celebrating the death penalty, the rabbis sound more like modern-day detractors.

Another example underscores this point. Perhaps the strangest death penalty commandment, and perhaps the most frequently cited in atheist criticism, is the injunction to execute the "wayward and defiant son." In Deuteronomy 21:18–21 the Bible states: "If a man has a wayward and defiant son, who does not heed his father or mother and does not obey them even after they discipline him, his father and mother shall take hold of him and bring him to the elders of his town at the public place of his community. They shall say to the elders of the town, 'This son of ours is disloyal and defiant; he does not heed us. He is a glutton and a drunkard.' Thereupon the men of his town shall stone him to death. Thus you will sweep out evil from your midst: all Israel will hear and be afraid." The atheists assume the Bible is here advocating the ultimate tough love for all rebellious teenagers. The Talmudic commentary on this passage argues just the opposite. Rabbi Shimon bar Yochai states in the

Babylonian Talmud Berachot 35b that the death penalty for a rebellious son "never happened and never will happen." In his view, this commandment was given to us to study hypothetically for moral purposes. The Bible was emphasizing that, in any instance that might have warranted investigation, the parents would have to present the case before a court. Such a process was a radical departure from the ancient world's normative practice, where parents could kill their children willy-nilly. As to the death penalty for ritual infractions, the rabbis also rendered this type of punishment virtually unenforceable. Entire books of the *Mishna*, such as *Seder Demai*, consist of finding legal work-arounds to permit farmers to continue practices contrary to the clean dictates of the ritual law.

The difference between rabbinic interpretations of the death penalty and ancient non-biblical practices reveals how much closer the ancient rabbis are to us moderns than to the idolatrous ancients. No equivalent of rabbinic opposition to capital punishment exists in other ancient societies.[9] In fact, there is a deafening silence from the ancients concerning this matter other than the voices of rabbinic tradition. The movement to abolish the death penalty on humanitarian grounds had to wait until the modern age to enter the world's consciousness.[10]

Where are the Witnesses?

> From my point of view, if it were not for God and people's belief in a just and fair God who has a plan for the universe, we would be in serious trouble. Martin Luther King said "The arc of the universe is long but it bends toward justice."
>
> —REVEREND DR. CALVIN BUTTS

The Bible and Talmudic traditions' tendencies to limit the death penalty is also apparent in their approach to judicial procedure. The Bible and rabbinic tradition are much more rational about judicial procedures than idolatrous ancient cultures.[1] Many of the early civilizations preferred exercising some type of ordeal to establish proofs for certain crimes. Examples included throwing a person in water or coercing oaths. These

---

1 For an overview of ancient justice, see Mark Jones and Peter Johnstone, *History of Criminal Justice* (Amsterdam: Elsevier, 2012); and John Sassoon, *Ancient Laws and Modern Problems: The Balance Between Justice and a Legal System* (Bristol: Intellect Books, 2005).

rituals rather than formal procedures, where a judge weighed the evidence with deliberation and reason, supposedly determined the accused party's guilt or innocence.[11] Not even the ancient Mesopotamians or Greeks and Romans, whose societies, indeed, relied on advocates and judges, developed in practice a fair or impartial system. In Mesopotamia, neither plaintiffs nor accused had access to professional advocates.[12] The Romans accepted hearsay as evidence, and affidavits could be submitted. The results of a case also depended largely on the oratorical skills of the advocates, who could liberally comment subjectively on the evidence.[13] The two advocates in a case might argue before a judge, upon whom both parties agreed, but only if he was of equestrian rank.[14] The entire system tilted toward the powerful. It often left the accused, whether guilty or innocent, facing a foregone verdict of execution.

In contrast to those of other ancient civilizations, Jewish legal procedures appear to have been remarkably rational and fair. The atheists' representation of biblical justice founders, yet again, on their lack of familiarity with biblical interpretation. The key to understanding biblical legal procedure is to consult the authoritative interpretation of these biblical passages according to the Oral Law as recorded in the Talmud. The Oral Law's interpretation is incredibly stringent.

Here are but a few examples. First, biblical law established that the evidence of at least two witnesses was required for conviction and punishment in criminal cases. (Deuteronomy 17:6, 19:15) In addition, the Oral Law stipulated that witnesses had to have warned the accused of the severity of the crime before he or she committed it. (Babylonian Talmud Sanhedrin 8b) Circumstantial evidence is simply inadmissible. Confessions are also not admissible as evidence—except in *favor* of the accused. (Babylonian Talmud Sanhedrin 42b, Rashi)

Second, the Oral Law places extremely stringent rules on the reliability of direct evidence: witnesses were cross-examined, informed that they could not rely on opinion or hearsay, and instructed to consider their responsibility—whether or not the death penalty was at stake. (Babylonian Talmud Sanhedrin 4:5) Witnesses were subject to cross-examination separately. Their evidence would not be accepted unless their respective testimonies were found to be consistent with each other. (Babylonian Talmud Sanhedrin 5:1–4 and Sanhedrin 12:1–3) In death penalty cases, if the evidence from the witnesses was found to be conclusive, the court was required to make a public announcement calling on anyone who had any evidence in favor of the accused to come forward. (Babylonian Talmud Sanhedrin 6:1) In addition, the ancient rabbinic court discharged the accused if it was not satisfied beyond a doubt of the accused's identification. This occurred even before the witnesses were examined on the merits of the case.[15] According to some scholars, the court also discharged the accused if the witnesses did not satisfactorily identify the victim.[16] Finally, the seriousness of bearing false witness in a capital crime was such that a witness was himself liable for the death penalty. As to appeals, the first chapter of Sanhedrin permits defendants to keep presenting arguments until the very last minute. It allowed executions to be carried out only when the court was available to meet. What is more, these procedures applied to other lesser crimes.[17] In biblical law, as supplemented by the Oral Law and understood by the ancient rabbis, the deck was stacked and the procedure framed, as we imagine it should be, in favor of the defendant.[18]

Better the Sanhedrin than the New York Supreme Court

If you still have doubts about the fairness of the biblical and Talmudic justice system, simply volunteer to sit on a grand jury for a month in Manhattan. The New York Supreme Court summoned me for this privilege several years ago. (In New York, the Supreme Court is the name of the trial division of the judiciary.) Though I did my best to fulfill my responsibility, I left the experience profoundly disappointed with the state of American criminal law, as well as criminal procedure. Unlike Jewish law, American law not only accepts circumstantial evidence, but such non-direct evidence, along with confessions (often under psychological duress), are the very oxygen of American justice, including capital cases.[19] Professor Brandon Garrett of the University of Virginia studied 250 cases in which innocent people were cleared by DNA evidence, including forty that were based on false confessions.[20] Because of the purported power of a confession, police may fail to order forensic evidence in a specific case. Or they may neglect to examine inconsistencies between the evidence and the confession, or even both.[21] American standards for identifying witnesses and accused are also less stringent than Talmudic ones. Garrett has demonstrated how 76 percent of convicted

persons ultimately exonerated by DNA evidence had been wrongly identified by eyewitnesses.[22] Other reasons for wrongful conviction include
shoddy investigation practices, official misconduct, inadequate legal
defense, false or fabricated forensic evidence, and perjury and incentiv-
ized testimony (i.e., snitches).[23] These procedural deficiencies led to 146
known cases of people wrongfully placed on death row.[24]

The American legal system also gives tremendous procedural advantages to the prosecutor. There is a strong incentive for prosecutors or
police to try to coax, coerce, or otherwise procure a confession from a
defendant in order to obviate any need for a trial. In the Biblical/Talmu-
dic justice system, it is impermissible that any accused person should be
convicted by their own confessions. In modern-day America, in addition
to confessions, prosecutors exploit an equally powerful tool (also prohibited under biblical law): multiple indictments for essentially the same
crime (in other words, giving the same crime different names so as to
multiply the potential incarceration time). It was hard for me to believe
how one basic crime could be characterized so many different ways by
assistant district attorneys' citing a host of different legal theories under
a host of different statutes. Recall the Abacus case in which the bank and
its owners were indicted 240 times for essentially the same crime.

This trend to compound previous convictions is now part of a terribly draconian law, the "three strikes" law. This law mandates severe
sentences, even life imprisonment, for someone who has been convicted
of three crimes, even if some or all of them are nonviolent and relatively
minor. These laws are a throwback to the days of *Les Misérables*, giving
modern prosecutors the ability to outdo Inspector Javert in adversarial
zeal.[25] In 1992, for example, Timothy L. Tyler was sentenced to life in
prison for possession of thirteen sheets of LSD, the third time he was
found guilty.[26] This tendency is now widespread. A sample of convictions in California demonstrates that 80 percent of the longest sentences
prior to the three strikes law were for previous violent crimes. After the
law, nonviolent crimes accounted for almost 50 percent of the longest
sentences.[27] In addition to these procedural issues, the American justice
system has increasingly replaced courtroom trials with alternate procedures altogether.

More than 95 percent of criminal cases brought in the United States
end in a plea bargain because of the power of prosecutors.[28] Plea bargains

consist of the defendant agreeing to plead guilty at the outset in return for some concession from the prosecutor, such as a lesser charge or a lenient sentence. Plea bargains thus change the very nature of legal procedure. Instead of proving the guilt or innocence of a party, lawyers are now occupied with agreeing on charges and sentencing that may very well be arbitrary. The problem has reached epidemic proportions, and the Supreme Court has finally taken notice. It has warned that plea incentives that were sufficiently large or coercive as to override defendants' abilities to act freely or used in a manner giving rise to a significant number of innocent people pleading guilty, might lead to concerns over constitutionality.[29] It is easy to see how people can be coerced into pleading guilty even if they had no involvement in a crime. The grand jury I happened to serve on was continuously instructed that we were not determining guilt or innocence; rather, we were to determine only if it was possible that the person charged *could have been* involved in the crime. This defendant typically was not present or even aware of the charges to refute them, but some bright assistant district attorney would be given the opportunity to come up with multiple legal theories germinating attaché cases full of indictments against the defendant. This potpourri of indictments would later result in the alleged crime carrying a gargantuan sentence. Through this threatening, wearying process, the defendant, guilty or innocent, is lured (beaten into submission is more like it) into "copping a plea."

Yes, plea bargains have been increasing in frequency, rising from 84 percent of federal cases in 1984 to 94 percent by 2001.[30] In addition, prosecutors today have added a shiny new coercive toy to their arsenal called "civil forfeiture."[31] Under this doctrine, a defendant may have his or her financial assets seized prior to appearing in court. Civil forfeiture thus punishes someone who has not yet been proven guilty. It also effectively reduces her or his chances of winning the case by forcing the defendant to rely on publicly funded, overworked, and underpaid public legal defense. To its great shame, the Supreme Court in *Kaley v. United States* upheld this unfair manipulation of the law.

Prosecutors also possess the coercive tool of pretrial incarceration for inability to make bail. With the backed-up court system, defendants can be held in county jails for months, even years, awaiting trial, losing their livelihood and contact with their families. Is it any wonder that innocent people facing these risks sometimes plead guilty?

And what about the right to an appeal? Is there a Sanhedrin always open for business and ready to accept new evidence? In the US, both state and federal appellate courts are only authorized to examine whether lower courts have made the correct legal judgments. They may not hear or reevaluate direct evidence or consider other mitigating facts, seriously limiting the defendant's case.[32] The only exception is if the appeals court finds the lower court's determination of facts to be entirely unreasonable. Not so in the Talmud, as we saw. Further, in most states, and in US federal courts, parties before the court are allotted just one appeal as a right. There is no guarantee that the Supreme Court will grant a further hearing should you have lost the first appeal. In addition, appeals are costly. Therefore, only a small proportion of trial court decisions give rise to appeals. *It is not surprising that the proportion of Americans behind bars is the highest on Earth.*[33]

CHAPTER 9

Biblical Inequality

Slavery: A Long, Sad Tale

Many readers may be prepared to accept the Bible's condemnation of idolatry and the just and egalitarian alternative it describes. But doesn't the Bible also include passages condoning hierarchies and practices that contradict its own overall message? The answer requires a contextualized reading of the text. The Bible was given to an ancient people steeped in idolatry and social, political, and economic inequalities. Its laws and message contend with this reality by design. The remarkable feature of the Bible is how it manages to combine an underlying universal message of equality and justice with practical laws that were tailored to unequal realities on the ground.

Yes, the Bible tolerates slavery. This is because it was so widespread in the ancient Near East. The proof of this is that there is no commandment to take slaves—you can check all 613 of them. In addition, the Bible also condemns and sharply limits its practice. In contrast to texts from surrounding ancient cultures, Israelite kings are not noted or noteworthy for possessing a retinue of enslaved eunuchs or a harem of slave girls; in fact, castration is forbidden.[1] Nor was the Temple serviced by slaves. Nor was forced labor for the king a feature of Israelite society.[1] Since

---

1 Snell, "Slavery in the Ancient Near East," in Bradley and Cartledge, *The Cambridge World History of Slavery*, vol. 1:17–18; and Mendelsohn, *Slavery in the Ancient Near East*, 100. While Bible attenuates slavery, both Snell and Mendelsohn rightly note that from the period of the monarchy and onwards Israelite elites did use slaves, possibly even temple slaves, though the nature of the group of people called Netinim, as Snell explains, is unclear.

the Bible did not advocate imperial conquests, it also limited the market in prisoner of war slaves. These unfortunates were another prominent source of labor in other ancient Near Eastern societies.[2] Chattel slavery is also absent from the Bible, though it was later used in Greece.[3] Nor does the Bible declare non-Israelites as slaves by nature, as the Greeks would do.[4] Nor does the Bible write pejoratively of the laziness of slaves as do the authors of ancient wisdom books. The Bible's disdain for slavery is at the heart of the Exodus narrative, the quintessential liberation narrative. And, it is also reflected in the laws demanded of the nascent nation of Israel, laws antithetical to all that Egyptian bondage signified.

A slave who desires to remain with his master rather than accept freedom after the sabbatical year is required to have his ear pierced with an awl. In this symbolic way, the Bible explains that he voluntarily gives up some of his humanity. (Exodus 21:5–6 and Deuteronomy 15:16–17) To voluntarily remain a slave is to debase oneself. The Bible expresses the same attitude to the practice of taking captive women. It requires the Israelite soldier to give the captive woman a period of mourning and requires that he free her if he does not desire to marry her and forbids him to sell her into slavery since he has dishonored her. (Deuteronomy 21:10–19) Yet again, nowhere does the text celebrate or encourage the taking of women in war, contrary to the rest of the ancient world where women captives were at the mercy of their captors. Nowhere does the Bible describe slaves as a different form of human being. Slavery is simply a legal status and one that can always be changed. *The Bible nowhere endorses slavery.*

The same basic thrust is true of the Qur'an and the Christian Scriptures. Neither promotes slavery, and both circumscribe the practice in comparison to other ancient societies and see freeing slaves as meritorious. The idolatrous Muslim and Christian slave trade contravened these teachings. In particular, with the rise of European chattel slavery, Popes issued numerous encyclicals condemning the institution.

"We Cannot All Succeed When Half of Us Are Held Back"— Malala Yousafzai

The Bible's approach to women is fundamentally egalitarian, but in this case, too, women's status reflects ancient realities. Atheist writers can

133

certainly point to inequalities between men and women in the Bible. There is no doubt that these inequities in the Scriptures contradict the overall moral arc, and there is, likewise, no denying the existence of a long tradition of interpreting many passages in a misogynist light. Eve's curse in the Book of Genesis is the prime example, where it is written: "I will make most severe Your pangs of childbearing; In pain shall you bear children. Yet your urge shall be for your husband, And he shall rule over you." (Genesis 3:16) Clearly this lends itself to misogynist interpretations, going so far as to suggest that patriarchy is embedded in the fabric of human society.[5]

Two further issues stand out in the Jewish oral tradition. Many Jewish thinkers point to the exclusion of women as witnesses in court cases and a prohibition against women holding public office as sexist.[6] The same can be said of the New Testament. In Paul's letter to the Ephesians he writes (5:22): "Wives, *be subject* to your own husbands, as to the Lord. For the husband is the head of the wife, as Christ also is the head of the church, He Himself *being* the Savior of the body. But as the church is subject to Christ, so also the wives *ought to be* to their husbands in everything."[2] The Qur'an contains similarly ambiguous passages: in Surah 4:34 it says: "Husbands should take good care of their wives, with [the bounties] God has given to some more than others and with what they spend out of their own money. Righteous wives are devout and guard what God would have them guard in their husbands' absence."[3] Strands of sexism in the Bible and the monotheistic traditions seem to confirm the atheists' point that modern political, social, and economic emancipation came later during a period of secularization that designedly confronted and went against biblical ideals.

Yet here, once more, they betray a deliberately narrow reading of the Bible. As described in part one, the Bible's description of the status

---

[2] For more on women and misogyny in the Christian tradition, see April D. De Conick, *Holy Misogyny: Why the Sex and Gender Conflicts in the Early Church Still Matter* (New York: Continuum, 2011).

[3] This is a very favorable translation. Other translations indicate "Men are in charge of women by [right of] what Allah has given one over the other and what they spend [for maintenance] from their wealth. So righteous women are devoutly obedient, guarding in [the husband's] absence what Allah would have them guard." For more on women and misogyny in the Muslim tradition, see Barbara Freyer Stowasser, *Women in the Qur'an, Traditions, and Interpretation* (New York: Oxford University Press, 1994); and Nicholas Awde, *Women in Islam: An Anthology from the Qur'an and Hadiths* (New York: St. Martin's Press, 2000).

and the legal rights of women far eclipsed those of the Greco-Roman world, for example.[4] Both men and women are created in the image of God. The very first description of the creation of man makes this point unequivocally: "male and female created He them. And when they were created, He blessed them and called them Man." (Genesis 5:2) Women are full members of the covenant. Women were present at the giving of the law and accepted it along with the male Israelites, embracing it with the words "we will do and we will hear." Women, thus, as part of the covenant, like men are held accountable for their decisions, the essential characteristic of human beings in the Bible.

Strikingly, women are often heroes in the Bible, in contrast to other ancient epics, where women are virtually absent. Women have little political role to play in Homer's *Odyssey*, for example, where the main female character's claim to fame is to ward off suitors. They are also conspicuously absent in the relief sculptures and written accounts of the exploits of ancient Near Eastern kings. In contrast, the women of the Hebrew Bible run the gamut from judges and matriarchs to warriors. The women of the Hebrew Scriptures challenge previous forms of oppression against women. The great leadership family in the Bible consists of Moses, Aaron, and Miriam, all of whom are prophets. In the Hebrew Bible, women such as Tamar and Hannah ensure the continuation of the Jewish people and the continuation of Jewish laws and principles at a time of total moral confusion. Rebecca, the wife of Isaac, according to the text, makes almost all of the consequential decisions for the couple. In fact, there is a pattern in the Pentateuch and in the Jewish Scriptures of women saving the day, whether by moral fortitude as in the case of Tamar, by cunning as in the case of Rebecca, by bravery as in the case of Yehoshavat, or even by sheer physical force as in the case of Judith and Yael.[7] The courage and do-it-yourself leadership of Deborah has been an inspiration to many women. As Tikva Frymer-Kensky writes, the world of the Bible may be patriarchal, but women are not represented as an evil other with particular defects. Nor does the Bible justify this subordination by a discourse on female inferiority. Rather, men and women share the same goals and employ the same strategies whether for good or evil.[8]

---

[4] For a good discussion of the status of women in the ancient world, and their accomplishments despite their status, see James and Dillon, *A Companion to Women in the Ancient World*.

Christian Scriptures also includes positive portrayals of women. In the words of Reverend Chloe Breyer:

> Looking at the New Testament, Jesus is clearly breaking so many taboos with His interaction with women in general and the woman at the well, who turns out to be the first Evangelist, or Mary Magdalene, who is among the first to find Jesus and goes and tells the Disciples. He eats with women, He heals women, He does so much that runs against the grain of the expectations in the society of the times. I, as a woman leader, find hope and inspiration from Deborah, Esther, and Miriam, and other great women from the Hebrew Bible who provide much hope.

The same can be said of female personalities in the Qur'an such as Fatima, Mohammad's wife. Most importantly, in all three monotheistic scriptures, women are moral agents who participate in the creation of a better society. They are far from powerless or convinced of their own inferiority.

Racism: Some Humans Aren't Human

In contrast to the question of slavery and sexism, which do have roots in the Bible, racism is totally absent. In fact, the Bible's universal view of humanity is truly astounding given the ancient context. That the atheists miss this point provides yet another instance of their selective reading of the Bible. We have already dealt with those who claim the Bible is racist in its discussion of the *herem*. Still, and the point cannot be stressed enough, the Bible claims that *all people are created in God's image*. Abraham's descendants are not racially superior. They are simply chosen to receive additional laws, in the hopes that they will act as an exemplary nation, and like all other peoples, are duly punished if they fail. The empires of the ancient Near East, as with the classical world, would conquer and even destroy other ethnic groups as par for the course.[9] The classical Greeks, for example, believed that all non-Greeks were inherently inferior. More to the point, anyone can join the Israelites. The Bible describes how David, King of Israel, is a descendant of Ruth, a convert from one of Israel's unfriendly neighbors, the Moabites. Not that other nations must become Israelites to be righteous. Moses's father-in-law, for example, the Midianite priest Jethro, not only abandons idolatry but becomes chief adviser to Moses, who accepts his wise counsel to train more judges to deal with questions of law, rather than attempt to deal with them all himself. Pharaoh's daughter Batyah, who rescues Moses, is a recognized hero in the Jewish tradition. In contrast, foreign heroes are hardly a feature of other ancient myths.

The Bible does, however, as we have seen, condemn various people and groups for their behavior, including of course the Israelites themselves. For example, Noah's son Cham is condemned for uncovering his father. According to the Bible, Noah curses his third son's son, Canaan, as a punishment for Cham's sin of uncovering his nakedness. "Cursed be Canaan; The lowest of slaves Shall he [notice the singular here] be to his brothers." (Genesis 9:25). This story has been used mainly by Christian racists as a justification for enslaving Africans.[10] The problem with this justification is that it is total nonsense based on gross distortion of the text. The origins of racism itself in the West are likely to be Greek and based on what the ancients considered "rational" observations.[11] The Bible's universalism is further evident in its laws about foreigners. In the ancient world, divide between the ruling imperial class, generally of a particular ethnic group, and foreigners among them was often stark depending on customs or the ruler's whims.[5] In contrast Israelites are admonished continuously to treat strangers justly. As in all ancient polities, Israelite laws favored Israelites in small ways, the provision of interest-free loans being one of them, the liberation of all Israelite slaves after seven years being another. Nevertheless, foreigners are protected by law in the Israelite polity, even granted citizenship without the necessity of full conversion, provided they follow the seven universal Noahide laws. Likewise, non-Israelite slaves can be freed and must be treated justly without any abuse.

---

[5] Ancient empires often had an ethnic hierarchy. See Cline and Graham, *Ancient Empires*. See also Anthony D. Smith, *The Cultural Foundations of Nations: Hierarchy, Covenant and Republic* (Malden: Blackwell Publishing, 2008), chapter 3.

CHAPTER 10

Monotheism and Violence

Idolatrous Wars

If the Bible is so just, what of all the wars caused by religion? The atheists narrowly focus on Jewish, Christian, and Muslim wars, and this distorts the historical record. The record clearly shows that idolaters, ancient and modern, have consistently surpassed monotheists in global destruction. As Matthew White, the author of *Atrocities: The 100 Deadliest Episodes in Human History* notes, only eleven out of the top one hundred atrocities in human history (including wars, mass slavery, and murder of civilians by dictatorial regimes) can be attributed to religion alone,[1] but let's take a closer look.

The largest war ever fought was that of the Mongol conquests. The global human population in the period preceding this war is estimated to have been in the range of three to four hundred million.[2] The Mongol conquests led to around forty million deaths[3]—the equivalent of somewhere between seven to nine hundred million people from today's world population, an unimaginable horror. It is indisputable that the motives for this campaign of conquest were sheer lust for power and greed.[4] The brutality and the enormity of the violence seem to be an early precursor to the Nazis, who centuries later caused the death of sixty-six million people during the Second World War, a larger number albeit a smaller percentage of the world's population.[5] There is a further logical problem with the atheist pseudo-syllogism, "wars are bad → religion causes wars → religion is bad." The nineteenth and twentieth centuries have seen numerous wars of independence.[6] Should we condemn freedom and political independence, too, because in these cases they were achieved by force of arms in the course of wars that ravaged three continents during the modern period?

All God is Saying is Give Peace a Chance

Monotheist cultures, unlike idolatrous cultures, formally championed the cause of peace and advanced the case for the moral limits of war, which, as described above, informed the development of modern international law. The medieval European clergy, for example, brought an end to the rampant warfare between petty barons and lords through the so-called Peace of God.[7] In the West, Christian thinkers such as Saint Augustine and Thomas Aquinas developed a just war theory, seriously limiting the justifications for starting a war as well as the means of waging it.[8] Rambam (Maimonides) famously wrote at length on the legitimate and illegitimate reasons for fighting a war.[9] Basing their views on the Talmud, he and subsequent Jewish commentators went so far as to wholly prohibit aggressive discretionary wars against ethical nations, only permitting war in the case of self-defense.[10] Like the Talmud and rabbinic writings, the Qur'an and Islamic texts, as interpreted by classical Islamic jurists, emphasized the limits on warfare, particularly the notions of last resort, legitimate authority, just cause, righteous intention, and aim of peace. Most of those concepts appear in modern Western just war theory.[11] Monotheists may not have followed their own teachings on peace, but at least they had formulated them.

Religious Violence: Taking God's Name in Vain

Atheists, finally, will claim that monotheists are still to be counted among history's greatest imperialists, and, for this reason alone, religion must be judged fatally flawed. The atheist writers often claim that monotheistic leaders, especially Christians and Muslims, have sought to convert others; they cannot tolerate difference. Jews have traditionally viewed their role as leading by example, though others contend that this is no less patronizing in intent, though given the Jews' lack of political sovereignty over most of the last two thousand years, the point has been moot. In the worst circumstances, the fervor to convert or dominate others has led to mass deaths and cultural destruction—think Crusades, the Muslim conquests on the Indian subcontinent, the Spanish Inquisition, modern European colonialism and, more recently, radical Islam and the subjugation of religious and national minorities in the Muslim Middle East. This accusation, as I have documented, is correct if we count all self-proclaimed monotheists, but wrong if we distinguish monotheists from idolaters in monotheistic garb. In the Fourth Crusade, greed so overcame the Crusaders that in the words of Bishop Murphy, "the whole thing got bollixed up. The Crusaders set out to reclaim the Holy Land. They got to Constantinople and there was this glittering city of the eastern empire. They decided that they were going to go after Byzantium on their way and they did their best to sack Constantinople. Christians fighting Christians. For what? Not for God." These instances of deadly excesses arose from human leaders who usurped monotheism and took it upon themselves to become spokespeople for God. This act of self-deification is expressly forbidden by the commandment of taking God's name in vain. It has all too often led monotheists to make the fateful shift from being demonstration nations to domination nations. In contrast, the Scriptures are clear: monotheists should be presenting principles to the world by example and allowing others to adopt them if they so choose, not imposing them on others, especially for one's own benefit.

Yet, it must be admitted that such a danger arises because biblical morality is not relativistic, nor is that of the Christian Scriptures and the Qur'an. Monotheism claims that such things as absolute justice, right and wrong, and an all-good/all-knowing God truly exist and are worth fighting for. This God advocates a world of just and mutual relationships both with and between all people. The Bible and monotheistic texts take a harsh stand against idolaters, and particularly idolatrous empires, because they are the true impediment to a just world. But in theory, this harsh stand is always as a last resort when all chances of achieving a just society have passed. In practice, this harsh stand against nonbelief has unfortunately been first resort rather than last resort throughout much of history. Abraham's descendants could use a greater dose of humility to restrain themselves from acting as self-appointed agents of God in the world; instead, they should work on cleaning out the idolatry within.

Despite the legitimate criticism of monotheistic imperialists, they cannot be accused, as atheists do, of being uniquely domineering. The view, held by many, that polytheistic peoples never went to war for their gods, making them more tolerant, is unrelated to the historical reality of ancient empires. First of all, it is not totally true. The Assyrian king Ashurbanipal, for example, insisted that the gods commanded conquest. In contrast, the Greeks insisted the gods did not care either way.[12] But, more importantly, it is beside the point. Idolatrous states and tribal groups throughout history have been interested in war and expansion. There is no difference whether this was achieved through total destruction as with the Mongols, through pillage as with the Vikings, or through various forms of imperial subjugation from Assyria to Rome. Idolatrous societies made war for the sake of expanding their own power and amassing material wealth. Having achieved power through subjugating others, it meant little to them if the conquered people continued to worship their local gods in private. Such freedom of worship had little to do with tolerance and much more with indifference, once power had been achieved.

CHAPTER 11

The Bible
and Modern Freedom

I think that the idea of liberation is central to God's saving activity is at the heart of my faith and I think the faith of a lot of people.

—REVEREND CHLOE BREYER

Aren't Modern Progressive Movements Secular?

If monotheism was meant to defeat idolatry and usher in a social blueprint of justice and equality, the picture was not looking good among the most powerful monotheistic nations at the beginning of the modern period. In the seventeenth century, the fervently Catholic King Louis XIV of France, known as the Sun King, claimed to rule by divine right and took royal absolutism to new heights. He declared himself "without equal" (at least Muhammad Ali, aka the Greatest, was, indeed, the greatest boxing champion). To prove it he brought the power of the nobles and churchmen under his rule using dependency, control, and courtly pomp. At Versailles, his sycophantic courtiers watched him perform an all-night ballet to demonstrate his power.[1] He revoked the Edict of Nantes, which had guaranteed freedom of religion for Protestants. He imposed mercantilist policies, which turned Saint-Domingue (Haiti), where slaves literally died producing sugar for his court, into the most lucrative colony of the Americas. He took possession of most of the territory of France outright, and he collected taxes by fiat. Not once did he call the Estates General into session. Unabashed by his own lust for power, he declared, "I am the State."[1] Under this king, the most important Catholic country in Europe exhibited all the social, political, and economic earmarks of the idolatrous empires of old.

Less than a hundred years later, inspired by the enlightened application of objective reasoning to worldly affairs, French revolutionaries called for a meeting of the Estates General. Moved to action by the suffering of the people and inspired by the writings of secular philosophers such as Diderot, who wrote, "No man has received from nature the right to command his fellow human beings," they proclaimed a credo of liberty, equality, and fraternity. Soon, the revolutionaries had created the National Assembly, issued a Declaration of the Rights of Man and of the Citizen, abolished feudal privileges, created a constitution, granted freedom of religion, abolished slavery, nationalized the church's great wealth, declared a French republic, and, last but far from least, beheaded the king.[2]

For many, the story of France's revolution serves as the axiomatic example of the liberating force of secularism.[2] Most recently Steven Pinker has made this case, citing the Enlightenment as *the turning point* for a human rights revolution, which ushered in the period of greatest peace the world has known. In other words, rational argument alone had inspired freedom and justice against Christian kings, who claimed religion-instigated power by divine right, and wealthy bishops who promised salvation in the next world while creating misery in this one. The values of the Enlightenment would further animate the emancipation of workers, the poor, women, and colonized nations in the nineteenth and twentieth centuries, giving birth to the secular emancipatory ideologies of nationalism, liberalism, socialism, anti-colonialism, and human rights

---

[1] For more on Louis XIV and absolutism, see John M. Merriman, *A History of Modern Europe: From the Renaissance to the Present*, 3rd ed. (New York: W. W. Norton, 2010), 242–261. For a psychological portrait of the king and a more detailed description of his politics, see Anthony Levi, *Louis XIV* (New York: Carroll & Graf Publishers, 2004).

[2] Even John Merriman, to whose work I refer, writes: "The French Revolution mounted the first effective challenge to monarchic absolutism on behalf of popular sovereignty." Merriman, *A History of Modern Europe*, 435.

that have since taken over not only Europe but the globe.[3] As Pinker sees it, thanks to reason we humans by and large no longer support capital punishment, cruel punishments, slavery, despotism, and major wars, and we have granted rights to all people, women, and children.

Not that all historians concur. Significant scholars dispute Pinker's view that the Enlightenment was a source of progress. They cite widespread examples of racism, support for slavery, exploitation of labor, and sexism based on "rational" and "scientific ideas."[3] Others posit that we moderns have not really progressed at all. What good, after all, is the right to vote if the politicians put into office are kleptocrats who also sell permits to their cronies' corporations to use our oceans as garbage dumps? What about countries run by despots who rig elections so votes don't really count? Universal human rights? If this is the present progress, imagine a standstill. As if this were not confusion enough, authors such as Yuval Harari dismiss the question of progress altogether. Taking a radically relativistic and biological view, Harari argues that according to nature, "sapiens" is not such an honorific for the human race. Historical developments can be described with little sense of greater destiny and with the same detachment as one would employ in examining how the finch's beak grew shorter over evolutionary time. In Harari's opinion, the modern period is simply a time of exponential growth in our scientific knowledge and amassed power as a species.

There is an alternative view.

The Biblical Revolution

Once we are talking about a world in which a republican constitution is seen as a requirement of legitimacy, in which the state uses its coercive power to redistribute wealth, and in which broad toleration is the rule, we are recognizably talking about the modern world. And if that world was, to an important degree, called into being, not by the retreat of religious conviction, but rather by the deeply held religious belief that the creation of such a world is

---

[3] See Andrew Vincent, *Modern Political Ideologies* (Oxford: Blackwell, 1992), 266. Vincent describes the importance of the French Revolution as a catalyst for modern ideologies. He also deems liberalism, nationalism, socialism, and Marxism as secular.

God's will, then the traditional narrative will have to be significantly revised, if not discarded.

—ERIC NELSON, *The Hebrew Republic*

The entire premise that the abandonment of religion ushered in an age of modern freedoms is entirely wrong. Both the experience of injustice and the increase of rational thinking about justice also played roles in spearheading the modern emancipation movements. As did the Bible. The turn toward political emancipation and equality did not begin in the "century of light," as the French call the eighteenth-century Enlightenment, but in the "Biblical century," burgeoning one hundred years prior—not with the French Revolution, but with the English Civil War and the Dutch Revolt.

As the scholar Eric Nelson argues in his book *The Hebrew Republic: Jewish Sources and the Transformation of European Political Thought*,[4] the first European thinkers to advance the political sovereignty of the people in the modern period turned to Jerusalem. Thinkers such as John Selden, John Milton, and Thomas Hobbes in England, Hugo Grotius and Petrus Cunaeus in Holland, and even Wilhelm Schickard in Germany neither turned to Athens and Rome, as did the Renaissance predecessors, nor did they rely on reason or pragmatism alone, as later Enlightenment thinkers would do. Instead, they considered the "Hebrew Republic," the polity described in the Bible, as an ideal political model—the demonstration nation to learn from—and writings on this model became the dominant political genre in the century.[5] In his republican writings, John Milton, for example, referred to the rabbinic sources that described the Israelites' call for monarchy as a sin, because the monarchy was a form of idolatry.[6] Thomas Paine, in his republican pamphlets during the American Revolution, referred to the argument of kingship as a form of idolatry.[7] The Bible, particularly the covenant tradition—which emphasized the people's acceptance of the law—also inspired the handmaiden of republicanism, constitutionalism, particularly the form and content of the American Constitution, as Donald Lutz argues.[8] The preamble to the American Constitution clearly expresses these ideas:

> We the People of the United States, in Order to form a more perfect Union, establish Justice, insure domestic Tranquility, provide for

the common defense, promote the general Welfare, and secure the Blessings of Liberty to ourselves and our Posterity, do ordain and establish this Constitution for the United States of America.

In Catholic France, it was a priest, Abbe Sieyes, who authored the pamphlet *What Is the Third Estate?* which led to the creation of the National Assembly,[9] a turning point in the French revolution. These thinkers, like their secular counterparts, used monotheistic ideas to attack the political privileges of the king and nobility.

The Bible Says Be Tolerant

As counterintuitive as it may seem, the thinkers of the biblical century were also among the first to advocate toleration of religious difference and separation of church and state. Key students of the Hebrew Republic, such as John Selden[10] and Hugo Grotius[11] (both active in the heated political debates regarding toleration in England and the Dutch Republic, respectively, and both widely read in their time), based their defense of religious pluralism on the Bible and the Talmud. According to Selden and Grotius, the Hebrew Republic permitted those who did not follow the Law of Moses to remain residents and citizens under full legal protection, provided they observed basic moral standards.[12] As a result, other than an elemental belief in God and adherence to central ethical practices, few doctrinal and ritual issues could be deemed as criminal unless they were used to create civil unrest. Therefore, no religious coercion in these matters should be implemented or tolerated by the state.[13] Ironically, these thinkers used the Bible itself to counter the clergy who wished to maintain their political power. They would later be joined by secular thinkers who would appeal to freedom of conscience or even secularism as reasons to separate church from state.

The Bible Wants to See Everyone Prosper

We can also thank the thinkers of the biblical century for their critiques of monopoly, the economic underpinning of political domination. As Eric Nelson writes, Roman republican thinkers had railed against land distribution in favor of the hoarding and monopoly of large landholders. In contrast, European thinkers inspired by the Bible, such as James

Harrington, squarely set blame for the decline of the Roman Republic on such plutocracy.[14] Following up, Harrington noted the Bible's approving description of allotting land to different tribes and redistributing inherited wealth during the jubilee, which occurred every fifty years. Not to put too fine a point on it, but there were no real-estate tycoons in search of off-desert accounts in ancient Israelite society. A modern adaptation of such principles, Harrington believed, would lead to a wider distribution of political power and laws to ensure a beneficial social balance.[15] As Nelson indicates, Harrington succeeded in his argument. The concept of agrarian redistribution became axiomatic in republican thought from Montesquieu to Rousseau, Jefferson to Tocqueville.[16] Biblical and monotheistic ideas also inspired another critique of monopoly: that of trade.[4] In his influential book on the international law of the seas, *Mare Liberum*, Hugo Grotius argued that the seas were God's dominion and that all men, Christian or not, were subject to natural law. Both principles dictated that men should be able to travel and trade freely.

Grotius further argued, based on the common descent of man in the Bible, that even idolaters who owned property did so rightfully. Therefore Christians could not expropriate it. This critique delivered a strong blow against financially motivated and distorted Christian justifications for colonialism.[17] According to Grotius's global vision, God had preordained that the different lands ruled by different nations would contain different natural and human resources. Trade and ownership, it followed, were part of God's providential plan to unite humankind in friendship and mutual exchange.[18] Grotius's anti-monopoly ideas would have a profound influence on Adam Smith, the first articulator of modern liberal economic theory.[19] Smith would add to Grotius's thought by warning that merchants' monopolies might easily replace government ones if they were not properly regulated. He wrote scathingly: "But the mean rapacity, the monopolizing spirit of merchants and manufacturers, who neither are nor ought to be the rulers of mankind, though it cannot perhaps be corrected, may very easily be prevented from disturbing the tranquility for everybody but themselves."[20] Smith, in fact, even foresaw that unfettered global trade

---

[4] As Europeans gained the technology to sail to distant lands, European thinkers took up the question of trade and conquest. For the historical context, see Merriman, *A History of Modern European*, chapter 5 and 6; and Raudzens, *Empires: Europe and Globalization*, chapters 4 and 5.

could very well unleash a race to the bottom and the utter destruction of national production. Such critiques of monopoly and appeals for laws and regulations would increasingly be made without appeals to God's providential plan.

The Bible Says Work It Out Nicely

Our modern Western ideas about international law and human rights can also be traced to the influence of the Bible, although this, too, may come as a surprise to many readers. After all, according to the atheists' narrative, the Jews, Christians, and Muslims sought power and domination over others, not their protection. Hugo Grotius, the remarkable Dutch jurist, established the basis of much of international law in his influential work *De Jure Belli ac Pacis.* In it, he advanced the idea that all human societies were bound by certain laws of war and justice,[5] regardless of their faith or culture. Grotius based his notions about international law on the idea that some laws both originate in nature and are repeated in the Scriptures. These are therefore universally applicable to all mankind.[21] As historian of human rights Micheline Ishay notes, the Enlightenment's secular formulation of human rights rested on ethical precepts drawn from Judaism and Christianity.[22] Over the course of the eighteenth century, these arguments for universal laws would, like the other progressive movements, increasingly be articulated without reference to the Bible. Indeed, the Bible's arguments for tolerance, against monopoly, and for international law, were so rational that they stood on their own without divine authority.

The thinkers and leaders who inspired these initial moves toward emancipation in the seventeenth and eighteenth centuries largely ignored women, the working classes, the enslaved, and peoples outside of Europe, whether colonized by the Europeans or living under other empires. In the nineteenth and twentieth centuries, however, the story of emancipation finally went global and encompassed the diversity of humankind.

---

[5] For a history of international law, see Stephen C. Neff, *Justice Among Nations: A History of International Law* (Cambridge: Harvard University Press, 2014); and for material on Grotius's religious views specifically, see Christoph A. Stumpf, *The Grotian Theology of International Law: Hugo Grotius and the Moral Foundations of International Relations* (Berlin: Walter de Gruyter, 2006).

The Bible—An Inspiration to Struggles for Human Rights

Modern enslaved peoples who fought for their own freedom certainly did not need Christian or secular philosophical inspiration to rise up against the slavery they so personally and bitterly experienced.[6] As Harriet Jacobs wrote of the hated institution, "What does he know of the half-starved wretches toiling from dawn till dark on the plantations? of mothers shrieking for their children, torn from their arms by slave traders? of young girls dragged down into moral filth? of pools of blood around the whipping post? of hounds trained to tear human flesh?"[23] Yet African American slaves nonetheless found inspiration in the Bible to fight for their freedom. They turned often to the biblical text to challenge their oppressors. Nat Turner, who led a Virginia slave rebellion, regularly used the language of the Exodus of the Israelites to describe the plight of African Americans.[24] Frederick Douglass, a prominent African American preacher and abolitionist, challenged those Southern whites who abused the Bible to defend slavery. He called them wolves in sheep's clothing.[25] Abolitionists in Britain and the United States, among them the eighteenth-century British Quaker Thomas Clarkson, drew inspiration from their Christian faith.[26] Jews such as Rabbi Gustav Gottheil, among others, openly preached against alleged biblical and Jewish justifications for slavery.[27] In India, Sayyid Ahmad Khan turned to the Qur'an and Islamic law to advocate the total abolition of slavery.[28] These thinkers understood the Bible and monotheistic thought too well to be deceived by those who conspired to manipulate the Bible to justify oppression.

Likewise, women did not need to learn the bitterness of injustice against themselves from the Bible. They felt it in their own daily lives. Yet, biblically inspired Protestants such as the Quakers demanded religious reform. The insistence of their demands became one of the sparks for modern feminism.[29] Prominent religious abolitionists such as Frances Willard, who also served as president of the National Council of Women of the United States, the first women's rights group in the

---

[6] On slave revolts and African American abolitionism, see Manisha Sinha, *The Slave's Cause: A History of Abolition* (New Haven: Yale University Press, 2016); and João Pedro Marques, Seymour Drescher, and P. C. Emmer, *Who Abolished Slavery? Slave Revolts and Abolitionism: A Debate with João Pedro Marques* (New York: Berghahn Books, 2010). For a history of African American life, including their life under and resistance to slavery, see Darlene Clark Hine, William C. Hine, and Stanley Harrold, *African Americans: A Concise History* (Boston: Pearson, 2012).

country, [7] became founders of the early organized women's movement.[30] For Willard, the same biblical notions of equality that had influenced their stance on slavery served as an inspiration for her feminism.[31]

Isms, Schisms, and Wisdoms

The atheists will still argue that the further political gains of the people in the nineteenth and twentieth centuries are attributable to secular "isms"—nationalism, liberalism, socialism, and anti-colonialism. All these ideologies sought in different ways to extend political, economic, and legal emancipation to those whom the elites formerly excluded from power.[32] But here again they would be wrong, because the influence of monotheism had endured and even informed these "isms." The leaders of the modern nineteenth- and twentieth-century emancipatory movements echoed key concepts of monotheism in their battle cry for political sovereignty and human rights. Two of the most important leaders of the Mexican Revolution, Miguel Hidalgo y Costilla and José María Morelos, were Catholic priests. They fought for independence from Spain and for the rights of people of mixed ancestry and indigenous people on the basis of Christian teachings.[33] In the twentieth century, monotheistic teachings combined with secular ideologies to inspire leaders in anti-colonial struggles.[34] The father of Indonesian independence, Mohammad Hatta, was a devout Muslim who took the road of peace in his fight to overthrow Dutch rule.[35] Likewise, Abdul Hamid Khan Bhashani, who fought for Bangladeshi independence, was widely referred to by the title of *Maulana*, the honorific for Islamic scholars on the Indian subcontinent.[36] When visiting Mohandas Gandhi's place of residence in Mumbai, I noted that he had just three books in his bedroom: a Bible, the Qur'an, and a Hindu holy text. Though Nelson Mandela rarely quoted Scriptures, deliberately so as to avoid divisions with secular anti-apartheid activists, he wrote, "I saw that virtually all of the achievements of Africans seemed

---

[7] Kathryn Kish Sklar, *Women's Rights Emerges within the Antislavery Movement, 1830–1870: A Brief History with Documents* (New York: Bedford/St. Martin's, 2000). As an undergraduate, I spent two years living in a residential college at Northwestern named for Francis Willard, who was best known to us as a founder of the Women's Christian Temperance Union. She also served as dean of the Women's College at Northwestern. During my undergraduate years, we staged a lively and very spirited party each fall at the residential college in celebration and remembrance of her birthday, if not of her temperance beliefs.

to have come about through the missionary work of the Church."[37] Dr. Martin Luther King Jr., a personal hero of mine, constantly made reference to the Bible. In 1968, he declared, "I just want to do God's will. And He's allowed me to go to the mountain. And I've looked over, and I've seen the Promised Land! I may not get there with you, but I want you to know tonight that we as a people will get to the Promised Land."[38] Christian groups were among the most important human rights advocates in the post-World War II period.[39]

The nineteenth- and twentieth-century movements for economic justice and equality were inspired in part by the Bible and monotheism. In the climate of the extreme exploitation of the nineteenth century, even Karl Marx, who famously labeled religion "the opium of the masses," praised the Anabaptists and other Christian sects as early socialists.[40] Moses Hess, Marx's contemporary and a fellow 1848 revolutionary, wrote of how the biblical and prophetic tradition informed his socialist ideas.[41]

Not that the Bible rejects the market economy. To the contrary, reliance on religious ideas could also be found by those who upheld the market economy but required it be regulated to the benefit of all investors, entrepreneurs, and workers, not just the heads of monopolies. Pope Leo XII's publication of *Rerum Novarum*, for example, declared the Church's open support for trade unions and called for more economic justice through proper regulations.[42] The story continues in the twentieth century. In Latin America, priests who worked with some of the most disenfranchised peasants in the world expounded on a theology of liberation. Peruvian priest Gustavo Gutiérrez described the Exodus story as a foundational text for anti-imperialism. "In Egypt," he wrote, "work is alienated and, far from building a just society, contributes rather to increasing injustice and to widening the gap between exploiters and exploited."[43]

Similar sentiments animated the Islamic world. In post-independence Indonesia and Bangladesh, Mohammad Hatta and Abdul Hamid Khan Bhashani merged Islamic ideas about economic and social equality with concepts inspired by European socialism. Their objective was creating a more just economy in both countries.[44] Like their Christian counterparts, twentieth-century Muslim liberals and socialists across North Africa, the Middle East, and Southeast Asia turned to the principles of economic and social justice in the Qur'an. They considered that these not only concurred with but even predated contemporary secular concepts of economic, political, and social emancipation.[45] Though not all of these thinkers rejected trade or demanded collective property, they did all reject outright the monopolies and exploitation of oligarchies and imperialists.

Many young people today are still motivated to create a better world. It is up to faith leaders to make the connection between social justice and monotheism for the new generation. As Reverend Dr. Katharine Henderson argues, "Millennials are very interested in social justice issues. They are interested in creating a better world and putting that together in some way with them, not for them, but with them, with spiritual traditions, with our religious traditions, which are very compelling."

The world is far from a perfect place, but at least in principle, people from Anchorage to Cape Town, Siberia to the Andes, have come to embrace the concept of political, social, and economic equality and justice—even if it is not yet fully in practice where they live.

The Bible Stands for Personal Freedom

I mean, you can go back and tell me about all the tragedies of people who have violated the tenets of religion, but look at all the positive things that have happened as a result of religion—the schools for the deaf and the disabled, the efforts of Mother Theresa, the work of Martin Luther King Jr., who was a minister, when you look at the airlifting of the Falasha out of Ethiopia by the Jewish people and transported them back to Israel. And I am just scratching the surface. We are talking about the tip of the iceberg here in terms of examples.

—REVEREND DR. CALVIN BUTTS

Today's prominent atheists also fail to grasp how much the Bible reinforces personal freedom and departs from ancient strictures. By focusing on the Bible's condemnation of Sabbath desecration, the atheists miss how much of human growth and endeavor the Bible entrusts to the people (never mind that it is thanks to the Sabbath that we don't have a seven-day workweek today). The Bible does not stipulate what choices people should make as to what kind of house they should live in, where they should live, whom they should befriend, and most of the other daily freedoms of will that we all take for granted. Nor does the Bible prescribe which talents we ought to develop, or what hobbies to take up. Most limits on personal freedom, which thinkers in the modern period have rightfully tried to abolish, have largely been imposed social customs. These, in turn, were based on power relations that relied upon outmoded and immoral hierarchies of class, gender, and race. In other words, just because your father says you should be a doctor doesn't mean you have to apply to medical school.

Contrast the Bible to Plato's *Utopia*. In the latter, class and social hierarchies are radically maintained, and therefore personal freedom is truly limited. The very fact that many biblical heroes are fringe figures, whether the prostitute Rachav or King David himself, underscores the centrality of moral freedom over social customs and constraints. Modern experiments in social engineering and rational and scientific thought, as reasoned as they may seem, have almost always curtailed people's freedom, restricting the choice of jobs available to them or controlling the number of children allowed per family. Modern critics of bourgeois culture, from Sartre to Dylan, have called for eliminating these culturally-based conventions.[46] The idea that a person might claim superiority based on class or taste runs contrary to the biblical idea that man is made in the image of God. Moreover, it appears nowhere in the biblical writings, which repeatedly emphasize righteous deeds—not custom, class, or even intelligence as the main criteria of character. Yet, sadly, even today everything from dress to taste in music can point to our power and social status, creating a culture of keeping up with the Joneses.[47] The atheist authors, and sadly some religious practitioners too, yet again misread the Bible and, most importantly, misunderstood how the Bible's emphasis on justice rather than power creates radical implications for personal freedom.

CHAPTER 12

The Bible and Monotheism Today

Incomplete Progress

This brief tour of the important influence the Bible and monotheism have exerted on the progressive movements of the modern period should dispel any idea that the modern world has made progress only when it cast off the shackles of religion. So, too, should the tally of global wars banish any notion that religion is the greatest source of war. Still, we must acknowledge that, despite many examples of leaders who drew their inspiration from the Bible in their fight for political, social, and economic emancipation, there are also examples of others who used the Bible to justify oppression. Southern plantation owners, for example, cynically cited the "curse of Ham" as justification for slavery, and the Roman Catholic bishop of Sarajevo, Ivan Šarić, debased the fundamental principles of his faith when he shamelessly declared, "[t]here is a limit to love. The movement of liberation of the world from the Jews is a movement for the renewal of human dignity. Omniscient and omnipotent God stands behind this movement."[1] Let us also not forget the many monotheistic leaders across the world who vehemently opposed giving women the vote and those in Europe in particular who wholeheartedly supported the colonial enterprise. Unfortunately, it is the words and actions of these monotheists that led many secular leaders of emancipation movements to denounce the creed of monotheism itself.

154

Yet, many secular thinkers do not have clean hands, either. Throughout the modern period, secular arguments were put forward to justify oppression, as well. Hence, exploiting workers made rational economic sense, women were irrational by nature, and biologically "inferior" people needed European "tutelage."[2] If secularism was accompanied by greater justice and equality in some instances, it was never pure and free of negative consequences. Secular communist leaders were no strangers to oppression, sending millions to their deaths.[3] Secular free market Machiavellians risked the economies of their countries by neglecting sensible regulation and tolerating environmental havoc.[4] Communist and free market Machiavellians alike defended their actions on rational grounds.

So, what are we to make of this muddled human history, in which both the path of the Bible and the path of reason might lead as easily to corruption and oppression as it might to progress and fulfillment? The political categories of right and left, conservative and liberal, are not particularly helpful since both could be oppressive. Would we really want to choose between the Khmer Rouge (Cambodian communists) and the Ustaše (Croatian fascists), both guilty of committing unspeakable atrocities? Both those on the right and those on the left deployed reason as their weapon. Consider that Ayn Rand and Rosa Luxemburg, leading theorists of the economic right and left respectively, were both outspoken atheists and rationalists. Likewise, the politics of left-wing social activist Father Daniel Berrigan could not be more different than those of Jerry Falwell, a leader of the Christian right, yet both are Christian clergy interpreting the identical Scriptures. A similar deep divide is apparent between the worldviews of the avowedly capitalist Saudi clergy and Muslim socialists like Hatta. Even if we try to categorize by class, the "good" guys are hard to separate from the "bad." After all, some of the working classes also cast enthusiastic votes for Hitler and some of the conservative Junkers (the land-owning elites) roundly rejected him. Indeed, this confusion is best encapsulated by the great number of twentieth-century secular French intellectuals, among them Michel Foucault, who, although steeped in Enlightenment values, nonetheless supported the Iranian mullah revolution in 1979 as a revolt against the injustice of secular monopoly capitalism and imperialism.[5] In fact, both were bad.

To clear up some of the confusion, we must closely examine the concept of idolatry and the political, social, economic, and legal systems that are created to support it. Wherever leaders establish laws that benefit a chosen few, deny equality before the law, repress religious freedoms where these do not harm others, promote a cult of personality, or support economic monopolies, we are dealing with manifestations of idolatry. It doesn't matter whether these leaders claim to be monotheists or secular, for the people or against them, left of center or right.

Looking at the current world scene with this in mind, a new picture begins to emerge. Just as modern emancipation movements have swept the globe, so too have a virulent variety of forms of idolatry. The Europeans who dominated global politics during the modern period spread *both* emancipatory ideas (inspired in part by monotheism, as we have seen) *and* systems of idolatry. It is understandable that on the continents of Africa, Asia, and the Americas, attitudes toward the West are ambivalent if not downright hostile.

On the one hand, the encounter with Western colonial powers and Christian missionaries across China, India, and various countries of Africa accelerated a process of Westernization that inspired locals to replicate their brothers in Europe and fight against injustice and inequality. Examples of this are the campaigns against the caste system in India, against the rigid social hierarchies in China, and against the absolute power of local chiefs in Africa. On the other hand, Western Europeans also introduced several sorts of secular idolatry that were adopted and replicated by elites across the world. Here we might point to the brutal and lawless exploitation of workers in Nigeria in the name of economic development, to the communist dictatorships of Cambodia in the name of social justice.

The encounters between the West and indigenous people in the Americas and Oceania have often persuaded these populations to question and abolish such heinous idolatrous practices as human sacrifice and intertribal warfare. Yet, at the same time, these same developing communities fell prey to the ravages of European greed and violence, if not outright attempts by European states to destroy their traditional cultures. The modern dominance of the Europeans has also led to paradoxical results in the Muslim world. While peoples within the Muslim world universally sought to free themselves from European colonialism, the encounter with the West could lead some Muslims to recover the more socially just aspects of their religion, as exemplified by Hatta's

Empires, Kingdoms, and Tribal Societies c. 1700CE

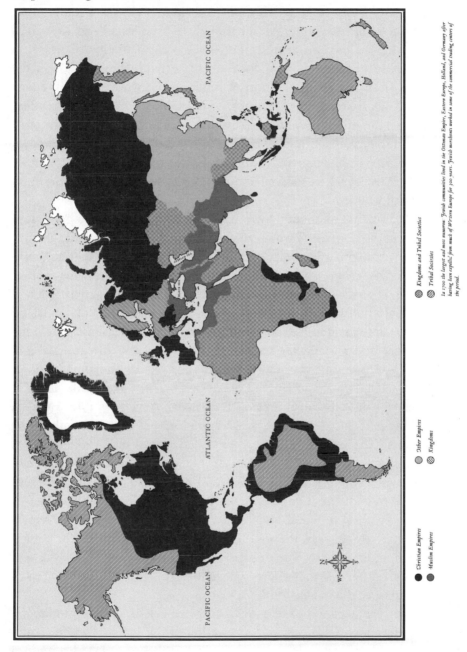

encounter with liberal socialist ideas in Holland, which encouraged him to search for similar ideas within Islam. But it could also prompt other Muslim leaders to adopt radical nationalist—even fascist—ideas such as Pan-Arabism and anti-Semitism, or economic exploitation of others, as occurred in Saudi Arabia in their encounter with similar ideas in the West. Thus, the Westernization of much of the world in the modern period has been a dual process. Yes, it has enabled many of the core ideas of the monotheistic revolution—even in secular form—to take root in the consciousness of humankind, but it has also empowered those who would propagate dangerous forms of secular idolatry at the expense of the social welfare to succeed in keeping the forces of oppression and inequality alive and well.

Indeed, not all moderns are equally confused about the good guys and bad guys, and it is from the clear-headed that we should take our cue. Over a winter break in 2016, I had the opportunity to go to South Africa. The scenery is breathtaking. But the trip was inspiring for another reason. I had the pleasure of meeting with anti-apartheid activist Thulani Mabaso, a political prisoner who arrived at the infamous Robben Island prison subsequent to Nelson Mandela's arrival. What Mabaso taught me was that under Mandela's leadership, activists across the political and religious spectrum, from atheist Marxists and secular humanists to pious Muslim, Christian, and Jewish liberals, were united against the idolatry of apartheid. Mabaso continued, "Our leaders kept us in line. Mandela and the others told us not to show depression but to try to smile at the warders." The leadership also stayed united against the common foe. At his arrival on Robben Island, Thulani saw fights between different factions within the prison, but they would not let the guards know about it. "We were different groups, ANC, PAN, and others. Mandela told us not to fight but to talk to each other. Even the warders knew Mandela was wise." By the way, the warders would come to Mandela for advice, according to Mabaso. The prisoners would hate it when a warder was transferred because they knew some new recruit would come in who was trained to be full of hate for them.

The participation of religiously-inspired activists in the anti-apartheid movement also required a rejection of the idolatry within South African Christianity. Mabaso explained to me that part of the fortitude of many of the prisoners came from their religious beliefs. He said he never missed a Sunday service: they brought in special priests and alternated between three denominations. Mandela was a Methodist, and that was one denomination, and the Dutch Reform Church was one of the others. Mabaso said that some of the warders were surprised that they attended all the different denomination services or even at all. Partially, church attendance was so high because it was a break from the backbreaking labor and harsh conditions.

Mabaso's mention of church got me wondering even more about the role of the Afrikaner Dutch Reformed Church (NGK) in apartheid. The policy of the NGK was clear up until 1857—as noted by the NGK synod of 1829, Holy Communion should be offered "simultaneously to all members without distinction of color or origin." How did the NGK deviate from this? In short, it was white member lay lobbying by congregants. The clergy did not hold strong and resist even though they might very well have known better. Instead, the NGK created special churches for blacks and Indians and subsequently developed a theology to justify apartheid. NGK members distorted biblical concepts to justify racism and oppression. Given this terrible history, it is a wonder any of the anti-apartheid activists remained Christian. The answer is simple. Leaders and activists from Mandela to Archbishop Desmond Tutu saw the NGK's distortion of Christianity for what it was. They rejected the idolatry that it disseminated. For its part, the NGK has still not fully merged with its black and Indian sister churches. I was told that a substantial number of former members of the NGK are in seeking mode for other churches, synagogues, and mosques that can meet their spiritual needs. Some of these folks just stopped being involved in organized religion.

It is amazing that the story of the transition from apartheid to majority rule took place peacefully in the end. Few on either side expected that outcome. I had relatives who left Cape Town for the US and Israel in the 1970s precisely because they detested apartheid. They fully expected a very bloody revolution at some point. The incredible recent history of South Africa is an example of how human action together with the silent helping hand of the divine can accelerate change in a positive way. Most importantly, it showed that atheists and monotheists can (and have) work together against idolatry. As I write these words, sadly, the corruption of economic idolatry seems to have taken hold of the African National Congress (ANC).

Across today's global landscape, the Bible's description of idolatry and the alternative society it proposes remain as relevant as ever. The indisputable influence of the Bible and monotheistic ideas on modern emancipation movements demonstrates that its message transcends its age. The Bible was written for ancient Israelites on one level, but on another, it is written for all peoples at all times. Yet the modern period provides ample evidence that, pun intended, we must not expect miracles from the Bible alone. That is to say, the Bible must be read in a dynamic relationship with our lived reality and with our ever-increasing knowledge of the world we inhabit. Those who justified slavery by recourse to the Bible, for example, did not simply use God's name in vain for personal advantage; they also chose to close their eyes to the reality around them, with all the horror and suffering it entailed. It is this attention to observed reality that makes it easier to separate the general and timeless principles and laws of the Bible from its concessions to ancient realities.

Further, biblical principles may have inspired members of the emancipation movements, but the power of reason provided rational strategies to make change happen. In the words of Timothy Cardinal Dolan: "Faith and reason are partners. They are not enemies. The sons and daughters of the Enlightenment would caricature religion as believing that reason is the enemy. Reason without faith can be an enemy, as faith without reason can be an enemy. To do what's best for humanity, God intends they both be used in conjunction." Thus, to advocate the importance of the Bible for people today is by no means to encourage fundamentalism, to demand that we re-create the social conditions of the era of the Bible, or to stop us from increasing our knowledge about the world we live in. Instead, it is *to include the Bible and the principles it communicates—equality before the law, economic justice, the value of all human beings—in our conversations about creating just societies in a complicated global reality. Of course, this conversation also requires us to bring reason to the table as well.* In essence, it is to continue to do what so many leaders like Martin Luther King Jr. have already done. If we lived in a world where there were no men like Kim Jong-un, no corrupt ministers selling state goods to the lowest crony bidder, no unaccountable corporatists subverting competition, and no corrupt union leaders diverting pension funds based on "logical" arguments, we might then be able to say we

The Constitutional Democracies and Dictatorships in the World Today

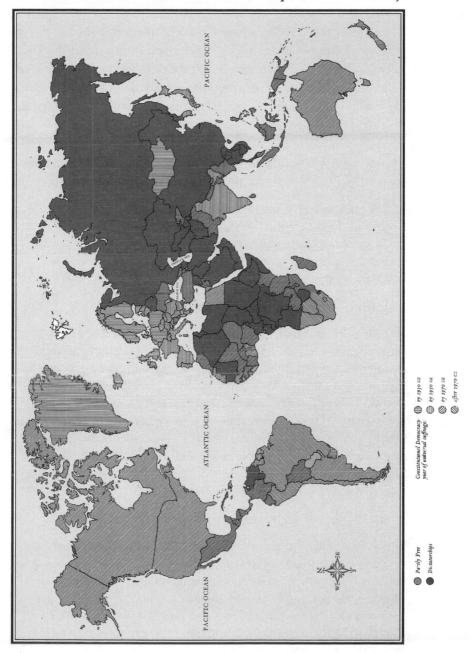

have learned our lesson, we don't need the Bible to remind us. But we clearly have not.

The work of recognizing idolatry and eliminating it should also be the priority of monotheistic groups themselves, both within the faiths and between them. Here too reexamining the Bible on this count can be useful. The proliferation of interfaith organizations today—which include not only the three monotheistic religions, but also some of the religions of India, Japan, and other parts of Asia, among others—indicates that the monotheistic faiths have come to recognize the idolatrous distortions that occur within religious streams that advocate domination and even religious violence.[6] In the words of Reverend Chloe Breyer:

> I think the Qur'an has the best answer to the question of why God created all the different religions of the world, which is so that we might know each other. But sometimes just to get to know people your diverseness is a prerequisite for discovering and exploring and experiencing other people for who they are.

Chaplain Tahera Ahmad offers similar words:

> Someone who is completely jaded could say that one of the reasons why religion is actually very problematic is because there are a number of people within different traditions that have particularized views not just on humanity, but on the relationship between God and a people. My response to that is, well, isn't that benefiting society? Or in other words, "Is it more harmful or is it more beneficial?" If a people believe that they have been given certain responsibility, I see that actually as a promotion, it is not regression. It is a progression because it gives people more reason to take an initiative and to work towards progress.

Imam Shamsi Ali emphasizes the personal choice involved:

> In my view, Islam in fact says their religion is theirs and yours is yours. It means Islam acknowledges the existence of other. So, for me, it is okay even though I may disagree in the way that they do what they do because I choose to be Muslim because I believe this is what is suitable for me. It is a very private and personal choice in choosing the way to go to God, and that is why there is no way for us to enforce our weight on others.

For many of these interfaith leaders, encounters with other religions, like the encounter with secular reason, forms an essential part of critically reexamining their faith traditions to eliminate the idolatry within them.

The Bible, as Timely as Today's Newspaper

As the atheists' accusations demonstrate, the Bible today remains an extremely contested text. There are still those who use it to blatantly excuse all sorts of injustice, from polygamy to white supremacy. Like the atheists' criticisms of God, their criticisms about the Bible serve a useful purpose, pointing out how monotheists themselves can obscure the Bible's timely and timeless messages through misreadings and distortions. Reading the Bible in good faith does not require one to believe in God; it just requires fairness and honesty on the part of both nonbelievers and believers alike.

Let us return to our friendly Martian. Imagine now that he was to have arrived 160 years ago, just as unionists/abolitionists and secessionists were in heated debates about whether the Constitution of the United States endorsed slavery. The abolitionists insisted that the original writers of the Constitution both acknowledged and permitted slavery as a necessary evil for the formation of the fledgling republic. But there is no endorsement of slavery in the Constitution. The test of history has validated that argument. Yet whether one was from the North or South or an abolitionist or not, everyone was reading the exact same words. It was all about the interpretation and the moral imperatives that emanated from the document. Indeed, if our Martian took a closer look at the Constitution even as it stood in 1860 (prior to amendments specifically providing equal protections without respect to race), even he could not help but feel the impulse for freedom and for universal rights. The atheists read the same Bible as do believers but interpret it very differently. Simply put, the atheists do not read the Bible as have Rambam (Maimonides), Mandela, King, Willard, Douglass, and the myriad of other leaders who referred to its ideas to fight for justice and equality. If we read the Bible as believers in the same spirit as these leaders, we have the best chance of making the world a much better place.

PART THREE

Is There Something About Evil?

Is Religion Useless or Is God Evil? Atheists Say It's One or the Other

We recognize it even as we recoil. Yet it holds a fascination over us unlike any other. It's the stuff of Hollywood slasher films, horror novels by Stephen King, and lurid tabloid headlines. But just what is this thing known as "evil" and what are its origins? Are we talking here about some eternal force of universal malevolence? Or are we merely confronting a set of cultural constructs that differ across time and space, the subject matter of a semester's social science syllabus? And what, if anything, is so special about the Bible's own take on evil? Is it insightful? Credible? Useful still in our modern world? Haven't Judaism, Christianity, and Islam historically defined evil as an ominous, supernatural force? Haven't they decried all manner of fun as evil and even accused man of being evil by nature? Haven't we all heard of, or witnessed, actions of self-declared monotheists that any rational person would designate as evil? Doesn't this suggest that monotheistic religions are getting at least something wrong themselves?

Recognizing religion's mixed results, maybe we should be turning to reason and science for a proper definition of evil. Why waste our time attending to the Bible's view of man as a moral agent endowed with free will, or traffic in its likely fictional stories of moral dilemmas? After all, we don't believe in Plato's noble lie that different men possess different metals mixed into their souls. Doesn't science teach us, instead, that all our choices hinge on evolutionarily and genetically pre-wired thought patterns, emotions, and behavioral processes? Do the Bible and monotheism really have anything of practical use to offer modern people concerned with confronting and containing evil? A final vexing question for believers and nonbelievers alike: Why would a good God create humanity with the capacity to do so much evil and subject us to so many natural disasters and pain?

None of these are easy questions. In my personal encounters with some avid atheists, these are the questions that bother them most. Yet, we will be finding that, contrary to the beliefs of many atheist writers, the Bible actually explains evil in a fashion compatible with our innate moral intuition and reason. Far from seeing evil as a supernatural force, the source of all of man's condemned desires, the Bible offers a straightforward definition. Evil is the act of doing unto others what one does not want done to oneself. Evil, in other words, entails transgressing what is commonly known as "the Golden Rule," a rational code of behavior well known across human cultures. The Bible thus locates evil in the actions we take toward others, not in our human nature. The gist of so many Bible stories is to effectively describe how evil operates by means of deception, self-deception, rationalizations, and force. The tenets and laws of the Bible are proposed as our means of combating evil and creating a good society. Little surprise that scientific studies of evil have come to confirm the Bible's approach.

But does any of this matter if we lack free will? We will claim, perhaps unexpectedly, that the Bible broadly concurs with science. While we retain some free choice, we are also yoked to the natural constraints of our brains and environment. Scientific research and knowledge of the nonconscious psychological and social factors that affect our decision-making can actually help us to become more moral. At the same time, the Bible and monotheistic traditions still make their own unique contribution to the moral scheme of things, for both believers in God and nonbelievers alike. The Bible's prohibition against idolatry (idolatry understood, as we have seen above, as lies about power and authority) is an axiom designed to upend the root of all evil. Without this prohibition, moral philosophy has the latitude to define morality in any number of ways suitable to some and harmful to others. Finally, and perhaps counterintuitively, we will claim that it is far more rational to believe in a God who is all good and who allows the existence of evil than to believe that the presence of evil constitutes God's limitations or, worse, God's own intrinsic evil. Evil, according to this argument, is the result of God hiding Himself from the world, thus granting humanity the foundational choice: to do good and perfect the world, or to do evil and harm it. As we shall explain in the form of the "Theosic principle," it is an ironic sign of His omnibenevolence that God gives us this choice. It is part of God's omniscience that He knows how to hide Himself. Indeed, in His omnipotence, God both runs the world and obscures His sovereignty over it.

Morality: It's in Our Genes

Atheists argue that religion is irrelevant to the question of evil. Science, they contend, amply demonstrates that morality, the difference between good and evil, derives simply from man's nature. For Harris, morality is the result of an innate biological characteristic: "Our ethical intuitions must have their precursors in the natural world, for while nature is indeed red in tooth and claw, it is not merely so. Even monkeys will undergo extraordinary privations to avoid causing harm to another member of their species."[1] Dawkins concurs, claiming that, just as evolutionary biology explains why we are selfish, it also explains why people are good, that is, altruistic: "First, there is the special case of genetic kinship. Second, there is reciprocation: the repayment of favours given, and the giving of favours in 'anticipation' of payback. Following on from this there is, third, the Darwinian benefit of acquiring a reputation for generosity and kindness. And fourth, if Zahavi is right, there is the particular additional benefit of conspicuous generosity as a way of buying unfakeably authentic advertising."[2] Or, back to Sam Harris, we just don't need religion to be good: "Concern for others was not the invention of any prophet. The fact that our ethical intuitions have their roots in biology reveals that our efforts to ground ethics in religious conceptions of 'moral duty' are misguided. Saving a drowning child is no more a moral duty than understanding a syllogism is a logical one. We simply do not need religious ideas to motivate us to live ethical lives."[3]

Not only is religion useless, according to the atheists, but its utterly irrational view of evil perverts our understanding of morality. As Dawkins describes it: "[Religion] invent[s] a separate evil god, call[s] him Satan, and blame[s] his cosmic battle against the good god for the evil in the world"[4] or it attributes evil acts to "possession by devils."[5] Or, worse, religion will claim that innocuous activities are so evil as to merit divine wrath, as witness, "Also, no doubt, many of those Asian holy men [who] blamed the 2004 tsunami not on a plate tectonic shift but on human sins, ranging from drinking and dancing in bars to breaking some footling Sabbath rule."[6] As atheists see it, religious ideas about man and evil impede our ability to make mature moral choices. Here Daniel Dennett adds: "Without the divine carrot and stick, goes this reasoning, people would loll about aimlessly or indulge their basest desires, break their promises, cheat on their spouses, neglect their duties, and so on. There are two well-known problems with this reasoning: (1) it doesn't seem to be true, which is good news, since (2) it is such a demeaning view of human nature."[7] As far as the atheist authors are concerned, we can only create a better world by using reason to further investigate the root of our ethical impulses and, with such information, devise codes of behavior and frameworks of seeing the world that will contribute to making it a better place. Reason alone, and not religious teaching, should be our guide. As Dawkins posits: "Moral philosophers are the professionals when it comes to thinking about right and wrong. As Robert Hinde succinctly put it, they agree that 'moral precepts, while not necessarily constructed by reason, should be defensible by reason.'"[8]

As their smoking gun, the atheists claim that the very existence of evil in the world—to say nothing of the ubiquity of evil—contradicts the notion of an omnibenevolent, omniscient, and omnipotent God. The ancient Greek philosopher Epicurus framed the problem succinctly: "Is God willing to prevent evil, but not able? Then he is not omnipotent. Is he able, but not willing? Then he is malevolent. Is he both able and willing? Then whence come evil? Is he neither able nor willing? Then why call him God?"[1] Mark Twain characterized the question with his trademark pithiness, "If there is a God, he is a malign thug."[9] The atheist writers assert that the argument about God could and should end right here. For Sam Harris, the plagues of nature not only prove God is imperfect, they demonstrate Him to be evil. "The perverse wonder of evolution is this: the very mechanisms that create the incredible beauty and diversity of the living world guarantee monstrosity and death. The child born without limbs, the sightless fly, the vanished species—these are nothing less than Mother Nature caught in the act of throwing her clay. No perfect God could maintain such incongruities. It is worth remembering that if God created the world and all things in it, he created smallpox, plague, and filariasis. Any person who intentionally loosed such horrors upon the earth would be ground to dust for his crimes."[10] Further, Harris claims that theodicy cannot be overcome. "The problem of vindicating an omnipotent and omniscient God in the face of evil (this is traditionally called the problem of theodicy) is insurmountable."[11]

Acknowledging the Problem of Evil

The question of evil has troubled me since I was a boy. In those days, I met many Holocaust survivors through my father, George, especially at the Chicago Jewish Lithuanian Club, which convened every so often at various synagogues, multipurpose rooms, and catering halls. The club members, mainly survivors like my father, got together to play cards, talk, argue, eat very tasty traditional foods (drenched in fried fats before we knew about cholesterol, so guilt-free as well), and, occasionally, host dance parties with live music. Most of the time, nobody talked of the war years or of the concentration camps. Listening to their conversations, it seemed to me as though Europe existed before the war, went into some sort of hibernation, and then reemerged in the form of displaced-persons camps. We, the children of survivors, knew to avoid topics that even touched on the Holocaust experiences of our parents. Anyway, they were focused on rebuilding their lives by raising families, working hard,

---

[1] Quotation attributed to Epicurus by David Hume. The attribution is disputed, but the sentiment is clear. David Hume, *Dialogues Concerning Natural Religion and Other Writings* (Cambridge: Cambridge University Press, 2007).

purchasing homes, dressing stylishly, and, of course, making certain that everyone always had plenty to eat.

But I do indelibly recall one evening—it was during a card game at the club—when one of the members sitting at the table with my father turned to a fellow survivor and said in a matter-of-fact voice: "How can you go to synagogue for the High Holidays? Where was God *when it counted* for the dead members of our families?" The dealer looked up, held the cards. Dead silence. And then came the responses, low-key as though the players were no more than mumbling "hit me" or raising the bets of the round. Their answers left me dumbfounded then, for a long while after, and they linger with me today.

I can't recall the exact wording, but their answers, which became seared into me, could be divided along the following lines. Some matter-of-factly denied God's existence: "There is no God, get over it, we're on our own." Others defended a God who simply meted out the punishment for disobedience: "We Jews suffered because of divine retribution. We didn't follow the commandments." One said that we can never really know what's at stake: "If it weren't for the Holocaust, the State of Israel would never have been voted into existence by the world. As bad as it was, the Holocaust led to a greater good." A last group blamed the rest of the world for letting the slaughter happen: "God was right there all the time, wondering why His children did nothing. Where were the Jews of the United States when we needed them?"

One more answer, and perhaps it was that of the majority, was not uttered out loud that evening. Or perhaps it was, hidden in the earlier initial silence that hung over the room. Afterward, I saw that answer all the time in action, though I could not articulate it until many years later. You see, there were certain friends of my father who went to synagogue on the High Holidays but never prayed. They would absolutely accept an *aliyah* (the honor of being called up to the Torah), and they would make sure that their sons were circumcised, that their children attended Hebrew school and completed their bar/bat mitzvah. But they would never pray. Instead, each would chat with the person next to him during the prayers, doze off during the sermon, congregate in the foyer at various points, schmooze during the collation after services, pay annual membership dues, and make customary donations to the synagogue. But, again, they would never pray. I later understood that these friends of my father believed in God, or, more accurately, *knew* that He existed. They even, somehow, *knew, for sure*, that it was hidden miracles had gotten them to the other side of the war and to the safety of Chicago. Yet they were too angry at God, for the sake of those He did *not* save, to show Him the courtesy of speaking to Him. I don't think there was a hint of uncertainty on either side of the relationship. I think God knew why these survivors were so angry, and He understood why they gave Him the silent treatment.

These same Holocaust survivors also struggled with their view of mankind. They displayed an array of attitudes toward Germans and other Europeans who participated in the mass murder of Jews. Occasionally, my father and his friends would talk about their Christian neighbors in Europe. While I would have expected them to have largely given up on the goodness of man in general—appalled by the cruelty they experienced—most actually directed their focus on specific groups, sometimes angrily and sometimes in bewilderment. Many had particular grievances against neighbors who stood by or worse, who participated in the murders of Jews or plundered the property of the murdered. Certainly, some survivors could name subsets of neighbors and other righteous individuals who risked their lives to provide these survivors with assistance along the way, but the majority of their neighbors looked the other way. My father told the story of his hometown of Švėkšna, Lithuania, where the locals stood by indifferently as Nazi invaders murdered many of the town's Jews before deporting the rest. In some witnessed cases, locals cheered on the actions of occupying soldiers, seizing the occasion to quickly seize their Jewish neighbors' land or possessions.[2] Most of my father's friends simply could not make sense of what happened, nor fathom how people could be or become so evil. Some remembered both those who helped and those who harmed them, and so they retained their faith in man, if barely. A few put the blame on long-held and deep-seated prejudices. A few attributed the unconcealed slaughter to the aggravating factors of

---

[2] A distant relative of mine who decided to visit Švėkšna was stunned to find little regret for what happened and was made to feel physically unsafe when she went to visit the property my father's family used to possess. In the early 1990s, after the fall of the Soviet Union and with the establishment of the EU, which Lithuania hoped to join, my father inquired at the Lithuanian consulate about reestablishing his Lithuanian citizenship. The consulate representatives made it clear he would need originals of the documents that no longer exist.

war and chaos. Many asked how so many of these people, presumably Christians, could forget the church's teachings of peace and love so easily and commit such heinous crimes. No one at the club came through the war with an unblemished picture of humankind.

As a teenager my confusion grew. My father, a carpenter-contractor, started working closely with a German carpenter, Hans, who had immigrated to the US after the war. The two men spoke German to each other, except when they addressed me. Often, my father would go for a beer with Hans after work. After all he had experienced at the hands of the Germans, my father's social drinking with a German émigré puzzled me enough that, one day, dropping my usual hesitation in these matters, I asked him about it point blank. My father began by telling me something that perplexed me even more; Hans had been a soldier during the war. But, he continued, Hans had been a conscript and had told my father that he was just one of many other German young men who were not Nazis and did not subscribe to Nazi ideology but were nonetheless forced to serve. Had they refused to serve, the SS would have shot them.[3] After the war, Hans determined to leave Germany for another place. Judging Germany as being morally bankrupt, he took the first opportunity he had to flee. He did not foresee that German society would abandon Nazism and democratize.

Hans's situation is not unlike that of the righteous, or at least less evil, inhabitants of the seven nations of Canaan that we discussed in part one. Within a corrupt society, one is forced to carry out the wishes of the corrupt state, which are the law, on penalty of death. Those who have the strength of character to turn their backs on their own corrupt societies stand a chance at redemption and a more virtuous life, but there are no guarantees. My father seemed to understand the world in this way: yes, there are substantial constraints, but the exercise of free will is available to all.

The events of the Holocaust, still present in living memory, bring into sharp relief the reality that man continues to perpetuate evil despite the millennia-old lessons of monotheism. Indeed, hadn't the Germans been Christian for more than a thousand years? In this respect, the atheists make a legitimate point. Why does man do evil if he knows how to be

---

[3] This was true particularly toward the end of the war, though deserters might be shot by the Feldgendarmerie (military police) and not the SS. For a discussion on consent and coercion in the German army, see Wolfram Wette, *The Wehrmacht: History, Myth, Reality*, trans. Deborah Lucas Schneider (Cambridge: Harvard University Press, 2006).

good? Or maybe we have the question all wrong? Does man really have the free will to choose between good and evil?

There was one more paradox to this story. Reading about the Holocaust in history books as an adult, I learned to my horror that the Nazis never considered themselves to be evil. If anything, they applied this term to the Jewish race. Concerning the Jews, Hitler writes in *Mein Kampf*: "Here he stops at nothing, and in his vileness he becomes so gigantic that no one need be surprised if among our people the personification of the devil as the symbol of all evil assumes the living shape of the Jew."[12] In the perverted worldview of the Nazis they were "saving" the German nation from the evil Jews, and, astonishingly, many Germans came to believe this.[13] While most people would assume that the Nazis simply spread lies about the Jews, some see in this example an extreme case of the fact that evil is in the eye of the beholder. Such a perspective opens the way to total moral relativism, leaving us without any meaningful definition of evil at all.[14] With no absolute and universally recognized criteria for judging evil, then not only the Nuremberg trials but any concept of crime and justice becomes irrelevant and useless. Thankfully, this is not the case. Most people today instinctively balk from such a radically relativistic stand. Instead, putting their faith in the innate moral intuition and reasoning power of human beings, thinkers across human cultures have adopted a similar view of good and evil that accords well with the Biblical view.[4]

The Bible's View of Evil

Contrary to common atheist accusations, the biblical view of evil is unrelated to supernatural satanic forces. The first mention of evil in the Bible appears in the story of Adam and Eve. In this story God famously forbids the pair to eat the fruit from the tree of the knowledge of good and

---

[4] A note on the references in part three. This section contains two types of references: references to generally accepted social-scientific theories and data and references to specific arguments about human thought and behavior. The first type of reference notes works in psychology, neurology, and the social sciences that I used to fact-check and/or expand my knowledge of specific social scientific data and theories. I also note books on the subject of theories that I mention in the text which readers may consult to broaden their knowledge. While the references are accurate, not all of the material in the books I use to fact-check, or as a general reference for further reading, necessarily accord with the arguments I make in this part of the book. The books that have influenced my own arguments are mentioned explicitly in the text as well as referred to in the notes. That being said, the authors of these works may or may not agree with my comparison between their arguments and biblical views.

evil (*tov* and *ra*, respectively in Hebrew). (Genesis 2:16–17) However, the snake comes along and tempts them to ignore this divine prohibition. With this story the Bible argues, as described in part one, that all humans are endowed with the knowledge of good and evil. The choice is up to us. This is not much different from the view expressed by atheists that we human beings have developed moral intuitions and a sense of ethics as part of our evolutionary makeup. Still, the story initially leaves the nature of evil rather up in the air. It is only in subsequent biblical episodes, as we follow the major characters in their epic moral struggles, that we get a clear sense of its meaning.

Introduced in the story of Adam and Eve,[5] the Hebrew word for evil "*ra*" reappears more than six hundred times in the Bible and prophetic books[15] primarily to describe harmful behavior toward others and not, as many atheists like to claim, with an obsessive focus on ritual or sexual misdemeanors. It appears in relation to the behavior of man before the flood (Genesis 6:5), to describe the men of Sodom (Genesis 13:13), and to depict the harm Laban wanted to do Jacob (Genesis 31:29), to choose but a few early examples within the founding stories of Genesis alone. The term *ra* also shows up again many times in a legal context in the book of Deuteronomy, where God reiterates to the Israelites the prohibitions against hurting others, all of which are described as evil. Instances here include bearing false witness (19:18–19), rejecting the judgment of an established court (17:12–13), adultery (22:22), kidnapping and enslaving (24:7), and other cases of people causing purposeful harm to others. Strikingly, the term is never used for Sabbath violation and ritual desecrations. It is also not applied to sexual misconduct except for such behaviors that threaten the quality of social and community standards, such as acts of adultery and giving an "evil name" through false accusations of a woman's lack of virginity or alternatively a woman falsely claiming virginity. (Deuteronomy 22:13–21). The Bible regularly employs the word *ra* for transgressions of those very rules that create social justice and a good society. Most importantly, it is also used to refer to idolatry, which, as we discussed in the first section and which we will further explain here, is inexorably tied to social injustice—whether

---

[5] To see when the word "ra" occurs in the Bible, you can look it up in any number of biblical concordances.

regarding the Israelites after the sin of the golden calf (Exodus 32:22) or in the repetition of the prohibition against idolatry in Deuteronomy (17:1–7). Make no mistake: the Bible's definition of evil is up front and center about our relationships and actions toward others.

Yet the word *ra* also appears in another context, which some atheist authors also note, namely the cruelty of nature and human suffering in this world, what philosophers call natural evil. *Ra* is used in the story of Joseph, for example, regarding the animal that Joseph's brothers' led Jacob to believe had killed him (Genesis 37:33). It occurs in relation to the harmful diseases and plagues that God visited upon Egypt (Deuteronomy 7:15) and which He also threatens to unleash upon the Israelites should they come to disobey him (Deuteronomy 28:59). Animals that are sickly, as appear in Pharaoh's dream, are also called *ra*. (Genesis 41:3–4) In biblical usage, thus, evil also refers to that which is lacking in blessing, to natural disaster and punishments from God. In this respect, the Bible recognizes the suffering man faces from nature as another source of evil.

Because the Bible's definition of evil so fully accords with human ethical intuition and reason, it resembles a view of evil found in many other cultures. The Bible's rational view of evil is not only evident throughout the Bible, but it underpins centuries of subsequent rabbinic interpretations collected in the Oral Law. It is summed up pithily by the sage Hillel: "That which is hateful to you, do not do to your fellow. That is the whole Torah; the rest is the explanation; go and learn." (Babylonian Talmud Shabbat 31a) Often called the Golden Rule, this fundamental principle is enunciated in all the major world religions and ethical traditions both monotheistic and those that have withstood the monotheistic revolution, such as the religions of India (Hinduism, Jainism, Buddhism), Zoroastrianism, and the religions of China (Confucianism, Taoism, Mohism). It is formulated as well in a number of secular ethical traditions in classical Greek and Roman philosophy[16] and in the proverbs of some traditional cultures,[6] even though these cultures were also, on the whole, idolatrous. The fact that human cultures have articulations for the Golden Rule while

---

[6] Some scholars argue that the Golden Rule developed in African societies independently of the African encounter with monotheism and that this is evident from traditional proverbs. For a discussion of these views see: Andrew M. Greenwell, "Golden Rule in African Proverbs," May 9, 2010, Lex Christianorum Blogpot, lexchristianorum.blogspot.co.il/2010/05/golden-rule-in-african-proverbs.html.

also advocating idolatry is a testament to our universal human moral intuition and reason despite a culture of entrenched lies about power and authority. But, as we shall demonstrate in this section, the more idolatrous a society, the more vociferously it actively rejects and suppresses the Golden Rule in theory not just in practice. Among secular thinkers in the modern period, Immanuel Kant, who tried to formulate a purely rational basis for ethics, devised the concept of "categorical imperative," which resembles the Golden Rule, though it is not exactly the same.[17] This rule remains one of the most important—though, as we shall see later, not the only—rational formulation of ethics.

It is important to note that not all discussions of evil in the traditions mentioned above limit their definitions to violation of the Golden Rule. Curious readers are invited to explore disagreements and different definitions in the references in the endnotes,[18] where they will discover that human reason can lead to other conceptions of evil. Nevertheless, all of these cultures endorse some form of the Golden Rule.

CHAPTER 13

Before Morality

What drives you? What gives you purpose? What gets you up in the morning? What keeps you going? It may be golf clubs, or money, it may be your stock portfolio, it may be your wife and family, it may be the thought of six martinis at the end of work, okay. There is some drive in life. We call ours God. And for us— Jews, Christians, and Muslims—He is a God who has told us about Himself. So He is not some impersonal deistic God. He is a God who is extraordinarily personal.

—TIMOTHY CARDINAL DOLAN

Given the near-universal consensus about evil, we must return to a question discussed by my father's friends. How and why could the Nazis ever conceive of the murder they carried out against the Jews if they knew and understood that killing was wrong? Is it that we humans are simply evil by nature, killers from birth? Do we need, as monotheistic preachers have railed in sermons across millennia, to exert gargantuan efforts in order to overcome our evil impulses? Atheist authors argue we should seek out science, not religion, in order to answer this critical question. I think we should look to both, as monotheists should never fear science.

Many people, not only the atheist writers, think that religion views evil as a diabolical force tempting us to indulge in physical pleasures. Historical examples are cited, like the stern Puritans decrying the evil of man's soul and deriding as evil the sort of harmless activities that we consider simple fun. Sour-faced orders of ascetic nuns, who spend solitary days repenting for being born, are brought to mind. Some people imagine firebrand preachers extolling abstinence from everything that delights, including vanilla ice cream on top of a brownie topped with chocolate liqueur. Or heavily bearded rabbis hunched in continuous study of oversized volumes of law, gaunt from fasting every Monday and Thursday. Or imams with growling faces clothed in headdresses and long robes on the hottest days, another not uncommon image.

Indeed, many people are truly convinced that monotheistic religions assert that man is inherently evil. That being the case, these religions seek to control the natural physical, emotional, and spiritual drives of people via an unrelenting regimen of restrictions and expiatory practices. I have heard stories of pious men in *shtetels* who would sleep nights on wooden floors to repent for any unintentional wrongdoings committed by day, and my Catholic friends recount similar anecdotes. Tablighi Muslims also describe feats of renunciation that seem from another era, sleeping on the ground as did Mohammad, for example. In the minds of many people, religion seeks to turn man's honest, natural vitality into something morally repugnant and evil.[1] If secularism can be credited with anything, as Michel Onfray writes in his book *A Hedonist Manifesto*,[1] it is giving people their lives back. It has led to the affirmation that our natural needs and drives are neither evil nor need they be a source of embarrassment. While such excesses of asceticism and punitive expiation have punctuated the histories of all three monotheistic religions, they are not found in the biblical text. Readers can follow the development of such trends in the sources in the endnotes.[2] The Bible itself, in fact, describes

---

[1] Most of the atheist writers argue that all three monotheistic religions have contributed to a hatred of the body and of a vital life. This hatred of physical pleasure is yet another reason to get rid of religion.

[2] Asceticism, the abstinence of worldly pleasures (including sex, food, and even comforts like shelter or clothing), has been a practice in idolatrous cults and even in all of the monotheistic religions, as well as in the religions of India, including Hinduism, Buddhism, and Jainism. All of these religions see asceticism as a means of controlling physical appetites so to not only develop self-control but access greater wisdom. Though none of the great world religions advocate asceticism for everyone, at various times they have emphasized asceticism sometimes as the most important ideal. This emphasis has also been opposed by coreligionists. Further, the ascetic current in all of these religions has frequently been open to extremism and abuse—often as a means of empowering the priestly classes over others. For a discussion of asceticism in rabbinic Judaism, see Eliezer Diamond, *Holy Men and Hunger Artists: Fasting and Asceticism in Rabbinic Culture* (Oxford: Oxford University Press; 2004). For Christianity, see Leif E. Vaage and Vincent L. Wimbush, *Asceticism and the New Testament* (New York: Routledge, 1999); and George E. Demacopoulos, *Five Models of Spiritual Direction in the Early Church* (Notre Dame: University of Notre Dame Press, 2007). For Islam, see Jonathan Berkey, *The Formation of Islam: Religion and Society in the Near East, 600–1800* (New York: Cambridge University Press, 2003), chapter 16, "Asceticism and Mysticism"; and Nile Green, *Sufism: A Global History* (Chichester: Wiley-Blackwell, 2012).

creation and man's drives and aspirations in positive terms and with psychological depth and sensitivity unique among ancient texts.

Good According to the Bible

The Bible's concept of good is the opposite of its concept of evil. If harm and the suffering of creation are evil, justice and the flowering of creation are good. Indeed, before the book of Genesis mentions the tree of the knowledge of good and evil, it first describes all of nature, including human beings, as good. "And God saw all that He had made, and found it was very good. And there was evening and there was morning the sixth day." (Genesis 1: 31) Nothing could be more straightforward: creation is good, life is good. At the end of the Bible, the message is equally clear. If the Israelites follow the laws, they will experience blessing. They will live, and life is good. "I have put before you life and death, blessing and curse. Choose life [...]" (Deuteronomy 30:19) In such a way, the Bible equates following the laws that prevent evil with life, and life itself is good. The Bible's notion of that which is good, thus, locates evil in man's actions, not in his nature.

The Bible and contemporary science share much in common in their descriptions of man's nature. Both see man as a creature endowed with a vital nature that underpins his/her actions. Evolutionary biologists, psychologists, neurologists, anthropologists, and other social scientists have long been concerned with the question of defining human nature.[3] While scientists still debate the exact features of human nature, there is broad agreement that humans display what some call "drives," others "instincts," and others still "needs" and/ or "motivations" that direct and determine our behavior.[4] For the sake of simplicity, we will use drives as the operative term. Understood as "energizing forces directed towards a particular goal or objective, drives may be viewed as innate (physiological) or acquired (learned). In the former [i.e., physiological] case,

---

[3] The journal *Human Nature: An Interdisciplinary Biosocial Perspective* brings together scholars from all of these disciplines to study the question of human nature.

[4] There is no unified theory of human needs, drives, instincts, or motivations in either psychology or anthropology. Yet these concepts continue to have theoretical relevance in the social sciences. Evolutionary biologists have looked at drives and instincts to see the commonalities between animals and humans and to look at adaptations that further our survival. The concept of needs and motivations has been important in research in psychology and social psychology, as we shall see.

the term is sometimes used as an alternative to instinct—though drive suggests less pre-patterning of behavior."[2] Some of these drives, as we shall see, are common to both animals and humans.[5] Yet they make up the backdrop against which we make moral decisions. Science creates frameworks for these drives through study and experimentation. The Bible does the same through its many stories. The Bible explicitly and implicitly accepts these drives as part of our being, our life force, and it rejects any notion that they are inherently evil. These drives are part of the good of creation.

Below are brief descriptions of some of the forces that motivate us and how the Bible anticipated our modern understandings millennia ago. Indeed, it is worth exploring these human drives and their echoes in the Bible in some detail, precisely because of the corrosive effect of misplaced asceticism and privations in the history of religious views of evil.

I Will Survive

Evolutionary biologists and psychologists alike agree about the primacy of the drive to survive. Freud called this the life drive.[6] The fight-or-flight response, evidence for the most basic survival instinct, is common to all living creatures. As biologists now know, it is controlled by the automatic nervous system, which regulates such other vital functions as heart rate, respiratory rate, and digestion, among others, and is activated and modulated by the sympathetic and parasympathetic nervous system.[3] Evolutionary biologists and psychologists view most human adaptations as responses to the problem of survival.[4] Linked to the drive to survive among most vertebrates and even other simpler animals is the sex drive. The limbic system is a key player for our human sex drive, regulating our arousal when the opportunity presents itself.[5]

Not surprisingly, the Bible and the monotheistic traditions understand the drive to live, and they honor it in their many narratives. Biblical characters like Yocheved and Miriam fight for the life of their son and brother, Moses. King David battles the Philistines to protect his people.

---

[5] A good reference for animal behavior is David McFarland, *Oxford Dictionary of Animal Behaviour*, 2nd ed. (Oxford: Oxford University Press, 2016).

[6] Freud developed the concepts of the life drive (Eros) and the death drive (later described as Thanatos) in his book *Beyond the Pleasure Principle*.

Abraham leaves the land of Canaan to avoid a famine, even resorting to lies that Sarah was his sister to avoid misfortune. In the event of life-threatening danger, the monotheistic traditions permit committing certain crimes, such as stealing or damaging property, provided that they are compensated at the earliest possibility. (Babylonian Talmud Sanhedrin 74a and Bava Kama 60b) Further reinforcing the importance of the drive to live, the Bible singles out murder as the most evil among all crimes. In so doing, it defies its ancient context and neighboring civilizations where human sacrifice was common. Monotheistic traditions, in fact, permit almost any law to be broken for the saving of a life. (Babylonian Talmud Sanhedrin 74a) The Talmud rules that one is required to save one's own life over that of another (Babylonian Talmud Bava Metzia 62a), not unlike the routine flight safety instruction to "please put on your own oxygen mask before assisting others." As for the sex drive, the command to be fruitful and multiply says it all. (Genesis 1:28, 9:1, 9:7) The Talmud paints a dramatic picture of how the destruction of the sex drive would end civilization. (Babylonian Talmud Sanhedrin 64a)

Why Your Toddler Insists the Crayon Is Hers

Biologists and social scientists also describe our instinct and drive to possess.[6] This, too, we share with animals.[7] Evolutionary biologists and ethologists (people who study animal behavior) show that animals hoard food as an instinctive behavior against scarcity. More than that, primatologists have located the desire to own property among nonhuman primates. They both maintain possession and show ownership of objects that they do not possess, the central features of property. Animals display the concept of possession, the simplest form of property; thus, ravens expect to be able to eat food in their possession even in the presence of a more dominant animal. Squirrels also demonstrate ownership of their hidden food items, which they retrieve when needed.

We, too, have this drive, which motivates us not only to accumulate objects but to possess and own them as our property. Yet property is also something that is far more developed in humans than in other species. Children as young as eighteen months show inferences about property. These inferences later become the basis for learning conflict resolution and morality.[8] Not only are we driven to possess; we are also driven to consume.[9] The fictional villain Gordon Gekko in the classic movie *Wall Street* (1987) concisely made the case for greed: "Greed, for lack of a better word, is good. Greed is right. Greed works. Greed clarifies, cuts through, and captures the essence of the evolutionary spirit." While the Gekko character clearly displayed abhorrent, over-the-top greed, did he have some point that greed is still the part of our nature that seeks bounty, comfort, and property? It is useful, for it motivates us to trade and thereby to explore, face conflict, and develop socially. Were it not for greed, we would still probably be primates. Remember, even hunter-gatherers who subsisted on roots and berries and painted on the cave walls in the evening owned and traded possessions.

The human drive for property and wealth also features in the Bible and monotheistic teachings. The Bible recognizes the human need for property. Just after the flood story, God declares that "the devisings of man's mind are evil [*ra* again] from his youth" (Genesis 8:21), yet in this very same verse God vows never again to destroy humanity. In the subsequent verses, He gives the earth and beasts to man as a possession, while also demanding he establish a system of justice. (Genesis 9:2–6) From these passages we understand that the Bible accepts that the desire for property is a part of human nature, though it needs to be mitigated with a system of justice because man is prone to harm others. The desire for wealth is also portrayed in positive terms, as wealth is called a blessing. Abraham and his descendants all accumulated wealth. As the Bible describes in Genesis: "'The Lord has greatly blessed my master [Abraham], and he has become rich.'" (Genesis 24:35) King Solomon acquired riches too. And as explained in part one, the Bible takes great pains to make sure *all Israelites* enjoy property in the form of land and material blessing. In this regard, the Bible and the monotheistic traditions view the opposite of wealth—poverty—as tragic. As the Midrash declares: "If all the sufferings and pain in the world were gathered on one side of a scale, and poverty was on the other side, poverty would outweigh them all." (Exodus Rabbah 31:14) Judaism, Christianity, and Islam emphasize widespread material prosperity to ensure that society does not descend into destitution and that wealth is not monopolized by a privileged few. That being said, the major monotheistic traditions warn against the ways in which one may misuse one's wealth and the power it confers, however bounty in itself is not evil.

Love, Love Me Do

The human need for love and companionship, often called attachment, is also universally acknowledged by scientists.[10] Human beings seek emotional bonds, first as children with caregivers, later with peers and then with romantic partners. There is even growing evidence that animals crave love and feel attachment, though their need for love is not as strong as among humans.[11] Psychologists further show that there are many aspects to love—ranging from attraction and passion to intimacy and commitment—that are now being explored at the neurological level.[12] Strap yourself into an MRI these days and find out whether you really love your partner or merely desire him/her, as revealed by your neural networks! Pioneering work on infants also examines what happens when we don't get love and how a mother who is unable to properly love and care for her child can make all other love relationships tremendously difficult for that child.[7] Our need for love from individuals is, of course, also related to our human desire for community, a sense of belonging, and a home,[13] which is common across cultures.[14]

The biblical text celebrates our need for human love. It describes instances of loss of love, unrequited love, desire, and the happiness of companionship. Isaac is able to overcome the loss of his mother and find comfort in his happy marriage to Rebecca. (Genesis 24:67) In the story of Leah and Rachel, Leah is devastated by her husband Jacob's lack of love and attention for her. (Genesis 30:15) Jacob could not be comforted for the loss of his son Joseph. (Genesis 37:35) Abraham and Sarah share a compassionate marriage (Genesis 16), while David is overcome with lust for Batsheva. (2 Samuel 11:2–4) The ancient rabbinic commentaries on the Bible relate how Yocheved, Moses's mother, succeeded in concealing Moses for three months (Exodus 2:2), disguising herself to be a nursemaid so as to continue to feed and care for Moses in Pharaoh's court. (Exodus 2:7, *Sotah* 12b) David and Jonathan love one another as the closest of friends, whose loyalty leads to self-sacrifice. (1 Samuel 31:1–6) The Bible is one of the richest ancient texts in exploring the many forms of love and attachment we humans need and want.

---

[7] There is widespread agreement that infants' attachment style even affects their ability to form bonds and healthy relationships as an adult. See various articles in Cassidy and Shaver, *Handbook of Attachment*.

R.E.S.P.E.C.T.

Respect, otherwise known as validation, is considered by psychologists and sociologists to be a central human need.[8] It is closely related to the need for love and consists in itself of a need to be recognized as a human being valued by others.[15] According to attachment theory—developed by John Bowlby, Mary Ainsworth, and other psychologists—and now confirmed in experiments for decades—respect and validation in the form of adult responsiveness to children are key to the development of a strong sense of self-worth.[16] Psychologists describe the devastating effects that the lack of respect and validation can have on a child or adult.[9] Shaming and humiliation are particularly destructive forms of psychological and social violence. They denigrate a person's standing with others and undermine a person's sense of self-worth.[17] The distress from shaming is astounding. As psychologists note, self-respect is essential for individuals to flourish.[18] In order for slaves to be inspired to rebel, for oppressed workers to rise up, and for women to demand the vote, each group needed to believe in its own worth. Internalized shame leads to political submission.

Respecting others is a central concept in the Bible and monotheistic teachings. Biblical heroes are characterized by their respectful behavior. Abraham is presented as hosting strangers with the utmost respect (Genesis 18:1–17), despite not knowing them, in contrast to the custom of

---

[8] Psychologists have addressed the concept of validation in a number of ways. Clinical psychologists, following the lead of Marsha Linehan, increasingly argue that validating individuals' emotions and feelings is an essential part of helping them heal from childhood abuse. See Kelly Koerner, *Doing Dialectical Behavior Therapy: A Practical Guide* (New York: Guilford Press, 2012). Indeed, researchers and clinicians focused on attachment theories have also noted the role of validation in emotional health. A mother's appropriate cues to her child serve as the most basic form of validation. See Cassidy and Shaver, *Handbook of Attachment*. Psychologists and sociologists have researched the devastating effect of constant disrespect/rejection on individuals, due to abusive parenting or bullying, and/or in groups, due to prejudice based on race, age, gender, and so forth. For the psychological impact of endemic disrespect, see for example Ellen DeLara, *Bullying Scars: The Impact on Adult Life and Relationships* (New York: Oxford University Press, 2016); and Alvin N. Alvarez, Christopher T. H. Liang, and Helen A. Neville eds., *The Cost of Racism for People of Color: Contextualizing Experiences of Discrimination* (Washington: American Psychological Association, 2016) and for a more sociological and political discussion of respect, see Cillian McBride, *Recognition* (Cambridge: Polity, 2013).

[9] One of the impacts of a consistent lack of validation and respect is chronic shame, which has a debilitating effect on a person's quality of life and relationships. See Patricia A. DeYoung, *Understanding and Treating Chronic Shame: A Relational/Neurobiological Approach* (New York: Routledge, 2015).

Sodom, where strangers were, according to legend, tortured. (Genesis 19:5) By contrast, Pharaoh is shown to be an autocrat who respects no one, to the point of asking the magicians to replicate the plagues, thereby killing his own citizens just to revel in his power. (Exodus 7:11, 22, and 8:14) Moses's personal relationships are characterized by respect, dialogue, and reason. He welcomes his father-in-law with dignity and defers to his wise counsel. (Exodus 18:7 and 14–27) He listens to the needs and concerns of the daughters of Zelophehad, who request to inherit the property of their father. (Numbers 27:1–11) He even counters Korach's accusations by defending the honor of God and his brother Aaron. (Numbers 16:8–11) Likewise, Joshua treats the prostitute Rachav with complete deference, despite her profession. (Joshua 2) Stories of reconciliation in the Bible are largely about newfound respect. Thus, Judah repents from his disrespectful behavior toward Tamar (Genesis 38:26), as he does toward Joseph. (Genesis 44:18–34) The Bible's concept of the essential equality of all human beings underpins all of these interactions. As we are all images of God, we should not disrespect each other in the first place. For this reason, the Talmud warns that shaming and embarrassing a person is tantamount to murdering them. (Babylonian Talmud Bava Metzia 58b) In fact, shaming someone publicly is one of the few sins for which the rabbis said a person forfeits his place in the world to come. (Babylonian Talmud Bava Metzia 59a) Think about that before you write in the next comments sections you come across online.

Empowerment Before Tony Robbins

Psychologists help us understand the universal human desire for power and self-actualization.[10] Power, as we have discussed, is the ability to assert and/or impose one's will in a given situation.[11] We learn about power at a very early age: the terrible twos is the time that children test the boundaries of their power over adults and their environment. They process learning to know and assert their will, and thereby their selfhoods, as distinct from their mothers.[19] Recall again the mixed emotions with which

---

[10] While again there is no one dominant theory on our need for power or self-actualization, these concepts appear in the works of many theorists and are used in clinical settings.

[11] Research on how power works is a central concern of the social sciences. For an examination of power in different fields, see Keith M. Dowding, *Encyclopedia of Power* (London: SAGE, 2011).

God notes "the devising of man's mind are evil from his youth." (Genesis: 2:21) The need to assert our will and power is related to both development of the self and the more basic necessity of overcoming physical dangers.[20] The psychologist Alfred Adler theorized that our will to power and our desire to master our environment was a primal urge.[21] Abraham Maslow and Carl Rogers discussed the need to realize one's capabilities, being fully oneself or individuating, generating ambition, growth, and change.[22] Americans have spent millions of dollars on self-help books about "empowerment." And for good reason. What if Winston Churchill had just stopped believing in himself and retired from politics instead of remaining in Parliament after all his many setbacks? Or, worse, if he had felt unworthy or incapable of fighting Nazi Germany? My mother had a phrase for resilience, "Don't be a *shmatta*," a rag in Yiddish. By which she meant, don't let people step on you or use you.

The Bible and monotheistic traditions affirm the necessity of discovering and asserting our personal power. The formative stories of the Bible are about unlikely characters who rise to the occasion and make history. Thus Moses, who suffers a speech impediment, becomes the greatest spokesperson for God. (Exodus 4:10) David, a scrawny lad almost outcast from his family (1 Samuel 16:1–13), defeats the warrior Goliath and later is crowned king. In the course of his reign, David fights against personal fears and doubts as well as palace intrigues and enemy assaults. (1 and 2 Samuel) The prophets of the Bible, such as Jeremiah, speak truth to power despite death threats and public ridicule. Deborah puts her talents as a teacher and military general to use to serve her people and nation. Other women, like Hannah, enjoying little encouragement, find it within themselves nonetheless to raise leaders of the Jewish people among forsaken generations. In texts within the monotheistic traditions, we are inspired to exert our own will by discovering and developing our own talents. By cultivating our own powers, we serve as examples to others to do the same. In the Talmud (Babylonian Talmud Shabbat 122a) it is written: "One man's candle is light for many." So many athletes ascribe their achievements to the example of previous athletic heroes. As the words of Matthew (5:16) indicate: "Let your light so shine before men, that they may see your good works." A gospel song cherished by civil rights activists goes, "This little light of mine, I'm gonna let it shine." The candle is an apt metaphor for such power. Just as a candle that is used to light another candle doesn't lose its own light, so, too, genuine personal power inspires others, neither diminishing them nor being diminished. The Bible recognizes and wants us to harness our human desire to strive for goals and succeed.

Far from offering a negative view of man's internal drives or seeking to suppress them through penitential solitude and a diet of bread and water, the Bible celebrates man's vital physical, emotional, social, and spiritual nature.

Is It All in Your Selfish and Altruistic Genes?

Atheists, particularly Dawkins, believe that morality emerges from an evolutionary drive to act altruistically toward members of the same species. Such an argument does not, however, stand up in light of our rational definition of good and evil. Indeed, rather than set selfishness in opposition to altruism, it is more useful to consider both altruism and selfishness along with their companion activities, cooperation and competition, as *neutral strategies*. Humans and animals use these strategies with each other to get basic needs met in their respective societies.[12] Each has evolutionary functions and, hence, each is necessary for survival. On the biological level, competition ensures the survival of the most robust genes, while in human cultures, it has often led to greater heights of intellectual and artistic expression, which can benefit all parties involved. Yet, neither strategy necessarily conforms to the Golden Rule. Among primates, competition between alpha males can be deadly,[23] while seemingly more benign cooperation can devolve into various forms of coercion, where one party is *forced* to cooperate with another.[24] In many cases both humans and primates create coalitions and alliances in order to compete more effectively against other groups.[25] The effects of hierarchy on cooperation are even observed in studies of primates.[26] Dawkins rightly points out that much altruistic behavior among primates is limited to

---

[12] For a discussion of cooperation as an essential strategy for survival, see eds. Kim Sterelny, Richard Joyce, Brett Calcott, and Ben Fraser, *Cooperation and Its Evolution* (Cambridge: MIT Press, 2013), introduction. For a cross-cultural perspective, see Richard E. Blanton and Lane Fargher, *How Humans Cooperate: Confronting the Challenges of Collective Action* (Boulder: University Press of Colorado, 2016). For a discussion of competition as an essential strategy for survival, see Paul A. Keddy, *Competition* (Dordrecht: Kluwer Academic, 2001).

their in-group. Many human and primate activities fit the definition of cooperation—work toward a common goal—but it is far from egalitarian and just.[27] Both cooperation and competition often find ways of quickly degenerating into killing and exploitation.

The Bible understands the basic amorality of selfishness and altruism and of competition and cooperation. Investing in one's own education may be selfish, yet many of the heroes of the Bible, such as David, spend time studying both as a form of personal enrichment and in service to the people. Total selflessness is not a virtue. Likewise, the Bible sees cooperation and competition as morally neutral. Hence the people's cooperation in building the Tower of Babel or in fashioning the golden calf is considered evil, while the competition between the rabbis of the *Mishna* was good, inspiring them to further heights of prayer and study. (Babylonian Talmud Bava Batra 22a) The competition between Korach and Moses was evil, as Korach simply wished to depose Moses for his own gain. The cooperation between Jacob's sons to sell Joseph into slavery was evil as well. However, their cooperation to save their father from further loss put an end to the estrangement between them and, thus, was good. Likewise, selfishness can sometimes become an asset as a survival mechanism; case in point, Jacob, who keeps food and livestock for his family as he flees in the face of Laban's treachery. (Genesis 31:10–18) And improper altruism can reveal itself to be an act of evil, as is self-evident in the story of Sodom, where Lot offers up his daughters to placate the mob that wants to abuse his guests. (Genesis 19:8) These strategies, like the drives they serve, are also fundamentally amoral in that, based on our definition of evil as a transgression of the Golden Rule, they can be either evil or good dependent upon circumstances and context.

The definition by the Bible and so many cultures of the nature of good or evil action thus involves a different dynamic of choice and reflection than simply altruism and cooperation. Here the Bible, too, offers some useful insights that again conform to our reason.

CHAPTER 14

Rational Morality
in the Bible

Evil Step by Step

Far from supernatural or irrational in its outlook, the Bible's view of evil is downright rational. It can be broken down logically into a series of conditions implicit in the Bible's laws and stories that find echoes among secular moral philosophers. First and foremost, in order to determine whether we have crossed the threshold from neutral strategy to evil action, one factor must be taken into account—is consent present or absent? In order for people to fulfill their personal, physical, emotional, and existential needs in society without doing harm to others, they need the willing and mindful consent of others. Consent between two individuals or two groups, then, is the rational prior condition of following the Golden Rule, do unto others what you would have done unto you, or in the Talmudic version, don't do to others what you would not want them to do to you.[1]

Let me explain. The Golden Rule is intended to prevent people from doing things to others, whether by coercion, force, or violence, that these others have *not* consented to. Stealing and murder are obvious examples

---

[1] For a discussion of consent and the Golden Rule, see Harry J. Gensler, *Ethics and the Golden Rule* (New York: Routledge, 2013).

based on a lack of consent. A person who willingly gives you something is not a victim of theft. If two persons willingly consent to a sexual relationship, neither of them is a victim of rape. If a person goes along with sex because of an unequal power relationship in which one party fears the consequences of dissenting, that is not consent, that is coercion. (The extreme case of a person who consents to let you kill him is not an example of consent, since you have to doubt the state of mind of that person. Much of the debate about euthanasia revolves around what constitutes uncoerced consent.) The complete prohibition against euthanasia in monotheistic religions is, in part, a function of the doubt over uncoerced consent in such a final act. In another example, if we agree that you'll go hunt for berries while I go hunt for bananas and then we'll share, you are not exploiting me. But the idea of consent goes much further. Consent is at the heart of fulfilling our emotional and existential needs.[1] Respect, for example, is often earned by demonstrating that one cannot be coerced. The need for connection is best fulfilled by consensual attachment. This rational approach is implicit in the Bible's understanding of evil. Most actions that the Bible labels as evil are, in fact, transgressions of consent regarding our bodies or our property. So mutual consent, that is our mindful, willing choice to participate in any particular relationship, is the basis of healthy relationships between people. Through this consent, we ensure that we are not doing to others what we don't want done to us. Modern secular explorations of the consent theory of ethics take this approach in one form or another.[2]

If consent is the precondition for avoiding evil, then knowing what one is consenting to and doing so freely are the preconditions for consent. Here too the Bible depicts this precondition narratively.

Evil Feeds on Lies

The logic behind the biblical narratives is that coercion and deception are the two prevalent means used to pervert consent, whether in our personal or our business relationships. Both means, ultimately, are based on lies, though they work somewhat differently. Coercion is simply a form of forced consent, thus not consent at all, and in that sense, it is deceptive.[3] The slave "consents" to doing her work because the choice is to work, or to face a beating or death. Yet coercion is also very real, since threats to one's life can be genuine. Therefore, the power of an unjust ruler is no mere illusion; it is very real and very evil. How does such a ruler derive the right to unfettered power? In the case of Pharaoh, it derives from *a lie*—the false claim that his will is more valid than all other Egyptians. The coercive power of unjust rulers like Pharaoh thus depends on swaying the masses to embrace this lie, thereby ensuring that they are followed, sometimes even blindly. One of the key strategies these rulers use to makes this lie convincing is to claim supernatural power. Here we see again how idolatry is a lie about power and authority and how psychological mechanisms underlie its success. Deception, like coercion, encourages false consent and can be exploited in all manner of ways.[2] A person might be falsely promised a reward for participating in something, thus influencing their consent. Using false threats is an example of combining coercion and deception in order to obtain consent. A pervasive culture of idolatry can hold an entire citizenry in its nefarious grip, convincing people that they are supposedly inferior, hence obligated to consent to living under systems that work against their very interests and dignity.[4] Thus is formed the basis of internalized sexism and racism.

The Bible consistently describes the centrality of deception in evil. Take the story of Jacob and Laban. Laban is an archetypical biblical villain. Father of Rachel and Leah, he negotiates a deal with Jacob, offering Rachel's hand in marriage in exchange for seven years of Jacob's labor. The eager suitor consents, but when the wedding day arrives Laban substitutes Leah for Rachel and unilaterally demands of Jacob another seven years labor as a revised bride price for Rachel. The story further notes how Laban craftily changes Jacob's wages many times. The celebrated story of Israelite bondage in Egypt does not deny the reality of the Egyptian nation's political, military, and social supremacy. But the Exodus demonstrates that the might of Egypt was based on a fundamental lie that the pharaoh was a divine being whose will was to be obeyed and that, by divine right, the Israelites were meant to be his slaves. Deception is one of those devious tools that people use to inflict harm and take from others while claiming to be cooperating.

---

[2] Much of the discussion around deception and consent today is about informed or uninformed consent. Outright deception nullifies consent in most legal contexts today, but the question of how much information a person was given affects the nature of their consent. Informed consent is particularly relevant in medicine and research today.

The Reason for Divine Law

Because of the centrality that deception and coercion play in the perpetration of evil, the Bible legislates absolute laws essential to stamping out such perverse practices. Atheist critics of religion and evil argue that the very notion that moral goodness derives from adherence to God-given laws is offensive and infantilizing. The power of human reasoning affords us ample ability, atheists claim, to distinguish between good and evil by our own wits and, if need be, to generate laws and social contracts for ourselves. The atheists are not all wrong. The biblical text, too, acknowledges without reservation that human beings are capable of reasoning their way to ethical behavior and moral efficacy. One rabbinic legend suggests that Abraham intuited all the laws of the Torah centuries before the revelation to Moses at Mount Sinai. (Yoma 28b) The Bible's laws are not some set of novel rules that shatter our human notion of good and evil, but rather, are codifications to stabilize society in light of human frailty. God, as an all good and all true force, revealed a set of absolute laws. In doing so, He gave us an option: Do we obey a higher set of principles, or do we capitulate in the face of overwhelming social pressures throughout history to obey other, very real, powers?[3] This dichotomy of choice appeared all the more pronounced in the ancient world, when idolatrous leaders wielded their power with gusto. But it remains equally true today. Those who choose to be guided by divine law are striving toward truth and justice. They reject any idea of loyalty and service to fallible and self-interested human beings. This is why the Bible equates serving God with obedience to His law (Deuteronomy 10:12–13), and this is why the Bible prohibits serving anything or anyone else as idolatry. The codification of these laws also provides us with a concrete reminder, a steadfast ethical compass should our imagination ever tempt us to act deceptively. The laws act as a kind of reality check, but only because they are rational. As the Bible explains in Deuteronomy 4–6, they are accessible to all, indeed downright user-friendly to global citizens who care to advance justice and equality and to better the world.

---

[3] Resistance to dominant powers is not only about power strategies, but about the belief that resistance is worthwhile. For an examination of resistance, see John M. Jermier, David Knights, and Walter R. Nord, *Resistance and Power in Organizations* (London: Routledge, 1994).

Hell, No: Reward and Punishment Revisited

The Bible's rational view of good and evil extends to its view of reward and punishment, contrary to the claim of atheists. The Bible considers reward and punishment to be primarily the rational consequences of good and evil behavior and secondarily a metaphysical force. Atheist authors contend that fear of postmortem retribution is, at best, a weak motive for doing good. They are both right. The biblical concept of reward and punishment is much more tied to man's choices and the result they carry than any hellfire after death. When man chooses to harm others, he contributes to creating an evil society. Living in such a society is a punishment in itself. However, the Bible makes a further point. The Bible in Deuteronomy explains this by depicting our actions as forever a stark choice between a blessing and a curse. (Deuteronomy 11:26–28) When a majority of people consistently choose to do evil they eventually destroy the entire fabric of society. Understood in rational terms, an unjust society inevitably degenerates into a weak society. This is why the Bible describes the resultant society as cursed: vulnerable to invasion, implosion, and/or deprivation. (Deuteronomy 28) Historically, empires under the sway of corrupt and evil political leadership, as is the nature of imperial rule, did not ultimately last, and so fell the Egyptian, Roman, and colonial European regimes.[5] Once man creates a truly just society on earth, that society will last forever.

Since monotheists understand justice and truth as being in line with God, then, naturally, when our actions prove out of sync with justice and truth, the results ripple across our relationships and politics, thereby coming back to rebound upon us one way or another.[4] This understanding is not unlike what is known in some Asian cultures as karma.[6] The fact that injustice does not always lead to a boomerang effect is a topic

---

[4] The biblical concept of punishment is described in national terms. If the Israelites do not create a just society, then that very injustice will itself lead to suffering for all who live in it. Subsequent Jewish thought describes the result of accumulated acts of evil on an individual person. The rabbinic notion that a transgression begets another transgression and a good deed begets another good deed (Sayings of the Fathers 4:2) suggests that these acts, in addition to affecting our relationships, also transform us. There is psychological evidence that we become habituated to doings good and doing bad. For a description of the role of habituation to evil, see Christopher R. Browning, *Ordinary Men: Reserve Police Battalion 101 and the Final Solution in Poland* (New York: HarperPerennial, 1998); and Philip G. Zimbardo, *The Lucifer Effect: Understanding How Good People Turn Evil* (New York: Random House, 2007).

we will explore at the end of part three, when we address the question of why God allows evil in the first place. But the fact remains that we should often expect to see effects of our transgressions of the Golden Rule in our own lifetimes, just as Jacob, Moses, and David found.

CHAPTER 15

Bad Men and Women

By applying rational biblical notions of evil and the mechanisms that underpin it to our contemporary world, we can more easily recognize the forms of evil that people commit and begin to answer two of the most vexing questions posed by my father's Holocaust survivor friends:

- How can people who know the difference between good and evil descend to such depths of evil as the Nazis did?
- More shockingly, how could they claim that their victims were actually the evil ones?

Spotting Evil Today: No Shortage of Candidates

Based on the Bible's definition, people and nations today are still steeped in evil enterprises. I know, like Claude Rains in *Casablanca*, you must be shocked, shocked! Nonetheless, it is worth analyzing contemporary forms of evil.

We can subdivide our recent transgressions of the Golden Rule by the types of harm to others we commit, why we commit it, and how we commit it. The first category, *exploitative* evil, occurs when people cheat or rob others of what is rightfully theirs, whether property or reward. The second, *abusive* evil, represents harming another's body and mind physically, sexually, or emotionally. The third, *raging* evil, is the result of people hating others to such a degree that they seek to exploit, abuse, dominate, or destroy them. Finally, the fourth is *cowardly* evil, people complying with the dictates of an authority figure to exploit, abuse, dominate, or even destroy others. All four of these types of evil are evident in modern societies for which the Golden Rule and monotheism are supposedly respected standards. Social scientists who study these behaviors provide insights into their prevalence, why we do them, and how we justify them despite recognizing that, even if in theory, they are evil.

Please Don't Steal This Book: Exploitative Evil

Let's face it, we live in a world where people steal, cheat, and deceive each other regularly. The first chapter of the bestselling book by Steven Levitt and Stephen Dubner, *Freakonomics*,[1] provides small-scale examples of how Americans cheat and steal today. A group of Chicago public school teachers, for example, cheated in order to improve their students' results on standardized testing; two University of Georgia basketball coaches offered a bogus course to make it easier for their players to maintain academic eligibility; and then there were the sumo wrestlers who sought to manipulate the wrestling rankings. If such anecdotes of cheating and stealing seem harmless ethical nitpicking, consider the fact that larger-scale government and corporate stealing have wreaked economic havoc in the last century and continue to ravage countries today.[2] The problem has become so acute in certain countries that they have been dubbed, ignominiously, *kleptocracies*.[3] Russian president Vladimir Putin, for one, is said by some estimates to hold assets estimated anywhere between seventy billion dollars and two hundred billion dollars.[4] Other leaders, such as Mobutu Sese Seko, have incurred "odious debt" by borrowing vast amounts of money (twelve billion dollars in Seko's case, of which he pocketed four billion dollars) in the name of the government but, in reality, for private purposes.[5] Corporate officials, like Yasuyoshi Kato, who embezzled over eighty-five million dollars over six years from Day-Lee Foods Inc. through fraudulent checks, have been known to steal similarly huge amounts.[6]

Contemporary forms of corporate and government cheating also rely on more indirect forms of deception and coercion such as circumventing market mechanisms or the rules of fair trade.[7] My personal wake-up call to this came as a college student, when a Senate committee reported that members of the Lockheed board paid upwards of twenty-two million dollars in bribes to foreign government officials in order to secure sales of their aircrafts.[8] To make matters worse, if that were possible, this scandal took place after the American government had bailed Lockheed out of close to two hundred million dollars in defaulted bank loans at the expense of America's taxpayers. Lockheed management argued that this was just the cost of doing business. I discussed this with some other undergraduates, of whom a portion agreed that—yes indeed—this was simply business as usual.

Related to bribery is the selling of state industries below market value, another form of cheating that took place in the 1990s in Latin America and the former Communist countries.[1] This cheating created a class of wealthy state officials and tycoons while impoverishing citizens.[9] Such collusion between the government and corporations also included subsidies, cash grants, and tax breaks—a variation of cheating based on creating "rules" meant to benefit the few at the expense of the many. States are not innocent of such corrupt practices either, having used the law to expropriate private industries, often at a tremendous loss to foreign investors who developed local industries,[2] often, again, for the sole benefit of the governing class. Companies, in turn, have cheated by forming cartels—whether legally or illegally—fixing prices to the detriment of consumers on items as prosaic as Christmas trees to milk and pharmaceuticals.[10] Massive fraud and Ponzi schemes have been made notorious by Bernie Madoff, ZZZZ Best, WorldCom, and Enron, who apparently competed for the prize of con artist of the millennium.[11] Citizens and consumers from first world to third world have been cheated out of billions of dollars and, too often, even out of a future. Social scientists show that, for most thieves and cheats, motives can be found among the many human drives and needs, whether for respect, possessions, or power.[12] Cheating and stealing are often an expedient means to meet these needs, especially when people have little fear of getting caught. The benefits are so large, in fact, that murder is not unthinkable as a strategy to protect perpetrators of large-scale cheating and stealing. The bigger question is not to what end people cheat—we know that—but why they cheat at all if they know it is wrong?

---

[1] For a discussion of such dishonest privatization, see Joseph E. Stiglitz, *Globalization and Its Discontents* (New York: W. W. Norton, 2003).

[2] See, for example, Idi Amin's nationalization of Ugandan business without paying any compensation whatsoever. In other instances, such as in the case of Hugo Chavez in Venezuela, compensation was partial.

Research shows that people generally cheat and steal because they have justified their behavior to themselves.[13] Few cheaters and thieves admit to harming others; rather, they simply lie to themselves. Levitt and Dubner, for example, describe how many bagel thieves rationalized that the supplier, a Mr. Feldman, would lose little money on his or her individual bagel, hence they were not really harming him.[14] Many business leaders and statesmen involved in selling companies below market value simply hid the information from the public or claimed deceptively that such expedient "privatization" would be good for the economy.[3] Companies involved in exploitative monopolies have similarly rationalized their status based on "efficiency" or on the jobs they create.[4] These are modern versions of "the noble lie." Middle-class Americans who cheat on taxes commonly rationalize their behavior as moral: "Why pay taxes if the whole system is rigged to benefit the rich anyway and my friends in cash businesses can hide some of their income?"[15] Some wealthy Americans, meanwhile, rationalize their own cheating as fair: "Why should I pay so much in taxes? I made my money myself, and the system just milks the wealthy." Some especially corrupt officials, whether corporate or government, don't even bother with rationalizations, relying on their power not to get caught, or, in the event of being discovered, to silence those who would expose their corrupt practices.[16] These folks are no better than gangsters who openly admit to being criminals, bragging that power and violence is the way of the world. In countries where people know good from evil, rather than tough braggadocio, most stealing and cheating is veiled through the lies and self-deception I so often heard in those car rides on my way from 96th Street to Wall Street. Facilitating the task enormously is the fact that in modern society many people live in communities where they are removed from the people they are cheating or stealing from.[17]

If You Read Just One Chapter of the Bible, Make it Leviticus 19

The Bible prohibits stealing and cheating outright. Further, it confronts the underlying lies we tell ourselves and others in order to rationalize our behavior. The Bible prohibits stealing categorically. The eighth

---

[3] For many examples of this, see Stiglitz, *Globalization*; and Steger and Roy, *Neoliberalism*.
[4] For many examples. see Utton, *Cartels and Economic Collusion*.

commandment says it all: do not steal. Virtually every biblical injunction against stealing and cheating reaffirms that we are *all* accountable to higher principles of truth and justice. A few examples from Leviticus 19 will illustrate this point: "You shall not steal; you shall not deal deceitfully or falsely with one another. You shall not swear falsely by My name, profaning the name of your God: I am the Lord." (Leviticus 19:11–12) "You shall not defraud your fellow. You shall not commit robbery. The wages of the laborer shall not remain with you until morning [...] You shall fear your God: I am the Lord." (Leviticus 19:13–14) The use of the word "you" could not be clearer; it means each person. The use of "I am the Lord" could be substituted with "this is truth and justice." Indeed, believing that all of our actions are measured against a set of absolute standards to which we are held accountable sensibly guides us to behave properly.

I believe that the modern founder of classical economics, Adam Smith, integrated in his writings this biblical message to guard against self-deception with an apt metaphor. In *The Wealth of Nations*, Smith used the term "the invisible hand" to describe the force within the free-market economy that creates prices. Guided by this force, the market supplies needs efficiently and in the most optimal manner without the need for a central planner to intervene.[18] When all externalities are appropriately priced into a transaction, Smith's logic generally holds true. Smith, however, first used the term in *The Theory of Moral Sentiments*,[19] a work of ethics and philosophy. Scholars debate as to what Smith meant with his concept of the invisible hand, which he never defined. Let me offer a homiletic reading of this concept, which to me seems congruent with his overall view of the relationship between economics and morality. The invisible hand is not just a wonderfully productive economic mechanism, but rather it is required to be present at every transaction in order to ensure morality and social order in the face of the lies one might tell oneself.[5] Indeed, Smith was well aware of how commercially-focused businessmen might be tempted to exploit others. As he put it, merchants and manufacturers are "an order of men whose interest is never exactly the same with that of the public, *who generally have an interest to deceive* [my emphasis] and even oppress the public and who accordingly have,

[5] My homiletic reading is in part inspired by the view is taken by Robert L. Heilbroner, who wrote the preface to the 1986 edition of Smith's collected works.

201

on many occasions, both deceived and oppressed it."[20] Given Smith's view on merchants, the invisible hand can refer indirectly to the absolute principles of truth and justice that ought to accompany transactions and therefore prompt one's conscience to be honest, occasionally also giving it a hard smack. While Adam Smith's exact religious beliefs are unknown (and some argue he was a deist),[21] it is hard to read chapter 19 of Leviticus, which is the heart of the Bible, without thinking that Smith must have at least reflected on this text, even if he did not actually intend to create the invisible hand as an analogy. In the words of Reverend Dr. Katharine Henderson:

> God doesn't just make things easier, God also makes things harder. God is related to conscience, God is our North Star moral framework. Particularly in the business world or any other ethical setting, a relationship with God and the belief that there is a moral dimension to human life means that due to your relationship with God, He will ask you to wrestle with things. It is the pinprick of conscience that will keep you from acting unethically to the people that you manage and supervise or to accounting principles or any other number of business practices for example. It is the knowledge of knowing and being known by a God who cares.

The Jewish texts offer a frightening image in further confronting the lies we tell ourselves in order to steal. As the Talmud records: "Rabbi Yochanan said, one who steals from a friend even the smallest coinage of money is like he takes from him his soul." (Babylonian Talmud Bava Kama 119a) In this way, thieves are like J.K. Rowling's description of "dementors."

Fatal Attraction: Abusive Evil

Sadly, we cannot turn to the news today without hearing another story of people who abuse others. In the United States alone, six and a half million children are abused every year.[22] Every day in the US, an average of three women and one man are murdered by their partner.[23] Sexual assault and abuse injure both the body and soul of their victims. According to the National Violence Against Women Survey, one in six American women and one in thirty-three American men have experienced an attempted or completed rape.[24] That comes to at least three girls in an average high school class. Even in the generally peaceful and law-abiding country of New Zealand, one in three women experience some form of abuse.[25] Around the world, 8 percent of men and 20 percent of women have been sexually abused before the age of eighteen.[26] Victims often never fully recover. In some cases, such abuse also ends in murder. Women are more likely to be murdered by an abusive partner or family member than any other person.[27] Emotional and verbal abuse also destroy lives by damaging the abused person's sense of self, thereby casting a shadow over their other relationships.[6] The US Workplace Bullying Institute released a report in 2010 that indicated that 35 percent of workers surveyed reported they had been bullied on the job.[28] One in four American children are bullied at schools.[29] According to current studies in domestic violence, emotional abuse can be more harmful than physical abuse.[30]

Further, across the world, whether in the form of forced labor or human trafficking, people combine exploiting and abusing others for their own profit: it is called slavery.[31] According to the Global Slavery Index, there are over *forty-five million people* in the world today who are enslaved, whether as sex slaves or for forced labor.[32] More than five million of these slaves are children. While not technically slavery, extreme poverty in some cases comes close enough. According to the International Labour Organization, in 2013 an estimated 375 million workers, who are officially free, lived on less than 1.25 US dollars a day.[33] This is not only a third world problem. In the United States, 13.3 percent of service-sector workers alone fell below the US poverty line.[34]

As with stealing, people abuse to fulfill their needs, often for love and power, or even money and possessions. In her book on men who abused women physically, verbally, and emotionally,[35] the batterer intervention counselor Sara Elinoff Acker describes through her interviews with abusive men how many batterers abuse women as a means of feeling powerful or in control. As domestic violence expert Donald Dutton explains, men who abuse their wives are often victims of early childhood abuse themselves (though not all victims of abuse go on to be abusers). Abusers grow up dependent on parents who did not provide the

---

[6] For a general discussion of violence and abuse in the world today, see Angela Browne Miller, *Violence and Abuse in Society: Understanding A Global Crisis* (Santa Barbara: Praeger, 2012).

necessary love and respect.[36] As a result of these deep childhood wounds, they use coercive means to maintain their adult relationships; in other words, to get love. Likewise, when asked why they bullied, many bullies replied that "it makes me feel stronger, smarter, or better than the person I'm bullying," while others said they had been bullied at home.[37] Thus, as with stealing and cheating, the question is not for what purpose people abuse, but rather why they do it, if they too know it is wrong.

Just like cheaters and stealers, abusers continue harming others by rationalizing their abuse. Many abusers will simply say their victims were asking for it or provoked them.[38] Verbal and emotional abusers may rationalize their behavior: they were speaking the truth or saying what they felt, denying that they had done wrong. Others will argue that their victims—whether women or a specific ethnic group—do not deserve any better, justifying their abuse with prejudices. As one of the batterers describes in an interview: "Men throughout the world think of women and children as chattel, that women are merely here to serve. My dad treated my mother that way. [...] I had a major attitude adjustment to make, in terms of valuing women and seeing them as equals."[39] Not that abuse is a male prerogative. As Dutton demonstrates, women who abuse their husbands exhibit similar patterns of self-deception.[40] Whether consciously or not they simply don't believe they can be loved or feel powerful without harming others.[41] As parts I and II clearly described, slave owners across history, including in the US, routinely abused their slaves physically, sexually, and emotionally. They justified this abuse based on the lies of the slave's "inferiority," whether in terms of gender, race, or nationality. As for those who enslave others today, they too rationalize their behavior, claiming to be giving their slaves a livelihood, or even cynically saying that those who were trafficked should have known better.[42]

Love Your Neighbors Even If You Don't Like Them

The Bible, again, not only prohibits abuse but emphasizes the importance of human worth. Biblical laws forbid harming others, whether by cruel words, physical abuse, sexual abuse, or labor exploitation. In simple terms, the Bible exhorts, "Do not wrong another, but fear your God; for I am the Lord your God," (Leviticus 25:17) or perhaps even more bluntly, "Do not murder." The laws against stealing and other prohibitions are addressed to everyone. The Bible conceives all creatures to be made in God's image and, thus, denies the lie that underpins most abuse. One commandment is mentioned in the Pentateuch—thirty-six times, to be exact—and that is "to treat the stranger well because we were strangers in Egypt." We are even required to extend good treatment to people we dislike. The Bible instructs, "When you encounter your enemy's ox or ass wandering, you must take it back to him." (Exodus 23:4) How many people suing their neighbor for property infringement would assist them in changing a flat tire? We are also forbidden from rejoicing at the downfall of an enemy, even if their fall from grace is deserved. Thus the Israelites were not allowed to rejoice at the death of the Egyptians. Or as described in Proverbs: "If your enemy falls do not exult; if he trips, let your heart not rejoice [...]" (Proverbs 24:17) By emphasizing the need to treat people who are different than us with respect, the Bible and Talmud make it perfectly clear that we cannot rationalize abusing anyone because of their status, gender, or ethnicity.

CHAPTER 16

Blaming Others

Love to Hate You: Raging Evil

The twentieth century saw an outpouring of hate between peoples, which often erupted into violence and even genocide.[1] This hatred occurred between populations at the grass-roots level and at the highest echelons of power. The German people actively encouraged the Nazi government to persecute the Sinti and Roma in their communities.[2] Other regimes fostered hatred of the victim populations above and beyond existing animosity and prejudice. The Nazis called Jews vermin and compared them to diseases.[1] They blamed the Jews for everything from Germany's failure to win World War I to its economic woes in the 1920s. They then propagated this mendacious version of history to all of the German people. Likewise, the Turkish[3] and Hutu-led Rwandan[4] governments unleashed intensely slanderous propaganda campaigns against the Armenians and Tutsis, respectively. The genocidal consequences of this hatred and these lies are incomprehensible to most people. Other cycles of mutual recrimination and violence also kept hatred alive, as happened in Eastern Europe between Slovenians, Croats, Serbs, and Bosnians. This conflict cost over one million lives during World War II (due not only to Nazi aggression but to fighting between ethnic and political groups within Yugoslavia as well) and some 140,000 lives in the Yugoslav wars of the 1990s.[5]

---

[1] For a good history of Nazi views, ideology, and practices in Germany, see Friedländer, *Nazi Germany and the Jews*.

Many of the victims of such hatred find it hard to talk about their experience. Thulani Mabaso, the anti-apartheid activist and former prisoner who graciously met with me and my family, told us that it was very difficult for him to continue to talk about his experiences. However, he wanted to talk because that is the only way for the world to know. His remarks reminded me of some Holocaust survivors who debated about whether to talk about their time in the concentration camps or to do their best to suppress the memories. For much of the 1950s and into the 1960s, most survivors were reluctant to retell their experiences. It was only toward the end of his life that my father was willing to open up, and then only somewhat. Although Mabaso did not put it this way, as he spoke I was struck by the danger that happens when some groups of people are just not considered human by their oppressors. When that happens, there is no end to the atrocities that can occur. Mabaso said, "We wondered why they tortured us. We were already in prison. They used electric prods. They put me and others in straitjackets and they lashed us in the rear so that we could not sit or lay down." He demonstrated the only way he could rest, uncomfortably on his side. "They used my private parts as an ashtray. They made me eat my own feces. They did everything to break us."

Western democracies are hardly immune from group hatred. It was not that long ago in the US when groups of white Americans hated African Americans enough to demand they drink from separate fountains and use separate bathrooms. The Ku Klux Klan and the alt-right still routinely blame America's ills on African Americans and Jews.[6] Racist movements today plague the United States, particularly white supremacy groups that have sadly enjoyed a lively resurgence and attracted broad audiences on the internet.[7] Perverse individuals plan hate crimes from comfortable suburban living rooms. The FBI reported over 5,700 hate crimes in 2012 in the United States; this is in a country whose motto declares *e pluribus unum*, out of many one, and where people try to teach respect and care for others.[8] Racism is not the only form of hatred we face in contemporary America. Over the past twenty years, disgruntled young men have experienced levels of hatred for their peers, their schools, and society, enough to go on unspeakable shooting rampages. From 2000 to 2017, the US has suffered nearly two hundred school shootings.[9] What motivates this sort of hatred?

In his book *Hatred*, Willard Gaylin, a psychiatrist who has spent a lifetime studying human emotions, explains that hatred derives from blaming others for one's pain.[10] Gaylin defines hatred as "a sustained emotion of rage that occupies an individual through much of his life, allowing him to feel delight in observing or inflicting suffering on the hated one."[11] Like all animals, humans experience fear and rage—root emotions beneficial to the survival of species. In addition to those traits, humans alone suffer guilt and shame.[12] Animals respond to physical threats, but human beings also respond to threats to their status, position, self-esteem, pride, face, and dignity. Gaylin claims that threats to these core needs are what produce the levels of shame and rage that lead to hatred.[13] Not that people have no right at times to feelings or grievances that are justified, but the key lies in how they understand these feelings, manage them, and address their causes. Honest folk may seek to defend themselves, taking action to address genuine assaults on their dignity or similar injustices, but Gaylin claims the dishonest person (or society, for that matter) simply "searches for a person or group on whom he can displace his rage and envy, similar to the way that the phobic displaces his anxiety," whether others have genuinely grieved him or her or not.[14] Little else is needed, then, for him or her to hate the external "source" of misfortune. Hatred thus trumps responsible action: we choose to hate because we lie to ourselves.

God Agrees, "Love Is All You Need"

The Bible echoes the social scientific view of the nature of hatred. As we have noted, the book of Genesis underlines that self-deception generates hatred and violence. These themes inform the story of Cain and Abel, as well as the interactions between Sarah and Hagar (Genesis 16), Jacob and Esau (Genesis 27, 32, and 33), and Joseph and his brothers. (Genesis 37, 39, 42–47) The entire arc of the Bible is left dangling until Joseph's brothers are reconciled with each other by abandoning self-deception and acknowledging the terrible fact that pernicious envy led them to sell Joseph into slavery. In another example, the Bible condemns Balak, the king of the Moabites, whose envy and hatred led him to curse the Jewish people (Numbers 22–24), even though the Israelites communicated their intentions to pass through Edom peacefully (Numbers

20:14–21) and were commanded not to conquer Moab. (Deuteronomy 2:9) The Bible clearly contrasts the self-deceptive hatred of those who are simply envious with the righteous actions of those who have been genuinely wronged. Thus, while the Bible condemns Korach for the envy and self-deception that led to his rebellion against Moses, Moses, who really was the victim of Korach's attacks, receives praise for seeking justice rather than responding with hate. (Numbers 16) The rabbinic concept of *sinat chinam,* or "baseless hatred," illuminates the false basis of hate. The Hebrew word *chinam,* which means freely, is also a play on the word *chen*—grace. Most hatred toward the grace—that is, particular beauty—of every other human being is a baseless lie. We have all seen those soccer moms who boo at other competing seven-year-olds and the dance recital dads who scowl at other dancers.

Broadly, the Bible emphasizes the importance of respecting the dignity of others and resolving conflicts so as not to foster hatred. In the biblical text, Moses calls on us to address genuine grievances that might lead to hatred in a constructive way: "'Hear out your fellow men, and decide justly between any man and a fellow Israelite or a stranger. You shall not be partial in judgment: hear out low and high alike. Fear no man, for judgment is God's. And any matter that is too difficult for you, you shall bring to me [Moses] and I will hear it.'" (Deuteronomy 1:16–18) Listening to your fellows is a vital first step in separating facts from lies in any conflict so as to resolve it justly. Listening means being honest about our own negative emotions. As a start, the Bible calls on people not to be envious: "You shall not covet your neighbor's house; you shall not covet your neighbor's wife, or his male or female servant, or his ox, or his donkey, or anything that is your neighbor's." (Exodus 20:14) A contemporary list might include your neighbor's Gucci bag, SUVs, or prime seats at Yankee Stadium. Jewish teachings go further, accepting that some people are particularly prone to becoming hateful. The Bible indicates the proper approach to such people, which is to both chastise and teach them. Following the verse "You shall not hate," the Bible continues: "You shall…reprove your kinsman but incur no guilt because of him." (Leviticus 19:17) The Bible advocates only one kind of hate, that of evil itself. Therefore, the Psalms and the Jewish teachings praise those who hate evil. "You love righteousness and hate wickedness; rightly has God, your God, chosen to anoint you." (Psalm

45:8) Without this "hate," we risk harming others. Thus, we are permitted to hate those who hate others, such as the Nazis or, in the biblical context, the Amalekites.

Why Everyone Agreed the Emperor Had Clothes: Cowardly Evil

St. Maximus the Confessor—we shall not only be judged for the evil we have done but for the good we have neglected.
—FATHER ALEXANDER KARLOUTSOS

The fourth primary form of contemporary evil occurs when people embrace the lies of authority figures who demand exploitation and abuse of others. Stanley Milgram, a social psychologist who pondered Adolf Eichmann's claim to simply be obeying orders, decided to create obedience experiments at Yale University in 1961. Volunteers were recruited and supposedly randomly divided between "teachers" and "learners." In fact, the learners were actually actors, unknown to the teacher volunteers. The "learners" were then supposedly hooked up to an electric shock

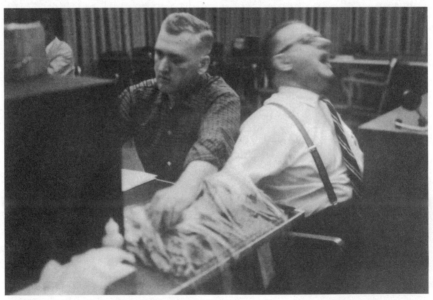

Milgram's obedience experiments.

device, in fact a harmless fake, and were informed by the experimenter in front of the teacher volunteers that they would be tested on word pairs. If they answered incorrectly, they would receive increasingly strong shocks of electricity. At this point, the actor would state that he just wanted to mention that he had a minor heart ailment. Though Milgram initially believed that the teacher volunteers would refuse to continue the experiments as the actors appeared to show greater distress, the results were surprisingly different. It is possible to watch films of these experiments on YouTube and to listen to the recorded actors' mounting shrieks and pleas after each shock. Although many of the teacher/volunteers exhibited stress as they pushed the buttons allegedly administering higher and higher levels of shock, and in most cases needed some encouragement from the experimenters to continue, in 65 percent of the cases the teacher/volunteers pushed the highest button.[15] Even among those who ceased pushing the button of their own accord, not a single one checked to see if the learner was okay.[16] The experiment has been replicated with women, in different countries, and over the past decades, with very little variance in the results.[17]

In the real world, where the stakes have been far higher, people have submitted to the will of the most nefarious authoritarian figures. They have complicitly endorsed their criminal actions, or gone so far as to commit murder and suicide themselves. One example is the 1978 Jonestown massacre in the jungles of Guyana, where Jim Jones convinced more than nine hundred followers—men, women, and children—to willingly drink cyanide-infused Kool-Aid.[18] Presumably all the followers knew at some level that both murder and suicide were wrong. Yet Jones persuaded his followers to give the poison to their children first. Examples of the willingness to commit mass suicide are surprisingly common, actualized either by the cult or when an outside authority approaches. These outrageous examples make the history of human sacrifice seem less far-fetched.

Similarly, in his groundbreaking book *Ordinary Men*, Christopher Browning directly explores the question that had so vexed my father and his friends: "How could the Nazis have killed so many Jews in cold blood?"[19] In it he shows how a group of policemen from Hamburg agreed to participate in the mass murder of Jews. They were neither die-hard Nazis nor SS men but rather older volunteer policemen.[20] Further, they

The Jonestown massacre of the People's Temple Cult in 1978.

came from one of the least Nazified parts of Germany. Yet, the majority engaged in point-blank shooting of women and children. How does such incredible behavior come about?

Whereas motives for stealing and abuse appear fairly straightforward, social scientists and historians attribute submission to evil authorities to a variety of personal needs and deep-seated beliefs about others. In her book *The Self Beyond Itself*, Heidi Ravven shows one group of participants who acted out of unquestioning respect for authoritative institutions and figures. The Milgram experiment participants explained that they were willing to hurt others for the cause of science.[21] They presumed the legitimacy of the institution conducting the experiment and, therefore, of the experiment itself.[22] A subset of this group described how their implicit faith in society led them to trust the leaders of the experiments when they assured them that no harm was done.[23] Still others in this group were convinced that they were just a part of the experiment and therefore bore no responsibility for it.[24] Another group acted out of fear. For some, politeness trumped morality; they felt uncomfortable and inhibited—that is to say fearful—about questioning the experimenter.[25] They likely also feared taking a stand against the collective power of the experimenters and the institution where the experiments took place. This became clear because participation rates dropped significantly when the participants received instructions by phone, which made the authority figures seem more remote and less imposing.[26]

Some acted out of fear of standing out, feeling pressured to conform. A variation of the initial experiment clarified this insight. In these experiments there were two fake co-teachers. When one fake co-teacher did not want to continue the shocks, 90 percent of real volunteers stopped administering the shocks. In other words, once one of two people in a position of authority changed course, it was easier for the volunteers to stop. As psychologist Philip Zimbardo explains, misplaced respect for authority and fear of shame or ostracism are stunningly powerful factors in controlling human behavior within groups.[27] But most importantly, most refused to accept responsibility, even though they clearly had the power to stop.[28]

Christopher Browning suggests that similarly complex needs and beliefs explain the behavior of the police battalion that participated in the mass murder of Jews. First came a sense of obedience to authority, only a small number—twelve out of five hundred of the battalion's men—asked to be transferred.[29] Most were socialized to accept authority. Indeed, one of the officers, though deeply disturbed by his orders, simply accepted that he had to do it. Peer pressure—the fear of seeming unmanly—also played a dominant role. Many soldiers believed that, should they refuse to follow orders, they would be looked down upon by their fellows in the battalion.[30] Since the others were acquiescing, many felt they, too, had to conform. According to Browning, propaganda also likely played a role, as top Nazis demanded that officers redouble propaganda efforts against the Jews. These other social factors loomed large and proved even more important than hatred.[31]

Those who comply with evil authorities often rationalize their own actions during and after events. Milgram's experiment was inspired by Adolf Eichmann's perverse trial defense that he was only doing what he was told, thereby absolving himself of personal responsibility for his deeds. After all, he claimed, he had no choice in the matter.[32] Yet, as scholars have shown, this was hardly the case.[2] Many people rationalize their

---

[2] In his biography of Eichmann, David Cesarani shows that Eichmann was a motivated anti-Semite who took initiative to murder Jews. Cesarani, *Eichmann: His Life and Crimes.*

failure to defy authorities by magnifying the risk they claim to have faced had they done so. This is certainly true of many Germans, who claimed they would have faced death if they obeyed Nazi orders, though historians have demonstrated that opting out rarely carried a death sentence.[33] Having said that, my father accepted as fact that Hans truly believed he would have been killed had he deserted the German army. Others rationalize their behavior by claiming to be ignorant of circumstances or misled by others. The failure to think about what one is being asked to do, the unwillingness to take a moral and courageous stand, and the subsequent justifications people invent all rely on distorted views about authority figures, about their responsibility, and about an individual's power to up and walk away. If evil authority figures are to emerge, let alone exert coercive power on others, they first need people to respect and fear them.[3]

Most psychologists agree that the way to encourage people to reject evil authoritarianism is to strengthen individual autonomy and sense of self.[34] This emboldens people to withstand peer pressure, the main form of social coercion[35] as well as to question ideas.[36] Affording children experiences early on in making choices; making mistakes and learning from them; finding solutions to their own problems; doing things for and by themselves; learning to hope; and, finally, voicing their own opinions all seem to encourage autonomy. By encouraging these things while providing love and guidance, parents help children learn to make good decisions and to face real-life situations on their own.[37] In studies of peer pressure, psychologists have found that children whose parents foster their self-worth and self-confidence are better able to withstand peer pressure.[38] These are the children who march to the beat of their own drums, even if it means taking up an unusual hobby, like duct-tape art. Such self-worth and self-confidence encourages children to think independently based on their own tastes, feelings, and values, thus making them more able to question the tastes, values, and feelings of others, if these conflict with their own. Such qualities let a person see the world through his or her own eyes, and not through those of others, and certainly combat the mind control exerted by evil authority figures. But,

---

[3] This is evident in the case of the Nazis, where Hitler gained power through both consent and coercion. Robert Gellately, *Backing Hitler: Consent and Coercion in Nazi Germany* (Oxford: Oxford University Press, 2001).

needless to say, a strong sense of autonomy must be combined with a clear sense of good and evil for people to make the right decisions.

Be Like Rosa Parks

In yet another instance, ancient biblical teachings anticipate the modern discovery of psychological mechanisms that lead us to be susceptible to evil authorities. The Bible understands well the power of misplaced respect and fear. As previously noted, in the story of the Tower of Babel, the Bible warned of the massive danger that one central authority can have. It can lead people to challenge God by deifying themselves. In rabbinic legends accompanying the story, it is told that if a person fell to his death while constructing the tower someone else replaced him immediately, but if a brick fell, the people mourned.[39] In its unquestioning faith in the legitimacy of authority, the only matter of import to the Tower of Babel generation was completing the task, just like the participants in Milgram's experiment.

The Bible is also extremely sensitive to the role that fear plays in our lives, whether it be simple inhibition, fear of losing face, or genuine fear of the repercussions of standing up for what is right. The Bible recognizes the psychology of fear, and many prayers, especially the Psalms, address this profound emotion. For example, Psalm 27:1 declares, "The Lord is my light and my help; whom shall I fear? The Lord is the stronghold of my life, whom shall I dread?" The Bible describes how even the leaders of each of the tribes of Israel, who spied upon the Promised Land before the conquest, became afraid of the power of the people living there. Only two of the twelve spies, Caleb and Joshua, demonstrated true courage in the face of perceived adversity. (Numbers 13 and 14) The biblical story of the golden calf also highlights the power of fear to unsettle a population. Though this aberrant instance of polytheistic worship was initiated by only a small group, most of the Israelites seem to have acquiesced. Despite their very recent liberation from Egypt by God, marked by miracles and divine majesty, they nonetheless lost faith in the miracle maker. Rather than boldly go, Starship *Enterprise*-style, where none had gone before, the Israelites whimpered. They whined that they preferred a return to the material certainty of servitude. Such is the danger of lost autonomy.

215

The Bible prescribes a sense of self-worth, courage, and fortitude as antidote against misplaced respect for and fear of authorities. Our human equality before God carries with it concomitant accountability before the law and individual responsibility for the choices we make. This is a far cry from the ways of idolatry. To accept that all people are made in God's image is to reject the dictates of those who assume authority through lies about the status of different groups. Later Jewish teachings expand on this point. As Hillel famously asks, "If I am not for myself, who will be for me? But if I am only for myself, who am I? If not now, when?" (Babylonian Talmud Pirkei Avot 1:14) Hillel explains that the choice to maintain a sense of self-worth and embrace life's responsibilities is ours alone. This responsibility ultimately extends to our behavior toward others. Hillel expands on this, counseling the duty to maintain autonomy and courage in the face of dire conditions: "In a place where there are no worthy individuals, strive to be worthy." (Babylonian Talmud Pirkei Avot 2:6) Circumstances, according to Hillel, would not excuse our actions or the lack thereof.

The Bible counsels faith in God and fear of God as the best weapons against evil authority. Facing their opponents in the Promised Land, God reminds the Israelites, "Be strong and resolute, be not in fear or in dread of them; for the Lord your God Himself marches with you: He will not fail you or forsake you." (Deuteronomy 31:6) On one hand, God informs the Israelites they can depend on Him for help. At the same time, they must never lose the fear of God. "Then the Lord commanded us to obey all these laws and to revere the Lord our God, for our lasting good and survival, as is now the case." (Deuteronomy 6:24) Those who choose to do the right thing in the face of human power can rely on the assistance of God. Those who choose to do wrong, who fear people more than the Lord, forfeit divine protection. (More on this in part VI.) For monotheists, God is the only true authority because He is omnibenevolent. For believers, such words are a great comfort. Even for nonbelievers, the notion that the only thing we truly have to fear is wandering off the path of justice and true action should be energizing as well.

The Bible's powerful message rang clear throughout history, inspiring many to confront tyranny and injustice with moral clarity and resolve. The Reverend Dr. Martin Luther King Jr. declared that we "must learn that passively to accept an unjust system is to cooperate with that system and thereby to become a participant in its evil."[40] Dr. King's 1963 "Letter from the Birmingham Jail" deserves quoting at greater length. In it King recognizes that to follow evil authority leads to the corruption all of God's creatures:

> I cannot sit idly by in Atlanta and not be concerned about what happens in Birmingham. [...] We are caught in an inescapable network of mutuality, tied in a single garment of destiny. [...] Whatever affects one directly, affects all indirectly. [...] We can never forget that everything Hitler did in Germany was "legal" and everything the Hungarian freedom fighters did in Hungary was "illegal." It was "illegal" to aid and comfort a Jew in Hitler's Germany. But I am sure that, if I lived in Germany during that time, I would have aided and comforted my Jewish brothers even though it was illegal. If I lived in a country today where certain principles dear to faith are suppressed, I believe I would openly advocate disobeying those anti-religious laws.[41]

These were not just words: Dr. King's faith led him to be able to stand away from the pack; to recognize authority for what it was, an entity of power, but not necessarily an entity of righteousness; and to have the courage to take a stand and oppose it.

The challenge for many of us today, particularly in affluent societies, is to reject idolatry even if we benefit from it. The story of Helen Suzman, an anti-apartheid activist and truly a Jewish woman of valor, shines as an example. I first heard of Suzman from Thulani Mabaso. He called Suzman "our mother." He described her "as a very powerful woman. She would come and yell at the warden and get us to have a blanket or some other necessity." Yet, in contrast to Mabaso's description, Suzman was not technically powerful. Her phone was constantly tapped and she was under 24/7 surveillance. For many years, she served as the sole member of the opposition in Parliament. It was the force of her unrelenting energy, to take personal risk and to speak truth to power in the regime, that gave her standing. She did not overturn apartheid by herself, but she stood at the intersection of what she could do and what could be done and did her best. What Thulani also did not mention is that Suzman was married to a prosperous doctor and could have spent her time sitting by the pool with maid servants bringing her all the piña coladas that she wished. Or, she could have set herself up at a country club, sunning herself with many prosperous white folks. But she did not become distracted by material wealth or by her near-term physical well-being. She took the hard path because that was the only one that met with the Godliness in her soul. She rejected the authority of the South African government because it was unjust and idolatrous, even if she herself did not suffer under its particular form of idolatry.

We as individuals need to evaluate authority, asking whether it is a force for good or evil. If it is for evil, we have a responsibility, or more correctly an obligation, to change that authority to a force for good. Challenging evil authorities in the name of justice is one of the most powerful ways we can banish idolatry in the world today.

Reverend Dr. Calvin Butts tells the following story:

> I went out on a tirade against alcohol abuse and I was saying how in the black community, there are too many liquor stores. Now, I didn't know at the time that one of the trustees of the church owned a liquor store. So after the sermon, we were downstairs at the time, and he was sitting in the back smiling and waiting for me to walk through the door and he says, "May I see you for a moment?" [He] closes the door and he says, "Nobody is going to tell me how to spend my money and run my business." And I said, "Yeah, you kind of sound like the guy who was dealing with human flesh. Had your mother, your grandmother, and great grandmother been in slavery and the minister was telling the owners that slavery was wrong, what would you think?" They were making so much money and doing so well, they didn't care what the minister said. But we have to persist even if that congregant walks out and takes his money with him. A lot of responsibility lies with us as religious leaders.

Idolatry: When a Lie Becomes the Truth

A society becomes idolatrous when the consensus is to accept the rationalizations given by both individuals and groups for exploiting, abusing, hating, and following evil leaders as the truth. Fake news, anyone? In part one, we discussed how elites used the coercive power of armies and the idolatrous myths of old to justify their abuse, exploitation, and hatred of others. These myths usually presented perverse practices as perfectly normal—after all, why would anyone think twice about murdering a servant girl so that she might accompany her dead master to the next world? Idolatry, we know, combined the power of falsehood and the power of coercion to muffle alternative views of the world. It is no coincidence that the most visibly idolatrous societies in the twenty-first century, such as North Korea, are not simply characterized by worship of the "beloved" leader via statues and myths. The leadership of North Korea exploits control of the media in order to prevent its citizens from learning anything contrary to the government line, encouraging fear of the leader as if he were God. Idolatrous societies deviously and precisely manipulate the ability of people to make what would be otherwise normal, day-to-day, individual decisions. Children raised in North Korea have no qualms about turning their parents in to the authorities for saying anything against the government, because that is what they have been taught to do. Normal human emotions of anger or empathy can be circumvented if an ideology suggests these are misplaced. In his book on evil,[42] Simon Baron-Cohen remarks that we do not have the same empathy for people we consider to act unfairly, or for a group we do not like. Idolatrous ideologies are designed to school individuals to fulfill their needs in ways

Kim Il-sung and Kim Jong-il.

that neither require consent nor follow rules that ensure justice. Little wonder, then, that a modern idolatrous leader, such as Libya's Colonel Muammar Gaddafi, had no problem abusing women or murdering his opponents. Idolatrous society silences the message of good as best it can and replaces it with acts of evil. In reality, it turns lies into truths, evil into good, and the rationalization of evil becomes the dominant ideology.

Most modern countries are not as blatantly idolatrous as North Korea. Most citizens, though perfectly capable of rationalizing evil, still manage to operate within a society where the underlying concepts of consent are still apparent, especially laws against stealing or murder. But there are many ways in which respecting consent and following rules are ignored. How many times a month do we hear of people who either try to circumvent the rules or bend them to unjust personal gain at the expense of others? Yet often we become mired in rationalizations for our behavior. We moderns can use reason and monotheistic concepts to make sure we stay on track and do not do to others what we would not want done to us. Anyone who tosses aside humanity's ethical compass and indulges in any of the four types of evil is guilty of serving either themselves or some political authority at the expense of others in society. He or she is, *ipso facto*, thus committing, by the definition we have suggested, a form of idolatry.

The Exodus from Egypt opposes the notion that unjust human power is fated to prevail. Eating my gefilte fish at seder one Passover, my thoughts turned to something that bothered me in the story of God taking the Israelites out of Egypt. Why couldn't the story have a mutually happy ending in which Pharaoh and the Egyptians recognize the evil they have been perpetrating, come to recognize God, and commit to changing their ways? Four glasses of wine later (at least), the seder nearing its end, the reason became clearer. Jewish tradition focuses on God's deliverance of the Israelites, which, while not against nature, as we shall describe in part four, resulted, nevertheless, from an unlikely combination of natural occurrences in their favor. Deliverance is an essential lesson of the narrative, conveying the practical idea that evil power, while real, is not insurmountable. It can be defeated. This is far from obvious. In a society where, evil leaders hold the monopoly on military power and control of the press, those fighting on the side of good have reason to despair. Once evil powers reach a critical mass, such as we have discussed in ancient

Egypt or in many evil dictatorships, it seems like the only option for the good person is to flee. One has difficulty imagining that a leader of the people who stood up to Kim Jong-il would be accepted and then, that he would prevail thanks to a series of natural occurrences. But, in fact, the story of the Exodus is not so far removed from contemporary history, and its message is not supernatural. Evil leaders, deify themselves as they might, are not in control of everything, least of all nature. There are always cracks in their power. Evil leaders are as powerless against nature as anyone else. They are always dependent upon the elites and the people's belief in their authority. These fissures can turn into chasms when even a few people choose to do good. At first Moses flees; only later does he return with a plan for organizing the Exodus. What the biblical text describes is an alternative (not fake) reality that exists, transcending the illusions of deceitful power that we can tap into if only we make the right decisions.

Is this too optimistic a view of humanity? What if, as some say, we don't really have a choice in matters at all?

CHAPTER 17

So Is It My Fault or Not?

Just Me and My Neurons

> *I was tempted to give up my priesthood to become a multi-millionaire like this guy. I was tempted. I saw a beautiful woman, I said, "Geez, what am I doing here?" I mean, my wife is beautiful, but these temptations were coming my way. My values held me back and my values stopped me from doing insane things. There was a rudder and there was a curb, but if I didn't have those values, there would be no curb or no rudder.*
>
> —FATHER ALEXANDER KARLOUTSOS

The Bible assumes human beings have the ability to make moral choices. But today, many scientists, particularly neuroscientists, have begun to question the idea that man possesses any such thing as "free will."[1] The Bible takes for granted that man knows the difference between good and evil, even if we are tempted to deceive ourselves. Scientists, in contrast, are not so certain. In the book *Free Will*, Sam Harris takes the position that free will is illusory.[1] At the same time, he recognizes, as do other neuroscientists, that as humans we can consciously deliberate and

---

[1] There are many books on this contentious topic. James B Miles, The Free Will Delusion: How We Settled for the Illusion of Morality (Leicester: Matador, 2015) and Paul Singh, Great Illusion: The Myth of Free Will, Consciousness, and the Self (Science Literacy Books, 2016) are just two recent examples.

222

make choices.[2] So what is the current debate on free will all about? As Heidi Ravven shows in her book *The Self Beyond Itself*,[3] the debate is about a very specific definition of free will. Scientists and many atheists reject the view that free will—that is, the power to choose what is right or wrong—is a kind of metaphysical power independent of our bodies and circumstances, which we consciously and completely control. Saint Augustine, Ravven argues, conceptualized this form of free will.[4] Since neuroscientists have begun to discover that our brains often make decisions before we consciously articulate the reason for our decision, or that emotions, hormones, and other external factors affect how we make decisions in ways we are not even conscious of, the Augustinian view of free will seems to hold less sway. Yet there is more.

Man's Reptile Brain

Atheists like Harris are not wrong to claim that many of our choices are automatic, but that is only part of the story. In another book on free will, *Who's In Charge?*,[5] neurologist Michael Gazzaniga defines the physical brain as a decision-making center.[6] Many of the brain's decision-making mechanisms are nonconscious. Gazzaniga describes, for example, how our instant human response to the threat of a rattlesnake is in actuality a multilayered process.[7] It starts with sensory and visual inputs to the thalamus, which then go to the cortex and prefrontal cortex, at which point the danger enters our consciousness. Then memory kicks in, reminding us that rattlesnakes are poisonous. Before our conscious mind begins to ponder what to do, our amygdala, the automatic danger center of the brain, leaps into action, leading to the fight-or-flight response, and therefore a jump out of the way. Only after we jump are we conscious of the whole situation and can then take further measures such as searching for a weapon to kill the snake. Thus, while much of our brain makes automatic choices, the left brain, called the interpreter, is the key to our conscious decision making. It takes input from the visual system, the somatosensory system, the emotions, and cognitive representations and tries to make sense of this input through the prism of cause and effect. Gazzaniga argues that as a result of these discoveries, we need to conceive of consciousness as an emergent property coming from the interpreter center in the left brain.[8] Crucially, Gazzaniga explains that the interpreter is a uniquely human function that generates beliefs, thoughts, and desires which in turn affect the nonconscious parts of our brain.[9] Thus we can have a belief about health that will constrain us from following our impulse to eat a doughnut. Yet the very ideas we have about the doughnut have been developed by the mental states, perceptions, memories, sensory stimuli, and automatic systems that the interpreter uses to create beliefs.

Here is where free will comes in. If we lived in a deterministic world, where all actions were caused by predetermined laws, we would be able to determine consciousness and its effects on other parts of the brain.[10] However, since consciousness is an emergent system, even if neuroscientists can prove that specific neuronal firing patterns will produce specific thoughts, we do not have deterministic rules for a nervous system in action.[11] Rather than thinking of neurons determining our thoughts, it would be better to think of our brains operating on multiple levels.[12] We find a parallel to this in physics: quantum mechanics, the rules for atoms, which are emergent systems, and Newton's laws, the rules for objects, which are deterministic. Neither is able to completely obviate the other. According to Gazzaniga, we should not give up on the concept of choice and responsibility, since "the reason we believe them, as with most emergent things, is because we observe them."[13] Further, scientists now understand many of the patterns at the "Newtonian" level of the brain, that of emotion and behavior, where we can observe automatic responses and the conscious overriding of such responses.

It Just Feels Right

Science teaches us that emotions, though neither reliably moral nor decisive, strongly influence our moral decision-making. A number of the atheist authors seek to locate morality in our emotions and behaviors, a line of inquiry that has a long history in Western thought, particularly in the works of David Hume and Adam Smith.[14] If we just cultivated empathy and sympathy, say, would we be more moral? In his book Judging Passions,[15] Roger Giner-Sorella explains that emotions serve four main purposes that help us survive individually and socially: (1) appraisal of the environment, (2) associated learning, (3) self-regulation, and (4) social communication.[16] These four functions can affect our choice to do good or evil. Emotions such as empathy and sympathy, however they are activated, whether through appraisal (this person is suffering, I feel bad for them); association learning (sad faces inspire empathy in me); perhaps even through social communication (this person is showing their suffering to me); or finally through self-regulation (if I don't feel bad about their suffering, I am a bad person) can prime a person not to harm someone else. Likewise, emotions such as shame and guilt can be activated, through appraisal or associated learning, to also ensure that we do not hurt others. But, just as Gazzaniga observed, Giner-Sorella agrees that our emotions are only as good as our input. Thus a person would naturally become angry if told that a specific person had stolen his savings, yet this anger, a result of our appraisal of a situation, would be misplaced if the information were false.[17] Further even empathy and sympathy, when based on bad information or when directed to someone who is dishonest, can lead to evil actions.[18] But it is not just a matter of false information; false beliefs affect our emotional life in far more subtle ways as well, through the mechanism of associated learning and social communication.

Deceptive Behaviors

Psychologists and sociologists also know a lot about the largely nonconscious effects of many behaviors on our decision-making. For example, psychologists have explored techniques of manipulative social communication[19] such as gaslighting (telling someone they are imagining something that is actually true in order to make them think they are insane), intermittent reward (creating dependence by giving someone a reward, then withdrawing it or only giving it irregularly), and repeated criticism, to name but a few examples. Such techniques are effective because, as Daniel Goleman explains in his book *Social Intelligence*,[20] they can reach non-decision-making centers in the brain, thus repeatedly shaming a person for making mistakes, which generates increases in cortisol, which in turn reduces memory and cognitive performance and leads to further mistakes.[21] Such techniques thus affect moral decision-making as well. Many experiments show that a person can unconsciously affect other people's decisions through socially constructed mechanisms. For example, in the West, the color black is associated with intelligence;

thus without being consciously aware of it, people will assume someone is more intelligent just by the color of their blouse![22] Indeed, sociologists explain that many socially constructed associations cause unconscious effects on our decision-making, from forms of dress, to taste in music, to discourses about certain groups. In his groundbreaking book *Distinction: A Social Critique of the Judgment of Taste*,[23] the sociologist Pierre Bourdieu describes how those in power construct these social associations in order to further assert their power. Thus, for example, when elites in a culture decide that being thin is somehow superior, or that going to the opera means you are smart, this association eventually affects people at an unconscious level so much so that it might change how someone is evaluated in a job interview, even if weight or taste in music is irrelevant to the job itself. Likewise, research on prejudice has shown how unconsciously susceptible even supposedly open-minded people are to making judgments based on race, age, or gender.[24] In a study about the popular dating website OkCupid, racial prejudices were devastatingly apparent, as some groups such as black women were at a considerable disadvantage, even though users were far from openly racist.[25] No one working in corporate America today is ignorant of the concept of groupthink, another powerful mechanism that unconsciously distorts our decision-making.[26]

Lifting the Veil Is Hard Work

Awareness of the unconscious effect of certain behaviors can help us to make more moral decisions, but not without individual and collective effort. In the book *Predictably Irrational*, Dan Ariely argues that irrational outcomes of our decision-making are actually quite predictable and can be easily manipulated.[27] Thus, for example, everyone knows you buy more at the grocery store on an empty stomach than on a full one. Nevertheless, the process of consciously addressing psychological and social factors that unconsciously affect our moral decision-making takes work. So, too, does our ability to uncover the truth of a given situation. This is especially so when we come up against internal emotional reactions. It is harder for a judge to send a gentle-looking, sobbing person to prison than to send the cruel-looking person, scowling up at the bench, even if the evidence against the former is greater.[28] Imagine how clouded judgment becomes in a society that dehumanizes the victim, such as Nazi

Germany. It is the difference between swimming with and against the current. But it is not impossible.

I Did It My Way

Like science, the monotheistic religions recognize the influence of other factors, while affirming our ability to make choices. The classic Talmudic statement on free will uses irony to make its point: "Everything is foreordained by heaven, except the fear of heaven." (Babylonian Talmud Berachot 33b) The conclusion of the saying affirms the optimistic monotheistic view that we are free to choose the good. At the same time, it acknowledges that we are subject to different circumstances and have a unique emotional and intellectual makeup over which we have little control. Or, as another sage puts it: "Whether man be strong or weak, richer or poor, wise or foolish depends mostly on circumstances that surround him from the time of his birth, but whether man be good or bad, righteous or wicked, depends upon his own free will." Another ancient sage, Rabbi Akiva, brings out the paradox even more saliently: "Everything is foreseen; yet free will is given." (Babylonian Talmud Pirkei Avot 3:15)

The Bible also understands the emotional aspects of decision-making. In an intriguing and well known passage of Exodus, God strips Pharaoh of his free will. The assault of ten plagues might, one by one, have ultimately brought Pharaoh to free the Israelites, but God hardened his heart. A classic explanation for God's intervention is that many decisions are no more than gut reactions with no moral basis; Pharaoh's repentance would not have been sincere, so God did not allow him to repent right away. The Bible recognizes the impact of psychological and sociological factors, and many of its stories center around individuals making moral decisions against the emotional and social tide. Esther agrees to try to speak with the king, despite the risk associated with such a meeting. Mordechai refuses to bow down to Haman, also in spite of intense social pressures. And Abraham departs his father's house and chooses a new life, with no social or psychological support system. The Bible's moral heroes are heroes precisely because they do good when their emotions and society are pushing them to do evil.

CHAPTER 18

Do We Still Need
the Bible to Be Good?

Using Reason to Be Good

The atheists are right. We *can* use all of our scientific knowledge about choice-making and reason in order to combat our habit of rationalizing evil. First and foremost, we can reason our way to establishing whether particular actions and rules fit the criteria of being consensual and just, as described above. We can ask whether deception is involved, whether anyone is coerced, whether people are being led to believe things about themselves or others that are untrue. Atheist, monotheist, or non-Abrahamic religious traditionalist, you can and should be doing this at home. Most contemporary initiatives that address issues of exploitation, abuse, and hate focus their efforts on educating people about the underlying elements of deception and coercion that precipitate injustice, and they follow through by encouraging a zero-tolerance approach. Evidence for this can be found in the many anti-fraud and anti-corruption measures established across the world, as well as in campaigns waged against rape, child abuse, and hate crimes.[1]

We can also reason with ourselves, opening internal dialogues with our personal emotional responses. This is something that many of us do

---

[1] Transparency International (https://www.transparency.org), the leading global anti-corruption NGO, advocates a zero-tolerance approach to corruption, encouraging states to create and enforce stricter anti-corruption laws. This approach has been taken by anti-trafficking and anti-violence groups across the world.

instinctively. If we become angry at another person's actions, we can ask, "Is my anger really justified? What might be its root cause?" The time-honored practice of counting to ten often dissipates our anger before we respond impulsively. Stop, apply the criteria of consent and just rules, and try to determine what you know to be true about an event. To return to the example of my father's life experience, if some of the Nazis who had been "incensed" by the destructive behavior of the Jews had taken the trouble to apply these criteria and to test the reality of the behavior of the Jewish community against the accusations that they were trying to destroy Germany, they may have in fact changed their mind. Or, if young German men who joined the Nazi Party had considered that they could satisfy their need for respect and power by building a just and humane society, the last century's history of Germany would certainly look different.

On occasions where dialoguing with our emotions is not enough, many forms of science-based therapies are available to assist us and provide us the skills to respond differently.[2] Some people will react to an angry outburst with panic or rage; others respond by defusing the situation. Prisoners of war describe the many counter-tactics they trained themselves to use in order to avoid falling prey to their torturers' tactics.[3]

As every poker player knows, there are more than a few ways to bluff. But your opponent can also call *your* bluff. Today we are more aware of the many forms of deception embedded in society that make people unconsciously consent to things that they don't really want to or feel emotions like guilt and anger in an unbalanced way.[4] Growing aware of our own emotions and thoughts, as well as learning to assess the truth of what society tells us are essential skills, enables moral decision-making. This may indeed mean admitting to darker impulses we did not think we had or discovering the emotional root of certain of our

---

[2] Cognitive-behavioral therapy is based, among other things, on comparing one's emotions to rational assessments of a given situation. See Judith S. Beck, *Cognitive Behavior Therapy: Basics and Beyond* (New York: Guilford Press, 2011).

[3] American and UK troops have been trained with a technique called resistance to interrogation, with the purpose of preparing soldiers to withstand interrogation techniques.

[4] For a discussion of the causes and effects of inappropriate guilt and shame, see June Price Tangney and Kurt W. Fischer, *Self-Conscious Emotions: The Psychology of Shame, Guilt, Embarrassment, and Pride* (New York: Guilford Press, 1995), 162–166 and throughout the book.

views. It is within the parameters of this investigation of emotions and false beliefs that we find the place for looking at idolatrous myths, which psychologists and anthropologists have convincingly argued express human fears, desires, and idealizations. For these myths can give us a mirror into the human psyche, though as explained in part one, they are devoid of moral content.

On a daily basis, the skills of negotiating and conflict resolution play a role in establishing consent so that people can fulfill their desires without harming others. Moral decision-making requires us to reflect on both the situation at hand and on our own reaction to it. We have all experienced the intensity of making a difficult decision, examining a situation from different angles, getting advice from people, and considering our own emotions. Social scientists in the last several decades have been writing more and more about the types of negotiation and conflict-resolution skills we need to fulfill our needs in a responsible and healthy fashion.[5] When people abuse or exploit others, they are not only living a lie that entitles them to profit at the expense of another, but they also fail to consider alternatives.[6] Since time immemorial, or at least since I attended business school, negotiation specialists have focused on helping people devise solutions that benefit everyone. The idea is to train people to think about how they can get what they want without exploiting or abusing others. In business, we seek to identify the "zone of potential agreement" (ZOPA),[7] taking into account each side's range of willing outcomes. Sometimes there is no apparent ZOPA, but more often than not, good negotiators will find one. Each side might not be thrilled, but they can leave the bargaining table content that they have reached an equable settlement. ZOPA can apply to emotional needs as well. Conflict resolution on a social scale applies ZOPA to help people reach an agreement about the conflict so that hatred does not brew and lead to further death

---

[5] The literature on conflict resolution is vast and covers conflicts between all manner of groups and individuals. For a good primer on conflict management in all relationships, see Susan Stewart, *Conflict Resolution: A Foundation Guide* (Hampshire: Waterside Press, 1998).

[6] The development of the win-win paradigm in business rejects the notion that success, whether in business or in personal relationships, can be to the benefit of all parties. See Steven J. Brams and Alan D. Taylor *The Win-Win Solution: Guaranteeing Fair Shares to Everybody* (New York: W. W. Norton, 1999).

and destruction. Yet zones of acceptable outcomes must be limited by the truth, so that, for example, a person who has stolen something from someone else cannot cite their legitimate need for that object and the other person's wealth as the basis for retaining it.

Moral Philosophy: Do We Need the Bible?

Though these sorts of rational deliberations can be of tremendous assistance in combating evil, rational approaches to ethics do not always automatically lead to the idea that one should *not* do onto others what one does not want done to oneself. Although human moral intuition and reason lead to the idea that one should generally adhere to the Golden Rule, philosophers do not always take this approach. In fact, many common, rational, secular ethical systems do not conform to the Golden Rule, and as a result suffer serious drawbacks even among *secular* critics.[2] Take, for example, consequentialism, the idea that one's actions should be judged by their consequences. Critics say that consequentialism can lead to the concept of the ends justifying the means, such as allowing a sick uncle to die faster so that his money will be given to charity (or to that most worthy charity, the niece or nephew).[3] Another common secular moral theory is utilitarianism, the idea of maximizing the total benefit for the most people. With this logic, utilitarianism might seem like good justification for people to cheat the few for the benefit of the many. We now turn to another secular concept: altruism, the idea that the moral value of one's actions depends upon its impact on others. Detractors say that it can lead to helping others at the expense of harming oneself, or it can take on a patronizing air, since one cannot always know what is good for another person.[4] Many people have that one aunt who had a nervous breakdown after too much selfless giving. Other theories, such as hedonism, living a life of maximum pleasure, also pose the problem of reconciling individual desires with a larger social good.[5] Another form of secular ethics, one especially favored by the atheists, is the science of morality, which promises that scientific investigation is sure to guide us to the best notion of the good. Many scientists, however, claim that science is, in fact, amoral—that it can only describe our biological impulses.[6] It cannot create norms.

Some Say Kant; Some Say God

What distinguishes the Bible and the monotheistic traditions from moral philosophy is the biblical principle that all men are equal before the law and the prohibition that no one may deify themselves. In contrast, every secular ethical system that we have examined earlier in this section requires some sensible person at some point to intervene to keep the system from going off the deep end. The same criticism has undoubtedly been made against monotheism: that radical groups can certainly hijack it in dangerous directions. *There is, however, a major difference between the two.* Monotheism possesses several pillars that should prevent distortions. It is not simply that the three monotheistic religions have a body of laws. They proclaim the following three tenets: (1) nothing can be deified, (2) we are made in God's image, and (3) we are accountable for our actions to the community and to a Higher Power. If a monotheist's behavior or views contradict either the laws or these three tenets, that individual's lapse becomes obvious. That is not to say that there are some criminals who claim to practice monotheism, but their right-thinking coreligionists would be absolutely correct to call them out as idolaters in religious garb. By contrast, the above-mentioned ethical systems are not beholden to these tenets. Finally, monotheistic tenets provide an antidote to the psychological and sociological mechanism of power that we mentioned above. Most important of these is the concept of loyalty to the law rather than to some person. This distinguishes monotheism from most moral philosophy, which leaves us vulnerable to either emotional and social distortions, or the whims of the powerful. By remembering never to deify any finite thing we have the best chance of going on the just path.

Without monotheistic guideposts, philosophy can quickly find itself in some gruesome places. For example, according to Dawkins and other scientifically-oriented secular thinkers, infanticide is acceptable under some circumstances. For instance, in the case of a mentally and physically challenged baby who will be a tremendous financial burden on the parents and society, the greatest good for the greatest number is to commit infanticide.[7] In other words, for a society to win, or succeed by saving its resources, it is defensible for it to kill useless infants, since there is no alternative that would benefit both the child and the larger community. From a societal perspective, probably 20 percent of the healthcare costs in the US would be "saved" by withholding all but routine care for those below thirty days old and above seventy-five years old. From a purely consequentialist perspective, there is no logical defeater to the conclusion that this policy will make society materially richer. Another case that would meet with consequentialist approval is the sterilization of the handicapped, a widespread practice in the West until the 1970s.[7]

What a telltale sign that Dawkins would justify as a commonplace such a classical idolatrous practice as infanticide. In doing so, he demonstrates that a "moral judgment" untethered from the bedrock principles of the monotheistic revolution only leads us back to the terrible, well-trodden territory of an ancient idolatrous world. There are many other rational arguments for adopting a win-lose strategy that compromises human dignity and dismisses the meaningfulness of relationships.

Idolaters in Religious Garb

We cannot blame the ideals that we believe in for our failure to follow those ideals.

—IMAM SHAMSI ALI

The Bible's definition of evil reminds us that monotheists are recognized by their behavior toward others, not by their ritual observance. Indeed, atheists rightly point out that self-described monotheists have been guilty of many forms of evil. I will never forget a meeting I attended in the 1990s in Glastonbury, Connecticut, as part of a group that had bought assets from the Resolution Trust Corporation, a government

---

[7] In his 2009 interview with Peter Singer, Richard Dawkins argues in favor of infanticide: "Another example might be suppose you take the argument in favor of abortion up until the baby was one year old, if a baby was one year old and turned out to have some horrible incurable disease that meant it was going to die in agony in later life, what about infanticide? Strictly morally I can see no objection to that at all, I would be in favor of infanticide but I think I would worry about, I think I would wish at least to give consideration to the person who says 'where does it end?'" Peter Singer, "The Genius of Darwin: The Uncut Interviews—Richard Dawkins" (2009), richarddawkins. net/2009/06/peter-singer-the-genius-of-darwin-the-uncut-interviews-richard-dawkins-2/.

agency that liquidated problem loans from failed savings and loans. We were sitting in a review meeting when we came to a certain loan for an office-building project named for a biblical site and owned by a person who dressed in the garb of a sect of Orthodox Jews. The loan had gone bad for reasons that were not originally apparent. It turned out that this superficially devout individual had been embezzling money from the project and continued to do so during the period following the declaration of bankruptcy of the entity holding the property. The lawyer on the team had been at this individual's deposition by the bankruptcy trustee a few days before this review meeting. Under oath during the deposition, the man admitted to taking the money. After his admission, one of the lawyers asked him the following question (and I paraphrase): "You dress in a way that indicates that you are a religious person, and yet you just admitted that you both lied and stole. Doesn't that violate two of the Ten Commandments?" This supposedly religious person responded that for very technical reasons the commandments did not apply to this situation. His answer shocked the lawyer. The embezzler not only showed no remorse, but he seemed to think his actions were permitted for "technical" reasons. After the lawyer recounted this man's answer, everyone in the review meeting turned toward me, almost in unison. (It could have been a scene out of a situation comedy, except it was not funny at all.) The reason they looked to me was clear: although I don't wear any sort of distinctive dress, everyone knew I was Jewish. My first instinct was to recoil in horror and hide under the table. But, after thinking about it for a moment, I informed everyone that this person was not a religious Jew.

He might have been dressed like a very traditional Orthodox Jew and he might have even observed the ritual commandments, like keeping the Sabbath, eating kosher food, and going to synagogue three times a day. But, since he missed the biggest part of Bible about justice, honesty, and concern for others, he could not be considered an observant Jew. He was a thief with a certain sort of wardrobe. By dressing in this way, he sadly cast aspersions on truly religious individuals.

Externally religious and internally evil people are nothing new. They existed in biblical times and were the subjects of stern warnings from the prophets. In the words of Reverend Dr. Calvin Butts:

Now the prophets come along. You are powerful, you have everything going for you. "If you are going to be strong, this is what you have to do. Don't forget the poor among you. All these festivals, the high temple days, don't care too much about that. Make sure the hungry are fed, make sure that the poor have justice. You have all this wealth, make sure you share it with those less fortunate because if you don't, you are going to get messed up." They got messed up. But that is a universal thing. That is not only for the Jews, that it is for the Muslims, it is for the Christians, and it flows everywhere.

Isaiah famously directs harsh words to the Jews in Judah at the end of the First Temple period. To the words of Isaiah, those of Amos could be added.

> I loathe, I spurn your festivals,
> I am not appeased by your solemn assemblies.
> If you offer Me burnt offerings—or your meal offerings—
> I will not accept them;
> I will pay no heed
> To your gifts of fatlings.
> Spare Me the sound of your hymns,
> And let Me not hear the music of your lutes.
> But let justice well up like water,
> Righteousness like an unfailing stream. (Amos 5:21–24)

But this emphasis is not just biblical. The later ancient rabbis, the first interpreters of the Bible, saw matters in the same way. The Talmud contains the following statement:

> Rava said when they escort a person to his final, heavenly judgment after his death, the Heavenly tribunal says to him: "Did you conduct your business/personal transactions faithfully? Did you set aside fixed times for biblical study? Did you engage in procreation? Did you wait in hope for the Messianic salvation? Did you delve into wisdom? When you studied the Bible, did you learn it deeply, inferring one thing from another?" (Babylonian Talmud Shabbat 31a)

Note the first question in the list: "Did you conduct your business/personal transactions faithfully?" Not "Did you attend synagogue? Did you fast on Yom Kippur?" If fear of God was this person's "storehouse," then yes, his judgment is favorable, and if it was not, then no, his judgment is not favorable. (Babylonian Talmud Shabbat 31a) Each of the statements in this Talmudic passage can be extensively unpacked, but for our purposes suffice it to say that Jews do not benefit from fasting on Yom Kippur, abstaining from leavened products on Passover, or refraining from ham-and-cheese sandwiches if at the same time they are less than completely honest in their business transactions and relationships. Therefore, the distinctly-garbed, ritually-observant Jew discussed above, who probably spent at least sixteen years in a yeshiva (religious seminary), either received a totally deficient religious education, or chose to ignore the core of Judaism. This person only learned about certain trees and didn't even know that he was in a forest.

This problem doesn't only affect Orthodox Jews. Rabbi Barry Star, a rabbi at a Conservative synagogue in Sharon, Massachusetts, was indicted for embezzlement and larceny for using synagogue funds to pay off a man allegedly blackmailing him for having an affair with a teenage boy. Christians have known their own fair share of financial scandals. Famously, the televangelist Jim Bakker lost his entire ministry after having been indicted for accounting fraud and facing accusations of rape. No number of prayer services or charitable donations can make up for his dishonesty. Muslims have been embarrassed by repeated scandals such as that at the Dubai Islamic Bank, which resulted in six convictions,[8] and the 1MDB in Malaysia.[9] Indeed, religious people have been found guilty of all four types of evil. From sexually abusive priests and rabbinical Peeping Toms to imams who beat their wives, there are many documented cases of religious people known to have abused others. Some purportedly religious folk also fail to stand up to unjust authorities, as was the case of the many Catholic bishops, archbishops, and cardinals who perpetrated the cover-ups of sexual abuse of children by parish priests. By flouting every fundamental monotheistic teaching about honesty, courage, respect for others, and building a decent society, such failed religious leaders demonstrate that their belief in the monotheistic God is no more than lip service and their relationship with Him nil. A fundamental tenet of monotheism measures true religiousness by adherence to God's precepts, not by the wearing of clerical clothes.

Sunday Schools Get an F

The Abrahamic faiths need to do a better job of explaining evil and the ways that monotheism teaches us to do good in our everyday life. As Reverend Dr. Katharine Henderson explains:

> I don't think traditional religious communities know how to be supportive and help people in their congregations to integrate the religious life with the professional life. I think that business people or professional people or people in the work world often don't feel as if their rabbi or minister really understands their workday world. So pulling these pieces of faith and work together in a more intimate way, I think both from the religious and professional side, is very important.

If we in the faith community do not explain our definition of evil and the ways in which monotheistic tenets and laws help to combat it, why should people take monotheism seriously? In the words of Father Alexander Karloutsos:

> When Moses went and got the Ten Commandments, what were the Jews doing? They were building an idol. So what you need to do is constantly go back, because what man is going to do is always go back to create the idol. So what we need to do as a church community is, we should be prophetic rather than pathetic. And the tragedy is we have become pathetic and instead we need to constantly go out there like Nelson Mandela.

This means a radical revamping of religious education. Fraudsters, exploiters, and criminals comprise a small minority of the members affiliated with religious organizations. The blame remains mainly with religious institutions for not doing a better job teaching about good and evil. The fault is certainly not with God. As it is sometimes said at Jewish conversion ceremonies, God is perfect and the Torah is perfect, but the Jewish people are not yet perfect. Just because one might encounter an incompetent doctor does not mean one should reject medicine.

As Imam Shamsi Ali has said:

> The challenge right now for people who believe in a religion is to be honest to their faith and implement the ideals that they believe in, and this is really the challenge for the Muslims particularly in

this modern time. We claim that Islam is a peaceful and civilized religion. I think the challenge is how to implement those concepts in our practical life.

Faith communities should also be invited to consider the historical failures of so-called monotheistic societies and leaders, such as the perpetration in God's name of catastrophes like colonialism and genocide. Religious educators can also highlight the lives and works of those believers who held fast to their monotheistic tenets when most of their coreligionists abandoned them. Dietrich Bonhoeffer was jailed and subsequently executed for his unflagging opposition to Nazism, even as many of his fellow Lutheran priests enlisted in the Nazi movement. Evaluation of historical failures has already begun in some communities, but there is so much more to do. Likewise, no Sunday school curriculum should be complete without including an examination of the nature of religious leadership—good, bad, and ugly—and the psychological and social factors that have led religious leaders to fail. The importance of teaching and reteaching ethics as part of religious education cannot be underestimated. For some faith communities, this also means rethinking the emphasis placed on ritual observance above moral behavior, and the potential conflict of renunciation and obedience to religious authorities versus fulfilling social responsibilities.

For most strands within Judaism, Christianity, and Islam, the first order of business should be returning to the Biblical understanding of evil (also expressed in the New Testament and Qur'an) and emphasizing it. It means reading the biblical stories in light of the question of what *they* teach about freedom of choice, as most were meant to be read. Finally, it also means teaching about how we can use our reason and ethical intuition to combat evil.

CHAPTER 19

Why Do Bad Things Happen to God's People?

The fact that science and religion concur more than is generally recognized about the nature of human evil and how to combat it does not, however, provide a satisfying answer to our final question, "Why does evil exist in the first place?"

Good God, Bad Man?

The problem of innocent sufferings: you are a good God, you are a merciful God, you are a loving God, you are a tender God. Help me to understand why those who do Your will suffer. Help me understand why the innocent suffer and on the flip side of that, dear God, help me to understand why more often than not that those who hate You and disobey You seem to flourish in this world. That is how it is framed, isn't it? And I tell you I don't have the answer to that. If I did, I would be able to pay for the restoration of St. Patrick's Cathedral. I could go on the road and make a mint. So I don't know if there is a clean, clinical, scientific answer to that, but I do know that there are certain nudges or hints that can help us understand it or accept it. One of them you already mentioned is free will. Free will that of course would only apply to human decisions that cause innocent suffering. So you might say, "Why

would a God allow a little child to be beaten up by an abusive
father, by a drunken father?" That is as tragic as it is, and as much
as we would grimace and maybe throw up over the whole idea,
at least we would say because that father made a terribly tragic
choice that hurts not only that little child but causes our God tears
as well. Because that is not the way He intended, but He has given
us the gift of free will that can unfortunately be abused. Because
He didn't create robots, He didn't create automatons. He created
rational, free human beings, and the only thing He wants from us
is trust and love. And those can never be coerced, so He had to give
us free will, and that tragically can be misused. That, at least, can
kind of explain why human tragedies happen.

—TIMOTHY CARDINAL DOLAN

Monotheistic religions teach that God created all things, including evil, and that evil has to exist. In the monotheistic account of creation, the knowledge of good and evil appears at the outset. "And the Lord God commanded the man, saying, 'Of every tree of the garden you are free to eat, but as for the tree of the knowledge of good and evil, you must not eat of it; for as soon as you eat of it, you shall die.'" (Genesis 2:16–17) In essence, man's first choice was to bring evil into the world. A number of Jewish sages, however, have taken the view that while man had the choice to eat of the forbidden tree, it was God's will that he did so.[1] By eating from the tree, man activated his freedom to have a meaningful life. This teaching is evident in the words of the story itself.

As described at the beginning of this part of the book, the concepts of good and evil (*tov* and *ra*) need some unpacking. While the antonym of *ra* in Hebrew, *tov*, is universally translated as "good," a more suitable translation might be "complete" or "completed" or "completeness." An alternative English word that fits several contexts is "functional," a definition that works even in connection with the sacrifices. Only *tov* animals could be sacrificed, which meant "unblemished" animals or those totally complete/functional. As God created the various aspects of the universe, he declared them *tov*, or complete or functional seven different times. (Genesis 1:4, 10, 12, 18, 21, and 25) When God finished the whole of the world, He declared it *tov meod*, or very complete/very functional. (Genesis 1:31) In other words, He no longer had to tinker with it. Nature was complete and could operate on its own; the goal of creation would inevitably lead to humanity partnering with God. Humanity's greatest role is to witness the absolute harmony of God's complete and perfectly functional creation just as a heavenly angel might. So, counterintuitively, the only way that the world can become complete for humanity's sake is for humanity to play a starring role in making the world complete in its goodness. For this to occur, it was necessary that evil exist in the world and that man have the ability to reject that evil and *freely choose* the good.

As difficult as it may be to accept, life would be meaningless without free choice, and free choice impossible without persistent evil, even in the face of good. As Isaac Bashevis Singer noted, "We have to believe in free will—we have no choice."[2] Imagine for a moment a world in which lightning strikes the perpetrator every time an evil act is committed. Where would be our free choice? Even those with a natural inclination to do evil would refrain just to avoid death. Everyone would behave the same. There would be no need to teach children to be moral, no need to teach adults the path to justice. The world would be a utopia. The only catch is that we would be automatons, not human. Without evil—that is to say, both human suffering and the lack of blatant divine justice—we cannot develop a moral sensibility. Without evil, we cannot contribute to making this world a better place through our own choices. In the words of Imam Shamsi Ali:

> So if God created everything else just on the red carpet easily without any struggle or strife, then what does it mean for us to be the most noble creation of God as human beings? And I think the difference between humans and other life lies in how we live our life more responsibly. And so, we see the challenges of this life as very evident and the question is not where God is; the question is where are we, what we do in taking that responsibility and making sure that those challenges are faced wisely and overcome by our responsibilities.

The Bible provides us with a story which illustrates this point beautifully. The Book of Esther is a provocative account of the hiddenness of God despite His power in the world. It is the only book in the Bible in which God's name is not mentioned once. There are two ways to read the book. The first is as a book of coincidences, some of which are amusing.

The second, in the manner of ancient rabbis, is as a book of human initiative. In this second interpretation, God will help in a hidden way if the righteous take action.

In chapter 4 of the Book of Esther, Mordechai learns that the Jews of the Persian Empire are all to be killed by government decree. He contacts Esther, the queen, who is also a Jew, to ask her to intervene. After hearing of Esther's reluctance to get involved, he sends her the following searing message: "Do not imagine that you, of all the Jews, will escape with your life by being in the king's palace. On the contrary, if you keep silent in this crisis, relief and deliverance will come to the Jews from another quarter, while you and your father's house will perish. And who knows, perhaps you have attained to a royal position for just such a crisis." (Esther 4:13–15) Interestingly, Esther not only responds by taking up the challenge, but does so both by fasting and praying to God, and by using various forms of physical and psychological power at her disposal to achieve her ends. Indeed, she employs the very same forms of power that the king himself had used to prop up his hegemony, including dressing regally. She presents herself to the court, thus allowing the king to summon her but at the risk of her life. (Esther 5:1) Thus we are not only called to make the right choice but to use all of our wisdom and knowledge to do so, even at a moment's notice.

Mordechai is fully aware that one can't opt out of making a choice between good and evil. Moral behavior is second nature to him and he knows instinctively that our choices have consequences. Perhaps our status, our job, our other responsibilities, make us "feel" that we can opt out of taking action or just avert our gaze. And, yes, we *can* do so, but not without consequence. As Rava said, opt out and you lose the "fear of God as a storehouse." And how will we feel then if we make the wrong decision hoping that "relief and deliverance will come…from another quarter?" How will we feel if, as Reverend Dr. Calvin Butts put it, we choose to be pathetic instead of prophetic? How will we feel when, more often than not, we subsequently face a community that will rightly point its finger and ask, "Where were you?"

In his book *The Dawn*,[3] Yoram Hazony interprets the Book of Esther in a way that addresses my father's friends' discussion that evening at the Jewish Lithuanian Club. When Hitler rose to power, there were no Mordechais or Esthers with whom God could partner to avert the evil that transpired. No leader with the ability to make a difference grasped the full consequences of the Holocaust that was about to happen. No leader cared enough to take the kind of action that would have prevented the full horror from occurring.[4] Some outstanding individuals did make a difference, but most, including the American Jewish community, averted their eyes. As Hazony puts it, "Relief and deliverance did come, in the form of the United States, in the form of the Soviets, and the life of the Jews as a people and an idea was indeed saved,"[5] though so much of the damage had already been done. God did not do His part because we did not do ours. As we were not merciful, so He was not merciful. This notion brings our discussion of human evil to a conclusion.

The Volcanic Eruption at Eyjafjallajökull

There is one last point for us to deal with, which is the issue of why nature and disease harm and kill innocent people.

As you may recall, the 2010 Eyjafjallajökull eruption caused a major disruption to European and transatlantic airline traffic. Many thousands were stranded and forced to cancel vacations, or found themselves unable to return home by plane. As inconvenient as this may have been for travelers, nobody died and little property damage occurred. Certainly, the 2010 eruption was unlike the 2004 Indian Ocean earthquake and tsunami, which killed approximately 280,000 people. Nor was it like the tsunami that wreaked havoc on large swaths of Japan in 2011, killing almost 16,000 people and causing more costly property damage than any natural disaster in history. Why can't illness be limited to the common cold or the flu? Why do cancer, heart disease, and stroke have to exist? Both natural disasters and disease are artifacts of God's creation.

The answers to all of these questions go back to the nature of God's chosen hiddenness. From the outset, the goal of this book has been to demonstrate the compatibility of reason and the universe as we know it with belief in a personal God, not to prove the existence of God. To believe in such a universe-compatible God, we need to conceptually reverse-engineer certain components of our relationship with Him. As we have explained above, God cannot strike someone down with lighting as an immediate reaction to the person doing an evil act. If God did so, we would have no choice—we would have to believe. If volcanoes never erupted, floods never overran riverbanks, the trillions of cells in our body never malfunctioned, God would, by that very fact, not be hidden. His revealed goodness would permeate all of nature. For God to appear so patently visible would have the same impact as immediate divine punishment. So to believe in a God that makes any sense, He must be hidden.

This phenomenon is an exposition of what I call the Theosic principle, which seeks to fill in the other side of the equation, *assuming* a personal God exists. The Theosic principle is a theocentric equivalent to the anthropic principle, a concept explored by certain physicists, particularly John Barrow and Frank Tipler.[6] The anthropic principle is the notion that the universe must exist in such a way that man can observe and understand it. Beyond that, the anthropic principle holds that the universe is compelled to create life and man. But instead of focusing on the universe's relationship to man, consider its relationship to God. If you posit that there is a God, then what would creation *have* to look like? Following the logic of the anthropic principle, the universe would have to be in harmony with God. It would have to comply with God's omnipotence, omniscience, and omnibenevolence. It would also have to be intelligible to us. The atheists would assert that this world is obviously not compatible with such a view of God, since it is full of suffering. But would a world without suffering really conform to our notion of an omnipotent, omniscient, omnibenevolent God?

In contrast to the atheist, a monotheist would say that this world, with all its imperfections, is actually more consistent with an omnipresent, omnipotent, and omnibenevolent God than a perfect world would be. If God had created a world where His presence was totally revealed and there was no suffering, whether man-made or natural, humans would have no free choice and we would be automatons. Elimination of evil would leave us with no room to grow in creativity and goodness, and the world could not be perfected. At a fundamental level, we would not be human. This would contradict God's goodness.

The Theosic principle also dictates that we need to be able to make sense of our world, since leaving us fundamentally in the dark would contradict God's omnibenevolence. Therefore, the universe must follow scientific principles, and not be tinkered with constantly, in order to make things work out for the best. The mechanisms of science are therefore an integral part of both concealing and revealing God's presence, power, and goodness. They make the world a massive "choose your own adventure" story. The very ambiguity of nature, its capacity to both provide for us and to harm us, yields the possibility of learning about and perfecting creation. Thus, according to the Theosic principle, nature must be both good and bad in order for God's presence to be partially hidden. The Theosic principle is a theological tenet that is rational, but not provable. When we properly apply the Theosic principle, the question of why evil exists disappears. Unsurprisingly, the Theosic principle is rational and therefore incompatible with an idolatrous worldview. In the idolatrous worldview, evil is simply the privilege of the gods. The rational view of the world is that nature and man are full of potential for both suffering and blessing. We must choose what we do with them.

While we can't explain sickness and natural disaster, we can partner with God in healing the sick and aiding the wounded and survivors of natural disasters. We can't leave the job for others, nor can we justify a smaller donation because others choose not to give their appropriate share. Perhaps we happen to find ourselves in a particular place just so we can do the right thing. Chaplain Tahera Ahmad shares an amazing story about taking the right action at the right time:

> A troubled student of mine came into my office with a story he had to tell me. He was on the expressway and deciding in which direction to go toward. He had two choices, one toward Chicago and the other toward his home in the western suburbs. He decided at the ramp that he was going to drive towards Chicago because he spontaneously thought he should go see his uncle. And just then, he sees on the side of the road a car that stopped. So he thinks that he should stop and help the lady in the car. He parks on the shoulder, a few feet from her, gets out to help her. It is an older lady who has two children with her. She says her car just failed, she did not know what was wrong and she was really, really cold, because it had gotten cold, as it does during Chicago winters. He says, "Okay I will help you." All four go and sit in his car and he starts to call 9-1-1. As he is on the phone looking through his rearview mirror he sees a drunk driver smash into her car. Her car is totaled to the curb. Fortunately, the lady and her children are with him, in his car safely. He is just in shock. The lady knows he has saved their

lives and tells him "you are my angel." Now in my office, he says, "I want to talk about God. I believe in something bigger or something higher." To him, this event was not a coincidence. He was having a very difficult time in his life, in his own personal narrative. But that incident re-shifted him. Could this have been some kind of random coincidence? As a person of faith, of course, I believe that there is something more there, but a skeptic would see it as coincidence. We should be open to an answer from either side.

It is appropriate to end this chapter with answers to Epicurus's questions based on what we have learned about evil through our explorations of science and monotheistic teachings. "Is God willing to prevent evil, but not able?" He is able, but to do so would remove the point of our humanity. "Is he able, but not willing?" No. He is willing to avert the ultimate disaster but he will do far more with us as His partners. "Is he both able and willing?" Yes, and if we follow the tenets and laws of the monotheistic faiths, we will find God will do His part as we do our part to prevent evil. "Is he neither able nor willing?" No. To say so is idolatry, and we already know what that leads to. Without the wellspring of the Bible and monotheism, society risks finding rationalizations to justify our drives and once again descending into idolatry.

PART FOUR

Does Science Make Belief in God Irrational?

Is Religion for Dummies?

An act of creation by an omniscient and omnipotent being? Is that believable? Atheists are fond of pointing out that advances in physics indicate the world came into existence from nothing. Don't biology and chemistry also teach us that the inception and evolution of life after creation contradict the Bible's account? This theory of irreconcilability casts a long shadow over the reliability and authority of the Bible. According to the atheists, the biblical version of creation is no different from any comparable ancient Near Eastern myth. The Genesis version therefore cannot possibly represent the literal words and actions of an all-powerful God. Furthermore, why posit the involvement of such an omnipotent and omniscient deity at all if nature perpetuates itself, with no need of divine intervention? Finally, how can belief in God be rational if it bases itself on an attendant belief in miracles, for which, the atheists claim, there is no existing or possible proof? It seems far more rational to explain that the universe(s) and all it encompasses is an awesome, wonderful, and perhaps infinite *physical* place.

Atheists consider advances in science to be their slam-dunk case against religion. Monotheists, however, remain unfazed by the atheists' motion to summarily dismiss their argument. On the contrary, they say, advances in science only make it more plausible than ever to credit God with the creation of the universe. Atheists maintain that the world came into being and continues to evolve through physical processes alone. Theists view the data from an equally valid, but different, perspective. Personally, I don't think that science represents the toughest challenge to believing in God, although the theist authors faithfully trot it out as their showstopper. *Far from being in perpetual conflict, the classic texts of monotheism—in stark contrast to creation legends from across the world—have influenced, fostered, and continue to be consistent with the very scientific thinking that inspired discoveries about the origins of the universe and of life.*

The atheist authors do not recognize this congruence because they totally misunderstand monotheism's relationship to empirical reality and logic. Nor do they get how monotheists traditionally interpret biblical texts. The fact is that neither these texts, when read properly, nor their interpretations contradict the findings of science. Rather, they affirm God's choice to operate through nature. It is theologically plausible to assert that God created the mechanics of nature as understood by contemporary science, that is to say the big bang and evolution. It is more likely, though not provable, that God is behind these mechanics.

Finally, as we shall see, both science and traditional biblical commentators have multiple views of creation. It is within the sphere of God's omniscience, omnipotence, and omnibenevolence to conceal such secrets and simultaneously make them amenable to discovery by humans through a long and protracted process, which ensures our readiness to grapple with this information. As the Reverend Dr. Calvin Butts describes:

> I got obsessed when I was an undergrad because light was created before the sun and the moon. What was primordial light like? The ancients were on to something. Now, when you say light, you think the sun, nuclear explosions, and all sorts of sources of visual light. But that is not the light I am talking about. So the ancients were trying to grapple with all this. The poor fellow writing that stuff down didn't know really, couldn't really know, what he was writing, but we know so much more and it just reveals to me the magnificence of God. It is the people who are trying to find out more about God and are discovering things about God that will benefit us as this discovering advances.

Were the Bible to have given us a clear, concise, and mathematically elegant set of equations describing creation, we human beings would have no free will. Perhaps more significantly, we would lack any ability to partner with God on our journey of discovery. Let's look at the atheists' claims one by one.

There Are No Miracles

According to the atheists, science discredits both the Bible and monotheism, and replaces them with a materialist view of the world. For Richard Dawkins, the theistic and atheistic views of creation are diametrically opposed:

> [...] I shall define the God Hypothesis more defensibly: *there exists a superhuman, supernatural intelligence who deliberately designed and created the universe and everything in it, including us.* This book will advocate an alternative view: *any creative intelligence, of sufficient complexity to design anything, comes into existence only as the end product of an extended process of gradual evolution.* Creative intelligences, being evolved, necessarily arrive late in the universe, and therefore cannot be responsible for designing it. God, in the sense defined, is a delusion; and, as later chapters will show, a pernicious delusion.[1]

Though Dawkins accepts that the creation of the world is improbable, he further claims that the theory of evolution reduces this improbability and debunks the argument for design:

> A deep understanding of Darwinism teaches us to be wary of the easy assumption that design is the only alternative to chance, and teaches us to seek out graded ramps of slowly increasing complexity. Before Darwin, philosophers such as Hume understood that the improbability of life did not mean it had to be designed, but they couldn't imagine the alternative.[2]

The fact that atheists attribute a materialist worldview to science is the reason why monotheistic groups so often take an anti-science stand. "The 'philosophical atom' has received the stamp of authenticity from the scientific—and in particular the nuclear—world. Nevertheless, the church to this day persists in its idealist, spiritualist, anti-materialist position that a reality irreducible to matter somehow exists in the human soul. It is no surprise, then, that materialism has been the fly in Christianity's ointment from the beginning."[3] The most salient example of the triumph of science, according to the atheists, is the debunking of miracles. As Hitchens writes: "Miracles have declined, in their wondrous impact, since ancient times. Moreover, the more recent ones that have been offered us have been slightly tawdry. The notorious annual liquefaction of the blood of San Gennaro in Naples, for example, is a phenomenon that can easily be (and has been) repeated by any competent conjuror."[4]

The atheists further argue that monotheists who accept evolution rely on what are essentially ancient views of creation. As Hitchens writes: "The very magnificence and variety of the process, they now wish to say, argues for a directing and originating mind. In this way they choose to make a fumbling fool of their pretended god, and make him out to be a tinkerer, an approximator, and a blunderer, who took eons of time to fashion a few serviceable figures and heaped up a junkyard of scrap and failure meanwhile. Have they no more respect for the deity than that?"[5] Hitchens further likens the biblical description of creation to all other creation myths. "The first point has already been covered. All the creation myths of all peoples have long been known to be false, and have fairly recently been replaced by infinitely superior and more magnificent explanations."[6] To sum up, the atheists claim that science and religion offer incompatible worldviews. Any attempts at reconciliation are ridiculous. Dawkins explains: "And whatever else they may say, those scientists who subscribe to the 'separate magisteria' school of thought should concede that a universe with a supernaturally intelligent creator is a very different kind of universe from one without. The difference between the two hypothetical universes could hardly be more fundamental in principle, even if it is not easy to test in practice."[7] The question is whether the atheists are right.[1]

---

[1] A note on the references in part four. There are two types of references in this section: those for specific data and scientific theories and those for arguments. I refer to sources I have used either to fact-check data or to learn about theories and look up data that I used to make my arguments. I also refer to sources that are useful guides for further understanding specific scientific theories I mention in the text. The authors of both of the sources for data and for theories may or may not agree with the arguments about religion and science I make in this section. Where I use the specific arguments of certain authors, I mention them in the text as well as in the references.

CHAPTER 20

Getting the Record Straight On Religion and Science

Monotheism and The Scientific Method: It's Not the Jets and the Sharks

There is a clear correlation between the rejection of idolatry and the development of science. Ancient Near Eastern societies developed certain technologies to serve practical and cultic needs. In fact, all animistic and idolatrous societies, past and present, developed specialized knowledge about the plant and animal life around them that enabled their survival. Scientists today are interested in testing much of this traditional knowledge. Many ancient cultures also achieved significant levels of astronomical, medical, and architectural know-how. Nevertheless, because of erroneous beliefs by ancient Near Eastern societies in the authority and supernatural powers of finite people and things, much of ancient Near Eastern astronomy and medicine in particular was riddled with superstitions. Historians have demonstrated that ancient Egyptian medicine was useless or worse.[1] In contrast to the ancient Near Eastern peoples, the Greeks made significant strides in the fields of mathematics, astronomy, and biology.[2] This progress reflects the Greek view of God and nature. As we saw in part one, precisely because the pre-Socratic philosophers were skeptics of idolatry—that is the deification or attribution of supernatural powers to nature and people—they were able to consider the workings of nature on its own terms, that is physical laws. They began, for example, to seek natural causes for events such as lightning and earthquakes, and they made conceptual advances in the study of science. We owe much of the basis of Western science to Greek philosophers such as Euclid, Pythagoras, and, of course, Aristotle and Plato. Aristotle, in particular, advanced the idea of natural causes and introduced the notion that truths about the natural world can only be arrived at by observation. All modern global advances in science stand on the shoulders of the Greeks. That being said, other classical cultures such as that of India, which invented our numerical system and zero in particular, and that of China, which invented the compass and paper, also revolutionized global science. Monotheists advanced Greek science because they shared the Greek view of nature as a physical reality that operated according to laws.

Many scholars now agree that monotheistic ideas promoted scientific advances. The Islamic view that God operates though natural means, and that learning about nature was a means to learn about God, contributed significantly to the flowering of scientific knowledge during the Islamic Golden Age. Medieval Islamic civilization not only preserved but also added to the knowledge of the Greeks.[3] Ibn al-Haytham, for example, is widely considered to be a founder of the experimental method, which departed from the Greek emphasis on observation and mathematics. Ibn Sina (Avicenna) developed experimental medicine, especially clinical trials, and discovered the contagious nature of infections. Muhammad ibn Musa al-Khwarizmi improved the Indian numerical system, particularly by adding decimals. Muslim chemists used the empirical method and influenced Roger Bacon, who brought this method to Europe. In addition, a number of prominent scientists were also great theologians, most notably Ibn Sina and Ibn Rushd (Averroes).

The same is true in the medieval West. The so-called Scholastic philosophers employed logical methods to test the truths of the Bible and were fond of philosophically arguing whether God existed.[4] The great Christian scientists of the medieval period, like their Muslim peers, were overwhelmingly clerics and included venerable theologians. Their advances during the Middle Ages paved the way for the scientific revolution. Contrary to the popular view, most of the scientific luminaries of the early modern period—when modern science took shape—such as Newton, Bacon, Copernicus, and Descartes, were pious Christians.

(Having invented calculus, Newton also indirectly caused many a freshman college student to utter their first prayers!) Few of these scholars considered that their scientific discoveries might put a dent into religious ideas. The three major monotheistic religions have especially welcomed scientific advances that benefit humanity. In the words of Reverend Dr. Calvin Butts:

> Our God is a God of understanding and science, and we should use science to benefit humankind and God's creation, not to enrich ourselves. If you have a cure for AIDS, don't want to sell it, give it away, quick. If you know how to grow food in the desert, don't sell it, give it away. Or if you do have to sell it in order to pay people, don't want to sell it at an exorbitant price, just make sure that people have food. Sadly, some people who are taking advantage of science are sitting in church on Sunday, or mosques on Friday and synagogues on Saturday, but they are actually sitting in temples to themselves.

It is a myth to think that enough study of science will persuade anyone conclusively that there is no God. Atheists like to claim that scientists are, by nature and training, more inclined toward atheism than belief.[5] Dawkins, Dennett, and Harris are themselves accomplished scientists, and they point to other high-profile atheist scientists, such as the physicists Stephen Hawking and Leonard Susskind, and the paleo anthropologist Richard Leakey, who share their beliefs. Atheist authors claim that the rejection of God by brilliant scholars implies a correlation between intelligence and skepticism of God.

Nevertheless, these claims by the atheists are exaggerated. A 2009 Pew Study revealed, in fact, that 51 percent of all scientists expressed a belief in God.[6] Many religious scientists confirm their belief in God as a result of their scientific inquiries. Vera Kistiakowsky, a physicist at MIT, writes, "The exquisite order displayed by our scientific understanding of the physical world calls for the divine."[7] Kistiakowsky is not alone. Arno Penzias, a Nobel Prize-winning physicist, suggests that "astronomy leads us to a unique event, a universe which was created out of nothing, one with the very delicate balance needed to provide exactly the conditions required to permit life, and one which has an underlying (one might say 'supernatural') plan."[8] A similar percentage of professors in all academic disciplines believe in God.[9] I still wonder how many of the 49 percent who deny the existence of God believe in a "force" instead or made a request to the universe for assistance before defending their dissertation.

True, on average a lower percentage of scientists believe in God than the general American public. However, this statistic hardly constitutes the correlation between intelligence and disbelief proclaimed by the atheists. Instead, the statistic demonstrates what one might expect, that among presumably rational and highly educated people, opinions differ about belief in God. This situation maintains even though the environment in academia is predisposed to secularism. "But why," we are obliged to ask, "should so many atheists, among them great scientists, think that science is, *ipso facto,* empirical and rational, while religion is incontrovertibly not?"

What Science and Monotheism Are About:
A Briefer than Brief Primer

Science engages in the empirical study of nature through observation and experimentation.[10] Science is primarily interested in understanding the mechanisms of natural processes, and it seeks to uncover and articulate rational tenets about the nature of reality.

The primary means by which scientists determine that they understand a natural process is their ability to reproduce it experimentally or predict its outcome. As we shall discuss, by applying the scientific method, some chemists, physicists, and biologists have attempted to re-create conditions for the origins of life. This is not to say, however, that scientists limit themselves to empirical investigations.

Scientists also engage in theorizing about the physical world, either through deduction—attempting to explain a process by the available evidence—or through mathematics and logic. Both methods are ways that cannot be proven experimentally. We shall explore how these processes apply to certain theories about the origins and nature of the universe. Finally, scientists develop and propose tenets about the cause and purpose of reality. The anthropic principle, for example, developed by physicists John D. Barrow and Frank Tipler, is one such tenet.[11] There are two versions of the principle, weak and strong, both unprovable. The weak form claims that only a world capable of supporting life would develop sentient beings capable of comprehending that world. The strong form claims that the universe was somehow fundamentally compelled to eventually support sentient humans. Likewise, Dawkins promotes notions that random, as well as natural, processes are self-generating and uncreated, and that the world has no inherent purpose. These tenets, likewise, though logical are yet also unprovable. Not all claims made by scientists have the same level of demonstrable truth. Some are empirically verifiable, some are logical and can be tested, and others are rational without being provable.

The monotheistic faiths primarily describe the nature of moral life and the nature of the world by means of rational tenets. In other words, monotheistic tenets ought not to contradict physical reality. As Chaplain Tahera Ahmad explains, the great philosophical questions we have about life remain as relevant today as ever:

> While we enjoy great technological advancement, the big questions still remain the same. So from the time 1,400 years ago when Islam was introduced in pre-Islamic Arabia, the questions about "where do you come from?" [and] "where are you going?" are the same. Essentially the questions boil down to "from where do you derive your values?", "what are you hopeful for?", and "how do you engage with a society with your values and hopes?" These questions remain the same and will continue to remain the same.

The three main monotheistic religions primarily teach us about the nature of the world and about the ideal relationships between God and man, man and man, and man and the world. Religious teachings must, however, conform with reality. Religious practices that falsely claim to be empirically valid are actually no more than superstitions. For this reason, both rational and monotheistic critics of polytheistic religions mocked practices such as wearing charms to ward off harm, and they rigorously rejected idolatrous notions that a human emperor could in any way be or become a god. Jewish texts are also brightly explicit in their qualification of commands, such as avoiding forbidden foods, as *not* rational or empirical, thus maintaining consistency about rational criteria.

The first monotheistic tenet applicable to science maintains that an omnipotent, omniscient, and omnibenevolent God—one who does not and would not deceive—is responsible for creating, organizing, and sustaining nature itself. This overarching tenet, coupled with the rejection of idolatry, explains why monotheistic religions traditionally support scientific inquiry. For monotheists, science is a means of both improving human life and expanding our collective knowledge of God and all creation. The second tenet maintains that our understanding of nature and the universe must follow the Theosic principle, which we first described in part three. If God had created a world where there was no evil, humans would not have free choice. The same would be true had God created a world where everything about creation and nature were revealed and known. The very fact that the mechanisms of nature and God's role in them are primarily hidden is, therefore, integral to God's plan for creating the world.

If, then, both religion and science possess similar empirical and logical components, why is there so pronounced an apparent conflict between the two? The simple answer is that, in fact, there isn't. Scientists and religious people don't clash over science. What they do disagree about, however, are the tenets relating to nature.

A Conflict About Tenets, Not About Science

If one is to claim that there is no mathematical proof of God, that just isn't valid, because not having proof of something [mathematically] doesn't necessarily mean that something doesn't exist.

—CHAPLAIN TAHERA AHMAD

There has never been anything that I have come across in these kinds of theories that would exclude the reality of God.

—BISHOP WILLIAM MURPHY

Monotheists view God as operating through nature, while scientists, to meet professional standards, are obliged to study nature as operating alone. Contrary to the dismissiveness of atheists, monotheistic religions do recognize natural processes and laws. The difference between monotheism and science is thus not a conflict over the workings of nature; rather it is a conflict over the specific logical tenets about nature. Tenets are principles, beliefs, or doctrines generally held to be true, and often espoused by members of a group or organization. Based on both the random and nonrandom mechanisms of nature, atheists extrapolate the tenet that these mechanisms are self-creating and self-perpetuating. Religious people, in contrast, extrapolate the tenet that these mechanisms were created and are perpetuated by God. Atheists claim that the more we know about the mechanisms of nature, the closer we are to writing God out of the picture. In contrast, monotheists claim that the more we know about the workings of nature, the more we come to know about God. For this reason, many monotheists, including this author, vociferously reject notions of irreducible complexity and the so-called God of the Gaps. We do so because, *as the atheists have correctly pointed out, rather than to reduce God, as they do, to those aspects of nature that cannot be explained, we, as monotheists, believe that God is behind all aspects of nature.*[12] In short, God created nature. The clash over tenets is, however, only part of the conflict. The second part is about biblical interpretation.

How to Read the Bible When It Comes to Science

Atheists take the Bible literally, but not seriously. Monotheists in contrast take the Bible seriously, but not literally.[1] Contrary to the atheists' view, there is a long tradition of nonliteral textual interpretation in Judaism, Christianity, and Islam, which reveals just how much the monotheistic faiths value logic and evidence. Atheists claim that the difference between the ancient biblical texts' account of creation and our cutting-edge scientific knowledge yields match point for science. The ironic problem is that the atheists' reading of the biblical text can be far more literal than the reading of many medieval scholars, let alone progressive modern ones. Monotheistic commentators generally accept the literal meaning of most parts of the Scriptures, but not all. For centuries, they have found instances where the preferred interpretation of portions of the Scriptures was allegorical or descriptive of something other than a physical reality. This tradition begins in the Talmud itself, which is keen on nuance and methodically takes pains to explain how certain biblical verses are to be understood. The most famous example is the Talmud's explanation that the biblical verse admonishing "an eye for an eye" is not to be taken literally. The tenth-century scholar Sa'adiah ben Yosef

---

[1] This expression of "seriously but literally and vice versa" is taken from an article by Selena Zito on Donald Trump: Selena Zito, "Taking Trump Seriously, Not Literally," *Atlantic*, September 23, 2016, www.theatlantic.com/politics/archive/2016/09/trump-makes-his-case-in-pittsburgh/501335/.

(882/892–942), often referred to as Sa'adia Gaon, referred to this as the argument from tradition.[2] This is the first category of biblical passages that the sages did not take literally. To this category of nonliteral interpretation, Sa'adia Gaon adds another three. The second occurs when one text appears to contradict another biblical passage. The third is when the text simply defies our senses. And the fourth is when the text confounds reason. Based on these rules, readers are not only permitted to bring common sense and reason to bear on the text, they are required to do so in order to uncover the hidden truth therein. These rules have long been reiterated and applied by such venerable sages as Menachem Meiri (1249–1310), Moses ben Maimon (1135/1138–1204), often called the Rambam (Maimonides), and Levi ben Gershon (1288–1344), also called Ralbag, among countless others. A familiar and well-received example is the nonliteral interpretation of descriptions of God's body in the text. Jewish tradition maintains that we find many theological concepts veiled in metaphors because Scriptures speak in "the language of men"; this is done on purpose in order to communicate the divine message in a way that humans can easily understand and appreciate.[13] Allegorical interpretation has long been applied to the book of Genesis in particular, as we shall see. Christian and Muslim scholars follow a similar course in their approach to texts.

Christian scholars such as Augustine of Hippo (354–430) and Origen Adamantius (184/185–253/254) explained that a biblical text should be interpreted according to its plain meaning unless it was contrary to reason and knowledge gained from science.[14] But more specifically, these Church Fathers also emphasized that the Bible was primarily a theological text.[15] The same principles apply for Islam. The Qur'an (3:7) declares that some passages are meant to be understood by their plain meaning, while others are metaphorical.

A number of classical Jewish, Christian, and Muslims commentators, though not all, included the Book of Genesis among those texts that could not be understood literally. Rambam wrote in *The Guide for the Perplexed*: "The account of creation given in Scripture is not, as is generally believed, intended to be literal in all its parts." (2:29) Additional

---

[2] This discussion about allegorical interpretation in Judaism is greatly inspired by Natan Slifkin's discussion of the same topic. Slifkin, *The Challenge of Creation*.

medieval commentators such as the Ralbag and Shem Tov ben Josef (1225–c. 1290) followed the Rambam's lead.[16] Some Christians also held similar views. Augustine, for example, did not consider the story of Genesis to be literally true in all its details, as he wrote in his work *On the Literal Interpretation of Genesis*:

> But simultaneously with time the world was made, if in the world's creation change and motion were created, as seems evident from the order of the first six or seven days. For in these days the morning and evening are counted, until, on the sixth day, all things which God then made were finished, and on the seventh the rest of God was mysteriously and sublimely signalized. What kind of days these were it is extremely difficult, or perhaps impossible for us to conceive, and how much more to say![17]

Origen also thought many elements in the text of Genesis to be contrary to reason and therefore best understood allegorically.[18] Muslim scholars have also been divided on the creation narrative in the Qur'an. For example, they do not agree whether God's command that creation "be" should be taken literally or metaphorically.[19]

That being said, until the modern period, many theologians also took the biblical passage about creation literally. And who could blame them, since rational science did not yet exist to contradict their views? Thus, Shlomo Yitzchaki (1040–1105), otherwise known as Rashi, for example, had no problem in accepting the six days of creation literally. Church Fathers such as Basil of Caesarea (329/330–379) and Ambrose of Milan also believed that the six days of creation were to be understood as actual days. Some Muslim scholars also took such an approach. One can only speculate whether their approach would be the same today given our current state of scientific knowledge. We will never know. The non-literal approach to the Bible not only erases the supposed divide between Scriptures and science—it helps to clarify the Scriptures' actual message about creation.

The second problem with the atheists' view of the conflict between Scriptures and science is that it ignores the vast monotheistic esoteric tradition about creation. Indeed, for many rabbis the esoteric tradition, not the literal words, might have something to say about the creation of the world. Monotheists have never relied solely on the plain meaning of the creation text. In fact, Jewish tradition has long considered the Book of Genesis to be full of secrets. According to the sages of the Talmud:

> One may not expound the laws of forbidden sexual relations before three people, nor the account of Creation before two, nor the Divine Chariot before one, unless he is wise and understanding from his own knowledge. Anyone who looks into four things would be better off if he had not come into this world: what is above, what is below, what is before, and what is after. And anyone who has no consideration for the honor of his Maker would be better off if he had not come into the world. (Babylonian Talmud Chagigah 2:1)

Further, the Talmud and Midrashim (biblical commentaries by the rabbinic sages) include commentaries on the Book of Genesis, which seem to contradict the plain meaning of the text and point to its esoteric secrets.[20] For example, the Talmud states: "Rabbi Katina said: The world will exist for six thousand years, and for one [millennium] will be destroyed." (Babylonian Talmud Sanhedrin 97a) Other mysterious commentaries include the statement: "This teaches that God was building worlds and destroying them, until He created this one, saying 'This Pleases Me; those did not please Me.'" (Midrash Bereshit Rabbah 3:7) There are a variety of colorful and contradictory commentaries on the description of creation that exist side by side in the Talmud and Midrash. Acknowledging the presence of these mysterious texts led many rabbis to reaffirm that the esoteric meaning of the text was hidden. In this way, they accounted for the multiple, often clashing, points of view among the rabbinic commentators. Rambam, for example, wrote in *The Guide to the Perplexed*:

> Now on the one hand the subject of Creation is very important, but on the other hand, our ability to understand these concepts is very limited. Therefore, God described these profound concepts, which His Divine wisdom found necessary to communicate to us, using allegories, metaphors, and imagery.[21]

Kabbalists, the name given to rabbis who specialize in the study of the mystical commentaries on the Bible, especially the Zohar, have expanded on the secrets of creation in countless books, rarely translated or available to the masses.[22] One is dedicated entirely to the first Hebrew letter in the Bible, at the beginning of the creation story. Christian and

Muslim scholars held the same views. The Church Fathers of the Alexandrian school of biblical interpretation focused on hidden meanings in the Book of Genesis.[23] Sufi scholars have also long expounded on the hidden aspects of creation.[24] There are some religious thinkers who believe that the more we learn in science the more credence esoteric teachings will have. Whether this is true or not remains to be seen. In the meantime, the primary message of the creation story rings clear.

Whether monotheistic scholars took a literal or allegorical approach to the creation story, whether they delve into its hidden secrets or not, they have agreed that it primarily communicates a timeless message about the relationship between God and the world. As Timothy Cardinal Dolan explains:

> This is a strand in the literature of the Old Testament that is used as a vehicle to teach a truth and is not meant by God to reveal everything. We find that with creation when scientists ask how can you believe that God created the world in six days? The truth is that God created the world, that the world is good. It is a gift from God. That's the truth of Genesis. How He did it, how long it took, when He did it, and where? We don't know and we are kind of interested and curious in what scientists find out because we think you scientists are part of God's plan, too. But the Bible in a carefully limited way, which, by the way, all of us are limited when trying to speak about God, expresses it in a beautiful style of literature and poetry. The style and poetry isn't meant to be literally true. The principle is forever true. The message and teaching are purely true. Atheists don't understand that because they think we are all, or would like to characterize us all as snake-biting rednecks who really take all of this literally.

Let's keep in mind this clarification of some atheist misunderstandings about monotheism's relationship to rationality, empirical truths, and Scriptures, as we check back to see if there really is a conflict between recent scientific discoveries and rational belief in God.

CHAPTER 21

Science, the Bible, and the Origins of the Universe

Scientists today have some pretty good ideas about the mechanisms of the universe, but their conjectures about what caused it all to happen, though not wild, are not yet proven. While I earlier promised no deep dives into Aquinas, Ibn Sina, or Rambam (Maimonides), we are about to dip a bit into some of the primordial waters of creation. For those who'd like to brush up on the big bang and string theories, or make a first acquaintance with quantum mechanics before the lifeguard shouts "everyone in the primordial pool," please visit the appendix at the end of the book and then rejoin us here. Most readers will probably find the information in the main text sufficient.

The Origins of the Universe—A Biblical Perspective: Genesis and the Big Bang

Unlike most creation myths, the simple meaning of the text of Genesis is consistent with the big bang theory in its description of the entire universe coming into being in a sudden action. Genesis, of course, attributes the action to God. Ancient retellings of the story of creation—with the notable exception of the views of the Greek philosophers—range from utterly fantastic to downright weird, from a scientific perspective. According to the Egyptian creation myth, the world rises out of prehistoric chaos in the form of a mound, from which various gods, and ultimately the sun god, appear.[1] Babylonian mythology envisions a battle among different gods preceding the creation of humankind.[2] These are two of the tamer versions. Greek myths, too—unlike Greek philosophy—record dueling deities.[3] Psychologists and anthropologists may study these creation texts as a window into a given culture's values and fears (especially those of the elites), or even into the psyche of man. These myths, however, personify and usually deify nature, and therefore negate the rational understanding of nature a something physical. The biblical text, in contrast, looks to one uniform, methodical, single beginning of our physical and natural—not supernatural or deified—universe. The Bible speaks in allegorical terms, not in mythical ones. The text does not explicitly indicate *how* God created the earth we inhabit. Its plain meaning is to simply insist that, gloriously, He created everything. "When God began to create heaven and earth" (Genesis 1:1)—this one simple phrase speaks to all generations, communicating the insight that God alone created nature.

The first verse of Genesis thus denies the deification of nature. This not only resembles our scientific view but has informed it. Beyond the message of the text that God and nature are separate but not equal, commentators have also teased out many details about the process of creation. Moses ben Nachman (1194–1270), one of the greatest medieval Talmudic scholars, biblical commentators, and kabbalists, expands on this verse based on his knowledge of Hebrew, kabbalistic sources, and Greek science. Commonly known by the abbreviation Ramban, he writes:

> Now listen to the correct and clear explanation of the verse in its simplicity. The Holy One, blessed be He, created all things from absolute non-existence. Now we have no expression in the sacred language for bringing forth something from nothing other than the word *bara* (created). Everything that exists under the sun or above was not made from non-existence at the outset. Instead He brought forth from total and absolute nothing a very thin substance devoid of corporeality but having a power of potency, fit to assume form and to proceed from potentiality into reality. This was the primary matter created by G-d; it is called by the Greeks *hyly* (matter). After the *hyly* He did not create anything, but He formed and made—things with it, and from this *hyly* He brought everything into existence and clothed the forms and put them into a finished condition.[4]

Ramban certainly knew nothing of Einstein's revolutionary equation $E = mc^2$, yet his description in his commentary resembles the concept of interchangeability of matter and energy proposed by twentieth-century physicists. Further in his commentary, on the last verse in the chapter, Ramban writes:

> At the briefest instant following creation all the matter of the universe was concentrated in a very small place no larger than a grain of mustard. The matter at this time was so thin, so intangible, that it did not have real substance and form to become tangible matter. From this initial concentration of this intangible substance in its minute location, the substance expanded, expanding the universe as it did so.[5]

Here Ramban also seems to anticipate the singularity that physicists describe as the start of the big bang, as well as the process of expansion that led to the universe as we now know it. More than eight hundred years before the nuclear age, Ramban portrays a process akin to the big bang, simply by contemplating the graceful words of Genesis and integrating esoteric traditions and the science of his time. Without the same precision, but in a similar vein, Augustine describes the earliest moment of creation as a dormant seed from which the rest of the world developed.[6]

A Young Earth or an Old Universe

Creation myths from around the world place the beginning of the universe in a primordial period beyond time.[7] In contrast, the Bible sees the beginning of time as coterminous with the beginning of nature. Nevertheless, there has been significant debate among monotheists as to when nature was created. Some literalist commentators in the three monotheistic traditions have advocated a young earth, while others have advocated a very old one. Channel-surfing between coffee and bagels on any lazy Sunday morning, you'll happen upon televangelists of both persuasions. Monotheistic tradition incorporates different calculations for the age of the universe and posits the notion that time is created and non-mythical. In Jewish tradition, the *Seder Olam* (*Order of the World*), a second-century Midrash (commentary) on the Book of Genesis, reads the chronology of Genesis literally and dates the world to less than six thousand years old based on a literal reading of the days of creation and of the genealogies after creation. Many rabbinic commentators have adopted this view. Other ancient sources claim that this chronology of six thousand years begins with the creation of Adam, and not the world, suggesting that the earth is older.[8]

Some Jewish sources point to a much older universe. For example, an early kabbalistic work, the *Sefer HaTemunah*, attributed to the first-century scholar Nehunya ben Ha-Kanah, passed down a secret teaching that six separate sabbatical cycles of seven thousand years each occurred before the creation of Adam. This is called the *shmittah* theory, which takes its name from the biblical command to let the land lie fallow every seventh year. While a number of renowned medieval scholars accepted the *shmittah* theory, including Ramban and his student, Rabbi Yitzchak of Acco, others did not. Among those who did, Rabbi Yitzchak of Acco argued that the universe was even older than forty-two thousand years based on the idea that the years before the creation of Adam had to be measured in divine years rather than human years. Referring to a psalm that states that a divine day is like one thousand years, Rabbi Yitzchak of Acco calculated that the universe would exist for 42,000 x 365,250 or 15.3 billion years. While Yitzchak of Acco's view was not widely accepted in his time, it is nonetheless noteworthy that he not only claimed that the universe was very old but that he calculated a time frame that is in the range of our modern understanding of the age of the cosmos.

Neither of the other monotheistic traditions has a firm hold on the age of the universe. Traditionally, some Muslim scholars affirmed that the earth was created in six days, but there has also long been a discussion of what this could mean. For a number of Muslim philosophers, a literal reading proved unacceptable based on observations in nature. Al-Biruni (973–1048) argued that the universe must be billions of years old based on observations of the movement of stars and planets and logic.[9] Other tenth-century scholars known as the Ikhwân al-Safâ', the Brethren of Purity, also considered the universe to be very old based of movement of stars.[10] And none other than Ibn Sina also thought the world to be very old based on observing mountains.[11] One Qur'anic verse indicates that a day is like a thousand years, another verse, more

The Creation of the Universe According to Modern Science & Pre-Modern Monotheistic Theologians

	Scientific	*Some Religious Thinkers*
15 *billion years ago*		Billions of Years
14 *billion years ago*		*Al Biruni (10th century Muslim) estimated that the universe was billions of years old based on the observation of the natural world and a non-literal reading of the days of creation.*
13.8 *billion years ago*	Generally accepted timing for creation of the universe	
		Titzchak of Acco (13th century Jewish scholar) estimated that the universe is 15.3 billion years old based on numerological calculations and a non-literal reading of the days of creation.
5 *billion years ago*		
4.6 *billion years ago*	Formation of our Sun	Very Old or Indeterminate
4.5 *billion years ago*	Formation of the Earth	*Augustine of Hippo (4th century Christian scholar) gave an indeterminate age for the universe based on an allegorical reading*
3.8 *billion years ago*	First life on Earth	*of genesis and commitment to natural philsophy.*
		Origen of Alexandria (3rd century Christian scholar) gave an indeterminate age of the universe based on an allegorical reading of genesis.
1.1 *billion years ago*	First sexually reproducing organisms	
		Ikhwân al-Safâ' (10th century group of Muslim scholars) estimated that the universe was extremely old based on the observation of the natural world and a nonliteral reading of the days of creation.
570 *million years ago*	First arthropods	
530 *million years ago*	First fish	*Ibn Sina (11th century Muslim scholar) estimated that the universe was extremely old based on the observation of the natural world and a non-literal reading of the days of creation.*
540 *million years ago*	The Beginning of the Cambrian Explosion	
200 *million years ago*	First mammals	*Rambam (12th century Jewish scholar) gave an indeterminate age for the universe based on a allegorical reading of genesis and commitment to natural philosophy.*
22 *million years ago*	Great apes	
8 *million years ago*	First humanoids	Under 6000 Years
3.5 *million years ago*	Use of stone tools	*Basil of Casaria (4th century Christian scholar) considered the world to be young based on a literal reading of the days of creation and the biblical genealogies.*
200 *thousand years ago*	Homo sapiens, 200–60 thousand years ago	
50 *thousand years ago*	Behaviorally modern humans	*Ambrose of Milan (4th century Christian scholar) considered the world to be young based on a literal reading of the days of creation and the biblical genealogies.*
6 *thousand years ago*		*Rashi (11th century Jewish scholar) considered the world to be young based on a literal reading the days of creation and the biblical genealogies.*
	* Estimates for these dates vary	

like fifty thousand. Other Islamic commentators have long considered the six days of creation to be eras.[12] The Church Fathers were similarly divided. While Ambrose of Milan and Basil of Caesarea[13] claimed that the earth was created in six days of twenty-four hours each, Origen advocated an allegorical reading of Genesis and therein argued against any clear indication of the duration of creation.[14] Augustine held the same view based on logic and the principles of natural philosophy.[15] Among the older religions, the Hindus stand alone to have universally advocated a very ancient universe based on accounts of creation in the texts of the Vedas and Puranas.[16]

Despite divided opinions among classical monotheistic scholars, the tradition of nonliteral interpretations of the creation story and its esoteric secrets has provided monotheists with an ancient precedent— totally unrelated to modern scientific knowledge—for unapologetically accepting that the universe is very old. In fact, given the current state of the evidence, to insist on the fact that God had created the world only six thousand years ago would require us to believe in a deceitful God, because the evidence so clearly points to the contrary. In my view, the so-called young earth arguments are a needless distraction to believing in God. Acknowledging that the description of creation in Scriptures is not to be taken literally was accepted by many theologians well before modern science.

Ancient Biblical Commentators Meet Quantum Theorists (Smart Casual Attire Suggested)

There are noticeable similarities between quantum theory's concept of a probabilistic universe and Jewish commentaries and monotheistic religious teachings. Most ancient, medieval, and modern idolatrous thought systems are based on the concepts of destiny or fate.[17] The gods or the stars were believed to determine the lives of humans, often in a spirit of supernatural whim. Ironically, in modern times, some scientists substitute natural laws as determinants of similar sorts of human behavior. Quantum physics has made a dent in this view without reducing the world to total chaos. Quantum mechanics paradoxically affirms the laws of nature without claiming they are deterministic. Because Jewish commentators accept the laws of nature, many have questioned how nature can coexist with the concept of reward and punishment. Rambam discusses this seeming paradox in his *Guide to the Perplexed*. In Rambam's view, the laws of nature operate at all times. Nevertheless, there exists within the framework of these laws the possibility for reward and punishment.

Rambam writes:

> This Universe remains perpetually with the same properties with which the Creator has endowed it...none of these will ever be changed except by way of miracle in some individual instances... (2:29)

Later, he adds:

> Divine Providence is connected with Divine intellectual influence, and the same beings which are benefited by the latter so as to become intellectual, and to comprehend things comprehensible to rational beings, are also under the control of Divine Providence, which examines all their deeds in order to reward or punish them. (3:17)

Rambam's solution to the problem of the possible coexistence of divine intervention and natural laws seems a lot like quantum theory in its denying determinism while simultaneously affirming that nature follows laws. The notion raised by quantum physics that the world is not material but rather a form of energy is akin to the kabbalistic idea that everything in the universe is actually part of the consciousness of God and His creative will. This is not to say that God and nature are one, but rather, to speak in kabbalistic terms, that nature is a concealed manifestation of God and His infinite light called *Ain Sof*. Such a kabbalistic view, which finds parallels in Christian and Muslim mysticism, ascribes a fundamental unity to creation.[18] Hindu and Buddhist mystics also refer to this fundamental unity: Hindus call it Brahman and Buddhists call it dharma.[19] It is not a coincidence that a number of prominent quantum physicists have become interested in mysticism. Father Alexander Karloutsos comments on this: "Einstein, who saw the interdependency of all things, would have appreciated that perspective because what is love, really? Love is the connective tissue of the universe. There is no, to use a Buddhist expression, there is no independent arising. We are all connected. We are all in a relationship."

270

Biblical Commentaries and String Theory

Mystical commentaries on the creation of the world also offer interesting parallels to modern string theory. The sixteenth-century kabbalist Rabbi Yitzchak Luria (1534–1572), called the Ari, developed certain kabbalistic doctrines about the creation of the universe,[20] which his student, Hayyim Vital (1542–1620), wrote down. According to the Ari, before the creation of the world, God withdrew His infinite presence in a process called *tzimzum* (contraction) in order to make space for creation. He then infused the world with a ray of light. This light, in turn, filled the "vessels" of ten spiritual dimensions called *sefirot* (emanations). All of the *sefirot* emanate from God and, taken together, they make up the fabric of the universe. While the first three *sefirot* were able to contain the light, the last seven shattered because of that divine light's tremendous energy. The remains of these shattered vessels persist in our universe in the form of tiny knots of energy. In the Ari's view, we humans repair these broken vessels through our good deeds and our expanding consciousness. This concept is referred to as *tikkun olam* (repair of the world).

What is surprising about the Ari's account of the creation of the universe is the homiletic parallel with string theory. In string theory, there are ten (though according to some formulations eleven) initial spatial dimensions, of which only three remain intact. The minute size of the shattered vessels, as well as their hidden but continued existence within the world, also offers a poetic parallel to string theory. As an aside, the kabbalists also argued that evil in the universe is able to exist only as long as the divine vessels remain shattered. In the Jewish tradition, the notion of *tikkun olam*, the repair of the world, refers to the restoration of the divine vessels. We can each help repair these vessels every time we choose to channel our drives and do good.

Mystical Teachings and Universes Beyond Our Own

A number of mystical commentaries speculated about physical universes before the big bang. Ancient creation myths occasionally presented other worlds, but these were the domains of the gods, remote and mythical.[21] Contrary to other ancient traditions, the Genesis text suggests that there is no such thing as mythical time; time is a part of creation and

271

the created world exists within that time. The commentaries on Genesis offer additional insights about our particular universe and the possibility of other universes. On the one hand, the plain meaning of the text, as described above, points to the notion of a creation *ex nihilo*. Yet a number of ancient rabbis read the creation story to suggest the possibility of universes before this one. (Midrash Bereshit Rabba 9:2) Another Midrash claims that God created and destroyed 974 worlds before this one. (Midrash Tehillim 90:13) As previously mentioned, a number of kabbalists advocated the so-called *shmittah* theory of seven cycles of creation. While these cryptic commentaries will probably never be deciphered, they nonetheless present these universes as created and specific like our own, rather than as mythical. Even the kabbalistic writings that describe other spiritual universes—such as *Atzilut*, the World of Emanation; *Beriah*, the World of Creation; and *Yetzirah*, the World of Formation, as well as our own world of action—delineate the specific characteristics of these universes and describe their relation to physical reality. They don't place them in a mythical realm. The Hebrew word for create, *bara*, which usually refers to a creation *ex nihilo*, can also mean a creation from something else. Thus, ancient rabbis read the plain text of the Bible in ways that pointed to the possibility that the world was either created from nothing or from something else. Science has also not resolved this question.

Disharmony in the Theological Choir

Just as scientists do not have the big bang, quantum, or string theory all figured out, no theological consensus exists about the mysteries of creation. Available texts on the secrets of creation are few and obscure.[1] Those that do exist often appear contradictory. How do we reconcile, for example, the Midrash that God created the world all at once with the Midrashim that the world developed over time?[22] The kabbalistic texts about the origins of the universe are so difficult to decipher that, for example, there are commentators who believe that the creation of the

---

[1] In his book, Natan Slifkin has unearthed many of the most important commentaries and/or books on this topic, though he has not included all of the kabbalistic commentaries. Nevertheless, commentaries on creation in the Jewish tradition are far less numerous than works on many other legal topics. Slifkin, *The Challenge of Creation*.

world initially happened on some sort of a spiritual plane, while others disagree.[23] Certainly, both those who insist that *bara* always means creation from nothingness and those who claim it does not can't both be right. Within kabbalistic circles, there is disagreement regarding the question of multiple universes. Among those who considered the cycle of worlds to be physical, there is also no consensus as to the world we are currently in. The author of the *Sefer HaTemunah*, on the *shmittah* theory, believed that we are currently in the second cycle; later kabbalists believed we are in the seventh.[24]

Like their Jewish peers, classical Muslim scholars held long debates about whether the world arose from nothing or whether it was created out of something else. The Muslim scholar Fakhr al-Din al-Razi (1149–1209) discusses the possibility of a multiverse based on this verse in the Qur'an: "All praise belongs to God, Lord of the Worlds." These are just a few examples of some of the disagreements that arose among monotheistic theologians long before the impact of modern physics. Just as we await a greater understanding of the scientific mechanics of creation, the secrets embedded in the monotheistic writings on creation still await a broadly accepted interpretation.

Congratulations, You Won the Lottery

While many physicists consider that the multiverse theory proves that we are here by chance, the probability of this fact is actually virtually nil. Of all the modern theories on the origins of the universe, the multiverse theory presents the biggest challenge to the notion of a creator God. Were there to exist an infinite number of universes, one could have arisen to accommodate life simply by chance.[25] But what are the odds of that being the case? Let me illustrate this with a short example. When I was in college, I took a statistics course in which we had an assignment to figure out the net present value of lottery tickets under different parameters. My professor was fond of saying that it was certain that someone would win the lottery and that it was also certain that it would not be one of us. (Recently, I heard that another statistics professor was still using a version of this joke. What are the odds of that?) The intended irony of the joke was that it is of course *not certain* that someone will win any particular lottery. That is one of the reasons why the net present value of a lottery ticket can change depending on the parameters. Some money from previous lotteries without winners can go back into the pot. It is also *not certain* that you or I will not win the lottery. Everyone who buys a ticket does have a chance, which is the reason people keep buying tickets.

In the case of the existence of a universe that can support life, the professor's joke is turned on its head. There is *no certainty* that *any* universe would have the exact combination of fine-tuned constants—in precisely the correct relationship with each other—and laws of physics so that there could be stars, planets, and the potential for life. Yet, it *is certain* that we won that lottery. Now what are the odds for that? In fact, they are beyond calculable. Unlike the lottery I referred to above, there is no money going into the pot. Each draw is entirely independent. Unlike a lottery requiring that a purchaser pick six or seven numbers, with lesser prizes for fewer numbers, here there is no second prize. Only getting many millions of numbers precisely right results in a universe with the potential for life. No matter how many times one buys a ticket, it is highly likely that there will be no winner. So I cannot say that it is impossible that the atheists' scenario is correct and that we are just fortunate to live in *the* universe in which everything worked out just right. With the precise dimensionless constants and the physical laws required for life, not only did we win one lottery, but we won an incalculable succession of lotteries. Thus, if you were offered a lottery ticket with those odds, I would advise you to save your money and buy a Bible.

While advances in physics over the last hundred years do not prove the existence of God, they hardly disprove it either. Current scientific discoveries have greatly improved our knowledge of how the universe functions. Yet they have not empirically proven the atheist tenet that the world arose by chance. As to whether God initiated the big bang and the mechanisms of nature, we may never know. Nevertheless, the probability that the universe began by natural mechanisms and developed in precisely the direction needed for life is microscopically minute, though not impossible. In addition, the singularity of the big bang conforms with the biblical concept that the world was created *ex nihilo*. Yet it is even possible to interpret the biblical text in line with those scientists who say that the world was created from something—whatever that something was. Thus, science has hardly disproven the tenet of a creator God as expressed in the Bible. It is not irrational to believe in an infinite, omniscient, and omnipotent God who initiated the creation of the universe and the mechanism that led to its shape. Likewise, it is not irrational to believe that the universe arose by chance and developed by chance.

The same reasoning is true with regard to quantum theory and string theory. While the kabbalistic parallels with string theory are not detailed and conclusive enough to convince a die-hard atheist, their surprising presence makes it rational to take monotheistic tenets about the creation of the universe seriously. Likewise, quantum theory has clearly put a dent in the conception of a totally deterministic universe. It is more rational than ever before to believe in some form of divine mind directing nature and providence. Yet, we are also a long way away from figuring out how quantum theory could be tied to notions of free choice or even God's providence.

Thus, it is rational both to consider the possibility of divine providence in nature and human interactions and to reject it. Finally, with regard to the multiverse, there is certainly too little proof to rule out a creator God and claim that our habitable universe is simply a random occurrence. None of the discoveries of the twentieth and twenty-first centuries have definitively proven either the atheist tenet that the world arose by chance as one of many outcomes or the monotheist tenet that it was created by an omniscient God. It is still a matter of personal belief. In the words of Imam Shamsi Ali:

> If we humans just ponder upon the universe itself, how much do we really know about this universe? According to some, it is no more than just 4 percent. How many billions of stars that we have, galaxies, and how many billions of stars in each galaxy, for example. How can we deny the possibility of the existence of a creator? It is not easy just to come to that conclusion that there is a creator or no creator. Both sides can argue forever.

It is clear that the vision of the creation of the universe in Genesis and the commentaries on this text conform more to the scientific vision of the creation of the universe than the atheist authors are willing to acknowledge.

CHAPTER 22

Science, the Bible,
and Evolution

Charles Darwin's Groundbreaking Idea

Darwin's world-shaking, and yet simple, hypothesis about the foundation and evolution of life is based on just two theoretical pillars. The first is that all life on earth descends from a common ancestor.[1] The second is that natural selection is the mechanism that leads to the diversity of life. Beneficial traits that contributed to survival and advantageous reproduction drove the complexity and range of life to achieve the mind-boggling differentiation it exhibits today. Darwin himself did not combine genetics with his theory, even though Gregor Mendel had already discovered heredity, since Mendel's writings remained obscure until the beginning of the twentieth century. Contemporary scientists link natural selection to the concept of genetic mutation, which produces diverse traits within a population of a particular species. Organisms that adapt best to the environment are able to propagate more, eventually giving rise to new species.

This synthesis between genetics and natural selection is called neo-Darwinism. Based on these two pillars, neo-Darwinists paint the following picture of life on earth. At some point about 3.8 billion years ago, life first appeared on earth as a single-celled organism. All life is descended from that single-celled common parent of us all. Life then burst forth, proceeding in accord with the second pillar of Darwinism. The accepted fossil record suggests that, for the next 2.8 billion years, all life on earth was microscopic. Over the same period of time, the composition of our atmosphere changed dramatically and the early, simple forms of life adapted to the shifting environment, developing ever-greater complexity. About one billion years ago, the earliest multicellular organisms emerged. Up until 580 million years ago, the most complex forms of life to be found on planet Earth were single-celled organisms, working together as colonies and some modest multicellular organisms. But commencing 580 million years ago, the forms of life on earth proliferated at an astounding pace. Within the next fifty to eighty million years, the ancestors of current life all came into existence, and they continue to adapt and evolve today.

I had the pleasure of retracing a few of Charles Darwin's steps while on vacation in Galapagos during 2014. There I experienced for myself the variety of finches across various islands, and saw the various ways in which they adapted to their circumstances. I was even able personally to spot four different finches during my stay—at least that is my story and I am sticking to it. The reigning experts on Darwin's finches are Professors (Emeriti) Peter and Rosemary Grant of Princeton University, who devoted forty years of study to observing adaptations in real time on the Galapagos Island of Daphne Major. In that time, they discovered a new lineage of finch, which they claim is a new species differing from others in size and song, among other characteristics.[2] The Grants' work offers us only one example in a mountain of data that has accumulated in favor of evolution. And so far, other than those proponents who stick fast to the idea of a six-thousand-year-old earth, almost everyone else would agree that Darwin's two pillars make sensible science. Nevertheless, many questions remain about the process of evolution itself.

The Evolution of Man

Darwinism also revolutionized our understanding of the evolution of man. Based on the fossil record and DNA evidence, evolutionary biologists and anthropologists believe that humans evolved from an ancestor common to other primates.[3] The family of hominids, from which man derives, diverged from other primates around fifteen million years ago.

277

Hominids themselves branched out into different species, among them the species *Homo*, the word for "man" in Latin. The species *Homo* in turn branched into several different species, including *Homo erectus* and *Homo ergaster*. Many of the species migrated out of Africa, spreading across Asia and Europe. Nevertheless, modern humans trace their ancestry to the species *Homo sapiens*, which evolved in Africa between two hundred thousand and sixty thousand years ago. That being said, recent genetic findings suggest that some Neanderthals may have mixed in with the *Homo sapiens* population in Europe and *Denisova hominins* with the *Homo sapiens* population in Australia, though at a very low rate of 1 to 10 percent. Others contest the idea that the various *Homo* species inter-mated, suggesting that they are just genetic remnants from a common ancestor. According to the "Recent Out of Africa Model" of human evolution, the *Homo sapiens* who migrated out of Africa largely replaced the other species of *Homo* living at the time. Geneticists have posited that modern humans shared a common male ancestor dating from 270,000–140,000 years ago and a common female ancestor dating from 200,000–100,000 years ago. Thus, while a number of controversies still remain about the nature of early humans (what are we to make, for example, of the discovery of "hobbit-like" persons in Indonesia?), a great deal of consensus exists about the common origins of modern humans. Most anthropologists consider humans to have become behaviorally modern around 50,000 years ago. The characteristics of behavioral modernity include complex symbolic thought; the development of art and language; creation of finely-made tools; skills in cooking, dance, and music; burial customs; and sharing between groups. All extant human civilizations on planet earth today, even those that have not developed metal tools, are considered behaviorally modern.

The Emergence of Life

Scientists have made some impressive advances in our understanding of the origins of life. Currently, no scientific evidence identifies the way that the first spark of life came to be.[4] Scientists certainly are considering a number of hypotheses. The first theory I learned in freshman biology class at Sullivan High, a Chicago public school, was based on a famous experiment conducted by Professors Stanley Miller and Harold Urey.

The two biochemists mixed gases of chemicals believed to have been on earth's surface some four billion years ago into a vessel with water. They then employed electrodes to pass an electric current through the mixture—a laboratory simulation of lightning—in an attempt to replicate the process by which life might first have appeared. This process yielded several amino acids. I remember going up to my teacher, Mr. Dubin, at the end of bio class and, knowing that he was Jewish, asking him how this all squared with the Bible's account of creation. While his answer was indecipherable, I do remember the shrug part well. Inevitably perhaps, the question stayed with me, and it was one of the compelling reasons I decided to transfer to the Ida Crown Jewish Academy in my junior year of high school. It was there that I learned Biblical Hebrew and began to study the Bible in a serious way.

Since Miller and Urey's experiment in the 1950s, later researchers eventually discovered all twenty-two standard amino acids, the building blocks of proteins. Scientists have also been able to create the chemical components of RNA in lab conditions. Professor Gerald Joyce of the Scripps Research Institute has gone so far as to create an RNA molecule capable of reproducing itself.[5] Unlike amino acids, RNA can both store information, like DNA, and serve as an enzyme-like protein. Some scientists believe that such findings are bringing us ever closer to the possibility of the spontaneous generation of life. In typical fashion, marketers no longer think of DNA and RNA as the ingredients of the universe, but rather as the solution for thinning hair, crow's feet, and other modern-day maladies. I am not sure how much of an advance this is over the magic potions described in part one. Despite these advances in our knowledge of Darwin's two main pillars, the road to definite conclusions about the origins and evolution of life is still fraught with pitfalls.

Blips In the Fossil Record

The Cambrian explosion of species was a fifty- to eighty-million-year period starting about 580 million years ago, during which time the diversity of life literally exploded well beyond what can be reconciled with Darwinian evolution.[6] According to the Darwinian model, the fossil record should reflect a gradual evolution of species. Yet, by the end of the Cambrian explosion, with few exceptions, the entire major phylum we have today had appeared out of nowhere. From the Cambrian explosion onward, the fossil record does indeed accord with the expectations of neo-Darwinian evolution, but it is difficult to reconcile this with the record in pre-Cambrian times. Darwin himself hoped that the advance of science would lead to the resolution of some of these difficulties. Still, the dilemma of the Cambrian explosion remains a challenge. In 1970s, biologists and paleontologists Stephen Jay Gould and Niles Eldredge purported to solve the problem, proposing a hypothesis they called "punctuated equilibrium."[7] According to their hypothesis, large species could have engendered small groups of subspecies, small enough to rapidly inculcate changed characteristics. These small groups would then either become viable—with the result that they would separate out from their parent species or simply differentiate from them—or would die out, though leaving us with no fossil record due to their small size. The larger species, in contrast, would go through long periods of equilibrium. This hypothesis would thereby explain the fossil record, which does in fact evidence long periods of no change.

My personal path to taking Judaism seriously in high school might be taken to illustrate the idea of punctuated equilibrium as well. At the time I asked Mr. Dubin my question, I had acquired the "mutation" of wondering about the role of God in the creation of life. That mutation lay dormant for the better part of two years, but when other influences and the opportunity to change schools presented itself, I made the change. Similarly, the Biblical Hebrew and Jewish texts I learned lay dormant in me until my equilibrium became "punctuated" and I wrote this book. An outside observer could not have easily guessed when or if these "mutations" would have the opportunity to cause a change in me. Had circumstances been different, perhaps they would not have manifested themselves in transforming my development at all. The scientific community continues to debate punctuated equilibrium, because the theory has created as many questions as it proposes to answer.[8] Similarly, my family and friends also struggle at times to make sense of me.

Wayward Species

The Cambrian explosion is not the only logical inconsistency facing Darwin's theory of speciation. In a sense, neo-Darwinism might be considered flawed in the same way as creationism. The reason we find no record of pandas, penguins, polar bears, or buffalo migrating from Noah's ark to their present locations is because that certainly did not happen. At the same time, there is also, as of yet, no accepted explanation for how species such as monkeys made the intercontinental journey from Africa to South America.[9] According to genetic studies, Old and New World monkeys seem to have split up thirty to fifty million years ago. Yet the continents of Africa and South America separated far earlier than that, over a hundred million years ago. The same issue arises with a host of other animals and plants.[10] The idea that plants and animals exist in diverse places because of continental drift is called vicariance. Vicariance is the currently ruling hypothesis, but it is not a totally satisfying one, since genetic and fossil dating don't completely square with the data on continental drift. Sure, some plants and animals may have made some very unlikely journeys to concur with principles of vicariance. But it might also be possible that something else, not yet understood, is at work here. I, for one, certainly don't believe that monkeys of various sorts popped into existence, like so many jack-in-the-box toys, on different continents at the same time in some sort of supernatural way, even though the fossil record as it stands seems to indicate that they did. Nor, of course, do scientists suggest this. Yet scientific research into evolution is inhibited for the unstated reason that it might yield data that gives succor to the creationists. The fear is that any addendum to the theory of evolution that is not airtight leaves room for creationists to much overstate it as a proof-text. Much more likely than providing proof of creationism, from a scientific perspective there are still unexplained phenomena at work. Future progress in evolutionary biology will, in all probability, lead to reasonable explanations down the research road.

Genetic Puzzles: I'm Not Just Your Sister's Brother's Brother

Genetic evidence has also baffled some proponents of natural selection.

Before we possessed extensive knowledge of DNA, biologists assumed that natural selection would lead more advanced species to exhibit a greater number of genes.[11] They further assumed that these genes would differ, since they would be the result of multiple mutations over time. However, as scientists began to map DNA, they discovered the astonishing fact that humans, the most complex of animal species, actually exhibit far fewer genes than predicted. Humans, the planet's most advanced species by far, in fact are close to mice in terms of their number of genes! What's the explanation?

Part of the answer to this conundrum was provided by experiments on *E. coli*, which demonstrated that genes have repressors that can be turned on and off.

This discovery solved a long-standing problem in biology concerning the question why genes operated differently in different cells. But it had important consequences for evolution as well. As scientists learned more about embryos, they discovered that certain genes, called Hox genes, possessed an ability to turn other genes on and off. Scientists are now of the opinion that the diversity of life is also the direct result of different patterns in how genes turn on and off, rather than just the diversity of genes themselves. These new developments in genetics afford us insights into the mechanism of evolution, but, more importantly, they make clear how much we still do not know about the process at a genetic level.

Competition or Cooperation

Biologists have also raised questions regarding the evidence that natural selection alone is the primary motor for speciation. In the 1970s, Lynn Margulis, an evolutionary theorist who started her academic career as an outcast but later became a hero, challenged certain elements of Darwin's theory of natural selection.[12] Though thoroughly committed to evolution, Margulis became convinced that natural selection and genetic mutation alone could not account for speciation. Margulis offered the theory of symbiogenesis to explain speciation. In other words, new species emerge through the symbiotic relationship between two or more organisms. For Margulis, the primary agents of symbiogenesis are bacteria. In fact, according to Margulis, cells with nuclei evolved through a symbiotic relationship with bacteria. This is no small claim since cells with nuclei make up all cells in the human body. But Margulis took this idea a step further. The juvenile slug, for example, could not originally accomplish photosynthesis. Nevertheless, after ingesting algae chloroplasts, it became green. According to Margulis, the slug then laid eggs, which were capable of photosynthesis. In other words, they had acquired the gene for photosynthesis from the algae and transmitted it to future generations. In Margulis's view, long-term symbiosis thus led to new intracellular structures and therefore new species. While Margulis's ideas about cell evolution are generally accepted, her theories about symbiosis and speciation remain more controversial. Some scientists believe that Margulis's theory works better for speciation in plants than in animals. In any event, Margulis added to a number of authoritative scientific voices that believe that natural selection alone cannot account for evolution.

From all of these examples, it is clear that neo-Darwinism seems to be simultaneously both correct, and yet, unable to account for important data. Problems with the theory of evolution can be compared to problems with particle physics after physicists discovered that Newton's theory of gravitation was inconsistent with discoveries about the speed of light. Perhaps we are awaiting the Einstein of evolution but with more evolved hair.

The Meaning of the Story of Genesis and Evolution

Although a literal reading of the text of Genesis seems to contradict the theory of evolution, it also reveals conceptual hints that creation evolved in a natural process and describes a more naturalistic vision of the living world than do ancient myths. In other words, unlike ancient myths it does not attribute supernatural qualities to or deify nature, or invent mythical creatures. Ancient myths in contrast are completely creationist, often fantastic, and rarely provide details about different types of often mythical species involved in or resulting from creation. That being said, at first glance, a literal reading of the biblical text seems to contradict the key pillars of Darwin's theory of evolution.

First of all, the biblical text appears to suggest that God created all of the species *ex nihilo*. Second, the text does not strictly follow the order of evolution. As Natan Slifkin shows, while there is some overlap, the biblical text claims that the sun and the moon were created on day four, after the trees, which were created on day three, when according to science they were created before trees.[13] This has never really bothered me since the universe is at least 13.8 billion years old and our sun (which is a third-generation star) was not formed until 4.6 billion years ago. This is close enough to the "fourth day" or stage from a metaphysical perspective. Not that the order is completely out of sync: the heavens and the universe (the Hebrew word for earth could certainly also be understood as "universe") are created before living things, and fish and insects are created before more complex mammals, including man.[14] The last difficulty for the ancients was, of course, with the duration of creation itself. These discrepancies led many ancient commentators to read the text allegorically. While I personally embrace such an allegorical reading, even the plain meaning of the text introduces the concept of natural progression, and therefore makes an important conceptual point about the nature of creation. For example, verses 1:11–13 of Genesis contain language that suggests a natural process:

"And God said, '*Let the earth sprout vegetation*: seed-bearing plants, fruit trees of every kind on earth that bear fruit with the seed in it.' And it was so. *The earth brought forth vegetation*: seed-bearing plants of every kind, and trees of every kind bearing fruit with the seed in it. And God saw that this was good." (Genesis 1:11–13)

A similar process is described in verses 1:20–22: "God said, 'Let the waters bring forth swarms of living creatures, and birds that fly above the earth across the expanse of the sky.' God created the great sea monsters, and all the living creatures of every kind that creep, which the waters brought forth in swarms, and all the winged birds of every kind. And God saw that this was good." (Genesis 1:20–22)

The text also offers other clues to its interpretation. For example, the text uses the verb *yatzar*, rather than *bara*, to indicate the creation of most species. The early modern commentator Yitzchak Abarbanel (1437–1508), who could not have had evolutionary theory on his mind back in the fifteenth century, writes that the presence of the verb *yatzar* suggests that plants, animals, and man were not created *ex nihilo* but, rather, they were fashioned out of something else. This observation also points to the idea that the biblical text accords with evolution more than would appear at first glance.[15] A number of medieval biblical commentators, including Nissim ben Reuven, also known as Nissim of Gerona (1320–1380), and Abarbanel, believed that only the first act of creation, which included "the heaven and the earth," was *ex nihilo*.[16] Nissim of Gerona also wrote of the evolving of different subspecies from those species preserved by Noah on the ark.[17] To me this seems amazing, even if the time frame the Ran understood could clearly not accommodate any such serious speciation. In addition to such hints, the simple meaning of the biblical text clearly presents a realistic view of creation. In the plain "language of men," it describes the natural world as we know it, filled with the elements, plants, and animals, rather than with gods and mythical creatures. Among these creatures, it also allots man a special place and responsibility.

The Mysterious Origins of Life

Despite advances in understanding, we are still a long way from knowing if, and how, life could have formed spontaneously.

Granting the working hypothesis that RNA might be a step toward life, it is highly unlikely that any single amino acid would have survived long enough to meet up with some of the other twenty or so amino acids necessary in order to form the most basic protein molecule.[1] Amino acids are also water-soluble. Since the surface of the earth during the era of life's beginning was primarily water, the probability that these random amino acids would have survived to make it into a stable environment is remote.[18] Further, in order for these amino acids to produce RNA, they would not only have had to link up but would also have had to have done so in the very precise format of at least two binding chains. Some scientists address this problem by positing that these amino acids could have washed up near a volcanic shore and linked up with each other there. Others suggest that either ice, clay, or deep-sea vents might have provided the necessary environments for molecules to survive, and for critical reactions to take place so that amino acids could form RNA.[19]

Even if we allow for these suggestions, the RNA hypothesis exhibits other problems. We still don't know, for example, how, once formed, amino acids would propagate in such a way as to create life, since natural selection only takes place with life. Some scientists have suggested that, at an early point in the chain of life, perhaps even as soon as the formation of reproductive RNA and DNA, a more modest form of natural selection might have begun. Nevertheless, we still need to explain how molecules would have gotten to that point. To bolster this idea of "nonlife

---

[1] For a good discussion of the current criticisms of the RNA World hypothesis, see Rauchfuss, *Chemical Evolution*, 166.

survival of the fittest," scientists have pointed to prions that benefit from natural selection without RNA, but this still does not solve the problem.[20] The experiments of Professors Miller and Joyce, noted earlier, were not themselves random events, and therefore also did not solve the problem, arranged as they were, by definition, by intelligent designers. Because of issues with the RNA hypothesis, a number of scholars hypothesize alternatively that smaller, less-complicated molecules interacted with each other in capsules until the more-complicated molecules among them began to replicate more numerously and overtake the simpler molecules.[21] Some scientists have suggested a more exciting and colorful theory—rocks from Mars or asteroids containing microbes could have landed on earth and started life.[22] But this only transfers the same problem to another heavenly body. In my view, all these conjectures only serve to buttress the argument for some sort of proactive design to the start of life. No evidence has ever been found of amino acids spontaneously appearing, linking up, and creating a protein outside of a lab built by very intelligent creators.

The Bible and the Creation of Man

The Bible's message about the creation of man focuses on his special nature, knowledge, dignity, and responsibility, contrary to many creation myths, where he is often but an afterthought, the plaything of fickle gods and deified natural processes. In this respect, the Bible's message is in line with what we can observe from science, where man has been uniquely influential in changing nature. Yet it also hints at the evolution of man from animals. Ancient myths are filled with created hybrid creatures, god-men, such as Hercules, and animal-men, such as centaurs. In contrast, the biblical text offers a different and subtler message about man's relationship to animals. As with the rest of creation, the creation of man seems at first glance to be a separate event from the creation of animals and appears to be brought about through direct divine action:

> And God said, "Let us make man in our image, after our likeness. They shall rule the fish of the sea, the birds of the sky, the cattle, the whole earth, and all the creeping things that creep on earth." And God created man in His image, in the image of God He created him; male and female He created them. (Genesis 1: 26–27)

There is the added complication that man is created twice in the biblical narrative. In the second instance, he is created from dust and woman is taken from man's rib. Most commentators have struggled with this repetition. For some medieval commentators, the solution to this conundrum bears a resemblance to the binary history of man. He is both a creature descended from animals and different from them. Taking a nonliteral approach to the text, Rambam and Abarbanel explain that man originally resembled an animal and was created along with the rest of creation before the sixth day.[23] The description of his creation on the sixth day indicates that he only later acquired the moral and spiritual faculties of being created in God's image. The record of man's humble origins remains in the text in order to show that he is still capable of descending to the level of an animal (as any person who has witnessed a Black Friday scramble for discounted flat-screen TVs in the United States can attest to). Other rabbinic commentators make this very point; still other rabbis have a different take. According to the Rambam, the second creation story should also not be understood literally. The text is actually describing the specific qualities and place of human beings in the world and their relationship with God; it is not interested in the mechanics of how man was actually created.[24] The Rambam even refers to sources in the Talmud to make the point.[25] Thus, in stark contrast to ancient creation myths, Genesis describes man's place at the apex of creation, his responsibility for the natural world within which he resides, and his moral character as a determinant of a good society. As Reverend Dr. Katharine Henderson writes:

> I don't think that the two notions of spiritual creation and physical creation of man are incompatible at all. Any kind of life form can fall within the privy or be part of God's greater plan. Whether you believe literally in an Adam and Eve, whatever that means, or evolutionary processes, I think these are different ways of understanding the same thing and that all of this is part of God's creation.

The commentaries on the text of man's creation thus offer more parallels with evolution than it would seem at first glance. My personal view of the Adam and Eve story is that God began His relationship with man when man developed consciousness and could distinguish moral interactions intellectually, and this was way before real science began. The creation story served its purpose for our ancestors, and its message of God's creation of nature and of all of us being the descendants of one couple is still relevant today. I view the text as begging for a nonliteral reading of creation, the Adam and Eve stories and of the entire first eleven chapters. How else could the only surviving child of Adam and Eve, namely Cain, meet up with a woman to marry and gather enough other people to start a city? The plain inconsistencies are all that were apparent to the ancient commentators, who were sure the texts contained deep secrets, even as they may have not possessed a conceptual framework to even understand their own inferences.

Evolution and God

I think evolution in Islam itself is acknowledged in the sense that everything is evolutionary. There is a process that happens. Human creation is part of evolution.

—IMAM SHAMSI ALI

Darwin's theory of evolution neither disproves the existence of God nor undermines the authority of the Bible. As we have seen, there are very ancient religious traditions that embrace a nonliteral approach to the first eleven chapters of the Bible. Let no one tell you that a nonliteral interpretation of the Bible is simply a form of modern apologetics. Properly understood, the plain meaning of the creation story in Genesis provides a clear theory of nature as a physical entity that cannot be deified and a rich interpretation of God's desires and of man's partnership role in fulfilling creation, far more than a dry mechanical blueprint for the emergence of biological life on earth. In this light, much of the perceived tension between monotheism and the theory of evolution is unnecessary, even perverse. At the same time, the biblical text presents a demystified view of life and humankind, which by virtue of the rejection of any deification of nature or man, is closer in spirit, and even scientific reasoning, to the theory of evolution than any of the ancient creation myths. It is not, as atheist writers argue, hypocritical, nor is it irrational for monotheists to both accept Darwin's theory of evolution and appreciate the biblical text at the same time. Of course, the theory of evolution also in no way excludes the possibility that God created the mechanism of evolution. There would be no apparent way of knowing if God gave the evolutionary process an undetectable (to human comprehension) nudge from time to time. Certainly, this would be one (admittedly nonscientific) explanation for the Cambrian explosion that continues to baffle scientists. It would not be beyond God to have gotten the evolutionary ball rolling by creating that first single-celled organism. Who would know? Atheists have hardly proven their case that life arose randomly, and, even if they discovered such a mechanism, there is no a logical reason why God could not have put that mechanism, randomness and all, in place. Always keep in mind that God created nature. He is not part of nature; He is outside of it.

CHAPTER 23

Natural Miracles

How People Think of and Experience Miracles

We usually use miracles in everyday speech to denote events that are *improbable*, which is very different from *inexplicable*. Most people use the word "miracle" to refer to an unexpected recovery or deliverance and often feel that *events unfolded unexpectedly in a precise way* to allow for this.

Such was the case with my father, who told me that he was saved during World War II in Europe by numerous miracles. The first of many low-probability events occurred when the Nazis and their local collaborators initially abducted him and my grandfather. Separated from my grandfather, my father frantically searched for him to no avail. A Nazi guard grabbed my father and heaved him into a different group than the one he had originally been put in. The Jews in the first group were murdered prior to deportation. For my father, this one action saved his life. If he had not searched for his father, he would have been murdered. If he had successfully found his father and joined him, my father would have been murdered. Had the Nazi guard thrown him in a different direction, he would have been murdered. Had the Nazi guard actually helped my father find and join his father, my father would have been murdered. Had he previously left Švėkšna to be with his uncles, he would have been murdered when the Nazis arrived in their community. And all of this occurred as so much of my father's journey went. There was an extremely narrow quantum path for him to have arrived alive in Chicago.

Imam Shamsi Ali considers his own amazing journey from a small village in Indonesia to the position of a prominent imam in New York City to be a miracle for the same reason:

> I don't find that it is really possible for me to deny the existence of God because I myself am a very proof of that existence. My path from my poor village to being in New York City is one piece of evidence. I never imagined that when I was a child I would be sitting here with you. I never imagined that I would even go to a big city to study. Then I went to Pakistan from my homeland and from there I went to Saudi Arabia. I was working in Saudi Arabia when the time came for Muslims to celebrate the hajj. It is something huge. I lived there for that, and now I am here, the capital of the world. I never imagined or planned my path.

Most people who experience what they describe as miracles feel either that a higher force guided the cluster of events that led to their deliverance or that they received emotional and spiritual strength from their faith in God to keep going despite the odds. Few people describe miracles that are genuinely contrary to nature.

Science and Miracles

Many modern philosophers and scientists dismiss miracles because they take a mechanistic view of nature and define them as impossible. David Hume, the famous philosopher and atheist, gave us a good working definition of a miracle when he described it as "a transgression of a law of nature by a particular volition of the deity or by the interposition of some invisible agent."[1] Hume thus considers miracles to be contrary to nature. Many scientists would agree with Hume's definition and maintain that such miracles, including those in the Bible, never took place and could not possibly ever take place. The atheist argument is that events seemingly contrary to nature are simply misunderstood or fabricated and are only viewed as miraculous due to ignorance, willful or otherwise. With regard to what ordinary people consider to be miracles, such as unforeseen medical recoveries, either scientists just don't yet know how to explain them or they actually fall within the range of probable outcomes, simply on the lower end. Some philosophers and even theologians, such as Maurice Wiles, criticize the notion of miracles on the basis that they represent a fault in God's omniscience. If God could really determine all events, why would He need to perform miracles? For Wiles, the lack of miracles does not eliminate the existence of God; he just does not see God having any use for them.

Quantum physics has actually given us a new way to view miracles and brings the concept closer to the way ordinary people might think of them. Quantum mechanics depicts a vast array of possible outcomes, some of them quite counterintuitive. Such a premise suggests that virtually nothing is impossible in the universe. For example, it is possible for you to walk through a brick wall, although the odds of you doing so by having the appropriate energy and wave function calibration are such that you might have to wait longer than the existence of the universe to experience that event. Further, there is no telling what you would look like after you pass through that brick wall. *But it is not impossible.* Quantum mechanics has also demonstrated that the action of observation impacts outcome. So, our observation—and I might add, our attitude— has a determining effect on what actually happens. We find instances of this in stories of yogis and other meditative mystics who seem to defy the laws of nature in various ways.

More concretely, there is a great deal of evidence, for example, that people who remained positive and envisioned themselves as liberated from the Nazi concentration camps at some point in the not-near future had a better chance of surviving than those who did not envision that future and lost the will to survive. Although this is not a hard-and-fast rule, Viktor Frankl, the famed psychologist and Holocaust survivor, describes this phenomenon in great detail. My father survived over four years of slave labor and concentration camps. He weighed only sixty pounds upon his liberation. Clearly, he had an enormous will to survive and an expectation that one day he would be liberated.

However, the implications of quantum physics on his experience run even deeper. Just as the human mind may be able to affect events, so too could the divine mind. Quantum mechanics certainly provides a plausible description of how God could engineer encounters and events within the bounds of nature and even seemingly "beyond" nature. Some scientists now view the biblical plagues in Egypt as natural, though highly improbable, events. They have identified algae, in particular protozoan and zooplankton, that can populate a body of water rapidly and cause it to become deoxygenated, undrinkable, and red, which fits the description of the first plague.[2] The deoxygenating of the river would have caused the death of the river fish and caused the frogs to flee from the Nile, a close description of the second plague visited upon the Egyptians. Further, since dry land is not all that hospitable for frogs, they died en masse and as their carcasses piled up, these dead frogs then became a natural breeding ground for the third and fourth plagues of gnats and flies. Not only can scientists describe the subsequent plagues in a similar manner, but they can even account for the most improbable plague, that of the death of the first-born. This plague could have arisen from the acute spoiling of food due to a food system overstressed under these highly unsanitary conditions and lacking the use of modern food-preservation technologies and techniques. The specific cause might have been mycotoxin fungi, of which many varieties have led to the death of those who had the bad luck of eating foods contaminated with them. Given the condition of the food chain in an environment that had been infiltrated by insects and disease, the first foods removed from the storage areas may have been the most infected. Because the first-born were honored by being fed first, they would have likely eaten the most contaminated food. In contrast, these diseases may not have fully spread to the food removed from deeper levels of storage and given later to lesser members of the family.[3] The ten plagues can thus be seen as a series of natural events orchestrated by God, whose order can be accounted scientifically. However, as we discussed in part two, the Bible takes poetic license and it is therefore also possible that the Bible might have taken some poetic license in describing the nature and number of the plagues.

Monotheism and Miracles

"Praise be to God and not our own strength for it."
—KING HENRY IN WILLIAM SHAKESPEARE'S *HENRY V*

The Jewish tradition regarding miracles more closely resembles the popular and quantum view of miracles than a supernatural or magical approach. The most common Hebrew word for miracle is *nes*, which means an outstanding event that inspires amazement.[4] Therefore, most miracles in Judaism are not, in fact, contrary to nature, but rather fall within the realm of possible events, though they often consist of highly beneficial and improbable ones. This definition fits very well with the common-sense usage of the word "miracle"—for example, in the case of a critically ill patient who recovers. Other miracles also result from a string of encounters or events that lead to a positive individual or historical outcome. The Jewish tradition, echoed in the writings of the venerable Rambam, sees miracles as low-probability events within nature. This definition is also a far cry from idolatrous notions of magic as the total subversion of the natural order at the will of human beings. The main distinguishing feature between Jewish and secular views regarding low-probability coincidences is, therefore, not that such incidents are contrary to nature, but rather that they are due to divine intervention, often combined with positive human initiative. According to Rambam, as we have seen, it is precisely within the range of possible events in nature for God to exercise divine providence based on a person's behavior.[5] Essentially, God just has to stack the deck, load the dice, or perform whatever other quantum sleight-of-hand He chooses in order for events to turn out the way He wants. We learn from the biblical narrative that, since the time of Esther, God has worked exclusively via hidden miracles. As is indicated in the Book of Proverbs: "It is the glory of God to conceal a matter, and the glory of a king to plumb a matter." (Proverbs 25:2) Judaism does, however, sharply distinguish between hidden miracles, or low-probability events, and revealed miracles that seem to openly defy the rules of nature. The latter are, however, very few and far between.

Miracles in the Bible

According to the rabbis, the very few events in the Bible that count as miracles contrary to nature were encrypted in nature from the beginning of time. After the event of the burning bush, the Bible describes big public miracles—the staff of Moses turns into a snake, for example—and more widely witnessed events like the ten plagues and the parting of the Sea of Reeds. We might certainly imagine that the Jewish tradition would celebrate all of these as open miracles. In fact, the ancient rabbis did not view the ten plagues themselves as unnatural. Rather, in the *Mishna*

Pirkei Avot (5:8), the rabbis explain that ten things were created especially at the end of creation:

> Ten things were created between the suns [taken to mean just before creation ended]. They are: the mouth of the earth, the mouth of the well, the speech of the ass, the rainbow shown to Noah, the manna, the rod [which Moses used in Egypt], the shamir worm [a worm that, legend has it, cut through rocks], the script [the Hebrew alphabet], the writing of the Tablets and the Tablets themselves.

All of these objects share the characteristic of leading to open miracles contrary to nature. Of all of them, the manna is perhaps the most famous. In order to explain these miracles, the rabbis argued that they were embedded in creation itself. In essence, these rabbis anticipated the questions of both Hume and Wiles, mentioned above. Outward miracles that are beyond the realm of possibility are awkward, if on rare occasion necessary. But an omniscient God can anticipate these eventualities and embed their possibility into the nature of creation, given that God transcends creation and is not part of it. In fact, Wiles' view that miracles are unnecessary is in general agreement with the ancient rabbis: an omniscient God does not make miracles extemporaneously, but rather foresees them and embeds them into nature at creation. Most importantly for Jewish thinkers, open miracles contrary to nature serve to bolster faith among the faithless. Many commentators have explained that this was the purpose of the manna: the Israelites needed to fully integrate the notion of God's sovereignty in the desert, since they were still strongly influenced by idolatry. Many Jewish thinkers have argued that, if human beings had a better understanding of God and nature, they would not need miracles to reinforce their devotion. Nature is itself a proof of God's greatness.

Islam and Christianity, like Judaism, emphasize that open miracles are simply signs from God. They are not only rare, but also the result of tremendous piety rather than magical powers. Of the three monotheistic faiths, Christianity places the most emphasis on miracles. Christian Scriptures attribute four sorts of miracles to Jesus: cures, resurrection of the dead, exorcisms, and natural wonders such as transforming water into wine. Many of these miracle stories communicate a specific theological message. In particular, they emphasize the importance of faith to a positive outcome. When Jesus cures the lepers, for example, he declares, "Rise and go; your faith has saved you." (Luke 17:19) In this respect, Christians see miracles as both a sign of God's power and as an inspiration to live with hope and faith even if a situation seems bleak. The emphasis on the power of faith and thought also suggests a quantum view of miracles.

The Christian view that holy people can be agents of miracles because of their holiness is echoed in Buddhist and Hindu teachings. Buddhists believe that the Buddha obtained the capacity to defy the natural order through his years of deep meditation. Hindus also believe that through yogic practice, individuals can achieve visions and clairvoyance. The same powers are attributed to Sufi mystics and kabbalists in Islam and Judaism respectively. In all five cases, holiness or meditative practice allows practitioners to access possible outcomes that are highly improbable or otherwise beyond the usual—though not quantum—limits of space and time. Such powers, however, are different from magical ones, since these miracles are performed for the purpose of divine glory and with divine permission rather than to satisfy the desires of individuals.

This is also why many miracles in Christianity and other religions occur in the context of teaching people about faith or giving them hope, rather than of achieving personal power and glory. Nevertheless, all three monotheistic religions de-emphasize open miracles. Which saint was praying for the Mets in 1969, we don't know, but it certainly wasn't me in Chicago. That being said, a hundred years of prayers of local Cubs fans were indeed answered in 2016. Personally, I practically cried from joy. The Catholic Church vigorously investigates all purported miracles. Islam also attributes few miracles to Mohammad, its greatest prophet, other than receiving the Qur'an itself. All three monotheistic religions focus more on God's providence through nature than on his miraculous activities.

Miracles without a Hollywood Budget

The existence of miracles as understood according to the Jewish and monotheistic traditions presents no barrier to rational faith in God. Very few passages in the Hebrew Scriptures demand that we believe in events contrary to nature. Quantum mechanics is a set of laws that seems tailor made for the Theosic principle in that it neatly allows God to work in the world in a manner that is natural and invisible. Quantum mechanics also makes it even more rational to accept the hidden miracles we experience. More to the point, most miraculous events seem like fortuitous coincidences, but on closer review, depend to some degree on our efforts and vision. Quantum mechanics ordains that the outcome of an event is not resolved until observation is made. When it comes to history, we the observers are also the actors, and, as we shall discuss in part VI, we are the ones praying for certain outcomes. When we work in partnership with God in the same way Mordechai and Esther did in the Purim story, God might do His part to resolve the outcome of the event in a positive way. With hidden miracles, He can select from the myriad possible states of nature. We don't know how these mechanisms work, but they do make belief in miracles more plausible within the structure of the universe.

CHAPTER 24

Science, the Bible, and a Theory of Everything

A large number of scientists express confidence in the notion that scientific developments of the last century prove that materialism is not only a logical tenet, but also a fact. Our atheist authors are among those who believe the universe is composed of matter alone and that it developed by chance. They point to the very advances in physics and biology we have been discussing as proof that the world is completely material. They argue that the more we know about subatomic particles and the development of the universe and the evolution of life, the more we can rule out any form of divine consciousness. The revered late physicist Stephen Hawking, for example, publicly shared his conviction that there is no God. From his perspective, there is nothing beyond the universe, except perhaps other universes.

A corollary to materialism is that the world has no direction or purpose. For many scientists, since the world is simply the result of random physical and chemical reactions and processes, it has no specific reason for being, no directed goal in its development. For many atheists, the world is progressing neither biologically nor in terms of consciousness (understood not as subjective thought, but rather as shared knowledge). No, the world simply follows random and evolutionary mechanisms and will one day end.

That being said, some physicists do take an opposite view: quantum theory points to the power of the mind and opens the possibility that matter and the universe are not randomly assembled. Scientific advocates of the strong-form anthropic principle describe a purposeful process whereby the world was compelled to develop for man as an alternative to the multiverse theory. Atheists should not misrepresent their own views as speaking for all scientists.

The Bible, the Kabbalah, and the Material Girl

Monotheistic concepts of the supernatural and the natural are very different from atheists' presentation of God and nature. Both atheists and monotheists, in contrast to idolaters, view nature as separate from God, which of course atheists do not believe in, so nature certainly must stand on its own. However contrary to what atheists may claim, monotheistic views of nature and God resemble quantum views that the world consists of information. The Bible describes the creation of the world through God's words. God's ideas about the world, as it were, are translated into words and formed into matter. While the Bible hardly provides details about the mechanism of translation from thought → to word → to matter, the parallel is hard to deny. More to the point, many kabbalistic texts describe the world as a concealed manifestation of the divine mind. We might find parallels to such a view in Max Planck's notion of matter. The mystical view of the world as information is also closely tied to monotheism's view of the direction and purpose of the universe: that it was created for man. As Imam Shamsi Ali puts it:

> I disagree about the world being called random, because we see that everything is being organized in this life. Everything is very organized in this universe. There must be someone who organized it, there must be someone who is ultimately unlimited in his power and his knowledge to organize the existence of this universe. And that itself is quite enough evidence to dispute this notion that everything randomly happens. How can you imagine about humans, for example, our lives, and I mean that personally, that everything is just random?

The atheist view of purpose of existence is actually closer to the idolatrous view than to the monotheistic view. In both the idolatrous and atheist view, there is no purpose to the world. Monotheists believe that the world is ultimately tending toward a utopian end, which God is directing. Among the characteristics of this utopian finale is an end to suffering and a greater understanding of all the mysteries of life. While there is no religious consensus on the details of what arriving at this finale might look like, this utopian goal has more to do with motivating man to take an active role in improving the world than in its precise outcome.

The Bible: On Purpose

Monotheistic texts present the view that humankind's purpose in this world is to create a better world through expanding consciousness. Such a task takes prodigious time. While the first eleven chapters of the Bible include some of the cognitive skills and technology of "modern" man, the main focus is on moral rather than technological consciousness. In these chapters, man is challenged to maintain his God-consciousness, though he often fails in practice. As noted, God's intervention with man only begins after man achieves consciousness. After the first eleven chapters, the Bible focuses on one group of people who also often backslide. The Israelites need a good forty years in the desert, under highly unusual circumstances, just to be able to adopt the new non-idolatrous consciousness—even in that, they don't fully succeed. Rambam writes that God allowed for the rites of sacrifices, since this was the custom of all the idolatrous nations, and both the Jews and the world could not be weaned away from idolatry if the change to monotheism were too abrupt. In other words, they needed training wheels. Likewise, according to the Talmud, the Jews had to figuratively receive the Torah a second time, voluntarily, after the hidden miracles of Purim, because they didn't really "get it" the first time. Progress is not a forward march in the Bible; it is more a Viennese waltz for beginners. Thinkers such as Rabbi Abraham Isaac Kook argue that God chooses the precise time for certain concepts to be known in the world so that man can advance in consciousness. Thus, man did not recognize the true dimensions of the vastness of the universe until the idea of his own importance and responsibility was firmly culturally implanted. If this had not been the case, he might have reverted to the idolatrous view that he was simply one cog in a big cosmic wheel.

From a mystical point of view, all information is already in the world, waiting to be actualized, when we are ready for it. As Father Alexander

Karloutsos asks, "Did you know twenty years ago, twenty-five years ago that you could do an instant text? Did you know that in the universe there was something called emails or the internet? Those energies have always existed in the universe. The ability to do that, all of that potential existed; we were just not enlightened enough." Or as Reverend Dr. Calvin Butts states it: "No, no, no, this is a wonderful world, and our search for God continues to reveal more about it."

God and Materialism

I feel like there are a lot of things in our everyday experience, such as caring for a loved one who is dying, to the more mundane experiences which have a spiritual dimension that explain things happening to people that science cannot explain and doesn't have answers for, and on a very day-to-day level. After 9/11, I was working at the Cathedral of St. John the Divine and we put together some services every evening for the first week after 9/11 and people just poured into the cathedral. I just question if anyone has really found that science has an answer to everything.

—REVEREND CHLOE BREYER

Our increasing knowledge about the mechanics of the world can lead to either greater materialism or greater faith in God. The question of whether the world is purely material or not is, as I have mentioned, at the core of the supposed divide between religion and science.

Clearly, many scientists remain convinced of the tenet that the universe is entirely material, even after taking into account quantum physics, while there are many who are convinced of the opposite. This is certainly the view of monotheists, as Reverend Dr. Katharine Henderson explains:

Well, I think there are lots of things in our lives and in human life that are inexplicable—that is, not rational, that defies explanation, scientific or otherwise. I am a great believer and appreciate science and evolution and all of that, but how do you explain love? Human love of somebody that just comes from nowhere in a sense, it is not logical at all. Falling in love, being in love—human love is inexplicable. Take nature. If you look at nature around us, yes, there are a lot of scientific explanations for a lot of what happens in nature, but

301

all of the scientific explanations don't account for the beauty beyond scientific explanation. I mean, who thought that up, how did that happen? It is not just utilitarian; the universe in which we live that is based on natural law. There are so many things beyond. Who created that added value of the rainbow or the red bud in spring, or the chirp of the bird? You know nature. So beyond the rational, there are so many things that nobody is going to be able to explain.

For the time being, contrary to atheists' views, there is no winner in this debate.

The Gift of Modern Science to Belief

A medieval theologian offers us a powerful insight about the natural world that scientists are only now beginning to understand. Thomas Aquinas was a forward-thinking theologian—so much so that, seven hundred and fifty years later, it is still amazing to contemplate his philosophical discussion of contingency, which sounds like it could have been composed yesterday. Bishop William Murphy describes his thought: "It is of the nature of the world in which we live that we are finite beings. So that means, everything in this world is in some sense philosophically contingent; it depends on something else. It comes to a close because some other thing that either interferes with or within itself causes it to devolve into something further or even evolve into something further. That sense of contingency still is a reality." In sum, according to Aquinas, all existence, except for that of God, comes and goes. Nothing we can conceive of outside of God is fixed, motionless, definite, and absolute.[1] We now know that Aquinas was not just philosophically correct, but also physically correct.

We find ourselves living in a universe that is ever dynamic, ever changing. The atoms in our very bodies consist of protons, electrons, and neutrons moving at such speeds that they are or have properties of both matter and waves. We witness particles in different ways depending on our perspective as observers. Space, time, and light can all bend. Yet we can't observe 96 percent of the stuff in the universe. Every interaction on a subatomic level is subject not to certainty, but to probabilities. While we embrace science's description of our universe and accept it, we also stand aghast at how counterintuitive it all seems.

We don't at all experience time, our most precious and limiting resource, in the way that physicists tell us it appears in the universe. Our equations tell us that time is like space, and so we should be able to grasp its wholeness in chunks, the way we look at the sky. Yet, strangely, time does not feel that way. We can't take in the entirety of our lives or of our children's lives in one gaze. We take time event by event, effort by effort, and decision by decision, and we build our identities by how we choose to perceive the world and by what we accomplish. We don't perceive one big time-scape, as physics would seem to imply, in which we can maneuver and retrace our steps. It is as though the more we know about how time and space work, the more they remain awesome and beyond our full understanding.

Modern science's insight into the awesomeness and counterintuitive nature of our contingent universe is a gift to all believers. It is axiomatic to believers that God is beyond our comprehension. God's distance from us is clear from a paradoxical biblical passage. In the biblical text, Moses "sees" God and yet he also cannot see him fully: "You may stand on a rock. When My glory passes by…I shall shield you…until I have passed…and you shall see My back…but My face may not be seen." (Exodus 33:21–22) The text seems to suggest that we can get a hint of God's glory, but we are simply not capable of seeing His face. Science has given us a profound insight into this inability to see God's face. Our difficulty in truly understanding this contingent universe on an intellectual level, in contrast to the way we experience it, hints at the difficulty of understanding and experiencing a noncontingent God. As Father Alexander Karloutsos explains: "God is the creator, but He is more than the creator because there is no word that can describe God. We only have manifestations of His presence in the world. We cannot. Who are we? We are finite beings that want to describe the infinite."

Science does not disprove monotheism in any way, shape, or form. Science is, for me, not the toughest challenge to belief, but rather a great source of support.

PART FIVE

Is the Bible a Hoax?

Divine Plan or Devious Propaganda?

Those of us who believe in an omnipotent, omniscient, and omnibenevolent God face a good deal of pushback when it comes to the Bible. Countless academic Bible critics and biblical archaeologists, who are deeply familiar with the ancient world and its texts, have concluded that the people and events in the Bible are bogus. Surely, atheists would say, a real God would have provided more accurate information. Many biblical critics also claim that the Bible is far from a divinely inspired treatise on good and evil. Rather, like the myths of other ancient Near Eastern cultures, it was crafted by Israelite elites who made up the events and/or transformed old legends, hundreds of years after the fact, to vindicate their power.

As has been described in part one, elites across the ancient world concocted stories of gods, composed self-promoting histories, and manipulated traditional legends with the aim of boosting their power and justifying their authority. Why should the contents of the Bible be viewed any differently? As for religious Bible scholars and archaeologists who assert the truthfulness of the Bible, are they not merely blinded by their faith? Do they fudge the discoveries of science and archaeology to defend the indefensible? These are troubling questions. If the Bible really is historically false, those who accept the Bible's moral reasoning should reject its deceitful foundations. There would also be no point in giving the Bible moral authority or believing in God as the Bible describes Him. For belief in God to be rational, a modern person can't avoid asking whether the Bible is propaganda written by charlatans.

The Bible, as we discussed in part one, is not a history book in our modern sense. The Bible does, however, claim to recount the actual actions of God and different peoples in history. It also purports to recount the laws God has revealed to make the world a good, rather than an evil, place. In part two, I agreed with the atheists: if the sweep of events in the Bible were untrue, there would be no rational reason to privilege God's laws. Even those who embrace the Bible's vision as rational and just would still be justifiably offended that those teachings and laws were bestowed fictional divine sanction. Yet, contrary to the assertions of the atheist authors, I argue that the jury remains out on whether the events of the Bible actually occurred, or what academics call "historicity."

For one thing, scholars conversant in scientific methodology have come to widely divergent conclusions about the historicity of the Bible. These differences can't be wholly explained by political or religious preferences, though biases are evident across the board. Rather, there continue to be diverging views because of the nature of the evidence. We will likely never possess ironclad proof of the existence of the specific people and events of the Bible—a mention of Abraham's ancestral property in Ur, for instance; an Egyptian obelisk with carved hieroglyphs detailing the confrontation of Moses and Pharaoh by name, and subsequent events of the Exodus; an archaeological discovery of weaponry and blanched bones from the Israelites' confrontation with the Canaanites. This should not be surprising and is also true of other peoples and events of the ancient past.

Based on this situation, *I argue that for belief in the Bible to be rational, the events and people of the Bible only need to be plausibly compatible with our scientific understanding of ancient Near Eastern history. In other words, the events of the Bible, which claim to be historical, cannot, thus, be anachronistic or mythical.* Specifically, I will claim that, although in many instances written with literary flourish and poetic language, Biblical narratives are nonetheless conceivable based on available archaeological, philological, and historical evidence. At the same time, I fully accept that it is just as rational to remain skeptical of the Bible's historicity, and many academic scholars do indeed remain so, since in most cases, while there is plausibility, there is no direct proof.

With regard to the question of authorship, I will argue that it is rational to believe in revelation, the notion that God inspired the prophets who wrote down the Bible. Belief in revelation should not suggest that the Bible recounts all the details of every event, nor that it aspires to the journalistic accuracy of news reports, nor, most importantly, that its text has never undergone any modifications. In fact, contrary to what some atheist authors may claim, Jewish tradition openly attests to the use of literary devices in the Bible and to edits and other modifications to the text prior to canonization. At the same time, the assumption of revelation does mean rejecting the idea that, sometime during either the tenth, eighth, fourth, or even second centuries BCE, the Bible (and in particular, its first five books) was made out of whole cloth for the selfish political goals of specific elites.

The Bible: Please Reshelve in the Fantasy Section

As far as the atheist writers are concerned, the Bible is a made-up book of ancient political propaganda fabricated long after the invented events it chronicles. Christopher Hitchens presents a particularly pithy case against the Hebrew Scriptures: "There was no flight from Egypt, no wandering in the desert (let alone for the incredible four-decade length of time mentioned in the Pentateuch), and no dramatic conquest of the Promised Land. It was all, quite simply and very ineptly, made up at a much later date. No Egyptian chronicle mentions this episode either, even in passing, and Egypt was the garrison power in Canaan as well as the Nilotic region at all material times…all the Mosaic myths can be safely and easily discarded."[1] The atheist writers see the Bible as little more than a sloppy attempt at historical fiction, replete with contradictions, repetitions, and anachronisms that accrued over centuries of rewriting and editing. As Dawkins puts it: "To be fair, much of the Bible is not systematically evil but just plain weird, as you would expect of a chaotically cobbled-together anthology of disjointed documents, composed, revised, translated, distorted and 'improved' by hundreds of anonymous authors, editors and copyists, unknown to us and mostly unknown to each other, spanning nine centuries."[2] From the atheists' perspective, the Bible is no different from other ancient texts: "The Bible is a blueprint of in-group morality, complete with instructions for genocide, enslavement of out-groups, and world domination. But the Bible is not evil by virtue of its objectives or even its glorification of murder, cruelty, and rape. Many ancient works do that—*The Iliad*, the Icelandic Sagas, the tales of the ancient Syrians and the inscriptions of the ancient Mayans, for example. But no one is selling *The Iliad* as a foundation for morality. Therein lies the problem. The Bible is sold, and bought, as a guide to how people should live their lives. And it is, by far, the world's all-time best seller."[3] Or as Harris suggests: "The Bible and Qur'an, it seems certain, would find themselves respectfully shelved next to Ovid's *Metamorphoses* and the *Egyptian Book of the Dead*."[4] The atheists conclude that countless generations of Jews, Christians, and Muslims simply have been deluding themselves about this so-called Good Book.[1]

The Stakes of the Debate

After reading James Kugel's *How to Read the Bible*[5] for a second time, I came to understand that it really did matter whether the Bible was considered true or not. Kugel, a biblical scholar at Harvard and Bar-Ilan Universities and an observant Jew, discusses two ways of reading the Bible. The first is how traditional commentators read it, with all of their religious assumptions and oral traditions; the second is how modern biblical scholars read with scientific objectivity.

---

[1] A note on the references in part five. This section attempts to give an overall picture of the historical arguments of the three main schools of thought on the historicity and authorship of the Bible. There are scholars who will perhaps dispute this threefold grouping as being an overly simplified classification. While there are differences between scholars that may place them outside of the neat confines of these three groups, this threefold classification is nevertheless a fairly accurate representation of the general trends among scholars in the field of ancient Israelite history and is used as such. This section has sought to represent in a fairly clear manner the approach to evidence and the arguments of scholars in all three groups. Clearly it is a sample of their arguments and readers are given references to examine the evidence and arguments in greater detail. If you do decide to read these sources be aware that it will mean getting deep into the weeds. Don't say I didn't warn you.

These separate readings, Kugel argues, actually reveal two very different "Bibles." The ancient interpreters created a wise, timeless, and unified work of edification. The biblical critics discovered a compilation of fictitious, politically motivated texts (often contradicting each other). As Kugel writes:

> Far from uncovering "Holy Scripture, as given by divine inspiration to holy prophets"...modern scholarship has actually accomplished exactly the opposite, reducing Scripture to the level of any ordinary, human composition—in fact, arguing that it was in some cases even worse: sloppy, inconsistent, sometimes cynical, and more than occasionally deceitful.[6]

Kugel reviews all the major episodes of the Bible, offering his readers a sample of how modern biblical critics and ancient interpreters read the same texts and came up with separate Bibles. Thus, while the ancient interpreters find a divinely inspired moral tale in the story of Cain and Abel,[7] modern critics discover a politically motivated etiological (narrative of origin) story relating to the Kenites, a group with whom the Israelites were in conflict.[8] Where the ancient interpreters see the story of the golden calf as a tale about idolatry,[9] modern scholars discern an attack on the priesthood written by royal scribes at a much later date.[10] These two Bibles are irreconcilably different, Kugel claims,[11] though both are authoritative. In his view, the Bible of the religious interpreters is the creation of a group of later editors (working mainly in the two centuries BCE). They took the Bible's initial stories (stories modern scholars have finally exposed with all of their political ruses) and transformed them using oral traditions and interpretive assumptions into tales of wisdom.[12]

Many of my religious friends who read Kugel's book were troubled and confused. So was I. If the method of the Bible critics is as sound, scientific, and objective as it is made out to be, then by consequence their reading of the Bible they uncovered must be the true one. It also follows that the Bible of the interpreters, however edifying, must be an artificial facade. What perturbed me with this view was that it made the ancient Jewish commentators come off as crafty deceivers. Could the ancient interpreters really have accomplished such an extreme makeover? Kugel appeared to be arguing that they had made a sumptuous three-course dinner out of kitchen scraps. To me, he was congratulating the charlatans on their creativity. I was bothered deeply by this idea. Other friends did not share my concern, but for a very different reason.

As I learned while chatting with an acquaintance at synagogue one Sabbath morning over chocolate brownies at a collation after prayers, many monotheists today simply skirt this question about the Bible. He told me that he believed God considered certain stories vital because of the values they contained, not because they truly happened.[2] It also hardly matters, he added, echoing Kugel, whether the biblical stories were initially composed for political purposes (even contradictory ones), since the ancient interpreters collected and adjusted them in such a way as to give them lasting moral meaning.[13] Whether Moses or Judah ever existed is irrelevant; what really matters are the lessons that we learn from their lives and apply to our own. Proponents of this point of view rightly note that the Bible is not a history or a science book, but a book of life lessons about our partnership with God and man. For them, God chose the medium of stories, not history, to reveal a higher truth.

There certainly is a lot to say for the notion that certain stories of the Bible need to be pondered by humanity. Nevertheless, I vociferously disagree with those who reduce the Bible to divinely inspired historical fiction. Their argument suffers, ironically, from the same defect as literal creationism: it necessitates a God who deceives. Claiming an omnipotent being who passes off made-up stories as true history is no better than claiming a God who plants bogus dinosaur bones or fake patterns in the earth. Why would an omnibenevolent God play such pranks? In addition, while the first eleven chapters of the Bible beg to be read allegorically, as described in part four, nowhere does the Bible suggest that the stories that follow chapter 11 of Genesis are mythological. Abraham is not a demigod, but a man; the Israelites are not flown out of Egypt on giant winged griffins, and Joshua does not kill his enemies with fire from his nostrils or geothermal flatulence. Nor are the contradictions or repetitions in the Bible so glaring that they turn the book into a senseless patchwork.

Insisting that the Bible can be historically false and still meaningful is also, it turns out, unnecessary. Kugel, like the atheist authors, claims that there is no way around the problem of the Bible's deceitfulness. He cites a

---

[2] This is, of course, Kugel's approach and it is shared by many Christian and Jewish theologians.

consensus from biblical scholars and archaeologists that the events in the Bible (Abraham's life, the Exodus from Egypt, Joshua's conquest, and so forth) didn't happen. He does mention in passing that some believe these fables have grains of truth to them,[14] though he claims that archaeologists mostly dispute that the patriarchs existed, that the Exodus occurred, or that the Israelites conquered Canaan.[3] He agrees with the atheists that the Bible is also filled with vengeance and bloodthirsty destruction.[15] Moreover, he posits that Bible critics are mostly in agreement that the Bible is a compilation of different books written by different groups for their own political purposes.[4] This goes to explain the contradictions, repetition, and variations in Hebrew language that appear in the Bible.

In short, the Bible that the academic critics have discovered is not necessarily a book with which nonspecialists would want to curl up. Kugel would assert, unlike atheists, that the Bible of the interpreters is worth our time and efforts. I thought a long time about whether Kugel could be right, and this set me off on an investigation of the landscape of biblical archaeology and criticism. Had I known that this research would take a year of my life, I would have suggested that a warning label be added to Kugel's book.

In my view, Kugel's confidence in the achievements of modern biblical scholarship, which he calls "extraordinary," is overstated.[16] In fact, as I discovered, *How to Read the Bible* obscures the extent of disagreement in academic scholarship. Upon examination of the scholarship, it becomes clear that archaeologists and biblical critics are far from unanimous and much less certain about which conclusions to draw. As we shall see, some theories once considered authoritative have been dismissed. The cacophony of different voices in biblical criticism and biblical archaeology is close to deafening. The debate is not only far from over; as we shall see, it will likely never end.[17]

---

[3] Kugel mentions the skepticism of archaeologists regarding the patriarchal stories and the Exodus. He seems to personally think the patriarchs are an invention, but the Exodus is based on a kernel of truth. Kugel, *How to Read the Bible*, 101, 231, and 373.

[4] "Even if no absolute proof exists, they say, some theory of different authors is the most logical and parsimonious way to make sense of the evidence. As will be seen on the following pages, some elements of Wellhausen's approach have been modified over time, and of late a serious challenge has been mounted to its chronological ordering of things, but the basic idea of the Documentary Hypothesis has nonetheless survived the sustained scrutiny of scholars over the last century." Kugel, *How to Read the Bible*, 42.

The rest of part five will explore whether the evidence that modern biblical critics and archaeologists bring to bear on the historicity of the Bible really is as definitive as asserted by the atheists. We will deal exclusively with the Hebrew Scriptures. I will leave it to Christian and Muslim experts, far more familiar with their scriptural texts than me, to discuss the historicity of the Christian Scriptures and the Qur'an.

The Bible in 900 Words

The Bible begins with the creation of the world and the concept of mankind. Starting from the twelfth chapter in the Book of Genesis, the Bible describes the story of one people and its relationships with God and other peoples in historical time. At this point, the Bible becomes pretty clear about the time and place of the events and the cast of characters and their actions. Chapter 11 sets the stage for the shift in the narrative. It recounts the creation of a number of peoples specifically in the ancient Near East. Among them, Abraham the Hebrew, a man who came from Ur somewhere in Mesopotamia. God chooses Abraham to father nations and then promises him land for his descendants farther west and south, between the Jordan River and the Mediterranean. But before Abraham's descendants can set up camp, God forces them to leave because of a famine. They initially find refuge in Egypt because the Egyptian leader was once aided by a stray Hebrew, a man called Joseph, who was sold into slavery by his brothers. Yet when a new pharaoh takes the throne, he soon enslaves these previously welcomed guests. After just over two hundred years by the biblical count, God hears the cry of Abraham's oppressed descendants. He enables this people to flee by creating a series of natural disasters that weaken Egypt and decisively challenge the pharaoh's belief in his own divinity.

Abraham's descendants, now a confederacy of tribes, go on to form a people. They are given a set of laws and asked to commit to obeying these laws. This solidifies a covenant between God and the Israelites. The terms of this agreement are simple but profound. The Israelites must abandon idolatry and follow the laws God has revealed to them in order to enjoy the blessings of a good life. No sacrificial bribes or flattery will ensure prosperity, but rather only a just society. They are then commanded to conquer the land promised to their forefathers and slay the Canaanite inhabitants who refuse to flee. They are, however, forbidden from conquering any other land, since God has granted these lands to other peoples. Further, their lease on the land is conditional, just as it had been for the Canaanites who inhabited it. If they do good by following the laws, they will keep the land and prosper. If they do evil, they will lose it and sink into misery. The conquest of the land by Joshua and the Israelites is described in the Book of Joshua, the first book after the Five Books of Moses, which we refer to as the Bible.

The prophetic books that follow the Bible describe the Israelites' choices, both those of the leaders and those of the people. Over the course of about 150 years after Joshua's conquest of the land (as told in the Book of Judges), things go downhill—and fast. The Israelites make evil choices by ignoring the laws, and some of their leaders are corrupt. These bad choices weaken their society and leave them vulnerable to wars with their neighbors, the Moabites, the Amalekites, the Midianites, and the Philistines. Yet every so often, a good judge and/or leader such as Gideon, Samson, or Deborah comes along to guide the people.

The Israelites, however, protest that simply having judges is not enough. They need a king. Although this request reflects an abdication of collective responsibility, God grants it. Samuel, the prophet at the time, anoints the first king. Over the next one hundred years, the prophetic books describe the challenges of the Israelite kings. David faces enemies within the court and outside the Israelite borders. The kings themselves also make poor choices. Rebuked by prophets like Nathan and Gad, David faces the consequences of his actions. So too does his son, Solomon.

The Book of Kings then describes the breakup of the Israelite kingdom into two and the kings' actions in each land. We read of the kings' poor marriage choices, like Ahab's union with the evil Jezebel. We also learn about the upper classes' abuse of the poor and the rebukes they receive from prophets such as Amos. Other peoples are also held to account. The prophet Jonah warns the inhabitants of the Assyrian capital, Nineveh, to repent. They are spared; however, not long after, Assyrian leaders and their people again make bad choices. The Assyrians invaded the Northern Kingdom, itself steeped in idolatry and injustice. Its inhabitants were deported, never to return—these are the so-called Ten Lost Tribes. The Assyrians also get a swift interview with their maker as they are replaced by the Babylonians just a generation later. The Kingdom of Judah continues to stand its ground, but its inhabitants and leaders stray from God's laws. Some kings, like Hezekiah and Josiah, seek to reform the country and teach God's laws, which had been all but forgotten. These valiant attempts nevertheless come too late and are not ambitious enough. Jeremiah the Prophet, who had spoken truth to power and warned the kings, witnesses the exile of the Israelites to Babylon and the destruction of the First Temple, built by Solomon. Babylon also falls, as Jeremiah predicted, and Persia becomes the new empire in the neighborhood. Under Persian rule, the Jews are granted license to return to build a second temple and reestablish a kingdom. The Second Temple Judean state had its share of bad leaders and challenges, first under Greek and then Roman rule. The last of the prophets, Haggai and Malachi, wrote during this time and their words mark the end the Jewish biblical canon.

The stories of the Bible are meant to be a lesson for all peoples. They focus on the Israelites, but they describe moral dilemmas all people face.

Yet, did these events really happen?

CHAPTER 25

The Case of the Mysterious Bible

Imagine you're on vacation in a Middle Eastern country and are mistaken for Indiana Jones. You and your companion enter a *souk* (market). Casually perusing some supposedly antique items in one of the shops, you are beckoned by the merchant to view something very, very special in the back. Intriguingly, he unlocks first a cabinet and then a box within that cabinet. Carefully, the merchant removes wrapped plastic file folders and, with painstaking patience, theatrically withdraws the contents and whispers, "Come, look. Papyrus with ancient inscriptions…" Your companion, who, of course, studied ancient Semitic languages in graduate school, peruses the papyrus. "Dear father," she translates the first, concluding "…Your Loving Son, Isaac." Now the second, "Dear father," with its conclusion, "…Your Loving Son, Ishmael." These letters purport to be from the biblical Isaac and Ishmael, who have apparently each written a letter to their father, Abraham, about the blessings they received from him. The merchant tells you that he is sure that these letters are each about 3,800 years old. "Of course, I had never planned on selling them, but…" Because of his need to raise cash for his daughter's dowry, he is willing to part with the priceless documents for a far too modest sum. And, after all, you look like a very nice couple who would appreciate the value of the papyri. As you make your exit, turning slowly and then picking up the pace, the merchant pursues, calling after you,

"Perhaps a shard from the broken tablets of the Ten Commandments… in my garage…might be of interest?"

Such findings would answer the question of whether the Bible is a lie written by an imposter, were they not assuredly forgeries. Yet, does the fact that these objects cannot possibly exist cast doubt on the existence of Abraham, Isaac, Ishmael, or the Exodus? Does their absence confirm that prophesy is a ruse? The case of the mysterious Bible presents a double puzzle. The first mystery is whether the Bible is a false report or not. Does it accurately recount actual events (again, what scholars call historicity), or semi-historical or completely fictional events? The second mystery is whether the Five Books of Moses were written by their stated author for their stated purpose (again, what scholars call authorship). Was it authored by the divinely inspired prophet Moses for the purpose of teaching humans about good and evil as tradition indicates, or rather, was it a literary concoction written with political objectives? The two questions are linked since the greater its historical accuracy, the greater the legitimacy of the Bible's own claim to truth. Conversely, the more numerous its historical errors, the more it contradicts its own claims. So, what kind of evidence for the Bible's historicity and authorship can we hope for and how should it be weighed? We shall begin with the question of historicity.

The Evidence in the Case

Scholars, like good detectives, need various types of evidence to evaluate the historicity of the Bible. Over the past 150 years, archaeologists have been investigating whether the Bible is historically accurate. They conduct digs all over the Near East. They seek evidence of settlements, agricultural practices, burials, remnants of destruction, and the like. Their goal is to use their findings to reconstruct the nature of the economy, society, and politics of the region. In some cases, the remains are plentiful; in other cases, there is nothing.

Archaeologists then often check whether this data matches other sources for the history of the region. They may do so alone or cooperate with historians, who form another expert unit in the investigative team. These other sources include inscriptions (usually royal), letters (often government), steles (like official plaques), annals (histories of kings), religious documents (such as myths, spells, rituals, and epics about heroes), and administrative documents (temple accounts, for example). Unlike archaeological remains that are chance remnants of people's actions, these sources are deliberate human creations. As such, they may not be completely or even partially true and must be tested. Egyptian letters, for example, are verified against what we know from archaeological digs, other Egyptian sources and even non-Egyptian sources. Whether examining the Bible, an Egyptian relief, or a Moabite inscription, historians do not assume that one source is inherently more reliable than another. That being said, the degree of accuracy varies depending on the type of source. Take the following contemporary example. A college student is more likely to bend the truth in a letter asking mom for money than in writing a grocery list or, more seriously, in composing a criminal witness affidavit. The motive for writing the texts and the penalty for lying are different in each case. The type of source thus impacts reliability. Yet, historians differ themselves on how skeptically one should approach various written and visual sources.

The evidence scholars accumulate for any question, as in a police investigation, can be strong or weak. It can be direct or indirect, i.e., circumstantial or corroborating. Scholars are most satisfied (and often thrilled) when they find direct evidence for an event or for an author from another source, whether it be archaeological or written. Such direct evidence is the strongest support for verifying the historicity of the Bible's account, or any other account for that matter.

In the absence of direct evidence, scholars rely on indirect evidence. Does the description of the biblical text match up with the evidence we have about the culture, politics, and society of the time? Indirect evidence cannot prove that an event occurred and is therefore weaker than direct evidence, but it can demonstrate *plausibility*. For example, in the absence of direct evidence, a contemporary Irish American, let's call him Patrick O'Leary, could plausibly but not definitely claim that his ancestors were Irish famine victims if the indirect, i.e., circumstantial evidence matched. To wit: (1) O'Leary's ancestors arrived in the US in the late 1840s, (2) they lived in western Ireland, and (3) they had an Irish name used during the period of the famine. By contrast, a letter recounting the life of slaves on an Alabama plantation cannot be plausibly dated to the 1970s.

I will argue that for belief in God to be rational, it is sufficient to offer evidence of the plausibility of the Bible's account. *It is only irrational to believe something occurred if it is not only unproven, but also implausible.* In order to do this, there are actually two questions about the case of the mysterious Bible that have to be answered: (1) Are the accounts of events as described in the biblical stories *plausible* given what we know now about the time, people, and places they describe? (2) If the events described in the Bible match our evidence for the period and place, are there any groups of people writing at a later time that could have had sufficient knowledge of earlier epochs to write accurate historical fiction? The task seems straightforward enough, so why all the fuss?

The Stalemate

One might suppose that since archaeology, philology, and history are "rational" sciences, the case would be long solved. A bit of hard work should make it easy to ascertain whether the Bible accurately describes the past. With forensics and cross-checked data, the case should be closed and scholars should be undivided. Yet, this is clearly not what is going on. There are several reasons for the impasse.

The first has to do with the quality of the evidence. The more distant the history that we examine, the less of both direct and indirect evidence we possess. This is true for individuals, such as the personalities described in the Bible, and even for entire groups. Further, the evidence that we do have is often difficult to interpret. Indeed, consider what is left: crusts—rarely rolls—of papyrus or parchment in ancient tongues, scratched rocks written in obscure languages, pottery shards, bones, various other broken and decomposed materials, and the remnants of buildings. All of these are open to multiple interpretations. Imagine recreating your great-great-great grandparents' lives from the few bits and pieces of the objects that they used in their daily routines, which haphazardly remained in an abandoned and forgotten garbage dump or were discarded in the corner of their long-buried basement that has had two houses built over it.

The second issue is that dating evidence is also tricky. If all we have are a few papyri "crusts" in a long-lost, but now partly-deciphered language, how can we know how long this language was around? The evidence also can't tell us for sure if this language was spoken at the time that the objects date from. Maybe the evidence was created in one period, but describes another. For example, if an archaeologist from the fiftieth century were to discover only one blues record from the 1930s, how could she know whether people still listened to the blues in 2018 or listened to it only in the 1930s? Further, how could she know when the music itself first came on the scene?

Last comes the question of which data is sufficient to close the case. Here scholars also take different positions.[1] Some argue that the historicity of the Bible can only be proven by direct evidence (a mention in another ancient document). They claim further that a lack of direct evidence is itself a form of evidence against historicity. This is a tricky business. The validity of arguments based on the absence of evidence depends on one's view of how much evidence happened to withstand the winds of history and nature. In either case, it is a hypothetical endeavor. Others claim that these criteria are too strict. They emphasize that the historicity of the Bible can be verified through indirect and circumstantial evidence. They argue that the absence of evidence does not necessarily mean an event did not occur. It can mean that the evidence is lost (many environments are not conducive to preservation) or was even deliberately destroyed. For example, the Egyptians destroyed most of the evidence of the reign of the pharaoh Akhenaten so as to erase him from the record. I am in the camp that believes it is specious to claim that the historicity of documents such as the Bible must be always proven with direct evidence, whose modern existence depends on the vagaries of preservation and the behavior of ancient peoples.

As a result of these issues, scholars have come up with a wide range of views on the historicity of the Bible, though they can broadly be grouped into three camps. These include the so-called maximalists, who consider the central events in the Bible to be historically plausible based on words in the text, archaeology, and external evidence from other neighboring cultures, despite a lack of direct evidence. Another group are the so-called centrists, who consider *trace aspects* of the biblical story of these events to be historically plausible or true, but do not believe that the Bible describes them accurately and that there are later substantial additions and embellishments. The final group are the minimalists, who focus on the lack of direct evidence for the events of the Bible as proof that they are much later inventions with little or no historical basis. While various scholars fall into one or the other camp, other factors play a role, as well.

Cold Facts, Hot Politics

Unfortunately, the debate about the historicity and authorship of the Bible is not just about complicated evidence; a distinctly political tinge has accrued to the conversation. This politicization was not inevitable, but it does exist. Certainly, one can believe or not in the veracity of the Bible regardless of one's views about the current geopolitical situation in the Middle East. Nevertheless, there appears to be a link between one's political views and one's trust in the historicity of the Bible, particularly among the minimalists.

Most minimalists, for example, closely align with Palestinian nationalist claims, a political position that is best served were the historical link between ancient Israel and modern Israel to be a fiction. In 1991, Niels Peter Lemche published *The Canaanites and Their Land: The Tradition of the Canaanites*,[2] in which he rejects the history of Israelites as the central subject of historical studies of the region. Similarly, Philip R. Davies' 1992 book, *In Search of "Ancient Israel"*;[3] Keith Whitelam's 1996 book, *The Invention of Ancient Israel: The Silencing of Palestinian History*;[4] and Thomas L. Thompson's 1999 book, *The Mythic Past: Biblical Archaeology and the Myth of Israel*[5] also argue that ancient Israel did not exist as described in the Bible and, as a consequence, modern Jews have no right to claim Israel as their ancient national homeland. Some scholars have accused minimalists of "erasing" ancient Israel.[6]

The minimalists in turn accuse the maximalists of writing history to bolster modern Israeli nationalist or other religious claims. Most centrists and maximalists uphold ancient Israel as a real historical entity, some are openly Jewish or Christian, and some support Israel in the Israeli-Arab conflict. This, too, is clear from the titles of some books by maximalist authors—Iain Provan, V. Philips Long, and Tremper Longman's *A Biblical History of Israel* (2003)[7] or Kenneth Kitchen's *On the Reliability of the Old Testament* (2003),[8] or James Karl Hoffmeier's *Ancient Israel in Sinai: The Evidence for the Authenticity of the Wilderness Tradition* (2005).[9] The more cautious, though non-minimalist, position of centrist scholars include William G. Dever's *What Did the Biblical Writers Know, and When Did They Know It? What Archaeology Can Tell us about the Reality of Ancient Israel* (2001)[10] and Amihai Mazar, Israel Finkelstein, and editor Brian B. Schmidt's *The Quest for the Historical Israel: Debating Archaeology and the History of Early Israel* (2007).[11]

Political considerations also affect the standards of evidence scholars are willing to accept as proof of the Bible's historicity. Minimalists attack the very notion of plausibility when it comes to the Bible and will only accept direct proof of historicity.[12] In their view, confirming that the details of Madame Bovary's life are true to nineteenth-century France does not make the novel a biography. In some cases, minimalists even dismiss direct proof, asserting that these must be forgeries. Many centrists and maximalists argue that minimalists demand archaeological proof for anything in the Bible, but broadly accept non-biblical sources without any third-party confirmation.[13] It is as though the minimalists believe that the Hebrews were liars, but the Egyptians and Assyrians were pedantically precise with historical details. While just about all scholars claim neutrality, there is the risk of confirmation bias by scholars on all sides of the debate.

You Be the Judge

In the following chapter, I will offer a sample of the range of scholars' arguments about the historicity of biblical events and biblical authorship and let readers decide for themselves which arguments are most convincing.[14] Obviously, this is only a brief survey of a massive field. Curious readers can peruse the sources in the endnotes.

One final note: the following pages in which the various positions are outlined might seem like three-sided tennis to some readers. The minimalists serve to the centrists, who volley to the maximalists, or vice versa. In fact, it is a subtly even more complex volley, as each side uses different rules. So, the service box and baseline are vastly different for each of the three sides. Since the minimalists give little credence to indirect evidence, the reader will get a bit more material from the centrists and maximalists.

CHAPTER 26

Abraham, Isaac, and Jacob— Our Imaginary Friends

Minimalist scholars claim that the patriarchal narratives are stories that were invented at a later period. In unison with all archaeologists, minimalists point out that there is no direct external evidence for the existence of the patriarchs. However, they also dispute the contextual evidence that would make the patriarchal stories historically plausible. According to Thomas L. Thompson, nothing in the patriarchal stories indicates that they are based on real events from the period c. 1900–1500 BCE (the biblical time frame for the narratives).[1] Citing evidence from non-biblical ancient Near Eastern sources, especially from the cuneiform archives recovered at the ancient sites of Nuzi (Iraq) and Mari (Syria), the minimalists say, for example, that the names of the patriarchs are not specific to the second millennium BCE since they were also used as late as the neo-Assyrian Empire (c. 900–600 BCE).[2] They also note that the social customs described in the patriarchal stories, such as a barren wife providing a female slave to her husband, as Sarah did with Hagar, are likewise not unique to the second millennium BCE time frame.[3]

In addition, minimalists point to anachronisms in the text. For example, they claim that camels, which are mentioned in reference to Abraham, were not used by people in Canaan in the second millennium BCE.[4] For the minimalists, the references to camels turn the Bible into some sort of "Flintstones" type of outdated parody, as though Abraham and Jacob were said to be riding dinosaurs. Further, the Philistines, who are mentioned in the patriarchal stories, did not inhabit the area in the early second millennium.[5] The mention of such later neighbors is for the minimalists the kind of dead giveaway typical of the 1959 Hollywood movie *Ben-Hur*, in which characters allegedly wore wristwatches. Finally, they argue that a number of the sites, especially towns, mentioned in the narratives did not exist until later in the first millennium BCE.[6] Indeed, they say that the general patriarchal depiction of Canaan as a whole does not fit the second millennium period. The whole matter is akin to an Italian renaissance painting depicting Mary and Jesus in Florentine merchant attire relaxing on the lush grass in a sunlit Tuscan landscape. Therefore, there is no reason to believe that the text draws from actual stories from the time period it indicates. Finally, minimalists argue that the exaggerated ages of the patriarchs, among other details, place the stories squarely in the realm of founder myths rather than history.

Campfire Stories

Some centrist scholars view the patriarchal narratives as later stories that partially draw on earlier material. As do the minimalists, the centrist scholars agree there is no direct external evidence for the patriarchs. Some noted biblical archaeologists, such as Israel Finkelstein and Amihai Mazar, agree with the minimalists that a number of cities, peoples, and other details (such as the aforementioned camels) are anachronisms in the patriarchal narratives.[7] Nevertheless, Mazar, though not Finkelstein, also claims that there are too many indications of second millennium details in the text to argue that it is totally a first millennium invention. He mentions, for example, that the Bible's depiction of Canaan as a wealthy urban region only fits the second millennium reality.[8] These parallels are simply too numerous to be ignored.[9] It would be like arguing that American stories about Thanksgiving and the *Mayflower* are total fabrications with no historical basis, as opposed to heavily embellished stories of actual events. He also points to the Amorite origin of the names of the patriarchs as another indication of the story's second millennium origin,[10] since the Amorites were important figures in the second, not the first, millennium, even if they still existed later. For Mazar, the patriarchal narrative includes too many second millennium details to be viewed as pure myth.[11] Nevertheless, for Mazar, these stories also contain anachronisms that indicate they were edited and added to at a later period. He also notes that even if these stories contain kernels of historical truth, this does not prove the patriarchs were real historical figures.[12]

The Photo Is Faded but You Can Make Them Out

Maximalist historians argue that patriarchal stories best fit the second millennium. They could not have been invented later, though they were likely edited at a later time. Maximalists agree that there is no direct external evidence for the existence of the patriarchs. Nevertheless, they dispute many of the interpretations of the indirect evidence proposed by minimalists and centrist scholars. Kenneth Kitchen, for one, argues that the patriarchal names were most popular during the second millennium, even if they were in continued use later.[13] Aldwyn may rank among the most common Old English names still in use today, but to say it is as popular today as it was in the Middle Ages is a stretch. Maximalists also claim that the social customs depicted in the patriarchal stories, as well as in extra-biblical sources, were most popular in the second millennium. As an example, Kitchen points to Abraham's treaties and covenants as consistent with similar texts from the ancient Near East during the second millennium.[14] Similar to Mazar, the maximalists also argue that the patriarchal picture of Canaanite society only suits the second millennium period.[15] The pharaoh's residence in the East Delta during the period of 1970–1540 BCE coincides with the biblical time frame given for Abraham and Sarah's travels in Egypt, but not later.[16] The city or town of Nahor, which figures prominently in the stories of Isaac and Jacob finding wives (Genesis 24:10), seems to have flourished from about 2000 BCE, then disintegrated around 1300 BCE, only to reemerge around 700 BCE under another name.[17] The maximalists argue that the fact that the Bible gets these details right, as verified by outside sources, offers strong positive support for its veracity. A modern parallel would be someone attempting to authenticate letters purported to be from the California Gold Rush and finding that the wages mentioned in the letters indeed matched the wages that companies were advertising in newspapers at the time of the Gold Rush.

Maximalists also strenuously dispute the so-called "smoking gun"[1] anachronism in the patriarchal story—yes, those camels. Kitchen draws attention to two pieces of evidence from historical Canaan: a figure of a kneeling camel holding two jars in a tomb from the thirteenth century BCE, and a camel jaw found in a tomb from c. 1900–1550 BCE, suggesting that domesticated camels were not unknown, but rather a luxury item in the area. Consider the following parallel: future archaeologists examine the remains of Los Angeles and discover a few scraps of Maserati or Bugatti cars, not as many as the scraps of Fords and Toyotas, but then the former two comprise a quite rare portion of the modern-day auto fleet (even in Hollywood). Finally, Kitchen claims that other anachronisms in the text, such as mention of the Philistines and names of certain cities, can be explained by later editorial changes, just as we New Yorkers no longer refer to ourselves as living in New Amsterdam.[18] Though the patriarchal texts accurately described non-Canaanite Aegean peoples who lived in Canaan during the time, according to Kitchen, a later editor simply renamed them Philistines so that they would be recognizable to the later audience. Thus, while none of the maximalists claim that the patriarchal stories are specifically confirmable, they find them plausible enough.[19]

That the maximalists accept the plausibility of the patriarchal narratives does not mean that these accounts did not include poetic license. One of the factors that has led readers to view the patriarchs and matriarchs as mythical rather than historical is their purported ages in the Bible. In relation to this problem, some readers have attempted to harmonize the very long lives by arguing that the Mesopotamian number system probably revolved around a six-decimal system. According to this logic, it makes sense to divide all the ages from chapter 12 onward in Genesis by two and then they seem to be compatible with normal life spans. This strikes me as possible, but arbitrary as well.

The real meaning of the patriarchal life spans might be both more straightforward and more poignant. As we described in part two, from chapter 12 of Genesis onward, the Bible purports to describe real historical events while also using literary license and poetic tropes to do so. A variety of commentators note that all of the ages used in Genesis

---

[1] Yes, that is a pun. Those of us of a certain age who recall the advertising by Camel cigarettes will get this. For everyone else, just keep reading.

are multiples of five with the sacred number seven added occasionally for special situations. If you check the text, you will see that everything significant happens when the main characters are multiples of five years old or have seven tossed in the mix. Abraham leaves Haran when he is seventy-five, Isaac is born when Abraham is one hundred, and he dies at 175. Sarah was ninety when Isaac was born and dies at 127. The text itself points out that there is something formulaic about Sarah's age, as she is described as "100 years, plus 20 years, plus 7 years, these are the years of Sarah's life." (Genesis 23:1) All the significant events in Isaac's life also follow the five-year multiple system. Isaac marries Rebecca at forty, Jacob and Esau are born when he is sixty, Esau marries when Isaac is one hundred and dies at 180, and Jacob descends to Egypt at 130 and dies at 147, getting the extra seven for significance. Joseph also follows this template, being sold into slavery at ten plus seven years, rising to power at thirty years, and dying at 110. Finally, the overall ages of the patriarchs follow an interesting ascending/descending pattern that most certainly had literary significance to the ancient reader.[2]

Person	Life Span	Factors
Abraham	175	7×5^2
Isaac	180	5×6^2
Jacob	147	3×7^2

The Bible underlined these sorts of deep numerical connections when the text was trying to make a point of extra significance, such as when Sarah passed away and Rebecca was her rightful successor. The Bible gives Sarah's lifespan as 120 (a multiple of five) plus one seven for 127, but it indicates that Rebecca's age is 134, or that same 120 plus *two* sevens, or one more than Sarah, as Rebecca is Sarah's successor. Additionally, the number five itself could be viewed more as we moderns would use the terms "several," "a few," "many," "a lot," "numerous," "not insubstantial," or other such expressions. The ancients did not keep track of numbers in the precise ways that we are capable of doing so today, and

---

[2] This chart comes from Nahum M. Sarna, *Understanding Genesis* (New York: Schocken Books, 1966), 84. My understanding of the pattern of the ages of the patriarchs and matriarchs was also aided by a private conversation with Rabbi Hayyim Angel in August 2015.

a text that attempted to do so would have been quite alien to the reader. So, these patriarchal and matriarchal ages had a literary significance well beyond the isolated arithmetic through which we moderns attempt to analyze the text. We should never forget L. P. Hartley's famous statement that "the past is a foreign country; they do things differently there."

CHAPTER 27

So What Happened Next, Really?

No Exodus

Minimalists claim that the Exodus is a fantasy. They find no direct archaeological evidence—not for the Israelites' slavery, nor for their flight from Egypt, nor for forty years of sojourn in the Sinai desert.[1] Are we really to believe that two million wandering Jews would not have left any trace in the Sinai? The discrepancy between the evidence and the narrative is so great as to be ludicrous. Minimalists aver that the well-documented evidence of Semites living in Egypt and working on construction projects is no proof that these people were related to the Israelites.[2] It is like saying that just because a National League Central Division team wins the World Series, doesn't mean the Chicago Cubs won.[1] In fact, taking things one step further, where's the proof that Israelites existed at all as an ethnic group before the first millennium BCE?[3] Minimalists also tout the opinion of Egyptologist and archaeologist Donald Redford that the journey of the Israelites from Egypt through the Sinai desert would better fit the period of the first millennium.[4] Redford thinks the place name of Ramses, where the Israelites are said to have worked for the pharaoh, is an anachronism.[5] Again, minimalists find no proof that a people later

---

[1] I write this as I proudly wear my Cubs 2016 World Series Champions hat!

called the Israelites lived, slaved, and escaped from Egypt, nor is there anything in the Exodus that a first millennium writer could not have known. On this basis, the minimalists simply dismiss the story of the Exodus as myth. The good magician Moses fights the evil Egyptian magicians in a run-of-the-mill plot as common to ancient sagas as bad jokes and ill-fated romances are to second-rate American sitcoms.

Rumor Has It, Some Semite Slaves May Have Slipped Away

Centrist scholars consider the Exodus to be either sheer invention or based on much more modest historical processes. Israel Finkelstein reiterates many of the minimalist views and adds that Egyptian soldiers manned many forts in the Sinai at the time and could have doubtless driven the Israelites back, another fact to poke a hole in the story.[6] Unlike the minimalists, however, he does not discount the option that the Exodus story might very well include memories of an expulsion of Semitic populations from Egypt, possibly the Hyksos, who were thrown out in the sixteenth century BCE.[7]

In contrast to Finkelstein, Mazar accords more weight to second millennium parallels in the story. The Israelites' settlement in Goshen accords with what we know of communities of Semites who lived in that area during most of the second millennium.[8] Canaanites moved into Egypt during this period, though the Egyptians kept them away from Upper Egypt. Among these Canaanites, the Hyksos not only colonized Lower Egypt, but also ruled it during the Thirteenth and Fourteenth Dynasties, effectively creating the Fifteenth Dynasty (seventeenth and sixteenth centuries BCE). They were then expelled from Egypt in the mid-sixteenth century by the pharaoh Ahmose I and sent fleeing across the Sinai into Canaan. While scholars once hypothesized that the Hyksos might be the Israelites, few still believe this today. Nevertheless, for Mazar, the history of the Hyksos lends plenty of credence to the plausibility of a Semitic group establishing themselves in Egypt in just the manner the Israelites are said to have done, and then leaving.[9]

Mazar also considers it possible that the story of the Israelites' participation in building projects in Ramses reflects the historically documented participation of Semitic populations in the building of Pi-Ramses in the thirteenth century BCE.[10] In fact, Ramses II, later known as Ramses the

Great, was a known megalomaniac who significantly increased the scale and number of building projects in the area. He not only covered the land of Egypt from the Delta to Nubia as no pharaoh had before, but he even put cartouches of his name on buildings he himself did not build![11] He also established the capital Pi-Ramses, named after himself. Stalin (and many other autocrats with a similar inclination to modesty) would later copy the congenial idea of naming a city after yours truly. Ramses' building spree finds echoes in the Bible (Exodus 5), which describes how the burden of building for the slaves increased dramatically.

Mazar also notes Egyptian sources from the period that describe slave rebellions and escapes.[12] Fleeing slaves all seem to have followed a certain road called the Road of the Horus, which led from the Eastern Nile to Gaza and resembles the Road of the Philistines described in the Bible, which the Israelites were deliberately told to avoid. Since the Egyptians controlled most of Canaan during the time of the Exodus, it made sense that the fleeing slaves would not want to confront the Egyptian military presence along the common route from the two areas but would, as the Bible suggests, take a circuitous route. Such parallelisms suggest that the story is rooted in the experience of West Semitic slaves who fled from Egypt though the Sinai in the thirteenth century.[13] Mazar further suggests that, if the identification of the "Yam Suf," often incorrectly translated as the Red Sea, is in fact the Sea of Reeds located close to the Suez Canal, then it could corroborate the geographical plausibility of the Exodus story.[14]

Despite such parallels, Mazar stops short of concluding that the Exodus occurred as described in the Bible. He is bothered by the large number of people said to have been involved.[15] He also mentions several anachronisms, particularly the Kingdom of Edom, which did not exist until after the time of the Exodus, as further indications that the story did not happen as described in the Bible. Nevertheless, Mazar believes the Exodus story contains memories of real events.[16] The biblical authors simply took tremendous liberties with a modest memory of escape, not unlike the descendants of the Pullman Railroad strikers who describe their ancestors' actions as the greatest workers' revolution of all time. (It really was a pivotal event in American labor relations for its time, but not necessarily the most important ever.) From Mazar's perspective, groups of escaped Semitic slaves could have joined the Israelite confederacy, carrying with them memories of their experience with dashes of embellishment.[17]

Other scholars, such as Avraham Faust, claim that the story of the Exodus became a founding narrative for a mix of people who likely made up what would become ancient Israel because of the Egyptian dominance of Canaan, which lasted until 1150 BCE.[18] As a result, the Exodus story's anti-Egyptian focus appealed even to those whose ancestors had not been part of the group who left Egypt. Due to intermarriage, many of the mixed group could also count an ancestor who had been among those who originally fled Egypt.[19] Compare this to how the story of the *Mayflower* became a founding American narrative, even though the ancestors of most Americans found their way to America very differently.[2]

As Reported by Cecil B. Demille with Some Swagger

Maximalists consider the story of the Exodus as described in the Bible to be plausible because of details contained therein that, they argue, could not have been known by a later writer. They agree with minimalists and centrists that there is no direct evidence of the Israelites' stay in Egypt.[20] However, they argue that the mud and humidity in the Eastern Delta, along with other wilderness conditions, caused most of the non-permanent material culture from the journey to have been destroyed. Pharaoh, moreover, exerted unilateral control over the scribal classes (far more than autocrats today, who have known only mixed success in controlling the internet), and certainly, if anything, the pharaohs had personal interest in burying any record of this demoralizing defeat.[21] Maximalists claim that too many details about the setting of the story and its protagonists relate too precisely to mid-second millennium conditions in Egypt for the story to be an outside invention. Two cities that the Israelites are reported to have built, Pithom and Ramses, are likely to be references to the Egyptian cities of P(r)'Atum and P(r)R'mss. Both suit the biblical time frame of the Exodus, particularly since Ramses was abandoned by 1100 BCE.[22] In addition, the biblical description of the taskmasters and

---

[2] Kugel mentions the comparison, though unlike Katz, he says that it is used as a pious myth rather than as the history of an expanding number of America's inhabitants through intermarriage. Kugel, *How to Read The Bible*, 232.

the foreman; the use of bricks, targets, and quotas; and hard service are consistently attested to in Egyptian depictions and documents.[23]

The covenant at Sinai resembles Hittite treaties that established a contract, or covenant, between two kings based on mutual obligation, and which are numerous for the period of 1200 BCE.[24] Maximalists also claim that the ten plagues could have been natural occurrences, as I have described in part four. According to the maximalists, it might have been one thing for a fiction writer to list ten plagues, but to get them generally in such a scientifically plausible order would be astounding.[25] Likewise, if the "Red Sea" is properly understood as the Reed Sea, the story is plausible. There are two lake systems, the Ballah Lakes and the Bitter Lakes (where the Sea of Reeds exists), which the Israelites would have had to cross to get to Sinai. The Ballah Lakes were connected to the Mediterranean in the second millennium BCE by canals and the Bitter Lakes were connected by canals to the Gulf of Suez three thousand years ago, as opposed to the present sixteen-kilometer (7.25-mile) separation.[3] A transformation from a marshy area covered by water to dry land could have taken place rapidly, given the right tidal and other accommodating conditions.[26] Compare the crossing of the Sea of Reeds to a theoretical journey over ice from Milwaukee to Chicago. Generally, this is not possible, and if a reader 3,500 years from now studied a text describing such a journey, they could be confused about the names of both Chicago and Milwaukee, which might have changed over time. Due to changes in climate, as well, by then both cities could conceivably be under Lake Michigan or miles away from its ports and shores. Nevertheless, a future reader would still have to acknowledge such an ice crossing as plausible, particularly if she had ever experienced a Midwestern polar vortex. Kitchen also disputes Redford's view of the travels of the Israelites. Kitchen claims that their itinerary best matches second millennium conditions and locations in the area.[27]

Maximalists turn to philology to resolve a long-standing problem in the Book of Exodus. They share the centrists' skepticism about the extraordinary number of Israelites who left Egypt. Indeed, the logistics

---

[3] Kitchen considers a crossing anywhere between the Ballah and Bitter Lakes plausible. Kitchen, *On the Reliability*, 260–263. Hoffmeier considers the crossing to have occurred in the Ballah Lakes just north of the Bitter Lakes, which were also connected to the Mediterranean in the second millennium. Hoffmeier, *Ancient Israel in Sinai*, 108, figure 5.

The Maximalist Reconstruction of the Exodus & Sinai Desert Wanderings

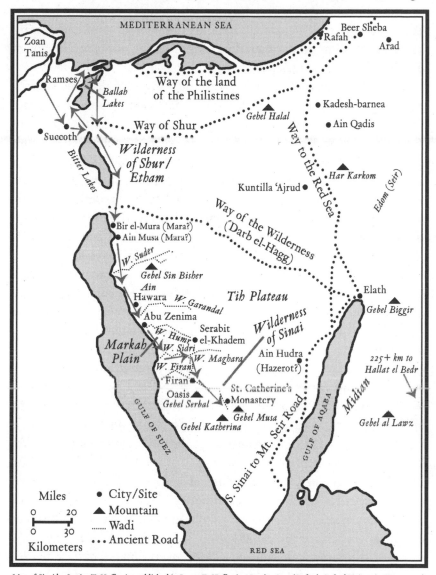

Map of Sinai by Jessica T. Hoffmeier published in James K. Hoffmeier, *Israel in Sinai* (Oxford: Oxford University Press, 2005)

of the Israelites' journey, the modes of communication depicted, and the activities of the Israelites described are all just too difficult to comprehend for two million people. Nor are maximalists alone in questioning these figures. Many others, including those who are not biblical scholars, have posed the same question.

Recently, I learned that one famous individual, Fidel Castro, chomped on many a cigar perplexed by this very question. On a Shabbat a few years ago, I was waiting with a friend for lunch in the lobby of the King David Hotel in Jerusalem. In walked Rabbi Yisrael Lau, a former chief rabbi of the State of Israel from 1993–2003, who by chance sat near us and engaged us in conversation. Luckily for us, Rabbi Lau's lunchtime companions were quite late, so the conversation went on for some time. Inspired by this encounter, I decided to buy Rabbi Lau's autobiography. In the book, he describes a 1994 visit to Cuba, where he was welcomed as the *gran rabino de Israel*. Rabbi Lau was scheduled to meet Fidel Castro at 10:00 p.m.—the leader was known for his late nights—and, for the next three hours, the two conversed on a wide range of topics. At one point during the discussion, Castro exclaimed that he had a question to ask the rabbi that had bothered him for a very long time: How was it that the Bible describes that seventy Israelites went down to Egypt and that, some four hundred years later, six hundred thousand Israelites left?

He continued. Assuming that there were thirty-five couples and rapid reproduction, this was still numerically very difficult to imagine. Rabbi Lau responded that the ancient rabbis had also been bothered by this question and had solved it by means of the legend that each Israelite woman gave birth to six babies at a time. This agitated Castro, who immediately checked the arithmetic—without a calculator—and promptly proclaimed that even this solution did not work. Rabbi Lau recognized the seriousness of his questioning and said that another verse explained the numeric discrepancy: "Moreover, a mixed multitude went up with them." (Exodus 12:38) Instantly, as Rabbi Lau wrote, "Castro gave a sigh of relief, as if I had lifted a burden of many years from his shoulders."[4] While Rabbi Lau provided the traditional answers to the

---

[4] Israel Meir Lau, *Out of the Depths: The Story of a Child of Buchenwald Who Returned Home at Last* (New York: Sterling, 2011), 327. The whole story can be found on pages 326–327.

question, which apparently satisfied the Cuban leader, maximalists try to resolve this issue philologically and more convincingly.

In the maximalist view, we have simply misunderstood the word *aleph*, which is translated as "thousand" in every edition of the Bible. Because the Bible did not contain vowels until Masoretic scholars added them in the Middle Ages, certain words would refer to more than one thing. In the case of the Exodus account, the word written with the letters *a l ph* could refer to *aleph* (1,000) or to *aluph*, which means leader or chieftain or squad. Maximalists argue that reading the word as *aluph* rather than as *aleph* transforms our understanding of the Exodus story. Rather than having to account for six hundred thousand men and their wives and children, this alternative reading leads to six hundred squads of around fifteen men, which would add up to around nine to ten thousand men.[28] This number makes consistent sense throughout the text. The assembling of all the folk, the lack of long lines in bringing sacrifices at the modest traveling tabernacle, and the pace of the Israelites' travels all demonstrate a lower population estimate. Pharaoh certainly would have needed to deploy more than six hundred chariots to subdue two million Israelites. If such a reading resolves so many issues, why is it new? The reason has to do with the difficulty of the text.

Consider the following illustration. When I was a newly minted freshman at Northwestern University, I was required to take an introductory English writing seminar. I attempted to register for my top choices, courses with such names as "Love and Lust," "Not Guilty," and "Strangers in Strange Lands." Alas, I was fated to be assigned to a class called "The Evolution of Poetic Statement in the Arthurian Material." I knew I was in trouble when I bought the course books and realized I was going to have to read the works of Sir Thomas Malory and other early writers in the original Middle English. My professor, David Campbell, insisted that we read and cite the materials in the original. He also tossed in a bit of *Beowulf* in Old English for good measure so we could write "compare and contrast" essays as well. The only way I could fathom getting through this class was by reading the texts out loud to myself with a Middle English dictionary at hand. Unfortunately, whenever I tried to speed up by skipping some words that I didn't quite understand, I frequently found myself way off course. But even with dictionary assistance, there were parts that were very difficult to comprehend due to the words' multiple potential definitions, or worse, unclear meanings. Here's just one random sentence of many that I had highlighted (for some now-obscure reason):

> For kynge Royns had purfilde a mantel with kynges berdis, and there lacked one place of the mantel; wherefore he sente for hys bearde, other ellis he wolde entir into his londis and brenne and sle, and nevir leve tylle he hathe the hede and the bearde bothe.[29]

Ancient Hebrew scribes trying to replicate older texts would have neither dictionaries nor vowels to aid their understanding. Just to give you a sense of the difficulty of working through a text without vowels, here's the same short passage from Malory without *a, e, i, o,* or *u*:

> Fr kng Rns hd prfld a mntl wth kngs brds, nd thr lckd n plc f th mntl; whrfr h snt fr hs brd, thr lls h wld ntr nt hs lnds and brnn nd sl, nd nvr lv tll h hth th hd nd th brd bth.

It seems pretty clear, then, how easy it is to misunderstand a word or to misinterpret its context. Even a reader a mere few decades away from Malory, in Shakespeare's time, might be forgiven for not understanding this text.

One can imagine that ancient Israelite scribes might well have made mistakes. This is why I don't get so worked up when I find an isolated point in the Bible that doesn't quite make sense to me. It probably also didn't quite make sense to the hapless scribe who was trying to transcribe and explain it in the Hebrew of his day. So, he might have tried to be "helpful" to future scribes by coming up with a meaning that made sense to him and passing it on.

As time passed, the meaning of the words has also become less apparent. Shortly after I finished writing these words, I was talking with my friend Michael Connelly, who has spent a good chunk of his life in China. During the conversation, I mentioned to him how I understood the word *aleph*. He asked me if I'd heard of Wang Wei. I had not. So he sent me the book *Nineteen Ways of Looking at Wang Wei*.[30] Wang Wei lived during the Tang Dynasty and wrote a poem around 760 CE in a literary Chinese dialect no longer spoken. *Nineteen Ways* portrays a variety of different ways that this poem can be construed, all based upon valid understandings of the words with a bit of literary license. We will never know precisely what Wang Wei had in mind in writing this poem, which is considered a masterpiece in China, but there is still tremendous wisdom in his words and insight into his Buddhist outlook. The meanings of some of the words are obscure after less than 1,300 years. How much more do we have to cut scribes and translators a bit of slack for a text over 3,000 years old?

The ancient rabbis also sent us a signal not to get too caught up on the translation of words signifying numbers that we might no longer comprehend. In the Passover Haggadah, there is a passage in which Rabbi Yosi, Rabbi Eliezer and Rabbi Akiva debate whether the ten plagues were really fifty, 200 or 250 plagues. In the Mechilta d'Rabbi Yishmael 13:18:3, there is a riff on the word "chamushim" that is used in Exodus 13:18 to describe the Israelites as they leave Egypt. Most traditional commentators translate this word as "armed," which fits the context. But the word "chamash" means five as well, and here it is used in a plural form. So, the Midrash suggests that perhaps only one in five, fifty, or five hundred of the Israelites left Egypt. The Ibn Ezra (Perush Ha-Aruch, on this verse) points out that, of course, we don't believe this because the numbers don't make any sense—no one thought that there were tens of millions or hundreds of millions of Israelites in Egypt. Rather the Midrash is being playful with the terms as it implicitly stipulates we can't be sure of the meaning of the word or of the numbers involved. I think that in all of these cases, the ancient rabbis are telling us to lighten up on these numbers issues. Yes, there were a number of Israelites who left Egypt. And that number was greater than zero. However, what precisely that number was, neither we, nor the ancient rabbis can be really sure.

For maximalists and for me, the most straightforward and clearest approach to understanding the meaning of the Exodus story is to recognize that, for at least two millennia, we have misunderstood the word *aleph* and mistakenly translated it as "thousand." Somewhere down the line, someone decided that the definite translation of the *alph* was *aleph* (1,000) and not *aluph* (a general or group) and ran with it. Just like someone decided that the fruit mentioned in the second chapter of Genesis was an apple—which is nowhere referenced in the text. (The later understanding of "apple" was probably based on a Latin pun.) While centrists simply dismiss these exaggerations in the Bible, maximalists are committed to testing the historicity of the text, including all its details. This has led them to an original and, in my estimation, a convincing interpretation. As unusual as the Exodus story might seem at first read-ing, maximalists argue that it contains too many second millennium details to be the vague remnant of an oral story, let alone a later fabrica-tion. For believers, that is about all we need to validate a rational belief in the historicity of this story. That is good enough for me. Yes, for mini-malists, only direct proof would be sufficient, and I freely concede that finding direct proof is highly unlikely.

CHAPTER 28

Fifty Thousand Canaanites
Walk Into a Bar

Minimalists claim that Israelites are simply Canaanites who migrated from the cities to the hills. They analyze the conquest narrative in light of archaeological surveys of the highland regions in the thirteenth century BCE and extra-biblical sources.[1] In their view, there is no evidence of mass destruction in Canaan to support the biblical time frame.[1] Only a few sites mentioned in the Book of Joshua, such as Bethel and Hazor, show any signs of destruction; others do not even appear to have been inhabited during the time the Israelites purportedly conquered the Canaanites.[2] If there is anything that archaeology can document with accuracy, it is mass destruction, ergo, no destruction, no conquest. It is that simple according to the minimalists. They nonetheless do agree that, during the thirteenth century, that area of the highlands where the Bible describes the Israelites settling did indeed become more populated than before, but they declare this a mere coincidence. The new inhabitants of the highlands were not a separate group, but rather indigenous Canaanites who developed a separate identity as Israelites, perhaps in the ninth century or even later.[3] For minimalists, the question of the emergence of Israel obscures the entire history of the area from

---

[1] The minimalists categorically refuse to use the Bible as a source for the history of ancient Israel on the basis that they believe it is a highly ideological text written at a later time. In contrast, most historians—even those who are skeptical about the Five Books of Moses—consider the Book of Judges to be a useful historical source. Moore and Kelle, *Biblical History*, 107–108 and 111.

1300 to 1000 BCE. They see this as a period primarily of changes within Canaanite society itself, a transition from city-states to small hinterland agricultural settlements.[4] This would be like historians discerning a distinct Czech nationality in the sixth century CE, when Slavic migrations to Eastern Europe had just begun and no distinct Slavic sub-nationalities yet existed. The Merneptah Stele, an Egyptian victory stele from the early 1200s BCE, depicts Egyptian campaigns and victories in Libya and Canaan and distinctly mentions a people called Israel:

> Canaan has been plundered into every sort of woe:
> Ashkelon has been overcome;
> Gezer has been captured;
> Yano'am is made non-existent.
> Israel is laid waste and his seed is not.

Minimalists consider this unimportant.[5] Thompson argues that this stele could just as well refer to a region or a group whose identity is not necessarily correlated to the later people called Israel. It therefore cannot be used to date the existence of an Israelite nation.[6]

The decline in trade in the thirteenth century BCE, which is evident from pottery remains, is not used to posit the existence of Israelite migrants, but rather to explain the Canaanites' retreat from the lowland cities to the hinterland.[7] Subsequent population growth in the area is attributed to increasing prosperity and new and better iron tools, which in turn led to better crop yields, which then resulted in a higher birthrate.[8] Robert B. Coote, for example, also claims that Egyptians, who controlled Canaan during much of the Late Bronze Age period, demanded taxes from the highlanders in exchange for protection and peace. The overall *Pax Egyptiana* would have led to increased economic prosperity, including higher crop yields, which as noted earlier could support an increase in population growth.[9] We can think of the thirteenth century BCE as a sort of extended baby boom, not unlike that which occurred during the much shorter post-World War II period, a phenomenon familiar to many of us.

In short, the minimalists claim that no Israelite nation arrived in Canaan as a separate group; rather, they were Canaanites who evolved a separate identity.

This Club Has No Bouncer

Centrists argue that a people of Israel populated the hill country and Transjordan (today Jordan), though they were likely a combination of Semitic slaves and local Canaanites. Unlike minimalists, centrists generally accept the Merneptah Stele as evidence that a people called Israel existed in the early 1200s BCE. They claim that, grammatically, the word "Israel" in the Merneptah Stele refers to an ethnic group and not a place, contrary to what Thompson suggests.[10] For centrists, the mention of a cigar is evidence of the existence of a cigar. Centrists also accept that the date of c. 1200 BCE for the Merneptah Stele corresponds more or less to the biblical chronology of the land of Israel conquest narratives.

Mazar claims that archaeological evidence of the destruction of sites such as Ai, which is mentioned in the Book of Joshua, suggests that the text does contain memories of real events.[11] He suggests that the archaeological evidence reveals signs of conflicts between Canaanite groups and between Israelites and urban Canaanites.[12] Mazar feels, however, that to label such battles a conquest might be hyperbole, agreeing as he does with minimalists that not all of the sites mentioned in Joshua were destroyed; some, like Lachish, never even existed during the period. Thus, for Mazar, the archaeological record suggests that the emergence of Israel was a complicated process, one which most likely involved Canaanites who moved to the highlands, either as pastoralists or refugees from the general political collapse of the period, and possibly some runaway slaves, called "Shasu" by the Egyptians, though archaeology cannot confirm these theories.[13] Other centrist scholars, such as Finkelstein, agree with the minimalists that the Israelites were most likely predominantly Canaanite pastoralists who gradually developed a distinct identity in their new region, since they lived in the hill country.[14] Nevertheless, he distinguishes them as a group at an earlier date than the minimalists, partly due to the near absence of pig bones in early Iron Age deposits from archaeological sites in the highlands.[15] Pigs were, of course, a forbidden animal for the Israelites.

"And That's the Way It Was" [2]

Maximalists claim that the Israelites were a separate nation who conquered the land, though they destroyed the cities incompletely.[16] They believe that some scholars overemphasize the purported level of destruction.[17] They point out that the Book of Joshua reports that only three cities were destroyed—Jericho, Hazor, and Ai—and those to varying degrees. There was every intent during the ongoing conquest to preserve the cities for the entering Israelites.[18] Thus they refute the claim that the lack of widespread destruction in the archaeological record wildly contradicts the biblical narrative. Maximalists consider the archaeological evidence for the cities named in the conquest narratives and those destroyed by Joshua to be largely consistent with the biblical narrative.[3] Joshua (chapter 8), for example, details a stratagem in which the defenders of Ai were lured out of the city and defeated in the fields, after which the city was burned down. The maximalist view is that such arson may or may not have caused total destruction to stone and mud structures, and this explains why the archaeological excavations of Ai do not reveal the total destruction of the site.[19] In addition, the excavation of Hazor seems to comport much more closely with the Joshua story (chapter 11) than previously maintained.[20] Similarly, evidence from Jericho is less conclusive than many scholars claim,[21] and various excavators of the site have held different views on the evidence for its destruction. While the first excavations in the 1930s seemed to corroborate the conquest story, Kathleen Kenyon's excavation of Jericho in the 1950s led to a radical redating of its destruction—indeed, she questioned whether Jericho was even populated in the biblically allotted time for the conquest.

In addition to reevaluating the convergence of the archaeological data and the narrative in the Book of Joshua, Kitchen argues that the substantial population growth of the late Iron Age cannot be accounted for by natural organic growth, and so some form of mass immigration

---

[2] For those of you who remember Walter Cronkite, and, yes, you can make a toast with prune juice spiked with rum. Believe me, it works.

[3] See Kitchen, *On the Reliability*, 183–190. Kitchen considers the evidence for Hazor to be the most compelling. As to Ai and Jericho, Ai is harder to locate and Jericho cannot be judged due to the conditions of the current site. Provan, Long, and Longman also agree that the evidence for Hazor is the most conclusive, while locating Ai is problematic. They consider the evidence for Jericho promising but inconclusive. See Provan, Long, and Longman, *A Biblical History of Israel*, 173–190; and Moore and Kelle, *Biblical History*, 100.

is needed to explain it.[22] Since virtually all archaeologists find proof of identifiable military activity from the time of the conquest period, max-imalists claim that it makes much more sense to accept the conquest narrative than to deny it.[23] They also argue that there is no single com-pelling counter-theory as to how the highlands became populated and the Israelites emerged. The population figures in the hill country is also broadly consistent with our amended count of Israelites being four to six times the approximately ten thousand men of military age.

Believers read Deuteronomy 7:22–24 as confirmation of an expected slow rate of conquest of the land. "The Lord your God will dislodge those peoples little by little; you will not be able to put an end to them at once, else wild beast would multiply to your hurt. The Lord your God will deliver them to you, throwing them into utter panic until they are wiped out." The conquest was never billed as a same-day cleaner's affair, and people who abandoned their homes in haste and utter panic would not have left destruction in their wake. This also comports well with the notion that the Bible assumes an Israelite population of fifty thousand or so versus two million, who would have massively swamped the numbers of people then living in Canaan.

Scholars also argue how the inhabitants of the highlands managed to live their lives according to the egalitarian ideology demanded by the Bible. As described in part one, the Bible introduced radically new forms of relationships between God and man, man and man, and man and the world. Archaeological discoveries about the highland societies underscore that the early Israelites, to a large extent, actually effected the social aspect of this vision in real life, especially during the period the Bible ascribes to the Book of Judges. As Avraham Faust describes it, from 1200 to 1000 BCE, the inhabitants of the highlands buried their dead very simply and in contrast to the common practices from con-temporary Egyptian and Canaanite societies.[24] Faust does not consider it plausible to explain this custom as due to the poverty or simplicity of the inhabitants, since even simple idolatrous societies buried their dead with possessions.[25] Instead, it is more likely evidence of an ideology of egali-tarianism, a viewpoint promoted in the early Five Books of Moses as an ideal and described in the later Book of Judges as in practice. Faust views this as further evidence linking the highlanders with the people of the

Bible, the Israelites. As he writes, the Israelites' material culture points to a "primitive democracy."[26]

The remains of the highland communities have revealed other aspects of their culture. The plainness of the highlanders' pottery and the ordinariness of their four-room houses—where no hierarchy in sizes of the rooms existed—indicate the society's egalitarian tendencies.[27] Within Israelite society, no one fights over the master bedroom or the fine china. Not so in neighboring Canaan, never mind Egypt, where idolatry and abusive hierarchy go hand in hand. For maximalist scholars, the parallels between the biblical ideal, the society it describes in the books of the prophets, and the archaeological record are too great to miss.

CHAPTER 29

The Clothes Have
No Emperor

Minimalists deny the existence of a United Monarchy under King David and King Solomon. They claim there is scarce evidence to back its historical existence centered in Jerusalem for the period.[1] They point out that there is a paucity of direct evidence of David and Solomon in Israel, but direct evidence is something one would certainly expect to find in abundance for kings: royal households should have produced Hebrew inscriptions or writing for the period, as well as external evidence for a period of monarchy in the form of great buildings or fortifications.[1] Some minimalists even doubt the usefulness of the few bits of direct external evidence that do exist, such as the ninth century BCE Tel Dan inscription that refers to the House of David. Instead, they claim that either the inscription is a forgery or the word "dwd" in the inscription, which is usually understood as House of David, can be read as a place-name rather than as a reference to the dynastic house of David[2] or the name of a temple.[3] They summarily dismiss this important and independent piece of textual evidence as highly idiosyncratic and useless.[4] They argue that a kingdom's remains would be more substantial

---

[1] It is generally agreed that direct extra-biblical evidence for the United Monarchy is scant. This is decisive for the minimalists. Direct extra-biblical evidence increases significantly for the divided monarchies. Moore and Kelle, *Biblical Israel*, 157.

than some mere provincial inscription, and one made by a conquering enemy, Hazael of Aram, at that.[5]

Minimalists also offer alternative interpretations of the archaeological evidence for the existence of a United Monarchy. They reject the idea that the monumental six-chamber gateway architecture of Hazor, Gezer, and Megiddo can be attributed to Solomon, arguing that these structures date from a later period, based on what is called the low chronology.[6] Similarly, minimalists also dispute that Jerusalem was an important capital city during the period of the United Monarchy. They find little evidence of scribal activity from the greater Jerusalem region, except for the Tel Zayit inscription (an alphabet from the tenth century) and the Gezer calendar (a list of seasons in the agricultural year from the tenth century as well).[7] Consequently, they claim that there existed no royal administration to support and regulate; therefore, the city could not have been a capital of kings.[8] An imperial capital in Jerusalem should also evidence some remains of monumental architecture, which the minimalists claim is nowhere to be found.[9] From the minimalist perspective, then, the Israelites, if they could even be called that at the time, never realized a United Monarchy or a grand empire.[10] They never formed more than a tribal confederation, and Jerusalem remained an insignificant town deep in the highlands, from which perhaps a tribal chieftain named David once modestly ruled.[11]

Mayor David and Governor Solomon of Jerusalem

In contrast, the centrists argue that David and Solomon existed in fact, although their kingdom may have been smaller than that described in the biblical depiction of the United Monarchy and perhaps later. Finkelstein and Mazar concur that David and Solomon were historical figures, both accepting the Tel Dan inscription mentioning Beit David [House of David] as a decisive piece of evidence for both their existence and the existence of the Davidic monarchic line.[12] Since the Tel Dan inscription was found during the excavation of the site, it is unlikely to be a forgery. This has been confirmed, since recent technological advances now make it possible to detect forgeries with even greater accuracy by determining whether the inscriptions were made with modern or ancient tools. Finkelstein argues that the archaeology of the highlands is consistent with the story of Saul's rule in that region.[13] Nevertheless, he claims that the United Monarchy did not exist in the tenth century and that David and Solomon ruled small chiefdoms at most. Proper monarchies might have existed, but only under the Omrides who ruled in Samaria during the ninth century BCE.[14] In Finkelstein's view, a United Monarchy is implausible because (a) structures previously dated to the tenth century and attributed to Solomon can be dated to a later period, and (b) no territorial states arose in this part of the ancient Near East before the expansion of the Assyrian Empire in the ninth century.[15] To further support his theory, Finkelstein claims that architectural features of the town of Megiddo resemble those of buildings in Samaria attributed to King Omri.[16] For Finkelstein, a skewed chronology led scholars to confuse the rather modest achievements of David—a more primitive ancestor—with the more robust accomplishments of his better-documented and more powerful descendants in Samaria and Judea. Nevertheless, Finkelstein argues that the geographical details of the story of David, like the prominence of the city of Gath, are consistent only with archaeology of the tenth century, not later.[17]

In contrast to Finkelstein, Mazar claims it is difficult to distinguish between ninth- and tenth-century structures. Thus, the structures of Megiddo could well have been constructed during the time attributed to the United Monarchy. External sources such as the campaign list of the Egyptian pharaoh Sheshonq I attest to many of the cities described in the Bible during the time of the United Monarchy.[18] Further, the only reason for Sheshonq I to have mentioned them would have been if they belonged to a political power that posed a genuine threat. This could only be Solomon's kingdom. Mazar, in contrast to Finkelstein, believes that the Large Stone Structure excavated in the City of David (Jerusalem) long ago by Kathleen Kenyon, which has no parallel in Israel between the twelfth and ninth centuries BCE, can be dated to the tenth century.[19] He shows that the use of large stones fits biblical description and is not attested to after the eighth century in the area. Evidence of urbanization and greater population density in the area, he adds, is sufficient to support the argument for a functioning state.[20] Mazar attributes the lack of extra-biblical written evidence for the United Monarchy to the widespread use of perishable writing materials. Finally, Mazar also mentions evidence for the urbanization of the Philistines and Edomites, peoples the Bible mentions as Israel's neighbors at the time.[21] Though the United Monarchy may have been no Roman Empire under Caesar or British Empire under Victoria, Mazar deems it quite possible that a charismatic leader such as David could unquestionably have created and successfully administered a smaller state.[22] Mazar claims that the United Monarchy was likely just such a small state,[23] though not the substantial kingdom of the Bible.

Their Majesties, King David and King Solomon of Israel

Maximalist scholars consider the biblical description of David to be largely historical. The Tel Dan inscription of a House of David is a decisive indication of the king's historical existence. Kitchen argues that, since no Mesopotamian rulers had direct contact with the area in the period,[24] and few Egyptian documents from the time survive,[25] one cannot expect much external direct evidence for the United Monarchy. Nevertheless, Sheshonq I's indication of "the heights of David" in a list created barely fifty years after the king's reign[26] is, as it is for Mazar, decisive.

For Kitchen, contextual factors are also important. David's kingdom resembled the other "mini" empires that existed in the region from the period of 1180–870 BCE.[27] Likewise, Solomon's foreign relations can best be understood as appropriate to the period of his reign. Kitchen also claims that the archaeology of Israel during the period suggests a unified state: the accepted dating of the monumental architecture in Hazor, Gezer, and Megiddo offers proof of the kingdom.[28] Eilat Mazar is joined by Avraham Faust and Amihai Mazar, as noted above, in upholding the interpretation of the Large Stone Structure as part of David's palace, suggesting that this offers direct evidence for a state at the period. Nor is the Large Stone Structure the only important recent find. Archaeologists led by Yosef Garfinkel have excavated a fortified city at Khirbet Qeiyafa, thirty kilometers southwest of Jerusalem on the main road from Philistia and the coastal plain to Jerusalem and Hebron in the hill country, which was a strategic location for the Kingdom of Judah. Using olive pits to date the site, Garfinkel argues that it is most certainly from the tenth century, possibly even the eleventh.[29] In addition, the planning and architecture of the site does not resemble a Philistine equivalent, and the site contained no pig bones, which makes it unlikely to be a Philistine settlement.[2] The existence of such a fortress, which only a small state could have constructed, is for Garfinkel further evidence that, indeed, there existed a kingdom in Israel under David.[30] Avraham Faust concurs.

The Israelites began to build cities in the twelfth and eleventh centuries BCE because of the threat of the Philistines. Without such fortifications and a state structure, the Israelites would not have been able to defend themselves. The people's plea for a king to organize their nation makes perfect sense in this context. Military imperatives transformed the Israelites from a relatively egalitarian society to a more hierarchical state structure.[31] Using comparative data, Kitchen shows how the description of Solomon's riches and gifts is largely accurate for the time.[32] Solomon kept up with the Joneses of the ancient Near East quite well.

Archaeological excavations further corroborate the narrative of David and Solomon's reign in what was then the territory of the Philistines. 2 Kings mentions the city of Gath, one of the Philistine city-states captured and destroyed by Hazael of Aram (Damascus). Recent excavations at the site of Tell es-Safi have confirmed that it was ancient Gath and that it was indeed destroyed in the mid-ninth century BCE, when Hazael would have rampaged through the region, according to the Book of Kings. The same recent excavations at the site have also demonstrated contact between the Philistines and Israelites at the time given for David's reign. For example, ostraca show that the Philistines wrote in Hebrew by the ninth century. Also, Philistine phallic symbols uncovered at the site are circumcised. This evidence points to Israelite cultural dominance in the areas, something only possible if Israel was, as the Bible describes it, an important regional power or state.

Relying on what they believe to be solid proof for ascribing buildings to the period of David and Solomon, maximalist scholars argue that the relative lack of remains of a monarchy only underscores the historical reality of what this book has called the monotheistic revolution. Archaeologists have long noted the relative absence of royal monuments, whether stately palaces, stele, inscriptions, and weights and seals in the land of Israel, not only in the more contested period of the tenth century, but even from the ninth to the seventh centuries BCE, when there is

---

[2] The planning of the city is typically Judean. Garfinkel and Ganor, *Khirbet Qeiyafa*, 4.

The Historicity of Biblical Events

	Minimalist	Centrist	Maximalist	Traditionalist
2000 BCE	Canaanites live in cities in Canaan	Canaanites live in cities in Canaan	Canaanites live in cities in Canaan	Canaanites live in cities in Canaan
1800 BCE			Migration of Mesopotamians to Canaan, plausibly Abraham	Abraham moves to Canaan
	Hyksos rule parts of Egypt	Hyksos rule parts of Egypt	Hyksos rule parts of Egypt	
1600 BCE				
				Children of Jacob move to Egypt
1400 BCE	Egypt rules Canaan and Canaanites live in Egypt as slaves	Egypt rules Canaan and Canaanites live in Egypt as slaves	Egypt rules Canaan and Canaanites including plausibly Abraham and his decendents live in Egypt as slaves	
		Decline in Canaanite cities, rise in rural populations, possible escape of Canaanite slaves from Egypt, emergence of Israelites, and Israelite Canaanite wars	Decline in Canaanite cities, escape of Israelite slaves from Egypt, return to Canaan and wars with Canaanites	Exodus from Egypt and conquest of Canaan
1200 BCE	Decline in Canaanite cities and rise in rural populations			Judges rule over Israel and war with Canaanites
		Possible emergence of Israelite chiefdom along with others chiefdoms such as the Edomite and Philistine. Canaanites assimilate to these chiefdoms	Israelite chiefdoms under Judges	
1000 BCE	Emergence of small Canaanite chiefdoms		Emergence of Israelite monarchy along with others monarchies such as the Edomite and Philistine city states to which Canaanites assimilate	Emergence of Israelite monarchy along with other monarchies such as the Edomite and Philistine city states to which Canaanites assimilate
	Neo-Assyrian Empire rules Canaan. Israelite may have emerged as a possible sub group among Canaanites, impossible to know.	Neo-Assyrian Empire rules over possible chiefdom/or kingdom of Israel and Judah as well as other chiefdoms/kingdoms	Israelite monarchy divides into two Kingdoms Judea and Israel	Israelite monarchy divides into two Kingdoms Judea and Israel
800 BCE			Neo-Assyrian Empire rules over Kingdom of Israel and Judah as well as other Kingdoms in the area	Neo-Assyrian Empire rules over Kingdoms of Israel and Judah as well as other Kingdoms in the area
		Assyrian deport populations from Chiefdom of Israel	Assyrian deport populations from Kingdom of Israel	Assyrian deport populations from Kingdom of Israel
600 BCE	Neo-Babylonian Empire rules Canaan	Neo-Babylonian Empire rules over Judea and exiles Judeans	Neo-Babylonian Empire rules over Kingdom of Judea and exiles Judeans	Neo-Babylonian Empire rules over Kingdom of Judea and exiles Judeans
	Persian Empire rules Canaan and a subgroup of Canaanites called Judeans build a Temple in Judea	Persian Empire rules over Kingdom of Judea and Judeans build a Temple in Judea as well as other areas of Levant	Persian Empire rules over Kingdom of Judea and Judeans build a Temple in Judea as well as other areas of Levant	Persian Empire rules over Kingdom of Judea and Judeans build a Temple in Judea as well as other areas of Levant
400 BCE				
	Greek Empire rules over Canaan including Judeans	Greek Empire rules over Judea	Greek Empire rules over Kingdom of Judea	Greek Empire rules over Kingdom of Judea
200 BCE				
	The Hasmonean Kingdom is founded in Judea	The Hasmonean Kingdom is founded in Judea	The Hasmonean Kingdom is founded in Judea	The Hasmonean Kingdom is founded in Judea
	Roman Empire conquers Judea and names it Palestine	Roman Empire conquers Judea and names it Palestine	Roman Empire conquers Judea and names it Palestine	Roman Empire conquers Judea and names it Palestine
0 CE				

much less debate about Israelite kingship (except from the über-minimalists). Some scholars argue that this is due to the primitive nature of the Israelite monarchy; others explain the evidence differently. For William Hallo, the absence of royal monuments testifies to the Israelites' respect for the Bible's understanding of relationships. The Israelite state stood in contrast to idolatrous cultures of the time whose kings were deified, as in the case of Egypt, or accorded almost superhuman honors, in the case of Babylon. In these cultures, monuments abounded. In fact, the main occupation of pharaohs or kings seemed to be nothing if not monumental self-aggrandizement. Not so for the rulers of the ancient kingdom of Israel, whose Bible does not even have a name for royal inscriptions.[33] The kings of the biblical period most likely also limited other monuments due to the Bible's negative view of graven images. As Hallo argues, we cannot attribute the lack of monuments to other factors. By this period, the Israelites were literate and monuments existed from surrounding Canaanite cultures of a similar economic level. The land of Israel has been thoroughly excavated. An absence of monuments lends archaeological weight to the argument that the Israelites adhered to a more egalitarian model of social and political relations, even during the period of the monarchy, which itself was a concession to social and political pressures.[34] For maximalist scholars, the monotheistic revolution, for all its incomplete character, has left clear archaeological traces.

So, both believers and nonbelievers can make a case that it is perfectly rational to believe in the historicity of the Bible. The general trend among contemporary scholars is increasingly to take the centrist position. At the moment, not many scholars hold the minimalist view that the Israelite monarchy is a fabrication; neither do many scholars hold the maximalist position that the Bible provides an accurate historical account of the lives of the patriarchs and matriarchs. Given the evidence we have seen for the plausibility of biblical events, evidence based on comparison with a wide range of outside sources, it makes more sense to me that the Bible is historically accurate while not being a history book. As a believer, I concede confirmation bias, but I rely on many esteemed scholars who affirm the plausibility of the biblical accounts. And the lack of convincing evidence to the contrary is sufficient for me to consider my belief in the Bible rational. With that, we can now move on to the second of our original questions—who wrote the Bible?

CHAPTER 30

When Shakespeare Became Marlowe and Friends

For a long time, people were satisfied that God revealed the first five books of the Bible to Moses and the later books to subsequent prophets. God's purpose was to teach us about how to live a good life. The Bible itself said so. No reason to doubt it. No mystery. No whodunit.

That universal confidence is certainly gone. In the seventeenth century, a number of thinkers, among them Thomas Hobbes and Baruch Spinoza, raised doubts about whether Moses had written all of the Bible. They did so based on passages, such as Deuteronomy 34:6, "no one knows of his [Moses's] burial place to this day," and Genesis 12:6, "and the Canaanites were then in the land," that suggested the text was written long after events it described. Traditionally, Jewish and Christian scholars attributed these anachronisms either to Joshua's hand or to Moses's prophetic powers. Hobbes and Spinoza saw them as evidence of multiple human authorships. During this time, scholars also began to study the transmission of and editorial changes in classical texts, such as the Homer's *Iliad* and *Odyssey*, by examining repetitions, contradictions, and anachronisms in those texts.

Scholars began to analyze the Bible in a similar way. Jean Astruc, a medical doctor by profession and biblical scholar by passion, used these new literary methods to argue that the different names of God and the repetitions of the same story in different parts of the Bible provided evidence enough that the Bible was a patchwork of different manuscripts. Yet, unlike Hobbes and Spinoza, he considered these to have been the texts Moses used to author the Bible! A subsequent generation of scholars, mainly Germans such as Johann Eichhorn and Wilhelm de Wette, carried Astruc's concept of multiple texts a step further. They claimed that each text was not only written by a different author, but was written at a different time. Thus began the biblical whodunit, the doggedly main focus of the discipline of modern literary biblical criticism.

As controversies go, "Who wrote the Bible?" has something in common with the mystery surrounding the Bard: "Who wrote the plays of Shakespeare?" Lots of questions arise from the very texts themselves. Some scholars argue that the different styles and sheer quantity of the Shakespearean oeuvre were such that one man could not have possibly written all the plays ascribed in the great folios to a singular Shakespeare. Yet there was no concrete evidence pointing to the other putative authors.

Biblical skeptics hypothesized about why, when, and how their hypothesized human authors might have written these different texts, as well as when they might have edited them together. Returning to our analogy of a police investigation, we require four things to determine plausible suspects: motive (why), means (how), opportunity (where), and the time it happened (when). A theologian turned biblical critic by the name of Julius Wellhausen espoused the so-called documentary hypothesis (DH). In it, he claimed that the Bible was written by four different authors, and for different purposes, as we will explore in greater detail. The DH became the most popular academic theory for human authorship of the Bible for most of the twentieth century.

Case Solved: The Documentary Hypothesis

For most of the late nineteenth and twentieth centuries, biblical critics considered that the DH answered questions of time, motive, means, and opportunity of the biblical authors.[1] Julius Wellhausen famously published the DH in 1876–1877. Relying on internal biblical data *only*, without recourse to archaeological, comparative, or manuscript evidence, he claimed to have discovered that the Bible was actually made up of four different sources written by four different authors at four different times, and for four different reasons which had later been put together by a final redactor (editor). According to this hypothesis, four individuals or groups of authors, designated by the initials J, P, E, and D, wrote the Bible. Each individual or group could be recognized by a unique style of writing and message. Each was motivated to preserve existing political power and to spread a particular vision of the world.

The author or authors of J, which stood for one particular name of God, Yahweh (which starts with J in German, hence the initial J), wrote in the tenth century in Solomon's court. As such, they emphasized the importance of Judah, the kingdom where they lived. They also described a world where God spoke to man directly and wrote in prosaic language. The author E, which stands for Elohim, another Hebrew name of God, wrote a prose that was not quite as stirring. E lived in the Northern Kingdom of Israel in the eighth century and spoke in positive terms about his kingdom, emphasizing encounters between God and man through events such as dreams. Critics, being critics, note the deficiency of E's style (but I digress). The text of D, for Deuteronomist, was allegedly written in King Josiah's court in Jerusalem in the seventh century. D argued that royal politics and administrative laws, like those propagated by Josiah, were necessary. P, which stands for the Priestly Code, was composed by priests in exile keen to exert their supremacy. Its greatest concern was to emphasize that God could be approached only via the priestly clan. P's writing is legalistic and dry.

After P's texts were completed, a final redactor (editor) compiled all the above sources into the book we now call the Bible. Wellhausen suspected that the different sources followed the progression and decline of Israelite religion. The authors of the J and E source were more primitive animists who imagined that God was close at hand; the writers of D developed an ethical outlook that represented the pinnacle of Israelite religion and later found echoes in Christianity.[1] The authors of P guided the degeneration of Israelite religion into empty ritual.[2] Wellhausen's DH accumulated so many academic supporters that it became, for a short while at least, virtually uncontested in the academy.

---

[1] Wellhausen's negative attitude to Judaism is well known. See Blenkensopp, "The Pentateuch" and also Gerdmar E. J. Anders, *Roots of Theological Anti-Semitism: German Biblical Interpretation and the Jews, from Herder and Semler to Kittel and Bultmann* (Leiden: Brill, 2009); and W. M. I. de Wette, *Judaism as Degenerated Hebraism*. De Wette's negative views influenced Wellhausen.

Reopening the Case: Dissing the Documentary Hypothesis

Wellhausen's DH did have some early detractors. Many religious people never bought into the DH, though few initially took the time to dispute it scientifically. Umberto Cassuto, an Italian rabbi and scholar, was an able exception. In the 1940s, Cassuto claimed that Wellhausen's argument was to a great extent hypothetical: different names for God, the repetition of a story, different theological messages, and different styles are not proof of different manuscripts or multiple authors. Instead, argued Cassuto, such variations were common enough in ancient Near Eastern writings known to be unitary documents.[3] Cassuto proposed an alternative: the authors of the Bible lived during the time of David and Solomon, and they composed the books of Genesis and Exodus based on Israelite oral traditions about actual events. Their motive? To write down the Israelites' national history and wisdom. Still, Cassuto's arguments changed the minds of few Bible critics.

The first cracks in the scholarly consensus over the DH appeared among biblical critics who accepted its premises, but not its specifics.[4] Those scholars who accepted the basic theory of multiple authorship no longer agreed with Wellhausen's theories regarding the number of authors or the time period in which they wrote. Some critics argued that J was a compendium of two or three authors and that E had a similar number of predecessor authors.[5] Others disagreed with Wellhausen's ideas and offered the alternative of the so-called supplementary hypothesis (SH).[6] This latter view had coexisted with the DH during much of the nineteenth century, but it had not come to equal prominence until the 1970s.[7] According to the SH, espoused principally by John Van Seters, the first book of the Bible is D.[8] D included the books of Joshua, Judges, and Kings. Scribes in King Josiah's court composed D as a history of Israel designed to justify the king's reforms. Writing during the Babylonian exile, a subsequent set of authors added to D in an attempt to explain the catastrophe of exile theologically. Even later authors, writing after the Babylonian exile, then simply supplemented the text of D, adding J as a prequel to the history of Israel in D and adding P as a religious supplement. Those in favor of the SH have a sequencing dispute. To make this clear, consider again our fiftieth-century archaeologist. This time, she finds the *Stars Wars* films and debates with her colleagues in what order the prequel, sequel, and original trilogies were produced.

The consensus concerning the premise of the DH crumbled irreversibly in the 1980s, mainly over the question of motive and means. Whereas previous critics had been focused on dating the different texts according to their content, Roger Whybray sought to examine the redactor's motives.[9] Why would a final redactor purposely include repetitions and unevenness in the text if the initial authors of the text avoided these inconsistencies and repetitions? Whybray also pointed out that, while the literary device of repetition might not appeal to our modern sensibilities, it was of no concern to the ancient authors. He suggests a more logical alternative, the so-called fragmentary hypothesis (FH). This theory posits that the Pentateuch was the product of a single author who used a series of fragments to compose the text. Scholars continue to offer different theories on biblical authorship with no agreement in sight. Just to mention a few more, Rolf Rendtorff and Erhard Blum also adopt a fragmentary model but, unlike Whybray, claim that the Bible emerged as the result of authors adding smaller units to an existing work over time.[10] These scholars also eliminated J and E as sources.

Other scholars add historical weight to Whybray's logical challenges to the question of motive and means. If, as Wellhausen believed, the different available groups of texts (i.e., laws, or two versions of the same story) were competing or even contradictory, why would the final editor of the Bible bring them all together as the DH posits? Scholars like Joshua Berman show this is not only illogical—it is unaccounted for.[11] Elsewhere in the ancient Near East, editors suppressed material they did not agree with. So how do we explain the contradictions in the text? For Berman, new versions of the same law were additions or adaptations to changing circumstances. They weren't in fact really contradictions, but complements. Further proof of this approach is that the books of prophets, which we can date much more easily, also contain echoes of two versions of a story. But Berman's critiques go further. In his view, only a careful comparative study of the text of the Bible with other ancient Near Eastern texts will reveal whether authors at any given period had the means to write the Bible as it has come down to us.

As it stands, the theories over biblical authorship have now multiplied on all points of the whodunit. The notion that there is at minimum an academic consensus about the multiple authors of the Bible, as Kugel claims, obscures the more problematic present state of biblical criticism. There are simply too many mutually exclusive hypotheses, none of which are provable.

The Evidence in the Case

The problem with resolving the biblical whodunit is that there are no physical biblical scrolls that would help scholars date the Bible. We must rely entirely on indirect evidence. The earliest full biblical manuscript comes from the ninth century CE. We do have earlier fragments of biblical texts—two silver scrolls excavated at Ketef Hinnom that date from c. 600 BCE; further fragments of biblical text are found in the Dead Sea Scrolls, which date from c. 300 BCE–100 CE. The Dead Sea Scrolls certainly yield evidence of slightly different versions of the biblical texts circulating at the time, though the origin of these versions among different Jewish sects in the Second Temple period is hotly debated. These biblical fragments still cannot tell us who wrote the Bible and when it was composed, since they are incomplete and date, according to all but the most radical minimalist accounts, from well after the Bible was first written. It is like trying to figure out the first publication date of Charlotte Brontë's *Jane Eyre* based only on a 2006 Penguin edition of the book.

In the absence of manuscript evidence, scholars must rely on internal evidence in order to date the Bible. They must compare Hebrew and foreign words, writing style, and content of the stories to other Hebrew language and ancient Near Eastern texts for which we have more certain dates. So, to take an example from the English language, when faced with the spelling "wyfe" for the word "wife," scholars know we are likely dealing with a text from before the eighteenth century. Another approach is to use evidence about the historicity of events in the Bible to date its writing. If certain events or places can be dated to fixed times, and not earlier or later, then this limits the time frame for the Bible's initial composition. While these methods for dating the Bible are perfectly rational, as we shall see below, they provide no consensus. Dating the Hebrew Bible remains the cornerstone to the question of authorships, yet it is not the only one.

Scholars have also worked hard on establishing the means, opportunity, and motive for putative writers of the Bible. Answering questions of means revolves first and foremost around dating the content of the text. Could putative authors at a given time have had knowledge about the events described? A historian who lived in the twentieth century, for example, would certainly be able to write a history of slave rebellion in Jamaica, but they would not be able to give a firsthand account of how its leaders planned and prepared it. This is the case because we only have descriptions of the rebellion from white planters as sources. Another key question for establishing the means is, "Did authors know how to write well enough to record the events at any particular time?" Can we, in fact, prove that literate people existed in a certain time and place? Finally, as to motive, scholars must consider writing conventions at various times in the region. They examine why other people in surrounding cultures committed particular ideas to writing. They analyze how their use of texts sheds light on their motive for writing something down. For example, a diary about a person's life is a different kind of book than Saint Augustine's *Confessions*, the former written for private reflection, the latter for public edification. Sometimes the motive for writing something down is evident, sometimes it is hidden. Here scholars are divided about how to treat the Bible, though proving their case is difficult either way.

So far, scholarly debate rages over every aspect of the whodunit, leading to a multiplication of theories. It is like a Rubik's Cube with numerous squares designated as "wild colors" that could signify any color. Multiple arrangements of the cube can be offered as possible perfect solutions. Thus, the jury is still out—and, quite frankly, more than a little confused. As regards the question of biblical authorship, scholars fall along the same continuum as on the question of historicity.

In the next chapter, we will follow the three-way tennis game of different academic approaches to who wrote the Bible, when, how, and why, and we will examine whether the Bible could have been written as tradition described.

CHAPTER 31

Dating the Bible—Something to Do on a Saturday Night

Historians try to date the writing of the Bible in order to determine its likely author/s. This is, again, similar to how the police attempt to determine the time and location of a crime. In addition to research on its historicity and external evidence for the events the Bible recounts (which can tell us if the Bible is accurate, but not necessarily when it was written down in its current form), researchers also analyze the linguistic evidence of the Bible itself—Hebrew writing and language.

The origins of the Hebrew language are obscure.[1] Working backward, linguists consider Hebrew to be part of the larger so-called Afro-Asiatic linguistic group, which includes many of the known languages of the ancient Near East such as ancient Egyptian, Akkadian, Ugaritic, Assyrian, and Moabite, among others.

Scholars can successfully trace changes in the Hebrew language and writing from the tenth century BCE onward. Most specialists agree that parts of the Bible contain archaic grammatical features that date anywhere between 1300 and 1000 BCE. Such archaic Hebrew could have been preserved in oral tradition or could have been written down in the common script used across the Levant. We just don't know. However, possibly in the ninth century and certainly by the eighth century BCE, Hebrew evolved new grammatical features and its own script, which scholars call Paleo-Hebrew (PH). This PH script is speculated to be one of many national scripts that arose in response to Assyrian political and linguistic imperialism.[2] The Hebrew language also changed in this period. Hebrew inscriptions from the ninth until the beginning of the sixth centuries BCE share enough common grammatical features that scholars call this version classical or standard Hebrew.[3] The Bible largely consists of these grammatical features. Hebrew grammar and writing would change again in the fifth century BCE, with features that would remain consistent until the third century BCE. Late Biblical Hebrew is also written in a different script, adopting the imperial Aramaic script that was then used across the Levant (from which the modern Hebrew script descends).[4] All of what we know about the history of writing in the region and the development of the Hebrew language and Hebrew writing has been central to how scholars date the Bible.

Deja Vu Deja Vu?

Minimalist scholars date the Bible to the Persian (fourth century BCE) and even Hellenistic (second century BCE) periods based predominantly on historical and linguistic evidence.[5] They make their claims according to the Bible's main contents. Minimalists argue that the Bible's overall message was devised after the Babylonian exile as a justification for the return of the Jews. In addition, they claim that it was only during the Babylonian exile that the Israelites gained enough exposure to a strong written culture to write a text like the Bible. Given the lack of evidence of scribal schools, they claim that too few Israelites knew how to write at all, let alone author complicated books. The kingdoms and courts of the ancient Near East generally guarded writing systems for their own use. They trained specialized scribes to use them for administrative and religious purposes. Based on this reasoning, Lemche, Whitelam, Davies, and Thompson argue that the Bible was predominantly invented and written down in the fifth and fourth centuries BCE to reflect a political agenda.[6] They emphasize the features of the biblical text that correspond to late Biblical Hebrew.

As further proof of a Babylonian influence, minimalists claim that much of the Bible consists of fictitious tropes that existed in other ancient Near Eastern cultures. Donald Redford argues that Moses's birth follows a literary motif common to the entire ancient Near East, not just Egypt.[7]

The Moses story is portrayed as akin to a contemporary archetype of the rags-to-riches story recycled in countless films from classics to Disney animations, not to mention supermarket novels. The minimalists, thus, use such contemporaneous texts as proof that the biblical stories were pilfered from Mesopotamian texts using similar methods and tropes. In their view, the priestly class then canonized the Bible not long after it was written.

The Never-Ending Story

Centrist scholars claim that the late dates proposed by minimalists make little sense. Linguist William Schniedewind argues that the Bible could not have been composed in the Persian period (fifth or fourth centuries) because, even if some portions of it show features of late Hebrew, most of it is written in classical Hebrew.[8] Further, the community that returned from Babylon was small and weak and did not produce very much writing, either.[9] In addition, during this time, Aramaic almost displaced Hebrew, making it even less likely that the whole Bible would have been written at that time as the minimalists claim.[10] As for dating it to the Hellenistic period, in Schniedewind's view, the Hebrew of the time was so different from that in the Bible that such an invention is hard to imagine.[11] Instead, Schniedewind claims that most of the Bible was written down during this period under Hezekiah's reign (late eighth century). In his view, the authors based their patriarchal narratives on oral traditions,[12] which explains some of the archaic features of some of the Biblical Hebrew. But Schniedewind considers it unlikely that these traditions were written down, since Israel was, in his view, mainly an oral society before the time of Hezekiah. In Schniedewind's view, the Bible was canonized in the Persian period (fifth and sixth centuries), but not written then.[13]

Other centrist scholars believe that the biblical text contains early material, though they argue that it was supplemented, edited, and altered over time. Many centrist scholars build their own theories, taking Wellhausen's dates as a point of departure. William Dever assigns much of the content of material in D to the period of 1000–600 BCE based on linguistic and thematic evidence.[14] In his view, the authors of D, scribes who resided in the court of the Kingdom of Judah, relied on both written material and oral traditions, some of which were archaic. If the Bible had been written in the Hellenistic period, Dever thinks it would have had very different content.[15] Alexander Rofé posits that P, for example, includes *both* archaic material from 1200–1000 *and* evidence of redaction from the Persian period (fifth to third centuries), like an eighteenth-century house with indoor plumbing installed.[16] Rofé has worked to separately identify, where possible, material from as early as the tenth century and layers of later editions. He is also known for his theory that much of the material from D can be dated back to tenth-century Shechem. Few centrists believe that the Israelites had the requisite writing technology or cultural sophistication to compose anything like the Bible earlier than the tenth century. Centrist scholars thus date parts of the Bible to a much earlier period than do the minimalists,[1] though most, like Dever and Rofé, claim that it was edited from before and after the Babylonian exile until the end of the Persian period to reflect the ideological preferences of the editors.

Looking Good for Your Age

Maximalist scholars consider much of the Hebrew Bible initially to have been written close in date to the events it describes, though they also accept that it was edited at later periods. Kitchen, Berman, and Provan rely on extensive evidence of treaty formats and covenants from the third to the first millennium in order to assume a date for the overall framework of the revelation at Sinai somewhere in the fourteenth and thirteenth centuries.[17] Likewise, he considers the laws in Deuteronomy to closely parallel second millennium legal materials from the area. In Kitchen's view, later authors could not have invented such close parallels. Likewise, both Kitchen and Berman note remarkable similarities between the Tabernacle and Ramses II's military tent during the Battle of Kadesh against the Hittites in the thirteenth century. The tent's form was depicted in monuments across the empire, including visual reliefs. Berman also points out striking literary parallels between the poem recounting the Battle of Kadesh and the Exodus story, which

---

[1] Mazar, for example, thinks that at least part of the Exodus story was conceived in the thirteenth century BCE. Finkelstein, Mazar, and Schmidt, *The Quest for the Historical Israel*, 61.

The Composition and Editing of the Bible

	Minimalist	Centrist	Maximalist	Traditionalist
2000 BCE				
1800 BCE			Oral traditions about Patriarchs	Oral traditions about Patriarchs
1600 BCE				
1400 BCE			Oral traditions about slavery in Egypt	Oral traditions about slavery in Egypt
				Composition of the Five Books of Moses
1200 BCE		Possible Oral traditions about the Slavery in Egypt and Exodus	Composition of the Five Books of Moses	
		Oral traditions about the time of the Judges	Composition of the Book of Judges	Composition of the Book of Judges
1000 BCE		Oral traditions / some writings about David and Solomon	Composition of the Book of Samuel and Book of Kings	Composition of the Book of Samuel and Book of Kings
800 BCE			Composition of the Prophets	Composition of the Prophets
	Possible oral traditions, but unrecoverable in the Bible	Composition of the Five Books of Moses and the Book of Judges, Samuel, and Kings as well as the Prophets incorporating earlier Writings		
600 BCE			Editing of all previously written books	Minimal editing of all previously written books
400 BCE	Composition of the Hebrew Bible and Book of Judges, Samuel, & Kings as well as the Prophets	Editing of Hebrew Scriptures	Editing of all previously written books	Minimal Editing of all previously written books
200 BCE	Canonization of the Hebrew Scriptures	Canonization of the Hebrew Scriptures	Canonization of the Hebrew Scriptures	Canonization of the Hebrew Scriptures
0 CE				

later authors would also have no knowledge of.[18] Faust argues that the Bible describes the Philistines as uncircumcised prior to the monarchic period, but not in texts that describe later periods. According to Faust, the archaeological record supports the text, as Philistines appear to have adopted circumcision after 1000 BCE.[19] Such small but significant details provide further proof that it would be very difficult for a later writer to simply have invented the text. For Kitchen, Faust, and Berman, the Bible demonstrates awareness of significant details related to Egyptian and local culture, suggesting that much of the Bible was written down contemporaneously with the events it described.

Further, Kitchen claims that it is perfectly plausible to consider that the biblical texts were written in a late Canaanite alphabet and then later updated. In addition, Kitchen argues that the biblical text is not particularly long and therefore could have been written on parchment, as mentioned in the Bible itself, and transported. Further, according to Kitchen, an update of the script, as well as certain names and grammatical usages, is a well-documented phenomenon by scribes in the ancient Near East.[20] This accounts for why most of the Bible is written in classical Biblical Hebrew.[21]

Consider the following example. There is the frequently told story that when Shakespeare's play *King Lear* was first produced by the Yiddish theater, it was advertised as "translated and much improved." This sort of transmission error via scribal "improvement" could have and, in my view, was very likely to have happened to some degree over time. It is plausible that the Yiddish "improved" version of Shakespeare actually made more sense to its particular audience, including passages that were inconsistent with the meaning of the original text because it deleted the parts that did not fit with the times. Nevertheless, it also does not mean that the whole original text was thrown out as an invention or just used to crib some possible plot lines in this improved Yiddish version. Yet, Kitchen considers it very likely that scribes puzzling over an antiquated word might have substituted a different word or passed down an understanding of the word that was absolutely incorrect. Thus, for Kitchen, words from a different century are intended clarifications even if they are mistaken. This is the case with the example of *aleph*, as we previously described.

CHAPTER 32

Motive, Please!

If the Bible's composition is "the crime," then motive is the key. Like binge watchers of *Game of Thrones*, scholars are incurably addicted to the biblical whodunit. Many historians specialize in the development of writing. They have extensively studied questions such as, "Why do societies across the world write particular texts? Who gets to be taught to read and write?"[1] Writing may have started as a form of bookkeeping, but it was eventually found useful for different reasons. In ancient Near Eastern societies, written texts were guarded as a means of exercising power, both administrative and symbolic. Courts trained royal scribes so that kings could communicate by writing with their conquered underlings, hence such documentary sources as treaties between the pharaohs and Hittite emperors or the Amarna letters. Other documents were employed exclusively in religious ceremonies. In fact, many of the myths composed by scribes were meant to be recited in front of idols. Kings also used writing to advertise their power. Kings would command craftsmen to engrave steles (carved large plaques) with texts to commemorate victories, like the Mesha Stele celebrating defeat over the Israelites in about 840 BCE. Scribes also composed wisdom literature, moral texts that often described the qualities of a good ruler. Similarly, they fashioned poetry describing the heroic deeds of a king in verse.

---

[1] For an exploration into the function of literacy in the ancient Near East, see Berman, *Created Equal*, chapter 4; and Alan K. Bowman and Greg Woolf, *Literacy and Power in the Ancient World* (Cambridge: Cambridge University, 1994).

Scribes would continue to copy these texts as scribal exercises, and many of them could be retransmitted for hundreds of years.

Let's Show Them Who's Boss

Minimalist scholars argue that the motive behind writing the Bible was to assert power and legitimacy. Israelite royal scribes authored the Bible after their return from Babylon, crafting an imagined history to accentuate their own power. The returnees would have had a strong need to justify their presence in the land, so they invented a history and promulgated it.[1] This invented history was meant to shore up the status of the royal houses and afford the people a tradition that they could turn to. The book was shot through with a theology meant to assure them that God had created all, favored their nation, and granted their leaders victory. So, the leaders of Israel wrote about themselves and—like leaders everywhere—indulged in self-glorification and promoted their own legitimacy. In the minimalists' view, the Bible is unremarkable.

One Book, Two Jews, Three Opinions

Centrist scholars contend that the Bible includes many different types of texts collected to explore many different issues. Schniedewind argues that Hezekiah wrote down the Bible to affirm the history and power of his kingdom. His view is that the Assyrian exile of the Northern Kingdom and the urbanization of the rural south catalyzed the writing activity of much of the Hebrew Bible.[2] Hezekiah wanted to integrate the refugees and restore the golden age of David and Solomon, and so he drafted much of the Bible for that purpose,[3] creating a literary idealization, a collection of works that included words of the prophets, priestly liturgies and ritual text, and some historical narratives.[4] Proof of this is adduced from the Book of Proverbs, which describes how the men of Hezekiah copied Solomon's proverbs.[5] Josiah then wrote additional portions of the Bible in which he chose to criticize Hezekiah's model, Solomon, and critique Hezekiah's vision of the monarchy and Judean society.[6] Some scholars believe that the Book of Deuteronomy through the end of Kings is a work of history that Israelite leaders composed after their exile to Babylon in order to give Jews hope for the future.[7] Others, like Rofé and

Dever, claim that the Bible is a combination of different types of ancient writings from etiological tales (the patriarchal narratives) to epics (the victory against Pharaoh) to laws (much of Deuteronomy), not unlike the sources found in neighboring cultures. Each genre possessed its own conventional motive: etiological tales to explain a people's origin, laws to demand norms of behavior, myth to explain how the world works, and history to glorify certain kings. In the case of the Bible, however, later editors compiled these various strands together into one book to bolster their own status, though they did not reduce the Bible to a work of political propaganda.

Teach Your Children

According to maximalist scholars, the Bible's motive was edification via a narrative of a nation's history and the origin of its laws. Kitchen argues that Israelites returning from Babylon would possess no knowledge of the Egyptian material in the Bible, and they would have no reason to write such a story as appears in the Bible.[8] The Bible attests to its own purpose— it was written to teach the Israelites. That the authors of the Bible claim divine inspiration is not exceptional, as many authors of wisdom texts from the ancient world made similar claims, as did many writers of Greek philosophy and law, according to Yoram Hazony.[9] Kitchen provides many indications that people in the ancient Near East wrote down laws and prophecies as a matter of practice rather than simply remembering them as oral traditions.[10] The biblical authors also shared many of the stylistic features of ancient Near Eastern texts, clearly indicating the text's purpose, whether it was as a set of laws or a prophetic pronouncement about God's will. Together they expressed a worldview for a good society, as did other ancient texts, though with a different message.[11] Yet, maximalist scholars also argue that the biblical authors had a distinctive vision.

Many maximalist scholars claim that while the biblical authors did, indeed, use the very literary conventions and styles common to the ancient Near East, their writings nonetheless contained a vision and message unique to their nation. Kitchen argues that the Bible uses many common literary conventions and implies that the Bible's message is different, but he does not elaborate on how these two aspects coexist. Berman picks up where Kitchen leaves off. He shows how the Bible borrows language previously used to extoll the pharaoh in the Kadesh poem in order to extoll God,[12] making the point that God is more powerful than the pharaoh. Like Kitchen, Berman also argues that the covenant at Sinai has much in common with Hittite treaties. But here again, unlike the Hittite treaties between two kings, the covenant at Sinai presents a treaty of mutual obligation between God and a people.[13] By using the familiar language of the treaty, the Bible presents a very new concept of God's relationship to man. By using the same language and style as other ancient texts, the Bible subverts common aspects of the ideology of other ancient Near Eastern societies.

But in Berman's view, the biblical texts also show important divergences from other ancient texts, divergences that underscore the author's educational motives. While the Bible describes the deeds of ancient forefathers and kings, it does so in far greater detail and with more criticism than other ancient writings. Berman shows that the very story of Moses's birth—which minimalists claim owes its origin to the Bible's commonality with other ancient texts—stands in bold contrast to the Sargon legend.[14] The latter is meant to glorify Sargon, whereas the story of Moses glorified God. Finally, in the Bible, Moses calls on the Israelites to teach their children the laws, to repeat them. This too indicates an educational motive for the entire people that is absent in other ancient texts. In short, the Bible as text, not just its message, differs from the texts that characterized ancient idolatrous societies.

"The Bible" (First Edition) by God, as Told to Moses (Copyright c. 1210 BCE)

The Bible records part of the story of revelation. Jewish tradition has it that the Israelites gathered at Mount Sinai and heard the first two commandments from God directly. Perhaps the people were too frightened to have even understood these first two utterances. The next eight were given only to Moses and then conveyed to the rest of the people. This version of the giving of the Ten Commandments derives from a close reading of the text in which the grammar moves from first person to third person between the second and third commandments. Subsequently, at five different junctures, the Bible states that Moses wrote something. In Exodus 17:14, God tells Moses to "Inscribe this document as a reminder." The text makes clear that this is a command to Moses to record Joshua's battle with Amalek. Exodus 24:4 tells us that "Moses wrote all the commands of the Lord." This presumably refers to the laws that God had given in the previous chapters from Exodus 20:21 to 23:33. Later in Exodus 34:28, it says that Moses "wrote down on the tablets the terms of the covenant, the Ten Commandments." Deuteronomy 31:9 states that "Moses wrote this Torah and gave it to the priests, sons of Levi, who carried the Ark of the Lord's Covenant, and to all the elders of Israel" and then seems to continue with verse 31:24–26, in which it is stated that "When Moses had put down in writing the words of this Torah to the very end, Moses charged the Levites, who carried the Ark of the Covenant of the Lord, saying: "Take this book of Torah and place it beside the Ark of the Covenant of your God [...]"" It is unclear from this command just what God intended to be written down. The term Torah could also mean "laws" or "teaching" in this context. Finally, as Moses nears his death and is warming up for a valedictory speech in Deuteronomy 32, the Song of Moses, Deuteronomy 31:22 states that "That day, Moses wrote down this poem and taught it to the Israelites."

Despite these hints, nowhere does the Torah internally explain its own transmission. Subsequent books of the Bible make mention of the Five Books of Moses, though they also mention a period of widespread idolatry among the Israelites, despite the presence of leaders and judges. The Book of Joshua makes reference to a Book of the Law (*sefer haTorah*): "Let not this Book of the Law cease from your lips, but recite it day and night, so that you may observe faithfully all that is written in it. Only then will you prosper in your undertakings and only then will you be successful." (Joshua 1:8)

Finally, and perhaps most intriguingly, the Book of Kings mentions how, during the reign of Josiah, the high priest Hilkiah found in the Temple a book of the Torah that had been long forgotten.

> Then the high priest Hilkiah said to the scribe Shaphan, "I have found a scroll of the Teaching in the House of the Lord." And Hilkiah gave the scroll to Shaphan, who read it. [...] When the king heard the words of the scroll of the Torah, he rent his clothes. And the king gave orders to the priest Hilkiah, and to Ahikam son of Shaphan, Achbor son of Michaiah, the scribe Shaphan, and Asiah the king's minister. "Go, inquire of the Lord on my behalf, on behalf of the people, and on behalf of all of Judah, concerning the words of

this scroll that has been found. For great indeed must be the wrath of the Lord that has been kindled against us, because our fathers did not obey the words of this scroll to do all that has been prescribed for us. (2 Kings 22:8–13)

Based on this discovery, Josiah reinstated the holiday of Passover, a commemoration that the Israelites would have certainly observed had they all along been reading the Bible! Imagine if a generation of Americans forgot that Independence Day was celebrated on July 4. Thus, the Bible itself hints as to how it was written and how it was subsequently forgotten as well. The Bible does not indicate the language in which it was written.

The Bible testifies, too, to its own fluidity. The prophetic books are the earliest internal sources referring to Biblical Hebrew, doing so by the name of the land in which the language was spoken, *Sfat Canaan*, the language of Canaan. (Isaiah 19:18) The Hebrew Bible also calls the language *Yehudit*, Judaean or Judahite. (2 Kings 18:26–28) In the Hellenistic period, Greek writings referred to the names *Hebraios* and *Hebraïsti* to describe the Israelites (Josephus, *Antiquities* I, 1:2, and so forth). In Mishnaic Hebrew, we find *Ivrit*, "Hebrew," and *Lashon Ivrit*, "Hebrew language." (Mishnah Gittin 9:8) As we shall see, the Talmud also describes two forms of scripts, Paleo-Hebrew and Aramaic Hebrew. Thus, the Bible and later Jewish writings both suggest the development of Hebrew in trace forms over time and witness the changing forms of Hebrew writing as well.

The early rabbis themselves puzzled over the Bible's transmission. The importance of the Bible to the ancient rabbis cannot be overstated. They cared more for the Bible than their own lives. For the rabbis, the Bible and the Oral Torah literally constituted the universe; everything emanated from these words of revelation. The ancient rabbis were acutely curious about the Torah's claim to authenticity. They did not hold one unanimous notion on how the Bible was transmitted, even as they were unanimously committed to Moses as its principal author. The Talmud (Babylonian Talmud Gittin 60a) offers two opinions. Rabbi Yochanan said that the Torah was given over the course of the forty years of wandering in the wilderness in a series of small scrolls, as hinted at in the biblical text. At the end of the forty years, Moses put it all onto one scroll. Rabbi Shimon ben Lakish held that the whole Torah was written at one time just before Moses's death and was based on what Moses heard from God over the forty years.

On the face of it, the Torah raises the puzzling question of how Moses could have written in past tense of his own death. Some rabbis held that he wrote it himself in a prophetic sort of way, while Rabbi Judah ben Ilai believed that Joshua wrote the final verses because Moses could not possibly have written "and Moses died." (Babylonian Talmud Bava Batra 15a and Menah 30a) After the writing of the Torah, the *Mishna* then confidently indicates a straight line of transmission. Moses received the Torah from Sinai and gave it over to Joshua. Joshua gave it over to the elders, the elders to the prophets, and the prophets gave it over to the Men of the Great Assembly. (Babylonian Talmud Pirkei Avot 1:1) However, the story is more complicated.

The ancient rabbis also recognized that the Bible went through a period of canonization and that editors made changes to it. The rabbis certainly recognized that Ezra, the last Jewish prophet who lived during the Babylonian exile (fifth century BCE) and led the Jews back to Israel, may have taken editorial/compilation license in bringing forward the biblical text to the returning Jews, perhaps, like the Yiddish *King Lear*, in a new and slightly "improved" version. While the ancient rabbis certainly didn't believe that Ezra authored the Bible, their commentary does highlight the fact that something very significant was going on with Ezra's editing. In the Talmud, Rabbi Yose (Babylonian Talmud Sanhedrin 21b) states: "Had the Torah not been revealed to Moses, it would have been revealed to Ezra." The rabbis also knew that the script of Hebrew had changed over the centuries and that the recoding of the letters itself may have required some editorial decisions. We find the following comment in the Talmud (Babylonian Talmud Sanhedrin 21b):

> Mar Zutra, or some say Mar Ukba, said, Originally the Torah was given to Israel in the Hebrew characters and Hebrew language. Later in the times of Ezra, the Torah was given in Ashurith (Assyrian Script) and Aramaic language. And even though the Torah was not given through him (Ezra), its writing was changed through him... It has been taught that: Rabbi (Rabbi Yehudah Ha Nazi) said, The Torah was originally given in Ashurith writing. When they (Israel) sinned, it was changed to Roatz. But when they repented, [Ashurith characters] were re-introduced.

Yet other rabbis disagreed. "Rabbi Simeon ben Elazar said...The writing [of the law] was never changed." Yet it is inescapable to miss the Talmud's broad hint that something significant was transpiring during the time of Ezra, minimally some editorial tinkering. The notion that wholesale new ideas or stories would be grafted onto the Torah might have been anathema to the ancient rabbis, but the Talmud nevertheless preserves traces of a collective repressed memory. Rabbi Professor David Weiss Halivni notes that the time period of Ezra, circa 600 BCE, is the same time many biblical scholars propose for the writing of the Bible.[15]

Some traditional scholars point out the Bible's mention of Israel's neglect of the Torah until its revival under Ezra. They see in this indirect evidence that the text could have been edited and revised. According to Halivni, because of the Israelites' many sins and strayings, the text became corrupted over time and different versions emerged.[16] Even if these included minor variations, it was still problematic. One consequence of some of these transmission errors is that the rabbis were certain some rules that were passed down orally were given as "Moses from Sinai"—in other words, they were beyond debate. Yet these particular rules did not appear in the text of the Torah. According to Halivni, such discrepancies are internal proof that some changes occurred. Halivni points out, too, that there are scribal markings of dots above the text in ten places in the Torah, which seem to indicate a question mark as to the correctness of those passages.

Jewish tradition ascribes these markings to Ezra. In *Bamidbar Rabbah* (3:13), the following story is recounted about Ezra and the Prophet Elijah, whom we have already encountered: "Ezra reasoned thus: If Elijah comes and asks, 'Why have you written these words?' [Why did you add these suspect passages?] I shall answer, 'That is why I dotted these passages.' And if he says to me, 'You have done well in writing them,' I shall erase the dots above them."[17] Thus, Halivni reveals further ways in which Jewish traditional sages, much to their own discomfort, acknowledged that changes had occurred in the text.

Other, later texts that are part of the biblical tradition attest to the canonization of the Bible sometime between the fourth and second centuries. The Talmud describes how the men of the so-called Great Assembly fixed the biblical canon, deciding which books were to be included and which not. Can tradition be reconciled with the academy?

Academy to Tradition: Call Me, Maybe

Kugel was certainly right in that modern scholars ask different questions than traditional scholars. Modern scholars have mainly been preoccupied with the case of the mysterious Bible due to their skeptical attitude to traditional commentators. But maybe the answer of tradition is less fanciful than Kugel argues. The traditional picture of revelation is both rational and plausible if one accepts a maximalist view of the dates of the events described in the Bible and of the writing of the biblical texts.

The traditional view posits that Moses spent forty days in deep communion and meditation with God. His situation was not unlike that of contemporary yogis who retreat in silence or artists who confine themselves in a room until they emerge with their literary masterpieces, inspired about what to write and how to write it. What this inspiration is in practice, whether connecting to a deeper consciousness or experiencing a eureka moment, whether it comes from within us or from outside, it is something artists can rarely explain. During this time, Moses received many of the laws. Perhaps God inspired him as to which vignettes and themes to memorialize that would depict the story of the patriarchs, the events of the Exodus, and entrance to the Promised Land. We don't know what portion of the Torah Moses received during those forty days and what he received in the subsequent forty years. Certainly, if great philosophers and novelists have been inspired to write hundreds, even thousands of pages over a period of several years, Moses could have done the same over a span of forty. In fact, the Bible is not a particularly long text. The traditional view is that Moses spoke to God and God spoke to him, though what this meant in practice is impossible to know. It is also possible that Moses wrote the Torah both under direct divine inspiration *and* with recourse to his knowledge of other ancient texts he had studied previously in the Egyptian court. In fact, there is no reason to assume that divine inspiration would lead to a foreign-sounding message. In other words, the wisdom he recorded could have been written in the style of ancient Near Eastern texts, but with variations to underpin its original message. As Imam Shamsi Ali says:

> There is a dialectic between what God reveals to the prophets and what we already know. The prophets did not come to teach us who God is because we know that essentially within our soul. What the

prophets initially came for is how to bring us to where we need to get. Their approaches differed in many ways.

For our purposes, the traditional view is that God indicated to Moses not only the laws, but also the way in which to describe the narrative of events so as to best convey their truth and their message. Moses must have also known about prior events from oral traditions. The text of the Bible, we know, consists of the beginning of creation, the recounting of the history of the Israelites, their laws, and their responsibilities in the Promised Land and their relationship to their neighbors. It can be rationally viewed as a book dictated by Moses over a forty-year period to the elders and scribes, accompanied by additional oral commentary and explanations of Moses. Moses then commanded them to be combined into one scroll.

Over the course of the generations after Moses, the Jews were frequently tempted by idolatrous practices, as the Books of the Prophets sadly recount when chronicling the deeds of Israelites and their leaders in relation to the covenant. During the reigns of King Hezekiah and later King Josiah, the biblical texts were updated to a more contemporary version of Hebrew, and they were edited to some extent to update names of places and to clarify (or mistranslate) words that had become arcane to readers of that time. When Ezra and his scribes brought the Jews back from Babylonia (then under Persian control), he further updated the grammar, changed the letters of the texts, canonized what was traditional, and judged what else might be necessary to add to the final text. In essence, Ezra took the opportunity to rename "New Amsterdams" to "New Yorks," and to update the word "cirichálgung" to "consecration of a house of worship." He may have been wrong in certain instances, or his alteration of words and narratives may have confounded the ability of modern scholars to accurately date the text purely from academic tools.

Such a description of the writing and transmission of the Bible harmonizes some maximalist academic views with traditional beliefs. The implication of the traditional picture is that the Bible is a coherent text whose narrative should be taken at face value. Much of what biblical critics view as editorial errors by the compiler of the Bible are understood by the ancient rabbis, from close reading, to be important and provocative clues regarding events otherwise described in quite sparing and economical prose.

The transmission of the Bible has likely been imperfect, and some meanings have been lost. We can easily imagine downtrodden Israelites losing their hold on individual words and contexts as their own vocabulary and even alphabet evolved. They would misunderstand words for the same reason I misunderstood the word *purfilde* in Malory, as I recounted earlier, when I did not realize it related to a garment trimmed with fur. Accepting the traditional view of the Bible thus means scrutinizing some traditional understandings of the text and being mindful of modern biblical scholarship, as modern discoveries can deepen our comprehension of the texts. As Reverend Dr. Katharine Henderson explains:

> I think that the Bible is a product of divine inspiration. I think that this is true for my own life. Divine inspiration means that our sacred text has validity as a completely sacred and special book inspired by God, that it is mediated and understood, and written in some fashion or told either as oral history or written history, oral story. Tradition absolutely goes through the process of human interpretation at every point in time and we know that. I think that this is the mystery and value of scholarship.

This is hard, intense, and frustrating work for anyone who takes these texts seriously. We may not, in fact, ever be capable of reconstructing our corrupted versions of the texts. The original text is not stored somewhere in an accessible hard drive. This is one profound tragedy of having the tradition of the Bible interrupted by generations that forsook the Bible. God's words may be in the Bible in ways that we can no longer comprehend. Some may have been excised. The ancient rabbis, sensing this, preserved certain oral traditions that they ascribed all the way back to Mount Sinai, despite the fact that these traditions were absent from the Bible itself. That being said, the Bible can reasonably be read as a document that describes a genuine history and whose narrative order is vital for its overall spiritual message. A brief examination of one biblical story can illustrate this point.

CHAPTER 33

How to Read the Bible, Take Two

Looking at Biblical Stories from Both Sides Now

Academic scholars continue to grapple with the Bible in different ways. Go to any liberal arts college and take a class on the Bible in ancient Near Eastern studies or in Judaic studies and you'll doubtlessly find yourself in the center of a debate about the great biblical whodunit. You'll learn to judge all sorts of external and internal evidence (none of it conclusive). Your professors will most likely endorse centrist or—to a lesser extent—minimalist stances.

If you study the Bible in a literature department, you'll have a remarkably different experience. There, you would analyze the style and themes of the Bible and perhaps explore its messages on particular topics. Or, as in the case of much comparative literature, you will read the Bible in light of other texts. A great example of this approach can be found in the work of Avivah Zornberg, who brings her deep knowledge of Western literature and literary theory to her readings of the Five Books of Moses. You'll find this approach in "famous book" curriculums as well.

Some scholars, like Yoram Hazony, think that the Bible belongs in philosophy departments alongside the classics of the discipline. The biblical texts deal with topics such as ethics, epistemology, moral philosophy, and even political theory, just like other ancient texts we learn. And just as some Greek philosophers claimed divine inspiration for their written works on politics and ethics, so too does the Bible. Chinese and Indian philosophers were masters at cultivating inspiration via meditation, which brought them new and deep insights. Artists of all sorts speak of metaphorical muses who inspire new ideas and approaches. Claims of divine inspiration are no reason to banish the Bible from philosophy departments. And, if you happen to take a Bible course in a religious studies department, you might get a mix of the above-mentioned university approaches.

If you study the Bible in a seminary or religious institution, you'll likely encounter a traditional interpretive apparatus or two. Christians and Jews may have different ways of reading the text of the Hebrew Bible, but they both approach the Holy Scriptures as a source of personal enlightenment and social justice. The historical critical approach is presently the dominant one in universities. In my view, that is a shame. There are so many layers to the biblical texts and so many approaches to studying it. The following example will illustrate why.

The Case of the Joseph Story

Though biblical critics divide the Joseph story into different episodes written at different times, the text makes eminently more sense taken as a whole. Critics claim that chapter 38 of the Joseph story, which recounts the story of Judah and Tamar, was a later addition to the text, and they offer a number of reasons for why the story was inserted. J. A. Emerton views the story as containing etiological (origin) motifs about the clans of Judah. Robert Alter feels that the Judah/Tamar story is connected to the unfolding of the Joseph story.[1] Most academic scholars consider the text to be an artificial addition, rather unrelated. Biblical critics are most concerned with the political message of the text.

The traditional view, by contrast, sees the Judah and Tamar episode as fundamental to the narrative, without which we lose the moral message of the text and its life lesson about relationships. The recounting of the story in the popular musical *Joseph and the Amazing Technicolor Dreamcoat* tells a logical, coherent, and entertaining story without any mention of Tamar. I should know—we played the movie version countless times in my home as an electronic babysitter for our children. Yet without Tamar, the story would not merit inclusion in the Bible and we would have no idea what to morally make of the Joseph story.

Let's take a closer look. In chapter 37, we learn of Joseph's impetuous behavior as a seventeen-year-old, which engendered the hatred of his brothers. He dreams of lording it over his brothers and, rather than keeping the dream to himself, bluntly proclaims it to his family. Failing to recognize the seething resentment of his brothers, he broadcasts the contents of a second dream to his family, one in which his father, too, now in addition to his brothers, pays him homage. Imagine what Joseph would have been like had Facebook and Twitter existed in his day. He would have Instagrammed all sorts of poses of himself in his coat.

No one is amused. His brothers are clearly steaming with hatred. Yet, his father Jacob, inexplicably insensitive to this advanced case of sibling rivalry, later sends Joseph to check on his brothers in the vicinity of Shechem. Joseph finds his brothers and most seek to kill him. Reuven plans surreptitiously to free him, but is late in doing so. Judah executes a more profitable plan of selling Joseph as a slave for twenty pieces of silver (which seems appropriate given our present historical knowledge). Both brothers are considered *ra*—not functional/incomplete in their actions toward Joseph.

Chapter 39 continues with Joseph's travails in the land of Egypt and the reconciliation and settlement of Jacob's family in Egypt as well. Chapter 38 seems to be shoehorned into the story, indicating it is an artifact retained by an inept editor that serves no real purpose. Some academics would argue that this Judah/Tamar story must have existed previously and needed to go somewhere. Perhaps this was the least bad place to put it in terms of the narrative. Reading from chapter 37 to the end of Genesis, while skipping chapter 38, certainly conveys the chronology of the tale flawlessly.

The problem is that this misses the whole point the Bible is making. The Bible was not written to recount the travails and battles of the Israelites the way a newspaper would, "just reporting the facts." The Bible represents a book of relationships between individuals and between individuals and God, and a key question always is whether individuals act as though God is a witness to their decisions and choices. Will they remember the Invisible Hand/Eternal Witness? When we understand the Bible as a book of relationships, chapter 38 becomes pivotal to understanding the subsequent reconciliation of the children of Jacob. It teaches, as well, how Judah goes from being a self-interested, self-centered, lying, deceptive grandee to a person willing to sacrifice himself for others. The narrative literally cannot be read without chapter 38 in the classical tradition.

The chapter begins with Judah leaving his brothers, becoming partners with a nonrelative, and marrying a Canaanite woman. To recap, Reuven, Shimon, and Levi are all on the outs with their father due to their misdeeds, and Judah has left (literally in Hebrew "went down") the family. So, the first four of Jacob's sons with Leah are at odds with their father, and Leah's daughter, Dinah, is a rape victim about whom we hear no more. Rachel, Jacob's only true love among his wives, is dead. Benjamin, Rachel's only child other than the presumed dead Joseph, is so coddled by his father that even as Benjamin ages, Jacob calls him a boy. He is frozen in Jacob's mind. In Genesis 37:35, Jacob seems to have written off his remaining sons: "[…] I will go down mourning to *my son* [my emphasis] in Sheol." No one else counts for anything. Fratricide, deception, death, depression, and no sense of responsibility or reliance on God characterize this family *in extremis* and in great pain. There is no place here for them to be redeemed. God will have to start over, perhaps through Joseph. Such a direction for the story also makes literary sense. In the prior two generations, only one son was the designated heir to the Abrahamic mantle. Perhaps for this generation, Joseph and all of his progeny could have been imagined as the ancestors of the Israelite people. Maybe that is what seventeen-year-old Joseph's dreams were all about.

After marrying Judah, Tamar bears three sons in quick succession. This is a bad sign in Genesis, as important births take a lot of effort and usually divine intercession. Further, throughout Genesis, intermarriage with Canaanites is seen in the poorest light. Abraham sends his servant back to Nahor to seek a spouse for Isaac. The marriage of Esau to a Canaanite woman distresses both Isaac and Rebecca, and Esau comes to realize it. Jacob himself has to go to the homeland of Abraham to find his brides. Shimon and Levi take the extreme and criticized act of killing all the Shechemite men rather than have their sister intermarry with the Canaanite prince.

Yet Judah, who marries a Canaanite, does not seem to fret over finding a wife for his eldest son. Her name is Tamar. Interestingly Tamar is not given any lineage, so we don't know if she is a full-fledged Canaanite. Her first husband, Judah's eldest son, is evil in the eyes of God and dies. Then Judah's second son takes Tamar as a wife in a levirate marriage. Levirate marriage is the obligation of the brother of a deceased man to marry the brother's widow, a common practice in the ancient Near East. In Deuteronomy, the Bible provides an out clause for levirate marriage. But at the time of Judah, levirate marriage was apparently broadly accepted. The idea was that the brother would have a responsibility to provide a son in the name of the deceased brother to carry on his name. Levirate marriage was at its essence the brotherly responsibility for the memory, legacy, and love of a brother. It should then be no surprise that the second son of Judah, Onan, did not see things that way and would not inseminate Tamar, as he knew that the firstborn would not count as his son. God ensured that Onan died quickly as well. His legacy in this world is to be the source of the word "onanism."

Judah does not want his third son to marry Tamar, as he is not aware enough to realize that it was actually the evilness of his first two sons that caused their deaths. He implicitly puts the blame on Tamar and is ready to give up his previous sons' legacy. Judah lies to Tamar and tells her to remain as a widow in her father's house until the third son, Shelah (literally in Hebrew "of her"), grows up. Judah deceives Tamar in the same way that he deceived his father and Joseph. He does not free Tamar from her obligation to marry Shelah, which he could have done, but sends her instead into an enforced captivity to her father's house that will presumably, in Judah's mind, never end. She must continue as a lifelong mourner like Jacob and as a prisoner with an indeterminate sentence like Joseph. Like Jacob, Tamar must remain in mourning while the existence of the person who can end that mourning is concealed by Judah in each case for his own motives. A long time passes and Judah forgets about Tamar. We don't know if Judah is also forgetting Jacob. But we do note that there is no mention in the text of Jacob in chapter 38. Wow, how low can Judah go? But it gets worse.

In the Bible, "remembering" and "forgetting" are both acts with ethical implications. Next in the story, Judah's wife dies. It seems that Judah's wife did not mean all that much to him either, as he was pretty quickly comforted and heads off a short while later to the sheep-shearing gala in Timnah with his now grown son, Shelah. When Tamar hears this, she throws off her widow's garb and heads straight for Judah and Shelah. She also covers her face with a veil, just as Rebecca wore a veil when she met Isaac, and she is described with the same words. Clearly wedding bells are ringing in Tamar's mind. She might have even opened her bridal registry at Bloomingdale's Timnah outlet. We are being prepared as readers for a potential covenantal marriage moment of the Hebrew patriarchs.

Rebecca, as previously mentioned, was the lead figure in the period of her marriage with Isaac. She made key decisions, such as deceiving Isaac by giving the birthright to Jacob. She did so not out of self-interest, but rather in the interest of perpetuating the patriarchal family. Rebecca was willing to do this at the great personal cost of sending away her beloved Jacob, whom she was never to see again, as well as alienating Esau from her irredeemably. Rebecca was not concerned about revenge or twenty silver coins. As much as Rebecca, Tamar is willing to sacrifice everything as Judah turns to her, not recognizing her behind the veil and assuming she is some sort of ritual prostitute. Judah's lack of perception may also stem from the fact that he perceives others as he perceives his environment. Judah is doing what Freud later called projection—because he uses other people, he assumes others are only out to use him. Tamar, quick on the uptake, asks what the payment would be. Judah says he will send a goat. Recall that Judah and his brothers slaughtered a goat and put the blood on Joseph's coat and asked Jacob, "Please examine this; is it your son's tunic or not?" (37:32) Tamar asks for a pledge until the goat is sent and she asks for his "seal, and cord and staff which you carry" (38:18), all three symbols of ancient kingship.

Judah has put his whole future and that of his progeny on the line with the same casualness with which Esau sold his birthright to Jacob for a bowl of soup. Judah and Tamar have intercourse and Judah wants to send a goat and redeem his personal symbols. But he cannot, as there is no cult prostitute to find. Judah does not want to become a "laughing-stock," so he quickly gives up looking for her and essentially abdicates his potential kingship and the lineage of his mother Leah. To our modern ear, it would be like someone giving up looking for a lost book bag that contained his wallet, the title to his house, keys to his car, and the key to his safe deposit box, all because he does not want to admit he lost them. This is the man whose descendants would be David, Solomon, and ultimately the Messiah. The Bible makes no sense if this is the case. The text is telling us that, at this point, Judah is not getting on the patriarchal train. Maybe Joseph is the rightful sole heir.

At this juncture in the story, we are again ready to break down and cry. For a book that is all about relationships, has Judah gone to the moral bottom? Is there anything in him that is redeemable? Yet there is still more! Tamar has become pregnant from the encounter, and three months later, she is showing. Judah is told and, exercising his right as the father of her prospective groom Shelah, Judah says, "let her be burned." (38:25) As she is to be brought out to be burned, she sends a private message to Judah that eerily echoes the message Judah delivered to Jacob. The Hebrew words are entirely parallel: "I am with child of the man to whom these belong…Examine these: whose seal and staff and cord are these?" Tamar is willing to be burned at the stake rather than embarrass her father-in-law. She cares enough about the continuity of the Abrahamic family not only to risk her life, but to put it entirely in the hands of Judah, who has shamelessly deceived her, forgotten her plight, and used her.

This is the pivotal point, which renders the entire remainder of Genesis understandable. Without this story, we could not hope to understand Judah's later redemptive actions of being willing to stand in the place of Benjamin, his half-brother. Judah looks at the staff, cord, and seal and, likely reminded of the circumstances of revealing Joseph's fraudulently blood-stained tunic, recognizes the enormity of what he did to Tamar and what he has made of his own life. He declares her to be more righteous then he is and lets the truth be known. Tamar gives birth to twins, who replace the two dead sons of Judah. The birth process recapitulates the process of Jacob and Esau's birth, each infant vying to be firstborn. One son sticks a hand out and has a crimson string placed on him, but withdraws, so his brother is then born first.

In case we miss the allusion, the second son out of the womb is named Zerah, which means bright, ruddy, just like Esau. Except here, both children are part of the covenantal chain.

Tamar has healed the breach in Jacob's family. Judah remembers Jacob and the rest of his family. Judah returns home, now with a new comprehension of his own responsibility because he has just been taught what responsibility is by Tamar. It is only now that we can understand why Judah rises to the occasion in Egypt and why we must take seriously Judah's pledge of his own life to Jacob. (43:8–9) What a radical reversal. Jacob, who had resisted earlier entreaties by the brothers to return to redeem Shimon and acquire food rations, instinctively understands Judah's sincerity. Jacob's trust is well placed, as Judah lives up to his word in 44:33, pleading to remain a slave to the viceroy in the place of Benjamin. Judah's sense of responsibility, as is his word that he gives to his father, is now more important to him than his own freedom. He has ethically traveled very far since the Timnah sheep-shearing gala. As a consequence, we can appreciate why the descendants of Judah and Tamar deserve the kingship. We can also recognize why the Kingdom of Judah will become the worthy surviving kingdom of the Israelites, even as the stronger, larger Northern Kingdom is destroyed and exiled, never to return.

The easy route is to assume that chapter 38 is unnecessary. The harder route is to grapple with the text in order to see what lessons are intended.[1]

Your Next Reading Group Selection: The Bible

Bible critics in the academy have focused on the biblical whodunit. For this purpose, they have analyzed the Bible's historical value, ideology, and literary style. This approach has often led to disregard of the moral, relational, and theological elements of the text. That is a pity, for these elements have no less resonance for readers today. But it has also led to even greater appreciation for the text. As scholars like Kenneth Kitchen, Joshua Berman, Avraham Faust, and many others have shown, the greater our historical knowledge about the time of the Bible and the cultures that surrounded it, the better our understanding of the revolutionary ideas the Bible introduced. There is no other book on earth as influential. It is the foundational text to the monotheistic revolution. It never fails to be relevant. I personally find something new and relevant every week.

---

[1] I learned about this approach to the story of Judah and Tamar, as well as Judah and his brothers, from Rabbi David Silber, founder of the Drisha Institute, when he taught a series of sessions at the Wexner Heritage Foundation in 1993 in New York City.

Unfortunately, today most people either do not read the Bible closely, tune it out, or adopt an academic approach to reading it. This is a shame. From the stories of the Exodus and the giving of the law to the wisdom and poetry of Job, Proverbs, Psalms, or the Song of Songs, the Bible is not easy reading, but it is well worth the time. Abraham, Rebecca, Judah, Tamar, Miriam, Moses, Devorah, Ruth, Esther, Ezra, and many other Biblical figures continue to inspire. Sometimes, we are so starved for heroes that we seek them among celebrities because they can sing or act or are good at sports or appeared on a reality television show. The characters of the Bible are almost all flawed individuals who also strive to choose good in a flawed world. This is what makes them so compelling. That being said, the Bible mostly reads as a tragedy. How could the Israelites have built the golden calf? How could they have been ready to negate the Exodus and revelation based on a few dispiriting words from the spies? Why couldn't they have remained loyal to God when they reached the Promised Land? Yet in the Bible, heroic acts by the humblest individuals turn out to be decisive.

To illustrate this point, let us return to the story of Hannah as we prepare for the final part of this book. The Bible story almost comes to an abrupt end as we open the first Book of Samuel. In Judges, which immediately precedes Samuel, we learned that the Israelite experiment was on the brink of collapse. Civil war raged between the tribes. Idolatry and corruption spread among the people. The conquest was stalled, incomplete, the priesthood was corrupt, and prophecy was rare. God was angry with the Israelites and the Ark of the Covenant was about to be captured by the Philistines, for the Ark itself could not abide with this sinful people. So, as we begin reading the first Book of Samuel, news from the Promised Land is pretty bad. And it's not fake news. Sad. The Bible is about to come to an abrupt end and society will have to reboot. It seems inevitable, but for one modest and otherwise anonymous person—Hannah, childless but devoted to the God of Israel. She takes a most radical step and, in the second chapter of Samuel, utters the first full-fledged prayer. Biblical scholars allege that this prayer is an early fragment, but it suits the text seamlessly. This prayer is her portal into the universe, into a relationship with the Almighty, into a relationship with those around her, and into a relationship with her people. Hannah's prayer fittingly teaches us all how to pray. Her humble prayer transforms everything for her, for the Israelites, and indeed for the world. Hannah bears a son, Samuel, who plays a significant role in purging the priesthood, returning the people to God, unifying the tribes, and anointing King David, whose descendants will advance humanity toward transcendence. One humble woman's prayer, from heart to heaven, can transform everything. This sort of prayer may be rare, but the Bible teaches us to strive for it. That is the magnificence, mystery, and challenge of the Bible to each of us. Read it with an open mind.

PART SIX

Why Have Faith and Why Pray?

INTRODUCTION

Is It Moral to Have Faith?

If there is no proof of God, why take the step of faith? Atheists argue that faith binds us in a straitjacket of irrational and immoral doctrines that constrain our every thought and action. In contrast, reason enables intellectual and personal freedom. Indeed, doesn't the very idea of having faith push adherents to blind obedience and to the abdication of their moral responsibility? Aren't the faithful susceptible to following irresponsible leaders who twist faith to feed their own hunger for power? How is faith even necessary to be a good person if we can decide to be moral based on our own rational choices?

And then, the notion of prayer. Preposterous! Even assuming faith, what's the point of praying? How dare we presume to devise better plans for an omniscient God? Who are we to convince Him, omnipotent as He is, to change the course of events? Shouldn't prayer be characterized as a copout, a magical way of thinking for the feebleminded who refuse to accept reality or take the initiative to better their own life?

If you have agreed with the reasoning of this book thus far, you presumably acknowledge that faith in the God of Abraham and the tenets of monotheism is not irrational. *Such faith is a decision to accept as true what is rationally possible (even likely by my reckoning of the evidence).* In other words, it is a step in one direction rather than another. All monotheists must take this step. Likewise, theists, who choose to doubt the existence of God, must also take this step of faith. The faith that atheists rightly criticize for being irrational and immoral is faith in idols. This faith is a belief in lies about the extraordinary power and authority of a finite thing, person, or class of people. Any choice to believe such a lie is bad faith. Because faith in idols is humanity's default mode, having faith is a fork in the road that every person takes, whether consciously or not. Every day through countless decisions, we choose to reject or accept the lies that constitute idolatry. Some reject idolatry by believing in one God, some without. Both are rational options. Acting according to the Golden Rule—not doing unto others what we don't want done to us—is the litmus test for rejecting all forms of idolatry or, in other words, lies about power and authority.

For those who choose monotheism, the Bible is the first text to teach us good faith: God alone is omnipotent, omniscient, and omnibenevolent. God's will is to partner with humanity to perfect the world. The Bible explains that we have the choice to imitate God and to partner with God in improving the world. But even those who choose monotheism face bad-faith pitfalls along the way. Monotheists have been known to park their reason at the door and embrace the leadership of "God's sole spokesperson," a dishonest purveyor of distorted tenets purportedly espoused in the Holy Books. In reality, such people are idolaters in monotheistic garb.

Atheists, too, are liable to find themselves entangled in their own webs of bad faith. They may choose to reason, as did my commuting companion from part one, that any means justify their desired ends. These atheists practice Machiavellian reasoning, relying on the false premise that only they themselves and those important to them matter, contemptuous of the truth that no human can fully judge the worth of others. This is no different than asserting one's own godhood in updated rhetoric. What really divides monotheists and atheists is not therefore the rejection of idolatry, which both can accept, but the step of believing in God and our ability to partner with Him as described in the Bible.

Faith in God is a prerequisite to prayer. Monotheistic prayer is a process of communication intended to help us actualize our individual role in God's plan. Idolatrous prayer, on the other hand, is different. Here, the atheist critique makes sense. Idolatrous prayer is irrational: it assumes that ceremonies and sacrifices can alter reality, whatever the request may be. Idolatrous prayer is immoral: it ignores the moral character and value (or lack thereof) of the petitioner and/or the request. Idolatrous prayer substitutes false belief for responsible action. Monotheistic prayer, in contrast, is a practice that clarifies our role in perfecting the world. And it requires belief in God's providence. The Bible describes prayer as our means of communicating our desires and aligning them with God's plan for perfecting the world. Monotheistic prayer is, thus, a request contingent on a process of moral reflection and our deepest, most honest reasoning.

Stories of prayer in the Bible teach us how to pray. Some biblical figures get it right; others fail. The Bible reveals that true prayer brings us to the junction of what we can do and what needs to be done to perfect the world, even if the answer to our prayers is often not yes.

The Perils of Faith and the Follies of Prayer

Atheists dismiss any act of faith—be it in the one God of Abraham or in a polytheistic pantheon—as indisputably contrary to reason and to morality. Harris writes, "Because most religions offer no valid mechanism by which their core beliefs can be tested and revised, each new generation of believers is condemned to inherit the superstitions and tribal hatreds of its predecessors."[1] Harris considers it inevitable that faith, in every case, thwarts rational thought: "Believing strongly, without evidence, [people] have kicked themselves loose of the world. It is therefore in the very nature of faith to serve as an impediment to further inquiry."[2] Worse still, religious faith bases itself on a feeling. For atheists, this constitutes a delusion constructed on a foundation of wishful thinking:

> I feel a certain, rather thrilling "conviction" that Nicole Kidman is in love with me. As we have never met, my feeling is my only evidence of her infatuation. I reason thus: my feelings suggest that Nicole and I must have a special, even metaphysical, connection— otherwise, how could I have this feeling in the first place? I decide to set up camp outside her house to make the necessary introductions; clearly, this sort of faith is a tricky business.[3]

Faith, as the atheists see it, is not only an intellectual failing; it is a moral one as well, an infantile and cowardly substitute for taking personal responsibility in the real world. As Dennett argues, "It is time for the reasonable adherents of all faiths to find the courage and stamina to reverse the tradition that honors helpless love of God—in any tradition.

Far from being honorable, it is not even excusable. It is shameful."[4] Onfray echoes this view: "Better the faith that brings peace of mind than the rationality that brings worry—even at the price of perpetual mental infantilism. What a demonstration of metaphysical sleight of hand—and what a monstrous price!"[5] Even more disturbing to the atheists, unquestioning faith in an idea or person is gravely dangerous. Dawkins quotes none other than the Nazis: "We believe that National Socialism is the sole saving faith for our people. We believe that there is a Lord God in heaven, who created us, who leads us, who directs us and who blesses us visibly. And we believe that this Lord God sent Adolf Hitler to us, so that Germany might become a foundation for all eternity."[6]

Atheists tolerate simply no intellectual or moral excuse for any act of absolute religious certainty. As a result, Dawkins even tempers his own atheism with a "step of faith," as I characterize it. Dawkins explains, "Atheists do not have faith; and reason alone could not propel one to total conviction that anything definitely does not exist."[7] Thus on a scale of one to seven, with one representing a committed theist and seven a committed atheist, each convinced respectively of God's existence or nonexistence, Dawkins places himself at six, "Very low probability, but short of zero. *De facto* atheist. 'I cannot know for certain but I think God is very improbable, and I live my life on the assumption that he is not there.'"[8] Dawkins portrays his step of faith from six to seven as an "assumption." Yet the rhetoric of atheist writers is that the only moral and rational way to live is by reason alone. We will see this attitude presents its own dangers.

Atheist writers exhibit a particular distaste for prayer, which they consider an abdication of reason and responsibility. Prayer is unreasonable because there is just no evidence that it works. More than simply being useless, prayer degrades human freedom and diminishes us as thinking beings. Michel Onfray classifies the petitioner in prayer as some combination of idiot and automaton. "The community is marked rather by the triumph of parrotlike repetition and the recycling of fables, with the help of well-oiled machinery that repeats but never innovates, which solicits not the intelligence but the memory. Chanting psalms, reciting, and repeating are not thinking."[9] Atheist writers contend that prayer is doubly irrational, inconsistent even with monotheism's own core tenets. Christopher Hitchens considers "[...] the man who prays [as] the one who thinks that god has arranged matters all wrong, but who also thinks that he can instruct god how to put them right."[10] Atheists think of prayer as a simpleminded superstitious practice, its sole purpose abdication of our responsibility to confront reality. As Onfray describes it, "the power of prayer, the effectiveness of ritual, the validity of incantations, communion with voodoo spirits, hemoglobin-based miracles, the Virgin's tears, the resurrection of a crucified man, the magical properties of cowrie shells, the value of animal sacrifices, the transcendent effects of Egyptian saltpeter, or prayer wheels…everywhere I look I saw how readily men construct fables in order to avoid looking reality in the face."[11]

In the eyes of atheists, prayer is a servile, demeaning substitute for taking responsibility and action. Hitchens chides, "The positions for prayer are usually emulations of the supplicant serf before an ill-tempered monarch. The message is one of continual submission, gratitude, and fear. Life itself is a poor thing: an interval in which to prepare for the hereafter or the coming—or second coming—of the Messiah."[12] Finally, Hitchens concludes, communal prayer also intensifies religious fanaticism and often incites violence. Describing a hypothetical group of men, he writes: "Now—would I feel safer, or less safe, if I was to learn that they were just coming from a prayer meeting? As the reader will see, this is not a question to which a yes/no answer can be given. But I was able to answer it as if it were not hypothetical. Just to stay within the letter 'B,' I have actually had that experience in Belfast, Beirut, Bombay, Belgrade, Bethlehem, and Baghdad. In each case I can say absolutely, and can give my reasons, why I would feel immediately threatened if I thought that the group of men approaching me in the dusk were coming from a religious observance."[13] While Dennett is open to the suggestion that prayer might provide psychological benefits, he finds that this is merely the result of the consolation comforting thoughts provide, whether they are true or not:

> People who are suffering, even if their morale is not improved in measurable ways, may well gain some solace from nothing more than the knowledge that they are being acknowledged, noticed, thought about. It would be a mistake to suppose that these 'spiritual' blessings have no place in the inventory of reasons that we skeptics are trying to assay, just as it would be a mistake to suppose that the nonexistence of an intercessory-prayer effect would show

that prayer is a useless practice. There are subtler benefits to be evaluated—but they do need to be identified.[14]

Beyond its possible placebo effects, atheists agree that prayer debases people intellectually and morally.[1]

---

[1] A note on the references and quotations in part six. The vast majority of quotations in this section have been gleaned from online quotation dictionaries like brainyquote, goodreads, and others. Longer quotations include a reference to their original source. I refer to various scientific studies in this section to bolster my arguments, though again those who conducted the studies may not agree with my view on religion. Finally, as with other parts, where I am referring to the arguments of a specific author, they are mentioned in the text as well as in the references.

CHAPTER 34

Faith in Idols

The atheists make their criticisms of faith in God based on a certain definition of faith. They define faith as the belief in the truth of an idea, being, or event that is either unproven or contrary to our senses and reason. In this formulation, it is precisely because faith is inherently irrational that it is so malignant and dangerous. This book has explained why monotheists share the atheists' critique of this sort of blind faith. Though proof is not a prerequisite to faith for monotheists, they do insist on consistency between faith and the evidence of our senses and reason. Faith in one Almighty God meets this criterion.

We Can All Mock Idolatrous Faith

Atheists and monotheists can agree on the irrationality of idolatrous faith. Idolatrous faith, the deification of finite things, people, or ideas, is, by any definition, contrary to our senses and reason. Jeremiah describes it thus:

> For it is the work of a craftman's hands. He cuts down a tree in the forest with an ax, He adorns it with silver and gold. He fastens it with nails and hammer, So that it does not totter. They are like scarecrows in a cucumber patch, They cannot speak, They have to be carried, For they cannot walk, Be not afraid of them, for they can do no harm; Nor is in them to do any good. (Jeremiah 10:3–6)

And the psalmist echoes, "The idols of the nations are silver and gold, made by human beings." (Psalm 135:15) In the words of Isaiah, "... their land is filled with idols; They bow down to the work of their hands, To what their own fingers have wrought." (Isaiah 2:8) Belief astrology is equally irrational. Jeremiah again: "And do not be dismayed by portents in the sky; Let the nations be dismayed by them! For the laws of the nations [magical customs] are delusions." (Jeremiah 10:2–3) What rational philosopher would object to such conclusions? Ancient nations might believe that Pharaoh was a god, attributing to his person powers beyond mortal financial, military, and human resources. Not so in the Bible, which dissents emphatically by describing a would-be god's all-too-human defeat, in Pharaoh's case by the plagues, and in Sennacherib's case by assassination.

Monotheists and atheists can agree it is immoral to believe in human beings as gods. Attribute special powers to specific individuals and, before you know it, you'll be attributing superiority to some people over others. Needless to say, once a leader or certain class of people is deemed superior, it's only a short distance to an autocratic society and a mandated legal code devoid of the Golden Rule. This is what occurred over the centuries in societies as different as ancient Egypt and Assyria, Stalinist Russia, and Jim Jones's Guyana dystopia. The tragedy of such societies is that people not only acquiesced to the injustices of their leaders, they actively collaborated on them. Consider what Jeremiah observes of the idolatrous imperial nations of the ancient world: "To You nations shall come from the ends of the earth and say, 'Our fathers inherited utter delusions, things that are futile and worthless.'" (Jeremiah 16:19)[1] Jeremiah here mocks the beliefs that underpin the entire mechanism of idolatrous injustice.

Monotheists and atheists can agree about the dangers of *uncritical belief*. The atheists' critique of belief is extremely important because *all idolatry depends on belief in lies*. This is the difference between idolatry's lies about power and authority and rational assessments about the two. A rational person might with justification consider someone or something as powerful. Certainly, the accumulation of power in whatever form—be

---

[1] I first discovered this quote in Hazony, *The Philosophy*, 176. Hazony's discussion of Jeremiah is highly informative.

it allies, money, arms, or the like—makes for a formidable opponent. Resistance requires resources, and, if your opponents hold the reins of government, many will die in the confrontation and victory will prove no more guaranteed than defeat. Still, no foe is invincible, given the right weapons, information, and alliances on your side. A rational person, likewise, might attribute authority to some figure based on her or his knowledge or experience, but would likely question that authority were he or she later to fail to conform to expectations. An idolater, on the other hand, believes above and beyond rational assessment, and contrary to evidence, that the power of a person or thing is unbeatable by human means or that this person has unquestionable authority. Atheists are right to ridicule the choice to believe mindlessly. In fact, monotheists, too, are encouraged to mock belief in idols, as all the biblical prophets do with contempt and as the Talmud explicitly encourages. (Babylonian Talmud Megillah 25b)

The decision to believe in something irrational is a human choice. Idolatry, however, obscures this notion of choice, whether it's to believe in the omnipotence of a charismatic leader or in the miracle-working capacities of manufactured statues. Recognizing a legitimate choice of options becomes highly difficult in cultures with a long history of idolatry, or where "idol worship" exists in a contemporary manifestation that is relentlessly reinforced by propaganda machines.

CHAPTER 35

God Is Not an Idol

Belief in the existence of the God of Abraham is different from belief in idols. The two are different. *You can be an avowed atheist and still grasp the difference between God and idols. Just read the texts.*

As we have noted throughout, the tenets of monotheism concerning God deliberately distinguish Him from idols. These tenets—omniscience, omnibenevolence, and omnipotence—derive from God's actions in the Bible and consist of the creation of world, the covenant with mankind, the covenant with Abraham, the defeat of the Egyptian empire and the Exodus, the covenant with the Israelites, and the revelations of the laws. The text is unambiguous about God's powers to intervene in nature, to alter the course of history, and to act for the good of humanity. By contrast, pick up any ancient polytheistic text at random and you will likely find an idol or god-king who is corrupt or corruptible.

God Directs the World

The Bible is predicated on God's possessing a plan and purpose for the world. The gods of polytheism are, by contrast, themselves subject to the whims and uncertainties of fate. God not only chooses Abraham, but He promises him that all nations will be blessed through him. God's promises to Abraham project into the distant future, a time of blessing for all humanity. The biblical prophets elaborate on this message. For instance, Isaiah declares, "In the days to come, the Mount of the Lord's House shall stand firm above the mountains and tower above the hills;

and all the nations shall gaze on it with joy." (Isaiah 2:2) This passage ends with the famous vision of global peace engraved on a wall outside the United Nations building in New York City: "Nation shall not take up Sword against nation; They shall never again know war." (Isaiah 2:4) Here is singular evidence, at once simple and profound, of God's vision of a perfect world, in which all peoples come together as partners in the divine enterprise. Idolatrous societies of the world proffer no such prophetic idyll to sustain humanity's hopes.

God Speaks to the World

God, thus, communicates with humans in the Bible in order to provide them the opportunity to join in perfecting the world. The most expansive of God's communiqués is the revelation at Sinai, delivered to the entire inchoate nation of Israel. But God also communicates with individuals. God makes a covenant with Abraham. God speaks to Isaac and Jacob in dreams. Nor does God address only the righteous. Laban, Jacob's wicked father-in-law, receives word from God in a dream as well, forewarning him that he will not be permitted to harm Jacob. God likewise cautions Bilaam, the prophet sent by the Moabite king Balak, that he will not succeed in cursing the Jews. Sometimes God delegates His message to prophets, urging a particular group to change their ways. God commands Jonah, for example, to caution the inhabitants of the Assyrian capital Nineveh to repent. Jeremiah warns the Israelites of their unconscionable moral lapses before the destruction of the First Temple. Numerous such stories fill the Bible.

Most of the time, however, God communicates with humanity more indirectly by setting up a situation to test our will and ability to choose good. The first most obvious instance of this is the setup in the Garden of Eden, when Adam and Eve are given a single rule and then tested to see if they would follow it. The biblical characters are constantly confronted with hard choices tailored to each person. Joseph can either go against his morals and have an affair with his boss's wife, or he can resist her and face the consequences. Judah is faced with publicly admitting his immorality or executing his daughter-in-law, Tamar. The ancient world called these encounters and challenges fate or chance. The Bible depicts them as setups, where God wants us to succeed. But these are not drills: failure is also possible and history altering. Only after the fact do we know if we have succeeded. Only after being reunited with his brothers does Joseph understand how he had been tested. As we read the subsequent chapters of the Bible, we grasp how these decisions have impacted human history.

Episodes in the Bible recount how heroes might struggle with God's communications. Abraham debates with God in the case of Sodom, questioning divine "justice." Knowing, at first, about God only from his parents, Jacob cannot hide a natural skepticism concerning the nature of God's justice and goodness; he pledges loyalty to Him, but on the condition that God see to his safe return home. Moses initially doubts the wisdom of God's decision to choose *him* for the job of leading the people. By contrast, in a later event, Moses figuratively throws his body in front of God in protest of a divine threat to destroy the Israelites. Jonah desperately seeks to evade his assigned mission to warn the people of Nineveh, because he considers God's plan a bad idea. The patriarchs and other biblical characters of the past exhibit the same sort of doubts and questions that we have today about God's message to us. These simple but sage folk of antiquity were no less perplexed about who God is and how He runs the world than we are today in our sophisticated digital age.

Why It's Not So Simple to Ask God His Name

Just like us, the biblical personalities wanted to better understand God. In his work *The Philosophy of Hebrew Scripture*,[1] Yoram Hazony analyzes the philosophical and ethical principles in the Bible. Hazony studies two major biblical personalities who wanted to know God and, to that end, asked Him His name. From these instances, Hazony argues that we can learn a lot about God.

Jacob is the first patriarch to ask about the nature of God, during the episode in which he wrestles with an angel. Moses, like Jacob—an heir to the traditions and knowledge of the God of Abraham—also asks God to identify Himself by name. Moses is initially more successful than Jacob. At the site of the burning bush in the desert wilderness near Mount Horeb, God answers him; however, as Hazony argues, God's reply, "I will be what I will be" is a highly ambiguous one.[2] Indeed, such an open-ended answer hardly differentiates God from the gods of the ancient world, who seem to show no consistency except their fickle desires and moods. The text suggests that Moses, like Hazony, is dissatisfied with God's response. Moses persists and again asks God for His name after the Exodus from Egypt, but before the episode of the golden calf. Still, God's answer is yet again ambiguous.[1]

> And the Lord said to Moses, "I will also do this thing that you have asked, for you have truly gained favor in my eyes and I have singled you out by name." ...And he answered, "I will make all My goodness pass before you, and I will proclaim before you the name of the Lord, and I will be gracious to whom I will be gracious, and I will have mercy on whom I will have mercy." (Exodus 33:17–19)

Hazony wonders if God is really saying that he arbitrarily chooses to be gracious to some and not to others.[3] He further argues that the words "I will have mercy on whom I will have mercy" sound a lot like the earlier "I will be what I will be."[4] Does it all mean that God, from whom we expect justice, actually offers us nothing more than the arbitrary and the meaningless?

Dissatisfied still with the apparent runaround he seems to be getting after the incident with the golden calf, Moses once again presses God to reveal His name. This time, God not only agrees, but specifies in great detail just what Moses must do to receive this news. Moses is to remain in the cleft of the rock, covered by God's hand, and God will pass before him and proclaim His name. At this point, God declares:

> The Lord, the Lord, a God merciful and gracious, longsuffering, and abundant in giving and truth [emet], storing up [the results of] righteousness to thousands [of generations], bearing iniquity and transgression and sin; but who will certainly not pardon [the guilty], visiting the iniquity of the fathers on the children, and on the children's children, to the third and fourth generation. (Exodus 34:5–7)

This description of Himself is the same that God gives to the Israelites in the second commandment:

> For I the Lord your God am an impassioned God, visiting the guilt of the parents upon the children, upon the third and upon the fourth generations of those who reject Me but showing kindness

---

[1] I have used Hazony's translations of the Hebrew texts that appear in his book on this topic.

to the thousandth generation of those who love me and keep my Commandments. (Exodus 20:5)

Hazony points out that, unlike the other names God gave Moses, this one emphasizes reward and punishment. So, what are we to make of these names? Hazony argues that through this series of responses to the question of His name, God reveals something more profound about His relationship to the world. While God may initially seem to rule the world arbitrarily, in fact, He does not. He rules with justice, though we cannot always see it because it is rarely immediate. Sadly, it is often our children who pay for our misdeeds.

Throughout its pages, the Bible teaches us many things about God and attributes many names to Him that we are not necessarily equipped to fully understand. Thus, these other names, many of which depict mere slivers of God's inexhaustible qualities—such as Majesty or Peace or Presence—are qualities that we as humans can relate to, but they are hardly descriptive of the wholeness of God. Islam holds a similar view:

> In Islam "theology," in the strict sense of the term—the study of the nature of God—does not exist. "Discourse about God" is limited by and to what the scriptural sources reveal. The Divine Names (*al-asmā'*) and attributes (*al-sifāt*) have been the subject of learned treatises and debate, as have the absolute knowledge of God and free will, faith and reason, in what is known as "*ilm al-kalām*."[5]

In Christianity, God's attributes were described with the language of Greek philosophy. Thus, the divine reason is called *Logos*.[6]

There Are Limits to Knowing God

The Bible informs us about God, but it also describes our human limits in knowing God. God does not even reveal himself fully to Moses, the greatest of all the prophets of Israel:

> And [God] said, "You will not be able to see my face, for no man can see me and live." And the Lord said, "Here, there is a place by me, and you will stand upon the rock. And it will be, when my glory passes by, I will put you in the cleft of the rock, and I will cover you with my hand until I have passed. And I will remove my hand and you will see my back, but my face you will not see." (Exodus 33:20–23)

As Hazony points out, even Moses could only see God after His Presence had moved on. In other words, as humans we only hope to obtain an inkling of God's providence, and this after the fact.[7]

We humans are therefore recipients of both knowledge about God *and* knowledge that we are innately limited in our ability to fully know God. Moreover, to even achieve an inherently limited understanding of God, we humans must pierce through layers of initial misunderstandings about God. In the words of Chaplain Tahera Ahmad:

> I prefer the term "divine" as opposed to the name God because I know that in our context we have students who don't necessarily follow all of the rituals of a particular faith tradition but still want to be connected to the idea of something higher, something that connects us all to the term God. That they first saw it in a particular scriptural sense often is a barrier to connecting to the term God or to the being of Jesus as understood in various faith traditions and is limiting and distracting. So coming up with other terminology of what God is or what is this Being is helpful, and we can just believe that the divine is there.

Father Karloutsos makes the following crucial point to which we will return:

> God is love but He is more than love. God is the Creator but He is more than the Creator because there is no word or words that can describe God. We only have manifestations of His presence in the world. We cannot truly understand Him; we are who we are. We are finite beings trying to describe the infinite.

Fully aware that an infinite God is beyond our comprehension, we must turn to the Bible to glean enough understanding to provide us with a starting point, so that we can glimpse manifestations of God's acts.

Humanity, the Image of God

In part one we described how the Bible's claim that humanity has common ancestry from Adam and Eve meant that all human beings were created equal in God's image (or, literally, "shadow" in Hebrew). The Bible proclaimed the idolatrous notion that some men are like gods, while others are not, is a lie. Crucially, monotheism actually makes a reverse claim as well, that *all people* possess within them some aspects of God's qualities. People can be faithful, can be true, can be just, can be kind. People can choose to do good. Man is the earthly creature with the most sophisticated consciousness and the capacity to see the world in terms of good and evil, exercise free will, and make principled decisions even against his own immediate interest. Yet we are also limited, finite beings. The Bible describes this paradox through the metaphor of the shadow of God.

The tenet that human beings are made as the shadow of God highlights the paradox that, as individuals, we are both all equal and yet each one of us is unique. This will be a crucial point later, when we get to our discussion of prayer. When a person's actions lead to greater justice, as did Abraham's in pleading mercy for inhabitants of Sodom, they are expressing the quality of divine justice. When a person's actions lead to greater beauty and harmony, as did Bezalel's in constructing the Tabernacle, they are expressing divine beauty. When a person's actions lead to forgiveness, as did Joseph when finally embracing his brothers, they are expressing divine compassion. We each possess unique elements of Godliness to impart. Our relationship to God intensifies each time we express those parts of ourselves that imitate God, otherwise known as *imitatio Dei*.

CHAPTER 36

Good Faith

Rational Belief in God

Faith in the God of Abraham, unlike belief in idols, does not demand belief in anything irrational. Nonetheless, we can only speak of faith in God, acknowledging that we have no path to direct knowledge of God. Monotheists these days are not like the ancient Israelites, who witnessed God's explicit acts of God in historical time. Nor do we possess conclusive archaeological proof or historical records to confirm that these biblical events did or did not happen, as discussed in part five. As a result, the existence of God is a matter of belief in the plausible rationality of the biblical description of God and our contemporary personal experiences of God. So yes, today one must *believe* in God; no one can be certain that He does or does not exist.

This book has endeavored to demonstrate that it is rational to believe in the veracity of monotheism's tenets. The Bible's concepts of God's omnipotence, omniscience, and omnibenevolence may not be provable, but they are reasonable. In part four, we argued that science has not disproven the notion that God created and maintains the universe. If anything, modern physics makes God's role more consistent than ever considering the evidence, though of course, still unprovable as the Theosic principle requires. Part one showed how the Exodus and the revelation at Sinai provided humankind with an alternative conceptual framework that challenged ancient idolatry and championed the option to *freely choose* to make the world more just and peaceful. The revelation is a clear sign of God's omnibenevolent care and respect for His creation. Part one also revealed that ancient philosophers arrived at their own critique of idolatry and support for monotheism through reason alone. Part two demonstrated the essential morality and universal relevance of God's laws, even if they were expressed at the time of their recording in a manner archaic and alien to us as moderns. Part three discussed how the gift of free will by its very nature depends on God withholding immediate administration justice in order to give us free reign in our actions. The consequences of evil are eventually apparent, a sign of His omnipotence. Father Karloutsos expresses it well:

> From Deuteronomy we learn that we shall love the Lord our God with all our heart, mind, and soul and love our neighbor as our self. This has three dimensions, and you can follow the view of Reverend Dr. Martin Luther King Jr. who said for him it was very important that his children be Trinitarian. He understood this as not just simply the Father, the Son, and the Holy Spirit but as his children's relationship with God, relationship with themselves, and relationship with their neighbors. If any one of those aspects are weakened, then the child's character is weakened. Similarly for us as community those are the three dimensions that have to be whole and complete.

Choosing to have faith in the God of monotheism necessitates a rational understanding of God as He is described in the Bible. To abdicate reason in making this choice is to court the danger of choosing childish or, worse, dangerous notions of God. This too is bad faith.

Faith as Loyalty

Faith in monotheism is grounded in the concept of loyalty. The word for "faith" in Hebrew is *emunah* and the verb for "to have faith" is *leha'amin*.[1] This noun can also be translated as "faithfulness" or "loyalty" and the verb as "to trust" or "to be loyal." The word "faith" first appears in the Bible in relation to Abraham, but it does not occur early in Abraham's journeys. After the war against an alliance of four of the kings of Canaan who kidnapped Lot, God comes to Abraham (who is still called Abram at this point in the Bible) in a vision. The following exchange is very instructive about the meaning of *emunah,* or "faith" in the Bible. To capture the particular nuance, I am using my own translation:

"Fear Not, Abram. I am a shield to you. Your reward will be very great." But Abram said, "Oh Lord God, what can You give me, seeing that I shall die childless, and the one in charge of my household is Dammesek Eliezer!" Abram said further, "Since you have granted me no offspring, my steward [Eliezer] will be my heir." The word of the Lord came to him in reply, "That one shall not be your heir, none but your very own issue shall be your heir." He took him outside and said, "Look toward the heaven and count the stars, if you are able to count them." And He added, "So shall your offspring be." And he put his trust/loyalty/faith in the Lord, and He reckoned it to his [Abram's own] righteousness. (Genesis 15:1–6)

In this exchange, we learn that Abram expects God to keep His word—yet he still has his doubts. He has acted according to God's instructions and, amazingly, has come to no harm in his adventures, but he still can't escape the fact that he has no heirs. Abram gently chides God that He is responsible for providing him with offspring. Yet it is precisely after Abram raises this doubt with God, voicing his desire for a child and receiving God's response—that he indeed will be a father—that Abram "put his trust/loyalty/faith in the Lord." It is when Abram sees that God is consistent over time that he believes in Him and considers Him truly just. The word "faith" appears in just two other occasions in the Five Books of Moses, both in the same sense of trust/loyalty/faith as a package.

In his discussion on the Bible's definition of truth, Yoram Hazony shows how the words *emet* ("truth") and *emunah* ("faith") have the same linguistic root in Hebrew and share a core meaning.[2] *Emunah,* or "faithfulness," means that something can be relied on and will not break under strain or over time,[3] just as something true can also be relied on. Thus, as Hazony explains, to speak of God as true (*emet*) and the gods as false (*sheker*)—as the Bible and the prophets do—is to affirm that they can be relied on in the sense of keeping commitments and promises. It also suggests that, after investigation, they can be relied on to be exactly what they claim to be: God is immutable, unchangeable truth, whereas all of the pantheons of gods are pliable. New gods could join the pantheon and/or they could change their names depending on circumstances and politics.

Christianity and Islam have developed a similar understanding of faith as loyalty to the principles of a relationship and, therefore, to action. Christians also define faith in terms of being true and loyal. The word "belief," which used to mean to be loyal and true as well as to consider something correct, has lost the first of these meanings.[4] Faith in Islam has been described as a relationship: "In a relationship of confidence and security with God, he who draws near is a 'friend of God' (*walī*). This is in turn one of the meanings of the word *imān*, most often translated as 'faith.'"[5]

Loyalty to God Requires Reason

To be loyal to God, or in secular terms, to be loyal to the principles of truth and justice, the Bible claims we need to rationally understand the moral choice we face. Atheists and monotheists can both unite in rejecting any faith that requires blind obedience. The Bible was perhaps the first book to espouse skepticism. If something doesn't make sense, then further investigation is appropriate. God never becomes angry with the Israelites over lack of faith, even before He reveals proof of the extent of His power through the Exodus. Atheists and monotheists share the critique of those who simply obey authority figures out of faith. As we have seen, loyalty to cult leaders and other forms of idolatry—whether in monotheistic garb or not—leads to blind obedience. One must establish truth. Acting on pure assumption is not acting faithfully. This is especially urgent in our current era of "fake news" or, more accurately, news that is manufactured with a motive, somewhat akin to the risk of false prophets in ancient days. Hazony points out that the Bible requires that a rumor or accusation of idolatry be investigated.[6]

A biblical inquiry is a rational procedure of obtaining at least two witnesses and seeking proof that must be considered conclusive.[7] This example extends to understanding all choices we face, since so many of our decisions are made within a haze of personal opinions, political affiliations, rationalizations, and emotions, both our own and those influenced by others. We must, in fact, use our reason in each and every instance in order to establish the truth—that is, the facts—of a given situation before we can act loyally to God.

It is difficult to be loyal to truth in a society where, as Stephen Colbert has mocked, "truthiness" pervades and lies are tossed out as "truth" to the crowd, like so many fish to seals in a zoo. Part three described how people rationalize to justify the evil they perpetrate. Idolatrous societies, we know, believe in inanimate idols and promote false views of man under the guise of truth. In most cases these beliefs are accompanied by a plethora of secondary and equally false beliefs that justify the actions of the powerful few. Idolatry becomes the basis for a fog of rationalizations, inevitably leading societies in dangerous directions. Only critical skills and reason can cut through these lies. This becomes all the more complicated when lying invokes moral categories, as when Hitler claimed that the Jews were an evil race. Here, too, the Bible and the prophets anticipate the problem. Deuteronomy describes a false prophet who claims to be God's true messenger. How can the Israelites distinguish a false prophet from a true prophet? The Bible's answer—a false prophet will invariably go against God's laws and, inevitably, what they predict will not come true. In other words, the words a person uses and the claims they make must be measured against known principles and observed reality. Our ability to discern if someone is taking God's name in vain derives from these very skills.

Loyalty to God and Self

Loyalty to God is a path to an authentic and just self. Atheists characterize the emphasis on faith as loyalty—and even more so when expressed in terms of humility and service—to be affronts to human dignity and freedom, a call to annihilate the self. And they are right when it comes to idolatrous faith. Being humble and servile to idols is dangerous and demeaning. Throughout history, idolatrous regimes sought to destroy the selfhood of people by stifling their freedom to speak, to choose the course of their lives, or even to escape. Paradoxically, humility and modesty in the face of absolute truth and goodness is liberating. The posture of humility and service is a call to expand the self. Arrogance, or the belief that one knows better or is better, closes off our mind to learning from others or seeking to improve ourselves. Humility, on the other hand, opens the door to striving—there is always more to learn, and the more we learn, the more we expand. Service to others demands not only autonomy, but putting to use our own particular aspect of Godliness to do something beyond ourselves, to seek more truth, more beauty, more justice, more kindness in the world. To be loyal to God means to strive to be the best and most just version of ourselves.

Good Faith and Love

Profound loyalty is the basis of love. In Roman Catholic and Anglican wedding ceremonies, the couples vow to hold fast "in sickness and in health…for richer or poorer…until death do us part," as an expression of absolute loyalty to one another. In Jewish and Muslim ceremonies, a contract is signed that affirms the responsibilities that the spouses have to one another. Marriage is all about loyalty. So too our relationship with God. Entering into marriage should be prefaced on a clear understanding of the nature of our spouse. In the case of our relationship with God, God knows us better than we know ourselves. He has instilled a spark of His divinity within us. He desires to have a relationship with us; otherwise, there would be no universe and certainly no "us." The most incongruous book in the Bible, the Song of Songs, testifies to this. Rabbi Akiva called the Song of Songs the most holy book of the Bible, akin to the Holy of Holies in the Temple. (*Mishna Yadayim* 3:5) As Father Karloutsos noted, once we figure out that God is love, many other things make sense… even if we can't fully articulate them. We have the awesome opportunity to be a partner in history with God. The question and goal of our lives is how we can best fulfill that. Love for God and our fellow man is a good place to start.

Our love is not blind or mindless. We need to exercise our reason to discern how to love our fellow humans, who are all similarly blessed with a spark of Godliness. We love our fellow humans by using logic, reason, and the principles of science to create new cures for diseases and new technologies to improve people's lives. We also demonstrate love by applying our reasoning powers to exploring and understanding our society and our history, in order to make it more just. Love of God compels us to be particularly vigilant of those who claim to speak for God. Here, too, we must effectively exploit our reason. Each person who claims to interpret and speak for God must demonstrate profound love for all of their fellow sparks of divinity, or else they must be called out as modern-day false prophets.

As the Bible says, "You shall love your God with all of your heart and with all of your soul and with all your might." (Deuteronomy 6:5) "Love your fellow as yourself." (Leviticus 19:18)

Love of God requires all of that which is the essence of good faith.

CHAPTER 37

The Faith of an Atheist?

Reason's Many Roads

The atheist critique of faith, as important as it is, obscures the fact that reason can lead in many directions and to differing conclusions. "Golden Rule atheists" reason that we often fail to recognize the worth of an individual, since people tend to contribute to society in so many personal, unique, or unrecognized ways. Therefore, if we make a considered effort to treat people as we ourselves wish to be treated, we increase the odds that everyone will benefit and society as a whole will flourish. "Machiavellian atheists," on the other hand, reason that we measure the worth of people in real time by assessing the power and authority that they wield. It follows, then, that the accumulation of power and authority is deemed a virtue, no matter the cost to others. The namesake of this view, Niccolò Machiavelli, said:

> For this has to be noted: that men should either be caressed or eliminated, because they avenge themselves for slight offenses but cannot do so for grave ones; so the offense one does to a man should be such that one does not fear revenge for it.[1]

To the Machiavellian atheist, accommodating oneself to the powers that be—even if it means treating others badly—is a perfectly rational decision. How many Germans joined the Nazi Party after 1933, for example, reasoning to themselves that by doing so they would preserve their jobs and provide for their families—even though it meant acquiescing to a regime that murdered others? Nowadays, some people have accepted complicity in bad actions, reasoning that they are unlikely to influence the course of events underway, so why lose out on a share of the profits from misdeeds at the expense of others?

Reason might suggest we judge the worth of other human beings based on a criterion like utility. This idea is not foreign to some contemporary atheist thinkers, Peter Singer prominent among them. Ethics professor at Princeton University, Singer has developed a utilitarian ethics that would result in unspeakable harm to the weakest members of society for, at first glance, failing to make a meaningful and fair contribution to the community at large. For starters, Singer endorses infanticide in the case of handicapped infants,[2] and is a proponent of euthanasia.[3] His explanations in this regard—which revolve around the suffering of individuals, their relative utility, and the cost to society—are entirely reasonable. Can you just imagine all the resources and money that would be saved if we eliminated the weakest members of our society rather than cared for them? A medical director of an insurance company once told me that we could dramatically decrease the cost of medical care in the United States if all we did was eliminate all but routine care for infants less than thirty days old and adults older than eighty years. So how would *you* initiate such a policy? Perhaps halt care for your newborn in the neonatal unit? Or, no, wait, maybe begin with your grandmother's physical therapy in the rehab center? Although, to be fair, Singer certainly does not argue for wholesale slaughter of the disabled (other than infanticide). Still, disability advocates recognize the dangers of sanctioned and enforced euthanasia, and they justifiably criticize the morality of Singer's conclusions.[1] Nonetheless, there are many clearheaded people who find the argument of the greatest good for the greatest number compelling, no matter the consequences to the minority. The more popular atheist writers are careful to avoid writing about these intuitively offensive and controversial logical extensions of atheism, but Dawkins is one who quite clearly, if conditionally, accepts infanticide.[4]

---

[1] The grassroots disability organization Not Dead Yet, a secular organization, strenuously opposes Peter Singer's views on euthanasia on social justice grounds. See their website, notdeadyet. org, and their analysis of an article on Singer in the *New York Times*, "Disabled Lives Worth Less, Hypothetically," July 17, 2009, notdeadyet.org/2009/07/peter-singer-in-ny-times-disabled-lives.html.

Another means of judging the worth of humans is "personism."[2] According to personism, those who make the decisions as to what constitutes "a person endowed with rights to life and liberty" should also decide just who gets to enjoy the benefits of being part of the species.[3] Thus, the person-in-charge decides who is a "person" and gets to impose his or her view on others, even in matters of life and death. Singer does not recognize some sort of universal responsibility between and among all human beings. But we have seen all too recently the consequences of one group deciding who is a person. Nazi medical schools taught their students medical ethics from Ärztliche *Rechts und Standeskunde* (*Medical Law and Health*), a textbook authored in 1942 by the physician Rudolf Ramm. Aspiring doctors were taught that "the Nazi physician's ethical obligation [was to be] responsible for ridding society of certain groups: Jewish people, disabled people and others who were deemed unable to contribute to society." The disabled should be disposed of by means of mercy killings, as "these creatures merely vegetate and constitute a serious burden on the national community. They not only reduce the standard of living of the rest of the family members because of the expense of their care, but also need a healthy person to take care of them throughout their lives."[5]

Unfortunately, reasonable people do not require embracing the extremes of Nazi philosophy in order to arrive at conclusions that are inherently incompatible with a believer's interpretation of the Golden Rule. My friend Morty Schapiro recounts the time that he was part of a team that authored a book produced by the World Bank entitled *Successful Development in Africa*. One chapter reviewed the partnership of seven West African nations, the World Bank, and other donors, in order to combat the dreaded illness of onchocerciasis (river blindness). Happily, the program was successful in substantially reducing river blindness in 90 percent of the targeted areas. Yet, because the World Bank's economic view of the program compared the costs versus the very low earnings of the people in the area (fifty-seven dollars to one-hundred and eight

---

[2] Helga Kuhse, Udo Schüklenk, and Peter Singer, *Bioethics: An Anthology*, 3rd ed. (Malden: Wiley-Blackwell, 2016). Harris develops his views on personism in Harris, *The Moral Landscape: How Science Can Determine Human Values* (London: Black Swan, 2012).

[3] For a discussion of personism and Singer's critics, see Dale Jamieson, *Singer and His Critics* (Oxford: Blackwell Publishing, 1999).

dollars per annum at the time), the program's net cost benefit analysis was "inconclusive." Morty argues, along with his coauthor Gary Morson, that viewing such questions from a purely economic perspective is not sufficient.[6] It is not only the World Bank that values human life in dollar terms. Every health and environmental regulatory agency in the United States compares the costs of the regulations it imposes with an assumed value of the lives that would be lost without the regulation. In practice, many economists, like Machiavellians and utilitarian philosophers, believe man's worth can be judged with some degree of certainty...in monetary terms.

We All Reason Based on Faith

The atheist critique of monotheism obscures the truth that those who choose to base their actions in the world on reason alone also, in fact, take a leap of faith. For example, people might find it reasonable to judge others on the basis of thoughtfully chosen criteria. I contend that judging anyone by metrics—not values—of power, utility, or cost is lying to oneself. When this happens on a society-wide basis, it can be fatal. Yes, power is real, whether in the form of influence, money, or talent; utility and costs are also real. Still, all of these are limited criteria. To believe that power, utility, or cost are more important than other qualities such as justice, kindness, and love is to demean the value of human experience, regardless of whether one considers—as monotheists do—that each of us contains a spark of Godliness. In practice, believing that we are all made in God's image means that we have to treat everyone according to the same laws.

I have argued throughout this book that monotheists and atheists align on many matters in their sincere intellectual search for truth. I hope by now, however, it is clear that this alignment exists only between true monotheists and Golden Rule atheists. Machiavellian atheists, in particular—but all atheists who reduce the worth of humans by applying the limited criteria outlined above—share with idolaters a fundamental uncritical belief. Machiavellian atheists uncritically believe in the primacy of their power to dominate; they are idolaters in their own special connection to a private pantheon of gods indifferent to the rest of humanity. Even certain monotheists, as we have seen, are known to shelve their ability to reason and blindly follow their leader as god-king, uncritical of the import of their actions, believing in the words of George Orwell that some people are more equal than others.

Golden Rule monotheists and Golden Rule atheists resist any soothing, uncritical certainty. Both groups recognize the profound immorality of treating fellow human beings as less than equal. In my view, true monotheists have the advantage—even over Golden Rule atheists—of remembering this rule through the tenet that man is made in the image of God.

CHAPTER 38

Living Faithfully

Faith as a Practice

Having faith in God is reflected in our choices. As former mayor of Newark and current New Jersey senator Cory Booker has written: "My simple point is that I judge a person's faith by how they live their life, not by the tenets of their religion. I've watched the holiest of people walk past somebody in need or treat their staff mean. To me, the beauty of faith is only seen when people live it consistently or struggle to do so." Yes, some believers may proclaim one thing and do another. Prize-winning Lebanese author Amin Maalouf observes: "I have the profoundest respect for people who behave in a generous way because of religion. But I come from a country where the misuse of religion has had catastrophic consequences. One must judge people not by what faith they proclaim but by what they do." Proclaiming one's faith without living by its monotheistic tenets is a betrayal.

Most of us today have simply grown acculturated to act according to these tenets. Indeed, force of habit can blind us to the integral link between our routine behaviors and our fundamental beliefs; between, say, not falsely billing overtime and faithfully believing in God. Faith shines most clearly in the face of circumstances that challenge it. We consider people like Nelson Mandela and Natan Sharansky, heroes precisely because they were faithful to their principles under impossible conditions in idolatrous environments that punished—rather than rewarded—them for their faith. The same holds true for agnostics and atheists who held honestly and fast to principles of justice or truth whether they believed in a personal God or not. Nonetheless, I argue that belief in a personal God profoundly transforms the nature and meaningfulness of these choices.

Free to Perfect the World

Faith in a personal God is a path to freedom to choose our role in perfecting the world. As Bishop William Murphy puts it:

> From Hegel, to Nietzsche, to Sartre, to Foucault, to the whole last two hundred years of philosophical thought in the West, that struggle about freedom time and again gets defined as a freedom from a god because the god will inhibit my freedom of choice as a human being, my sense of autonomy. And yet my sense of God is just the opposite. My experience of God is just the opposite. It frees me to be my best self and invites me to live in a certain way that give me a foundation for the way I should interact with other people, the way I should respect other people, the way I should see the world about me.

Believing in God and in His teachings is the counter-narrative to the shackles of idolatry. It frees us to build just societies as we saw in part one. It is no less liberating for individuals to discover their own path. As Rabbi Kook expresses it, "A person with a slave mentality lives his life and harbors emotions that are rooted, not in his own essential spiritual nature, but in that which is attractive and good in the eyes of others. In this way, he is ruled by others, whether physically or by social conventions." Belief in the personal God, who creates and sustains the world, creates and sustains each of us with our characteristics and particularities and motivates us to chart our own course independently and regardless of convention. A person of faith like Oprah Winfrey demonstrates this freedom. Raised in Mississippi, abused as a child, abandoned by her parents, and finding herself with few prospects in a culture that did not value black women, Oprah Winfrey dared to liberate herself from all the prejudice around her and to pursue her dreams as a journalist. "Understand," she says, "that the right to choose your own path is a sacred privilege. Use it. Dwell in possibility." She has forged her own path in perfecting the world and, in doing so, has become an inspiring example to millions of people across the globe.

Modern atheists who strove to reject Machiavellian idolatry have come to similar conclusions about the importance of freedom. Jean-Paul Sartre would certainly have agreed with Rabbi Kook that we are often enslaved by the expectations of others and of society. As Sartre famously said, "Freedom is what you do with what's been done to you."

Empowered to Protect the World

Faith in a personal God provides a source of strength and courage to perfect the world in the face of tremendous obstacles. Believing that God creates us with particular talents and that God possesses a plan for our world is a source of tremendous power. Faith has empowered the leaders of liberation movements to stand up to oppressive regimes. As Lech Wałęsa, the founder and head of the independent Polish trade union Solidarity in the Soviet bloc, once put it, "I'm a man of faith. I only fear God, and my wife—sometimes." These were not empty words, since Wałęsa was not only imprisoned but threatened with death for his activism to bring democracy and justice to Poland. Such faith in God can empower a person in more everyday situations, to stand up to an abuser or cruel boss, for example. Faith that God is omnibenevolent fosters conviction that it is possible for us to overcome even the greatest challenges. We can never know whether, or when, God might just cast the dice in our favor if we do the right thing. As Dr. Martin Luther King suggests in eloquent simplicity, "Take the first step in faith. You don't have to see the whole staircase, just take the first step." Faith liberates us from a labyrinth of social constructs that thwart us at every turn and prevent us from pursuing our dreams. As Helen Keller explained, "Faith is the strength by which a shattered world shall emerge into the light." Or as Reverend Dr. Calvin Butts expresses it, "When you begin to explore the depths of the faith community and the men and women who have tied their vision to God's understanding of how this world is supposed to be, you find many more examples of people making a better world than you do of those making the world worse off."

Faith and Life

Faith in a personal God means not only rolling with the punches but learning and growing from them. Timothy Cardinal Dolan wrestles with the question of faith and doubt:

> Saint Thomas Aquinas, who was one of our greatest thinkers, would say that "the act of doubt itself can become a very beautiful prayer," and like when Jesus responded to a question by saying, "What is necessary is faith," the questioner replied, "Lord, I do believe, help my lack of faith." So sometimes, one of the greatest prayers of all is to say "Lord, I don't understand this at all. As a matter of fact, I am very upset with You. As a matter of fact, I am tempted to tell You to go to hell, but right now You are all I've got, and You have gotten me through a lot in the past, and I am part of a tradition that says ultimately You are not going to let me down. And you know what else, Lord? I don't know where else I could go, because nothing else makes sense either. I can go through a fifth of Jameson or I can take that bottle of pills, but that isn't any better so right now I am sticking with You." It is all about humble acts of love and faith, and that is what animates the believer. It is not some cocky sureness that one says, "Oh, let me explain what God is doing here."

Humor often helps us to better understand and navigate our relationships with God and with life. It is the nature of jokes to always include some unexpected twist, an extra oomph that marks the punchline. Likewise, every life includes unexpected twists. Sometimes these twists can be positive—like missing a bus only to bump into an old friend because of it—or they can be negative, such as missing that bus and arriving late for a pricey Broadway show and not being seated until after the show-stopping scene. Random events are just that: random, and we'll never know their outcomes in advance. Several movies and plays, such as *Sliding Doors* (1998) and *If/Then* (Broadway production 2014), explore this theme, asking, for example, how so simple a random event as a train door closing one second earlier or later might lead to alternative lives. Sometimes, of course, life's twists turn out to be far more substantial with immediate impact on people's careers, family, or health. Recognizing these twists and turns as part of a larger pattern of divine providence encourages us to learn from them. In a letter to Eliza Gurney, Abraham Lincoln discussed the Civil War through the lens of his personal faith:

If I had my way, this war would never have been commenced. If I had been allowed my way, this war would have ended before this. But we find it still continues; and we must believe that He permits it for some wise purpose of His own, mysterious and unknown to us; and though with our limited understanding we may not be able to comprehend it, yet we cannot but believe, that He who made the world still governs it. We are indeed going through a great trial—a fiery trial. In the very responsible position in which I happened to be placed, being a humble instrument in the hands of our Heavenly Father, as I am, and as we all are, to work out His great purposes, I have desired that all my works and acts may be according to His will, and that it might be so, I have sought His aid.[1]

Sometimes we think of these events as unfortunate tests that we must undergo to fortify our faith. They may perhaps be easier to handle, however, if we accept them as unexpected twists and try to anticipate the surprise punch line. A person of faith, indeed, learns to roll with the punch lines and, as Zen philosophy counsels, to go unflustered with the flow. Oprah Winfrey understands this; "I believe," she says, "that every single event in life that happens is an opportunity to choose love over fear."

I have a friend, Herb Siegel, who was Lew Ranieri's driver for many years. Herb is a thoughtful, quiet sort of fellow. He was once expecting to work a certain week in 2002 when Lew changed his vacation plans, and so Herb had the week off. Since he happened to be at home, his wife asked him to do some shopping. Driving to the supermarket, Herb came upon a terrible scene—cars were pulled haphazardly off the road and a growing crowd of people stood anxiously watching the fiery spectacle of a burning house with flames spreading furiously out through charred windows and across a blackening roof. The fire department had not yet arrived. Herb told me that some sort of inner voice urged him to action. So, into a burning house he ran and found a young woman in the hall-way in a state of shock. He managed to rouse her and learn that she was the babysitter for two infants upstairs. Herb raced the steps into a room ablaze in flames and brought out the first child, whom he handed off to another person. Then Herb returned upstairs, braving the scorching heat and a wall of flames, reached into the crib, and retrieved the second child. Herb, slightly injured himself, passed the baby to an ambulance attendant outside…and then drove off. (Yes, he remembered to get the groceries.) For two days, everyone on Long Island sought the identity of the anonymous hero who risked his own life running into a burning house and saving three total strangers. Finally, one of Herb's daughters let word get out of her father's heroics, and Herb "fessed up." The insurance company that provided coverage for the house also provided Herb and his family with an all-expenses-paid trip to Disney World, so his daughter was convinced she had made a wise move unmasking her modest dad's selfless act of bravery. Fifteen years later, Herb himself still wonders how he was able to do what he did. As he told me the story again, he said he was not a religious man, yet he was convinced it was that voice—or as the Bible describes it, the still small voice—that empowered him to save three lives.

Choosing Faith

People choose to believe in a personal God for many reasons. For some, the path of reason leads to the leap of faith, like the case of Pascal's wager. For others, belief is an act of will; such people want to believe in God because it just makes the most sense to them. In some instances, an individual personally experiences Godliness so persuasively that the encounter deeply influences her or him to believe. This experience could be the result of intense wonder at the infinite, or in response to an unlikely deliverance from danger. Certain experiences might strengthen a person's faith, as her father's death affected Reverend Dr. Katharine Henderson:

> When my father died, we were with him as a family in the palliative care center in Louisville, Kentucky. I was in the room with my mother and my sisters and probably twenty others as we accompanied him on the death journey for a full day. We sang the hymns without a hymnal, we recited the passages from the Bible that meant the most to him. There was a shared experience of faith in the presence of God in the moment of my father's dying that I wouldn't give up for anything. I can't imagine how hard it would be to be without that whole repertoire that carries one through these sorts of moments of need. It that would be just inconceivable to me to get by relying on only myself and my other human travelers.

Dr. Henderson makes it clear to us that there is an undeniable void in our human experience that calls out for faith.

The choice of faith requires an act of free will. True, faith in idolatry as well as in monotheism can be passive, passed down culturally. Still, cultural heritage does not override the exercise of free will, individual choice, and critical reason, despite such a claim by some atheists. Many individuals have abandoned the faith in which they were born. Two of the greatest rabbis in the Talmud, Rabbi Akiva and Rabbi Meir, were the descendants of converts to Judaism. While himself Jewish by birth, Akiva felt no real connection to his religion until he turned forty. Similarly, the transition from polytheism to monotheism consisted initially of personal conversions. Many people have traveled on a winding journey through any number of different faiths. For one, the towering Western Church Father, Saint Augustine, grew up a Christian, became a Manichean, only to return later to Christianity as an adult. Reverend Chloe Breyer describes her own conversion experience:

> I went to visit a roommate in the Texas Panhandle and met this amazing ninety-two-year-old Presbyterian missionary who had been walking between villages in World War II in China. He was the real deal as far as missionaries are concerned, and he and his then eighty-seven-year-old wife and I stayed in contact until he was one hundred [years old]. It was that conversation and relationship that really got me thinking about following the calling of becoming a priest in the Episcopal Church. It was almost like a conversion, even though I was baptized and confirmed. So then I returned to college and graduated. I helped start a magazine in Washington and then went through the discerning process of applying for the ministry in the Episcopalian church. To do so you must get a committee of folks from your church to endorse you, as well as create and edit a sort of a spiritual autobiography that also sets out different lay directions and ordained directions that you could pursue. Then your bishop has to agree to send you to seminary, which sometimes he does and sometimes he doesn't, and that is how I ended up going to the General Theological Seminary in New York.

Nor do the faithful ever stop questioning. Many of the greatest religious thinkers, from Thomas Aquinas to Rambam (Maimonides) and Ibn Sina (Avicenna), spent their lives probing monotheistic tenets and exploring reasons for faith. Some of us may have been raised in a given faith, followed it as a child, only to lose it slowly by attrition, letting go over time, without ever a sign of overt rejection, no formal act or declaration of renunciation. One simply stops attending church, mosque, or synagogue. As Yogi Berra might have said, "If people don't want to go to church, how are you going to stop them?" (He actually did say this about baseball stadiums.) The range of people's attitudes toward faith and monotheistic tenets reflects people's free will and individual choice.

The Christian philosopher Søren Kierkegaard calls for a great leap to faith, but as Dr. King advises earlier in this chapter, it takes only a small step of faith in order to begin the process. Faith in the God of Abraham and in His tenets does not conflict with reason, despite what atheists claim. Consider again the following two assertions:

1. The Bible is rational.
2. Modern science by no means negates the concept of God.

If these two propositions are true, then faith is a step toward the rational acknowledgment of the possibility of the existence of God. The stakes are quite high in taking this step, as it commits us to holding ourselves accountable to the Almighty…who sees all. In the words of Bob Marley, "There is no hiding place from the Father of creation." The dividends are high as well. If we all live accountably, we will transform the world.

CHAPTER 39

Idolatrous Prayer

Prayer that Doesn't Have a Prayer

Atheists define prayer as the ridiculous ritualistic practice of requesting things from imaginary gods instead of taking action. Such a definition of prayer suits ancient idolatrous prayer well. In their temples, priests honored, flattered, and petitioned the gods so that their city would be blessed, the king would defeat his enemies, and the nation would conquer new lands.[1] At home, private petitioners offered their household idols food and drink and recited incantations specific to their circumstances. Requests could range from material blessings to malignant curses. For both public and individual prayers, precise adherence to ritual was vital. Idolatrous prayer is a kind of mechanism by means of which you flatter and please your god, and your god is nice to you in return.[2] These prayers are of a kind with magical incantations. Magic, as we discussed, subtracts the gods from the equation and hands over to individuals the power to control nature with words and formulas.

On a business trip to Japan, I had occasion to stay an extra day and a half to do some touring, in particular to visit some Shinto shrines and Buddhist temples. Both the Buddhists and the Shinto do ceremony very well, but the beautiful Shinto ritual for blessings stood out.

Seated at the edge of a small service at the Meiji Shrine, I was hoping to observe Shintoism in practice from somewhat of an analytical distance. That proved difficult. It was impossible, in fact, not to be mesmerized by the pageantry, regalia, melody, choreography, and encompassing sensuality of the services, all meticulously staged. The first priest entered intoning a complex chant. He was followed shortly by other priests who entered and took various positions. This staggered entrance transitioned seamlessly to a performance of synchronized chanting and drum beating, increasing over time in intensity. Additional priests then entered. One of them approached icons in the center of the stage, and then, once more in unison and with increasing intensity, all the priests beseeched the gods for blessings, some for particular people, and—in the service I happened to witness—for an entire company whose senior members were in attendance. The service continued with even more urgent chanting and emphatic drumming, if that seems possible. Thereafter, the priest in the center led priests and congregants together in bowing several times to the icons, while a staff was removed from the central icon and waved over all the participants to bless those who had requested blessings. Amulets purchased by certain attendees were also blessed. I was told that these blessings would last for the year. When I asked a participant if the blessings were conditional on the morality of the recipients' behavior, she looked at me perplexed. The company seeking a blessing could have been a tobacco producer or a health-care company; it would not have mattered.

The prayer I had witnessed in the Shinto temple was similar to the prayer in the idolatrous temples of old, only the sacrifices were missing.[3]

Atheists reject this sort of prayer as irrational and immoral. Many monotheists, for many of the same reasons, do the same. How can simple incantations negate the laws of nature or alter the course of events? Such a belief is not only demonstrably untrue, it's absurd on the face of it. If the spoken desires of even a single human being had the power to affect the course of history, human existence would become a jumble of chaotic events and confusing reversals, which it is clearly not. This becomes doubly absurd when we remark upon how irrational it is to believe that these gods even exist. Idolatrous prayer further feeds the irrational belief that dedicated action in the real world is less important than spurious prayer in some imaginary aether. This type of prayer is also immoral, prone as it is to unjust petitions in the form of entreaties for abusive powers and unfair distributions of wealth at the expense of others.

Monotheists would agree. The biblical psalmist knows that gods are but of wood and stone, and petitions to them are nonsensical. Monotheists concur that such prayer is immoral as well, pointing out two additional reasons. First, monotheists believe that immoral requests are not even considered valid prayer. Second, it is immoral to bestow blessings upon people whose personal behavior lacks merit and warrants no reward. Where monotheists and atheists disagree is on the rationality and morality of the monotheistic conception of prayer.

CHAPTER 40

Prayer in the Bible

Biblical Prayer

Prayer in the Bible does include requests to God. At first glance, this may not seem to be particularly different from pagan prayer. There exists a chasm of difference, however, between Abrahamic practice and idolatrous, and that is what determines the potential efficacy and validity of prayer.

In the Bible, God's consideration of answering a petition is contingent on the morality of the request and of the petitioner. Monotheism attributes to God alone the power to affect the course of nature and history, *and* it explains that He does so according to principles of good and evil. An early instance of prayer in the Bible, Abraham's petition to God on behalf of the innocent people of Sodom, illustrates this point. (Genesis 18:16–33) Abraham appeals to God's justice in the form of rhetorical questions in order to make his moral case. Abraham is granted standing to pray precisely because he is personally righteous. (Genesis 18:16–19) He asks, "Will you sweep away the innocent along with the guilty?" (Genesis 18:23) Following the sin of the golden calf, Moses likewise appeals to God's sense of justice and mercy: "Let not the Egyptians say, it was with evil intent that He delivered them only to kill them off in the mountains [...]" (Exodus 32:12) On a number of occasions in the Bible, people pray on behalf of others with God's encouragement. These examples demonstrate the importance of the petitioner's personal morality. God makes just this point in a dream to Avimelech, who has taken Abraham's wife and been struck with illness as a result: "And God said to him in a dream. 'I knew that you did this with a blameless heart, and so I kept you from sinning against Me. That was why I did not let you touch her. Therefore, restore the man's wife—*since he is a prophet, he will intercede to save you—to save your life* [my emphasis].'" (Genesis 20:6–7) The text finds it important that Abraham actively pray for Avimelech, as opposed to God simply effecting a cure on His own. Similarly, God tells Job's friends that they will not be forgiven unless they get Job to pray for them. Monotheists do recognize personal requests as a valid form of prayer, but with a catch. To be valid, prayers for seemingly personal outcomes must demonstrate that they make the world at large a better place.

Biblical prayer is never a form of mindless pleading that replaces a plan of action. Nor is it an exercise in changing God's mind, presenting new evidence, or convincing Him that we know better, as the atheists charge. Instead, it is grounded in deep reflection and personal commitment to change by applying our free will. The Hebrew word *lehitpalel* ("to pray") is a reflexive verb which means that the act of prayer is self-directed. The etymology of the word further indicates the root of prayer. The root of the verb is *pelel (pll)*, which has two core meanings: to "judge" or reflexively to "judge oneself" and "truth." At the intersection of self-judgment and truth about ourselves and our request, we arrive at prayer.

Reverend Dr. Calvin Butts says:

> I am not praying so much for God to change. I believe that God is the same yesterday, today and will be tomorrow. I believe that the plan for the universe is the same, at least from my little section of it, our little section of it, and I believe that when I pray for justice, it is not so much that God is going to come down and make justice happen; it is that I am being given the strength somehow, or realizing the strength that is already in me, to work for justice, fight for justice, argue for justice. So, that to me is what prayer does. If I want the sofa you are sitting on to be moved, I am not praying for God to miraculously move that sofa; my useful prayer is that God will give me the strength to move the sofa. I know that I have to put my hands on it to lift it.

In Abrahamic prayer we exercise self-judgment on many levels. We first learn to scrutinize the morality of our desires. Instead of praying for the destruction of an enemy, we might first pray that they repent. If we are praying to win a court case, we must consider if our cause is just. Second, we must examine our past and current actions. We cannot pray for blessings if we ourselves cause harm to others. The Biblical texts make it clear that our moral standing to pray hinges on the quality of our moral behavior. The Israelites at times abandoned this principle. Isaiah accuses the Israelites in God's name: "And when you lift up your hands, I will turn my eyes away from you; though you pray at length I will not listen. Your hands are stained with crime—Wash yourselves clean [...] Cease to do evil; Learn to do good." (Isaiah 1:15–17) Those who pray for the end of a conflict with a family member or friend should first consider their own responsibility for the situation. Prayer is an opportunity for us to dissect *why* we want what we want. Even if we are convinced that our prayers are for moral outcomes, monotheistic prayer puts up front that our judgment has limits. We do not have all the information, as we are not omniscient. Even if we decide we really do want to undertake a certain business partnership because it presents itself as the best opportunity after our rational assessment, we should still pray that the outcome should be in our best interest whatever it is. We should exercise self-judgment by praying that our personal outcome accord with the world's highest good or, if not, that we will be open to a change in direction. In the words of Imam Shamsi Ali:

> I embrace faith and rationality at the same time because I think that is what we believe Islam is; combining faith, belief, and rationality. When I pray to God and it turns out my request does not happen, I still do believe that I did the best because when I pray I don't mean to force God to do what I want but normally I say God I want this and if you see this is good, please do it. I have to trust that God has the best plan for the universe.

Abrahamic prayer combines requesting something from God while trying to discern His truth.

One could argue that self-judgment and truth can be achieved by thinking critically for oneself—no need to talk to God and certainly no need to ask God for the request in question. Monotheists say that while that sounds good, the only place we are capable of complete commitment to self-judgment and truth is when we stand in awe and fear in front of our Creator. Only in front of our Creator do we have nowhere to deflect the truth. When facing a boss, a friend, a counselor, or ourselves, we are prone to self-delusion for specific ends. *Biblical prayer places us at the intersection of what needs to be done and what we can do to achieve a better world in the light of perfect truth.* This is radically different than idolatrous prayer.

To illustrate this, let's return to our discussion of the most powerful institution in American society—namely, the legal system—specifically the prosecuting attorney. Consider the potential tragedies that could occur should a prosecutor allow other considerations to get in the way of loyalty to truth. As an advisory board member of the Medill Justice Project, I have reviewed a number of such cases. The Medill Justice Project (MJP) investigates instances of potentially wrongful convictions and of systemic issues in the criminal justice system. The cases that MJP takes up are not based on technicalities, but on indications that evidence for the conviction was not sufficient. MJP believes, as does the Bible, that to do justice one must use one's reason and seek the truth diligently. The student investigators do this due diligence even when the result does not overturn a conviction.

The response from the prosecutors involved is more complicated and falls into two categories. The first type of response is one of loyalty to power. Certain prosecutors consider the case being investigated to be closed and do not want to review evidence that might exonerate someone wrongly sent to prison. These prosecutors want to move on to other cases and cannot *believe* that they or their predecessors might have missed something, that their conviction scorecard might be impaired, or that the real culprit is still at large and needs to be found. Idolatrously, so to speak, they place their faith in the power of prior prosecutors, not in the truth. Like idolaters at some ceremony, they go through the process, but the outcome is determined. These same prosecutors charged with doing justice really only want to win at all costs, not to be embarrassed or forced to admit that they or their predecessors were wrong. They worry that any such admissions diminish the prestige of their office or proverbial priesthood.

Happily, there is a second type of response: loyalty to truth. These prosecutors willingly admit to error and are eager to see wrongfully convicted individuals set free. They also tend to keep politics and public sentiment outside the bounds of their decision-making.

As I write these words, the MJP has undertaken the case of Andre Gonzales, a Miami man sentenced to life in prison for a murder at a dance club. Gonzales was convicted based on the testimony of one witness who claimed to be "60 percent certain" the killer was Gonzales based on a photo shown to him more than nine months after the crime was committed. Another witness, the bouncer of the club, was never tracked down by prosecutors and, when later found by MJP student investigators, admitted he was unaware that anyone had even been charged with the murder. The bouncer subsequently signed an affidavit that Gonzales "was definitely not the man who shot the victim." Referring back to part two, based on the Bible's requirements, the prosecutors would not have possessed insufficient evidence to win a conviction against Andre Gonzales. From a Biblical perspective, prosecutors should have tracked down all the possible witnesses before bringing a case to trial. The prayer of a prosecutor should be that justice be done, not that he or she win a case. This is how prosecutors can situate themselves at the intersection of what needs to be done and what we can do to achieve a better world in the light of perfect truth.

The narrative arc of the Bible depicts how the relationship between God and man evolves into prayer. Genesis begins with God as the primary agent in the world who speaks plainly to individuals. In Exodus, too, God speaks directly to humans, although primarily to Moses. Throughout the Books of the Prophets, God communicates with a chosen few via voice or visions. By the time of the Writings, such as the Psalms or the Book of Esther, man is praying and God is listening, choosing when to intercede on a concealed basis. In other words, man begins to relate to God uniquely through prayer and a sensitivity to His presence.

It is perfectly rational to believe in a God that is involved in the world but does not listen to individual prayer. However, the possibility of prayer *must* exist if we rely on the Bible, as it describes God listening to man's pleas. For monotheists, prayer is our access to divine providence. It is our ability to willfully connect to the consciousness that wants the best for us. As we described in part four, a probabilistic quantum universe gives us a hint as to how proper prayer can be answered and not violate

Monotheistic Prayer

the laws of nature or disrupt the fabric of the cosmos.[1] The Bible gives us many examples of God partnering with human beings to improve the situation if the person in question is aligned with God's will. If the Biblical character is not aligned with God's will, or the request itself is not in sync with what needs to be done, the answer to the prayer is "no."

---

[1] In an online course for students called Prayer and Destiny (Lessons 2, 7), Sarah Yehudit Schneider describes the physics of prayer and magic. This course can be accessed on her website, www.astillsmallvoice.org. In brief, Schneider explains that all forms of thought and words grease natural quantum pathways, but that prayer accesses a level above nature.

When God Says Yes and When God Says No

The Bible provides a road map for how to pray properly. In the Bible, God both granted and denied Moses's prayers. Moses was the greatest conversant with God in the Hebrew Scriptures, having a direct prayer intercom to God. Although Moses started his career as a man of limited verbal skills, his implicit request for improved articulation abilities was answered through the lifework of his career. The whole fifth book of the Torah, Deuteronomy, is his eloquent valedictory speech. Throughout his career, Moses almost always grasped the intersection of what he could do and what needed to be done in conformance with God's will and with a deep love of the people. Thus, Moses's prayers were almost always in golden intersection and were thus almost always answered. Moses's requests in his prayers were also nearly always selfless. On the rare occasion that Moses's prayers did not meet this intersection, the consequences were shocking. As readers, we are stunned when Moses and Aaron lose the right to enter the Holy Land. Yet the reason is totally consistent with the rules of prayer in the Bible: they lost sight of what their relationship with God and the people must be.

In chapter 20 of Numbers, the original adult generation that left Egypt in the Exodus had largely died out while the new generation that was about to enter the land became ascendant, although still led by Moses and Aaron. Miriam, who was a heroine to the people and the symbol of water throughout her prophetic career, had just died. At this point the people were depressed and there was no water, which the Midrash commentary ascribes to the loss of Miriam's merit. The people complained, although a close reading indicates that these complaints were far less inflammatory than those of their parents. The people feared some would die from thirst, which is of course truly scary. God told Moses and Aaron to speak to the rock to yield water and, in this way, sanctify the name of God before this new generation, many of whom had not seen the miracles firsthand during the Exodus from Egypt. Moses and Aaron assembled the people before the rock, but they changed the script God had given them as the Bible describes: "Listen *you rebels, shall we* [emphasis mine] get for you water out of this rock? And then also at variance with God's command, Moses raised his hand and struck the rock twice with his rod. Out came abundant water." (Numbers 20:10–11) With these words

Moses and Aaron demonstrated that they lost the vision of what they had to do and what needed to be done, namely to "affirm the sanctity [of God] in the sight of the Israelites." (Numbers 20:12) Far be it from me to criticize Moses and Aaron, but at this point in the narrative it is clear that the use of "we" was inappropriate since it was God—and not them— who was to bring the water from the rock. Meanwhile, Moses and Aaron were simply human conduits calling the new generation, which thirsted to be taught to understand the sanctity of God, but the term "rebels" was counterproductive to their mission. Despite Moses and Aaron's errant presentation, the people do need water, and God does ultimately allow the water to flow, but the episode causes the beginning of the end of their leadership roles. The only open issue being succession.

The biblical story of Elijah also demonstrates circumstances in which prayer is effective, and those in which it is not. At the outset of his prophetic career in 1 Kings, chapter 17, Elijah's prayers are fulfilled to a tee by God, even though they negatively impact the people by creating a massive drought. The point of Elijah's harsh prayer is to induce King Ahab and Queen Jezebel to repent of their idolatry. Failing that, he hoped his prayer might at least induce the people to overthrow the crooked regime. In chapter 18, Elijah stages a reality television show-style sacrifice competition. During this showdown, the priests of Baal fail to see their sacrifice accepted by the god Baal, of course, whereas Elijah's sacrifice is immediately accepted in a dramatic heavenly fire despite the fact that it is offered up on a water-drenched alter.

So far so good. The people are impressed despite the intentions of Ahab and Jezebel to kill Elijah. Yet at that point, Elijah gives up and falls into despair notwithstanding God's help and protection. In chapter 19, he flees and asks God to take his life because he has no more to give. In response, God sends an angel to provide food and water and much needed sleep. In other words, God does everything to nourish and revive Elijah's spirits. Next, God sends him on a forty-day journey to Mount Horeb, traditionally identified as Mount Sinai, a journey meant to give Elijah time to meditate and revive his spirits. Hmm, forty days, a trip to Mt. Sinai, and food and water supplied by heaven. God's hint to Elijah is crystal clear: *be like Moses* and put yourself on the line for the people; don't just give up. The power of a prophet, just as the power of prayer, comes from a vision of the future that is helpful and not destructive or needlessly despairing.

In fact, despair never leads to any good in the Bible. No matter how dismal the situation, a hopeful prayer that envisions a better future should be in our hearts and on our lips, whether promptly answered or not. Incredibly, Elijah fails to take God's clear hint. He reiterates his claim that the people are no good; he considers himself the only righteous person left. Elijah reverses Moses's entreaty to erase himself, Moses, from the book of God if God does not redeem the people after the sin of the golden calf. Instead, Elijah asks for the people to be wiped out and for God to start all over with him. In response, God understandably commands Elijah to retreat down from the mountain and appoint a successor, Elisha.

After this second failure to heed God's call, Elijah is given early retirement; in other words, he had lost the vision of the intersection of what he could do and what needed to be done and therefore his prayer was denied. Elijah is then dramatically depicted in the beginning of 2 Kings as whisked off alive to heaven after anointing Elisha and—according to legend—gets to spend eternity being dispatched by God to witness Jews doing good deeds or to assist them in doing good deeds. In answer to his prayer to wipe out the people because of their evilness, Elijah is charged with witnessing the descendants of this evil generation conduct Passover seders until the end of time. This is one reason that a cup of wine is poured for Elijah each year at the Passover seder table and the door is opened to welcome him to the festivities. It is as if to say, "Never despair, Elijah; never give up on the people. You thought we were done for but here we are thousands of years later still conducting the Passover seder." Elijah was a very holy person whose prayers could have been answered as they were in the past, but he lost that privilege because his prayer was no longer at the intersection of what could be done and what God would have wanted done; he no longer prayed out of love for the people. God did not want to wipe out the Northern Kingdom of Israel, at least at that time.

Redemption was still possible, but now it would be up to Elisha.

The story of Hannah in the first Book of Samuel represents a classic example of God saying yes to a mortal's prayer. In the last section, we noted the pivotal role that Hannah played in the history and continuity of the Israelite nation. Hannah's key to success in prayer is that she does not suffer from self-deception—literally the only one with this virtue at the beginning of the book. Her husband Elimelech, her co-wife Peninah, Eli the high priest, and Eli's sons, all have succumbed to self-deception. In the story, no one but Hannah comprehends the gravity of the situation in which the Israelites find themselves; every other actor is nursing a self-absorbed life. There is simply no one to lead the people.

Hannah could have focused on indulging her justified anger and resentment. But she neither prays for revenge nor out of self-interest. Instead she is able to realize that the Israelites need a true leader. She prays to God to relieve her of her infertility, couching her words in terms of the service she can provide her people by bearing a child and molding that child to become the long overdue leader of the Israelites...a leader who would guide them back to the path of God and cleanse the priesthood of corruption to boot. She is willing to turn her child over to Eli in an act of self-sacrifice because her priority is getting the Israelites back on track. God, of course, does His part as well, curing Hannah of infertility and nurturing and communicating one-on-one with Samuel.

The text of Hannah's prayer in chapter 2 of 1 Samuel highlights the intertwining of her prayer for a child with that for a leader for the Israelites. Had she prayed solely for a child of her own or solely for a redeemer of Israel, those prayers would have been less effective. Hannah instinctively understands that the backsliding nation urgently needs a living prophet and that her purpose in life is to nurture just such an individual from birth. At the same time, had she not suffered infertility, Hannah might not be motivated to pray as she does or be willing to devote her child to the service of God. But Hannah connects the dots and her prayer is granted. Had Hannah not prayed, or not prayed in an effective way at that divine intersection, we can presume that sooner or later God would have ultimately intervened by reaching out or responding to someone else. However, an improved path for the Israelites might have taken more generations of succumbing to idolatry. It might have meant that many fewer Israelites would have survived to the time of that prophet, but, eventually, it would have happened.

The story of Esther also illustrates God answering prayer in the Bible. At first, Esther tries to deceive herself into believing that she will be just fine in the king's palace. Certainly, as queen she would personally survive Haman's planned destruction of the Jews. But she is in the right place at the right time to affect the outcome of events, and in response to her prayer, God affirms a partnership. As Mordechai told her, a redeemer would have come from elsewhere eventually, but many Jews might already have been murdered by that time. When Esther is jolted out of self-deception, she fasts, prays, and puts herself at risk. From that moment on, God acts as her partner in His own subtle, but decisive, manner.

Another earlier example—yet again from the career of Moses—reveals that unless a prayer takes into consideration what is best for the world, it will ultimately fail, even if initially answered. In Numbers chapter 10, Moses's father-in-law announces that he is departing home, creating a stressful situation for Moses, who finds that his father-in-law perhaps the only person he can relate to and confide in at this point, since Moses's prophetic role has created a rift between him and his siblings and wife, as alluded to in the text. By this juncture in the story, Moses presumably expected the Israelites to be dwelling in the Promised Land within a matter of weeks, a few months at most, and there he would continue to fulfill his role as their leader. The people's complaints and the sad episodes that occur in chapter 11 and beyond are still unknown to him.

But in chapter 11, the first generation of Israelites once again prove to be ingrates, and Moses tells God that there is nothing further he can do. Perhaps God has some magical solution. It comes as a shock to hear Moses himself personally complain about the weight of leadership. Rather than attempting to resolve matters as leader and role model by instructing and inspiring the fledgling nation, he instead prays for meat to feed the grousing people and asks for God to assign others as prophets to share his burden. Both requests were granted, but neither simple solution could work. The provision of the meat does not address the core of the problem, that the first-generation Israelites are incapable of psychologically adjusting to entering the Promised Land. Bestowing prophecy on random individuals unprepared for the responsibility guarantees that no genuine relationship could exist between the newly minted prophets and God or the people. In fact, the seventy freshly minted prophets did start prophesizing, but were poignantly never heard from again. This short-term solution was not of lasting value. The point of God granting Moses's inappropriate requests—with seemingly happy solutions that did not work—was to contrast with Moses's subsequent prayer after the scouts made their report that was answered in a tough way, but was best for the long term.

The problem was that self-deception was rife at this point in the Israelites' journey. The people were not ready to enter the land, and some serious remedial work needed to be done. The fact that the people wanted to send scouts ahead to the Promised Land was a sign that they still had not achieved trust in God, despite the miracles of the Exodus. A time-out, a retreat, was needed—not a surge forward. God did hint at this signal when he told Moses, "Send *for you* men to scout the land of Canaan, which *I am giving* to the Israelite people." (Numbers 13:1) God is not commanding that scouts be sent, as it were, but saying if you and the people want to do it, suit yourself. God makes the point by noting tersely that He is giving the land to the people. What more could be needed at this point? Certainly, Moses did not want the Israelites to wander forty years in the desert, but no other solution was really available.

Sadly, the incident of the scouts proved that this generation of Israelites could not have successfully entered the Promised Land. Had they simply marched straight to the land, the entrance might have led to an ignominy that would have tarnished the name of God and the monotheistic revolution for humanity. Moses pleaded for the people and was willing to blot out his own place in history in defense of the people; however, he did not argue that the people should immediately continue their direct journey to the land. Moses did accept that in due course the people would enter the land but that they needed the next thirty-eight years of teaching, development, and preparation in order to do so. Moses did not pray for immediate continuation of the journey because he recognized the truth that going forward was not the best course of action. Sometimes answers to prayers are long-term and not easy, but are the best available roads to ultimate redemption.

Why No Is Sometimes Better

We should not expect all of our many prayers to be answered affirmatively, and certainly not necessarily in accord with the specifics of our requests. First, we must learn from Moses and admit that the divine plan for the universe is beyond our intellectual purview. What we want may simply not fit into the great cosmic plan that only God knows. Sometimes the answer to even the most sincere, honest, and searing prayer is a simple "no" for reasons we cannot imagine. When God does answer a prayer with a no, He might provide a better alternative. We might propose a partnership with God that seems to us to suit the divine intersection, but God might still find it unacceptable for any one of many cosmic reasons beyond our comprehension. Should God possibly suggest a counteroffer, we ought to acknowledge it with gratitude, as Moses did after the debacle of the scouts. Sometimes we are unaware that our prayers actually have been answered, only in a manner different than what we had requested or expected.

When God Says, "Not Yet"

Often God does not answer prayers right away. Think of the well-known Broadway (and later movie) production of *Fiddler on the Roof* in which Tevye makes an impassioned prayer in the song "If I Were a Rich Man" for God to make an innocuous change to the universe to grant him wealth. Yet, who's to say? Had Tevye's prayer been answered at once, he might have devised a way to stay in Anatevka and not moved to America, the country where he or his progeny would become affluent, certainly by Anatevka standards. Further, fleeing to America saves them from the most likely scenario of those who remained back in the *shtetels* of Russia, which was murder by the Nazis and their accomplices. We have to accept the fact that we do not know what is in our long-term best interests when we pray.

As a New Yorker, I can recount my share of stories from the day the World Trade Center was attacked. One of my daughters was friends with the sister of a girl who had not wanted to go to summer camp in the worst possible way. In the end, she did go to camp, where she unfortunately ended up breaking her arm. Her cast was scheduled to be removed on the morning of September 11, 2001, and so her father arranged to take off the morning from his job at the World Trade Center to bring her to the doctor. His life was saved.

I had a business colleague who regularly took United Flight 93 from Newark to San Francisco. He was due to go to San Francisco on 9/11, but because of some annoying complications with his car, he had to change his reservation to a New York flight to San Francisco later that day. His life was saved.

By the same token, there are stories of people who were *at* the World Trade Center by happenstance on that fateful day. And there are the many stories of the heroes who went into the buildings to save lives after the airplanes had already struck. Nine firemen from the fire station near my home, FDNY Engine Company 22/Ladder 13, rushed into the buildings to save lives and never emerged.

A Better Punch Line

This concept is called Qadr in Arabic and it is what we call defined creed or defined destiny and it is something that you have to struggle for, work hard for, praying to God but at the end of the day, accepting that God decided what will be happening. In other words, I can plan what I would like in my life. I would like to be a businessman, I have to go to the university and study economics and then I plan my business and then have something happen that upends my whole plan, and still keeping faith. I believe that I have done everything right but God decided something else, and what gives me the pleasure is the satisfaction that I don't have to despair, I don't have to blame myself or someone else for what happens. If I did become a businessman that is also part of God's plan. I have done my part and God wants that to happen, so thank God. That is the importance of being grateful to Him. So always here there is a positive thing. Things happen either way.

—IMAM SHAMSI ALI

Sometimes prayer is about suggesting a better punchline. We know that God has a sense of humor. How else can we understand the story of chapter 22 of Numbers in which Balaam saddles his donkey and sets out on a journey to curse the Israelites of his own free will. In a most odd occurrence, Balaam's jackass speaks to him as "the Lord opened the ass's mouth." (Numbers 22:28) Balaam then gets into a verbal argument with the beast. Words fly back and forth in the original Hebrew version (*ATN* for the ass and *AT* for the definite article proceeding Balaam's name) in a way that the reader might infer that it is not clear which character is really the ass and which character is speaking from his ass. The narrative does not need the shtick to proceed but it makes its point.

To the discerning reader, the Bible is full of subtle jokes and ironies. As mentioned above, one thing Elijah prays for is to die rather than have to deal with his fellow Israelites. In response to Elijah's doubts about God's ability to protect him from King Ahab's wrath, God makes a show of bringing Elijah into the heavens via a celestial chariot, as if chuckling, "Elijah, how did you doubt *Me*?" There are multiple punchlines here. Elijah is lifted alive and well into heaven despite his plea for death, and—according to legend—as comeuppance for his complaints about the Israelites, Elijah receives the charge to spend an eternity witnessing descendants of the Israelites performing good deeds. In a final irony, Elijah must also announce the ultimate redemption at the beginning of the messianic age. He will be the messenger of the ultimate optimistic announcement.

Prayer Is Not Enough

Prayer is necessary but never sufficient. Prayer is really an entreaty for a partnership that requires human action according to the Bible. In Exodus (14:15), Moses prayed as the Israelites stood at the foot of the Reed Sea and "Then the Lord said to Moses, 'Why do you cry out to Me? Tell the Israelites to go forward.'" Someone had to lead the march into the Reed Sea so that others could follow. Action was needed, not words. A rabbinic legend has it that Nachshon ben Aminadav walked into the sea up to his neck in water before the seas parted. (Babylonian Talmud Sota 37a) Saint Augustine expressed the balance between prayer and action as follows: "Pray as though everything depended on God. Work as though everything depended on you."

One way to ensure an unanswered prayer is for the petitioner to refuse to do his or her part. There is the story of a woman who prays three times a day that she should win the lottery so that she can send her children to college. Over time she prays ever more fervently until, finally, after a few years, God calls out to her and says, "Can't you at least meet Me halfway and buy a lottery ticket?" Mere prayer itself is no substitute for right and righteous action. More seriously, if Nelson Mandela, Thulani Mabaso, and the other political prisoners on Robben Island had not maintained their dignity, strength, and very lives they would not have been prepared to seize the moment when the regime proved ready to negotiate. Undaunted courage and a fierce belief in a better future sustained the will to survive, and, so, their prayers and actions were profoundly aligned.

Permission for Prayer

We need the Bible to show us how to pray. Pure reason hits a brick wall when it comes to imagining a relationship with the divine. Like some ancient Greek philosophers, we can arrive at the concept of God without the Bible but we cannot logically rationalize praying to Him. The virtue of humility and a close reading of the Bible become our permission slips to pray. As discussed above, we must begin by acknowledging that we don't hold the answers to the secrets of the universe, or even to what is in our own best interest. Moses, who pursued the most successful prayer relationship with God, is legendary for his humility, as the Bible indicates, "Moses was a very humble man, more so than any other man on earth." (Numbers 12:3) Of course, Moses possessed self-awareness of the unprecedented nature of his particular leadership and prophetic roles. His humility existed in his very nature, his unreserved willingness to put others ahead of himself and to recognize that everything is in the hands of God. Moses's plea to God to write himself out of the Bible if God destroyed the people reveals that Moses recognized the decision was up to God and that all he could do was to control his own role and attitude via his free will.

CHAPTER 41

Why Pray?

Hallelujah

> *As Cardinal Newman said, shaping and defining belief is hard, as we don't know quite what we believe until we are on our knees in prayer. I very much believe that the prayer itself, whatever the outcome of the prayer may be, shapes who we are and how we feel about God. This is the core idea that prayer in fact shapes belief.*
>
> —REVEREND CHLOE BREYER

Praising God strengthens our faith. Many prayers in the monotheistic traditions are prayers that praise God's creation and deeds. Atheists often mock these prayers by asking why God would need our praises. Is He, at bottom, a narcissist? No, God does not *need* our praises: *we* need to make them. Praising God awakens in our hearts the greatness of God and of His creation. It inspires us with a sense of wonder and reminds us of God's omnipotence.

Don't Forget to Say Thank You

The practice of giving thanks cultivates our moral qualities and faith. While supplications spotlight what we lack, prayers of gratitude focus on the good in our lives. As Christian mystic Meister Eckhart declared, *"If the only prayer you ever say in your entire life is thank you, it will be enough.*" Thank-you prayers cultivate the important moral quality of being grateful. Gratitude is essential to all our relationships, and our relationship with God is no exception. Without gratitude, we lose perspective on our place in the world and our relationship to others.

We also need to be realistic and be prepared to express gratitude, even if only a portion of our prayer requests are answered. The comedian Myron Cohen tells of a grandmother at the beach with her grandchild when suddenly a great wave sweeps the child out into the ocean. The grandmother looks to heaven and cries with her whole heart, "Dear God, please save the life of my only grandchild!" Suddenly, a wave rushes in toward the shore and deposits the child back on the dry sand unhurt. Grabbing the child to her bosom, she again turns her eyes upward toward heaven and calls out, "He had a hat." Gratitude helps us to remember that what we have is really important. In the joke, the grandmother loses sight of what is important the minute she has her grandchild back. How often we, too, take the important things in life entirely for granted.

What We Want Matters

Like thought, communication, and action, prayer derives from our free will. Choosing to pray, like choosing to imagine a better future and acting to make it happen, is a sign of our free will. Prayer signifies our uniqueness, our humanity, and our spark of Godliness. As the British poet W. H. Auden wrote, "*In a world of prayer, we are all equal in the sense that each of us is a unique person, with a unique perspective on the world, a member of a class of one.*" Or as the Islamic mystic Rumi explains in similar words, "In prayer all are equal." Saint Augustine expresses it thus: "*The desire is thy prayers; and if thy desire is without ceasing, thy prayer will also be without ceasing. The continuance of your longing is the continuance of your prayer.*" When we speak our heart and discover our deepest longings, we discover what God wants for us.[1]

The Bible and monotheistic tradition encourage prayer as God's way of acknowledging that our wishes for ourselves and for others matter. Not only are we free to think the way we want and act the way we want, but we are also free to imagine what we want and ask God for help in achieving it. If the Bible were not revealed, we would be uncertain whether our free will was guaranteed and whether prayer mattered at all. Without the Bible's assurance, we might conclude that, in our lives, we merely play predestined roles on a vast stage, strangely incapable of flubbing our predetermined lines because we have no choice otherwise. A comforting thought for actors perhaps, but not for the rest of us.

The Bible resolves this dilemma by emphasizing that we are created in the image of God (Genesis 1:26) and, therefore, we have the right to change our minds, the right to argue with God, and the power to change history through our free choice of actions. This is not to say that the ancient rabbis did not puzzle over the mystery of free will. Rabbi Akiva encapsulated the paradox: "Everything is foreseen, yet freedom of choice is bestowed." (Babylonian Talmud Pirkei Avot 3:19) As previously discussed, except in cases of mental illness, the ancient rabbis believed that ultimate free will always exist, unless specifically overruled by God (as in the case of Pharaoh in Exodus). Prayer is a way we express our free will.

Our ability to formulate prayers also stems from the fluidity and freedom of our consciousness and our ability to access a higher consciousness. God's omnipotent aspect is crucial to prayer, and it flows both from God to us, and from us to God. As we have seen, it is a core monotheistic tenet that each human being is endowed with a spark of God and so we are conscious of a hint of omnipotence. No matter what our physical limitations, in our consciousness we can all imagine being Superman or Wonder Woman. Conscious imagination may be what fundamentally separates humanity from the animal world. This mysterious ability can be profound, as in the case of a political prisoner in a cell who imagines freedom for himself and his nation. During the moments that I visited Nelson Mandela's tiny cell, I stood there feeling vaguely claustrophobic, even with the door open, and I wondered how he could ever, in such imprisonment, have resolutely imagined a free South Africa. Natan Sharansky suffered similar conditions in the Soviet gulag, and yet he was able to imagine a Soviet Jewry free of its Communist shackles. Consider how a person sitting indoors in a room without recourse to a telescope or microscope can still imagine in his or her mind's eye the infinite aspects of the universe, or of quantum behavior at the Planck length too small to measure with our most precise equipment. In our consciousness we can change anything, be anything, do anything, exist in any society, alter our relationships with other individuals. We can imagine societies and countries that live in peace and freedom and mutual respect, despite more depressing realities in the world.

Prayer is a practice that enables us to expand our consciousness and frees us to be who we truly want to be, who we surely need to be. Prayer requires us to clear away all the underbrush of what others want for us or what we think they might want for us. Consciousness is a gift that can be turned, of course, towards an evil purpose as well. Consciousness could be wasted on trivia, such as daydreaming about craft beers. How many times do we want something simply because it is what society wants for us? Are we pining for a certain house or job because it can change our lives for the better, or do we just want it? Are we praying to get into a certain college because it is the most prestigious, or because its course of studies is best for us?

Many people turn to prayer when they feel the limits of their own vision. None other than Abraham Lincoln had this habit. In his own words, "I have been driven many times upon my knees by the overwhelming conviction that I had nowhere else to go. My own wisdom and that of all about me seemed insufficient for that day." Likewise, Dr. Martin Luther King Jr. habitually found inspiration in prayer:

> Saturday evening, as I began going over my sermon, I was aware of a certain anxiety. Although I had preached many times before having served as associate pastor of my father's church in Atlanta for four years, and actually doing all of the preaching there for three straight summers, I had never preached in a situation in which I was being considered for the pastorate of a church. In such a situation one cannot but be conscious of the fact that he is on trial. Many questions came to my mind. How could I best impress the congregation? Should I attempt to interest it with a display of scholarship? Or should I preach just as I had always done, depending finally on the inspiration of the spirit of God? I decided to follow the latter course. I said to myself over and over again, "Keep Martin Luther King in the background and God in the foreground and everything will be all right. Remember you are a channel of the gospel and not the source." With these words on my lips I knelt and prayed my regular evening prayer. I closed the prayer by asking for God's guidance and His abiding presence as I confronted the congregation of His people on the next morning. With the assurance that

always comes to me after sincere prayer, I rose from my knees to the comfortable bed, and in almost an instant I fell asleep.[2]

Prayer and Optimism

When I have had a good conversation with atheists, I will say to them, "Thank you for your candor and telling me you have lost your faith. Let me ask you this: Have you lost your hope?" I have never met a person who has said, "Yes, I have no hope." They will all say to me, "Well, of course I have hope." Then I say, "Well tell me what hope is? Hope is the trust that I have to get through the day, the drive that makes me go on. Well, tell me what it is?" They will mention a lot of things, most of them extraordinarily noble, and I'll say, "What happens when your spouse dies? What happens when your health goes? What happens when the stock market plummets?" As we talk about what if each reason for hope goes away, usually I know what they'll answer: "I don't know what I would do, but then there would be something else to hope in," and my response is, "Why don't we conclude and call that God?" There is always going to be a substratum of some bedrock, which we could call hope in and we could put a capital letter on it, call this phenomenon God. So sometimes I wonder if we should change the conversation about faith to a conversation about hope.

—TIMOTHY CARDINAL DOLAN

The practice of prayer leads us to adopt a posture of hope toward the world. We pray because we can imagine things could be better and we choose to put this vision into words. At the point of total despair, people no longer pray. As the expression goes, "You don't even have a prayer." We rarely have enough information to know if a situation is beyond hope or not.

Prayer helps us to exercise our hope muscle and also to put us in the mindset of imagining courses of action. In moments of despair during the Civil War, Abraham Lincoln turned to prayer to renew his hope and his strength to continue the fight: "When everyone seemed panic-stricken…I went to my room…and got down on my knees before

Almighty God and prayed…Soon a sweet comfort crept into my soul that God Almighty had taken the whole business into His own hands…"[3] The process of praying often requires us to forgive others and ourselves for our past actions. We may prefer to wallow in anger and view our situation as a dead end, but, truly, this leads nowhere. Louis Zamperini, survivor of forty-seven days in a life raft and subsequently captured and tortured by the Japanese in a POW camp for unregistered prisoners, wrote this of his experience: *"All I did was pray to God, every day. In prison camp, the main prayer was, 'Get me home alive, God, and I'll seek you and serve you.' I came home, got wrapped up in the celebration, and forgot about the hundreds of promises I'd made to God."*

Zamperini ultimately remembered his prayers and became a Christian Evangelical. Prayer forces us to seek alternatives. It demands that we look to transcend moods and circumstances, to abandon our resentment and anger toward others. Prayer is a genuine antidote to negative, nonconstructive thoughts.[4]

Imprisoned by Soviet authorities, as we've already noted, the refusenik Natan Sharansky drew tremendous strength from prayer when he could well have lost himself in despair instead. Sharansky recounts the following story in an interview:

> When I was arrested some days after this, I suddenly remembered about it [a psalm book], and I started fighting in order to get it. It took me three years to fight, to force authorities to give me this book. They gave it to me the day when they gave me, also, the telegram that my father passed away. I felt terrible, because I could not be with my mother, I could not support her in those days. So what can I do? I decided that what I'll do, I'll start reading this psalm book. It was difficult for me to read, with my [limited] knowledge of Hebrew, this ancient language where you cannot even understand where is the end of the sentence. It was difficult to understand, but when you are reading day after day, you understand a word here, a word there, a phrase here, a phrase there, you compare, and some moment you start understanding. I remember the first psalm which I suddenly understood, the phrase which I understood was, [Hebrew], "and when I go through the valley of death, I'll fear no evil, because you are with me." It was such a powerful feeling, as if King David himself, together with my wife, together with my

friends, came to prison to save me from this, and to support me. Suddenly all these connections of thousands of years are restored, and you feel exactly as King David, three thousand years ago, wrote this. This was sending me a message to be strong. So now, whatever I'll say, maybe I'll be influencing someone who will be sitting in prison in three thousand years, and suppose that he will know that "you are [with me]"…who's *you*? God or King David, or my wife, or the people of Israel? I don't know. All this together. That was a very powerful feeling, and it gave me a lot of strength.[5]

Prayer and Empowerment

Prayer empowers us to face challenges. At some stage, almost everyone fears that they are not up to the task of whatever challenge they face. By seeking to examine the situation and ourselves with complete truth, we sharpen our perception of what is going on and expand our capacity to respond critically. The practice of prayer yields determined resolve and galvanizes us for positive action. Prayer reinforces the tenet of faith that only God is omnipotent and therefore no person or situation is unnefeatable. Prayer sustains us intellectually and psychologically to confront our challenges rather than to avoid them. Many people pray for strength itself. Helen Keller famously wrote these words about prayer and power: "On Power: It is for us to pray not for tasks equal to our powers, but for powers equal to our tasks, to go forward with a great desire forever beating at the door of our hearts as we travel toward our distant goal."

Prayer and Honesty

The practice of prayer can help us to achieve greater levels of frankness and honesty about what we really want and why. Another valuable aspect of consciousness is that we are capable of examining our requests and dissecting our thought processes in a critical manner. Proper prayer cannot happen without self-assessment and self-honesty. We know, of course, that something that first appears as bad might, in reality, be good. But we also know that, inevitably, enough bad things do happen in life. In such cases, prayer reminds us that we are never meant to understand everything and are best served by turning our attention instead toward acquiring the strength to move on.

Real prayer has to have an honesty that is deeper than one has with a spouse or a psychotherapist for it to have a chance of being effective. We cannot fool God, and before God fooling ourselves becomes silly. The bright light of frankness that we must focus on our self and our motivations must be so fiercely piercing that our natural reaction is to squint and often to cringe, or perhaps to recoil and reconsider our supplication and plan of action out of sheer embarrassment.

Prayer also requires an honest appraisal of the morality of our petition. Do we want a business to succeed, a relationship to heal? But what if neither of these outcomes would actually lead to the moral betterment of the people involved? Would we pray for a certain athlete to win a competition without at least considering whether they might be cheating or not? (FYI, I did not pray for the Cubs to win the 2016 World Series, even though I really, really wanted them to win.)

A good example of the power of truth in prayer is the case of Bartolomé de las Casas, the Spanish priest who denounced the *encomienda* system (which rationalized the servitude of the Native Americans) and called for its end. De las Casas first realized his hypocrisy while writing a sermon, whose message he understood contradicted his actions. Through reflection, prayer, and meditation de las Casas fully understood the evil he had done and the evil of the whole *encomienda* system. People may close their eyes and bend the knee, but they simply are not meeting the definition of prayer if their moral GPS is turned off. The feminist abolitionist Angelina Grimké explains it this way: "I have not placed reading before praying because I regard it more important, but because, in order to pray aright, we must understand what we are praying for." Radical honesty is awfully frightening, but it is fundamental to petitionary prayer. Done right, petitionary prayer compels us to become more and more honest with ourselves and others. Idolaters would consider all of this all beside the point of their prayer.

When we pray, we reconsider our actions. It is traditional in monotheistic cultures that self-assessment precedes prayer. British philosopher Julian Baggini writes, "Prayer provides an opportunity to remind oneself of how one should be living, our responsibilities to others, our own failings, and our relative good fortune, should we have it. This is, I think, a pretty worthwhile practice and it is not something you can only do if you believe you are talking to an unseen creator." The Jewish liturgy for morning prayers includes the following sentiment: "A person should be God fearing in private as well as in public. He/she should always acknowledge/recognize the truth and speak the truth in his/her heart." [my translation]

In the context of prayer, we can now better understand the desecration that arises from treating our fellow human beings immorally. Someone who preys on fellow human beings but prays to God objectifies God, expecting Him to answer our prayers but ignore our deeds just because we fulfill some ritual formula and get the words right. This objectification is itself a camouflaged version of idolatry, as if we were expecting God to respond to us while we reserve the right to disrespect our relationship with Him. Would someone who has defrauded or robbed another expect attentive concern from his or her victim? Such prayers must be particularly vulgar to God, and religious education must bear the responsibility for educating its adherents. Schools and churches, mosques and synagogues must truly preach and teach that immorality destroys our relationship with God and that careless or malicious actions negate the efficacy of our prayers. Immoral people may well attend our religious institutions, and it is there and then that they should be exposed to instruction and inspiration to confront the self-deception and self-betrayal that comes from acting immorally. Instead, many congregants lean heavily on the scaffolding around prayer but ignore the hard part of self-assessment. These attempts at prayer will of course fail because they are not real prayer.

Prayer provides the venue for the radical honesty that can lead us to the action that will transform our relationships with others and God, and thereby change the world. If, after a penetrating self-examination of where we are situated and what actions we can take, we can present to God a better outcome for humanity, for our community, for our family in our small corner of the world, and if we *change our actions*, our prayer has a chance to be heard by an omnibenevolent God. Our change itself will be one step to bettering the world.

If through a courageous change in our actions we can hasten redemption, then it makes sense for an omnibenevolent God to act in partnership with us to make that outcome happen. The omniscient

God knows whether our contemplated intervention is better than the default outcome, and advances redemption. Through prayer and our willingness to act, we can aspire to persuade God to let us affect history whether it be for our family, our community or, on rare occasion, the world. That ability gives us a slender glimpse of the omnipotence of God in our own souls.

Ritualized Prayer

Because real prayer is so tremendously difficult to accomplish, the religious traditions have built scaffolding around its edifice. This scaffolding consists of liturgical arrangements of prepared prayers in the form of prayer books, hymns, processions, and rituals. Such scaffolding allows us to wade into prayer, so to speak, slowly and judiciously, careful to realize the goal of true prayer. Yet, over the centuries, the scaffolding has unfortunately become thick with dust, hardened and seemingly impenetrable. Ironically it has become in itself a wall around real prayer. Furthermore, ritual scaffolding often leads to confusing true prayer with idolatrous prayer. Nevertheless, few of us are capable of preparing or composing prayers of our own, neither on a daily nor an occasional basis. At the same time, let's face it, rote prayer is no rock concert, and it's not long before it can lose its hold on the soul. An over-reliance on institutional trappings also impairs the ability of prayer to inspire a sense of spirituality. People trying to pray in our modern-day religious institutions often find themselves submerged in the ritual. Many feel that they are not experiencing real prayer that touches the soul but, rather, something that might look like "praying" to an anthropologist or some other objective outside observer.

I cannot overstress this point. I have seen congregants drift away from synagogues because they find the service devoid of any spirituality. Others stick it out for a sense of community and shared mission, but they deeply yearn for a transcendent experience of true prayer. Some just don't "feel it" when they pray, and they've come typically to expect no more, end of story.

In response to this, leaders and educators in the monotheistic tradition need to reconsider how they approach prayer with congregants. Only after we really learn how to make prayer meaningful and effective for congregants in the twenty-first century can we succeed in reenergizing the ritualized form of monotheistic prayers. These ancient prayers were sagely composed to remind us to pray for what is truly important in life. Such formal prayers serve a real purpose. If they are introduced and practiced properly, they add potent force to our personal prayer experience. Communal prayers also express the particular spiritual sensitivity and customs of a community.

My Nominee for The Golden Fleece Award

As we now comprehend the true nature of prayer, we can observe that so-called studies of the efficacy of prayer are bizarre. Academics have attempted to measure prayer using alleged double-blind tests of intercessory prayer (praying for another, usually for healing). One famous study, which Dawkins has commented on extensively, was dubbed the "Great Prayer Experiment."[6] These studies typically involve asking strangers to pray for the recovery of individuals who are ill. In some instances, the individuals in question know that others are praying for them. In other cases, they are unaware or, in control cases, unsure. Further, in one study they received only first names and last initials.[1] Although there have been some exceptions, the person praying and the person being prayed for have no relationship outside of the study.

Obviously, these prayers do not fit the definition of monotheistic prayer. In fact, if God does laugh, He is having an Almighty good chuckle at these experiments. To think that we can measure the power of God by university- or foundation-underwritten man-made studies is like measuring the progress of salmon attempting to build a spaceship for a flight to Mars. The misunderstanding is so fundamental as to make this research no less inane. These studies might measure idolatrous prayer, which is equivalent to putting some prayer tokens into an imagined cosmic vending machine via some mechanism of a formulaic prayer for

---

[1] There have been a couple of meta-analyses of the studies of intercessory prayer. See John A. Astin et al., "The Efficacy of 'Distant Healing': A Systematic Review of Randomized Trials," *Annals of Internal Medicine 132*, no. 11 (June 6, 2000): 903–910; and Kevin S. Masters, Glen I. Spielmans, and Jason T. Goodson, "Are there Demonstrable Effects of Distant Intercessory Prayer? A Meta-Analytic Review," *Annals of Behavioral Medicine 32*, no. 1 (August 2006): 21–6. For a review of the major studies on prayer and healing, see David R. Hodge, "A Systematic Review of the Empirical Literature on Intercessory Prayer," *Research on Social Work Practice 17*, no. 2 (March 2007): 174–187.

people who don't know each other, and have no idea how their presence affects the world. This is more or less what I witnessed at the Meiji Shrine. These experiments possess no real control groups to ascertain the righteousness or deeds of the patients, or the worthiness of the people doing the praying. The divine intersection cannot be found because the person praying has no coordinates. As we have described, prayer emanates from relationships at all angles. This caricature of prayer stripped of relationships is not prayer. Further, unlike the omniscient God, we have no way of foreseeing how the future will pan out with the ill person's recovery so we cannot attempt to try to align ourselves with the Godly vision that is essential for prayer. These studies, therefore, have nothing to do with monotheistic prayer. (At least in Myron Cohen's joke the grandmother knew whom she was praying for and what the stakes were, so her initial prayer could be heartfelt.)

Imam Shamsi Ali illustrates this with a story:

There were two children, a brother and very devout sister. The brother and sister got into an argument and the brother broke the leg of his sister's doll. The brother asks the sister, "Now what are you going to do?" and she said, "I am going to pray to God that the doll's leg gets fixed." And so she goes off and prays and the brother waits for her as she comes back and the doll's leg is still broken. The brother asks, "Now what do you have to say for yourself? You prayed and the doll's leg is still broken." The sister replied, "Well I prayed to God and asked God to fix the doll's legs and God said no."
I think it is difficult to show that prayer affects things. I think it is even just as difficult to show that prayer doesn't affect things.

It seems about five million dollars was spent on the academic prayer studies noted above. The only difference between giving this money to people for digging ditches and then refilling them is that these studies employ people who work in air-conditioned offices and are possibly under the illusion that they are accomplishing something. Were any of these studies to come up with a positive outcome for prayer as they define it, I would reject those findings as a false positive. Finally, the Theosic principle implies that these studies must be worthless, as God would never reveal Himself in such a straightforward manner through such daft experiments. A much better use of the money used for these studies would be to redirect the funds to medical research or treatment for the ill.

There is a joke about a famous atheist professor who wrote popular books ridiculing the concept of God and denigrating believers. This fellow went to Yellowstone National Park to attend a convention of vocal atheists. One morning at dawn he got up to take a walk and ponder the wonder of nature that emerged from nothingness. Suddenly in the midst of his walk he saw a huge bear and started to run. The bear saw him and catapulted toward him. Unfortunately, the professor tripped and fell and as he turned face up, he saw the bear at his feet about to pounce on him.

The professor cried out, "O God! Please save me!" At that moment there was a clap of thunder and the bear froze in place, hovering in mid pounce. A voice called out from the heavens, "Professor, you have not walked in my ways but if you accept Me as God and go back to the convention and proclaim that you are now God-fearing, I will save you." Having regained his composure, the professor responded that accepting God would be okay but proclaiming himself as a believer to his colleagues at the convention would be very embarrassing. The professor proposed that a better solution would be to make the bear a God-fearing creature. Immediately there was another clap of thunder and the bear fell back on its knees. For a second the professor was relieved until he heard the bear solemnly say in perfect English, "O Lord, thank You for this meal of which I am about to partake."

In the joke, it seems that God thinks that what is best for the universe and what was worth making a miracle to accomplish was for the professor to publicly and privately acknowledge belief. The joke makes the point that the solution that the professor had proposed was not at the intersection of what was best for the humanity and God's plan and so there was another outcome, presumably the second-best outcome for the world.

Faith in a Personal God

Feeling and being in touch with God's presence and having an identity as somebody who repairs breeches in the world instead of creating them, a repairer of the breech, a restorer of streets in which we live. We have faith and we build the tangible, we build the infrastructure. It is not just putting food in the mouth of the hungry, it is clearing a path and creating an infrastructure for a just society.

—REVEREND DR. KATHARINE HENDERSON

You are free to choose God, but if you are really going to commit yourself to that relationship, as you would with your spouse, you are going to live up to that relationship and that relationship means you are not going to do other than try to right, to reach out to others who need you, to be charitable, to see others as God sees you and me. That means you live your life in a certain way.

—BISHOP WILLIAM MURPHY

I would like to invoke an individual who clearly did not believe in a personal God but whose words are sometimes distorted by atheists to abnegate God entirely, namely Albert Einstein. In an interview published in 1930 Einstein responded to the question whether he believed in God:

Your question [about God] is the most difficult in the world. It is not a question I can answer simply with yes or no. I am not an atheist. I do not know if I can define myself as a pantheist. The problem involved is too vast for our limited minds. May I not reply with a parable? The human mind, no matter how highly trained, cannot grasp the universe. We are in the position of a little child, entering a huge library whose walls are covered to the ceiling with books in many different tongues. The child knows that someone must have written those books. It does not know who or how. It does not understand the languages in which they are written. The child notes a definite plan in the arrangement of the books, a mysterious order, which it does not comprehend, but only dimly suspects. That, it seems to me, is the attitude of the human mind, even the greatest and most cultured, toward God. We see a universe marvelously arranged, obeying certain laws, but we understand the laws only dimly. Our limited minds cannot grasp the mysterious force that sways the constellations.[7]

With all humility, I would go beyond this statement of Einstein's to say that the Designer of that huge library—and the Author of one particular book in the library—has given our limited minds a trail of tremendous insights to follow. We can follow that trail if we have the courage. We have been graced with the Bible and with consciousness—therefore we have a guidebook and the capacity to relate to God. The Bible teaches us that we can pray, and that in doing so, can have a glimpse of the briefest hint at omniscience, omnipotence, and omnibenevolence in a relationship with no deception to the self or others. That is why prayer is the religious experience par excellence, and why true believers strive to achieve that state. Real faith in God takes courage—because even though it is only a small step to faith, that step can change everything. While faith can give our lives meaning and purpose, it also requires us to accept responsibility, an obligation that is not only to our families and ourselves but to all humanity. The sincerity of our prayer and our faith is seen in our actions.

That small step requires that we break away from the comfortable slogans and convenient excuses we tell ourselves. It means turning aside from the many ways we distract ourselves.

A Final Thought

This book would not have happened without the power of prayer. Prior to the lunch described in the introduction, I had been thinking for a long time about the state of monotheistic belief in the modern world and of the failure of religious education to cope with modernity. I worried even more as I witnessed idolatry under different banners reemerging in the world. As I read through the atheist books referred to herein, I became more and more convinced that a book on rational belief in God was very much needed to make this world a better place.

I did not, however, consider that I was the person to write that book.

Then, people kept having those "God conversations" with me. I thought about organizing a group and commissioning "an expert" to take on the writing of a book. For a long time, I was uncertain if I was capable of writing this book. As you know by now, I am not a rabbi, a theologian, or an academic, yet I believe that one need not be in any of these professions to understand or have a relationship with God. I would have to do a lot of study on the historicity of the Bible and really brush up on scientific developments in physics and biology.

Having said that, I have spent a lot of time reading the Bible and thinking about the issues that the book would need to cover. As I prayed and thought about it more and more, I kept having new experiences or thinking about my past experiences that would be useful in writing this book. Then, in the space of two months, my four children were all leaving for school or work and my wife was accepted as a PhD candidate. Suddenly, I went from living in an apartment with six people to just me most of the time. I would have some unaccustomed alone time. I started to think that writing this book could possibly be at the intersection of what I could do and what needed to be done. I also felt a bit of a tailwind. Prayer helped me clear away my comforting (and many) justifications for not taking on this project. Prayer helped me see that although writing this book was way out of my comfort zone, I could do it. By the time, I had my lunch conversation, I felt like I was being given a nearly physical shove.

This book has been about clearing away comforting confusions and pithy slogans for you so that you can freely decide whether to have faith. May you find the intersection of what you need to do, what you can do, and what needs to be done to better the world regardless of what you decide.

ACKNOWLEDGMENTS

Writing a few words of thanks seems remarkably inadequate to express my appreciation, debt, and gratitude toward friends, family, and others who generously extended themselves to offer help throughout my work on this book. I must begin with Carolyn Starman Hessel, who has somehow helped more authors than there are visible stars in the sky. When I first told Carolyn I was thinking about writing this book, she immediately instructed me to take out a pad of paper and then she started giving me an outline of my next steps. Among other points, Carolyn gave me the idea of conducting interviews with well-known faith leaders as a pillar of the book. She was also kind enough to read multiple drafts of key chapters, and to give me unwavering encouragement with digestible dollops of constructive criticisms.

I cannot overstate my thanks to Olga Kirschbaum, who was the research associate for the entire book. Olga acted as an intellectual sparring partner during the five years of my writing. She would never let me get away with an argument that might be a sleight of hand or avoid an issue that she thought needed to be addressed. She also played a vital role as occasional motivational coach at several key junctures. I feel I can confidently predict that Olga will do important things in the future. Keep an eye on her as an emerging intellectual talent and voice. It was indeed a privilege and pleasure to work with Olga on this project.

I was fortunate enough to have a variety of expert specialist readers agree to review specific sections of the book. I must promptly note that in no way should those who were benevolent enough to comment on certain sections be liable for the content, perspective, opinions, or errors expressed. With that caveat goes my entirely unreserved thanks to Dan Ariely, Gabi Barkay, Simon Goldhill, Haskel Greenfield, Marty Grumet,

Yarom Hazony, Gil Kahn, Jill Katz, Seth Newman, and Natan Slifkin for their thoughtful remarks and criticisms. I must separately thank David Gershon and Ben Rathus who gave me in depth tutorials on quantum physics and carefully reviewed multiple drafts of the text.

In addition, I need to thank certain friends, colleagues, and family members who read the bulk of the book, sometimes through multiple drafts. I doubt some appreciated what they were getting into when they graciously agreed to be readers, but some of the comments I received were invaluable and led to significant redrafting of various sections. Thank you to Calanit Dovere-Valfer, Alicia DePaolo, Audrey Lichter, Alan Barnett, Gerry Magaldi, Steve Salinger, Benjamin Shay, Ariel Shay, Mark Sigona, and John Tamberlane. I must spotlight my friend Ron Schienberg, who expended tremendous energy on his timely, insightful, and comprehensive comments on three different drafts of the book.

Making the complicated topics addressed *In Good Faith* accessible, clear, and as concise as possible was a high priority. So, I had two separate editors review and provide edits as well as editorial advice during the drafting. The first was Sam Friedman, whose comments and edits made it clear to me that I was further away from being able to offer the book to publishers than I had thought. Sam asked me if I wanted brutal honesty in his editing, and in a professional manner, he gave it to me. Sam's suggestions and comments lead me to substantially redraft certain sections and to the relegation of the more technical sections of part four to an appendix. The second editor was Alan Zelenetz, who began his relationship with the book as one of my friendly informal commentators. I realized that Alan's editing background and skills would be invaluable if he were to accept a more formal role for the book, which he agreed to do for the final draft of the book. Alan brought a fresh and incisive eye to each sentence. Thank you, Sam and Alan.

I must also note my gratitude to my friend Tobi Kahn who walked the floors of Barnes & Noble with me looking at book covers and thinking about the best cover for In *Good Faith* and for designing it. Tobi also relentlessly encouraged me over these five years, somehow never doubting I would finish the project.

My earnest thanks also go to the entire Post Hill Press team led by Anthony Ziccardi and Michael Wilson. It is a pleasure to work with these professionals. My sincere thanks also go to Jon Ford, my Post Hill Press editor, for his efficiency and clarity. I am truly amazed at how much Jon knows about such a variety of disciplines. Thanks also accrue to Maddie Sturgeon at PHP for staying on top of every detail. Also thanks to the editors of Post Hill Press who read the final draft of this book and still managed to whack a few moles of typos.

Rob LoMascolo was careful and thoughtful in making sure every map and chart was descriptive, complete, and elegant.

I would like to thank my lawyers, Charles Googe and Jennifer Murdoch (of Paul, Weiss, Rifkind, Wharton & Garrison), for guiding me through the complicated world of publishing contracts. While I presume uncommon for books on religion, I would like to thank my travel agents Kate Doty and Becca Glatz (of GeoEx) for arranging deeply meaningful spiritual and faith encounters during my trips to far flung lands.

I am also grateful to Lew Ranieri and Joe DePaolo, two of my business partners, for their encouragement and helpful suggestions along the way. I must also thank my longtime assistant Pat Burger, who manages my day so efficiently that she seemingly squeezes in extra minutes in the hour. Knowing that I could trust Pat to handle many administrative aspects of the book process was a great comfort to me.

In a non-ironic manner, I extend my thanks Richard Dawkins for his suggestion to all authors that he included in his preface to *The God Delusion,* specifically to employ professional actors to read one's book aloud prior to completion. As I was very impressed with Dawkins's rhetoric in *The God Delusion* as well as his other writings, I took advantage of being a member of the board of New York Theatre Workshop and asked for NYTW to identify several actors who would take on this project and read the entire book aloud to Olga and I. So my thanks go to Caroline Hewitt, Leigh Wade, Rowan Vickers, and Nikki Massoud-Moghaddam. When any of them would trip over a phrase or look puzzled after reading a paragraph, I knew that revision was in order.

As acknowledgments conclude, it is appropriate to focus on one's family. I am truly blessed. My wife Susan has been abundantly supportive during the entire writing of this book while she has been deeply engaged in pursuing a PhD. Susan has made so many things possible in my life that words truly cannot express my thanks and gratitude. I would also like to thank my children, Benjamin, Ariel, Alison, and Abigail. You are my inspiration and my most important legacy to the future.

I end by reciting a modified Jewish *Shehechiyanu* blessing. I thank the Almighty for giving me the life that I have, for preserving me, and for bringing me to this point in my life so that I could write and complete this book.

APPENDIX

This appendix was written with the assistance of Ben Rathaus and with heavy comments from David Gershon, both of whom have PhDs in physics. I want to acknowledge the invaluable help that both Ben and David so graciously gave to me.

In the framework of the "standard model of cosmology," our universe came into being by means of the big bang event, which marks the "beginning of time."[1] We do not know what got the big bang going, nor how large (or small) space was at that time. The energy density in the first stages of the universe was so high that it is believed that the laws of physics, as we know them today, were not in effect. The universe was comprised of energy, particles, and fields that we do not know, and of matter-antimatter pairs that seemed to appear "out of the blue" (actually from the energy present all around) and disappear into the thin air (in fact, back to the thin air).[2]

Then, for some reason, some billionth of a billionth of a billionth of a billionth of a second (or so) after the big bang, the universe entered a phase of inflation, during which space itself was inflated into being macroscopic (that is, visible to the naked eye).[3] Near the end of inflation (we don't exactly know when), some process had taken place that broke the symmetry between the matter and antimatter pairs, leaving us in a universe that is almost entirely made up of matter.[4] Only ten to twenty seconds after the Big Bang (which is also ten to twenty seconds after inflation had already been over), helium and lithium and some heavier nuclei formed.[5] It then took four hundred thousand years before our universe became electrically neutral—as free electrons and nuclei combined to form atoms. This was the queue for these atoms to start clumping[6] (before that the radiation pressure did not allow this).[1] It would take roughly two hundred million years more before the first stars were formed,[7] which would enrich galaxies with "heavy" elements (heavier than hydrogen), which, in turn, enabled the formation of Population II and I stars, like our own sun (which is a Pop I star).

These first-generation stars were unlike most of our stars in the Milky Way. Rather, they were very light stars that became incubators for our lightest elements: hydrogen, helium, and lithium, which in turn became raw fuel for the second generation of stars, since the first generation of stars exploded as they begat these materials. The second generation of stars next led to the creation of heavier elements and the stuff of matter that we recognize and that makes up our earth and its carbon-based life. A third generation of stars formed by capturing some of the matter of the previous generation, subsequently leading to the formation of planetary systems. Our solar system—with the sun, the moon, the Earth, and its other planets—is fortuitously placed in one of the Milky Way's spiral arms[8] that is hospitable to the formation of life. The theory of the big bang has led physicists to date the universe to about fourteen billion years old.

Quantum Theory

Here is where the primordial waters get murkier. Quantum mechanics has radically changed our understanding of matter, radiation, and physical interactions, of which the universe we inhabit is comprised.[9] Like the big bang theory, quantum mechanics is another one of the incredible achievements of the twentieth century.[10] In the late 1800s and early 1900s, classical physics faced a substantial crisis, as it failed to explain several microscopic phenomena.[11] The first breakthrough came in 1900 when German physicist Max Planck sought an explanation for the relation between the color (or, more accurately, the energy distribution of

---

[1] It should be noted that the lion's share of matter in our universe is actually what we call "dark matter"—matter that gravitates just like the matter we know from our everyday experience, but does not interact with electromagnetic fields. Consequently, dark matter started clumping before "ordinary matter" could clump, resulting in a nontrivial gravitational potential at the time in which ordinary matter was allowed to clump. The already-existing clumps of dark matter then attracted ordinary matter, thus giving the latter a "push" toward clumping. For a more elaborate explanation, see for example Dodelson, *Modern Cosmology*.

the emitted radiation) and the temperature of objects[2] in thermal equilibrium[3] with their surroundings (a phenomenon known as the famous "blackbody radiation"). In order to solve this problem, Planck had ingeniously hypothesized that the energy exchange between radiation and its surrounding takes place in discrete, or quantized, amounts.[12] With this hypothesis, Planck was able to reproduce experimental results of actual blackbody radiation. This put an end to one of the pressing problems that kept physicists awake at night and fired the opening shot in the establishment of quantum mechanics.[13]

Subsequent quantum mechanics developed quite rapidly. In 1905, Albert Einstein followed Planck's quantization of electromagnetic radiation and claimed that this principle should also be valid for light. He therefore posited that light itself is made of discrete energy quanta, called "photons." With this hypothesis, he was able to elegantly solve the photoelectric effect,[14] which had been observed by Heinrich Hertz in 1887, but which to date, had acquired no compelling explanation.[4] In 1913, Niels Bohr introduced his model for the hydrogen atom,[15] according to which atoms can be found only in discrete energy states, and according to which interaction of atoms with radiation can only take place if the energy exchange between the atom and the radiation is quantized properly. (For those of you chafing at the bit to know what "quantized" signifies, it means "according to the energy difference between the hypothesized allowed energy states of Bohr's atom.") This allegedly simplistic model has provided a satisfactory explanation to several pressing problems, the stability of atoms for one.[5]

---

[2] Not just any object, but a blackbody, which means an object that absorbs all the radiation that is radiated upon it.

[3] An object that is in thermal equilibrium is an object that emits exactly the same amount of energy as it absorbs.

[4] Albert Einstein was awarded the Nobel Prize in Physics in 1923 for the explanation of the photoelectric effect.

[5] According to the "classical picture," before the Bohr model, a hydrogen atom consists of a nucleus and an electron that orbits the nucleus. According to classical electromagnetism, however, an electric charge, such as an electron "on the move," radiates energy continuously. Therefore, classically, a hydrogen, or any other atom, could not be stable, as the electrons that keep orbiting the nucleus would radiate away their energy until they collapse into the nucleus. This inconsistency (with the observable world that forces us to the conclusion that matter is stable) was called the "ultraviolet catastrophe."

Another key concept of quantum mechanics was introduced in 1923–1924, by Louis de Broglie, who postulated that not only can radiation exhibit particle-like behavior (i.e., the exchange of discrete amounts of energy), but the opposite is also true—material particles can display wave-like behavior.[16] This concept was confirmed experimentally in 1927. In that same year, the German physicist Werner Heisenberg, one of the founding fathers of quantum mechanics,[6] published the uncertainty principle,[17] one of the field's key concepts. According to the uncertainty principle, one cannot simultaneously measure with equal precision both the momentum and position of a particle. The more precise the measurement of one value, the more flawed the measurement of the other. The uncertainty principle holds valid in all circumstance, but it is perceptible only for measurements of microscopic objects,[7] while measurements of macroscopic objects yield the results one would expect from classical physics.

This principle has had a profound impact on how we grasp matter, since the position of a particle is never accurately known. Particles in quantum mechanics are described by "wave functions," which can be used to calculate the probability of finding the particle at some little portion of space but can never yield the particle's exact position. This is what physicists mean when they say that our world is probabilistic rather than deterministic. Several approaches, one very different from the next, have been suggested to explain the probabilistic nature of quantum mechanics or, as it is euphemistically called, its counter-intuitiveness to our everyday experience.

Physicists are both perplexed and divided by this. For example, according to the Copenhagen interpretation (which is perhaps the most popular), originally formulated and advocated by Bohr and Heisenberg, at the moment of the measurement, the wave function described above collapses, and a single permissible quantum state is chosen. According to this interpretation, questions regarding the position, for example, of a particle prior to the measurement are meaningless. In contrast,

---

[6] Werner Heisenberg was awarded the Nobel Prize in Physics in 1932 "for the creation of quantum mechanics, the application of which has, inter alia, led to the discovery of the allotropic forms of hydrogen."

[7] Only for microscopic particles is the uncertainty in the position, for example, comparable to the de Broglie wavelength of the particles.

the many-worlds approach takes an entirely different point of view. According to this approach, the quantum wave function has an objective, deterministic reality, and upon making a measurement the universe splits into distinct universes within a single multiverse. Thus, despite its contribution to our understanding of nature, quantum mechanics has also added to the mystery our universe.

String Theory

The beginning of the twentieth century was an exciting time for physics, having given birth to the separate development of both quantum mechanics and the theory of relativity (special and general). Where quantum mechanics completely changed the way we think about matter,[18] Einstein's theory of relativity revolutionized our conceptions of space, time, and gravity.[19] Motivated by a long-standing question about the seemingly constant speed of light without regard to one's motion with respect to the beam of light, Albert Einstein formulated the special theory of relativity in 1905. In two papers,[20] Einstein investigated the dynamical and electromagnetic effects of the relative motion of matter in a "sterile" environment free of gravitational forces. On the basis of a couple of seemingly harmless assumptions,[8] Einstein had proven some very surprising truths of nature,[9] such as that the simultaneity of two events is in the eye of the beholder, and that matter and energy are interchangeable, as implied by probably the most famous equation in history: $E = mc^2$.

Despite this equation's success in solving important problems in physics, Einstein was not satisfied and immediately sought a generalization to his special theory of relativity, one that would incorporate the gravitational field. In 1915, he completed his general theory of relativity, which revised our understanding of gravity as a "geometric effect" of the distorting of space and time due to mass and energy rather than as a force.[10] Since the differences between the predictions of Newtonian

---

[8] The first assumption is that the laws of physics are identical in all inertial frames, and the second is that there always exists an inertial frame in which light propagates at constant speed.

[9] See for example Feynman, Leighton, and Sands, *The Feynman Lectures on Physics, Vol. 3: Quantum Mechanics*, or any book on special relativity.

[10] See Feynman, Leighton, and Sands, *The Feynman Lectures on Physics, Vol. 3: Quantum Mechanics*, for a simple description; or Rindler, *Relativity: Special, General, and Cosmological* for a more detailed description.

physics and Einstein's relativistic physics are minute with respect to our everyday experiences, it took some time for technology to catch up and confirm the general theory of relativity via experiments and observations.[21]

As scientists worked on quantum theory, they began to test its compatibility with other experimentally verified theories. They found that quantum theory appeared inconsistent with Einstein's theory of gravity—which could not be "quantized."[22] Even though attempts at the formulation of a standalone quantum gravity theory have been made, they have not been successful. One possible promising solution to these inconsistencies is String Theory. Many physicists believe this theory to be the missing piece in our description of the universe, our understanding of the standard model, and its connection to gravity.[23] This is due to the fact that string theory contains both standard model particles (which can be described as different excitations of a quantum string) and quantum gravity.

The most appealing property of string theory is that it reduces the constraints within the theory, such as the number of dimensions, while it also increases the parameters that emerge from string theory equations.[24] According to string theory, our universe has one temporal dimension, time, and six spatial dimensions, six of which are said to be "compactified" and are thus inaccessible to us.[25] In addition, there is more than just one version of string theory that may be valid, and several different versions have been proffered. All these different theories, however, can be considered part of an overarching "mother theory," dubbed M-theory.[11]

Despite the fascinating mathematics, string theory is not yet—and may not ever be—physically provable. While its critics say that it has no predictive power,[12] others argue that this is the first quantum theory to have predicted gravity and hope that string theory (or M-Theory) will

---

[11] M-Theory has ten spatial dimensions and one temporal dimension, unlike the five versions of string theory that have been mentioned that have 9+1. Zwiebach, *A First Course in String Theory*.

[12] In order for string theory to describe our universe, the laws of physics must have been obeyed in its early phases—when the universe was very hot and energetic—in a special symmetry, called supersymmetry, or SUSY for short. The fact that SUSY is not observed in physics today does not necessarily mean that it had never existed. In fact, physicists believe that SUSY had indeed been obeyed, but as the universe expanded, and therefore cooled down, this symmetry was broken, which is why we do not observe it today. Many physicists hope and believe that experiments at the Large Hadron Collider at Geneva will be able to reproduce the conditions to restore SUSY. Even though SUSY may exist independently of string theory, string theory cannot be valid without SUSY. Hence many consider this as our best shot at getting closer to proving string theory.

constitute the "Theory of Everything," a unified description of all forces and particles in the universe that will one day resolve the puzzle of how our universe came into being and why it looks the way it does.

Our Universe of Math

Though physics has the reputation of being a very complicated science (and not undeservedly), physicists have always favored "simple" theories over complicated ones. Simplicity is also considered a necessary condition for a theory to be considered "pretty."[26] A theory's simplicity cannot be tested, however, by means of the simplicity of its equations or the elegance of their solutions.[13] It should manifest itself in the principles, axioms, and assumptions that underpin its model. The general theory of relativity is an example of such a simple theory. Even though its equations are complicated to solve, requiring knowledge of very specific cases, and despite its far-reaching consequences, it stems, almost entirely, from the equivalence of gravity and inertia, known as the equivalence principle.

Another criterion for determining the prettiness of a physical theory is its naturalness and its inevitable conclusions, with few to no arbitrary inputs, initial conditions, or God-given numbers. Using general relativity as an example, granting the equivalence principle and Einstein's physical principles, general relativity naturally emerges. Other theories similarly strive to be natural. The inflationary paradigm strengthens the standard cosmological model, for without it, we would require a precise understanding of the initial conditions of the universe. String theory, as discussed above, also reduces the number of free parameters "of the universe." The dimensionality of space-time is emergent from the equations, as are the number of "elementary" particles, their masses, and their spins.

Nevertheless, some background numbers are still arbitrary, even from string theory's or cosmology's point of view.[14] These numbers may be crucial, and even if only one of them had a slightly different value, our

---

[13] As the German physicist Ludwig Boltzmann said, "If you are out to describe the truth, leave elegance to the tailor." This sentence is commonly misattributed to Einstein.

[14] See for example Martin J. Rees, *Just Six Numbers: The Deep Forces that Shape the Universe* (New York: Basic Books, 2000), which describes six dimensionless constants of particular values that are vital for our universe to consist of stars and planets as we know them. While some of them are accounted for by string theory, or Big Bang cosmology, some of them are not, at least not in string theory's current state of affairs.

universe would have been very different than it actually is and might not have been able to sustain life of any form.

One or Many Universes?

As if our universe was not complicated enough, some physicists hypothesize that ours is just one of many—perhaps infinitely many—universes. Although this hypothesis represents less than a consensus and is dismissed outright by some leading, highly distinguished physicists,[27] it also has its advocates in other leading physicists of the same caliber.[28] There are several many-universes hypotheses, which differ in the nature of the mechanisms that produce them. For example,[29] an infinite universe (and therefore an infinite space-time) gives rise to a quilted multiverse: due to the finiteness of the speed of light, we are able to observe only a small portion of this infinite universe. Since space is infinite, the quilted multiverse is composed of infinitely many "observable universes" that take on any possible configuration, and in which, any possible event occurs.[15]

A slightly different hypothesis leads to a very different multiverse, the inflationary multiverse. Imagine that, at every single moment, some portion of the vast universe may be going through a phase of inflation. Once inflation ends in that portion of space, the ending will give rise to a new "bubble" that may be similar to our own observable universe, but can also be substantially different. Another type of a multiverse is due to the many-worlds interpretation of quantum mechanics, as mentioned earlier. According to this theory, quantum wave function has an objective reality, and at every single "quantum junction" the universe splits into several universes, one for each junction arm. These "new universes" all share the same history, without having to go through it again, so that everything that could have happened in the past has taken place in at least one universe. For a more advantageous view of the multiverse, it

---

[15] Suppose one ape is given a keyboard and is allowed to hit it, one key at a time, for a very long time. This experiment will most likely result in a gibberish text. However, had there been infinitely many apes, doing just the same, all assumed to hit the keyboard randomly, then one of them would have eventually typed Tolstoy's *War and Peace* cover to cover. The same argument goes for universes: if there are infinitely many observable universes, any single configuration or event will take place somewhere across this multiverse.

would be nice if all the answers in a history multiple-choice exam were right somewhere at some time.

The striking commonality between all of these examples (and, in fact, all other many-universes types), which are otherwise very different from each other, is that somewhere in *our* universe the Milky Way, the solar system, the sun, and the Earth were formed and sustain life. While one approach to this commonality is that we are lucky to live in the universe that has produced us, the other approach is that if we had not been in this universe, we would not have been able to make this distinction or ponder about anything.

Echoes in the Big Bang

Even though the standard cosmological model explains quite rigorously many cosmological observations, some fundamental puzzles regarding our universe's content and history persist. One puzzle that has been around since the 1930s,[16] for example, is that observations indicate unequivocally[17] that the bulk of the matter in our universe, about 85 percent of it, in fact, is unfamiliar to us—meaning, it cannot be observed directly and does not participate in any "luminous interactions" that emit photons. This is the reason why physicists call it dark matter. Dark matter, however, is not the only "dark" component of our universe. A look at the universe's energy accounts reveals that while matter (luminous and dark) comprises roughly 30 percent of the energy in our universe,[18] the remaining share of the universe's energy is in "dark energy."[30][31] We still do not know what this dark energy is, but we can observe its effects. Our universe's expansion has been dominated by it for the last 3.5 billion years or so. Altogether, while the matter and radiation *we know* account only for 4 percent of the universe's energy budget, the remaining 96 percent

---

[16] The first suggestion that a significant fraction of matter is nonluminous was made by the Swiss astronomer Fritz Zwicky in 1933, due to observations of rotation velocities of galaxies within the Coma Cluster. See for example Fritz Zwicky, "On the Masses of Nebulae and of Clusters of Nebulae," *Astrophysical Journal* 86 (1937).

[17] Since 1933, many other instances of observational evidence have corroborated the existence of dark matter. See for example Mario Livio ed., *The Dark Universe: Matter, Energy, and Gravity* (Cambridge: Cambridge University Press, 2004).

[18] According to Einstein's Theory of Relativity, mass and energy are interchangeable. Therefore, when one considers the energy-budget of the universe, matter radiation and Dark Energy are considered on the same footing.

are in dark matter and dark energy, which are crucial to the standard cosmological model. They are necessary ingredients for the universe to have formed galaxies, stars, and planets, and to undergo accelerated expansion[19] in accordance to observations.

Other mysteries abound in the standard cosmological model, or the big bang cosmology. One of them lies at its very root—the big bang itself. Assuming that the general theory of relativity is the correct framework to describe the cosmological evolution of the universe, the conclusion is inevitable that our observable universe began from an infinitely dense and hot state, in a big bang event. Physicists also believe, however, that in some extreme conditions,[20] general relativity is no longer valid and serves inadequately to describe the big bang itself. Ironically, the big bang event and the radical question of what came before are beyond the scope of big bang cosmology.[32] A number of theories do address this topic,[33] but as of yet, they are speculative and offer no realistically testable predictions.

Questions about Quantum and String Theory

Although quantum mechanics has been confirmed experimentally,[21] a number of questions remain unanswered. These include the interpretation of quantum mechanics or, in particular, of the wave function. Different interpretations imply different views of nature. As mentioned above, within the framework of the Copenhagen interpretation, the wave

---

[19] In his original formulation of the general theory of relativity, Einstein had included a term, called the "cosmological constant," so that his equations would be consistent with a steady-state universe, which was favored at that time. After Edwin Hubble's detection of the expansion of the universe, Einstein discarded this term and according to some sources referred to it as "the greatest blunder of my life" (though other sources claim that he had never said that). Since the detection of the accelerated expansion of the universe, Einstein's cosmological constant had been reintroduced to the general relativity equations, as it accounts for the accelerated expansion, and many favor it as the right interpretation of dark energy.

[20] If we could play cosmic time backwards, then we would find that our universe contracts, its temperature and matter density increase, and except for the last 3.5 billion years (in which its energy is dominated by a cosmological constant or dark energy), so does its energy density. Had we been able to continue playing it backwards all the way until the Big Bang (infinite energy density), we would have necessarily gone through a period in which the energy density was extreme, so that general relativity would not be valid, yet finite.

[21] For example, by fluorescence of molecules, the Aharonov-Bohm effect, the photoelectric effect.

function that describes the quantum state of each particle in the universe collapses *only* upon measurement.

Many readers are aware of the illustrative story of Schrödinger's cat. In this story, a cat is in an apparatus, but it is unknown if the cat inside is dead or alive. According to the Copenhagen interpretation of quantum mechanics, the cat is both alive *and* dead prior to any individual checking. At the point of checking, the cat's universe collapses, resulting in the cat being either dead or alive. In this analogy, our universe may be seen as probabilistic. However, when the many-worlds interpretation is considered, in which a universal wave function exists, then all the outcomes happen somewhere. Therefore, it would be fair to say that not only do we know very little about the lion's share of the energy in the universe (the dark energy component that comprises approximately 70 percent of the universe), but furthermore, 85 percent of the rest of the stuff in the universe also somehow eludes direct measurement. In fact, there is no consensus on how to quantum-mechanically describe the 4 percent of the universe's matter that we *are* able to identify. Even if this were not the case and all physicists agreed on a single quantum mechanics interpretation, there would still be many other unsolved questions. Why is gravity so much weaker than the other forces? Why is the cosmological constant (or vacuum energy) so weak? What are the actual processes that broke the symmetry between matter and antimatter? New theories—such as cosmic inflation and string theory—potentially answer some questions, but they also raise new questions of their own. What, for example, are the actual equations that govern the string's behavior? What is the size of the extra-dimensions? Which field (or fields) drove inflation and at what energy?

The Mythical Multiverse

The various theories of the multiverse are exhilarating, but far from provable.

In fact, these so-called theories of the multiverse are not really in the category of theory, because in science the term "theory" denotes a system of ideas that explains some type of phenomena *based on evidence from observations*.[34] Calling these theories hypotheses is also being charitable, as a scientific hypothesis is a system of ideas that *can* be subjected to observation to gain evidence with which to evaluate the plausibility of the hypothesis.

The theory of the multiverse can be better classified as a logical conjecture based on physical and mathematical reasoning. There is nothing wrong with starting a scientific investigation with a conjecture, especially one based on logical possibilities. But one has to be modest in making bold statements about the implications of a certain guess until there is physical evidence, even if such guesses can one day be proven. However, we are a long way from such proof with regard to the multiverse and, in fact, we may never be able to get there. Indeed, some scientists who claim that it is impossible to prove the multiverse exclude these conjectures from legitimate scientific inquiry, placing them in the realm of philosophy.

For example, the prominent British physicist Paul Davies doubts the *scientific* value of the multiverse conjecture precisely because he does not think it can be tested.[35] Princeton cosmologist Paul Steinhardt also rejects the notion of the multiverse for being fatally flawed since it is untestable, unnatural, and assumes away key problems seeking a solution.[36] Even proponents who believe the multiverse can be proven acknowledge that we may be light years away, so to speak, from being able to prove or disprove it. Despite this lack of proof, some physicists have nonetheless referred to the multiverse theory to account for the origins of life based on probabilities, rather than on a conscious act of creation. It is on this slender reed of conjecture that many atheists base and close their case against a God of creation.

ENDNOTES

INTRODUCTION

1   A number deal with the atheists' scientific criticism of a creator God. See: Alvin
    Plantinga, *Where the Conflict Really Lies: Science, Religion, and Naturalism* (New
    York: Oxford University Press, 2011); Richard Grigg, *Beyond the God Delusion: How
    Radical Theology Harmonizes Science and Religion* (Minneapolis: Fortress Press,
    2008); Alister E. McGrath and Joanna Collicutt McGrath, *The Dawkins Delusion:
    Atheist Fundamentalism* (Downers Grove: InterVarsity Press, 2007); Antony Flew
    and Roy Abraham Varghese, *There Is a God: How the World's Most Notorious Athe-
    ist Changed His Mind* (New York: HarperOne, 2007); and Phillip E. Johnson and
    John Mark Reynolds, *Against All Gods: What's Right and Wrong About the New
    Atheism* (Downers Grove: IVP Books, 2010). Others deal with the atheists' views on
    the Bible. See: Paul Copan, *Is God a Moral Monster? Making Sense of the Old Testa-
    ment God* (Grand Rapids: Baker Books, 2011). Copan's perspective is also primarily
    Christian. Many are written from a uniquely Christian perspective. See David Bent-
    ley Hart, *Atheist Delusions: The Christian Revolution and Its Fashionable Enemies*
    (New Haven: Yale University Press, 2009); Mike King, *The God Delusion Revisited*
    (Eastbourne: Gardners Books, 2007); William Lane Craig and Chad V. Meister
    eds., *God Is Great, God Is Good: Why Believing in God Is Reasonable and Respon-
    sible* (Downers Grove: IVP Books, 2009); Rob Slane, *The God Reality: A Critique
    of Richard Dawkins' The God Delusion* (Leominster: Day One, 2008); and Andrew
    J. Wilson, *Deluded by Dawkins? A Christian Response to The God Delusion* (East-
    bourne: Kingsway Communications, 2007). Some responses are written in specific
    styles. For a philosophical exploration see Eric Reitan, *Is God a Delusion? A Reply to
    Religion* (Malden: Wiley-Blackwell, 2009). For a theological approach see James A.
    Beverley, *The God Solution: A Reply to the God Delusion* (Nashville: Thomas Nelson,
    2008) and Andrew David, Christopher J. Keller, and Jon Stanley eds., *"God Is Dead"
    and I Don't Feel So Good Myself: Theological Engagements with the New Atheism*
    (Eugene: Cascade Books, 2010). For a polemical approach see: David Aikman, *The
    Delusion of Disbelief: Why the New Atheism Is a Threat to Your Life, Liberty, and
    Pursuit of Happiness* (Carol Stream: Tyndale House Publishers, 2008); and John
    F. Haught, *God and the New Atheism: A Critical Response to Dawkins, Harris, and
    Hitchens* (Louisville: Westminster John Knox Press, 2008). For a liberal approach
    see Tina Beattie, *The New Atheists: The Twilight of Reason and the War on Religion*
    (Luton: Andrews UK Ltd., 2010). Finally, for books that seek to prove the existence

of God, see Keith Ward, *Why There Almost Certainly Is a God: Doubting Dawkins* (Oxford: Lion Hudson, 2008); Robert J. Spitzer, *New Proofs for the Existence of God: Contributions of Contemporary Physics and Philosophy* (Grand Rapids: William B. Eerdmans Pub., 2010); and Klaus Nürnberger, *Richard Dawkins' God Delusion: A Repentant Refutation* (Bloomington: Xlibris Corporation, 2010). This list is by no means exhaustive; however, it covers the main style of response to the atheists.

PART ONE INTRODUCTION

1 Richard Dawkins, *The God Delusion* (Boston: Mariner, 2008), 245.
2 Michel Onfray, *Atheist Manifesto: The Case Again Christianity, Judaism, and Islam*, trans. Jeremy Leggatt (New York: Arcade Publishing), 19–20.
3 Christopher Hitchens, *God Is Not Great: How Religion Poisons Everything* (New York: Twelve, 2007), 231.
4 Onfray, *Atheist Manifesto*, 150–151.
5 Dawkins, *The God Delusion*, 249–250.

CHAPTER 1

1 In Sumeria, the first ancient Near Eastern civilization, the first gods were likely deifications of elements in the physical universe, and then became deities of activities such as farming and metalworking. Graham Cunningham, "Sumerian Religion," in Salzman, *The Cambridge History of Religions in the Ancient World*, 31. In the ancient Near East, our written and archaeological sources for most of the gods of place already describe them in human form. The political instrumentalization of the gods in the ancient Near East is clear from the shifting importance of various gods depending on the changing political situation. Tammi J. Schneider, "Assyrian and Babylonian Religion," in Salzman, *The Cambridge History of Religions in the Ancient World*, 54. The earliest gods in Europe were not yet conceived of in human form, but were nature spirits, then as war became more important in Celtic society, war gods depicted with human characteristics emerged along with fertility and healing gods, though nature spirits remained. Dorothy Watts, "Celtic Religion in Western and Central Europe," in Salzman, *The Cambridge History of Religions in the Ancient World*, 366.
2 Tammi J. Schneider, "Assyrian and Babylonian Religion," in Salzman, *The Cambridge History of Religions in the Ancient World*, 54–55; and Joshua Berman, *Created Equal: How the Bible Broke with Ancient Political Thought* (Oxford: Oxford University Press, 2008), 21.
3 Glenn Stanfield Holland, *Gods in the Desert: Religions of the Ancient Near East* (Lanham: Rowman & Littlefield Publishers, 2009), 113; and Berman, *Created Equal*, 18.
4 Holland, *Gods in the Desert*, 112.
5 Gary Beckman, "Hittite Religion," in Salzman, *The Cambridge History of Religions in the Ancient World*, 91.
6 David P. Wright, "Syro-Canaanite Religions," in Salzman, *The Cambridge History of Religions in the Ancient World*, 136; and Cyrus Herzl Gordon and Gary Rendsburg, *The Bible and the Ancient Near East* (New York: W. W. Norton, 1997), 159.
7 Jennifer R. March, *The Penguin Book of Classical Myths* (London: Penguin, 2009), 50.

Endnotes

8   Prudence Jones and Nigel Pennick, *A History of Pagan Europe* (London: Routledge, 1995), 86.

9   Jones and Pennick, *A History of Pagan Europe*, 142.

10 Jones and Pennick, *A History of Pagan Europe*, 143.

11 Schneider, "Assyrian and Babylonian Religion," in Salzman, *The Cambridge History of Religions in the Ancient World*, 54–55; and Berman, *Created Equal*, 21.

12 Schneider, "Assyrian and Babylonian Religion," in Salzman, *The Cambridge History of Religions in the Ancient World*, 64.

13 Holland, *Gods in the Desert*, 168.

14 Homer, *The Iliad*, trans. M. S. Silk (Cambridge: Cambridge University Press, 2004), (Book XIV, Section I)

15 Holland, *Gods in the Desert*, 133.

16 Plato, *The Republic*, trans. Reginald E. Allen (New Haven: Yale University Press, 2006), (Book III, Section III)

17 Mitchel P. Roth, *An Eye for an Eye: A Global History of Crime and Punishment* (London: Reaktion Books, 2014), introduction and chapter 1.

18 Berman, *Created Equal*, 97.

19 Berman, *Created Equal*, 96.

20 Berman, *Created Equal*, 69.

21 Robert G. Hoyland, *Arabia and the Arabs: From the Bronze Age to the Coming of Islam* (London: Routledge, 2001), 121–123.

22 Roth, *An Eye for an Eye*.

23 Larry S. Milner, *Hardness of Heart/Hardness of Life: The Stain of Human Infanticide* (Lanham: University Press of America, 2000), 28.

24 Schneider, "Assyrian and Babylonian Religion," in Salzman, *The Cambridge History of Religions in the Ancient World*, 75.

25 Holland, *Gods of the Desert*, 172.

26 This is a list of sacrifices from the Sumerian city of Uruk: Google Sites, The Ancient Mesopotamia Project, sites.google.com/site/theancientmesopotamiaproject/religion. See also: Mario Liverani, *Uruk: The First City*, trans. Zainab Bahrani and Marc Van De Mieroop (London: Equinox, 2006).

27 Nigel Davies, *Human Sacrifice—In History and Today* (New York: Morrow, 1981), 36–37.

28 John Noble Wilford, "At Ur, Ritual Deaths That Were Anything but Serene," *New York Times*, October 26, 2009, www.nytimes.com/2009/10/27/science/27ur.html.

29 Miranda J. Aldhouse-Green, *Dying for the Gods: Human Sacrifice in Iron Age and Roman Europe* (Stroud: Tempus, 2001). On Celtic sacrifice see also: H. D. Rankin, *Celts and the Classical World* (London: Routledge, 1996).

30 Jones and Pennick, *A History of Pagan Europe*, 118.

31 Jones and Pennick, *A History of Pagan Europe*, 138.

32 A. Rosalie David, *The Ancient Egyptians: Beliefs and Practices*, rev. and expanded ed. (Brighton: Sussex Academic Press, 1998), 24.

33 Siegfried Morenz and Ann E. Keep, *Egyptian Religion* (London: Methuen, 1973).

34 Pyramid Texts 273–4, Old Kingdom translated by Jacob Rabinowitz.

35 Roger Tomlin and Barry Cunliffe, *Roman Inscribed Tablets of Tin and Lead from the Sacred Spring at Bath* (Oxford: Oxford University Committee for Archaeology,

1988) and John G. Gager, *Curse Tablets and Binding Spells from the Ancient World* (New York: Oxford University Press, 1992).

36 Jones and Pennick, *A History of Pagan Europe*, 151.

37 Jones and Pennick, *A History of Pagan Europe*, 151.

38 Jones and Pennick, *A History of Pagan Europe*, 152.

39 See: Denise M. Doxey, "Egyptian Religion," in Salzman, *The Cambridge History of Religions in the Ancient World*; and A. Rosalie David, *Religion and Magic in Ancient Egypt* (London: Penguin Books, 2002).

40 Ulla Jeyes, "Divination as a Science in Ancient Mesopotamia," *Jaarbericht "Ex Oriente Lux,"* 32 (1991–92): 23–41.

41 Schneider, "Assyrian and Babylonian Religions," in Salzman, *The Cambridge History of Religions in the Ancient World*, 76.

42 See: Jörg Rüpke, "Roman Religion Through the Early Republic," in Salzman, *The Cambridge History of Religions in the Ancient World*; and Robin Lorsch Wildfang and Jacob Isager, *Divination and Portents in the Roman World* (Odense: Odense University Press, 2000).

43 Marcus Tullius Cicero, *On the Republic and On the Laws*, trans. David Fott (Ithaca: Cornell University Press, 2014), (Book II, 31).

44 Hoyland, *Arabia and the Arabs*, 154.

45 Jones and Pennick, *A History of Pagan Europe*, 149.

46 Jones and Pennick, *A History of Pagan Europe*, 149.

47 Jones and Pennick, *A History of Pagan Europe*, 150.

48 For an exploration of how powerful elites and states emerged in the ancient Near East see: Diane Bolger and Louise C. Maguire, *The Development of Pre-State Communities in the Ancient Near East: Studies in Honour of Edgar Peltenburg* (Oxford: Oxbow Books, 2010) and Liverani, *Uruk: The First City*.

49 Berman, *Created Equal*, 78.

50 Berman, *Created Equal*, 27.

51 Berman, *Created Equal*, 90.

52 Thomas R. Martin, *Ancient Greece: From Prehistoric to Hellenistic Times* (New Haven: Yale University Press, 2013), chapter 5.

53 Martin, *Ancient Greece*, chapter 5.

54 Martin, *Ancient Greece*, chapter 5.

55 Martin, *Ancient Greece*, chapter 5.

56 Martin, *Ancient Greece*, chapter 7.

57 Martin, *Ancient Greece*, chapter 9; and Richard Stoneman, *Alexander the Great* (London: Routledge, 1997).

58 Jones and Pennick, *A History of Pagan Europe*, 130.

59 Jones and Pennick, *A History of Pagan Europe*, 128.

60 Nancy T. de Grummond, "Etruscan Religion," in Salzman, *The Cambridge History of Religions in the Ancient World. vol. 1*; and Holland, *Gods in the Desert*.

61 Jones and Pennick, *A History of Pagan Europe*, 29.

62 Rebecca Langlands, *Sexual Morality in Ancient Rome* (Cambridge: Cambridge University Press, 2006).

63 See: Eric H. Cline and Mark W. Graham, *Ancient Empires: From Mesopotamia to the Rise of Islam* (Cambridge: Cambridge University Press, 2011).

64 Albert Kirk Grayson, *Assyrian and Babylonian Chronicles* (Locust Valley: J. J. Augustin; 1975, [1970]).

65 Adam Jones, *Genocide: A Comprehensive Introduction*, 2nd ed. (London: Routledge, 2011), chapter 1; and Cline and Graham, *Ancient Empires*.

66 Holland, *Gods of the Desert*; and Cline and Graham, *Ancient Empires*.

67 Malcolm Moore, "Hittites Used Germ Warfare 3,500 Years Ago," *The Telegraph*, December 8, 2007, www.telegraph.co.uk/news/worldnews/1571927/Hittites-used-germ-warfare-3500-years-ago.html.

68 Jones and Pennick, *A History of Pagan Europe*, 42.

69 Jones and Pennick, *A History of Pagan Europe*, 81.

70 Cline and Graham, *Ancient Empires*; and Paul Veyne, *The Roman Empire* (Cambridge: Belknap Press of Harvard University Press, 1997).

71 Ira M. Lapidus, *A History of Islamic Societies* (Cambridge: Cambridge University Press 1988), chapter 1.

72 Roy W. Perrett, *An Introduction to Indian Philosophy* (Cambridge: Cambridge University Press, 2016).

73 Andrew Gregory, *The Presocratics and the Supernatural: Magic, Philosophy, and Science in Early Greece* (New York: Bloomsbury, 2013), 14.

74 Aristophanes, *Clouds; Wasps; Peace*, ed. and trans. Jeffrey Henderson (Cambridge: Harvard University Press, 2014).

75 Gregory, *The Presocratics*, 107.

76 For a summary of Plato and Aristotle's ideas as they relate to monotheism see: Adam Drozdek, *Greek Philosophers as Theologians: The Divine Arche* (Aldershot: Ashgate, 2007).

77 Ryan K. Balot, *Greek Political Thought* (Malden: Blackwell Publishing, 2006).

78 Balot, *Greek Political Thought*, chapter 6.

79 Balot, *Greek Political Thought*, chapter 7.

80 James Thrower, *Western Atheism: A Short History* (Amherst: Prometheus Books, 2000).

81 Plato, *The Republic*, eds. and trans. C. J. Emlyn-Jones and William Preddy (Cambridge: Harvard University Press, 2014), (Book III, 24b).

82 Balot, *Greek Political Thought*, 189.

83 For a discussion of God and ethics in Hinduism, see Kim Knott, *Hinduism: A Very Short Introduction* (Oxford: Oxford University Press, 2016).

84 For a discussion of ethics in Buddhism, see Damien Keown, *Buddhism: A Very Short Introduction* (Oxford: Oxford University Press, 2000).

85 Richard Heywood Daly and Richard B. Lee, eds., *The Cambridge Encyclopedia of Hunters and Gatherers* (Cambridge: Cambridge University Press, 1999).

86 Steven Pinker, *The Better Angels of Our Nature: Why Violence Has Declined* (New York: Viking, 2011), 44, 55, and 57.

87 Jones and Pennick, *A History of Pagan Europe*, 37.

88 Jones and Pennick, *A History of Pagan Europe*, 92.

89 Hoyland, *Arabia and the Arabs*, 137.

CHAPTER 2

1 Berman, *Created Equal*, 47.
2 Berman, *Created Equal*, 22.
3 Berman, *Created Equal*, 22.
4 Berman, *Created Equal*, 47.
5 Berman, *Created Equal*, 54.
6 Berman, *Created Equal*, 70–71.
7 Berman, *Created Equal*, 70.
8 Berman, *Created Equal*, 69.
9 Berman, *Created Equal*, 68.
10 Berman, *Created Equal*, 68–70.
11 Berman, *Created Equal*, 55–56.
12 Berman, *Created Equal*, 82.
13 Berman, *Created Equal*, 90.
14 Berman, *Created Equal*, 91.
15 Berman, *Created Equal*, 95.
16 Berman, *Created Equal*, 93.
17 Berman, *Created Equal*, 97.
18 Berman, *Created Equal*, 99.
19 Berman, *Created Equal*, 102.
20 Berman, *Created Equal*, 80.
21 Berman, *Created Equal*, 51.
22 Berman, *Created Equal*, 84.
23 This was not the case elsewhere in the ancient world. See Roth, *An Eye for An Eye*.
24 Menachem Elon, *Jewish Law: History, Sources, Principles* (Philadelphia: Jewish Publication Society, 1994).
25 Berman, *Created Equal*, 114.
26 Berman, *Created Equal*, 117.
27 Berman, *Created Equal*, 115.
28 Berman, *Created Equal*, 124.

CHAPTER 3

1 B.S.J. Isserlin, *The Israelites* (London: Thames and Hudson, 1998), 84.
2 Rainer Kessler, *The Social History of Ancient Israel: An Introduction*, trans. Linda M. Maloney (Minneapolis: Fortress Press, 2008), 109.
3 Seth Schwartz, *The Ancient Jews from Alexander to Muhammad* (Cambridge: Cambridge University Press, 2014), 24.
4 Schwartz, *The Ancient Jews*, 31.
5 Schwartz, *The Ancient Jews*, 40.
6 Schwartz, *The Ancient Jews*, 42.
7 Schwartz, *The Ancient Jews*, 46.
8 Schwartz, *The Ancient Jews*, 47.
9 Schwartz, *The Ancient Jews*, 52.
10 Schwartz, *The Ancient Jews*, 66.
11 Schwartz, *The Ancient Jews*, 79.

Endnotes

12 Louis H. Feldman, *Jew and Gentile in the Ancient World: Attitudes and Interactions from Alexander to Justinian* (Princeton: Princeton University Press, 1993), 312.

13 Feldman, *Jew and Gentile*, 206.

14 Feldman, *Jew and Gentile*, 226

15 Feldman, *Jew and Gentile*, 226.

16 Feldman, *Jew and Gentile*, 203.

17 Feldman, *Jew and Gentile*, 235.

18 Feldman, *Jew and Gentile*, 151.

19 Feldman, *Jew and Gentile*, 128.

20 Feldman, *Jew and Gentile*, 133.

21 Feldman, *Jew and Gentile*, chapter 10.

22 Feldman, *Jew and Gentile*, 441.

23 Feldman, *Jew and Gentile*, 336.

24 Veyne, *The Roman Empire*.

25 Averil Cameron, *The Later Roman Empire, AD 284–430* (Cambridge: Harvard University Press, 1993), 43–44.

26 F. E. Peters, *The Monotheists: Jews, Christians, and Muslims in Conflict and Competition*, vols. 1 and 2 (Princeton: Princeton University Press, 2003).

27 Jacob Lassner and Michael David Bonner, *Islam in the Middle Ages: The Origins and Shaping of Classical Islamic Civilization* (Santa Barbara: Praeger, 2010), 4–6.

28 Christopher Bryan, *Render to Caesar: Jesus, the Early Church, and the Roman Superpower* (Oxford: Oxford University Press, 2005), 78–82.

29 Cameron, *The Later Roman Empire*, 127.

30 Carolyn Osiek and Kevin Madigan, *Ordained Women in the Early Church: A Documentary History* (Baltimore: Johns Hopkins University Press, 2005).

31 Cameron, *The Later Roman Empire*, 124.

32 Cameron, *The Later Roman Empire*, 129.

33 Larry Steven Milner, *Hardness of Heart/Hardness of Life: The Stain of Human Infanticide* (Lanham: University Press of America, 2000), 33.

34 Cameron, *The Later Roman Empire*, 130.

35 Cameron, *The Later Roman Empire*, 129.

36 Lapidus, *Islamic Societies*, 29–30. See also Surah 4:3.

37 Lapidus, *Islamic Societies*, 29–30. See also Surahs 81: 8–9 in the Qur'an.

38 Judith Reesa Baskin, *Midrashic Women: Formations of the Feminine in Rabbinic Literature* (Hannover: University Press of New England, 2002).

39 Schwartz, *The Ancient Jews*.

40 Freeman, *A New History of Early Christianity*, 294.

41 Freeman, *A New History of Early Christianity*, chapters 22 and 24.

42 Freeman, *A New History of Early Christianity*, chapter 26.

43 Cameron, *The Later Roman Empire*, 77–78.

44 Lassner and Bonner, *Islam in the Middle Ages*, 85. See also: Lapidus, *Islamic Societies*, chapter 1.

45 Lassner and Bonner, *Islam in the Middle Ages*.

46 Lapidus, *Islamic Societies*, chapter 1.

47 Lapidus, *Islamic Societies*, chapters 1–22.

48 Peters, *The Monotheists*, 135–137 and 268–272.

49 Peter Brown, *The Rise of Western Christendom: Triumph and Diversity, AD 200–1000* (Malden: Blackwell, 1997).

50 Lapidus, *Islamic Societies*, chapter 3 and 4. See also Hoyland, *Arabia and the Arabs*.

51 Peters, *The Monotheists*, vol. 1, 92 and 132.

52 Alan Brill, *Judaism and Other Religions: Models of Understanding* (New York: Palgrave Macmillan, 2010).

53 Barbara H. Rosenwein, *A Short History of the Middle Ages*, 4th ed. (Toronto: University of Toronto Press, 2014), 121–149; and Nora Berend, ed., *Christianization and the Rise of Christian Monarchy Scandinavia, Central Europe, and Rus', c. 900–1200* (Cambridge: Cambridge University Press, 2007).

54 Berend, *Christianization and the Rise of Christian Monarchy*.

55 Rosenwein, *A Short History*, 133, 203–204, and 208.

56 Jonathan Elukin, *Living Together, Living Apart: Rethinking Jewish-Christian Relations in the Middle Ages* (Princeton: Princeton University Press, 2007).

57 Berend, *Christianization and the Rise of Christian Monarchy*.

58 Rosenwein, *A Short History*, chapter 4 and 5.

59 Lapidus, *Islamic Societies*, see chapters 3, 4, and 8.

60 Rosenwein, *A Short History*, 132.

61 Rosenwein, *A Short History*; and Kevin Madigan, *Medieval Christianity: A New History* (New Haven: Yale University Press, 2015).

62 Rosenwein, *A Short History;* and Jonathan Simon Christopher Riley-Smith, *The Oxford History of the Crusades* (Oxford: Oxford University Press, 2002).

63 See Rosenwein, *A Short History;* and Samuel Kline Cohn, *Popular Protest in Late Medieval Europe: Italy, France, and Flanders* (Manchester: Manchester University Press, 2004).

64 Lassner and Bonner, *Islam in the Middle Ages*.

65 Lassner and Bonner, *Islam in the Middle Ages*; and Murray Gordon, *Slavery in the Arab World* (New York: New Amsterdam, 1989).

66 Kevin Terraciano, "Religion and the Church in Early Latin America," in *A Companion to the Reformation World*.

67 Michel Foucault, *"Society Must be Defended": Lectures at the Collège de France, 1975–76*, eds. Mauro Bertani and Alessandro Fontana and trans. David Macey (London: Penguin Books, 2004).

68 On the Lollards and the Hussites, see Euan Cameron, "Dissent and Heresy," in *A Companion to the Reformation World*, Po-chia Hsia, ed.

69 William Roscoe Estep, *Renaissance and Reformation* (Grand Rapids: W. B. Eerdmans Pub. Co., 1986), 64.

70 Euan Cameron, "Dissent and Heresy," in *A Companion to the Reformation World*.

71 On Luther, see Robert Kolb, "Martin Luther and the German Nation," *A Companion to the Reformation World*.

72 On the German Peasants' War, see Tom Scott, "The Peasant's War," in *A Companion to the Reformation World*.

73 Estep, *Renaissance Reformation*, 116.

74 Estep, *Renaissance Reformation*, 88. On Erasmus and the Bible, see also Joke Spaans, "Reform in the Low Countries," in *A Companion to the Reformation World*.

75 Estep, *Renaissance Reformation*, 92.

76 Miriam Bodian, "Jews in a Divided Christendom," in *A Companion to the Reformation World,* and see also Nicholas Terpstra, *Exiles and Religious Refugees in the Early Modern World: An Alternative History of the Reformation* (New York: Cambridge University Press, 2016).

77 Alison Rowland, "The Conditions of Life for the Masses," in Cameron, *Early Modern Europe: An Oxford History.*

78 Steven Gun, "War, Religion, and the State," in *Early Modern Europe: An Oxford History.*

79 See: R. A. Houston, "Colonies, Enterprises, and Wealth: The Economies of Europe and the Wider World," in *Early Modern Europe: An Oxford History.*

80 Thrower, *Western Atheism,* chapter 7.

81 Thrower, *Western Atheism,* chapter 7.

82 Thrower, *Western Atheism.* chapter 7.

83 Thrower, *Western Atheism,* chapter 9.

84 Thrower, *Western Atheism,* chapter 8.

85 Thrower, *Western Atheism,* chapters 7–9.

86 Niccolò Machiavelli, *The Prince,* 2nd ed., trans. Harvey C. Mansfield (Chicago: University of Chicago Press, 1998).

CHAPTER 4

1 On Hitler and Germanic "neo-Pagan" ideology, see Simon Taylor, *Prelude to Genocide: Nazi Ideology and the Struggle for Power* (New York: St. Martin's, 1985).

2 Neil MacFarquhardec, "Saddam Hussein, Defiant Dictator Who Ruled Iraq with Violence and Fear, Dies," *New York Times,* December 30, 2006, www.nytimes.com/2006/12/30/world/middleeast/30saddam.html?pagewanted=all&_r=0. See also Joseph Sassoon, *Saddam Hussein's Ba'th Party: Inside an Authoritarian Regime* (New York: Cambridge University Press, 2012).

3 Timothy Ryback, "Hitler's Forgotten Library," *Atlantic,* May 2003.

4 See: Bernard Diederich and Al Burt, *Papa Doc & the Tontons Macoutes* (Princeton: Markus Wiener Publishers, 2005).

5 See Bernice Glatzer Rosenthal, *The Occult in Russian and Soviet Culture* (Ithaca: Cornell University Press, 1997).

6 See Page Smith, *Tragic Encounters: The People's History of Native Americans* (Berkeley: Counterpoint, 2015).

7 Phil Zuckerman, *Society Without God: What the Least Religious Nations Can Tell Us About Contentment* (New York: New York University Press, 2008).

8 Moshe Halbertal and Avishai Margalit, *Idolatry* (Cambridge: Harvard University Press, 1992).

PART TWO INTRODUCTION

1 Onfray, *Atheist Manifesto,* 178.

2 Dawkins, *The God Delusion,* 280.

3 Onfray, *Atheist Manifesto,* 195.

4 Dawkins, *The God Delusion,* 283.

5 Hitchens, *God Is Not Great,* 100.

6 Dawkins, *The God Delusion*, 279.
7 Dawkins, *The God Delusion*, 81.

CHAPTER 5

1 Dawkins, *The God Delusion*, 268.
2 Dawkins, *The God Delusion*, 272–273.

CHAPTER 6

1 John F. A. Sawyer, *The Blackwell Companion to the Bible and Culture* (Oxford: Blackwell, 2006); Michael J. Gilmour and Mary Ann Beavis, eds., *Dictionary of the Bible and Western Culture* (Sheffield: Sheffield Phoenix Press, 2012); Dee Dyas, Esther Hughes, and Stephen Travis, eds., *The Bible in Western Culture: The Student's Guide* (London: Routledge, 2005); Jonathan A. Jacobs, *Judaic Sources and Western Thought: Jerusalem's Enduring Presence* (New York: Oxford University Press, 2011); and Gabriel Said Reynolds, *The Qur'an and its Biblical Subtext* (London: Routledge, 2010).

CHAPTER 7

1 Michael Walzer, "Commanded and Permitted Wars," in *Law, Politics, and Morality in Judaism*, ed. Michael Walzer (Princeton: Princeton University Press, 2006), 161.
2 For more on ancient empires see: Eric H. Cline and Mark W. Graham, *Ancient Empires: From Mesopotamia to the Rise of Islam* (Cambridge: Cambridge University Press, 2011); and Ian Morris and Walter Scheidel, *The Dynamics of Ancient Empires: State Power from Assyria to Byzantium* (Oxford: Oxford University Press, 2009).
3 Amélie Kuhrt, *The Ancient Near East, c. 3000–330 BC, vol. 1* (London: Routledge; 1995), 598; see also Cline and Graham, *Ancient Empires*, chapter 4.
4 For ancient genocides, see Frank Robert Chalk and Kurt Jonassohn, *The History and Sociology of Genocide: Analyses and Case Studies* (New Haven: Yale University Press, 1990), 65; and Jones, *Genocide: A Comprehensive Introduction*.
5 See: Cline and Graham, *Ancient Empires*, chapter 9. For ancient warfare, see also Christon I. Archer et al., *World History of Warfare* (Lincoln: University of Nebraska Press, 2002).
6 Thucydides, *History of the Peloponnesian War*, trans. Richard Crawley (London: J. M. Dent, 1993), chapter 17; and Cline and Graham, *Ancient Empires*, 138–140.
7 John H. Walton, *Ancient Near Eastern Thought and The Old Testament: Introducing the Conceptual World of the Hebrew Bible* (Grand Rapids: Baker Academic, 2006), 247.
8 Katell Berthelot, Joseph E. David, and Marc G. Hirshman, *The Gift of the Land and the Fate of the Canaanites in Jewish Thought* (Oxford: Oxford University Press, 2014).
9 For a good survey on European imperialism, see Raudzens, *Empires: Europe and Globalization*; and James R. Lehring, *European Colonialism Since 1700* (Cambridge: Cambridge University Press, 2013).
10 See Page Smith, *Tragic Encounters: The People's History of Native Americans* (Berkeley: Counterpoint, 2015).

11 Jones, *Genocide*, 73–75.

12 Smith, *Tragic Encounters*.

13 Margaret D. Jacobs, *White Mother to a Dark Race: Settler Colonialism, Maternalism, and the Removal of Indigenous Children in the American West and Australia, 1880–1940* (Lincoln: University of Nebraska Press, 2009); and John Sheridan Milloy, *A National Crime: The Canadian Government and the Residential School System, 1879–1986* (Winnipeg: University of Manitoba Press, 1999).

14 P. M. Holt and M. W. Daly, *A History of the Sudan: From the Coming of Islam to the Present Day* (Harlow: Longman/Pearson, 2011).

15 Arthur Goldschmidt, *Modern Egypt: The Formation of a Nation-State* (Boulder: Westview Press, 2004). And for a general history of the Arabization of Sudan (Nubia), see Holt, *A History of the Sudan.*

16 Anthony G. Pazzanita and Alfred G. Gerteiny, *Historical Dictionary of Mauritania* (Lanham: Scarecrow Press, 1996).

17 Walter T. K. Nugent, *Habits of Empire: A History of American Expansion* (New York: Alfred A. Knopf, 2008).

18 Adams, *Genocide*, 73.

19 Adams, *Genocide*, 73.

20 Adams, *Genocide*, 71.

21 Taner Akçam, *A Shameful Act: The Armenian Genocide and the Question of Turkish Responsibility* (New York: Metropolitan Books, 2006), 24.

22 Alex Cruden, *The Rwandan Genocide* (Farmington Hills: Greenhaven Press, 2010).

23 Adams, *Genocide*; and Adam Jones and Nicholas A. Robins, *Genocides by the Oppressed: Subaltern Genocide in Theory and Practice* (Bloomington: Indiana University Press, 2009).

24 Adams, *Genocide*, 29.

25 Adams, *Genocide*, 29.

26 Adams, *Genocide*, 29.

27 Walton, *Ancient Near Eastern Thought*, 108.

28 Walton, *Ancient Near Eastern Thought*, 244–247.

29 Walton, *Ancient Near Eastern Thought*, 250–251.

30 For a discussion of Noah that references traditional rabbinic commentaries, see Jonathan Sacks, *Covenant & Conversation Genesis: The Book of Beginnings* (New Milford: Toby, 2009); and Aviva Gottlieb Zornberg, *The Beginning of Desire: Reflections on Genesis* (New York: Schocken Books, 2011).

CHAPTER 8

1 Roth, *An Eye for an Eye*; and Michael Kronenwetter, *Capital Punishment: A Reference Handbook*, (Santa Barbara: ABC-CLIO, 1993), 11–13.

2 *The Code of Hammurabi*, trans. L. W. King (1915), www.general-intelligence.com/library/hr.pdf. For an exploration of ancient Near Eastern law, see Raymond Westbrook and Gary M. Beckman, *A History of Ancient Near Eastern Law* (Boston: Brill, 2003).

3 Roth, *An Eye for an Eye*, chapters 1 and 2. For a study of the relations between politics and the law in the ancient Near East and Mediterranean, see Dominique Charpin and Jane Marie Todd, *Writing, Law, and Kingship in Old Babylonian*

Mesopotamia (Chicago: University of Chicago Press, 2010); Lin Foxhall and A. D. E. Lewis, eds., *Greek Law in Its Political Setting: Justifications not Justice* (Oxford: Oxford University Press, 1996); and Richard A. Bauman, *Crime and Punishment in Ancient Rome* (London: Routledge, 1996). For more general sources on the law in these regions, see, Westbrook and Beckman, *A History of Ancient Near Eastern Law*; David J. Cohen, ed., *The Cambridge Companion to Ancient Greek Law* (Cambridge: Cambridge University Press, 2006); and David Johnston ed., *The Cambridge Companion to Roman Law* (New York: Cambridge University Press, 2015).

4   Wolfgang Behringer, *Witches and Witch-Hunts: A Global History* (Cambridge: Polity Press, 2004).

5   John G. Youger, *Sex in the Ancient World: From A to Z* (London: Routledge, 2005), 60, 125–126.

6   Paul Chrystal, *In Bed with the Romans* (Stroud: Amberley, 2015), chapter 7.

7   Chrystal, *In Bed with the Romans*, chapter 14.

8   *The Code of Hammurabi*, trans. L.W. King (1915).

9   Roth, *An Eye for an Eye*, chapters 1 and 2.

10   Roth, *An Eye for an Eye*, chapters 8 and 9.

11   Sassoon, *Ancient Laws and Modern Problems*, 40–41 and 47.

12   Sassoon, *Ancient Laws and Modern Problems*, 32.

13   Jones and Johnstone, *History of Criminal Justice*, 32.

14   J. A. Borkowski and Paul J. du Plessis, *Textbook on Roman Law* (Oxford: Oxford University Press, 2005), 69; and Roth, *An Eye for an Eye*, chapter 1.

15   Elon, *The Principles of Jewish Law*, 600.

16   Elon, *The Principles of Jewish Law*, 600.

17   Elon, *The Principles of Jewish Law*, 599.

18   Elon, *The Principles of Jewish Law*, 600.

19   William J. Stuntz, *The Collapse of American Criminal Justice* (Cambridge: Belknap Press of Harvard University Press, 2011).

20   Brandon L. Garrett, *Convicting the Innocent: Where Criminal Prosecutions Go Wrong* (Cambridge: Harvard University Press, 2011).

21   Garrett, *Convicting the Innocent*, 35.

22   Garrett, *Convicting the Innocent*, chapter 3.

23   Garrett, *Convicting the Innocent*, 7–9.

24   For more information see: "The Innocent List," Death Penalty Information Center, www.deathpenaltyinfo.org/innocence-list-those-freed-death-row.

25   Stuntz, *The Collapse of American Criminal Justice*, chapter 9.

26   For more on the three strikes law, see Jennifer Edwards Walsh, *Three Strikes Laws* (Westport: Greenwood Press, 2007).

27   Franklin E. Zimring, *Punishment and Democracy: Three Strikes and You're Out in California* (New York: Oxford University Press, 2001), 20.

28   For a general critique of plea bargaining, see Stuntz, *The Collapse of American Criminal Justice*. For more specific discussion of plea bargaining referred to here, see Jacqueline E. Ross, "The Entrenched Position of Plea Bargaining in United States Legal Practice," in *World Plea Bargaining: Consensual Procedures and the Avoidance of the Full Criminal Trial*, ed. Stephen Thaman (Durham: Carolina Academic Press, 2010), 107.

29 Lucian E. Dervan, "Bargained Justice: Plea Bargaining's Innocence Problem and the Brady Safety-Valve," (*Utah Law Review* 2012), 1: 51–97.

30 George Fisher, *Plea Bargaining's Triumph: A History of Plea Bargaining in America* (Stanford: Stanford University Press, 2003), 220–221. See Stuntz, *The Collapse of American Criminal Justice*, chapter 9.

31 "The Grabbing Hand of the Law," *Economist*, November 2, 2013, www.economist.com /news/united-states/21588915-how-prosecutors-seize-assets-innocent-grabbing-hand-law.

32 On appeal courts, see William M. Richman and William L. Reynolds, *Injustice on Appeal the United States Courts of Appeals in Crisis* (Oxford: Oxford University Press, 2013). For a broader discussion of American criminal justice, see Stuntz, *The Collapse of American Criminal Justice*; and Joseph F. Spillane and David B. Wolcott, *A History of Modern American Criminal Justice* (Thousand Oaks: SAGE Publications, 2013).

33 Roy Walmsley, *World Prison Population List,* 10th ed. (London: International Centre for Prison Studies, 2013).

CHAPTER 9

1 Isaac Mendelsohn, *Slavery in the Ancient Near East: A Comparative Study of Slavery in Babylonia, Assyria, Syria, and Palestine, from the Middle of the Third Millennium to the End of the First Millennium* (New York: Oxford University Press, 1949); and Daniel C. Snell, "Slavery in the Ancient Near East," in Keith Bradley and Paul Cartledge, eds., *The Cambridge World History of Slavery, vol. 1* (Cambridge: Cambridge University Press, 2011).

2 Mendelsohn, *Slavery in the Ancient Near East*, 3.

3 Niall Mckeown, "Resistance Among Chattel Slaves in the Classical Greek World," in Bradley and Cartledge, *The Cambridge World History of Slavery,* vol. 1.

4 Peter Hunt, "Slaves in Greek Literary Culture," in Bradley and Cartledge, *The Cambridge World History of Slavery,* 35–38.

5 Judith Reesa Baskin, *Midrashic Women: Formations of the Feminine in Rabbinic Literature* (Hannover: University Press of New England, 2002).

6 I. S. D. Sassoon, *The Status of Women in Jewish Tradition* (New York: Cambridge University Press, 2011).

7 Tikva Simone Frymer-Kensky, *Reading the Women of the Bible* (New York: Schocken Books, 2002).

8 Frymer-Kensky, *Reading the Women of the Bible*, xiv–xvi.

9 Ton Derks and Nico Roymans, eds., *Ethnic Constructs in Antiquity the Role of Power and Tradition* (Amsterdam: Amsterdam University Press, 2008), introduction.

10 George M. Fredrickson, *Racism: A Short History* (Princeton: Princeton University Press, 2002), 39; and David M. Goldenberg, *The Curse of Ham: Race and Slavery in Early Judaism, Christianity, and Islam* (Princeton: Princeton University Press, 2005).

11 For a discussion of the history of Western racism, see Benjamin H. Isaac, *The Invention of Racism in Classical Antiquity* (Princeton: Princeton University Press, 2004).

CHAPTER 10

1 Matthew White, *Atrocities: The 100 Deadliest Episodes in Human History* (New York: W. W. Norton, 2013), 544.

2 "How Many People Have Ever Lived on Earth?" Population Reference Bureau, www.prb.org/Publications/Articles/2002/HowManyPeopleHaveEverLivedonEarth. aspx.

3 White, *Atrocities: The 100 Deadliest Episodes*, 529.

4 Stephen R. Turnbull, *Genghis Khan & the Mongol Conquests, 1190–1400* (New York: Routledge, 2003).

5 White, *Atrocities: The 100 Deadliest Episodes*, 529.

6 Andreas Wimmer, *Waves of War: Nationalism, State Formation, and Ethnic Exclusion in the Modern World* (Cambridge: Cambridge University Press, 2013).

7 Richard Allen Landes and Thomas Head, *The Peace of God: Social Violence and Religious Response Around the Year 1000* (Ithaca: Cornell University Press, 1992).

8 Sohail H. Hashmi, *Just Wars, Holy Wars, and Jihads: Christian, Jewish, and Muslim Encounters and Exchanges* (Oxford: Oxford University Press, 2012), 4–8.

9 Reuven Firestone, *Holy War in Judaism: The Fall and Rise of a Controversial Idea* (Oxford: Oxford University Press, 2012).

10 Aviezer Ravitzky, "Prohibited Wars," in *Law, Politics, and Morality in Judaism*, 170–171.

11 John Kelsay, *Arguing the Just War in Islam* (Cambridge: Harvard University Press, 2007), chapter 3, especially 102–103.

12 Graham and Cline, *Ancient Empires*, 140.

CHAPTER 11

1 Jennifer Homans, *Apollo's Angels: A History of Ballet* (London: Granta, 2010), 13.

2 Merriman, *A History of Modern Europe*, chapter 12.

3 See for example Silvia Sebastiani, *The Scottish Enlightenment: Race, Gender, and the Limits of Progress*, trans. Jeremy Carden (New York: Palgrave Macmillan, 2013). See also: Sarah Knott and Barbara Taylor, eds., *Women, Gender, and Enlightenment* (New York: Palgrave Macmillan, 2005); and Emmanuel Chukwudi Eze ed., *Race and the Enlightenment: A Reader* (Cambridge: Blackwell, 1997).

4 Eric Nelson, *The Hebrew Republic: Jewish Sources and the Transformation of European Political Thought* (Cambridge: Harvard University Press, 2010).

5 Nelson, *Hebrew Republic*, 17.

6 Nelson, *Hebrew Republic*, 36 and 46.

7 Nelson, *Hebrew Republic*, 53.

8 Donald S. Lutz, *The Origins of American Constitutionalism* (Baton Rouge: Louisiana State University Press, 1988), 7 and chapter 3.

9 Merriman, *A History of Modern Europe*, 443.

10 Nelson, *Hebrew Republic*, 115.

11 Nelson, *Hebrew Republic*, 106.

12 Nelson, *Hebrew Republic*, 106

13 Nelson, *Hebrew Republic*, 120.

14 Nelson, *Hebrew Republic*, 78.

15 Nelson, *Hebrew Republic*, 79.

Endnotes

16 Nelson, *Hebrew Republic*, 86.

17 Johannes Thumfart, "On Grotius's Mare Liberum and Vitoria's De Indis, Following Agamben and Schmitt," *Grotiana* 30 (2009), 73.

18 Thumfart, "On Grotius's Mare Liberum," 78.

19 Thumfart, "On Grotius's Mare Liberum," 68.

20 Laurence J. Malone and Robert L. Heilbroner, eds., *The Essential Adam Smith* (New York: W. W. Norton, 1986), 323–324.

21 Stumpf, *The Grotian Theology of International Law*, section III.

22 Micheline Ishay, *The History of Human Rights: From Ancient Times to the Globalization Era* (Berkeley: University of California Press, 2004), chapter 1.

23 Harriet Jacobs, *Incidents in the Life of a Slave Girl: Written by Herself*, eds. Jean Fagan Yellin and Lydia Maria Child (Cambridge: Harvard University Press, 2000), 74.

24 For more on Turner, see Sinha, *The Slave's Cause*; and Paul Finkelman, *Encyclopedia of African American History, 1619–1895: From the Colonial Period to the Age of Frederick Douglass* (New York: Oxford University Press, 2006).

25 Paul Finkelman, *Encyclopedia of African American History, 1619–1895: From the Colonial Period to the Age of Frederick Douglass Three-volume Set* (Oxford: Oxford University Press, 2006), 129. See the entry on Frederick Douglass.

26 See: Christopher Leslie Brown, *Moral Capital: Foundations of British Abolitionism* (Chapel Hill: University of North Carolina Press, 2006); Brycchan Carey, *From Peace to Freedom Quaker Rhetoric and the Birth of American Antislavery, 1657–1761* (New Haven: Yale University Press, 2012); and J. R. Oldfield, *Transatlantic Abolitionism in the Age of Revolution: An International History of Anti-slavery, c. 1787–1820* (Cambridge: Cambridge University Press, 2013).

27 Saul S. Friedman, *Jews and the American Slave Trade* (New Brunswick: Transaction Publishers, 1998).

28 W. G. Clarence-Smith, *Islam and the Abolition of Slavery* (London: Hurst & Co., 2006), 196 and 203–204.

29 Sarah Apetrei, *Women, Feminism and Religion in Early Enlightenment England* (Cambridge: Cambridge University Press, 2010); and Sue Morgan, *Women, Religion, and Feminism in Britain, 1750-1900* (New York: Palgrave MacMillan, 2002).

30 See: Jean Fagan Yellin, *Women & Sisters: The Antislavery Feminists in American Culture* (New Haven: Yale University Press, 1989); and Sklar, *Women's Rights Emerges*.

31 Sklar, *Women's Rights Emerges*.

32 For world history in the nineteenth and twentieth centuries, see Jürgen Osterhammel, *The Transformation of the World: A Global History of the Nineteenth Century*, trans. Patrick Camiller (Princeton: Princeton University Press, 2014); and J. A. S. Grenville, *A History of the World from the 20th to the 21st Century* (London: Routledge, 2005).

33 John Lynch and R. A. Humphreys, *Latin American Revolutions, 1808–1826: Old and New World Origins* (Norman: University of Oklahoma Press, 1994).

34 On the relationship between Islam and social movements, see Ervand Abrahamian, Lapidus, and Edmund Burke, *Islam, Politics, and Social Movements* (Berkeley: University of California Press, 1988).

35 See: Grenville, *A History of the World*, chapter 38; and Adrian Vickers, *A History of Modern Indonesia* (Cambridge: Cambridge University Press, 2005).

36 Grenville, *A History of the World*, chapter 66; and Willem van Schendel, *A History of Bangladesh* (Cambridge: Cambridge University Press, 2009).

37 Nelson Mandela, *Long Walk to Freedom: The Autobiography of Nelson Mandela* (Boston: Little, Brown, 1994).

38 Martin Luther King Jr., *A Call to Conscience: The Landmark Speeches of Dr. Martin Luther King, Jr*, eds. Clayborne Carson and Kris Shepard (New York: IPM, 2001).

39 Samuel Moyn, *Christian Human Rights* (Philadelphia: University of Pennsylvania Press, 2015).

40 For a general discussion of the effects of Christianity on social and labor movements, see William Smaldone, *European Socialism: A Concise History with Documents* (Lanham: Rowman & Littlefield Publishers, Inc., 2014). See also Robert Service, *Comrades! A History of World Communism* (Cambridge: Harvard University Press, 2007), 15–16.

41 For the influence of Hess on Marx, see Smalldone, *European Socialism*, 57–58; and Shlomo Avineri, *Moses Hess, Prophet of Communism and Zionism* (New York: New York University Press, 1985).

42 Merriman, *A History of Modern Europe*, 792–793.

43 Gustavo Gutiérrez, *A Theology of Liberation: History, Politics, and Salvation* (Maryknoll: Orbis Books, 1973), 90.

44 Schendel, *A History of Bangladesh*, 205–6; and Vickers, *A History of Indonesia*, 94.

45 John L. Esposito, *The Oxford Dictionary of Islam* (Oxford: Oxford University Press, 2003), 298.

46 See Arthur Marwick, *The Sixties: Cultural Revolution in Britain, France, Italy, and the United States*, c. 1958–c. 1974 (Oxford: Oxford University Press, 1998).

47 Pierre Bourdieu, *Distinction: A Social Critique of the Judgment of Taste*, trans. Richard Nice (London: Routledge, 2010).

CHAPTER 12

1 Quoted in: Michael Hayer, *The Catholic Church and the Holocaust, 1930–1965* (Indianapolis: Indiana University Press, 2000), 35.

2 Lehning, *European Colonialism*, 242–247.

3 Grenville, *A History of the World*. See chapter 64 on Mao for example.

4 Grenville, *A History of the World*, chapter 89.

5 Janet Afary and Kevin Anderson, *Foucault and the Iranian Revolution Gender and the Seductions of Islamism* (Chicago: University of Chicago Press, 2005).

6 Kate McCarthy, *Interfaith Encounters in America* (New Brunswick: Rutgers University Press, 2007).

PART THREE INTRODUCTION

1 Sam Harris, *The End of Faith: Religion, Terror, and The Future of Reason* (New York: W.W. Norton, 2004), 172.

2 Dawkins, *The God Delusion*, 251.

3 Harris, *The End of Faith*, 172.

4 Dawkins, *The God Delusion*, 135.

5 Dawkins, *The God Delusion*, 209.

6 Dawkins, *The God Delusion*, 269–270.

7 Daniel Dennet, *Breaking the Spell: Religion as a Natural Phenomenon* (New York: Viking, 2006), 279.

8 Dawkins, *The God Delusion*, 265.

9 Samuel Langhorne Clemens, *Letters from the Earth* (New York: Harper & Row, 1962).

10 Harris, *The End of Faith*, 172.

11 Harris, *The End of Faith*, 173.

12 Adolf Hitler, *Mein Kampf*, trans. Ralph Manheim (Boston: Houghton Mifflin, 1971), 324.

13 Saul Friedländer, *Nazi Germany and the Jews, 1933–1945*, trans. Orna Kenan (New York: Harper Perennial, 2009).

14 For a good discussion of moral relativism, see Steven Lukes, *Moral Relativism* (New York: Picador, 2008).

15 *Bible Study Tools*, s.v. "ra," www.biblestudytools.com/lexicons/hebrew/kjv/ra.html.

16 Jacob Neusner and Bruce Chilton, eds., *The Golden Rule: The Ethics of Reciprocity in World Religions* (London: Continuum, 2008).

17 Kant himself claimed that the categorical imperative differed from the Golden Rule, though subsequent scholars minimize this difference. See Jeffrey Wattles, *The Golden Rule* (New York: Oxford University Press, 1996), chapter 7.

18 For a discussion of the variations on the definitions of evil in world religions, see Peter Koslowski, *The Origin and the Overcoming of Evil and Suffering in the World Religions* (Dordrecht: Springer Netherlands, 2001).

CHAPTER 13

1 Michel Onfray, *A Hedonist Manifesto: The Power to Exist*, trans. Joseph McClellan (New York: Columbia University Press, 2015).

2 Gordon Marshall, *A Dictionary of Sociology*, 3rd rev. ed., (2009), s.v. "drives."

3 Ari Berkowitz, *Governing Behavior: How Nerve Cell Dictatorships and Democracies Control Everything We Do* (Cambridge: Harvard University Press, 2016).

4 Jennifer Vonk and Todd K. Shackelford, *The Oxford Handbook of Comparative Evolutionary Psychology* (New York: Oxford University Press, 2012).

5 Helen E. Fisher, *Anatomy of Love: A Natural History of Mating, Marriage, and Why We Stray* (New York: W. W. Norton, 2016).

6 Hildy S. Ross and Ori Friedman eds., *Origins of Ownership of Property: New Directions for Child and Adolescent Development*, no. 132 (San Francisco: John Wiley & Sons, 2011).

7 Sarah F. Brosnan, "Property in Nonhuman Primates," in *Origins of Ownership of Property*. The following examples about animals are all taken from this article.

8 Philippe Rochat, "Possession and Morality in Early Development," in *Origins of Ownership of Property*.

9 Gad Saad, *The Consuming Instinct: What Juicy Burgers, Ferraris, Pornography, and Gift Giving Reveal About Human Nature* (Amherst: Prometheus Books, 2011).

10 Jude Cassidy and Phillip R. Shaver eds., *Handbook of Attachment: Theory, Research, and Clinical Applications* (New York: The Guilford Press, 2016).

11 Carl Safina, *Beyond Words: What Animals Think and Feel* (New York: Henry Holt and Company, 2015).

12 Fisher, *Anatomy of Love*.

13 John S. Allen, *Home: How Habitat Made Us Human* (New York: Basic Books, 2015).

14 Peter B. Smith, Ronald Fischer, Michael Harris Bond, and Vivian L. Vignoles, *Understanding Social Psychology Across Cultures: Engaging with Others in a Changing World* (London: SAGE, 2013); and Susan T. Fiske, *Social Beings: A Core Motives Approach to Social Psychology* (Hoboken: J. Wiley, 2010).

15 The concept of validation recurs throughout discussions of attachment. See: Cassidy and Shaver, *Handbook of Attachment;* and Koerner, *Doing Dialectical Behavior Therapy.*

16 Cassidy and Shaver, *Handbook of Attachment.*

17 DeYoung, *Understanding and Treating Chronic Shame.*

18 DeYoung, *Understanding and Treating Chronic Shame.*

19 T. Brazelton, *Toddlers and Parents: A Declaration of Independence* (New York: Delacorte Press/S. Lawrence, 1974).

20 T. Brazelton, *Toddlers and Parents.*

21 Michael Wertheimer, *A Brief History of Psychology* (New York: Psychology Press, 2012), 198. See also Jon Carlson, *Alfred Adler Revisited* (New York: Routledge, 2012).

22 Wertheimer, *A Brief History of Psychology,* 215. See also Carl R. Rogers, *Carl Rogers on Personal Power* (New York: Delacorte Press, 1977); and Abraham H. Maslow, *Motivation and Personality,* 3rd ed. (New York: Harper and Row, 1987). The theories of Rogers and Maslow are still influential today.

23 Keddy, *Competition.* See also: Richard W. Wrangham and Dale Peterson, *Demonic Males: Apes and the Origins of Human Violence* (Boston: Houghton Mifflin, 1996).

24 Paul A. M. Van Lange, *Social Dilemmas: The Psychology of Human Cooperation* (Oxford: Oxford University Press, 2014), 86; and Blanton and Fargher, *How Humans Cooperate.*

25 F. B. M. de Waal, *Coalitions and Alliances in Humans and Other Animals* (Oxford: Oxford University Press, 1992).

26 Peter M. Kappeler and Carel van Schaik, *Cooperation in Primates and Humans: Mechanisms and Evolution* (Berlin: Springer, 2006), 126, and de Waal, *Coalitions and Alliances.*

27 Van Lange, *Social Dilemmas.*

CHAPTER 14

1 There is a strong relationship between consent and the development of the self and autonomy. See Tom L. Beauchamp, "Autonomy and Consent," in *The Ethics of Consent Theory and Practice,* eds. Franklin G. Miller and Alan Wertheimer (Oxford: Oxford University Press, 2010).

2 Miller and Wertheimer, eds., *The Ethics of Consent Theory and Practice* (Oxford: Oxford University Press, 2010).

3 For a discussion of valid consent, see John Kleinig, "The Nature of Consent," in Miller and Wertheimer, *The Ethics of Consent.*

4 For a discussion of why people believe ideologies or people who make them act against their own interests see *Encyclopedia of Power,* s.v. "domination."

5 Cline and Graham, *Ancient Empires;* and Martin Shipway, *Decolonization and Its Impact: A Comparative Approach to the End of the Colonial Empires* (Malden: Blackwell Publishing, 2008).

6   For a discussion of the concept of karma, see Stephen II. Phillips, *Yoga, Karma, and Rebirth: A Brief History and Philosophy* (New York: Columbia University Press, 2009).

CHAPTER 15

1   Steven D. Levitt and Stephen J. Dubner, *Freakonomics: A Rogue Economist Explores the Hidden Side of Everything* (New York: William Morrow, 2006).

2   Laurence Cockcroft, *Global Corruption: Money, Power, and Ethics in the Modern World* (London: I. B. Tauris, 2012).

3   See: Katherine Hirschfeld, *Gangster States: Organized Crime, Kleptocracy, and Political Collapse* (New York: Palgrave Macmillan, 2015).

4   Adam Taylor, "Is Vladimir Putin hiding a $200 billion fortune? (And if so, does it matter?)" *Washington Post*, February 20, 2015.

5   Michael Kremer and Seema Jayachandran, "Odious Debt: When Dictators Borrow, Who Repays the Loan?" Brookings Institution, March 1, 2003, www.brookings.edu/research/articles/2003/03/spring-development-kremer. For more detailed studies, see Yvonne Wong, *Sovereign Finance and the Poverty of Nations: Odious Debt in International Law* (Cheltenham: Edward Elgar, 2012); and Léonce Ndikumana and James K. Boyce, *Africa's Odious Debts: How Foreign Loans and Capital Flight Bled a Continent* (London: Zed Books, 2011).

6   Nancy Rivera Brooks, "Executive Gets 5 Years in Embezzlement Case," *Los Angeles Times,* October 7, 1997, articles.latimes.com/1997/oct/07/local/me-40026, accessed December 18, 2016; Henry N. Pontell and Gilbert Geis, eds., *International Handbook of White-Collar and Corporate Crime* (New York: Springer, 2007); and John Minkes and A. L. Minkes, eds., *Corporate and White-Collar Crime* (Los Angeles: SAGE, 2008).

7   Mark Pieth, Lucinda A. Low, and Peter J. Cullen, eds., *The OECD Convention on Bribery A Commentary* (Cambridge: Cambridge University Press, 2007).

8   William D. Hartung, *Prophets of War: Lockheed Martin and the Making of the Military-Industrial Complex* (New York: Nation Books, 2011).

9   Manfred B. Steger and Ravi K. Roy, *Neoliberalism: A Very Short Introduction* (Oxford: Oxford University Press, 2010).

10 M. A. Utton, *Cartels and Economic Collusion: The Persistence of Corporate Conspiracies* (Cheltenham: Edward Elgar, 2011).

11 See Samuel W. Buell, *Capital Offenses: Business Crime and Punishment in America's Corporate Age* (New York: W. W. Norton, 2016).

12 David Callahan, *The Cheating Culture: Why More Americans Are Doing Wrong to Get Ahead* (Orlando: Harcourt, 2004), chapter 1.

13 Terry L. Leap, *Dishonest Dollars: The Dynamics of White-Collar Crime* (Ithaca: ILR Press/Cornell University Press, 2007).

14 Levitt and Dubner, *Freakonomics*, 44.

15 Callahan, *The Cheating Culture*, 23.

16 To give examples from two regions: James F. Petras and Henry Veltmeyer, *Social Movements in Latin America: Neoliberalism and Popular Resistance* (New York: Palgrave Macmillan, 2011); and Sung Chull Kim and N. Ganesan, *State Violence in East Asia* (Lexington: University Press of Kentucky, 2013).

17 Leap, *Dishonest Dollars*, chapters 3 and 4.
18 The reference to the invisible hand is in book IV, chapter 2 of *The Wealth of Nations*.
19 The reference to the invisible hand in part four, chapter 1 of *The Theory of Moral Sentiments*.
20 Smith, *Wealth of Nations*, 227.
21 Ian Simpson Ross, *The Life of Adam Smith* (Oxford: Oxford University Press, 2010).
22 "Child Abuse Statistics and Facts," Childhelp, www.childhelp.org/pages/statistics.
23 "Domestic Violence/Abuse Statistics," US Department of Justice Figures, Statics Brain, www.statisticbrain.com/domestic-violence-abuse-stats/.
24 "Victims of Sexual Violence: Statistics," Rape, Abuse & Incest National Network, www.rainn.org/statistics/victims-sexual-violence.
25 "Domestic Violence," Women's Refuge, womensrefuge.org.nz/domestic-violence/.
26 Global Prevalence of Child Sexual Abuse," Journalist's Resource, journalistsresource .org/studies/government/criminal-justice/global-prevalence-child-sexual-abuse.
27 "Female Victims of Violence," US Department of Justice, Bureau of Justice Statistics, Selected Findings, September 2009, www.bjs.gov/content/pub/pdf/fvv.pdf.
28 "Results of the 2010 WBI U.S. Workplace Bullying Institute." www.workplacebully-ing.org/wbiresearch/2010-wbi-national-survey/.
29 School Bullying Statistics, www.bullyingstatistics.org/content/school-bullying-statistics.html.
30 Joseph Pittman, "What's Worse: Physical Scars or Mental Scars?" Domes-tic Violence Statistics, July 12, 2012, domesticviolencestatistics.org/whats-worse-physical-scars-or-mental-scars/.
31 Austin Choi-Fitzpatrick and Alison Brysk, *From Human Trafficking to Human Rights: Reframing Contemporary Slavery* (Philadelphia: University of Pennsylvania Press, 2012).
32 "Global Findings," Global Slavery Index, www.globalslaveryindex.org/.
33 "Global Employment Trends 2014," International Labour Organization, www.ilo. org/global/about-the-ilo/newsroom/news/WCMS_234030/lang--en/index.htm.
34 "A Profile of the Working Poor, 2013," US Bureau of Labor Statistics, www.bls.gov/ opub/reports/working-poor/archive/a-profile-of-the-working-poor-2013.pdf.
35 Sara Elinoff Acker, *Unclenching Our Fists: Abusive Men on the Journey to Nonvio-lence* (Nashville: Vanderbilt University Press, 2013).
36 Donald G. Dutton, *The Abusive Personality Violence and Control in Intimate Rela-tionships* (New York: Guilford Press, 2007).
37 "Why Do Kids Bully?" Stomp Out Bullying, www.stompoutbullying.org/index.php/ information-and-resources/about-bullying-and-cyberbullying/why-do-kids-bully/.
38 Dutton, *The Abusive Personality*, 228.
39 Elinoff Acker, *Unclenching Our Fists*, 44.
40 Dutton, *The Abusive Personality*, chapter 10.
41 Dutton, *The Abusive Personality*, chapter 7.
42 Margaret Haerens, *Human Trafficking* (Detroit: Greenhaven Press, 2012).

Endnotes

CHAPTER 16

1 See Eric D. Weitz, *A Century of Genocide Utopias of Race and Nation* (Princeton: Princeton University Press, 2003); and Dale C. Tatum, *Genocide at the Dawn of the Twenty-First Century: Rwanda, Bosnia, Kosovo, and Darfur* (New York: Palgrave Macmillan, 2010).

2 Guenter Lewy, *The Nazi Persecution of the Gypsies* (Oxford: Oxford University Press, 2000).

3 Ronald Grigor, "*They Can Live in the Desert But Nowhere Else*": *A History of the Armenian Genocide* (Princeton, New Jersey: Princeton University Press, 2015).

4 Gérard Prunier, *The Rwanda Crisis: History of a Genocide* (New York: Columbia University Press, 1995).

5 John R. Lampe, *Yugoslavia as History: Twice There Was a Country* (Cambridge: Cambridge University Press, 2000).

6 For a description of the threat of the KKK in the twenty-first century, see David Cunningham, "The Ku Klux Klan in History and Today," Oxford University Press blog, blog.oup.com/2015/01/klansville-usa-david-cunningham-ku-klux-klan/.

7 Adam Klein, *A Space for Hate: The White Power Movement's Adaptation into Cyberspace* (Duluth: Litwin Books, 2010).

8 "2012 Hate Crime Statistics," Federal Bureau of Investigation, www.fbi.gov/about-us/cjis/ucr/hate-crime/2012/topic-pages/incidents-and-offenses/incidentsandoffenses_final.

9 Joshua A, Krisch, "The U.S. Has Suffered Nearly 200 School Shootings Since 2000," *Fatherly*, November 15, 2017, www.fatherly.com/health-science/map-of-school-shootings-since-2000/.

10 Willard Gaylin, *Hatred: The Psychological Descent into Violence* (New York: Public Affairs, 2003).

11 Gaylin, *Hatred*, 34.

12 Gaylin, *Hatred*, 38.

13 Gaylin, *Hatred*, 46.

14 Gaylin, *Hatred*, 108.

15 Zimbardo, *The Lucifer Effect*, 271.

16 Heidi M. Ravven, *The Self Beyond Itself: An Alternative History of Ethics, the New Brain Sciences, and the Myth of Free Will* (New York: New Press, 2013), 102.

17 Ravven, *The Self Beyond Itself*, 97–98.

18 David Chidester, *Salvation and Suicide: Jim Jones, the Peoples Temple, and Jonestown* (Bloomington: Indiana University Press, 2003).

19 Christopher R. Browning, *Ordinary Men: Reserve Police Battalion 101 and the Final Solution in Poland* (New York: HarperPerennial, 1998).

20 Browning, *Ordinary Men*, chapter 8.

21 Ravven, *The Self Beyond Itself*, 97.

22 Ravven, *The Self Beyond Itself*, 107.

23 Ravven, *The Self Beyond Itself*, 99.

24 Ravven, *The Self Beyond Itself*, 100.

25 Ravven, *The Self Beyond Itself*, 108.

26 Ravven, *The Self Beyond Itself*, 103.

27 Zimbardo, *The Lucifer Effect*, 294–296.

28 Ravven, *The Self Beyond Itself*, 100.
29 Browning, *Ordinary Men*, chapter 8.
30 Browning, *Ordinary Men*, chapter 8.
31 Browning, *Ordinary Men*, 72–73.
32 David Cesarani, *Eichmann: His Life and Crimes* (London: W. Heinemann, 2004).
33 Browing, *Ordinary Men*, 74–75.
34 Zimbardo, *The Lucifer Effect*, chapter 12.
35 Zimbardo, *The Lucifer Effect*, chapter 12.
36 Christopher Winch, *Education, Autonomy, and Critical Thinking* (London: Routledge, 2006).
37 See Madeline Levine, *Teach Your Children Well: Parenting for Authentic Success* (New York: Harper, 2012).
38 Levine, *Teach your Children Well*, chapter 3.
39 Pirkei De Rabbi, *Midrash,* Eliezer 24:7.
40 Martin Luther King Jr., *Letter from the Birmingham Jail* (San Francisco: Harper San Francisco, 1994).
41 King, *Letter from the Birmingham Jail*, 15
42 Simon Baron-Cohen, *The Science of Evil on Empathy and the Origins of Cruelty* (New York: Basic Books, 2011).

CHAPTER 17

1 Sam Harris, *Free Will* (New York: Free Press, 2012).
2 Harris, *Free Will*, 21.
3 Ravven, *The Self Beyond Itself*.
4 Ravven, *The Self Beyond Itself*, chapter 4.
5 Michael S. Gazzaniga, *Who's In Charge? Free Will and the Science of the Brain* (New York: HarperCollins, 2011).
6 Gazzaniga, *Who's In Charge?*, 127.
7 Gazzaniga, *Who's In Charge?*, 76–78.
8 Gazzaniga, *Who's In Charge?*, 102–103.
9 Gazzaniga, *Who's In Charge?*, 107.
10 Gazzaniga, *Who's In Charge?*, 129–130.
11 Gazzaniga, *Who's In Charge?*, 131.
12 Gazzaniga, *Who's In Charge?*, 130.
13 Gazzaniga, *Who's In Charge?*, 134.
14 Joseph Duke Filonowicz, *Fellow-Feeling and the Moral Life* (Cambridge: Cambridge University Press, 2008); and Roger Crisp ed, *The Oxford Handbook of the History of Ethics* (Oxford: Oxford University Press, 2013).
15 Roger Giner-Sorolla, *Judging Passions Moral Emotions in Persons and Groups* (New York: Psychology Press, 2012).
16 Giner-Sorolla, *Judging Passions*, 24.
17 Giner-Sorolla, *Judging Passions*, 22.
18 Giner-Sorolla, *Judging Passions*, 138–141.
19 Susan Forward and Donna Frazier, *Emotional Blackmail* (London: Bantam, 1998).
20 Daniel Goleman, *Social Intelligence: The New Science of Human Relationships* (New York: Bantam Books, 2006).

21 Goleman, *Social Intelligence*, 230–233.

22 Michel Pastoureau, *Black: The History of a Color* (Princeton: Princeton University Press, 2009).

23 Pierre Bourdieu, *Distinction: A Social Critique of the Judgment of Taste*, trans. Richard Nice (London: Routledge, 2010).

24 Rupert Brown, *Prejudice: Its Social Psychology* (Malden: Wiley-Blackwell, 2010), chapter 7.

25 Allison P. Davis, "New OKCupid Data on Race Is Pretty Depressing," *The Cut*, September 11, 2014, nymag.com/thecut/2014/09/new-okcupid-data-on-race-is-pretty-depressing.html.

26 Paul 't Hart, *Groupthink in Government: A Study of Small Groups and Policy Failure* (Baltimore: Johns Hopkins University Press, 1994).

27 Dan Ariely, *Predictably Irrational: The Hidden Forces that Shape Our Decisions* (New York: Harper, 2009).

28 Dennis J. Devine, *Jury Decision Making: The State of the Science* (New York: New York University Press, 2012), especially chapter 5.

CHAPTER 18

1 See the chapter on ZOPA in Roy J. Lewicki, David M. Saunders, and John W. Minton, *Negotiation: Readings, Exercises, and Cases* (Boston: Irwin/McGraw-Hill, 1999).

2 John Deigh, *An Introduction to Ethics* (Cambridge: Cambridge University Press, 2010).

3 Deigh, *An Introduction to Ethics*, 101–103.

4 For a discussion of some of the problems of altruism, see Jonathan Seglow ed., *The Ethics of Altruism* (London: Frank Cass, 2004).

5 Deigh, *An Introduction to Ethics*, 41–42.

6 Sam Harris is a big advocate of the science of morality. For a discussion of science and ethics, see Adam Briggle and Carl Mitcham, *Ethics and Science: An Introduction* (Cambridge: Cambridge University Press, 2012).

7 Forced sterilization occurred all over the world. Alison Bashford and Philippa Levine, *The Oxford Handbook of the History of Eugenics* (New York: Oxford University Press, 2010).

8 Bassam Zázá, "Six Convicted of Dh1.8b Bank Fraud," *Gulf News*, April 27, 2011, gulfnews.com/news/uae/crime/six-convicted-of-dh1-8b-bank-fraud-1.799770.

9 Bradley Hope, "1MDB Scandal: Talks Between Malaysia, Abu Dhabi Over Missing Money Break Down," *Wall Street Journal*, January 20, 2017, www.wsj.com/articles/1mdb-scandal-talks-between-malaysia-abu-dhabi-over-missing-money-break-down-1484941644.

CHAPTER 19

1 Sarah Yehudit Schneider, *You Are What You Hate* (Jerusalem: A Still Small Voice, 2009).

2 Stefan Kanfer, "Isaac Singer's Promised City," *City Journal*, Summer 1997, www.city-journal.org/html/isaac-singer%E2%80%99s-promised-city-11935.html.

3 Yoram Hazony, *The Dawn: Political Teachings of the Book of Esther* (Jerusalem: Genesis Jerusalem Press, 1995).
4 For a discussion of how the Allies responded to the news of the Holocaust see Shlomo Aronson, *Hitler, the Allies, and the Jews* (Cambridge: Cambridge University Press, 2004).
5 Hazony, *The Dawn*, 264.
6 John D. Barrow and Frank J. Tipler, *The Anthropic Cosmological Principle* (Oxford: Oxford University Press, 1986).

PART FOUR INTRODUCTION

1 Dawkins, *The God Delusion*, 52.
2 Dawkins, *The God Delusion*, 139.
3 Onfray, *Atheist Manifesto*, 84–85.
4 Hitchens, *God Is Not Great*, 141–142.
5 Hitchens, *God Is Not Great*, 85.
6 Hitchens, *God Is Not Great*, 205.
7 Dawkins, *The God Delusion*, 82.

CHAPTER 20

1 J. F. Nunn, *Ancient Egyptian Medicine* (London: British Museum Press, 1996).
2 Tracey Rihll, *Greek Science* (Oxford: Oxford University Press, 1999).
3 John Freely, *Light From the East: How the Science of Medieval Islam Helped to Shape the Western World* (London: I. B. Tauris, 2011).
4 Edward Grant, *The Foundations of Modern Science in the Middle Ages: Their Religious, Institutional, and Intellectual Contexts* (Cambridge: Cambridge University Press, 1996).
5 Dawkins, *The God Delusion*, 125.
6 Pew Research, "Scientists and Belief," May/June 2009, www.pewforum.org/2009/11/05/scientists-and-belief/.
7 H. Margenau and R. A. Varghese, eds. *Cosmos, Bios, and Theos* (La Salle: Open Court, 1992), 52.
8 Margenau and Varghese, *Cosmos, Bios, and Theos*, 83.
9 In their article on the religiosity of university professors, N. Gross and S. Simmons calculate that the overall percentage is 52. See N. Gross and S. Simmons, "The Religiosity of American College and University Professors," *Sociology of Religion: A Quarterly Review* 70, no. 22 (2009): 101–129.
10 Hugh G. Gauch, *Scientific Method in Brief* (Cambridge: Cambridge University Press, 2012).
11 Barrow and Tipler, *The Anthropic Cosmological Principle* (Oxford: Oxford University Press, 1986).
12 For a good explanation of the theological problems with the God of the Gaps, see Natan Slifkin, *The Challenge of Creation: Judaism's Encounter with Science, Cosmology, and Evolution* (Ramat Bet Shemesh: Zoo Torah, 2010).
13 Slifkin, *The Challenge of Creation*, chapter 7 and 206–210.
14 Paul M. Blowers, *Drama of the Divine Economy: Creator and Creation in Early Christian Theology and Piety*, (Oxford: Oxford University Press, 2012), 107.

Endnotes

15 Blowers, *Drama of the Divine Economy*, 104.
16 Slifkin, *The Challenge of Creation*, 194.
17 R. W. Dyson ed., *Augustine: The City of God Against the Pagans* (Cambridge: Harvard University Press, 1998), Book 11, chapter 6.
18 Origen, *Homilies on Genesis and Exodus*, trans. Ronald E. Heine (Washington: Catholic University of America Press, 2002), 75.
19 Husām Muhyī ăd-Dīn al-Ālūsī, *The Problem of Creation in Islamic Thought* (Baghdad: National Printing and Publishing, 1965), 29.
20 Many of these references to the Talmud or to specific scholars are taken from Slifkin, *The Challenge of Creation*.
21 Slifkin, *The Challenge of Creation*, 98.
22 For just a sample of the vast kabbalistic literature on this topic, see Sarah Schneider, *Evolutionary Creationism: Kabbala Solves the Riddle of Missing Links* (Jerusalem: A Still Small Voice, 2005).
23 Hanneke Reuling, *After Eden: Church Fathers and Rabbis on Genesis 3:16-21* (Leiden: Brill, 2006), 51.
24 Seyyed Shahabeddin Mesbahi, *Method and Mysticism: Cosmos, Nature, and Environment in Islamic Mysticism* (Louisville: Fons Vitae, 2011).

CHAPTER 21

1 Byron E. Shafer, John Baines, Leonard H. Lesko, and David P. Silverman, *Religion in Ancient Egypt: Gods, Myths, and Personal Practice* (London: Routledge, 1991).
2 W. G. Lambert, *Babylonian Creation Myths* (Winona Lake: Eisenbrauns, 2013).
3 Dirk L. Couprie, *Heaven and Earth in Ancient Greek Cosmology: From Thales to Heraclides Ponticus* (New York: Springer, 2011).
4 Ramban, *Commentary on the Torah*, trans. Charles B. Chavel (New York: Shilo Publishing House, 1971), 23.
5 Gerald Schroeder, *Genesis and the Big Bang Theory: The Discovery of Harmony between Modern Science and the Bible* (New York: Bantam Books, 1990), 65. This is Schroeder's distillation of the Ramban's commentary, which somewhat simplifies the original text.
6 Alister McGrath, "Augustine's Origin of Species: How the Great Theologian Might Weigh in on the Darwin Debate," *Christianity Today*, May 8, 2009, www.christianitytoday.com/ct/2009/may/22.39.html.
7 David Adams Leeming and Margaret Adams Leeming, *A Dictionary of Creation Myths* (Oxford: Oxford University Press, 1995).
8 Aryeh Kaplan, *Immortality, Resurrection, and the Age of the Universe: A Kabbalistic View* (Hoboken: Ktav Publishing, 1993).
9 T.O. Shanavas, *Creation and/or Evolution: An Islamic Perspective* (Philadelphia: Xlibris Corp., 2005), 87. Chapter 4 of Shanavas's book discusses Islamic views of the age of the universe.
10 Shanavas, *Creation and/or Evolution*, 83–84.
11 Shanavas, *Creation and/or Evolution*, 87.
12 Osama Ali al-Khader, *The Qur'an and the Universe: From the Big Bang to the Big Crunch* (Beyrouth: al-Maktaba al-A'sryiyah, 2005).
13 Blowers, *Drama of the Divine Economy*, 106–107 and 112.

14 Origen, *Homilies on Genesis*, 75.
15 Dyson ed., *Augustine: The City of God*, Book 11, chapter 6.
16 Kalpana M. Paranjape, *Ancient Indian Insights and Modern Science* (Pune, India: Bhandarkar Oriental Research Institute, 1996).
17 Sarah Iles Johnston, *Ancient Religions* (Cambridge: Belknap Press of Harvard University Press, 2007).
18 Bernard McGinn, *The Mystical Thought of Meister Eckart: The Man from Whom God Hid Nothing* (New York: Crossroad, 2001); Nidhal Guessoum, *Islam's Quantum Question: Reconciling Muslim Tradition and Modern Science* (London: I. B. Tauris, 2011); and Mesbahi, *Method and Mysticism*.
19 Gavin D. Flood, *An Introduction to Hinduism* (New York: Cambridge University Press, 1996); and Knott, *Hinduism*.
20 Lawrence Fine, *Physician of the Soul, Healer of the Cosmos: Isaac Luria and His Kabbalistic Fellowship* (Stanford: Stanford University Press, 2003).
21 Leeming and Leeming, *A Dictionary of Creation Myths*.
22 Slifkin, *The Challenge of Creation*, 157 and chapter 13, especially 180.
23 Sarah Schneider, *Evolutionary Creationism: Kabbala Solves the Riddle of Missing Links* (Jerusalem: A Still Small Voice, 2005).
24 Slifkin, *The Challenge of Creation*, 171–173.
25 P. C. W. Davies, *Cosmic Jackpot: Why Our Universe Is Just Right for Life* (Boston: Houghton Mifflin, 2007).

CHAPTER 22

1 Kostas Kampourakis, *Understanding Evolution* (Cambridge: Cambridge University Press, 2014).
2 Peter R. Grant and B. Rosemary Grant, *40 Years of Evolution: Darwin's Finches on Daphne Major Island* (Princeton: Princeton University Press, 2014).
3 Douglas Palmer, *The Origins of Man* (London: New Holland Publishers UK, 2007).
4 For a short primer on the origins of life on earth, see Michael. J. Benton, *The History of Life: A Very Short Introduction* (Oxford: Oxford University Press, 2008). For a good exposition of the different theories, see Horst Rauchfuss, *Chemical Evolution and the Origin of Life* (Berlin: Springer, 2008). For some more technical up-to-date research, see Joseph Seckbach, *Genesis—In the Beginning: Precursors of Life, Chemical Models, and Early Biological Evolution* (New York: Springer, 2012); and Muriel Gargaud, Purificación López-Garcìa, and Hervé Martin, *Origins and Evolution of Life: An Astrobiological Perspective* (Cambridge: Cambridge University Press, 2010). For research on the fossil records of early life, see Suzanne D. Golding and Miryam Glikson, *Earliest Life on Earth: Habitats, Environments, and Methods of Detection* (London: Springer, 2010).
5 T. A. Lincoln and G. F. Joyce, "Self-sustained replication of an RNA enzyme," *Science* 323, no. 5918 (2009): 1229–1232.
6 Stephen Jay Gould, *The Structure of Evolutionary Theory* (Cambridge: Belknap Press of Harvard University Press, 2002).
7 Gould, *The Structure of Evolutionary Theory*.
8 M. D. Brasier, *Darwin's Lost World: The Hidden History of Animal Life* (Oxford: Oxford University Press, 2009).

9 Alan de Queiroz, *The Monkey's Voyage: How Improbable Journeys Shaped the History of Life* (New York: Basic Books, 2014).

10 De Queiroz, *The Monkey's Voyage.*

11 Sean B. Carroll, Jennifer K. Grenier, and Scott D. Weatherbee, *From DNA to Diversity: Molecular Genetics and the Evolution of Animal Design* (Malden: Blackwell Publishing, 2005).

12 Lynn Margulis, *Symbiosis in Cell Evolution: Microbial Communities in the Archean and Proterozoic* (New York: Freeman, 1993); and Boris Mikhaylovich Kozo-Polyansky, Victor Fet, and Margulis, *Symbiogenesis: A New Principle of Evolution* (Cambridge: Harvard University Press, 2010).

13 Slifkin, *The Challenge of Creation*, 189.

14 Slifkin, *The Challenge of Creation*, 189.

15 Slifkin, *The Challenge of Creation*, 267–268.

16 Slifkin, *The Challenge of Creation*, 297–298.

17 Slifkin, *The Challenge of Creation*, 302.

18 Rauchfuss, *Chemical Evolution*, 166. Some people have proposed solutions to this problem. One of them is that the presence of lipids from meteorites could have protected the RNA. "Scientist Suggests Comet and Meteorite Impacts Made Life on Earth Possible," *Astrobiology*, November 6, 2013, www.astrobio.net/meteoritescomets-and-asteroids/scientist-suggests-comet-and-meteorite-impacts-made-life-on-earth-possible/.

19 For some of these different options in brief, see Michael Marshall, "First Life: The Search for the First Replicator," *New Scientist*, August 10, 2017, www.newscientist.com/article/mg21128251-300-first-life-the-search-for-the-first-replicator/.

20 Scripps Research Institute, "Lifeless Prions Capable of Evolutionary Change and Adaptation," *Science Daily*, January 3, 2010, www.sciencedaily.com/releases/2009/12/091231164747.htm.

21 Rauchfuss, *Chemical Evolution*, 167–178.

22 "Scientist Suggests Comet and Meteorite Impacts Made Life on Earth Possible," *Astrobiology*, November 6, 2013, www.astrobio.net/meteoritescomets-and-asteroids/scientist-suggests-comet-and-meteorite-impacts-made-life-on-earth-possible/#sthash.TRKQNMmT.dpuf.

23 Slifkin, *The Challenge of Creation*, 359–360.

24 Slifkin, *The Challenge of Creation*, 372.

25 Slifkin, *The Challenge of Creation*, 372.

CHAPTER 23

1 David Hume, *An Enquiry Concerning Human Understanding*, ed. Tom L. Beauchamp (Oxford: Oxford University Press, 1999).

2 Patricia Tester, "Harmful Marine Phytoplankton and Shellfish Toxicity Potential Consequences of Climate Change," *Annals of the New York Academy of Sciences* 740, no. 1 (1994): 69–76.

3 John S. Marr and Curtis D. Malloy, "An Epidemiologic Analysis of the Ten Plagues of Egypt," *Caduceus* 12 no. 1 (1996).

4 Slifkin, *The Challenge of Creation*, 65.

5 Slifkin, *The Challenge of Creation*, chapter 4.

CHAPTER 24

1 Robert E. Barron, *Catholicism: A Journey to the Heart of the Faith* (New York: Image Books, 2011), 64–66.

PART FIVE INTRODUCTION

1 Hitchens, *God Is Not Great*, 102–103.
2 Dawkins, *The God Delusion*, 269.
3 Dawkins, *The God Delusion*, 293 quoting John Hartung.
4 Harris, *The End of Faith*, 24.
5 James L. Kugel, *How to Read the Bible: A Guide to Scripture, Then and Now* (New York: Free Press, 2007).
6 Kugel, *How to Read the Bible*, 667.
7 Kugel, *How to Read the Bible*, 59–61
8 Kugel, *How to Read the Bible*, 63–68.
9 Kugel, *How to Read the Bible*, 282–283.
10 Kugel, *How to Read the Bible*, 314–316.
11 Kugel, *How to Read the Bible*, see chapters 1 and 36.
12 Kugel, *How to Read the Bible*, see chapter 36.
13 Kugel, *How to Read the Bible*, see chapter 36.
14 Kugel, *How to Read the Bible*, 101 and 231.
15 Kugel, *How to Read the Bible*, 674.
16 Kugel, *How to Read the Bible*, 662–663.
17 Joshua Berman, "Diachronic Study of the Hebrew Bible: A Field in Crisis," *HIPHIL Novum* 1, no. 1 (2014).

CHAPTER 25

1 Moore and Kelle, *Biblical History*, 95.
2 Niels Peter Lemche, *The Canaanites and Their Land: The Tradition of the Canaanites* (Sheffield: JSOT Press, 1991).
3 Philip R. Davies, *In Search of "Ancient Israel"* (Sheffield: JSOT Press, 1992).
4 Keith W. Whitelam, *The Invention of Ancient Israel: The Silencing of Palestinian History* (New York: Routledge, 1996).
5 Thomas L. Thompson, *The Mythic Past: Biblical Archaeology and the Myth of Israel* (New York: Basic Books, 1999).
6 Baruch Halpern, "Erasing History—The Minimalist Assault on Ancient Israel," *Bible Review* 11, no. 6 (1995): 26.
7 Iain W. Provan, V. Philips Long, and Tremper Longman, *A Biblical History of Israel* (Louisville: Westminster John Knox Press, 2003).
8 Kenneth A. Kitchen, *On the Reliability of the Old Testament* (Grand Rapids: W. B. Eerdmans, 2003).
9 James Karl Hoffmeier, *Ancient Israel in Sinai: The Evidence for the Authenticity of the Wilderness Tradition* (Oxford: Oxford University Press, 2005).
10 William G. Dever, *What Did the Biblical Writers Know, and When Did They Know It? What Archaeology Can Tell Us about the Reality of Ancient Israel* (Grand Rapids: W. B. Eerdmans, 2001).

11 Israel Finkelstein, Amihai Mazar, and Brian B. Schmidt, *The Quest for the Historical Israel: Debating Archaeology and the History of Early Israel* (Leiden: Brill, 2007).

12 Thompson for example argues that no contextual evidence from other cultures in the region from the time period is relevant. Many of the arguments used by the minimalists and maximalists are taken from Megan Bishop Moore and Brad E. Kelly, *Biblical History and Israel's Past* (Grand Rapids: Eerdmans, 2011). For the discussion of the minimalist approach to contextual evidence see: Moore and Kelle, *Biblical History*, 58 and 64–64 and again 94–95.

13 Thomas L. Thompson, *The Historicity of the Patriarchal Narratives: The Quest for the Historical Abraham* (New York: W. de Gruyter, 1974).

14 Many of the centrist arguments are taken from: Israel Finkelstein, Amihai Mazar, and Brian B. Schmidt, *The Quest for the Historical Israel*.

CHAPTER 26

1 Thompson first made this argument in his book *The Historicity of the Patriarchal Narratives*. See also John Van Seters, *Abraham in History and Tradition* (New Haven: Yale University Press, 1975).

2 Moore and Kelle, *Biblical History*, 59.

3 Moore and Kelle, *Biblical History*, 59.

4 Moore and Kelle, *Biblical History*, 59.

5 Moore and Kelle, *Biblical History*, 61.

6 Moore and Kelle, *Biblical History*, 60.

7 Finkelstein, Mazar, and Schmidt, *The Quest for the Historical Israel*, 41 and 45–47.

8 Finkelstein, Mazar, and Schmidt, *The Quest for the Historical Israel*, 59.

9 Finkelstein, Mazar, and Schmidt, *The Quest for the Historical Israel*, 59.

10 Finkelstein, Mazar, and Schmidt, *The Quest for the Historical Israel*, 57.

11 Finkelstein, Mazar, and Schmidt, *The Quest for the Historical Israel*, 59.

12 Finkelstein, Mazar, and Schmidt, *The Quest for the Historical Israel*, 59.

13 Kitchen, *On the Reliability*, 341–342.

14 Kitchen, *On the Reliability*, 322 and 324.

15 Kitchen, *On the Reliability*, 319–322 and 333–335.

16 Kitchen, *On the Reliability*, 318–319.

17 Kitchen, *On the Reliability*, 317.

18 Kitchen, *On the Reliability*, 339–341.

19 See Kitchen, *On the Reliability*, chapter 9 and 10. Kitchen's position is held by Provan as well. See Provan, Long, Longman, *A Biblical History of Israel*, chapter 1.

CHAPTER 27

1 Moore and Kelle, *Biblical History*, 81.

2 Moore and Kelle, *Biblical History*, 95.

3 Moore and Kelle, *Biblical History*, 96

4 Moore and Kelle, *Biblical History*, 91. See: Donald B. Redford, *Egypt, Canaan, and Israel in Ancient Times* (Princeton: Princeton University Press, 1992), 407–408.

5 Redford, *Egypt, Canaan, and Israel*, 409.

6 Finkelstein, Mazar, and Schmidt, *The Quest for the Historical Israel*, 52.

7 Finkelstein, Mazar, and Schmidt, *The Quest for the Historical Israel*, 52.

8 Finkelstein, Mazar, and Schmidt, *The Quest for the Historical Israel*, 59.
9 Finkelstein, Mazar, and Schmidt, *The Quest for the Historical Israel*, 59–60.
10 Finkelstein, Mazar, and Schmidt, *The Quest for the Historical Israel*, 59.
11 Joyce A. Tyldesley, *Ramesses: Egypt's Greatest Pharaoh* (London: Penguin, 2001).
12 Finkelstein, Mazar, and Schmidt, *The Quest for the Historical Israel*, 59–60.
13 Finkelstein, Mazar, and Schmidt, *The Quest for the Historical Israel*, 60.
14 Finkelstein, Mazar, and Schmidt, *The Quest for the Historical Israel*, 60.
15 Finkelstein, Mazar, and Schmidt, *The Quest for the Historical Israel*, 60–61.
16 Finkelstein, Mazar, and Schmidt, *The Quest for the Historical Israel*, 60.
17 Finkelstein, Mazar, and Schmidt, *The Quest for the Historical Israel*, 60.
18 Avraham Faust, "The Emergence of Iron Age Israel: On Origins and Habitus," in *Israel's Exodus in Transdisciplinary Perspective: Text, Archaeology, Culture, and Geoscience*, eds. Thomas Evan Levy, Thomas Schneider, and William Henry Propp (Cham: Springer, 2015), 477.
19 Faust, "The Emergence of Iron Age Israel," 478.
20 Moore and Kelle, *Biblical History*, 89.
21 Kitchen, *On the Reliability*, 245–246.
22 Moore and Kelle, *Biblical History*, 89.
23 Hoffmeier, *Israel in Egypt: The Evidence for the Authenticity of the Exodus Tradition* (New York: Oxford University Press, 1999), 112–114.
24 Moore and Kelle, *Biblical History*, 84.
25 Kitchen, *On the Reliability*, 249–254.
26 Kitchen, *On the Reliability*, 261–263. Hoffmeier, *Ancient Israel in Sinai*, 108 and figure 5.
27 Kitchen, *On the Reliability*, 255–261.
28 Joshua Berman, "Was There an Exodus?," *Mosaic*, March 2, 2015, mosaicmagazine.com/essay/2015/03/was-there-an-exodus/.
29 Thomas Malory, *The Works of Sir Thomas Malory*, 2nd ed., ed. Eugene Vinaver (Oxford: Oxford University Press, 1971), "The Tale of King Arthur," 56.
30 Eliot Weinberger, Wei Wang, and Octavio Paz, *Nineteen Ways of Looking at Wang Wei: How a Chinese Poem is Translated* (Mount Kisco: Moyer Bell, 1987).

CHAPTER 28

1 Moore and Kelle, *Biblical History*, 99.
2 Moore and Kelle, *Biblical History*, 99.
3 Moore and Kelle, *Biblical History*, 113.
4 Moore and Kelle, *Biblical History*, 115 and 117.
5 Moore and Kelle, *Biblical History*, 116.
6 Thompson, *The Mythic Past*, 79.
7 Moore and Kelle, *Biblical History*, 120–121.
8 Moore and Kelle, *Biblical History*, 121.
9 Moore and Kelle, *Biblical History*, 121.
10 Finkelstein, Mazar, and Schmidt, *The Quest for the Historical Israel*, 74.
11 Finkelstein, Mazar, and Schmidt, *The Quest for the Historical Israel*, 39
12 Finkelstein, Mazar, and Schmidt, *The Quest for the Historical Israel*, 39–40
13 Finkelstein, Mazar, and Schmidt, *The Quest for the Historical Israel*, 95.

Endnotes

14 Finkelstein, Mazar, and Schmidt, *The Quest for the Historical Israel*, 81–83.
15 Finkelstein, Mazar, and Schmidt, *The Quest for the Historical Israel*, 79.
16 Moore and Kelle, *Biblical History*, 100.
17 Moore and Kelle, *Biblical History*, 100; see notes 25 and 26.
18 Moore and Kelle, *Biblical History*, 100; see notes 25 and 26. See Richard S. Hess, "The Jericho and Ai of the Book of Joshua," in *Critical Issues in Early Israelite History*, eds. Richard S. Hess, Gerald A. Klingbeil, and Paul J. Ray (Winona Lake: Eisenbrauns, 2008); Kitchen, *On the Reliability*, 183–190; and Proven, Long, and Longman, *A Biblical History of Israel*, 173–190.
19 Kitchen, *On the Reliability*, 160–163 and 188–189.
20 Kitchen, *On the Reliability*, 184–185.
21 Kitchen, *On the Reliability*, 187–188.
22 A number of scholars share this view. See Moore and Kelle, *Biblical History*, 119.
23 Kitchen, *On the Reliability*, 189–190.
24 Faust, "Early Israel: An Egalitarian Society," *Biblical Archaeology Review*, 39, no. 4 (2013): 45–63.
25 Faust, "Early Israel," 46.
26 Dever, "How to Tell a Canaanite from an Israelite" in *The Rise of Ancient Israel*, ed. Hershel Shanks (Washington: Biblical Archeology, 1992), 54.
27 Faust, "Early Israel," 48 and 49.

CHAPTER 29

1 Moore and Kelle, *Biblical Israel*, 175 and 210.
2 This is the view taken by the minimalist Niels Peter Lemche. Lemche, *The Israelites in History*, 38–44. See also Thompson, *The Mythic Past*, 203–205.
3 Thompson, *The Mythic Past*, 203–205.
4 Lemche, *The Israelites in History*, 38–44. See also Thompson, *The Mythic Past*, 203–205.
5 Thompson, *The Mythic Past*, 206–207.
6 Moore and Kelle, *Biblical Israel*, 211–213.
7 Moore and Kelle, *Biblical Israel*, 216–217.
8 Moore and Kelle, *Biblical Israel*, 217–218.
9 Moore and Kelle, *Biblical Israel*, 238.
10 Moore and Kelle, *Biblical Israel*, 175 and 240.
11 Moore and Kelle, *Biblical Israel*, 220 and 225–228.
12 Finkelstein, Mazar, and Schmidt, *The Quest for the Historical Israel*, 114–115, and 139.
13 Moore and Kelle, *Biblical Israel*, 230.
14 Finkelstein, Mazar, and Schmidt, *The Quest for the Historical Israel*, 101.
15 Finkelstein, Mazar, and Schmidt, *The Quest for the Historical Israel*, 115.
16 Finkelstein, Mazar, and Schmidt, *The Quest for the Historical Israel*, 115.
17 Moore and Kelle, *Biblical History*, 240.
18 Finkelstein, Mazar, and Schmidt, *The Quest for the Historical Israel*, 133.
19 Moore and Kelle, *Biblical Israel*, 235.
20 Finkelstein, Mazar, and Schmidt, *The Quest for the Historical Israel*, 104.

21 Finkelstein, Mazar, and Schmidt, *The Quest for the Historical Israel*, 105.
22 Finkelstein, Mazar, and Schmidt, *The Quest for the Historical Israel*, 105.
23 Finkelstein, Mazar, and Schmidt, *The Quest for the Historical Israel*, 138–139.
24 Kitchen, *On the Reliability*, 88.
25 Kitchen, *On the Reliability*, 89.
26 Kitchen, *On the Reliability*, 157.
27 Kitchen, *On the Reliability*, 157.
28 Kitchen, *On the Reliability*, 158.
29 Yosef Garfinkel and Saar Ganor, *Khirbet Qeiyafa*, vol. 1 (Jerusalem: Israel Exploration Society, 2009), 3.
30 Garfinkel and Ganor, *Khirbet Qeiyafa*, 4 and 13.
31 Faust, *The Archaeology of Israelite Society in Iron Age II*, trans. Ruth Ludlum (Winona Lake: Eisenbrauns, 2012), chapter 9.
32 Kitchen, *On the Reliability*, 157.
33 William W. Hallo, "The Bible and Monuments," in *Context of Scripture, 2: Monumental Inscriptions from the Biblical World*, eds. Hallo and K. Lawson Younger (Leiden: Brill, 2003), xxiv.
34 Hallo, "The Bible and Monuments," xxvi. This point about the lack of monumental architecture lends weight to Berman's argument that the Bible spread a radical message of equality. Berman, *Created Equal*.

CHAPTER 30

1 Joseph Blenkinsoopp, "The Pentateuch," in *The Cambridge Companion to Biblical Interpretation*, ed. John Barton (Cambridge: Cambridge University Press, 1998); and Robert Kugler and Patrick Hartin, *An Introduction to the Bible* (Grand Rapids: W. B. Eerdmanns, 2009).
2 Umberto Cassuto, *The Documentary Hypothesis and the Composition of the Pentateuch: Eight Lectures*, trans. Israel Abrahams (Jerusalem: Magnes Press, 1961).
3 Cassuto, *The Documentary Hypothesis*, 21–26.
4 For a brief description of different hypotheses with regard to the Bible's composition, see R. N. Whybray, *Introduction to the Pentateuch* (Grand Rapids: W.B. Eerdmans, 1995), chapter 2.
5 Kugler and Hartin, *An Introduction to the Bible*, and Whybray, *Introduction*, chapter 2.
6 Kugler and Hartin, *An Introduction to the Bible* (Grand Rapids: W. B. Eerdmans, 2009), 49.
7 Kugler and Hartin, *An Introduction to the Bible*, 47–50.
8 John van Seters, *The Pentateuch: A Social-Science Commentary* (Sheffield: Sheffield Academic Press, 1999).
9 Whybray, *The Making of the Pentateuch: A Methodological Study* (Sheffield: JSOT, 1987).
10 Kugler and P. J. Hartin, *An Introduction to the Bible,* 49.
11 See Berman, "Diachronic Study of the Hebrew Bible."

Endnotes

CHAPTER 31

1 William M. Schniedewind, *A Social History of Hebrew: Its Origins Through the Rab-binic Period* (New Haven: Yale University Press, 2013).

2 Schniedewind, *A Social History of Hebrew*, 79.

3 Schniedewind, *A Social History of Hebrew*, 79.

4 Schniedewind, *A Social History of Hebrew*, 79.

5 See Philip R. Davies, *In Search of "Ancient Israel"*; Keith W. Whitelam, *The Invention of Ancient Israel*; Thompson, *The Mythic Past*; and Lemche, *The Israelites in History*.

6 Davies, *In Search of "Ancient Israel"*; Whitelam, *The Invention of Ancient Israel*; Thompson, *The Mythic Past*; Lemche, *The Israelites in History*; and Niels Peter Lemche, *Biblical Studies and the Failure of History* (Sheffield: Equinox, 2013).

7 Redford, *Egypt, Canaan, and Israel*, 410.

8 Schniedewind, *How the Bible Became a Book: The Textualization of Ancient Israel* (Cambridge: Cambridge University Press, 2004), 82.

9 Schniedewind, *How the Bible Became a Book*, 166–168.

10 Schniedewind, *How the Bible Became a Book*, 174.

11 Schniedewind, *How the Bible Became a Book*, 181.

12 Schniedewind, *How the Bible Became a Book*, 81.

13 Schniedewind, *How the Bible Became a Book*, 18.

14 Dever, *What Did the Biblical Writers Know*, 101–102.

15 Dever, *What Did the Biblical Writers Know*, 275–277.

16 Alexander Rofé, *Introduction to the Composition of the Pentateuch* (Sheffield: Sheffield Academic Press, 1999).

17 Kitchen, *On the Reliability*, 289; Joshua Berman, "Was There an Exodus?," *Mosaic*, March 2, 2015, mosaicmagazine.com/essay/2015/03/was-there-an-exodus/and Provan, Long, and Longman, *A Biblical History*, 134.

18 Berman, "Was There an Exodus?"

19 Faust, "The Bible, Archaeology, and the Practice of Circumcision in Israelite and Philistine," *Journal of Biblical Literature* 134, no. 2 (2015): 288.

20 Kitchen, *On the Reliability*, 306.

21 Kitchen, *On the Reliability*, 304–306.

CHAPTER 32

1 See the works of Thompson, Lemche, and Davies as cited previously.

2 Schniedewind, *A Social History*, 77.

3 Schniedewind, *A Social History*, 76.

4 Schniedewind, *A Social History*, 77.

5 Schniedewind, *How the Bible Became a Book*, 75.

6 Schniedewind, *How the Bible Became a Book*, 192.

7 Schniedewind, *How the Bible Became a Book*, 77; and Martin Noth, *The Deuterono-mistic History* (Sheffield: Sheffield Academic Press, 2001).

8 Kitchen, *On the Reliability*, chapter 10.

9 Hazony, *The Philosophy of Hebrew Scripture* (Cambridge: Cambridge University Press, 2012).

10 Kitchen, *On the Reliability*, chapter 8.

11 Kitchen, *On the Reliability*, 283–306 and chapter 8.

12 Berman, "Was There an Exodus?"
13 Berman, *Created Equal*, chapter 1.
14 Berman, *Created Equal*, chapter 5.
15 David Weiss Halivni, *Revelation Restored: Divine Writ and Critical Responses* (London: SCM, 2001).
16 Halivni, *Revelation Restored,* 4–5.
17 Halivni, *Revelation Restored,* 17.

CHAPTER 33

1 Robert Alter, *Genesis: Translation and Commentary* (New York: Norton, 1997), 217 and chapter 38.

PART SIX INTRODUCTION

1 Harris, *The End of Faith*, 31.
2 Harris, *The End of Faith*, 45–46.
3 Harris, *The End of Faith*, 64.
4 Dennett, *Breaking the Spell*, 298.
5 Onfray, *Atheist Manifesto*, 1.
6 Dawkins, *The God Delusion*, 277–278.
7 Dawkins, *The God Delusion*, 74.
8 Dawkins, *The God Delusion*, 76.
9 Onfray, *Atheist Manifesto*, 52.
10 Christopher Hitchens, *Mortality*, 21–22.
11 Onfray, *Atheist Manifesto*, xvi.
12 Hitchens, *God is Not Great*, 73–74.
13 Hitchens, *God is Not Great*, 18.
14 Dennett, *Breaking the Spell*, 276–277.

CHAPTER 35

1 Hazony, *The Philosophy of Hebrew Scripture* (New York: Cambridge University Press, 2012).
2 Hazony, *The Philosophy of Hebrew Scriptures*, 245.
3 Hazony, *The Philosophy of Hebrew Scriptures*, 245.
4 Hazony, *The Philosophy of Hebrew Scriptures*, 245.
5 Tariq Ramadan, *Islam: The Essentials*, trans. Fred A. Reed (London: Penguin Books, 2017), 58.
6 Armstrong, *A History of God*, chapter 3.
7 Hazony, *The Philosophy of Hebrew Scriptures*, 187 and 247.

CHAPTER 36

1 Part of this discussion was informed by a similar discussion in Hazony, *The Philosophy of Hebrew Scriptures*, chapter. 7.
2 Hazony, *The Philosophy of Hebrew Scriptures*, 196.
3 Hazony, *The Philosophy of Hebrew Scriptures*, 196–199.
4 See Karen Armstrong, *The Case for God* (New York: Alfred A. Knopf, 2009), chapters 4, 87 and 88.

5   Ramadan, *Islam*, 134–135.
6   Hazony, *The Philosophy of Hebrew Scriptures*, 212.
7   Hazony, *The Philosophy of Hebrew Scriptures*, 214.

CHAPTER 37

1   Niccolò Machiavelli, *The Prince*, 2nd ed., trans. Harvey C. Mansfield (Chicago: University of Chicago Press, 1998).
2   Helga Kuhse and Peter Singer, *Should the Baby Live? Problem of Handicapped Infants* (Aldershot: Gregg Revivals, 1994).
3   Peter Singer, *Practical Ethics* (Cambridge: Cambridge University Press, 2011).
4   David Jenkins, "Richard Dawkins on infanticide," YouTube Video, 0:29, April 1, 2010, www.youtube.com/watch?v=YWkJ6cZ0FY8.
5   Florian Bruns and Tessa Chelouche, "Lectures on Inhumanity: Teaching Medical Ethics in German Medical Schools Under Nazism," *Annals of Internal Medicine* 166, no. 8 (April 2017).
6   Gary Saul Morson and Morton Owen Schapiro, *Cents and Sensibility: What Economics Can Learn from the Humanities* (Princeton: Princeton University Press, 2017), 26–29.

CHAPTER 38

1   President Abraham Lincoln, letter to Eliza Gurney, October 6, 1862, in *Abraham Lincoln: Speeches and Letters* (Rutland, VT: C. E. Tuttle, 1993).

CHAPTER 39

1   Holland, *Gods of the Desert*, 168.
2   Holland, *Gods of the Desert*, 168.
3   Shinto is among the most ritualistic religions still practiced today. See Helen Hardacre, *Shinto: A History* (New York: Oxford University Press, 2017).

CHAPTER 41

1   Sarah Yehudit Schneider, Prayer and Destiny, Lesson 2, 7.
2   Martin Luther King Jr. *The Autobiography of Martin Luther King, Jr.*, ed. Clayton Carson (New York: Grand Central Publishing, 1976).
3   New World Encyclopedia, 2016, s.v. "Abraham Lincoln," accessed December 31, 2017, www.newworldencyclopedia.org/p/index.php?title=Abraham_Lincoln.
4   Sarah Yehudit Schneider, Prayer and Destiny, Lesson 16, 3.
5   Natan Sharansky and Stefan Hoffman, *Fear No Evil: A Memoir* (London: Hodder and Stoughton, 1989).
6   H. Benson et al., "Study of the Therapeutic Effects of Intercessory Prayer (STEP) in Cardiac Cypass Patients: A Multicenter Randomized Trial of Uncertainty and Certainty of Receiving Intercessory Prayer," *American Heart Journal* 151, no. 4 (April 2006): 934–42.
7   George Sylvester Viereck, *Glimpses of the Great* (New York: Macaulay Company, 1930), 372–373.

APPENDIX

1 Scott Dodelson, *Modern Cosmology* (San Diego: Academic Press, 2003).

2 V. F. Mukhanov, *Physical Foundations of Cosmology* (Cambridge: Cambridge University Press, 2005).

3 Andrew R. Liddle and D. H. Lyth, *Cosmological Inflation and Large-Scale Structure* (Cambridge: Cambridge University Press, 2000).

4 Mukhanov, *Physical Foundations of Cosmology.*

5 Dodelson, *Modern Cosmology.*

6 Dodelson, *Modern Cosmology.*

7 Houjun Mo, Frank Van den Bosch, and S. White, *Galaxy Formation and Evolution* (Cambridge: Cambridge University Press, 2010).

8 James Binney and Scott Tremaine, *Galactic Dynamics* (Princeton: Princeton University Press, 1987).

9 Stephen Gasiorowicz, *Quantum Physics* (Hoboken: Wiley, 2003).

10 A. Zee, *Quantum Field Theory in a Nutshell* (Princeton: Princeton University Press, 2010).

11 Nouredine Zettili, *Quantum Mechanics: Concepts and Applications* (Chichester: Wiley, 2001).

12 Max Planck, *Acht Vorlesungen über Theoretische Physik, Gehalten an der Columbia University in the City of New York im Frühjahr 1909* (Leipzig: S. Hirzel, 1910). For an English translation, see Max Planck, *Eight Lectures on Theoretical Physics*, trans. Peter Pesic (Mineola: Dover, 1998).

13 Zettili, *Quantum Mechanics.*

14 Albert Einstein, "Über einen die Erzeugung und Verwandlung des Lichtes betreffenden heuristischen Gesichtspunkt," *Annalen der Physik* 17, no. 6 (1905): 132–148.

15 Niels Bohr, *On the Constitution of Atoms and Molecules*, trans. E. S. Johansen (London: The Philosophical Magazine, 1913).

16 Louis de Broglie, "Waves and Quanta," *Nature* 112 (1923): 540.

17 Werner Heisenberg, "Über den anschaulichen Inhalt der quantentheoretischen Kinematik und Mechanik," *Zeitschrift für Physik,* 43, nos. 3–4 (1927): 172–198.

18 Richard Phillips Feynman, Robert B. Leighton, and Matthew L. Sands, *The Feynman Lectures on Physics, Vol. 3: Quantum Mechanics* (Reading: Addison-Wesley, 1963–1965).

19 Wolfgang Rindler, *Relativity: Special, General, and Cosmological* (Oxford: Oxford University Press, 2001).

20 Albert Einstein, *"Zur Elektrodynamik bewegter Körper,"* *Annalen der Physik* 17, no. 10 (1905): 891–921; and Albert Einstein, *Ist die Trägheit eines Körpers von seinem Energieinhalt abhängig?* (Leipzig: J. Barth, 1905).

21 J. B. Hartle, *Gravity: An Introduction to Einstein's General Relativity* (San Francisco: Addison-Wesley, 2003).

22 Michael Edward Peskin and Daniel V. Schroeder, *Introduction to Quantum Field Theory* (Reading: Addison-Wesley, 1995).

23 Michael B. Green, E. Witten, and John H. Schwarz, *Superstring Theory* (Cambridge: Cambridge University Press, 1987).

24 Barton Zwiebach, *A First Course in String Theory* (New York: Cambridge University Press, 2004).

Endnotes

25 Green, Witten, and Schwarz, *Superstring Theory*.

26 Steven Weinberg, *Dreams of a Final Theory* (New York: Pantheon Books, 1992).

27 See for example Dan Falk, "Science's Path from Myth to Multiverse," *Quanta*, May 14, 2015, www.scientificamerican.com/article/science-s-path-from-myth-to-multiverse/; Paul Davies, "A Brief History of the Multiverse," *New York Times*, April 12, 2003; Davies, *The Goldilocks Enigma: Why Is the Universe Just Right for Life?* (London: Allen Lane, 2006); Paul Steinhardt, "Theories of Anything," edge. org, 2014, www.edge.org/response-detail/25405; Viatcheslav Mukhanov, "Inflation without Self-Reproduction," *Fortschritte der Physik*, 63, no. 1 (2015): 36–41; George Ellis and Joe Silk, "Scientific Method: Defend the Integrity of Physics," *Nature* 516, no. 7531 (2014): 321–323; and Davies, "Taking Science on Faith," *New York Times*, November 24, 2007, www.nytimes.com/2007/11/24/opinion/24davies.html.

28 For example, Bernard Carr ed., *Universe or Multiverse?* (Cambridge: Cambridge University Press, 2007), particularly the chapter by Stephen Hawking, "Cosmology From the Top Down"; Brian Greene, "A Physicist Explains Why Parallel Universes May Exist," Fresh Air NPR, January 24, 2011, www.npr. org/2011/01/24/132932268/a-physicist-explains-why-parallel-universes-may-exist; Max Tegmark, "Parallel Universes," in *Science and Ultimate Reality: Quantum Theory, Cosmology, and Complexity*, eds. John D. Barrow, P. C. W. Davies, and Charles L. Harper (Cambridge: Cambridge University Press, 2004); Andrei Linde, "Inflation in Supergravity and String Theory: Brief History of the Multiverse," 2012, www.ctc.cam.ac.uk/stephen70/talks/swh70_linde.pdf; and R. Bousso and L. Susskind, "Multiverse Interpretation of Quantum Mechanics," *Physical Review Journals D—Particles, Fields, Gravitation, and Cosmology* 85, no. 4 (2012).

29 Brian Greene, *The Hidden Reality: Parallel Universes and the Deep Laws of the Cosmos* (New York: Alfred A. Knopf, 2011).

30 Dodelson, *Modern Cosmology*.

31 Dark energy has been added to the standard cosmological model in 1998—after independent observations that proved that the expansion of our universe is accelerating—by groups led by Adam Riess, Saul Perlmutter, and Brian Schmidt, who have won the Shaw Prize in Astronomy (2006) and Nobel Prize in Physics (2011).

32 See for example: "Foundations of Big Bang Cosmology," NASA, map.gsfc.nasa.gov/universe/bb_concepts.html.

33 See for example George Musser, "Gravitational Waves Reveal the Universe Before the Big Bang: An Interview with Physicist Gabriele Veneziano," *Scientific American*, April 3 2014, blogs.scientificamerican.com/critical-opalescence/2014/04/03/gravitational-waves-reveal-the-universe-before-the-big-bang-an-interview-with-physicist-gabriele-veneziano/.

34 Carr, *Universe or Multiverse?*; and Tegmark, *Our Mathematical Universe*.

35 Davies, "A Brief History of the Multiverse," *New York Times*, April 12, 2003.

36 Steinhardt, "Theories of Anything," www.edge.org/response-detail/25405.

INDEX

516

Index

Index

Index

Index

ABOUT THE AUTHOR

Scott A. Shay has had a successful business career spanning Wall Street, private equity, venture capital, and banking. He co-founded Signature Bank of New York and has served as its Chairman since its formation. He has been a provocative commentator on many financial issues, including, among others, how the banking system should best function to help society, the implications of a cashless world, and tax reform. Scott called for the re-imposition of Glass-Steagall and breaking up the big banks at a TEDx talk at the NY Stock Exchange in 2012. Throughout his life, he has been a student of religion and how religion ought to apply to the world outside of the synagogue, church, or mosque. In addition to authoring articles relating to the Jewish community, Scott authored the bestselling *Getting Our Groove Back: How to Energize American Jewry* (Second Edition, Devora 2008).